The Relations of Dwight D. Eisenhower

His Pennsylvania German Roots

2nd Edition

by

Lawrence Knorr

SUNBURY PRESS

Mechanicsburg, Pennsylvania   USA

Published by Sunbury Press, Inc.
105 South Market Street
Mechanicsburg, Pennsylvania 17055

SUNBURY
PRESS

www.sunburypress.com

For information about special discounts for bulk purchases, please contact Sunbury Press Orders Dept. at (855) 338-8359 or orders@sunburypress.com.

To request one of our authors for speaking engagements or book signings, please contact Sunbury Press Publicity Dept. at publicity@sunburypress.com.

ISBN: 978-1-62006-730-7 (Trade Paperback)

Library of Congress Control Number: 2016932777

SECOND SUNBURY PRESS EDITION: March 2016

Product of the United States of America
0 1 1 2 3 5 8 13 21 34 55

Set in Bookman Old Style
Designed by Lawrence Knorr
Cover by Lawrence Knorr
Edited by Lawrence Knorr

Continue the Enlightenment!

"Soldiers, Sailors and Airmen of the Allied Expeditionary Force: You are about to embark upon the Great Crusade, toward which we have striven these many months. The eyes of the world are upon you. In company with our brave Allies and brothers-in-arms on other Fronts you will bring about the destruction of the German war machine, the elimination of Nazi tyranny over oppressed peoples of Europe, and security for ourselves in a free world. I have full confidence in your courage, devotion to duty and skill in battle. We will accept nothing less than full victory! Good Luck! And let us all beseech the blessing of Almighty God upon this great and noble undertaking."

Dwight D. Eisenhower
Order of Day
June 4, 1944

Table of Contents

Preface to the 2nd Edition

The Eisenhowers: From the Saarland to Elizabethville, Pennsylvania

Imagine you are on a ship, tossed in a gale. The winds howl. The bow pitches and yaws. You are stowed below with dozens of other immigrants, trapped in the dank and putrid air. The ship moans and creaks and shudders as the contents not lashed down rolls back and forth.

The immigrant Gottlieb Mittelberger, bound for Philadelphia, described a similar trip across the Atlantic in Summer of 1750:

...during the voyage there is on board these ships terrible misery, stench, fumes, horror, vomiting, many kinds of sea sickness, fever, dysentery, headache, heat, constipation, boils, scurvy, cancer, mouth rot, and the like, all of which come from old and sharply-salted food and meat, also from very bad and foul water, so that many die miserably.

Add to this want of provisions, hunger, thirst, frost, heat, dampness, anxiety, want, afflictions and lamentations, together with other trouble, as e.g., the lice abound so frightfully, especially on sick people, that they can be scraped off the body. The misery reaches a climax when a gale rages for two or three nights and days, so that everyone believes that the ship will go to the bottom with all human beings on board. In such a visitation the people cry and pray most piteously.

Mittelberger was aboard the *Osgood*, which arrived in Philadelphia in September of 1750 with 486 (surviving) persons aboard, 145 of whom were adult men. He further described the plight of the women and children:

No one can have an idea of the sufferings which women in confinement have to bear with their innocent children on board these ships. Few of this class escape with their lives; many a mother is cast into the water with her child as soon as she is dead. One day, just as we had a heavy gale, a woman in our ship, who was to give birth and could not give birth under the circumstances, was pushed through a loophole (porthole) in the ship and dropped into the sea, because she was far in the rear of the ship and could not be brought forward.

Children from one to seven years rarely survive the voyage; and many a time parents are compelled to see their children miserably suffer and die from hunger, thirst, and sickness, and then to see them cast into the water. I witnessed such misery in no less than thirty-two children in our ship, all of whom were thrown into the sea. The parents grieve all the more since their children find no resting place in the earth, but are devoured by the monsters of the sea. It is a notable fact that children who have not yet had the measles or smallpox generally get them on board the ship, and mostly die of them.

Johann (Hans) Nicholas Eisenhauer (1691 - c. 1760)

A ship similar to Europa floundering in a storm.

Johann Nicol (Hans Nicholas) Eisenhauer and his family were aboard *Europa,* having left Rotterdam in August of 1741. By late November, they were nearing the mouth of the Delaware Bay. According to the list of those taking oaths in Philadelphia, there were 46 surviving men aboard -- considerably less than the *Osgood.* Given the ratio of souls on the *Osgood,* there were likely about 100 others aboard *Europa* -- the women and children.

According to the official records, we are left with a very obscure and mundane statement that the *Europa* ran aground off of Lewes, Delaware, and Captain Lumsdaine and a cabin boy perished. The 120 surviving passengers later arrived in Philadelphia aboard three shallops, which were smaller sailing vessels. The details of the shipwreck are lost to time. But what happened that November? How many others perished besides the Captain and the cabin boy? Did the ship run aground in a storm, or was he an incompetent navigator? Regardless, the end of the harrowing voyage from Rotterdam was nearly a tragic one for the line of Eisenhauer who would later produce the Supreme Commander of Allied Forces in Europe, and our 34th President, Dwight David Eisenhower.

This lucky immigrant, Johann Nicol Eisenhauer, according to some records, was born in Forbach, near Saarbrucken, in the Saarland, in 1691. In other records, he was born in Eiterback, about 8 miles from Heidelberg. He was the son of Hans Peter Eisenhauer and his second wife, Anna Catharina Mildenberger. He was a *potaschbrenner* by trade (someone who renders potash, a material used as fertilizer and in gunpowder). In 1722, he was working at the Sophienhutte glass factory near Forbach, where his oldest son, Johann Peter, was christened. The next year, he moved to Karlsbrunn, a village near Forbach. He married Anna Margaretha Strobel, his second wife, circa 1725. The couple resided in Karlsbrunn. The Johann Nicholas had eleven children, the first two likely from his first wife, the rest from Anna Margaretha:

Johann Peter, born in Forbach 3/15/1722
Johann Martin, born 9/25/1723
Johann George Adam, 2/28/1725
Maria Margaretha, 5/28/1726
Johannetta Margaret Elisabeth, 9/29/1727
Johann Martin, 6/19/1729
Catherine Margaret, 11/18/1731
Anna Catharina, 8/30/1732
Maria Magdalena, 11/7/1735
Catherine Elisabeth, 2/15/1738
Anna Margaretha, 10/25/1739

An early view of the colonial city of Philadelphia.

Anna Margaretha's brother, Friedrich Strubel/Strobel, had emigrated to Pennsylvania, arriving on September 11, 1731. He settled in Lebanon County (then Lancaster), and lived there for ten years before returning to find a wife. At their wedding at Neuenheim, across the Neckar River from Heidelberg, on April 18, 1741, Friedrich persuaded his brother-in-law, Johann Nicholas Eisenhauer, and his wife to join him in America.

According to the Church Book at Karlsbrunn, the parents and seven children, Johann Peter (1), Johann Martin (2), Johann Martin (6), Anna Catherina (8), Maria Magdalena (9), Catherine Elisabeth (10), and Anna Margaretha (11) left the area in 1741, bound for Pennsylvania.

Four Eisenhauer men were qualified as debarking from the ill-fated *Europa* in November, 1741 These were Hans Nicol (age 50), Johan (age 28), Johann Peter (age 25), and Johannes (age 16). All but Johannes took the Oath of Allegiance on November 20. The accuracy of some of the ages given is definitely in question.

The couple settled in Bethel Township, Lebanon County, Pennsylvania, near Anna's brother, Friedrich Strubel. The land lay northwest of Fredericksburg on a gentle slope looking towards the Blue Mountain. On January 20, 1753, Hans Nicholas had 168 acres (Deed Book A55-224) surveyed near Fredericksburg, Bethel Township, Lebanon County.

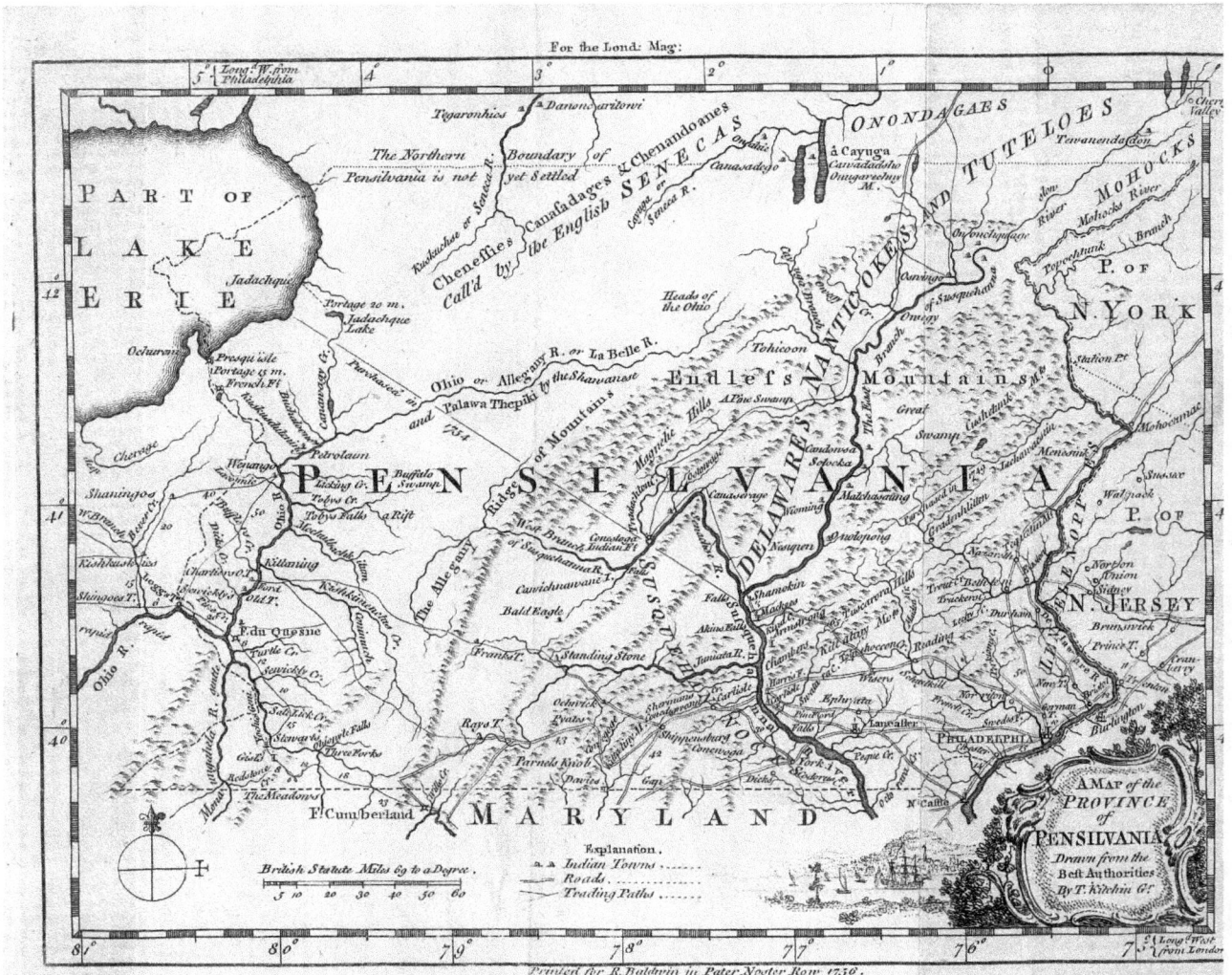

1756 map of Pennsylvania.

Not soon after the family made their home, the French and Indian War began (1754 - 1763). Once again, Hans Nicholas faced potential tragedy. *The Pennsylvania Gazette* reported on 12 August 1756 that Indians had burned his home:

> *By a letter from Fort Henry in Berks County, dated August the 7th, there is advice that the Indians are hovering about that neighborhood, some of them being seen almost every day, and that they burned the house of Nicholas Eisenhauer.*

The following year, September 30, five children of Peter Wampler were kidnapped by Indians. This family was on the *Europa* with the Eisenhauers and lived just south of their farm. This house was also later burned.

It is not long afterward that Nicholas faded from the scene. On September 13, 1759, he deeded this tract to his son, Peter who subsequently deeded it to Jacob Meiley, with whom there was a relation or close friendship. On December 19, 1759, he witnessed the will of his son Martin and attested his signature on the will on March 27, 1760. This is the last known written record in his name. Although no graves are known, it is believed Hans Nicholas and his wife Anna Margretha are buried near Fredricksburg, Pennsylvania.

Johann Peter Eisenhauer (1721/22 – 1802)

Born on the Ides of March in 1721/22 in Forbach, Lorraine, France, Johann Peter Eisenhauer emigrated with his parents in 1741, and subsequently inherited their lands near Fredericksburg. Peter was a blacksmith, gunsmith, prominent merchant, and landowner in Bethel Township, Lebanon County, Pennsylvania, where he also served as constable in 1777. He married three times and fathered nineteen children:

with Elizabeth Ann Graff (1720 - c. 1764) of Dauphin County:

Peter (9/6/1745), died 1795.
Maria Barbara (8/22/1747), died 1808 in Rowan, North Carolina.
John Nicholas (5/6/1749), died 1802.
George Michael (8/4/1751)
Anna Margaretha (2/14/1753), married Christian Meyer.
John Frederick (10/6/1753), died April 10, 1777, at Rising Sun, Germantown,
   Pennsylvania.
Phillip (12/19/1754)
Maria Magdalena (3/7/1756)
Anna Maria Elizabeth (4/25/1759)
Samuel (11/25/1763)

Elizabeth's sister, Anna Barbara Graff, was the wife of Peter's brother, Johannes Martin. They were daughters of Hans George and Catherine Graff, shopkeeper, of Lancaster County, Pennsylvania. These Graff sisters were daughters of Hans Graff as indicated by their record in Deed Book D, page 369, deed recorded May 20, 1756 in Lancaster County, Pennsylvania.

with Anna Maria Elizabeth Schmidt (b. 1725) married August 21, 1770 at Bethel Township, Lebanon County:

John (2/5/1774), died June 21, 1861.

with Anna Margaret Dissinger (c. 1750 - 1815), daughter of Peter Dissinger, of Stouchsburg, Berks County, Pennsylvania, married January 29, 1777 at Stouchsburg:

John Jacob (4/13/1777), married Nancy Anna McDonald.
Catherine (1780)
Ann (1781)
Christina (1783)
Barbara (1784)
Margaret (1787)
John Peter (1/4/1790)
Frederick (7/15/1794), died March 13, 1884 in Belle Springs, Kansas

1790 census listing Peter "Isinhower"

After deeding his lands to the Meileys, he subsequently settled in Lower Paxton Township, Dauphin County, near the village of Linglestown. The 1790 Census placed Peter Isenhower in Dauphin County. The household contained one male over 16, 3 males 16 and under, and 4 females. This would indicate that two of the daughters had perished prior to the census.

The 1800 Pennsylvania Census listed Peter Eisenhauer in Lower Paxton Township, in Dauphin County.

Peter is buried at Wenrich's Cemetery in Linglestown, PA.

Frederick Eisenhower (1794 - 1884)

As the youngest of 19 children, Frederick did not likely know his father, who passed while he was a boy. He married Barbara (Raysor) Miller (1789 - 1862) of Elizabethville, the daughter of John and Susanna (Raysor) Miller. The couple initially lived near Linglestown.

The 1820 Census from Lower Paxton Township, Dauphin, County, Pennsylvania, tallied four individuals in the household, including the parents and two daughters under 10.

The couple had six children:
Polly (8/15/1817)
Anna (8/25/1819)
John David (6/23/1821)
Catherine (7/11/1824)
Jacob Frederick (9/19/1826)
Samuel (2/4/1831)

1800 census for Lower Paxton Township

By the 1840 Census, the family had moved to Upper Paxton Township, near Millersburg, west of Elizabethville, Pennsylvania. There were 8 in the household, including the parents, 1 male 5 to 9, 1 male 10 to 14, 1 male 15 to 19, 1 female 15 to 19, 1 female 20 to 29, and additional female between 50 and 59. Given Barbara's roots near Elizabethville, it is likely this move had something to do with her family -- the passing of a brother or brother-in-law or her parents.

The 1850 Census lists Fred and Barbara, Catherine Novinger, aged 4, and Elizabeth Miller, aged 56, who is noted as "insane." The young girl is likely a granddaughter. The insane Elizabeth is likely Barbara's sister. Did Fred and Barbara move to Upper Paxton to care for

1820 census of Lower Paxton

NAMES of HEADS OF FAMILIES.																												
Jacob Keefer		1			1								2		1		1			1								
Frederick Eisenhower	1	1	1		1												1	1		2								

1840 census for Upper Paxton

22			Wm Cramer	16	m			
23	49	49	Jacob Eisenhower	23	m	farmer		500
24			Rebecca	23	f			
25			John H	2	m			
26			Mary Ann	1	f			
27			Jacob Hecht	11	m			
28	50	50	Benjamin Miller	42	m			
29			Mary	32	f			

1850 census for Lower Paxton

their insane sister? Curiously, son Jacob Frederick was living on the Lower Paxton farm at this time, with his wife Rebecca, and three young children.

Jacob Frederick Eisenhower (1826 - 1906)

The young farmer, Jacob Frederick tilled his father's farm in Lower Paxton Township, near Linglestown. His bride, Margareta Rebecca Matter (1825 - 1890) was the daughter of Heinrich Matter and Anna Deitrich of Mifflin Township, Dauphin County, Pennsylvania, near Berrysburg. The couple had 14 children:

John H. (3/7/1848)
Mary Ann (9/2/1849)
Catherine Ann (3/19/1851)
Jacob F. (9/3/1852)
Samuel F. (9/30/1853)
Susanna (10/29/1854)
Peter A. (11/27/1855)
Lydia A. (8/27/1857)
Emma Jane (12/3/1859)
Amanda Hannah (12/11/1861)
David Jacob (9/23/1863)
Abraham Lincoln (7/22/1865)
Clinton (7/30/1867)
Ira A. (7/30/1867)

1860 census for Washington Township

By 1860, the couple, Father Frederick, Aunt Elizabeth, and four children were living in Washington Township, Dauphin County, in Elizabethville, Pennsylvania. Tragically, baby Emma Jane had passed away only the month before the census, which was tallied in June. All of the boys--John, Jacob, Samuel, and Peter had succumbed as well-- all but John as infants. More details about Elizabeth Miller are provided, noting she was "insane caused by fright."

Eisenhower homestead in Elizabethville

In 1870, the family was still living in Washington Township. Mother Barbara had passed, and father Frederick was living elsewhere. He reappears in the 1880 census in Kansas, where the family was to move next.

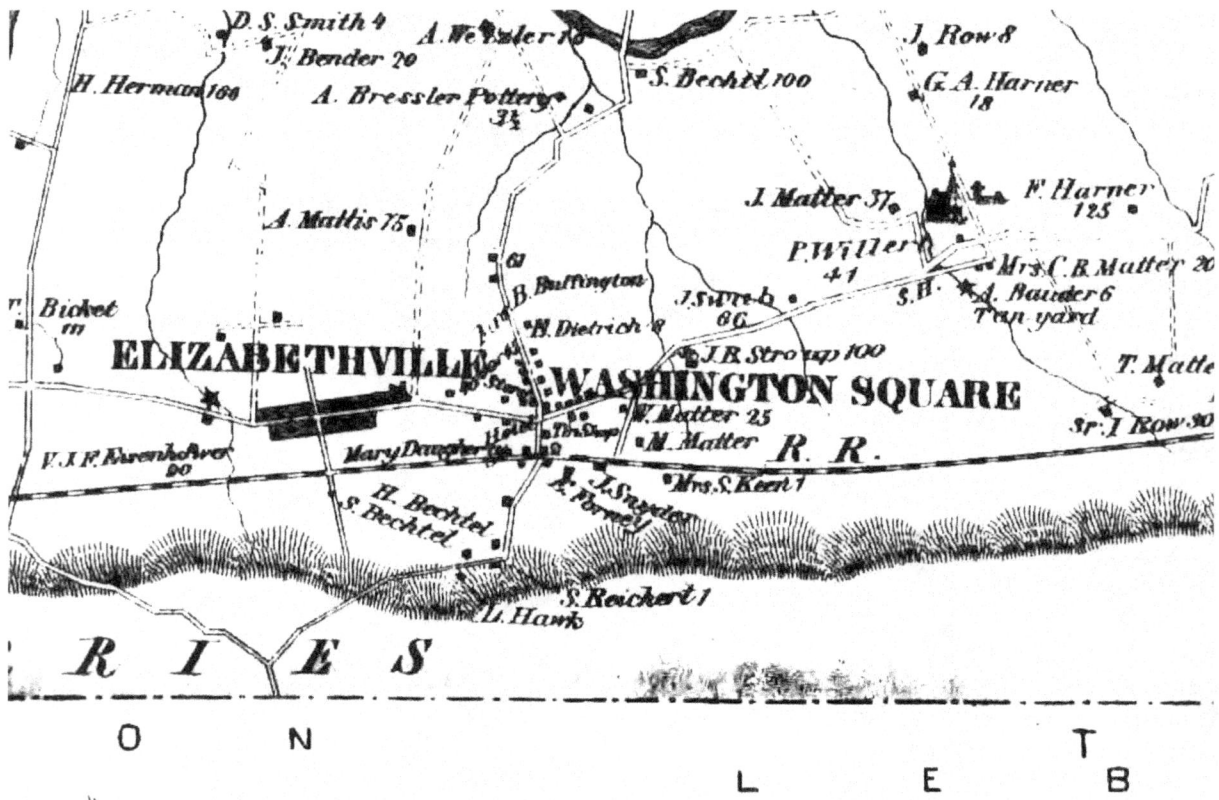

1875 map of Elizabethville area. Eisenhower property is on the bottom left.

The oldest house in Karlsbrunn.

Location of the former Eisenhower tract in the village of Karlsbrunn.

Thus, for over 130 years, the Eisenhower line lived and thrived in Pennsylvania. They survived a shipwreck and hostile natives to establish the lineage for one of our most important Americans, Dwight D. Eisenhower.

On my (the author's) recent trip to Karlsbrunn and Forbach in July of 2015, I was taken by the beauty of the place and its similarity to Pennsylvania. The locals were very proud. Karlsbrunn had recently won an award as one of the loveliest German villages. While little remains of the Eisenhower connection to this village, the citizens are aware of it, and are very proud. But, the real gem is the nearby cemetery at St. Avold, France, also known as the Lorraine American Cemetery. It is the largest cemetery in Europe for US soldiers—even larger than the cemetery at Normandy. It is a grim reminder of the severe cost of war, situated snugly in France, right at the German border – just like the Eisenhowers of old. Is this a coincidence?

Lorraine American Cemetery, Saint Avold, France, minutes from Forbach.

Introduction

Two thousand years from now, when historians look back on the 20th century, they will look upon us not unlike how we study Roman history. It will be apparent that there was an age when the American super power reigned. The great men and women who contirbuted to this nation's history will be reviewed similarly to how we review the lives of Julius Caesar, Cicero, Crassus, Hadrian, Augustus, Marcus Antonius, etc. Among those Americans who will stand out will be Dwight D. Eisenhower - as leader of the D-Day invasion and as a two-term president who led the nation through an era of peace and prosperity.

The late historian Stephen Ambrose opened his biography of Dwight David Eisenhower (1990) by stating that he was "a great and good man". Such accolades are not without merit. If anything, they are understated. Dwight D. Eisenhower was a son, husband, father, athlete, coach, successful military leader, two term president, and grandfather. When reviewing his life, it is hard to fathom that one is reading about the same person and not some amalgamation of distinctly separate lives. In other words, few have had the opportunities, abilities and accomplishments that Eisenhower possessed. He is truly one for the ages.

This book is not an attempt to rehash the history of this great man. This has been done numerous times by more gifted authors. Rather, this book shall serve as a record of the lineage of Dwight Eisenhower as well his relations. While others have documented well "Ike's" ancestors, this book attempts to record the many extended relations of the great general and president. Most specifically, the focus is on the family lines that had some connection to Pennsylvania.

Like many individuals of primarily Pennsylvania German descent, Eisenhower was descended from hardy emigrants who left the Palatinate or other German lands to seek a new life in the American colonies. Most of these settlers came through Philadelphia seeking economic and religious freedom following the difficult 30 Years War. Many of these immigrants to Pennsylvania eventually moved inland into Berks, Lancaster, Dauphin & Lebanon counties. Descendents of these families then spread out across the nation in search of opportunities. Eisenhower's paternal ancestors lived in the Elizabethville, PA area until 11 years before he was born. At that point, they and a number of other families from the area moved to Abilene, Kansas. However, left behind were many of Dwight's close and more distant cousins.

Additionally, the Eisenhower's shared an English ancestor of note who settled in Exeter Township, Berks County, PA. by the name of Boone. A grandson of this line was Daniel Boone, the famous frontiersman. Again, the Boones are an example of Pennsylvania settlers who subseuqently expanded into the wilderness of the south and west, while many Boone's remained in the region.

Eisenhower was always conscience of his Pennsylvania German roots. He corresponded with people in the area concerning his lineage. His return to Pennsylvania was marked by the purchase of a farm in Gettysburg that served as a presidential retreat and is now an historic site. Eisenhower had "Pennsylvania" in his blood. This book is a compilation of those blood relations.

Lawrence Knorr (2005)

Ancestors of Dwight David Eisenhower

Generation No. 1

1. Dwight David Eisenhower, born 14 Oct 1890 in Denison, Grayson, Texas; died 28 Mar 1969 in Washington, District Of, Columbia. He was the son of **2. David Jacob Eisenhauer** and **3. Ida Elizabeth Stover**. He married **(1) Mary Geneva Doud** 01 Jul 1916 in Denver, Denver, Colorado. She was born 14 Nov 1896 in Boone, Boone, Iowa, and died 31 Oct 1979 in Washington, D.C.. She was the daughter of John Sheldon Doud and Elivera Mathilda Carlson.

Notes for Dwight David Eisenhower:

****** 34th President of the United States of America * 1953-1961 ******

NOTE: WEBSITE: Eisenhower Center: http://www.ukans.edu/heritage/abilene/ikectr.html

Born October 14, 1890, at Denison, Texas, third of seven sons of David Jacob and Ida Elizabeth Stover Eisenhower. The family returned to
Abilene, Kansas, in 1892. Graduated from Abilene High School, 1909. Worked at Belle Springs Creamery, 1909-1911. Entered United States Military Academy, West Point, New York, June 14, 1911, and graduated June 12, 1915. Commissioned a Second Lieutenant, September 1915.

Married Mamie Geneva Doud of Denver, Colorado, July 1, 1916. First son, Doud Dwight, born September 24, 1917, and died January 2, 1921 . Second son, John Sheldon Doud, born August 3, 1922. Served with the Infantry September 1915 to February 1918 in Ft. Sam Houston, Camp Wilson and Leon Springs, Texas and Ft. Oglethorpe, Georgia. Served with the Tank Corps, February 1918 to January 1922 in Camp Meade, Maryland, Camp Colt, Pennsylvania, Camp Dix, New Jersey, Ft. Benning, Georgia, and Ft. Meade, Maryland. Promoted to First Lieutenant on July 1, 1916; Captain on May 15, 1917; Major (temporary) on June 17, 1918; and to Lieutenant Colonel (temporary) on October 14, 1918. Reverted to permanent rank of Captain on June 30, 1920 and was promoted to Major on July 2, 1920.

Volunteered to participate as a Tank Corps observer in the First Transcontinental Motor Convoy from July 7, 1919 to September 6, 1919.
Assigned as executive officer to General Fox Conner, Camp Gaillard, Panama Canal Zone, January 1922 to September 1924. Served in various capacities in Maryland and Colorado until August 1925. Entered Command and General Staff School, Ft. Leavenworth, Kansas, August 19, 1925, graduated first in a class of 245, June 18, 1926. Served as battalion commander, 24th Infantry, Ft. Benning, Georgia,
August 1926 to January 1927. Next assigned to American Battle Monuments Commission, directed by General John J. Pershing. January to August 1927 served in W ashington, D.C. office, writing a guidebook to World War I battlefields. In charge of guidebook revision and European office, Paris, France July 1928 to September 1929. August 27, 1927, entered Army War College, Washington, D.C. and graduated
June 30, 1928. Served as executive officer to General George V. Moseley, Assistant Secretary of War, Washington, D.C., November 1929 to February 1933. Served as chief military aide to General Douglas MacArthur, Army Chief of Staff, until September 1935. September 1935 to December 1939 assigned to General MacArthur as assistant military advisor to the Philippine Government. Promoted to Lieutenant Colonel, July 1, 1936. Assigned to General DeWitt Clinto n, Commander, 15th Infantry, for a short term in Ft. Ord, California, and then permanently to Ft. Lewis, Washington as regimental executive, February 1940 to November 1940. Chief of Staff for General Thompson, Commander, 3rd Division, Ft. Lewis until March 1941. Served as Chief of Staff to General Kenyon Joyce, Commander 9th Army Corps, Ft. Lewis, until June 1941. Designated Chief of Staff to General Walter Kreuger, Commander 3rd Army, Ft. Sam Houston, Texas, June
1941 to December 1941. Promoted to Colonel (temporary), March 11, 1941, and to Brigadier General (temporary), September 29, 1941.

Assigned to General Staff, Washington, D.C., December 1941 to June 1942. Named Deputy Chief in charge of Pacific Defenses under Chief of War Plans Division, General Leonard Gerow, December 1941. Designated as

Chief of War Plans Division, February 1942. In April 1942, appointed Assistant Chief of Staff in charge of Operations Division for General George Marshall, Chief of Staff. March 27, 1942, promoted to Major General (temporary).

Conducted mission to increase cooperation among World War II allies, London, England, May 1942. Designated Commanding General, European Theater, London, England, June 1942. Named Commander- in-Chief, Allied Forces, North Africa, November 1942. Promoted to Lieutenant General (temporary), July 7, 1942 and to General (4 stars) (temporary), February 11, 1943. He was appointed Brigader General (permanent) on August 30, 1943 and was promoted to Major General (permanent) on the same date.

Appointed Supreme Commander, Allied Expeditionary Forces, December 1943. Commanded forces of Normandy invasion, June 6, 1944. December 20, 1944, promoted to General of the Army (5 stars). Shortly after the German surrender, May 8, 1945, appointed Military Govemor, U.S. Occupied Zone, Frankfurt, Germany. On April 11, 1946, wartime rank of General of the Army converted to permanent rank.

Designated as Chief of Staff, U.S. Army, November 19, 1945. Inaugurated as President, Columbia University, New York City, June 7, 1948. Named Supreme Allied Commander, North Atlantic Treaty Organization, Europe, and given operational command of Treaty Organization, Europe and given operational command of U.S. Forces, Europe, December 16, 1950. Retired from active service, May 31, 1952 and resigned his commission July 1952.

Announced his candidacy for the Republican Party nomination for President on June 4, 1952 in Abilene. Was nominated at the Republican convention and elected on November 4, 1952.

Served two terms as President of the United States, January 20, 1953 to January 20, 1961. Saw end of Korean War, promoted Atoms for Peace, and dealt with crises in Lebanon, Suez, Berlin , and Hungary in foreign affairs. Saw Alaska and Hawaii become states. Was concerned with civil rights issues and the interstate highway system in domestic affairs.

In March 1961, by Public Law 87-3, signed by President John F. Kennedy, returned to active list of regular Army with rank of General of the Army from December 1944. Maintained office at Gettysburg College and residence at his farm near Gettysburg, PA, January 1961-March 1969.

General Dwight D. Eisenhower died on March 28, 1969 at Walter Reed Army Hospital in Washingto n, D.C. He was buried in the Place of Meditation at the Eisenhower Center, Abilene, Kansas on April 2, 1969.

Eisenhower, Dwight D
  Age: 39 Year: 1930
  Birthplace: Texas Roll: T626_297
  Race: White Page: 1B

  State: District of Columbia ED: 195
  County: Washington Image: 0534
  Township: Washington

Born David Dwight Eisenhower. Most entries have Dwight David Eisenhower. He changed it at West Point.

======
Located across from the Eisenhower Home is the final resting place of Dwight D. Eisenhower, 34th President of the United States. In November 1979 Mamie Doud Eisenhower was interred in the building. The Eisenhower's first born son, Doud Dwight was interred in 1966. The Place of Meditation was built with private funds under the auspices of the Eisenhower Presidential L ibrary Commission.

Other outstanding elements of the interior design of the building are the richly colored windows, the Travertine marble wall panels, the walnut woodwork, and the large embroidered hanging, which carries the words of the prayer that President Eisenhower wrote for his first Inaugural Address, on January 20, 1953. There is a meditation portion of the building where, according to General Eisenhower's wishes, it was hoped that visitors would reflect upon the ideals that made this a great nation and pledge themselves again to continued loyalty to those ideals.

Casket - $80 government issue requested by Eisenhower the only difference between his casket and those furnished for any soldier buried by the Army is an inner glass seal that cost an extra $115. It was lined with tailored eggshell crepe. Vault - bronze and cement both DDE and MDE graves are covered with a marble slab Markers - 11 3/4" x 8" x 3/4" bronze Marker Inscriptions:

DWIGHT D. EISENHOWER
BORN OCTOBER 14, 1890
DIED MARCH 28, 1969

DOUD DWIGHT EISENHOWER
BORN SEPTEMBER 24, 1917
DIED JANUARY 2, 1921

MAMIE DOUD EISENHOWER
BORN NOVEMBER 14, 1896
DIED NOVEMBER 1, 1979

General Dwight D. Eisenhower was buried in his World War II uniform. It consists of "pink" trousers and the green "IKE" jacket that he made famous. Although he was one of the most decorated military men in history, his uniform had only the following medals: Army Distinguished Service Medal with three oak leaf clusters, Navy Distinguished Service Medal, and the Legion of Merit.

There were four gun salutes during the Eisenhower funeral ceremonies.

1. When the body was taken to the Capitol, a saluting battery (1 officer and 13 enlisted me) fired a 21 gun salute at 5 second intervals.
2. When the body arrived at Union Station, saluting battery (1 officer, 13 enlisted men) fired a 21 gun salute beginning when the hearse entered Delaware Avenue with the last shot fire d as hearse stopped at entrance at Union Station.
3. Before benediction in Place of Meditation, six howitzers manned by 2 officers and 36 enlisted men delivered a 21 gun salute.
4. After benediction, a firing party (8 members) discharged three volleys.

Honorary Pall Bearers
Washington, DC

General Omar Bradley
Admiral Arthur Radford
General Lauris Norstad
Edgar Eisenhower
Milton Eisenhower
General J. Lawton Collins
General Wade H. Haislip
General Alfred M. Gruenther
M/Sgt. John Moaney
Col. G. Gordon Moore

Honorary Pall Bearers
Abilene, Kansas

Edgar Eisenhower
Milton Eisenhower*
General Omar Bradley
General J. Lawton Collins
General Lauris Norstad

General Wade H. Haislip
General Alfred M. Gruenther
General Leonard Heaton
Admiral George W. Anderson
Admiral Lewis Strauss
Col. G. Gordon Moore
M/Sgt. John Moaney

*Milton Eisenhower became ill and was hospitalized. General Andrew Goodpaster substituted for him as an honorary pall bearer.

Special Honor Guard in Abilene

Major General Linton S. Boatwright, Commanding General of the 24th Infantry Division, Fort Ri ley, Kansas
Major General B. G. Owens, , Assistant Chief of Staff United States Marine Corps
Major General J. T. Robbins, Commanding General of the Twelfth Air Force, Austin, Texas
Rear Admiral H. A. Renken, Commandant of the Ninth Naval District, Cleveland, Ohio
Rear Admiral R. R. Waesche, Commander of the Second Coast Guard District, St. Louis, Missouri

Notes for Mary Geneva Doud:
http://history.cc.ukans.edu/heritage/abilene/ikedoud.html

Mamie Doud Eisenhower

Mamie Geneva Doud was born in Boone, Iowa, on November 14, 1896, the daughter of John Sheldon and Elivera Mathilda Carlson Doud. When Mamie was nine months old, in August 1897, the family moved to Cedar Rapids, Iowa. At age six, she moved with her family to Pueblo, Colorado, an d then to Colorado Springs. They lived in each of these places only a short time, and in 1905 moved to Denver. The house at 750 Lafayette remained in the family until after the death of Mamie's mother in 1960.

Mamie Doud attended Denver public schools and Miss Wolcott's, a private finishing school attended by daughters of many prominent Denver families. Mamie met the then Second Lieutenant Dwight D. Eisenhower in October, 1915 while visiting friends at Fort Sam Houston, in Texas. The Douds had rented a house in San Antonio for the winter. The young officer, just out of West Point, courted Miss Doud and on February 14, 1916, they formally announced their engagement. The engagement ring was a miniature copy of Ike's West Point ring, amethyst set in gold.

Dwight D. Eisenhower and Mamie Doud were married at noon on July 1, 1916, in the Doud family home in Denver--the same day Ike received his first army promotion. They had a ten-day honeymoon, spending the first days in Colorado, then a few days visiting the Eisenhower family in Abilene, Kansas.

The newlyweds established their first home in Ike's two-room bachelor quarters at Fort Sam Houston. The First Lieutenant's pay was $161.67 per month. They had only an improvised kitchen , consisting of a hot plate, percolator, chafing dish, etc.--appliances that could be hidden away behind curtains and in closets. Mrs. Eisenhower admitted that at the time she was married she could make only fudge and mayonnaise, and that Ike taught her to cook.

Two sons were born to the Eisenhowers. The first, Doud Dwight Eisenhower, was born on September 24, 1917. "Little Icky", as he was nicknamed, died of scarlet fever on January 2, 1921. The second son, John Sheldon Doud Eisenhower, was born in Denver on August 3, 1922. On July 10 , 1947, he married Barbara Jean Thompson. They had four children: Dwight David Eisenhower II , born March 31, 1948; Barbara Anne, born May 30, 1949; Susan Elaine, born December 31, 1951 ; and Mary Jean, born December 21, 1955. There are eight Eisenhower great-grandchildren.

General and Mrs. Eisenhower lived in various army posts in the United States and around the world. From their small quarters at Fort Sam Houston, they moved to their first real home--a white pillared fraternity house at

Gettysburg, Pennsylvania, where Ike commanded the Tank Corps Training Center at Camp Colt. After Camp Colt they were transferred to Camp Meade, Maryland , and then to Camp Gaillard in the Panama Canal Zone.

In 1924, they returned to Camp Meade, and then to Fort Logan, Colorado. Eisenhower then received an appointment to the Command and General Staff School at Fort Leavenworth, Kansas, from which he graduated first in his class, in 1926. After Fort Leavenworth, they spent a few months at Fort Benning, Georgia, before Ike was named to serve with the American Battle Monumen ts Commission. With this new assignment, they took an apartment in Washington, D.C., where Mamie remained until 1936, except for a short stay in Paris.

When Ike was transferred to the Philippines in 1935, Mamie elected to remain with son John in the United States for a year before joining Ike in Manila. They returned to the U.S. in 1941. When the Pearl Harbor attack occurred, Ike was Chief of Staff of the Third Army at Fort Sam Houston in San Antonio, Texas. He was called to Washington immediately and Mrs. Eisenhower established living quarters at the Wardman Park Hotel, where she lived almost continuously throughout the war and General Eisenhower's service overseas. During the General's absence , Mamie shunned publicity and the social whirl by doing volunteer work at servicemen's canteens in Washington and for the Red Cross.

When the General served as Army Chief of Staff, 1946-48, they resided in Quarters Number 1 on Fort Myer in the Washington area. The next major move was to 60 Morningside Drive in New York City where they lived from 1948 to 1950 while Ike was president of Columbia University. In 1950 the General was recalled to active duty to serve as head of the NATO military forces as Supreme Allied Commander, Europe. They lived in Paris until 1952 when Eisenhower returned to the U.S. to campaign for the presidency. Mamie was a gracious and popular First Lady--so much so that, beginning in 1952, she appeared every year on the Gallup Poll's list of the Ten Most Admired Women in America.

After eight years in the White House, 1953-1961, the Eisenhowers retired to the farm they had purchased in 1949. This home at Gettysburg, Pennsylvania, was the first one they actually owned. After the General's death, Mamie continued living on the farm, with extended winter vacations in California and Georgia, until she took an apartment in Washington, D.C. when her health began to fail in the late 70's.

Although she lived and traveled all over the world, Mrs. Eisenhower always remained a person who was most happy at home surrounded by her family. She enjoyed babysitting her grandchildren. Playing canasta, mahjong, or bridge with her friends was a favorite pastime. She had a lifelong interest in fashion and developed a flair that was strictly the "Mamie Look"--from her feminine dresses to her trademark bangs. In her later years, Mrs. Eisenhower enjoyed answering the many letters she received from the public and assisted in fund-raising activities for several institutions and charities, including the Eisenhower Memorial Hospital in Palm Springs, California.

Mrs. Mamie Doud Eisenhower died on November 1, 1979, in Washington, D.C. and was buried beside her husband and first son in the Place of Meditation at the Eisenhower Center in Abilene, K ansas.

Marriage Notes for Dwight Eisenhower and Mary Doud:

_UID4AB4111EA0010549ACBCD687EEA2BF83B3B8

Generation No. 2

   2. David Jacob Eisenhauer, born 23 Sep 1863 in Elizabethville, Dauphin, Pennsylvania; died 10 Mar 1942 in Abilene, Dickinson, Kansas. He was the son of **4. Jacob Frederick Eisenhauer** and **5. Margareta Rebecca Matter**. He married **3. Ida Elizabeth Stover** 23 Sep 1885 in Hope, Dickinson, Kansas.
   3. Ida Elizabeth Stover, born 01 May 1862 in Mt. Sidney, VA; died 11 Sep 1946 in Abilene, Dickinson Co , Kansas. She was the daughter of **6. Simon P Stover** and **7. Elizabeth Ida Link**.

Notes for David Jacob Eisenhauer:
From Eisenhower Birthplace site:
http://www.eisenhowerbirthplace.org/family.htm

Progenitors of both David J. and Ida Elizabeth Eisenhower landed in America just before the middle of the 18th century. the Eisenhower name was originally spelled "Eisenhauer" and the Stover name "Stoever." The Eisenhowers settled in Pennsylvania, and the Stovers in Virginia.

David J. Eisenhower went to Kansas in 1878 with his father, grandfather and other members of the family, and Ida Elizabeth Stover went to Kansas to join her brother about the year 1883 . They met at Lane University in Lecompton, Kansas, a school which has since disappeared.

(2) 1.10 David Jacob 90 EISENHOWER
Birth Date: 23 Sep 1863
Birth Place: Elizabethville, Pennsylvania
Death Date: 16 Mar 1942
Death Place: Abilene Cem. , Dickinson Co. Kan.
Occupation: Machinist, Farmer, Merchant
Religion: River Bretheren Church

Notes:
Leader with his father in the River Breathern church settlement near Abilene, Kansas. Upon his marriage in 1885, was co-partner in a general merchandise store in Hope, Kansas. The store failed in the drought and hard times of 1888 and he moved his family to Denison, Texas to work in the Cotton Belt Railroad repair shop. His third son, Dwight David, was born there in 1890. In 1892, he moved his family back to Abilene to work in the Belle Springs Creamery as a maintainance man..

Research:
Sarah A Wetzel, grand-daughter of David Jacob stated that Jacob Frederick gave each of his sons, a bible, 160 Acres of land and a gift of $2000 to get started in life. David Jacob declined the land but took the cash and the bible as he could not abide farming for a living.

Notes for Ida Elizabeth Stover:
Spouse: Ida Elizabeth Stover
Birth Date: 1 May 1862
Birth Place: Mount Sidney, Virginia (near Staunton, VA)
aka Place: d/o Simon Stover & Elizabeth Link
Death Date: 11 Sep 1946
Burial Place: Both buried in Abilene Cem. Dickinnson Co. Kans.
Religion: Evangical Lutherans
Spouse Father: Simon P. Stover (1822-1873)
Spouse Mother: Elizabeth Ida (Juda) Line (1822-1867)

Spouse Notes:
The name was originally spellled Stauffer. The Stauffers owe their origin to a generation of knights called Stauffacher at Hohenstauffer before the year A.D. 1000, of Alsatian ancestry. The last of the house, Conrad, was beheaded on 29 Nov 1268. Ida is descended of Swiss immigrants who settled in the Shenandoah Valley of Virginia, mid 18th century. She and her two brothers moved to Dickinson County Kansas four years after her future husband (1883) to live with relatives.

Ida Elizabeth was the daughter of Simon P. and Elizabeth Ida (Juda) Line Stover.

Marriage Date: 23 Sep 1885
Marriage Place: Lane University, Lecompton, Kansas

Children: Arthur Bradford 1892
Edgar Newton 1893
Dwight David "Ike" 1894
Roy Jacob 1895
Paul Dawson A.

Earl Dewey 1896
Milton Stover 1897

Marriage Notes for David Eisenhauer and Ida Stover:

_UIDDA06C04DE9DDAC43A2915B8105B4AB596E6E

Children of David Eisenhauer and Ida Stover are:
- i. Arthur Bradford Eisenhower, born 11 Nov 1886 in Hope, Dickinson, Kansas; died 26 Jan 1958; married (1) Alida B ?; born 17 Feb 1889; married (2) Louis Sondra Grieb 03 Sep 1926.

  Notes for Arthur Bradford Eisenhower:

  Occupation: Banker[JJMiller.ged]

  Ancestral File Number:<AFN> 1GD8-MTR

- ii. Edgar Newton Eisenhower, born 19 Jan 1889 in Hope, Dickinson, Kansas; died 12 Jul 1971 in Tacoma, Pierce, Washington.

  Notes for Edgar Newton Eisenhower:

  Ancestral File Number:<AFN> 1GD8-MV0

1 iii. Dwight David Eisenhower, born 14 Oct 1890 in Denison, Grayson, Texas; died 28 Mar 1969 in Washington, District Of, Columbia; married Mary Geneva Doud 01 Jul 1916 in Denver, Denver, Colorado.
- iv. Roy Jacob Eisenhower, born 09 Aug 1892 in Abilene, Kansas, Kansas; died 17 Jun 1942; married Edna Alice Shade 18 Nov 1917 in Ellsworth, Ellsworth, Kansas; born 13 Sep 1891 in Ellis City, Ellis, Kansas; died 26 Jun 1989 in Denver, Denver, Colorado.

  Notes for Roy Jacob Eisenhower:

  Occupation: Pharmacist[JJMiller.ged]

  Ancestral File Number:<AFN> 1GD8-MW6

- v. Paul Dawson A. Eisenhower, born 12 May 1894 in Abilene, Dickinson, Kansas; died 16 Mar 1895.

  Notes for Paul Dawson A. Eisenhower:

  Ancestral File Number:<AFN> 1NPV-JT3

- vi. Earl Dewey Eisenhower, born 01 Feb 1898 in Abilene, Dickinson, Kansas; died 18 Dec 1968 in Scottsdale, Maricopa, Arizona; married Kathryn McIntyre Snyder 29 Apr 1933 in Connellsville, Pennsylvania; born 15 Aug 1909 in Charleroi, Washington, Pennsylvania; died Sep 1986 in Scottsdale, Maricopa, Arizona.

  Notes for Earl Dewey Eisenhower:

  Ancestral File Number:<AFN> 1GD8-MXD

- vii. Milton Stover Eisenhower, born 15 Sep 1899 in Abilene, Dickinson, Kansas; died 02 May 1985 in Baltimore, Maryland; married Helen Elsie Eakin 12 Oct 1927 in Washington, District Of, Columbia; born 14 Aug 1904 in Manhattan, Riley, Kansas; died 10 Jul 1954.

  Notes for Milton Stover Eisenhower:

Generation No. 3

4. Jacob Frederick Eisenhauer, born 19 Sep 1826 in Elizabethville, Washington Twp., Dauphin Co., PA; died 20 May 1906 in Abilene, Dickinson Co , Kansas. He was the son of **8. Frederick Eisenhauer** and **9. Barbara Miller**. He married **5. Margareta Rebecca Matter** 25 Feb 1847 in Dauphin , Pennsylvania.

5. Margareta Rebecca Matter, born 18 Mar 1825 in Mifflin Twp, Dauphin, PA; died 22 Jun 1890 in Abilene, Dickinson Co , Kansas. She was the daughter of **10. Heinrich Matter** and **11. Anna Marie Deitrich**.

Notes for Jacob Frederick Eisenhauer:
(1) 1. Jacob Frederick 40 EISENHOWER ,16 (Eisenhauer)

Birth Date: 19 Sep 1826
Birth Place: Elizabethville, Dauphine Co. Pennsylvania
aka Place: Moved To Kansas 1879
Death Date: 20 May 1906
Death Place: Both buried in Belle Springs River Brethern Cem.
Burial Place: 12 Miles South of Abilene, Dickinson Co. Kan.
Occupation: Preacher, Farmer
Religion: Bretheren In Christ, Not Aka Dunkards

Born Eisenhauer. In the 1850 Lower Paxton Twp., Dauphin Co. Census, he was listed as John Frederick Isenhour. Hereafter the spelling is Eisenhower. In 1854, he built a 9-room brick house at # 530 West Main Street, Elizabethville. It was insured against fire with Lykens Vally Mutual Fire Ins. Co. which is still in business at # 8 West Main Street. He, like most Eisenhauers of the day were Lutheran but he changed to the Church of the Brethern in Christ, the Faith of his wife when they married and became very active in its activities. He and his father moved to Dickinson County, Kansas, in 1879, where they became leaders in the River Brethern Settlement, a Mennonite Sect, near Abilene, Kansas. This denomination was formed in Pennsylvania in 1770 among Swiss immigrants who lived along the Sesquehanna River. All of his children were born in Elizabethville. Grand-father of D. D. Eisenhower.

Notes for Margareta Rebecca Matter:
Spouse: Margareta Rebecca E. 'Margaret' Matter
Birth Date: 18 Mar 1825
Birth Place: Elizabethville, Mifflin Twp. Dauphine Co. Penn
Death Date: 22 Jun 1890
Death Place: Abilene, Kan.
Burial Place: Belle Springs River Brethern Cem.
Religion: Brethern In Christ
Spouse Father: Henrick (Henry) Matter (1796-1868)
Spouse Mother: Anna Mary "Polly" Dietrich (1803-1865)

Spouse Notes:
Margareta Rebecca Matter was the 3rd daughter of Henry Matter b. 26 Dec 1796 and d. 01 Oct 1868, [b/d in Dauphin Co. Penn.] and Anna Mary "Polly"Dietrich, b. 1803.

Baptized May 29, 1825, in St. John's Lutheran Church, Berrysburg, Mifflin Twp., Dauphin Co., PA. Buried in the River Brethern Cemetery, Belle Springs, Dickenson Co., KS. Source: Roger Cramer.

Ancestral File Number:<AFN> LMGK-6Q

Marriage Notes for Jacob Eisenhauer and Margareta Matter:

Children of Jacob Eisenhauer and Margareta Matter are:

    i.   John H. Eisenhauer, born 07 Mar 1848 in Elizabethville, Dauphin Co, PA; died 10 Apr 1857 in Elizabethville, Dauphin Co, PA.

    ii.   Mary Ann Eisenhauer, born 02 Sep 1849 in Elizabethville, Dauphin, Pennsylvania; died 27 Apr 1893 in Abilene, Dickinson, Kansas; married John J Witter; born Jul 1840 in Prussia; died 1918 in Abilene, Dickinson Co, KS.

Notes for Mary Ann Eisenhauer:

IGI - Death: 1893

    iii.   Catherine Ann Eisenhauer, born 19 Mar 1851 in Elizabethville, Dauphin, Pennsylvania; died 03 Apr 1924 in Ramona, Marion, Kansas; married Samuel B. Haldeman; born 11 Jan 1846 in Bainsbridge, PA; died 21 Oct 1928 in Abilene, Dickinson Co, KS.

    iv.   Jacob F. Eisenhauer, born 03 Sep 1852 in Elizabethville, Dauphin Co, PA; died 02 Oct 1852 in Elizabethville, Dauphin Co, PA.

    v.   Samuel F. Eisenhauer, born 30 Sep 1853 in Elizabethville, Dauphin Co, PA; died 11 Jun 1854 in Elizabethville, Dauphin Co, PA.

    vi.   Susanna Eisenhauer, born 29 Oct 1854 in Elizabethville, Dauphin, Pennsylvania; died 14 Jun 1932 in York, PA; married Aaron Wetzel; born 1849; died 03 Jul 1947 in York, PA.

Notes for Susanna Eisenhauer:

    vii.   Peter A. Eisenhauer, born 27 Nov 1855 in Elizabethville, Dauphin Co, PA; died 04 Aug 1856 in Elizabethville, Dauphin Co, PA.

    viii.   Lydia A. Eisenhauer, born 27 Aug 1857 in Elizabethville, Dauphin Co, PA; died 15 Nov 1874 in Elizabethville, Dauphin Co, PA.

    ix.   Emma Jane Eisenhauer, born 03 Dec 1859 in Elizabethville, Dauphin Co, PA; died 08 May 1860 in Elizabethville, Dauphin Co, PA.

    x.   Amanda Hannah Eisenhauer, born 11 Dec 1861 in Elizabethville, Dauphin Co, PA; died 25 Aug 1951 in Abilene, Dickinson Co, KS; married Christian O Musser; born 10 Nov 1863 in Mt. Joy, PA; died 14 Apr 1950 in Abilene, Dickinson Co, KS.

Notes for Amanda Hannah Eisenhauer:

Ancestral File Number:<AFN> 1WCZ-LFS

2   xi.   David Jacob Eisenhauer, born 23 Sep 1863 in Elizabethville, Dauphin, Pennsylvania; died 10 Mar 1942 in Abilene, Dickinson, Kansas; married Ida Elizabeth Stover 23 Sep 1885 in Hope, Dickinson, Kansas.

    xii.   Dr Abraham Lincoln Eisenhauer, born 22 Jul 1865 in Elizabethville, Dauphin Co, PA; died 23 Dec 1944 in Upland, CA; married Anna Long 1886; born 1865.

Notes for Dr Abraham Lincoln Eisenhauer:
1900 United States Federal Census about Abraham L Eisenhower
Name: Abraham L Eisenhower
[Abraham Elsenhowen]
Home in 1900: Deer Creek, Custer, Oklahoma
Age:34
Birth Date: Jul 1865
Birthplace: Pennsylvania
Race: White
Gender: Male
Relationship to Head of House:Head
Father's Birthplace: Pennsylvania
Mother's Birthplace:Pennsylvania
Spouse's name: Anna D

Marriage Year: 1886
Marital Status: Married
Years Married: 14
Residence : Deer Creek Township, Custer, Oklahoma Territory
Occupation: View on Image
Neighbors: View others on page
Household Members:
Name Age
Abraham L Eisenhower 34
Anna D Eisenhower 35

California Death Index, 1940-1997 about Abraham L Eisenhower
Name: Abraham L Eisenhower
Social Security #: 0
Sex: MALE
Birth Date: 22 Jul 1865
Birthplace: Pennsylvania
Death Date: 13 Dec 1944
Death Place: San Bernardino
Mother's Maiden Name: Kefauver
Father's Surname: Eisenhower

  xiii.   Clinton Eisenhauer, born 30 Jul 1867 in Elizabethville, Dauphin Co, PA; died 10 Aug 1867 in
           Elizabethville, Dauphin Co, PA.
  xiv.   Ira A Eisenhower, born 30 Jul 1867 in Elizabethville, Dauphin, Pa; died 28 Mar 1943 in Los Angeles,
           CA; married Katherine E Dayhoff 08 Sep 1885 in Abilene, KS; born 02 Sep 1865 in PA; died 30 Dec
           1930 in Shawnee Co, KS.

           Notes for Ira A Eisenhower:
           Ancestral File Number:<AFN> 1WCZ-LH7

   6. Simon P Stover, born 28 Sep 1822 in Augusta Co, VA; died 11 Dec 1873 in Augusta Co, VA. He was
the son of **12. Daniel Stover** and **13. Mary Hannah.** He married **7. Elizabeth Ida Link** 31 Dec 1848 in
Augusta Co, VA.
   7. Elizabeth Ida Link, born 19 Nov 1822 in Augusta Co, VA; died 28 Mar 1867 in Augusta Co, VA.

Notes for Simon P Stover:
S. P. was born 28 Sept 1822 in Augusta Co. Va. and died 11 Dec 1873.

Notes for Elizabeth Ida Link:
(6)Elizabeth Link was the daughter of William & Ester Charlotte Schindler Link and granddaughter of Adam
Schindler. (5) Wm. Linc descended from (4)Peter and Judith Burkett(Burkhardt) Linc;

(3)John Matthias Link, b. 11 Feb c1736, Berks Co. Penn., d. 08 Feb 1915, Augusta Co. Va. married to Anna
Mary Christina Schmit.

(2.) Johann Jacob Link, b. 20 Oct 1682, Grossgartach, Germany and died April 1738, Berks Co. Penn , s/o (1)
Hans Bernhard Linckh, b. c1647, Grossgartach, Germany, d. c1708, Germany & Anna Catharine Schummann .
Johann J. Link was married to Anna Maria Magdalena Neuwirth, d/o Jeremias & Margareta Christ Neuwieth.

Mt. Sidney, VA

Child of Simon Stover and Elizabeth Link is:
      3   i.   Ida Elizabeth Stover, born 01 May 1862 in Mt. Sidney, VA; died 11 Sep 1946 in Abilene, Dickinson
                       Co , Kansas; married David Jacob Eisenhauer 23 Sep 1885 in Hope, Dickinson, Kansas.

Generation No. 4

8. Frederick Eisenhauer, born 15 Jul 1794 in Linglestown, Dauphin, Pennsylvania; died 13 Mar 1884 in Belle Springs, Dickinson, Kansas. He was the son of **16. Hans Peter Eisenhauer** and **17. Anna Margaret Dissinger**. He married **9. Barbara Miller** 1816 in Linglestown, Dauphin, Pa.

9. Barbara Miller, born 27 May 1789 in Elizabethville, Dauphin, Pa; died 01 Jan 1862 in Millersburg, Dauphin, Pa. She was the daughter of **18. John Miller** and **19. Susanna Raysor**.

Notes for Frederick Eisenhauer:
(1) 1. Fredrick 16 EISENHOWER , 02 Eisenhauer

Birth Date: 15 Jul 1794
Birth Place: Linglestown, Dauphin Co. Penn.
Death Date: 13 Mar 1884
Death Place: at Jacob Frederick's home, one mile north of the cemetery.
Burial Place: Belle Springs River Brothern Cem. 12 miles south of Abilene
Occupation: Farmer and weaver of bed spreads
Religion: Converted to wife's Church, a Mennonite Sect.

Change of spelling from Eisenhauer (Isenhour) to Eisenhower occured with this generation and is mostly confined to the decendents of this family group. Frederick 's father was 78 years old at the time he was born. he is the Great-grand-father of D. D. Eisenhower.
In the 1820 and 1830 Census, he lived in Lower Paxton Twp, Dauphin Co. Penn. He had moved to Upper Paxton Twp by 1840. In the 1850 Upper Paxton Twp. Census, page #444, his granddaughter Catherine NOVINGER and Elizabeth MILLER (Barbara's sister?) were living with Frederick and his wife. In 1860, at age 66, he were living with son, Jacob Frederick, in Washington Twp near Elizabethville, Dauphin Co.
In 1878, he moved with Jacob and Samuel to Hope, Dickerson Co. Kansas. Catherine and Samuel Pike (Pyke) followed shortly and also bought land near Abilene.

In 1878-1879 a colony of several hundred (Susquehanna River Brethren from Pennsylvania}arrived in the old time corrupt cow town of Abilene, Kan. They brought with them fifteen carloads of household and farming equipment, and more than a half-million dollars in cash. With this stuff they at once began to organize homes and fields on virgin land purchased from the Kansas Pacific Railroad.
The old railhead cow towns of Kansas rapidly died away as railroads extented west and south to where the cattle were raised and civilizaion rapidly erased that era of history.

Notes for Barbara Miller:

Ancestral File Number:<AFN> LMGK-83Spouse: Barbara Miller
Birth Date: 27 May 1789
Birth Place: Elizabethville, Dauphin Co.Penn.
aka Place: d/o John & Susanna Rayson Miller
Death Date: 1 Jan 1862
Death Place: Millersburg, Dauphin Co. Penn.
Burial Place:

Spouse Notes:
Daughter of John Miller and Susan Raysor. [Originally Millerin]. Mrs. Richardson's book has her burial in the Keefer Cemetery near the Free Grace Bretheran Church which is half-way between Millersburg and Elizabettville, Dauphin Co., Penn.
She stated to her daugher, that the Eisenhauer family lived near the borderline of France and some came from Alsace, France. Also, that a number of the family went to Canada to live. She also noted the story from her mother Susanna Miller, about British soldiers breaking into their home and running sabres thru the feather beds looking for hiding American soldiers during the Rev. War. She also noted that the family was related to Gen. Winfield Scott who became commander of the American Forces in the Mexican-American War.

Marriage Date: 1816

Marriage Place: Linglestown, Dauphin Co. Penn.

Children: Polly 37
Anna 38
John David
Catherine 39
Jacob Frederick 40
Samuel Peter 41

Marriage Notes for Frederick Eisenhauer and Barbara Miller:

_UID23AD096C8B01B447A011C0FAF9CA8DE66D7E

Children of Frederick Eisenhauer and Barbara Miller are:

    i.   Polly Eisenhauer, born 13 Aug 1817 in Elizabethville, Dauphin, Pennsylvania; died 09 Dec 1863; married Benjamin Miller.

        Notes for Polly Eisenhauer:

        Ancestral File Number:<AFN> 1WCZ-K9S

    ii.   Anna Eisenhauer, born 25 Aug 1819 in Elizabethville, Dauphin, Pennsylvania; died 26 Dec 1849 in Elizabethville, Dauphin, Pennsylvania; married Joseph Novinger 1839 in ,Dauphin , Pennsylvania; born 08 Feb 1810 in Upper Paxton Twp, Dauphin Co, PA.

        Notes for Anna Eisenhauer:

        Ancestral File Number:<AFN> 2160-T9W

        Notes for Joseph Novinger:

    iii.   John David Eisenhauer, born 23 Jun 1821 in Elizabethville, Dauphin, Pennsylvania; died 13 Dec 1840 in Dauphin Co, PA.

        Notes for John David Eisenhauer:

        Ancestral File Number:<AFN> 2160-TB4

    iv.   Catherine Eisenhower, born 11 Jul 1824 in Elizabethville, Dauphin Co, PA; died 07 Nov 1907 in Abilene, Dickinson, Kansas; married Samuel Pyke 30 Mar 1848 in Pennsylvania; born 06 Apr 1825 in York, PA; died 26 May 1887 in Abilene, Dickinson Co, KS.

        Notes for Catherine Eisenhower:

        Ancestral File Number:<AFN> 2160-QCS

        Notes for Samuel Pyke:

4   v.   Jacob Frederick Eisenhauer, born 19 Sep 1826 in Elizabethville, Washington Twp., Dauphin Co., PA; died 20 May 1906 in Abilene, Dickinson Co , Kansas; married Margareta Rebecca Matter 25 Feb 1847

in Dauphin , Pennsylvania.

vi. Samuel P Eisenhower, born 04 Feb 1831 in Elizabethville, Dauphin, Pennsylvania; married (1) Lydia Orndorff; married (2) Mary Ann Orndorff 21 Oct 1855 in ,,Pennsylvania; born 1839; died 1932.

Notes for Samuel P Eisenhower:
1900 United States Federal Census about Samuel P Eisenhower
Name: Samuel P Eisenhower
Home in 1900: Ridge, Dickinson, Kansas
Age:69
Birth Date: Feb 1831
Birthplace: Pennsylvania
Race: White
Gender: Male
Relationship to Head of House:Head
Father's Birthplace: Pennsylvania
Mother's Birthplace:Pennsylvania
Spouse's name: Liddian
Marriage Year:1855
Marital Status: Married
Years Married: 45
Residence : Ridge & Union Townships, Dickinson, Kansas
Occupation: View on Image
Neighbors:View others on page
Household Members:
Name Age
Samuel P Eisenhower69
Liddian Eisenhower 61
James M Eisenhower 21

10. Heinrich Matter, born 26 Dec 1796 in Elizabethville, PA; died 01 Oct 1868 in Lykens, PA. He was the son of **20. John Michael Matter** and **21. Anna Maria Romberger**. He married **11. Anna Marie Deitrich** in PA.

11. Anna Marie Deitrich, born 15 Mar 1803 in Lykens, Dauphin, PA; died 11 Nov 1865 in Lykens, Dauphin, PA. She was the daughter of **22. Jacob Deitrich**.

Notes for Heinrich Matter:
(6) Henrick (Henry) Matter, father of Margareta Rebecca Matter
Birth Date: 26 Dec 1796, Dauphine Co. Penn.
Death Date: 01 Oct 1868, Dauphine Co. Penn.
Spouse: Anna Mary "Polly" Dietrich, d/o Jacob & Anna Magdalena Dietrich
Birth Date: 15 Mar 1803, Lukens, Penn
Death Date: 11 Nov 1865, Dauphine Co. Penn.

Marriage Date: 25 Feb 1847
Marriage Place: Elizabethville, Dauphin Co. Penn.

Children: John H. 86
Mary Ann
Catherine Ann 87
Jacob F.
Samuel F.
Peter A.
Lydia A.
Emma Jane
Hannah Amanda ' Mandy' 89
DAVID JACOB 90
Abraham Lincoln

Isaac

Ira

Clinton

Susanna M. 88

Baptized January 29, 1797, in St. John's Lutheran (Hill) Church, Berrysburg, Dauphin Co., PA. Buried in the Motter Family Cemetery, Elizabethville, Dauphin Co., PA.   Source: Roger Cramer.   Source: Roger Cramer.

Notes for Anna Marie Deitrich:

Baptized in St. John's Church, Berrysburg, Dauphin Co., PA. Buried in the Motter Family Cemetery, Elizabethville, Dauphin Co., PA.   Source: Roger Cramer.

!Data from St John's, Mifflin Twsp, Dauphin County, Pa, transcribed by Robert M Howard.

Children of Heinrich Matter and Anna Deitrich are:

    i.   Elisabeth Matter, born 06 Feb 1820 in Dauphin Co., PA; died 09 Feb 1891 in Dauphin Co., PA; married (1) David Sheesley Abt. 1838 in Dauphin Co., PA; born 14 Feb 1813; died 23 Aug 1845; married (2) George Gilbert Aft. 1845; born 31 Dec 1813 in PA; died 10 Nov 1869; married (3) Philip Bowman Aft. 1850.

        Notes for Elisabeth Matter:

        Baptized April 16, 1820, in St. John's Church, Berrysburg, Dauphin Co., PA. Buried in the Motter Family Cemetery, Rlizabethville, Dauphin Co., PA.   Source: Roger Cramer.

        Notes for David Sheesley:

        Source: Roger Cramer.

    ii.   Thomas Matter, born 20 Apr 1821 in Dauphin Co., PA; married (1) Margaretha ?; born 22 Jul 1831 in Dauphin Co., PA; died 09 Jul 1863 in Pennsylvania; married (2) Lovina ?; born 28 Aug 1840 in Pennsylvania; died 25 Feb 1892 in Dauphin Co., PA.

        Notes for Thomas Matter:

        Baptized in St. John's Church, Berrysburg, Dauphin Co., PA. Relocated to Washington Twp., Dauphin Co. PA, prior to 1850. Buried in the Motter Famikly Cemetery, Elizabethville, Dauphin Co., PA. Source: Roger Cramer.

        Notes for Margaretha ?:

        Buried in the Motter Family Cemetery,m Elizabethville, Dauphin Co., PA.   Source: Roger Cramer.

    iii.   Catharina Matter, born 29 Jan 1823 in Dauphin Co., PA; died 13 Mar 1915 in Dauphin Co., PA; married Phillip Wilbert; born 29 Oct 1821; died 02 Nov 1893 in Dauphin Co., PA.

        Notes for Catharina Matter:
        Baptized in St. John's Lutheran Church, Berrysburg, Mifflin Twp., Dauphin Co., PA. Buried in the Motter Family Cemetery, Elizabethville, Dauphin Co., PA.   Source: Roger Cramer.

        Notes for Phillip Wilbert:
        Son of PETER and MARY (ENDERS) WILGERT. Burried in the Motter Family Cemetery, Elizabethville, Dauphin Co., PA.   Source: Roger Cramer.

5   iv.   Margareta Rebecca Matter, born 18 Mar 1825 in Mifflin Twp, Dauphin, PA; died 22 Jun 1890 in Abilene, Dickinson Co , Kansas; married Jacob Frederick Eisenhauer 25 Feb 1847 in Dauphin , Pennsylvania.

v. Nicholas Matter, born 07 Dec 1826 in Dauphin Co., PA; died 23 Jun 1865; married Mathilda Lebo; born 31 May 1827 in Dauphin Co., PA; died 27 Aug 1917.

Notes for Nicholas Matter:

Baptized March 4, 1827, in St. John's Lutheran Church, Berrysburg, Mifflin Twp., Dauphin Co., PA. Source: Roger Cramer.

Notes for Mathilda Lebo:

Source: Roger Cramer.

vi. Sarah Matter, born 1830; married George R. Williard.

Notes for Sarah Matter:

Source: Roger Cramer.

Notes for George R. Williard:

Source: Roger Cramer.

vii. George Washington Matter, born 16 Jan 1832 in Elizabethville, Dauphin Co., PA; died 26 Sep 1878 in Dauphin Co., PA; married Margaret Cumbler 08 Sep 1857 in Washington Twp., Dauphin Co., PA; born 22 Jul 1829; died 30 Aug 1898 in Washington Twp., Dauphin Co., PA.

Notes for George Washington Matter:

Buried in the Motter Family Cemetery, Elizabethville, Dauphin Co., PA.   Source: Roger Cramer.

Notes for Margaret Cumbler:

Source: Roger Cramer.

viii. Moses Matter, born 1834 in Elizabethville, Dauphin Co., PA; died 1836 in Elizabethville, Dauphin Co., PA.

Notes for Moses Matter:

Source: Roger Cramer.

ix. Mary Ann Matter, born 25 May 1841 in Elizabethville, Dauphin Co., PA; died 09 Feb 1904.

Notes for Mary Ann Matter:

Source: Roger Cramer.

12. Daniel Stover, born Abt. 1780 in Augusta Co, VA; died 18 Jan 1862 in Augusta Co, VA. He was the son of **24. Daniel Stover.** He married **13. Mary Hannah** 30 Mar 1803 in Augusta Co, VA.
13. Mary Hannah, born Abt. 1781 in Augusta Co, VA; died Abt. 1852.

Notes for Daniel Stover:
He was born c1760 in Augusta Co. Va. & died there on 18 Jan 1862. HIs father was also called Daniel.

Child of Daniel Stover and Mary Hannah is:

6   i.   Simon P Stover, born 28 Sep 1822 in Augusta Co, VA; died 11 Dec 1873 in Augusta Co, VA; married Elizabeth Ida Link 31 Dec 1848 in Augusta Co, VA.

Generation No. 5

16. Hans Peter Eisenhauer, born 1716 in Palatinate District of Germany; died 10 Jun 1801 in Lower Paxton Township, Dauphin, Pennsylvania. He was the son of **32. Hans Nicholas Eisenhauer** and **33. Anna Struble.** He married **17. Anna Margaret Dissinger** 29 Jan 1777 in Stouchsburg, Berks, Pennsylvania.

     17. Anna Margaret Dissinger, born Abt. 1750 in Christ Lutheran, Stouchsburg Berks Co, PA; died 18 Nov 1815 in Lower Paxton, Dauphin, PA. She was the daughter of **34. Peter Dissinger**.

Notes for Hans Peter Eisenhauer:

Various entries have it spelled Eisenhower/Eisenhauer/Eisenhouer prior.
======
Johann Peter Could be Hans, Peder; Petrus, Peter;
Palatine Nat 11 Apr 1752
Total 17 children;
Hans' place of residence Am. 17 Nov 1741 Swarta Tp. Dauphin, PA
======
IGI BD 1716 Weschnitz, Starkenburg, Hessen
======
--Lutheran Church Records
(Johannes)
======

Children of Hans Eisenhauer and Anna Dissinger are:

      i.   John Jacob Eisenhauer, born 13 Apr 1777 in ,Berks, Pennsylvania; married Nancy Anna McDonald 09 Jun 1803 in ,Dauphin, Pennsylvania.

           Notes for John Jacob Eisenhauer:

           Lutheran Church Record;

     ii.   Catherine Eisenhauer, born 1780 in ,Berks, Pennsylvania.
    iii.   Ann Eisenhauer, born 1781 in ,Berks, Pennsylvania.
    iv.   Christina Eisenhauer, born 1783 in ,Berks, Pennsylvania.
     v.   Barbara Eisenhauer, born Mar 1784 in ,Berks, Pennsylvania; married Conrad Knepley 04 Aug 1801 in ,Dauphin , Pennsylvania.

           Notes for Barbara Eisenhauer:

           Barbara Christened in Shoops Reformed Church;

    vi.   Margaret Eisenhauer, born 1787 in Berks, Pennsylvania; married George Leininger 08 Oct 1808 in ,Dauphin, Pennsylvania.

           Notes for Margaret Eisenhauer:
           Married in Salem Reformed Church

   vii.   John Peter Eisenhauer, born 04 Jan 1790 in ,Berks, Pennsylvania.
8   viii.   Frederick Eisenhauer, born 15 Jul 1794 in Linglestown, Dauphin, Pennsylvania; died 13 Mar 1884 in Belle Springs, Dickinson, Kansas; married Barbara Miller 1816 in Linglestown, Dauphin, Pa.

18. John Miller, born Abt. 1755 in Pa; died 04 Mar 1788 in Pa. He was the son of **36. John Jacob Miller**. He married **19. Susanna Raysor** in Pa.

19. Susanna Raysor, born Abt. 1759.

Notes for John Miller:

Ancestral File Number:<AFN> 15T1-0N7

Marriage Notes for John Miller and Susanna Raysor:

_UID099D70832A74D84D8C7DEF83728BCEB55751

Children of John Miller and Susanna Raysor are:

      i.   Anna Miller, born Abt. 1781 in Pa.

         Notes for Anna Miller:

         Ancestral File Number:<AFN> 15T1-0QM

      ii. Jacob Miller, born Abt. 1783 in Pa.

         Notes for Jacob Miller:

         Ancestral File Number:<AFN> 15T1-0RT

      iii. John Miller, born Abt. 1785 in Pa.

         Notes for John Miller:

         Ancestral File Number:<AFN> 15T1-0S2

      iv. Elizabeth Miller, born Abt. 1787 in Pa.

         Notes for Elizabeth Miller:

         Ancestral File Number:<AFN> 15T1-0T8

9   v.   Barbara Miller, born 27 May 1789 in Elizabethville, Dauphin, Pa; died 01 Jan 1862 in Millersburg, Dauphin, Pa; married Frederick Eisenhauer 1816 in Linglestown, Dauphin, Pa.

    20. John Michael Matter, born 03 Oct 1763 in Lancaster Co, PA; died 12 Feb 1852 in Dauphin Co, PA. He was the son of **40. Johannes Adams Matter** and **41. Anna Barbara Arnhold**. He married **21. Anna Maria Romberger** in Probably, Dauphin County, Pa.

    21. Anna Maria Romberger, born 12 Jun 1771 in Lancaster Co, PA; died 18 Mar 1866 in Dauphin Co, PA. She was the daughter of **42. Balthaser Romberger** and **43. Anna Maria Traut**.

Notes for John Michael Matter:
LDS AFN:37F4-Q8.
JOHN MICHAEL MATTER, son of JOHANNES and ANNA (ARNHOLD) MATTER, was baptized on November 21, 1763, in the Trinity Evangelical Lutheran Church, New Holland, Lancaster Co., PA. John Michael, known as "Big Mike," farmed part of the original Matter farm for most of his life. John Michael married ANNA MARIA ROMBERGER. Twenty children, including three sets of twins, were born of this

union. He was buried in the St. John's (Hill) Church Cemetery, Berrysburg, Dauphin Co., PA.   Source: Roger Cramer.

(5) Michael Matter
Birth Date: 03 Oct 1763
Death Date: 01 Feb 1852, Luken Valley, Penn.
Spouse: Anna Marie Romberg,
Birth Date: 12 Jun 1771, Lukens Valley, Penn, d/o Balthasar Romberg
Death Date: 26 Feb 1838, Dauphine Co. Penn.
Notes: Mrs Richardson-Taylor's book had Henry and Elizabeth Romberger as her parents as does gaulch@iag.net, but, Anne Marie Traut, b.1749, d. c1785 & Balthasar Raumberger were her parents (by two Ancestry.com submitters);

Notes for Anna Maria Romberger:

!Data from St John's, Mifflin Twsp, Dauphin County, Pa, transcribed by Robert M Howard. One f amily history gives death date shown, but St Johns give DOB and DOD as Jan 12 1770, and Feb 2 4 1838, the Feb 26 could be the burial date.

Buried in St. John's Lutheran Cemetery, Berrysburg, Mifflin Twp., Dauphin Co., PA.   Source: S-164.

Children of John Matter and Anna Romberger are:
  i.   Johannes Matter, born 04 Jul 1788 in Dauphin, Pa; died 16 Feb 1816 in Dauphin Co., PA; married Anna Maria Paul; born 01 Jul 1789 in Dauphin Co., PA; died 18 Mar 1866 in Dauphin Co., PA.

       Notes for Johannes Matter:

       !Data from St John's, Mifflin Twsp, Dauphin County, Pa, transcribed by Robert M Howard. Bapti smal sponsers were Johannes Matter, Sr, and A. Catherina.

       Baptized July 20, 1788, in St. John's Lutheran (Hill) Church, Berysburg, Dauphin Co., PA.   Source: Roger Cramer.

       Notes for Anna Maria Paul:

       ANNA MARIA PAUL, daughter of JOSEPH and ANNA (MATTER) PAULand wife of JOHANNES MATTER, is buried in the St. John's Church Cemetery, Berrysburg, Dauphin Co., PA.   Source: Roger Cramer.

       !Data from St Johns Luthern Church, Dauphin County, Pa, transcribed by Robert M Howard.

  ii. Anna Maria Matter, born 21 Jan 1790; died 29 Jan 1871; married Peter Minnich 21 Feb 1808 in Mifflin Twp., Dauphin Co., PA; born 11 Sep 1785 in Upper Paxton Twp., Dauphin Co., PA; died 25 Sep 1855 in Washington Twp., Dauphin Co., PA.

       Notes for Anna Maria Matter:
       Daughter of MICHAEL and ANNA MARIE (ROMBERGER) MATTER, baptized in St. John's Lutheran (Hill) Church, Berrysburg, Dauphin Co., PA, on February 14, 1790. Buried in Rife, Dauphin Co., PA.   Source: LDS AFN:LMGG-J2.

       Notes for Peter Minnich:
       Buried in Rife, Dauphin Co., PA.   Source: LDS AFN:LMGG-HV.
       Peter Minich was a soldier during the War of 1812.   Source: Gratz History p. 786.

  iii. Johann Michael Matter, born 29 Mar 1791 in Dauphin, Pa; died 11 Feb 1838 in Dauphin, Pa; married (1) Anna Catherina Cooper 25 Sep 1814 in Dauphin, Pa; born 17 Oct 1792 in Dauphin, Pa; died 07 Nov 1824 in Dauphin, Pa; married (2) Margaret Rebecca Kiehner 29 Mar 1825 in Mifflin Twp., Dauphin Co., PA; born 17 Mar 1805 in Dauphin Co., PA; died 07 May 1854 in Dauphin Co., PA.

Notes for Johann Michael Matter:
Data from St John's, Mifflin Twsp, Dauphin County, Pa, transcribed by Robert M Howard. Baptismal sponsors were Michael Enderlein and Elizabeth.

JOHANN MATTER, son of JOHANN MICHAEL and ANNA MARIE (ROMBERGER) MATTER, was baptized April 14, 1791, in St. John's Lutheran (Hill) Church, Berrysburg, Dauphin Co., PA. On September 25, 1814, he married first, ANNA CATHARINA COOPER. daughter of JOHN and CHRISTINA (SCHOTT) KUPPER/COOPER. On March 29, 1825, he married second MARGARET REBECCA KIEHNER, daughter of PHILIP and MARIA MAGDALINA KIEHNER. Johann Matter is buried in St. John's Lutheran Church Cemetery, Berrysburg, Dauphin Co., PA. Source: Roger Cramer.

Notes for Anna Catherina Cooper:

!Data from Salem Luthern, Killingers, Dauphin County, Pa, transcribed by Robert M Howard. I b eleive these are the right parents. Baptismal sponsors were Ludwig Schott and Catharina. O n a tomessbone the birth is 1793. this is impossible since the baptism was 1793.

ANNA CATHARINA COOPER, daughter of JOHN and CHRISTINA (SCHOTT) KUPPER/COOPER and first wife of JOHANN MICHAEL MATTER, is buried in St. John's Lutheran Church Cemetery, Berrysburg, Dauphin Co., PA. Source: Roger Cramer.

iv. Johann George Matter, born 16 Feb 1793 in , Dauphin, Pa; married Susanna Catharine Reigle; born 17 Mar 1771.

Notes for Johann George Matter:

!Data from St John's, Mifflin Twsp, Dauphin County, Pa, transcribed by Robert M Howard.

Source: Gratz History p. 179.
Baptized March 10, 1793, in St. John's Lutheran (Hill) Church, Berrysburg, Dauphin Co., PA. Source: Roger Cramer.

Notes for Susanna Catharine Reigle:

Source: Gratz History p. 179.
Source: Roger Cramer.

v. Balthasar Matter, born 07 Jul 1795 in , Dauphin, Pa; died 21 Dec 1871 in , Dauphin, Pa; married Catherine Ritzman in No Data, Probably, Dauphin County, Pa; born 12 Feb 1797 in Dauphin Co., PA; died 17 Oct 1864 in Gratz, Lykens Twp., Dauphin Co., PA.

Notes for Balthasar Matter:

!Data from St Johns, Lykins Twsp, Dauphin County, Pa, transcribed by Robert M Howard.

Baptized in St. John's Lutheran (Hill) Church, Berrysburg, Dauphin Co., PA. According to 1870 Census, was living with son Edward at that time. Buried in Union Cemetery, Lykens, Lykens Twp., Dauphin Co., PA. Source: Roger Cramer.

Notes for Catherine Ritzman:

Daughter of PETER and CATHARINE ELISABETH RITZMAN, baptized May 14, 1797, in Zion (Klinger's) Church, Erdman, Dauphin Co., PA. Sponsors: Friederich and Anna Dibentorf. Source: K-16.
Buried in the Simeon Church Cemetery, Gratz, Lykens Twp., Dauphin VCo., PA. Source: Roger Cramer.

!Data from St Johns, Lykins Twsp, Dauphin County, Pa, transcribed by Robert M Howard.

10   vi.   Heinrich Matter, born 26 Dec 1796 in Elizabethville, PA; died 01 Oct 1868 in Lykens, PA; married Anna Marie Deitrich in PA.

vii.   Anna Catherina Matter, born 14 Feb 1798 in , Dauphin, Pa.

Notes for Anna Catherina Matter:

!Data from St John's, Mifflin Twsp, Dauphin County, Pa, transcribed by Robert M Howard.

Baptized March 25, 1798, in St. John's Lutheran (Hill) Church, Berrysburg, Dauphin Co., PA.   Source: Roger Cramer.

viii.   Georgianna Matter, born 14 Feb 1798 in Dauphin Co., PA.

Notes for Georgianna Matter:

Baptized March 25, 1798, in St. John's Lutheran (Hill) Church, Berrysburg, Dauphin Co., PA.   Source: Roger Cramer.

ix.   Elisabeth Matter, born 16 May 1799 in Dauphin Co., PA; died 16 Nov 1837 in Gratz, Lykens Twp., Dauphin Co., PA.

Notes for Elisabeth Matter:

Baptized July 7, 1799, in St. John's Lutheran (Hill) Church, Berrysburg, Dauphin Co., PA.   Source: Roger Cramer.

!Data from St Johns, Mifflin Twsp, Dauphin County, Pa, transcribed by Robert M Howard. Baptis mal witneses were Johannes Matter and Elisabeth.

x.   Anna Catharina Matter, born 07 Oct 1800 in Mifflin Twp, Dauphin Co., PA; died 13 Aug 1852 in Jefferson Twp., Dauphin Co., PA.

Notes for Anna Catharina Matter:

Baptized November 2, 1800, in St. John's Lutheran (Hill) Church, Berrysburg, Dauphin Co., PA. Source: Roger Cramer.

xi.   Catherine Matter, born 07 Oct 1800 in , Dauphin, Pa; married Johannes Ritzman; born Abt. 1815.

Notes for Catherine Matter:

!Data from St John's church records, Mifflin Twsp, Dauphin County, Pa, transcribed by Rober t M Howard.s

xii.   Sophia Matter, born 07 Oct 1800 in Mifflin Twp, Dauphin Co., PA.

Notes for Sophia Matter:

Baptized November 2, 1800, in St. John's Lutheran (Hill) Church, Berrysburg, Dauphin Co., PA. Source: Roger Cramer.

xiii.   Jonas Matter, born 18 Apr 1802 in , Dauphin, Pa.

Notes for Jonas Matter:

!Data from St John's church records, Mifflin Twsp, Dauphin County, Pa, transcribed by Rober t M Howard.s[Romberger.FTW]

Baptized May 9, 18002, in St. John's Lutheran (Hill) Church, Berrysburg, Dauphin Co., PA.   Source: Roger Cramer.

xiv.   George Daniel Matter, born 03 Nov 1803 in Dauphin Co., PA; died 01 Oct 1873 in Beaver Twp., Jefferson Co., PA.

Notes for George Daniel Matter:

Baptized Januaryr 2, 1804, in St. John's Lutheran (Hill) Church, Berrysburg, Dauphin Co., PA. Source: Roger Cramer.

!Data from St Johns, Mifflin Twsp, Dauphin County, Pa, transcribed by Robert M Howard.

xv.   Michael Matter, born Abt. 1805; died 1838; married Catherine Kupper; born Abt. 1805.

xvi.   Johann Solomon Matter, born 03 Mar 1806 in Mifflin Township, Dauphin, Pa; died 13 May 1877 in , Dauphin, Pa; married Isabella Row in No Data, Probably, Dauphin County, Pa; born 30 Apr 1810 in , Dauphin, Pa; died 27 Jan 1857 in , Dauphin, Pa.

Notes for Johann Solomon Matter:

!Data from St Johns, Mifflin Twsp, Dauphin County, Pa, transcribed by Robert M Howard.

Baptized April 7, 1806, in St. John's Lutheran (Hill) Church, Berrysburg, Dauphin Co., PA.   Source: Roger Cramer.

Notes for Isabella Row:

!Data from St Johns Luthern, Lykens, Dauphin County, Pa, transcribed by Robert M Howard.

xvii.   Infant Matter, born 05 Oct 1807 in Dauphin Co., PA; died Oct 1807 in Dauphin Co., PA.

Notes for Infant Matter:

Baptized December 3, 1807,in St. John's Lutheran (Hill) Church, Berrysburg, Dauphin Co., PA. Source: Roger Cramer.

!Data from the St John's, Mifllin Twsp, Dauphin County, Pa, transcribed by Robert M Howard.

xviii.   Eva Matter, born 16 Jan 1810 in , Dauphin, Pa; died Abt. 1850.

Notes for Eva Matter:

!Data from St John's, Mifflin Twsp, Dauphin County, Pa, transcribed by Robert M Howard.

Baptized January 28, 1810, in St. John's Lutheran (Hill) Church, Berrysburg, Dauphin Co., PA. Source: Roger Cramer.

xix.   Adam Matter, born 01 Apr 1812 in , Dauphin, Pa; died 14 Sep 1889 in Rosecrans, Clinton Co., PA.

Notes for Adam Matter:

!Data from St John's, Mifflin Twsp, Dauphin County, Pa, trancribed by Robert M Howard.

Baptized April 10, 1812, in St. John's Lutheran (Hill) Church, Berrysburg, Dauphin Co., PA.   Source: Roger Cramer.

xx.   Jacob Matter, born 02 Jul 1813 in , Dauphin, Pa; died 12 Feb 1875 in Dauphin Co., PA.

Notes for Jacob Matter:

!Jonathan lived at Campbelltown, and had ten children, with data from the Koppenhoffer Famil y History, transcribed by Robert M Howard.

Baptized August 14, 1813, in St. John's Lutheran (Hill) Church, Berrysburg, Dauphin Co., PA. Source: Roger Cramer.

xxi.   Regina Matter, born 25 Sep 1815 in Dauphin Co., PA; died Bef. 1852; married Joseph Rowe.

Notes for Regina Matter:

Baptized October 23, 1815, in St. John's Lutheran (Hill) Church, Berrysburg, Dauphin Co., PA. Source: Roger Cramer.

Notes for Joseph Rowe:

Source: Roger Cramer.

xxii.   Susanna Matter, born 25 Sep 1815 in , Dauphin, Pa; died 12 Aug 1903 in Gratz, Lykens Twp., Dauphin Co., PA.

Notes for Susanna Matter:

!Data from St John's, Mifflin Twsp, Dauphin County, Pa, transcribed by Robert M Howard.

Baptized October 22, 1815, in St. John's Lutheran (Hill) Church, Berrysburg, Dauphin Co., PA. Source: Roger Cramer.

22. Jacob Deitrich, born Abt. 1777 in Berrysburg, PA.

Child of Jacob Deitrich is:
11   i.   Anna Marie Deitrich, born 15 Mar 1803 in Lykens, Dauphin, PA; died 11 Nov 1865 in Lykens, Dauphin, PA; married Heinrich Matter in PA.

24. Daniel Stover, born 1750 in Augusta , Virginia; died 1826 in ,Augusta, Virginia. He was the son of **48. Abraham Stover** and **49. Sarah ?**.

Notes for Daniel Stover:
Son of Jacob of German- Swiss descent who married Mary Hannah.

Child of Daniel Stover is:
12   i.   Daniel Stover, born Abt. 1780 in Augusta Co, VA; died 18 Jan 1862 in Augusta Co, VA; married Mary Hannah 30 Mar 1803 in Augusta Co, VA.

Generation No. 6

32. Hans Nicholas Eisenhauer, born 1691 in Weschnitz, Starkenburg, Hesse; died Bef. 27 Jul 1802 in Dauphin, PA. He was the son of **64. Hans Peter Eisenhauer** and **65. Anna Catherina Mildenberger**. He married **33. Anna Struble** Abt. 1725.
33. Anna Struble, born Abt. 1700 in Germany; died in PA. She was the daughter of **66. ? Strubel**.

Notes for Hans Nicholas Eisenhauer:

Hans: Death after Mar 1750 Bethel Twp. now Lebanon Co. PA;
Residence: Frederickburg, PA ;
======
One record shows BP Weschnitz, Starkenburg, Hesse
"   "   "   DOD Bef 27 1802 Jul DP, Dauphin, Pennsylvania

======
http://www.eisenhowerbirthplace.org/family.htm
Hans Nicol Eisenhower arrived in America in 1741 aboard the "Europa" with his son John Pete r Eisenhower
grandson Frederick Eisenhower 1794 -1884

Children of Hans Eisenhauer and Anna Struble are:
      i.   Martin Eisenhower, born 1725 in Palentine District of Germany; died 1760 in during skirmish with Indians probably Shawnees.
      ii.   Johanna Eisenhauer, born in Germany.
16   iii.   Hans Peter Eisenhauer, born 1716 in Palatinate District of Germany; died 10 Jun 1801 in Lower Paxton Township, Dauphin, Pennsylvania; married (1) Elizabeth Graff in of Dauphin, Pennsylvania; married (2) Anna Maria Elizabeth Schmidt 21 Aug 1770 in Bethel, Dauphin, Pennsylvania; married (3) Anna Margaret Dissinger 29 Jan 1777 in Stouchsburg, Berks, Pennsylvania.
      iv.   Maria Magdalena Eisenhauer, born in Weschnitz, Starkenburg, Hesse, Germany; married Michael Fischer 01 Mar 1757 in ,Dauphin/Berks, Pennsylvania.
      v.   Johannes Eisenhauer, born 24 Jun 1725 in Weschnitz, Starkenburg, Hesse; died 01 Feb 1789 in , Lebanon, Pennsylvania.
      vi.   Martin Eisenhauer, born 1729 in Germany.

          Notes for Martin Eisenhauer:

          Lutheran Church Records

34. Peter Dissinger, born Abt. 1724 in Lower Paxton Twp, Dauphin Co, PA; died Abt. 1781 in Stumpstown, PA.

Child of Peter Dissinger is:
17   i.   Anna Margaret Dissinger, born Abt. 1750 in Christ Lutheran, Stouchsburg Berks Co, PA; died 18 Nov 1815 in Lower Paxton, Dauphin, PA; married Hans Peter Eisenhauer 29 Jan 1777 in Stouchsburg, Berks, Pennsylvania.

36. John Jacob Miller, born 24 Sep 1728 in Germany; died 02 Mar 1767 in Pa. He was the son of **72. Jacob Mueller** and **73. Catherine Charlotta.**

Notes for John Jacob Miller:

Ancestral File Number:<AFN> 15T0-07D

Children of John Jacob Miller are:
18   i.   John Miller, born Abt. 1755 in Pa; died 04 Mar 1788 in Pa; married Susanna Raysor in Pa.
      ii.   David Miller, born Abt. 1758 in Pa.

          Notes for David Miller:

          Ancestral File Number:<AFN> 15T0-L8P

      iii.   Abraham Miller, born 1761 in Somerset, Pa; died 24 Apr 1834 in Brothersvalley T, Somerset, Pa;

married Anna Maria Troutman Abt. 1817 in Brothersvalley Twp., Somerset Co., PA; born 08 Sep 1783 in Greenwich Twp, Berks, Pa; died 05 Nov 1869 in Somerset County, Pa.

Notes for Abraham Miller:

Ancestral File Number:<AFN> 15T0-0C7

40. Johannes Adams Matter, born 24 Jan 1731/32 in Altdorf, Alace-Lorraine Germany; died 26 May 1802 in Upper Paxton Twp, Dauphine Co. Penn.. He married **41. Anna Barbara Arnhold**.
    41. Anna Barbara Arnhold

Notes for Johannes Adams Matter:
(1) Hans Matter
Birth Date: 1614, Alsace-Lorraine, France
Death Date: 20 Feb 1681, Eckendorf, Alsace-Lorraine, France
Spouse: Catherina ? b. 1616, d. 06 March 1698, Eckendorf, Alsace-Lorraine, France.

(2) Diabold Matter
Birth Date: 1647, Eckendorf, Alsace-Lorraine,France
Death Date: 18 Feb 1728, Altdorf, Alsace-Lorraine, Germany
Spouse: Margaratha Kueffer
Birth Date: 1656, Eckendorf, Alsace-Lorraine, France
Death Date: 08 Nov 1726, Altdorf, Alsace-Lorraine, Germany
Notes: d/o Christmann Kueffer, d. 06 Mar 1698, Eckendorf, Alsace-Lorraine, France & Catharina Gautzberg, b. 1633, Alsace-Lorraine, France, d. 01 Oct 1688, Eckendorf, Alsace-Lorraine, France. Catharina's parents were Anna & Melchoir Gautzberg, b. 1607, Alsace-Lorraine, France

(3) Johannes Hans Matter
Birth Date: 11 May 1692, Alsace-Lorraine, France
Death Date: 06 May 1736, Altforf, Alsace-Loraine, Germany
Spouse: Anna Christina Keiser
Birth Date: 1656, Eckendorf, Alsace-Lorraine, France
Death Date: 08 Nov 1726, Altdorf, Alsace-Lorraine, Germany

(4) 1.1.1.1 Johannes Hans Matter , [Spelled Mather in older records].
Birth Place: Altdorf, Alsace-Lorraine, Germany
Death Date: 26 May 1802, Upper Paxton Twp, Dauphine Co. Penn.
Spouse: Salome Staklschmidt
Birth Date: 1737, Altdorf, Alace-Lorraine Germany

Children of Johannes Matter and Anna Arnhold are:
  20   i.   John Michael Matter, born 03 Oct 1763 in Lancaster Co, PA; died 12 Feb 1852 in Dauphin Co, PA; married Anna Maria Romberger in Probably, Dauphin County, Pa.
          ii. Johannes Matter, born 17 Aug 1759 in New Holland, Lancaster Co, PA; died 30 Jun 1832 in Lykens Valley, Dauphin Co, PA; married Elizabeth Bergner; born 16 Apr 1762 in Lykens Valley, Dauphin Co, PA; died 18 Dec 1832 in Lykens Valley, Dauphin Co, PA.

42. Balthaser Romberger, born 1736 in Franconia, Bavaria; died 1838 in Mifflin Twp, Dauphin Co, PA. He was the son of **84. Johann Bartholomus Romberger** and **85. Elizabeth Matter**. He married **43. Anna Maria Traut** Abt. 1770 in Lebanon Co., PA.
    43. Anna Maria Traut, born 1753; died Bef. 1797 in Mifflin Twp, Dauphin Co, PA.

Notes for Balthaser Romberger:

Source: Roger Cramer.

Notes for Anna Maria Traut:

Daughter of JOHANN and MARIA (WALTER) TRAUT.   Source: Roger Cramer.

Children of Balthaser Romberger and Anna Traut are:

21   i. Anna Maria Romberger, born 12 Jun 1771 in Lancaster Co, PA; died 18 Mar 1866 in Dauphin Co, PA; married John Michael Matter in Probably, Dauphin County, Pa.

    ii. Heinrich Romberger, born 12 Jul 1773 in New Holland, Lancaster Co, PA; died Bef. 31 Jan 1822; married Elizabeth Hoffman Bef. 1798; born Abt. 1777.

     Notes for Heinrich Romberger:

     Source: Roger Cramer.

   iii. Adam Romberger, born 03 Jun 1775 in Hew Holland, Lancaster Co., PA; died 17 Aug 1868 in Uniontown (Pillow), Dauphin Co., PA; married (1) Anna Maria Werner Abt. 1794; married (2) Anna Catharina Paul Abt. 1808; born 14 Apr 1788 in Dauphin Co., PA; died 09 May 1862 in Dauphin Co., PA.

     Notes for Adam Romberger:

     Source: Brian Barr Wiest.
     Source: "Hoffman's Ancestral Family Record."
     Buried in the Pillow Grandview Cemetery, Mifflin Twp, Dauphin Co., PA.   Source: S-135.

     Notes for Anna Maria Werner:

   iv. Anna Catharina Romberger, born 19 Mar 1777 in New Holland, Lancaster Co., PA; died 03 Jul 1851 in Wiconisco, Dauphin Co., PA; married John George Matter; born 16 Jan 1771 in Dauphin Co., PA; died 11 Oct 1855 in Dauphin Co., PA.

     Notes for Anna Catharina Romberger:

     Source: Roger Cramer.

     Notes for John George Matter:

     JOHN GEORGE MATTER, son of GEORGE and ANNA CATHARINA (ARNHOLD) MATTER, was confirmed in the Salem Evangelical Lutheran Church, Killinger, Dauphin Co., PA. He served in the Army during the War of 1812.   Source: Roger Cramer.
     He married CATHARINE ROMBERGER. This union produced fourteen children eight sons and 6 daughters. John George Matter is buried in the St. John's Lutheran Church Cemetery, Berrysburg, Dauphin Co., PA.   Source: S-164.

   v. Balthaser Romberger, born 28 Dec 1778 in New Holland, Earl Twp., Lancaster Co., PA; died 16 Jun 1839 in Mifflin Twp, Dauphin Co., PA; married Elizabeth Sierer 25 Dec 1802 in Dauphin Co., PA; born 15 Nov 1782 in Lancaster Co., PA; died 02 Feb 1858 in Dauphin Co., PA.

     Notes for Balthaser Romberger:

     BALTHASER ROMBERGER Jr is buried in St. John's Church Cemetery, Berrysburg, Mifflin Co., PA.
     Source: Roger Cramer. [Note: Date of death recorded as 1839 in Egles Notes & Queries.   BTH]

Notes for Elizabeth Sierer:

ELIZABETH SIERER was the daughter of JOHN and ANNA (STAUCH) SIERER. She is buried in St. John's Church Cemetery, Berrysburg, Mifflin Co., PA. Source: Roger Cramer.

vi. Johannes Romberger, born 29 Nov 1783 in Lancaster Co., PA; died 1840 in Porter Twp., Dauphin Co., PA; married Eva Hand.

Notes for Johannes Romberger:

Source: Roger Cramer.

Notes for Eva Hand:

Source: Roger Cramer.

48. Abraham Stover, born in Oley Township, Berks, Pennsylvania. He was the son of **96. Jacob Stover** and **97. Sarah Boone.** He married **49. Sarah ?.**
49. Sarah ?, born in <Oley Township, Berks, Pennsylvania>.

Children of Abraham Stover and Sarah ? are:
       i. Jeremiah Stover, born in Virginia; died in Wilkesco North Carolina; married Mary ?.
      ii. Henry Stover, born 1741 in Franklin , Virginia; died 1798 in Franklin , Virginia; married Anna Kline.
24   iii. Daniel Stover, born 1750 in Augusta , Virginia; died 1826 in ,Augusta, Virginia.

Generation No. 7

64. Hans Peter Eisenhauer, born Abt. 1650 in Eiterbach, Odenwald, Germany; died 28 Feb 1728/29 in Karlsbrun, Saar, Germany. He was the son of **128. Hans Eisenhauer.** He married **65. Anna Catherina Mildenberger** 1677 in Heidelbert, Eiterbach, Germany.
65. Anna Catherina Mildenberger, born 1655 in Heidelbert, Eiterbach, Germany.

Notes for Hans Peter Eisenhauer:

Source: http://worldconnect.rootsweb.com/cgi-bin/igm.cgi?op=GET&db=:1325956&id=I22287
According to the book
Hans Peter Eisenhauer worked as a farm hand for Hans Brand and his wife, who had three childr en.
Hans was killed in a clearing accident on the land and Hans Peter later married Hans Brand' s wife, Anne Beckenbach Brand.

Together Peter and Anne had three sons. Anne died in 1677.

Peter later married Anna Catharina Mildenberger.
By his two wives, Hans Peter had ten children.

The names of the children were not given in the book.
======

Children of Hans Eisenhauer and Anna Mildenberger are:
32   i. Hans Nicholas Eisenhauer, born 1691 in Weschnitz, Starkenburg, Hesse; died Bef. 27 Jul 1802 in Dauphin, PA; married Anna Struble Abt. 1725.
      ii. Elizabeth Catharina Eisenhauer, born in <Weschnitz, Starkenburg, Hesse, Germany>.
     iii. Anna Margaretha Eisenhauer, born in <Weschnitz, Starkenburg, Hesse, Germany>.
     iv. Maria Sara Eisenhauer, born in <Weschnitz, Starkenburg, Hesse, Germany>.

66. ? Strubel

Children of ? Strubel are:
- i. Frederich Strubel
33   ii. Anna Struble, born Abt. 1700 in Germany; died in PA; married Hans Nicholas Eisenhauer Abt. 1725.

72. Jacob Mueller, born 22 Oct 1697 in Germany; died 18 Dec 1772 in Bern Twp, Berks Co., PA. He married **73. Catherine Charlotta**.
73. Catherine Charlotta, born 11 Oct 1699.

Notes for Jacob Mueller:
Jacob is the immigrant ancestor of this Miller family. He Was born in Germany and came to Philadelphia, Pa. on the ship "Pink Johnson" on 19 Sep 1732. He was a farmer and tanner In Berks Co. Pa. His tannery continued in the family for 150 years. He and many of the family are buried in the Christ Little Tulpehocken Church cemetary near Bernville, Pa. There are six more children not named in the will of 1766. They may have died before the will was made. The four known children include Matthias Miller.

Note: Jacob & Catherina were married 53 years.

Children of Jacob Mueller and Catherine Charlotta are:
36   i. John Jacob Miller, born 24 Sep 1728 in Germany; died 02 Mar 1767 in Pa; married in Pa.
    ii. Johannes Miller, born 09 Nov 1733.
    iii. Mary Elizabeth Miller, born 09 Sep 1736.
    iv. Mattias Miller, born 18 Oct 1743; died 1805 in Rockingham, VA.

84. Johann Bartholomus Romberger, born 04 May 1716 in Franconia, Bavaria; died 25 Sep 1800 in Lebanon, Lebanoh Co., PA. He married **85. Elizabeth Matter** Abt. 1739.
85. Elizabeth Matter, born Abt. 1720 in England; died Bef. 1753. She was the daughter of **170. Richard Mather**.

Notes for Johann Bartholomus Romberger:

Arrived in Philadelphia on board the ship Neptune, from Rotterdam, but last from Cowes, on September 24, 1753.
Married first, ELIZABETH MATHER, daughter of RICHARD MATHER. Married second. ANNA SABRINA HAAS, daughter of MICHAEL HAAS, on March 31, 1761, in the Trinity Evangelical Lutheran Church, New Holland, Lancaster Co., PA.
Johann Bartholomus Romberger is buried in the Evangelical Lutheran (Hill) Church Cemetery, Quitapohalia (near Anneville), Lebanon Co., PA. Source: Roger Cramer.

Notes for Elizabeth Matter:

Daughter of RICHARD MATHER. Source: Roger Cramer.

Children of Johann Romberger and Elizabeth Matter are:
42   i. Balthaser Romberger, born 1736 in Franconia, Bavaria; died 1838 in Mifflin Twp, Dauphin Co, PA; married (1) Anna Maria Traut Abt. 1770 in Lebanon Co., PA; married (2) Susannah Lehman 15 Jun 1798 in Harrisburg, Dauphin Co., PA.
    ii. Adam Romberger, born 1740 in Franconia, Bavaria; died Nov 1800 in Anneville, Lebanon Co., PA; married Esther Cray 04 Jul 1765 in Earl Twp., Lancaster Co., PA.

       Notes for Adam Romberger:

       Source: Roger Cramer.

Notes for Esther Cray:

Source: Roger Cramer.

      iii.   Maria Eva Romberger, born 1740 in Franconia, Bavaria; married Peter Cray 29 Sep 1765 in New Holland, Lancaster Co., PA; born Abt. 1740.

Notes for Maria Eva Romberger:

Source: Roger Cramer.

Notes for Peter Cray:

Source: Roger Cramer.

96. Jacob Stover, born in Switzerland; died 24 Jun 1741 in , Orange, Virginia. He was the son of **192. Christian Stover** and **193. ? Stover.** He married **97. Sarah Boone** 15 Mar 1714/15 in Christ Church, Philadelphia, Philadelphia, Pennsylvania.
    97. Sarah Boone, born 29 Feb 1691/92 in Bradninch, Exeter, Devonshire, England; died 20 Nov 1743 in Virginia. She was the daughter of **194. George Michael Boone** and **195. Mary Maugridge.**

Children of Jacob Stover and Sarah Boone are:
      i.   ? Stover, born in North Carolina>; married ? ?.
      ii.   Jacob Stover, born in Christ Church, Philadelphia, Pennsylvania; died in South Carolina>; married (1) Elizabeth Ruffner in Stoverstown, Shenandoah, Virginia; married (2) Catherine ?.
      iii.   Barbara Stover, born in Philadelphia Pennsylvania; died in Massanutten, Augusta; married (1) Martin Kauffman in Lancaster, Pennsylvania; married (2) Martin Nissly; married (3) John Lionberger in Augusta , Virginia.
48   iv.   Abraham Stover, born in Oley Township, Berks, Pennsylvania; married Sarah ?.

Generation No. 8

128. Hans Eisenhauer, born Abt. 1600 in Hedesbach, Odenwald, Germany.

Child of Hans Eisenhauer is:
64   i.   Hans Peter Eisenhauer, born Abt. 1650 in Eiterbach, Odenwald, Germany; died 28 Feb 1728/29 in Karlsbrun, Saar, Germany; married (1) Anne Beckenbach 08 Oct 1672 in Lichtenklinger Hof, Starkenburg, Hessen; married (2) Anna Catherina Mildenberger 1677 in Heidelbert, Eiterbach, Germany.

170. Richard Mather

Notes for Richard Mather:

Source: Roger Cramer.

Child of Richard Mather is:
85   i.   Elizabeth Matter, born Abt. 1720 in England; died Bef. 1753; married Johann Bartholomus Romberger Abt. 1739.

192. Christian Stover, born 1662 in Switzerland. He married **193. ? Stover.**
    193. ? Stover, born 1666 in , Switzerland>.

Child of Christian Stover and ? Stover is:

96   i.   Jacob Stover, born in Switzerland; died 24 Jun 1741 in , Orange, Virginia; married (1) Margaret ?; married (2) Ruth ?; married (3) Sarah Boone 15 Mar 1714/15 in Christ Church, Philadelphia, Philadelphia, Pennsylvania.

194. George Michael Boone, born 19 Mar 1665/66 in Stoke, Exeter, Devonshire, England; died 07 Aug 1744 in Exeter Township, Berks, Pennsylvania. He was the son of George Boone II and Sarah Uppey. He married **195. Mary Maugridge** 16 Aug 1689 in Stoke, Canon, Devonshire, England.

195. Mary Maugridge, born 23 Dec 1668 in Bradninch, Exeter, Devonshire, England; died 02 Feb 1739/40 in Exeter, Berks, Pennsylvania. She was the daughter of John Milton Maugridge and Mary Susan Mean Milton.

Notes for George Michael Boone:

http://www.data-wales.co.uk/boone2.htm

George Boone was a weaver by trade and a Quaker by religion. He was born in 1665 in the hamlet of Stoak near Exeter in Devonshire, England. In his time the Quakers were oppressed and George Boone therefore sought information of William Penn, his co-religionist, regarding the colony which Penn had established in America. In 1712 he sent his three children, George, Sarah , and Squire to spy out the land. Sarah and Squire remained in Pennsylvania, while their brother George returned to England with glowing reports. On August 17, 1717, George Boone went first to Abingdon, the Quaker farming community. Later they moved to the northwestern frontier hamlet of North Wales, a Welch community which a few years previously had turned Quaker.

(Ref. "Pioneers of the old Southwest" by Skinner ; 24-25)

George Boone's wife was Mary Milton Maugridge. (Ref. "The Boone Bulletin" and "The American Pioneer Records")

In 1718 George Boone took up 400 acres in Olay in the subdivision to be later called Exeter and there lived in a log cabin. He died in 1744. He left 8 children, 52 grandchildren and 10 great grandchildren, English, German, Welsh and Scotch blended into one family of Americans.

Children of George Boone and Mary Maugridge are:

      i.   George Boone, born 24 Jul 1690 in Bradninch, Exeter, Devonshire, England; died 20 Nov 1753 in Exeter, Berks, Pennsylvania; married Debrah Howell 17 Sep 1713 in Abington, Philadelphia, Pennsylvania, Pennsylvania.

97   ii.   Sarah Boone, born 29 Feb 1691/92 in Bradninch, Exeter, Devonshire, England; died 20 Nov 1743 in Virginia; married Jacob Stover 15 Mar 1714/15 in Christ Church, Philadelphia, Philadelphia, Pennsylvania.

      iii.   Mary Boone, born 26 Sep 1694 in Bradninch, Devon, Eng; died 20 May 1696 in Bradninch, Exeter, Devonshire, England.

      iv.   Squire Boone, born 25 Nov 1696 in Bradninch, Exeter, Devonshire, England; died 02 Jan 1765 in Salisbury, Rowan, North Carolina; married Sarah Morgan 27 Jul 1720 in Owyne, Berks, Pennsylvania; born in Exeter, Berks, Pennsylvania; died 01 Jan 1777 in ,Rowan, North Carolina.

Notes for Squire Boone:

One record says mariage 23 Sep 1720, North Wales, Montgomery, PA

======

Squire and Sarah Morgan Boone are both buried in Joppa Cemetery, Davie County, NC. They are my 5X great grandparents. I have been to their graves. --Geraldine Ingersoll

======

http://www.americanrevolution.com/DanielBoonesMovetoKentucky.htm

Daniel 1713 Boone's father, Squire, arrives in Philadelphia from England.

======

http://www.data-wales.co.uk/boone2.htm

It was in North Wales hamlet, Pennsylvania, that Squire Boone met Sarah Morgan and married he r in 1720 in a Quaker meeting house. Their children were: (Record obtained from The Boone Fam ily by Hazel Attervury Spraker, published by the Tuttle Co., Tutland, VT., 1922 Edition)

Notes for Sarah Morgan:

Sarah: Other info; Born Bala, Wales
======

Marriage Notes for Squire Boone and Sarah Morgan:

http://www.americanrevolution.com/DanielBoonesMovetoKentucky.htm
1720 Squire Boone and Sarah Morgan marry in the Friends' meetinghouse in Gwynedd, Pennsylvani a.

   v.   Mary Boone, born 23 Sep 1699 in Stoak, Exeter, Devonshire, England; died 16 Jan 1774 in Reading, Berks, Pennsylvania; married John Webb 13 Sep 1720 in Berks , Pennsylvania.

  vi. John Boone, born 14 Jan 1701/02 in Bradninch, Exeter, Devonshire, England; died 10 Oct 1785 in Bradninch, Exeter, Devonshire, England.

Notes for John Boone:

Never Married.

 vii. Joseph Boone, born 05 Apr 1704 in Stoak, Exeter, Devonshire, England; died 30 Jan 1776 in Reading, Berks, Pennsylvania; married (1) Mary ?; married (2) Catherine 30 Jan 1776 in Exeter Township, Berks , Pn.

Notes for Joseph Boone:
!Spraker. Apparently he married a Catherine, outside the Quaker faith.

viii. Benjamin Boone, born 16 Jul 1706 in Bradninch, Exeter, Devonshire, England; died 17 Oct 1762 in ,Exeter, Berks, Pennsylvania; married Ann Farmer 28 Sep 1726 in Abington, Bucks, Pennsylvania; born in Saffron, Walden, England.

  ix. James Boone, born 18 Jul 1709 in Stoak, Exeter, Devonshire, England; died 01 Sep 1785 in Exeter Township, Berks, Pennsylvania; married (1) Mary Foulke 26 May 1735 in Exter, Berks, Pennsylvania; married (2) Anne Griffith 20 Oct 1757 in Pennsylvania.

   x. Samuel Boone, born 07 Jul 1711 in Stoak, Exeter, Devonshire, England; died 06 Aug 1745 in Reading, Berks, Pennsylvania; married Elizabeth Cassel 29 Oct 1734 in Philadelphia, Philadelphia, Pennsylvania.

David Eisenhower and Ida Stover
Wedding Portrait, September 23, 1885

Arthur
Roy
Edgar
Dwight

Four Eisenhower Brothers, 1893

Note: David was the last generation originally from the Elizabethville, PA area.

Photos courtesy of www.dwightdeisenhower.com

Dwight
Edgar
Earl
Arthur
Roy
David
Ida
Milton

1902

The Eisenhower Family, 1902

36

Ike's Abilene High Baseball team - rear 2nd from right.
http://www.nps.gov/eise/gallery3.htm

Other photos courtesy of www.dwightdeisenhower.com

Dwight D. Eisenhower
Abilene High School Graduate, 1909

West Point Graduation, 1915

Just Married, 1916

Ike addressing the troops
http://www.nps.gov/eise/gallery6.htm

General of the Army (right)
http://www.history.navy.mil/photos

Bottom photos courtesy of:
www.dwightdeisenhower.com

Photo # NH 71005-KN   1948 portrait of General of the Army Dwight D. Eisenhower

**40th Wedding Anniversary
Gettysburg Farm
1956**

**The 1956 Campaign for re-election
Washington, D.C.,
Nov. 1**

Mamie, Doud Dwight, Dwight, 1919

Inauguration Day, 1957

Upper right: Dwight & Mamie at theur Gettysburg Home

http://www.nps.gov/eise

Remaining photos are courtesy of www.dwightdeisenhower.com

The Eisenhowers,
Palm Desert, California
mid 1960's

Descendants of Hans Nicholas Eisenhauer

Generation No. 1

1. Hans Nicholas³ Eisenhauer (Hans Peter², Hans¹) was born 1691 in Weschnitz, Starkenburg, Hesse, and died Bef. 27 Jul 1802 in Dauphin, PA. He married **Anna Struble** Abt. 1725, daughter of ? Strubel. She was born Abt. 1700 in Germany, and died in PA.

Children of Hans Eisenhauer and Anna Struble are:

2	i.	Martin⁴ Eisenhower, born 1725 in Palentine District of Germany; died 1760 in during skirmish with Indians probably Shawnees.
3	ii.	Johanna Eisenhauer, born in Germany.
+ 4	iii.	Hans Peter Eisenhauer, born 1716 in Palatinate District of Germany; died 10 Jun 1801 in Lower Paxton Township, Dauphin, Pennsylvania.
5	iv.	Maria Magdalena Eisenhauer, born in Weschnitz, Starkenburg, Hesse, Germany. She married Michael Fischer 01 Mar 1757 in ,Dauphin/Berks, Pennsylvania.
6	v.	Johannes Eisenhauer, born 24 Jun 1725 in Weschnitz, Starkenburg, Hesse; died 01 Feb 1789 in , Lebanon, Pennsylvania.
7	vi.	Martin Eisenhauer, born 1729 in Germany.

Generation No. 2

4. Hans Peter⁴ Eisenhauer (Hans Nicholas³, Hans Peter², Hans¹) was born 1716 in Palatinate District of Germany, and died 10 Jun 1801 in Lower Paxton Township, Dauphin, Pennsylvania. He married **(1) Elizabeth Graff** in of Dauphin, Pennsylvania. She was born in ,,,Germany. He married **(2) Anna Maria Elizabeth Schmidt** 21 Aug 1770 in Bethel, Dauphin, Pennsylvania. She was born 1725 in Of, Pennsylvania. He married **(3) Anna Margaret Dissinger** 29 Jan 1777 in Stouchsburg, Berks, Pennsylvania, daughter of Peter Dissinger. She was born Abt. 1750 in Christ Lutheran, Stouchsburg Berks Co, PA, and died 18 Nov 1815 in Lower Paxton, Dauphin, PA.

Children of Hans Eisenhauer and Elizabeth Graff are:

+ 8	i.	Peter⁵ Eisenhauer, born 06 Sep 1745 in Bethel, Dauphin/Berks, Pennsylvania; died 1795.
+ 9	ii.	Maria Barbara Eisenhauer, born 22 Aug 1747 in Bethel, Dauphin, Pennsylvania; died 1808 in Rowan, North Carolina.
+ 10	iii.	John Nicholas Eisenhauer, born 06 May 1749 in Lancaster, Lebanon/Berks, Pennsylvania; died 1802 in ,,Pennsylvania.
+ 11	iv.	George Michael Eisenhauer, born 04 Aug 1751 in Berks, Pennsylvania.
12	v.	Anna Margaretha Eisenhauer, born 14 Feb 1753 in , Berks, Pennsylvania. She married Christian Meyer 05 Jan 1772 in , Berks, Pennsylvania.
+ 13	vi.	John Frederick Eisenhauer, born 06 Oct 1753 in ,Berks, Pennsylvania; died 10 Apr 1777 in Rising Sun, Germantown, Pennsylvania.
14	vii.	Philipp Eisenhauer, born 19 Dec 1754 in ,Berks, Pennsylvania.
15	viii.	Maria Magdalena Eisenhauer, born 07 Mar 1756 in ,Berks, Pennsylvania.
16	ix.	Anna Maria Elizabeth Eisenhauer, born 25 Apr 1759 in ,Berks, Pennsylvania; died 19 Nov 1847. She married Wood.
+ 17	x.	Samuel Eisenhauer, born 25 Nov 1763 in Berks, Pennsylvania.

Child of Hans Eisenhauer and Anna Schmidt is:

+ 18	i.	John⁵ Eisenhauer, born 05 Feb 1774 in ,Berks, Pennsylvania; died 21 Jun 1861.

Children of Hans Eisenhauer and Anna Dissinger are:

19	i.	John Jacob⁵ Eisenhauer, born 13 Apr 1777 in ,Berks, Pennsylvania. He married Nancy Anna McDonald 09 Jun 1803 in ,Dauphin, Pennsylvania.
20	ii.	Catherine Eisenhauer, born 1780 in ,Berks, Pennsylvania.
21	iii.	Ann Eisenhauer, born 1781 in ,Berks, Pennsylvania.

22	iv.	Christina Eisenhauer, born 1783 in ,Berks, Pennsylvania.
+ 23	v.	Barbara Eisenhauer, born Mar 1784 in ,Berks, Pennsylvania.
+ 24	vi.	Margaret Eisenhauer, born 1787 in Berks, Pennsylvania.
25	vii.	John Peter Eisenhauer, born 04 Jan 1790 in ,Berks, Pennsylvania.
+ 26	viii.	Frederick Eisenhauer, born 15 Jul 1794 in Linglestown, Dauphin, Pennsylvania; died 13 Mar 1884 in Belle Springs, Dickinson, Kansas.

Generation No. 3

8. Peter⁵ Eisenhauer (Hans Peter⁴, Hans Nicholas³, Hans Peter², Hans¹) was born 06 Sep 1745 in Bethel, Dauphin/Berks, Pennsylvania, and died 1795. He married **Anna Maria Fisher** 07 May 1765 in Bethel, Dauphin, Pennsylvania. She was born 1750 in Of Dauphin, Pennsylvania.

Children of Peter Eisenhauer and Anna Fisher are:

27	i.	Peter⁶ Eisenhauer, born 1776 in , Dauphin, Pennsylvania. He married Anna Margaret Early Oehrle 24 Aug 1794.
28	ii.	Joseph Eisenhauer, born 1778 in , Dauphin, Pennsylvania. He married Catherine.
29	iii.	Anna May Eisenhauer, born 1780 in , Dauphin, Pennsylvania. She married Abraham Wolf 1800.
30	iv.	Johannes Eisenhauer, born 1782 in , Dauphin, Pennsylvania. He married Christine Maria Krebs 30 Oct 1798.

9. Maria Barbara⁵ Eisenhauer (Hans Peter⁴, Hans Nicholas³, Hans Peter², Hans¹) was born 22 Aug 1747 in Bethel, Dauphin, Pennsylvania, and died 1808 in Rowan, North Carolina. She married **Christian M. Mikel** 05 Mar 1765 in Bethel, Dauphin, Pennsylvania. He was born in Pennsylvania, and died in Rowan, North Carolina.

Children of Maria Eisenhauer and Christian Mikel are:

31	i.	?⁶ Mikel. She married ? ?.
32	ii.	Barbara Mikel, born in Pennsylvania. She married Elisha Barber.
33	iii.	John Mikel, born in , Rowan, North Carolina.
+ 34	iv.	David H. Mikel, born 04 Apr 1772 in ,Pennsylvania; died in Missouriravian Springs, Wilkes, North Carolina.

10. John Nicholas⁵ Eisenhauer (Hans Peter⁴, Hans Nicholas³, Hans Peter², Hans¹) was born 06 May 1749 in Lancaster, Lebanon/Berks, Pennsylvania, and died 1802 in ,,Pennsylvania. He married **Mary Myers** 19 Apr 1773 in ,Rowan, North Carolina. She was born 1752 in ,,Pennsylvania, and died 09 Aug 1832 in Gold Hill, Rowan, North Carolina.

Children of John Eisenhauer and Mary Myers are:

+ 35	i.	George Michael⁶ Eisenhauer, born in Radell, Alexander, North Carolina.
36	ii.	Martin Eisenhauer, born in Iradell, Alexander, North Carolina.
+ 37	iii.	John Nicholas Eisenhauer, born in Iradell, Alexander, North Carolina.
+ 38	iv.	Peter Eisenhauer, born 1774 in Iradell, Alexander, North Carolina; died 1850 in Gold Hill, Rowan, North Carolina.
39	v.	Mary Eisenhauer, born 1776 in Iradell, Alexander, North Carolina.

11. George Michael⁵ Eisenhauer (Hans Peter⁴, Hans Nicholas³, Hans Peter², Hans¹) was born 04 Aug 1751 in Berks, Pennsylvania. He married **Catherine ?** 1772 in Jonestown, Lebanon , Pennsylvania.

Children of George Eisenhauer and Catherine ? are:

+ 40	i.	George W.⁶ Eisenhauer, born in Fredricksburg, Lebanon, Pennsylvania.
+ 41	ii.	John Michael Eisenhauer, born 28 Aug 1774 in Fredricksburg, Lebanon, Pennsylvania; died 17 May 1850 in ,,Virginia.
42	iii.	Catherine Eisenhauer, born 1775 in Fredricksburg, Lebanon, Pennsylvania. She married John Webb.
43	iv.	Marie Elizabeth Eisenhauer, born 01 Sep 1776 in Fredricksburg, Lebanon, Pennsylvania; died 29 Dec 1855.
+ 44	v.	J. Jacob Eisenhauer, born 21 Sep 1778 in Fredricksburg, Lebanon, Pennsylvania.
+ 45	vi.	Johannes Eisenhauer, born 10 Feb 1781 in Fredricksburg, Lebanon, Pennsylvania; died 16 Nov 1861 in

13. John Frederick[5] Eisenhauer (Hans Peter[4], Hans Nicholas[3], Hans Peter[2], Hans[1]) was born 06 Oct 1753 in ,Berks, Pennsylvania, and died 10 Apr 1777 in Rising Sun, Germantown, Pennsylvania. He married **Hannah Kleinan**. She was born 1754 in ,Berks, Pennsylvania.

Children of John Eisenhauer and Hannah Kleinan are:

+ 46   i.   Hannah[6] Eisenhauer, born in , Dauphin, Pennsylvania; died in Columbiana, Columbiana, Ohio.
+ 47   ii.   Sarah Eisenhauer, born in ,Dauphin, Pennsylvania.
   48   iii.   Susannah Eisenhauer, born 1777 in Dauphin, Pennsylvania. She married David Allen.

17. Samuel[5] Eisenhauer (Hans Peter[4], Hans Nicholas[3], Hans Peter[2], Hans[1]) was born 25 Nov 1763 in Berks, Pennsylvania. He married **Elizabeth**. She was born 1768 in Botetourt, Virginia.

Children of Samuel Eisenhauer and Elizabeth are:

   49   i.   Elizabeth[6] Eisenhauer, born 1785 in ,Botetourt, Virginia. She married ? ?.
   50   ii.   Susannah Eisenhauer, born 1788 in Botetourt, Virginia. She married Francis Camper 20 May 1811.
+ 51   iii.   Jacob Eisenhauer, born 1790 in ,Botetourt, Virginia; died 1853 in ,,Virginia.

18. John[5] Eisenhauer (Hans Peter[4], Hans Nicholas[3], Hans Peter[2], Hans[1]) was born 05 Feb 1774 in ,Berks, Pennsylvania, and died 21 Jun 1861. He married **Catherine Plank**. She was born 25 Feb 1770 in ,Berks, Pennsylvania, and died 17 Jul 1843.

Children of John Eisenhauer and Catherine Plank are:

+ 52   i.   Catherine[6] Eisenhauer, born 14 Apr 1796 in Linglestown, Dauphin , Pennsylvania; died 17 Feb 1855.
+ 53   ii.   Marie Elizabeth Eisenhauer, born 03 Nov 1797 in Linglestown, Dauphin, Pennsylvania.
+ 54   iii.   John David Eisenhauer, born 27 Sep 1799 in Linglestown, Dauphin, Pennsylvania; died 17 Sep 1827 in Greensburg, Pennsylvania.
   55   iv.   Maria Magdalena Eisenhauer, born 06 Nov 1802 in Linglestown, Dauphin, Pennsylvania; died 28 Mar 1838. She married Samuel Seig.

23. Barbara[5] Eisenhauer (Hans Peter[4], Hans Nicholas[3], Hans Peter[2], Hans[1]) was born Mar 1784 in ,Berks, Pennsylvania. She married **Conrad Knepley** 04 Aug 1801 in ,Dauphin , Pennsylvania.

Children of Barbara Eisenhauer and Conrad Knepley are:

   56   i.   Jefferson[6] Knepley, born 1803 in Annville, Lebanon, Pennsylvania.
   57   ii.   Jacob Knepley, born 1805 in Annville, Lebanon, Pennsylvania.
   58   iii.   William Knepley, born 1807 in Annville, Lebanon, Pennsylvania.
   59   iv.   Mary Knepley, born 1810 in Annville, Lebanon, Pennsylvania.

24. Margaret[5] Eisenhauer (Hans Peter[4], Hans Nicholas[3], Hans Peter[2], Hans[1]) was born 1787 in Berks, Pennsylvania. She married **George Leininger** 08 Oct 1808 in ,Dauphin, Pennsylvania.

Child of Margaret Eisenhauer and George Leininger is:

   60   i.   George[6] Leininger, born 10 Jan 1814 in Harrisburg, Dauphin, Pennsylvania.

26. Frederick[5] Eisenhauer (Hans Peter[4], Hans Nicholas[3], Hans Peter[2], Hans[1]) was born 15 Jul 1794 in Linglestown, Dauphin, Pennsylvania, and died 13 Mar 1884 in Belle Springs, Dickinson, Kansas. He married **Barbara Miller** 1816 in Linglestown, Dauphin, Pa, daughter of John Miller and Susanna Raysor. She was born 27 May 1789 in Elizabethville, Dauphin, Pa, and died 01 Jan 1862 in Millersburg, Dauphin, Pa.

Children of Frederick Eisenhauer and Barbara Miller are:

+ 61   i.   Polly[6] Eisenhauer, born 13 Aug 1817 in Elizabethville, Dauphin, Pennsylvania; died 09 Dec 1863.
+ 62   ii.   Anna Eisenhauer, born 25 Aug 1819 in Elizabethville, Dauphin, Pennsylvania; died 26 Dec 1849 in Elizabethville, Dauphin, Pennsylvania.

63	iii.	John David Eisenhauer, born 23 Jun 1821 in Elizabethville, Dauphin, Pennsylvania; died 13 Dec 1840 in Dauphin Co, PA.
+ 64	iv.	Catherine Eisenhower, born 11 Jul 1824 in Elizabethville, Dauphin Co, PA; died 07 Nov 1907 in Abilene, Dickinson, Kansas.
+ 65	v.	Jacob Frederick Eisenhauer, born 19 Sep 1826 in Elizabethville, Washington Twp., Dauphin Co., PA; died 20 May 1906 in Abilene, Dickinson Co , Kansas.
+ 66	vi.	Samuel P Eisenhower, born 04 Feb 1831 in Elizabethville, Dauphin, Pennsylvania.

Generation No. 4

34. David H.[6] Mikel (Maria Barbara[5] Eisenhauer, Hans Peter[4], Hans Nicholas[3], Hans Peter[2], Hans[1]) was born 04 Apr 1772 in ,Pennsylvania, and died in Missouriravian Springs, Wilkes, North Carolina. He married **Lucinda Doty** 19 Aug 1794 in , Rowan, North Carolina. She was born 01 May 1772 in New Jersey>, and died in Missouriravian Springs, Wilkes, North Carolina.

Children of David Mikel and Lucinda Doty are:

67	i.	Mikel[7], born in ,Wilkes, North Carolina.
68	ii.	Mikel.
+ 69	iii.	Hannah Mikel, born 22 Aug 1794 in , Rowan, North Carolina; died 28 Feb 1885 in , Johnson, Missouri.
+ 70	iv.	John S. Mikel, born 07 Jul 1799 in , Rowan, North Carolina; died 07 Jan 1865 in Missouri.
+ 71	v.	Sarah Mikel, born 30 Jul 1803 in ,Wilkes, North Carolina; died 10 Apr 1894 in Neosho, Kansas.
+ 72	vi.	David Hugh Mikel, born 04 Aug 1806 in Wilkesboro, Wilkes, North Carolina; died 02 Jan 1855 in Greentop, Schuyler, Missouri.
+ 73	vii.	Lucinda Mikel, born 12 Feb 1809 in Wilkesboro, Wilkes, North Carolina; died 25 Feb 1843.
+ 74	viii.	Moses Loren Mikel, born 13 Aug 1813 in ,Wilkes, North Carolina; died 16 Oct 1899 in San Jose, California.
+ 75	ix.	Rebecca Mikel, born 16 Dec 1819 in , Wilkes, North Carolina; died 24 May 1908 in Boone, Watauga, North Carolina.

35. George Michael[6] Eisenhauer (John Nicholas[5], Hans Peter[4], Hans Nicholas[3], Hans Peter[2], Hans[1]) was born in Radell, Alexander, North Carolina. He married **Barbara Agleston** 1799 in ,Rowan, North Carolina.

Children of George Eisenhauer and Barbara Agleston are:

76	i.	Mary[7] Eisenhauer, born 1800.
77	ii.	Elizabeth Eisenhauer, born 1802.
78	iii.	Daniel Eisenhauer, born 1805; died 1865. He married Susanna Barringer.
79	iv.	Barbara Eisenhauer, born 1807.
80	v.	Catherine Eisenhauer, born 1809.
+ 81	vi.	George Michael Eisenhauer, born 1811; died 1872.
82	vii.	G. Adam Eisenhauer, born 1815; died 1857. He married Barbara Goodnite.
83	viii.	John A. Eisenhauer, born 1816; died 1897. He married Rosanna Overcash.
84	ix.	Margaret Eisenhauer, born 1816.

37. John Nicholas[6] Eisenhauer (John Nicholas[5], Hans Peter[4], Hans Nicholas[3], Hans Peter[2], Hans[1]) was born in Iradell, Alexander, North Carolina. He married **Elizabeth Null**. She was born 1788 in Taylorsville, Alexander, North Carolina, and died 1871.

Children of John Eisenhauer and Elizabeth Null are:

85	i.	Mary[7] Eisenhauer.
86	ii.	Joseph Eisenhauer, born 1804; died 1809. He married (1) Elizabeth Gallimore. He married (2) Alphonia.
87	iii.	Martin Eisenhauer, born 1805. He married (1) Margaret Hayr. He married (2) Jane Reed. He married (3) Jane Preshill Bentley.
+ 88	iv.	Sarah Jane Eisenhauer, born 1807; died 1851.
89	v.	Catherine Eisenhauer, born 1813.
90	vi.	Elizabeth Eisenhauer, born 1815.
91	vii.	Alexander Caleb Eisenhauer, born 1818 in Alexander, North Carolina. He married Mary Ann Fox.
92	viii.	Ann Eisenhauer, born 1820 in ,Alexander, North Carolina.

| 93 | ix. | John Eisenhauer, born 1821 in ,Rowan, North Carolina. He married Margaret Hunsucker; born 1823 in ,,North Carolina. |
| 94 | x. | Christine Eisenhauer, born 1823. |

38. Peter[6] Eisenhauer (John Nicholas[5], Hans Peter[4], Hans Nicholas[3], Hans Peter[2], Hans[1]) was born 1774 in Iradell, Alexander, North Carolina, and died 1850 in Gold Hill, Rowan, North Carolina. He married **Mary Kenup** 1801. She was born 1781 in Of, Rowan, North Carolina, and died 1842 in Gold Hill, Rowan, North Carolina.

Children of Peter Eisenhauer and Mary Kenup are:

	95	i.	Elizabeth[7] Eisenhauer, born 1803 in ,Rowan, North Carolina.
	96	ii.	Caty Eisenhauer, born 1804 in ,Rowan, North Carolina.
	97	iii.	Mary Eisenhauer, born 1806 in ,Rowan, North Carolina.
	98	iv.	Anna Eisenhauer, born 1808 in ,Rowan, North Carolina.
	99	v.	Sally Eisenhauer, born 1810 in ,Rowan, North Carolina.
	100	vi.	Jacob Eisenhauer, born 1812 in Rowan, North Carolina. He married Elizabeth L. Leopald 30 Nov 1841 in ,Rowan, North Carolina.
+	101	vii.	Daniel Eisenhauer, born 19 Jun 1814 in ,Rowan, North Carolina; died 10 Nov 1895 in ,Cabarrus, North Carolina.
	102	viii.	Rachel Eisenhauer, born 1816 in ,Rowan, North Carolina.
	103	ix.	Susannah Eisenhauer, born 1817 in ,Rowan, North Carolina.
	104	x.	Phillipina Eisenhauer, born 1819 in ,Rowan, North Carolina.
	105	xi.	Henry Michael Eisenhauer, born 1822 in ,Rowan, North Carolina. He married Caty Dry.

40. George W.[6] Eisenhauer (George Michael[5], Hans Peter[4], Hans Nicholas[3], Hans Peter[2], Hans[1]) was born in Fredricksburg, Lebanon, Pennsylvania. He married **Jennet Walker** 31 May 1810 in , Rockbridge, Virginia.

Children of George Eisenhauer and Jennet Walker are:

+	106	i.	Timothy N.[7] Eisenhauer.
+	107	ii.	Alexander Eisenhauer.
+	108	iii.	George W. Eisenhauer.
	109	iv.	John W. Eisenhauer.
	110	v.	Matilda C. Eisenhauer, born 1822. She married Harvey L. Goode.
	111	vi.	James Harvey Eisenhauer, born 1825. He married Margaret McCorkle.

41. John Michael[6] Eisenhauer (George Michael[5], Hans Peter[4], Hans Nicholas[3], Hans Peter[2], Hans[1]) was born 28 Aug 1774 in Fredricksburg, Lebanon, Pennsylvania, and died 17 May 1850 in ,,Virginia. He married **Isabella Mitchell** 18 Feb 1804 in ,Botetourt , Virginia. She was born 1783.

Children of John Eisenhauer and Isabella Mitchell are:

	112	i.	Andrew[7] Eisenhauer, born 1804.
	113	ii.	Margaret Eisenhauer, born 1806.
	114	iii.	Isabella Eisenhauer, born 1808.
	115	iv.	Michael Eisenhauer, born 1811; died 1864. He married Durcilla Mann.
	116	v.	Mary Eisenhauer, born 1813.
	117	vi.	Sarah Eisenhauer, born 1815. She married Henson.
	118	vii.	William Mitchell Eisenhauer, born 1820; died 1860. He married Rachel Anderson.

44. J. Jacob[6] Eisenhauer (George Michael[5], Hans Peter[4], Hans Nicholas[3], Hans Peter[2], Hans[1]) was born 21 Sep 1778 in Fredricksburg, Lebanon, Pennsylvania. He married **Annie Robinson** 21 Sep 1820 in ,Rockbridge , Virginia. She was born 1792, and died 1877.

Children of J. Eisenhauer and Annie Robinson are:

+	119	i.	Samuel L.[7] Eisenhauer, born 1822; died 1893.
	120	ii.	James V. Eisenhauer, born 1825; died 1885.
	121	iii.	Jacob Burns Eisenhauer, born 1827.

45. Johannes[6] Eisenhauer (George Michael[5], Hans Peter[4], Hans Nicholas[3], Hans Peter[2], Hans[1]) was born 10 Feb 1781 in Fredricksburg, Lebanon, Pennsylvania, and died 16 Nov 1861 in Ringtown, Schuylkill, Pennsylvania. He married **Eva** 16 Dec. She was born 1783, and died 1862.

Children of Johannes Eisenhauer and Eva are:

	122	i.	Peter[7] Eisenhauer, born 1804; died 1874. He married Elizabeth.
+	123	ii.	John J. Eisenhauer, born 1807; died 1864.
	124	iii.	Jacob Eisenhauer, born 1813; died 1815.
	125	iv.	Elizabeth Eisenhauer, born 1815.
	126	v.	Isaac Eisenhauer, born 1821. He married Polly.
	127	vi.	Abraham Eisenhauer, born 1822.

46. Hannah[6] Eisenhauer (John Frederick[5], Hans Peter[4], Hans Nicholas[3], Hans Peter[2], Hans[1]) was born in , Dauphin, Pennsylvania, and died in Columbiana, Columbiana, Ohio. She married **Jesse Allen**. He was born in Ohio, and died in Salem Ohio.

Children of Hannah Eisenhauer and Jesse Allen are:

	128	i.	Felena[7] Allen, born in Columbiana, Columbiana, Ohio.
+	129	ii.	Clarkston Allen, born in Columbiana, Columbiana, Ohio.
	130	iii.	Willburface Allen, born in Columbiana, Columbiana, Ohio.
	131	iv.	Elizabeth Allen, born in Columbiana, Columbiana, Ohio.
	132	v.	John Allen, born in Columbiana, Columbiana, Ohio. He married Hull.

47. Sarah[6] Eisenhauer (John Frederick[5], Hans Peter[4], Hans Nicholas[3], Hans Peter[2], Hans[1]) was born in ,Dauphin, Pennsylvania. She married **David Allen**.

Children of Sarah Eisenhauer and David Allen are:

| 133 | i. | Synthia Ann[7] Allen. She married Henry Swaggart. |
| 134 | ii. | Hiram Allen, born 1797. |

51. Jacob[6] Eisenhauer (Samuel[5], Hans Peter[4], Hans Nicholas[3], Hans Peter[2], Hans[1]) was born 1790 in ,Botetourt, Virginia, and died 1853 in ,,Virginia. He married **Esther Lantz** 03 Feb 1810 in ,Rockbridge, Virginia. She was born 1793.

Children of Jacob Eisenhauer and Esther Lantz are:

135	i.	Mary Ann[7] Eisenhauer, born 1812.
136	ii.	Jonathan Eisenhauer, born 1815. He married (1) Elizabeth Croply. He married (2) Jane A. Hamilton.
137	iii.	Eliza M. Eisenhauer, born 1817. She married John Walker.
138	iv.	Agnes Eisenhauer, born 1819. She married Patrick Guaen.
139	v.	Joseph J. Eisenhauer, born 1820; died 1880. He married Elizabeth Nichols.
140	vi.	Catherine Eisenhauer, born 1822. He married John Smith.
141	vii.	Margaret Eisenhauer, born 1825. She married William Alexander McNabb.
142	viii.	Jacob H. Eisenhauer, born 1827; died 1909. He married Francis Goodrich.

52. Catherine[6] Eisenhauer (John[5], Hans Peter[4], Hans Nicholas[3], Hans Peter[2], Hans[1]) was born 14 Apr 1796 in Linglestown, Dauphin , Pennsylvania, and died 17 Feb 1855. She married **David Unger**. He was born 1792.

Child of Catherine Eisenhauer and David Unger is:

| 143 | i. | John George[7] Unger, born 1817. |

53. Marie Elizabeth[6] Eisenhauer (John[5], Hans Peter[4], Hans Nicholas[3], Hans Peter[2], Hans[1]) was born 03 Nov 1797 in Linglestown, Dauphin, Pennsylvania. She married **Jacob Bludhart**. He was born 1793.

Children of Marie Eisenhauer and Jacob Bludhart are:

144	i.	Margaret[7] Bludhart, born 1816.
145	ii.	Elizabeth Bludhart, born 1820.

54. John David[6] Eisenhauer (John[5], Hans Peter[4], Hans Nicholas[3], Hans Peter[2], Hans[1]) was born 27 Sep 1799 in Linglestown, Dauphin, Pennsylvania, and died 17 Sep 1827 in Greensburg, Pennsylvania. He married **Elizabeth M. Gearhart**. She was born 1804.

Child of John Eisenhauer and Elizabeth Gearhart is:

+ 146   i.   Jane Catherine[7] Eisenhauer, born 1827; died 1907.

61. Polly[6] Eisenhauer (Frederick[5], Hans Peter[4], Hans Nicholas[3], Hans Peter[2], Hans[1]) was born 13 Aug 1817 in Elizabethville, Dauphin, Pennsylvania, and died 09 Dec 1863. She married **Benjamin Miller**.

Children of Polly Eisenhauer and Benjamin Miller are:

147	i.	John[7] Miller, born 1837.
148	ii.	Susan Miller, born 1840.

62. Anna[6] Eisenhauer (Frederick[5], Hans Peter[4], Hans Nicholas[3], Hans Peter[2], Hans[1]) was born 25 Aug 1819 in Elizabethville, Dauphin, Pennsylvania, and died 26 Dec 1849 in Elizabethville, Dauphin, Pennsylvania. She married **Joseph Novinger** 1839 in ,Dauphin , Pennsylvania. He was born 08 Feb 1810 in Upper Paxton Twp, Dauphin Co, PA.

Children of Anna Eisenhauer and Joseph Novinger are:

149	i.	James[7] Novinger.
150	ii.	John D. Novinger, born 21 Dec 1840 in Dauphin Co, PA. He married Leah Jane Orndorff.
151	iii.	Samuel P. Novinger, born 11 Oct 1842. He married Catherine Shaffetall.
152	iv.	Mary Ann Novinger, born 1844. She married William Stauffer.
153	v.	Catherine Novinger, born 19 Jul 1846. She married Eubert Dufler.
154	vi.	Elizabeth Novinger, born 25 Aug 1848 in Dauphin Co, PA; died 06 Jun 1938. She married John Abraham Keifer.

64. Catherine[6] Eisenhower (Frederick[5] Eisenhauer, Hans Peter[4], Hans Nicholas[3], Hans Peter[2], Hans[1]) was born 11 Jul 1824 in Elizabethville, Dauphin Co, PA, and died 07 Nov 1907 in Abilene, Dickinson, Kansas. She married **Samuel Pyke** 30 Mar 1848 in Pennsylvania. He was born 06 Apr 1825 in York, PA, and died 26 May 1887 in Abilene, Dickinson Co, KS.

Children of Catherine Eisenhower and Samuel Pyke are:

+	155	i.	John David[7] Pyke, born 14 Jul 1849; died 1904.
+	156	ii.	Jacob Frederick Pyke, born 16 Oct 1851; died 1896.
	157	iii.	Susan Pyke, born 17 Jul 1853.
	158	iv.	Mary Ann Pyke, born 26 Mar 1855; died 1856.
+	159	v.	Sarah Catherine Pyke, born 29 Nov 1856; died 1930.
	160	vi.	Samuel Peter Pyke, born 23 Jul 1860; died 1880.
+	161	vii.	Anna Jane Pyke, born 22 May 1864.
+	162	viii.	Elizabeth Rebecca Pyke, born 09 Apr 1869 in Millersburg, PA; died 1895.

65. Jacob Frederick[6] Eisenhauer (Frederick[5], Hans Peter[4], Hans Nicholas[3], Hans Peter[2], Hans[1]) was born 19 Sep 1826 in Elizabethville, Washington Twp., Dauphin Co., PA, and died 20 May 1906 in Abilene, Dickinson Co , Kansas. He married **Margareta Rebecca Matter** 25 Feb 1847 in Dauphin , Pennsylvania, daughter of Heinrich Matter and Anna Deitrich. She was born 18 Mar 1825 in Mifflin Twp, Dauphin, PA, and died 22 Jun 1890 in Abilene, Dickinson Co , Kansas.

Children of Jacob Eisenhauer and Margareta Matter are:

	163	i.	John H.[7] Eisenhauer, born 07 Mar 1848 in Elizabethville, Dauphin Co, PA; died 10 Apr 1857 in Elizabethville, Dauphin Co, PA.
+	164	ii.	Mary Ann Eisenhauer, born 02 Sep 1849 in Elizabethville, Dauphin, Pennsylvania; died 27 Apr 1893

in Abilene, Dickinson, Kansas.

+ 165   iii. Catherine Ann Eisenhauer, born 19 Mar 1851 in Elizabethville, Dauphin, Pennsylvania; died 03 Apr 1924 in Ramona, Marion, Kansas.

166   iv. Jacob F. Eisenhauer, born 03 Sep 1852 in Elizabethville, Dauphin Co, PA; died 02 Oct 1852 in Elizabethville, Dauphin Co, PA.

167   v. Samuel F. Eisenhauer, born 30 Sep 1853 in Elizabethville, Dauphin Co, PA; died 11 Jun 1854 in Elizabethville, Dauphin Co, PA.

+ 168   vi. Susanna Eisenhauer, born 29 Oct 1854 in Elizabethville, Dauphin, Pennsylvania; died 14 Jun 1932 in York, PA.

169   vii. Peter A. Eisenhauer, born 27 Nov 1855 in Elizabethville, Dauphin Co, PA; died 04 Aug 1856 in Elizabethville, Dauphin Co, PA.

170   viii. Lydia A. Eisenhauer, born 27 Aug 1857 in Elizabethville, Dauphin Co, PA; died 15 Nov 1874 in Elizabethville, Dauphin Co, PA.

171   ix. Emma Jane Eisenhauer, born 03 Dec 1859 in Elizabethville, Dauphin Co, PA; died 08 May 1860 in Elizabethville, Dauphin Co, PA.

+ 172   x. Amanda Hannah Eisenhauer, born 11 Dec 1861 in Elizabethville, Dauphin Co, PA; died 25 Aug 1951 in Abilene, Dickinson Co, KS.

+ 173   xi. David Jacob Eisenhauer, born 23 Sep 1863 in Elizabethville, Dauphin, Pennsylvania; died 10 Mar 1942 in Abilene, Dickinson, Kansas.

174   xii. Dr Abraham Lincoln Eisenhauer, born 22 Jul 1865 in Elizabethville, Dauphin Co, PA; died 23 Dec 1944 in Upland, CA. He married Anna Long 1886; born 1865.

175   xiii. Clinton Eisenhauer, born 30 Jul 1867 in Elizabethville, Dauphin Co, PA; died 10 Aug 1867 in Elizabethville, Dauphin Co, PA.

+ 176   xiv. Ira A Eisenhower, born 30 Jul 1867 in Elizabethville, Dauphin, Pa; died 28 Mar 1943 in Los Angeles, CA.

66. Samuel P[6] Eisenhower (Frederick[5] Eisenhauer, Hans Peter[4], Hans Nicholas[3], Hans Peter[2], Hans[1]) was born 04 Feb 1831 in Elizabethville, Dauphin, Pennsylvania. He married **(1) Lydia Orndorff**. He married **(2) Mary Ann Orndorff** 21 Oct 1855 in ,,Pennsylvania. She was born 1839, and died 1932.

Children of Samuel Eisenhower and Mary Orndorff are:

177   i. William Henry[7] Eisenhauer, born 1858; died 1926. He married Alice Hoover.

178   ii. Eisenhauer, born 1859; died 1859.

+ 179   iii. Mary Ann Eisenhauer, born 1860 in Elizabethville, Dauphin Co, PA; died 1918.

180   iv. Leah Jane Eisenhauer, born 1864; died 1865.

181   v. Elizabeth Eisenhauer, born 1868; died 1875.

182   vi. Sarah Ellen Eisenhauer, born 1873; died 1942. She married Abram Book.

183   vii. John Franklin Eisenhauer, born 1874. He married Mabel Blanche Beasler.

+ 184   viii. Emma Bertha Eisenhauer, born 23 Jul 1876 in Millersburg, PA; died 1941.

185   ix. James Monroe Eisenhauer, born 1878; died 1941. He married Josephine Gastbend.

186   x. Simon Peter Eisenhauer, born 1880. He married Edythe Rager.

Generation No. 5

69. Hannah[7] Mikel (David H.[6], Maria Barbara[5] Eisenhauer, Hans Peter[4], Hans Nicholas[3], Hans Peter[2], Hans[1]) was born 22 Aug 1794 in , Rowan, North Carolina, and died 28 Feb 1885 in , Johnson, Missouri. She married **Micajah I. Hampton** 01 Dec 1813 in , Wilkes, North Carolina. He was born in , Wilkes, North Carolina, and died 29 Aug 1868 in , Johnson, Missouri.

Children of Hannah Mikel and Micajah Hampton are:

187   i. Hampton[8], born in , Wilkes, North Carolina.

+ 188   ii. Mary Hampton, born in , Wilkes, North Carolina.

189   iii. Hampton, born in , Wilkes, North Carolina.

+ 190   iv. Noah Hampton, born in , Wilkes, North Carolina.

+ 191   v. John Hampton, born in , Wilkes, North Carolina; died in , Wilkes, North Carolina.

+ 192   vi. Rufus Hampton, born in , Wilkes, North Carolina; died in , Johnson, Missouri.

193   vii. Lorenzo Hampton, born in , Wilkes, North Carolina. He married Olive Minerva Cobb.

194   viii. William James Hampton, born in , Wilkes, North Carolina.

195   ix. Hampton, born in , Wilkes, North Carolina.

196   x. Hampton, born in , Wilkes, North Carolina.

197   xi. ? Hampton, born in , Wilkes, North Carolina.

+	198	xii.	David Hampton, born 22 Jul 1822 in , Wilkes, North Carolina; died 16 Sep 1904 in , Johnson, Missouri.
+	199	xiii.	Silas Hampton, born 20 Jun 1832 in , Wilkes, North Carolina; died 27 Oct 1911 in Tekamah, Burt, Nebraska.
+	200	xiv.	Romlour Agustus Hampton, born 24 May 1839 in Wilkes, North Carolina; died 25 Oct 1908 in Johnson, Missouri.

70. John S.[7] Mikel (David H.[6], Maria Barbara[5] Eisenhauer, Hans Peter[4], Hans Nicholas[3], Hans Peter[2], Hans[1]) was born 07 Jul 1799 in , Rowan, North Carolina, and died 07 Jan 1865 in Missouri. He married **(1) Sarah Whitacre** 29 Jun 1803 in ,Rowan, North Carolina. She was born in North Carolina, and died in , Muhlenberg, Kentucky. He married **(2) Louisa Bethany Mintum** 19 Dec 1825 in Wilkesboro, Wilkes, North Carolina. She was born 27 Aug 1812 in Wilkesboro, Wilkes, North Carolina, and died 15 Apr 1900 in Kirksville, Adair, Missouri.

Children of John Mikel and Sarah Whitacre are:
+	201	i.	Samuel[8] Mikel, born in , Schuyler, Missouri.
+	202	ii.	John S. Mikel, born in Kentucky; died Aft. 1860.
	203	iii.	Ned Edward? Mikel.
+	204	iv.	Whitaker W. Mikel, born in Kentucky.
+	205	v.	Hugh Frank Mikel, born 09 Mar 1807 in , Rowan, North Carolina; died 06 Jun 1884 in Polk Township, Adair, Missouri.

Children of John Mikel and Louisa Mintum are:
	206	i.	Benjamin F.[8] Mikel, born 17 Sep 1830 in North Carolina; died 22 Nov 1835 in , Wilkes, North Carolina.
+	207	ii.	William Silas Mikel, born 09 Jan 1833 in Wilkesboro, Wilkes, North Carolina; died 28 Feb 1903 in Leavenworth, Leavenworth, Kansas.
	208	iii.	James P. Mikel, born 21 Nov 1834 in North Carolina; died 22 Oct 1864 in Greentop, Greentop, Schuyler, Missouri.
	209	iv.	Rebecca Adaline Mikel, born 01 Oct 1837 in North Carolina; died 01 Oct 1888. She married (1) Mark B. Patterson; born 20 Jan 1829 in Belfast, Waldo, Maine; died 27 Nov 1905. She married (2) Elias Brower 15 Dec 1852 in ,Schuyler, Missouri; born 18 Feb 1818 in ,,Ohio; died 17 Apr 1872 in Queen City, Schuyler, Missouri.
+	210	v.	Mary Jane Mikel, born 01 May 1841 in Greentop, Schuyler, Missouri; died 10 Jul 1923.
	211	vi.	Abraham Lee Mikel, born 28 Apr 1849 in ,,Missouri; died 03 Nov 1857.

71. Sarah[7] Mikel (David H.[6], Maria Barbara[5] Eisenhauer, Hans Peter[4], Hans Nicholas[3], Hans Peter[2], Hans[1]) was born 30 Jul 1803 in ,Wilkes, North Carolina, and died 10 Apr 1894 in Neosho, Kansas. She married **Shadrack Minton** 12 Feb 1829 in Tennessee. He was born 06 Nov 1805 in , Wilkes, North Carolina, and died 23 Jan 1841 in , Marshall, Tennessee.

Children of Sarah Mikel and Shadrack Minton are:
| + | 212 | i. | Lucy[8] Minton, born 08 Feb 1832 in ,,North Carolina; died Aft. 1865. |
| + | 213 | ii. | Martha Elizabeth Minton, born 21 Dec 1837 in ,,Kentucky; died 25 Dec 1924 in Chanute, Kansas. |

72. David Hugh[7] Mikel (David H.[6], Maria Barbara[5] Eisenhauer, Hans Peter[4], Hans Nicholas[3], Hans Peter[2], Hans[1]) was born 04 Aug 1806 in Wilkesboro, Wilkes, North Carolina, and died 02 Jan 1855 in Greentop, Schuyler, Missouri. He married **Margaret Minerva Swinney** 13 Jan 1831 in Missouriravian Springs, Wilkes, North Carolina. She was born 12 Nov 1815 in , Wilkes, North Carolina, and died 16 Mar 1889 in , Schuyler, Missouri.

Children of David Mikel and Margaret Swinney are:
	214	i.	William[8] Mikel, born in ,,North Carolina.
	215	ii.	Susan Mikel, born in ,,North Carolina.
+	216	iii.	Betheny Louisa Mikel, born 03 Feb 1840 in ,,Tennessee; died 14 Jan 1912.
+	217	iv.	David Hugh Mikel, born 13 Aug 1841 in , Perry, Tennessee; died in Missouri.
	218	v.	John Mikel, born 1844.
	219	vi.	Thomas M. Mikel, born 10 Nov 1846 in ,,Tennessee; died 03 Apr 1929. He married Mary J. Scott.

220   vii.   Nancy J. Mikel, born 1848 in ,,Tennessee.

221   viii.   James Mikel, born 1854.

73. Lucinda[7] Mikel (David H.[6], Maria Barbara[5] Eisenhauer, Hans Peter[4], Hans Nicholas[3], Hans Peter[2], Hans[1]) was born 12 Feb 1809 in Wilkesboro, Wilkes, North Carolina, and died 25 Feb 1843. She married **Christian Myers** 1829 in ,,Wilkes, North Carolina.

Child of Lucinda Mikel and Christian Myers is:

+   222   i.   Henry[8] Myers, born 07 Nov 1830 in ,Wilkes , North Carolina; died 08 May 1914.

74. Moses Loren[7] Mikel (David H.[6], Maria Barbara[5] Eisenhauer, Hans Peter[4], Hans Nicholas[3], Hans Peter[2], Hans[1]) was born 13 Aug 1813 in ,Wilkes, North Carolina, and died 16 Oct 1899 in San Jose, California. He married **Nancy Catherine King** in ,Wilkes, North Carolina. She was born 20 Dec 1821 in , Ashe, North Carolina, and died 11 Jan 1906 in San Jose, Santa Clara, California.

Children of Moses Mikel and Nancy King are:

   223   i.   Martha America[8] Mikel, born in , Wilkes, North Carolina; died 08 Apr 1929 in , Santa Clara, California. She married W. H. Hamilton; born in Florida.

   224   ii.   Sidney Mikel, born in ,,North Carolina.

   225   iii.   Joseph Mikel, born in North Carolina.

   226   iv.   Joseph N. Mikel, born in ,,North Carolina.

+   227   v.   James King Mikel, born in ,Wilkes, North Carolina.

   228   vi.   Sydney Fulton Mikel, born in ,Ashe, North Carolina; died 13 Mar 1901 in Oakland California. He married Mary Ann Rossiter 27 Dec 1871 in ,Ashe, North Carolina.

   229   vii.   Judith Isabell Mikel, born in Missouriravian Falls, Wilkes, North Carolina; died 18 Aug 1945. She married George Park Burkett 27 Dec 1876 in ,Ashe, North Carolina.

+   230   viii.   Charles Milton Mikel, born 07 Feb 1855 in Moravian Falls, Wilkes, North Carolina; died 17 Dec 1936 in Everett, Snohomish, Washington.

75. Rebecca[7] Mikel (David H.[6], Maria Barbara[5] Eisenhauer, Hans Peter[4], Hans Nicholas[3], Hans Peter[2], Hans[1]) was born 16 Dec 1819 in , Wilkes, North Carolina, and died 24 May 1908 in Boone, Watauga, North Carolina. She married **Samuel Brown** 01 May 1837 in , Wilkes, North Carolina. He was born 21 Nov 1807 in , Wilkes, North Carolina, and died 14 Mar 1897 in Boone, Watauga, North Carolina.

Children of Rebecca Mikel and Samuel Brown are:

   231   i.   William[8] Brown, born in , Wilkes, North Carolina. He married Martha E. Brown; born in North Carolina.

+   232   ii.   Mary Brown, born in , Wilkes, North Carolina.

   233   iii.   Sarah Brown, born in , Wilkes, North Carolina. She married Ben Ashley.

+   234   iv.   John W. Brown, born in , Wilkes, North Carolina.

   235   v.   Maria Brown, born in , Wilkes, North Carolina. She married Tom Story.

+   236   vi.   Joseph Brown, born in , Wilkes, North Carolina.

   237   vii.   Lucy Brown, born in , Wilkes, North Carolina. She married Asa Gilbert.

   238   viii.   Martha Brown, born in North Carolina. She married James Osborn.

   239   ix.   Julia Brown, born in North Carolina. She married Jim Day.

   240   x.   Benjamin F. Brown, born in North Carolina. He married Myra Johnson.

   241   xi.   Martishe R. Brown, born in North Carolina. She married Kimber Johnson.

   242   xii.   Laura E. Brown, born in North Carolina.

+   243   xiii.   David A. Brown, born in North Carolina.

81. George Michael[7] Eisenhauer (George Michael[6], John Nicholas[5], Hans Peter[4], Hans Nicholas[3], Hans Peter[2], Hans[1]) was born 1811, and died 1872. He married **(1) Mary Barringer**. She was born 1813, and died 1845. He married **(2) Esther Ridenhour**.

Children of George Eisenhauer and Mary Barringer are:

   244   i.   ?[8] Eisenhauer.

   245   ii.   Daniel Monroe Eisenhauer, born 1836.

   246   iii.   Barbara S. Eisenhauer, born 1842.

88. Sarah Jane^7 Eisenhauer (John Nicholas^6, John Nicholas^5, Hans Peter^4, Hans Nicholas^3, Hans Peter^2, Hans^1) was born 1807, and died 1851. She married **Hugh Franklin McCoy**. He was born 1803.

Children of Sarah Eisenhauer and Hugh McCoy are:
- 247   i.   Martin Lee^8 McCoy, born 1843; died 1928.
- 248   ii.   Washington McCoy, born 1843.
- 249   iii.   Matilda Josephine McCoy, born 1850; died 1923.

101. Daniel^7 Eisenhauer (Peter^6, John Nicholas^5, Hans Peter^4, Hans Nicholas^3, Hans Peter^2, Hans^1) was born 19 Jun 1814 in ,Rowan, North Carolina, and died 10 Nov 1895 in ,Cabarrus, North Carolina. He married **Leah Boger**. She was born 1823.

Children of Daniel Eisenhauer and Leah Boger are:
- 250   i.   Margaret^8 Eisenhauer, born 1845.
- 251   ii.   John Eisenhauer, born 1847; died 1923.
- 252   iii.   Amanda Leah Eisenhauer, born 1850; died 1935.
- 253   iv.   Frank Eisenhauer, born 1852.

106. Timothy N.^{7} Eisenhauer (George W.^{6}, George Michael^5, Hans Peter^4, Hans Nicholas^3, Hans Peter^2, Hans^1) He married **Lena V. Vandine**. She was born 1804.

Children of Timothy Eisenhauer and Lena Vandine are:
- 254   i.   Selina V.^{8} Eisenhauer, born 1835.
- 255   ii.   James Co. Eisenhauer, born 1837.

107. Alexander^7 Eisenhauer (George W.^{6}, George Michael^5, Hans Peter^4, Hans Nicholas^3, Hans Peter^2, Hans^1) He married **Eleanor Schoonover**.

Children of Alexander Eisenhauer and Eleanor Schoonover are:
- 256   i.   Mary A.^{8} Eisenhauer.
- 257   ii.   David G. W. Eisenhauer.
- 258   iii.   Virginia F. E. Eisenhauer.
- 259   iv.   Adeline Eisenhauer.
- 260   v.   John Eisenhauer.

108. George W.^{7} Eisenhauer (George W.^{6}, George Michael^5, Hans Peter^4, Hans Nicholas^3, Hans Peter^2, Hans^1) He married **Julia Ann Goode**. She was born 1826.

Children of George Eisenhauer and Julia Goode are:
- 261   i.   ?^{8} Eisenhauer.
- 262   ii.   Elijah J. Eisenhauer, born 1845.

119. Samuel L.^{7} Eisenhauer (J. Jacob^6, George Michael^5, Hans Peter^4, Hans Nicholas^3, Hans Peter^2, Hans^1) was born 1822, and died 1893. He married **Mary E. Stith**. She was born 1823, and died 1872.

Children of Samuel Eisenhauer and Mary Stith are:
- 263   i.   John Edward^8 Eisenhauer.
- 264   ii.   Lucy Ellen Eisenhauer, born 1840.
- 265   iii.   Richard L. Eisenhauer, born 1843.
- 266   iv.   Ann Eliza Eisenhauer, born 1848.
- 267   v.   William L. Eisenhauer, born 1849.
- 268   vi.   Eisenhauer, born 1851; died 1851.
- 269   vii.   Jacob Burns Eisenhauer, born 1855.
- 270   viii.   James H. Eisenhauer, born 1857.

271   ix. Emma L. Eisenhauer, born 1862.

123. John J.[7] Eisenhauer (Johannes[6], George Michael[5], Hans Peter[4], Hans Nicholas[3], Hans Peter[2], Hans[1]) was born 1807, and died 1864. He married **Susannah**. She was born 1808, and died 1837.

Children of John Eisenhauer and Susannah are:
272   i.   Susanna[8] Eisenhauer, born 1832; died 1910.
273   ii.   John J. Eisenhauer, born 1833; died 1905.
274   iii. Polly Eisenhauer, born 1835; died 1902.
275   iv.   Jacob Eisenhauer, born 1837. He married Elizabeth Bowman.

129. Clarkston[7] Allen (Hannah[6] Eisenhauer, John Frederick[5], Hans Peter[4], Hans Nicholas[3], Hans Peter[2], Hans[1]) was born in Columbiana, Columbiana, Ohio. He married **Anna Devitt**. She was born in , Ohio>.

Children of Clarkston Allen and Anna Devitt are:
276   i.   Adelaide[8] Allen, born in Columbiana, Columbiana, Ohio.
277   ii.   John Allen, born in Columbiana, Columbiana, Ohio.
278   iii. Allendal Allen, born in Columbiana, Columbiana, Ohio.

146. Jane Catherine[7] Eisenhauer (John David[6], John[5], Hans Peter[4], Hans Nicholas[3], Hans Peter[2], Hans[1]) was born 1827, and died 1907. She married **Andrew J. Stephens**. He was born 1819, and died 1891.

Children of Jane Eisenhauer and Andrew Stephens are:
279   i.   J. David[8] Stephens, born 1861; died 1899.
280   ii.   Harry C. Stephens, born 1863; died 1869.
281   iii. Orlanda Stephens, born 1863; died 1869.
282   iv.   Ella Stephens, born 1868; died 1869.
283   v.   Scott Stephens, born 1871; died 1871.

155. John David[7] Pyke (Catherine[6] Eisenhower, Frederick[5] Eisenhauer, Hans Peter[4], Hans Nicholas[3], Hans Peter[2], Hans[1]) was born 14 Jul 1849, and died 1904. He married **Anna Lesher**. She was born 1846, and died 1904.

Children of John Pyke and Anna Lesher are:
284   i.   Abraham Solomon[8] Pyke, born 1873; died 1954.
285   ii.   William Franklin Pyke, born 1875; died 1964.
286   iii. Isaac Lesher Pyke, born 1878; died 1962.
287   iv.   John Albert Pyke, born 1879; died 1968.
288   v.   Rhoda Leah Pyke, born 1881; died 1920.
289   vi.   Franklin Milton Pyke, born 1883; died 1967.
290   vii. Samuel Wesley Pyke, born 1888; died 1963.
291   viii. Ernest James Pyke, born 1894; died 1970.

156. Jacob Frederick[7] Pyke (Catherine[6] Eisenhower, Frederick[5] Eisenhauer, Hans Peter[4], Hans Nicholas[3], Hans Peter[2], Hans[1]) was born 16 Oct 1851, and died 1896. He married **Susan Jane Bowers**. She was born 1848, and died Aft. 1880.

Children of Jacob Pyke and Susan Bowers are:
292   i.   Anna C[8] Pyke, born 1873.
293   ii.   Lilly M Pyke, born 1874.
294   iii. Harry M Pyke, born 1876.
295   iv.   Catherine E Pyke, born 1879.
296   v.   Samuel Frederick Pyke, born 1882; died 1965.
297   vi.   Elizabeth Pyke, born 1883.
298   vii. Cora Pyke, born 1885.
299   viii. Susan Pyke, born 1889; died 1904.
300   ix.   Jacob Herb Pyke, born 1894; died 1982.

159. Sarah Catherine[7] Pyke (Catherine[6] Eisenhower, Frederick[5] Eisenhauer, Hans Peter[4], Hans Nicholas[3], Hans Peter[2], Hans[1]) was born 29 Nov 1856, and died 1930. She married **John Henry Romberger**. He was born 1857, and died 1930.

Children of Sarah Pyke and John Romberger are:

301	i.	Charles Oscar[8] Romberger, born 1887; died 1980.
302	ii.	James Frank Romberger, born 1888; died 1950.
303	iii.	Mary Elizabeth Romberger, born 1889; died 1949.
304	iv.	Mabel Catherine Romberger, born 1890; died 1946.
305	v.	Thomas Pyke Romberger, born 1894; died 1968.

161. Anna Jane[7] Pyke (Catherine[6] Eisenhower, Frederick[5] Eisenhauer, Hans Peter[4], Hans Nicholas[3], Hans Peter[2], Hans[1]) was born 22 May 1864. She married **Alfred Henry Fair**. He was born 30 Dec 1863 in Pennsylvania, and died 21 Sep 1929.

Children of Anna Pyke and Alfred Fair are:

306	i.	Alice[8] Fair, born Bef. 1888.
307	ii.	Mabel Fair, born 1888.
308	iii.	Maude Fair, born 1890.
309	iv.	George Fair, born 07 Jun 1894.

162. Elizabeth Rebecca[7] Pyke (Catherine[6] Eisenhower, Frederick[5] Eisenhauer, Hans Peter[4], Hans Nicholas[3], Hans Peter[2], Hans[1]) was born 09 Apr 1869 in Millersburg, PA, and died 1895. She married **William Harvey Bentzel**. He was born 24 Aug 1864, and died 23 Dec 1892.

Children of Elizabeth Pyke and William Bentzel are:

+	310	i.	Harry I[8] Bentzel, born 1891 in Abilene, Dickinson Co, KS.
	311	ii.	Ida Viola Rosabel Bentzel, born Abt. 1893.

164. Mary Ann[7] Eisenhauer (Jacob Frederick[6], Frederick[5], Hans Peter[4], Hans Nicholas[3], Hans Peter[2], Hans[1]) was born 02 Sep 1849 in Elizabethville, Dauphin, Pennsylvania, and died 27 Apr 1893 in Abilene, Dickinson, Kansas. She married **John J Witter**. He was born Jul 1840 in Prussia, and died 1918 in Abilene, Dickinson Co, KS.

Children of Mary Eisenhauer and John Witter are:

+	312	i.	Martha Rebecca[8] Witter, born 27 Sep 1871 in Millersburg, PA; died 20 Aug 1955 in Upland, CA.
	313	ii.	Harry Witter, born 1873 in PA.
	314	iii.	Amanda Witter, born 1877 in PA; died Nov 1883 in KS.
	315	iv.	Bessie Witter, born 19 Sep 1880; died 28 Sep 1883 in Abilene, Dickinson Co, KS.
	316	v.	Sadie Witter, born 01 Jan 1883 in Enterprise, KS; died 14 Jun 1982 in Abilene, Dickinson Co, KS. She married Lewis Steckley 27 May 1958 in Navarre, KS; died 16 Sep 1977.
	317	vi.	Susie A Witter, born 28 Jan 1885 in Enterprise, KS; died 23 Jul 1956 in Modesto, CA. She married Noah B Martin Abt. 1924 in CA.
	318	vii.	Johnnie Witter, born 18 Oct 1887 in Abilene, Dickinson Co, KS; died 06 Feb 1888 in Abilene, Dickinson Co, KS.
	319	viii.	Mamie Stella Witter, born 25 Nov 1888 in KS; died 29 Sep 1969 in KS.
	320	ix.	Ray I Witter, born 19 Jan 1891 in Enterprise, KS; died 26 Jan 1967 in Abilene, Dickinson Co, KS. He married Ruth V Book 18 Feb 1914; born 29 Dec 1894; died 02 Nov 1980 in Mechanicburg, PA.

165. Catherine Ann[7] Eisenhauer (Jacob Frederick[6], Frederick[5], Hans Peter[4], Hans Nicholas[3], Hans Peter[2], Hans[1]) was born 19 Mar 1851 in Elizabethville, Dauphin, Pennsylvania, and died 03 Apr 1924 in Ramona, Marion, Kansas. She married **Samuel B. Haldeman**. He was born 11 Jan 1846 in Bainsbridge, PA, and died 21 Oct 1928 in Abilene, Dickinson Co, KS.

Children of Catherine Eisenhauer and Samuel Haldeman are:

321	i.	Hattie Jane[8] Haldeman, born 19 Jun 1872; died 1883.
322	ii.	Mary Rebecca Haldeman, born 1874.
323	iii.	Lydia Ann Haldeman, born 1875.
324	iv.	John Thaddeus Haldeman, born 1876; died 1901.
+ 325	v.	Lillian Elizabeth Haldeman, born 27 Aug 1878.
326	vi.	Jesse Ira Haldeman, born 1879 in PA.
327	vii.	Abraham Lincoln Haldeman, born 02 Feb 1882; died 1883.
+ 328	viii.	Katherine Ann Haldeman, born 20 Jul 1883 in Hope, KS; died 28 Nov 1959 in Abilene, Dickinson Co, KS.
329	ix.	Samuel Walter Haldeman, born 17 Dec 1884 in Hope, KS; died 23 Feb 1949 in Topeka, KS. He married Grace Johnson 15 Aug 1909.
+ 330	x.	John Henry Haldeman, born 09 Jun 1886 in Hope, KS; died 12 Dec 1969.
331	xi.	Milo Edward Haldeman, born Dec 1887.
+ 332	xii.	Harry Milton Haldeman, born 22 Apr 1889 in KS; died 04 Jul 1968 in Hillsboro, KS.
333	xiii.	Ora Blanche Haldeman, born Aug 1892 in KS. She married m Button.
334	xiv.	Delilah Haldeman, born 1895 in KS. She married m Book.

168. Susanna[7] Eisenhauer (Jacob Frederick[6], Frederick[5], Hans Peter[4], Hans Nicholas[3], Hans Peter[2], Hans[1]) was born 29 Oct 1854 in Elizabethville, Dauphin, Pennsylvania, and died 14 Jun 1932 in York, PA. She married **Aaron Wetzel**. He was born 1849, and died 03 Jul 1947 in York, PA.

Children of Susanna Eisenhauer and Aaron Wetzel are:

335	i.	Harper[8] Wetzel, born 1872; died 1873.
336	ii.	Janny R. Wetzel, born 1874; died 1881.
337	iii.	Franklin Jacob Wetzel, born 1876; died 1940.
338	iv.	Sarah A. Wetzel, born 1878.
339	v.	Raymond Wetzel, born 1880; died 1905.
340	vi.	Minnie M. Wetzel, born 1883.
341	vii.	Otto Robert Wetzel, born 1885.
342	viii.	Grace Pearl Wetzel, born 1888.
343	ix.	Della Mae Wetzel, born 1890; died 1902.
344	x.	Vernon Wetzel, born 1894; died 1913.

172. Amanda Hannah[7] Eisenhauer (Jacob Frederick[6], Frederick[5], Hans Peter[4], Hans Nicholas[3], Hans Peter[2], Hans[1]) was born 11 Dec 1861 in Elizabethville, Dauphin Co, PA, and died 25 Aug 1951 in Abilene, Dickinson Co, KS. She married **Christian O Musser**. He was born 10 Nov 1863 in Mt. Joy, PA, and died 14 Apr 1950 in Abilene, Dickinson Co, KS.

Children of Amanda Eisenhauer and Christian Musser are:

345	i.	Beulah E[8] Musser, born 11 Jun 1887 in Abilene, Dickinson Co, KS; died 28 Nov 1945 in KS. She married Abram E Brechbill 1931; born 15 Nov 1881 in Abilene, Dickinson Co, KS; died 07 Aug 1964 in Abilene, Dickinson Co, KS.
346	ii.	Florence Musser, born 19 Mar 1895 in KS; died Apr 1969 in KS. She married A Ray Etherington.

173. David Jacob[7] Eisenhauer (Jacob Frederick[6], Frederick[5], Hans Peter[4], Hans Nicholas[3], Hans Peter[2], Hans[1]) was born 23 Sep 1863 in Elizabethville, Dauphin, Pennsylvania, and died 10 Mar 1942 in Abilene, Dickinson, Kansas. He married **Ida Elizabeth Stover** 23 Sep 1885 in Hope, Dickinson, Kansas, daughter of Simon Stover and Elizabeth Link. She was born 01 May 1862 in Mt. Sidney, VA, and died 11 Sep 1946 in Abilene, Dickinson Co , Kansas.

Children of David Eisenhauer and Ida Stover are:

+ 347	i.	Arthur Bradford[8] Eisenhower, born 11 Nov 1886 in Hope, Dickinson, Kansas; died 26 Jan 1958.
348	ii.	Edgar Newton Eisenhower, born 19 Jan 1889 in Hope, Dickinson, Kansas; died 12 Jul 1971 in Tacoma, Pierce, Washington.
+ 349	iii.	Dwight David Eisenhower, born 14 Oct 1890 in Denison, Grayson, Texas; died 28 Mar 1969 in Washington, District Of, Columbia.
+ 350	iv.	Roy Jacob Eisenhower, born 09 Aug 1892 in Abilene, Kansas, Kansas; died 17 Jun 1942.
351	v.	Paul Dawson A. Eisenhower, born 12 May 1894 in Abilene, Dickinson, Kansas; died 16 Mar 1895.
352	vi.	Earl Dewey Eisenhower, born 01 Feb 1898 in Abilene, Dickinson, Kansas; died 18 Dec 1968 in

Scottsdale, Maricopa, Arizona. He married Kathryn McIntyre Snyder 29 Apr 1933 in Connellsville, Pennsylvania; born 15 Aug 1909 in Charleroi, Washington, Pennsylvania; died Sep 1986 in Scottsdale, Maricopa, Arizona.

353   vii.   Milton Stover Eisenhower, born 15 Sep 1899 in Abilene, Dickinson, Kansas; died 02 May 1985 in Baltimore, Maryland. He married Helen Elsie Eakin 12 Oct 1927 in Washington, District Of, Columbia; born 14 Aug 1904 in Manhattan, Riley, Kansas; died 10 Jul 1954.

176. Ira A[7] Eisenhower (Jacob Frederick[6] Eisenhauer, Frederick[5], Hans Peter[4], Hans Nicholas[3], Hans Peter[2], Hans[1]) was born 30 Jul 1867 in Elizabethville, Dauphin, Pa, and died 28 Mar 1943 in Los Angeles, CA. He married **Katherine E Dayhoff** 08 Sep 1885 in Abilene, KS. She was born 02 Sep 1865 in PA, and died 30 Dec 1930 in Shawnee Co, KS.

Children of Ira Eisenhower and Katherine Dayhoff are:

+   354   i.   Mary Rebecca[8] Eisenhower, born Oct 1886; died 29 May 1937 in Topeka, KS.
      355   ii.   Simon L Eisenhower, born 03 Dec 1895 in Abilene, Dickinson Co, KS; died 03 Dec 1895 in Abilene, Dickinson Co, KS.
      356   iii.   Clinton Eisenhower, born Aft. 1895; died 1943.

179. Mary Ann[7] Eisenhauer (Samuel P[6] Eisenhower, Frederick[5] Eisenhauer, Hans Peter[4], Hans Nicholas[3], Hans Peter[2], Hans[1]) was born 1860 in Elizabethville, Dauphin Co, PA, and died 1918. She married **Alfred Peter Buffington** 1878, son of John Buffington and Elizabeth Fight. He was born 1856 in Elizabethville, Dauphin Co, PA, and died 1902.

Children of Mary Eisenhauer and Alfred Buffington are:

      357   i.   Annie E[8] Buffington, born 29 Aug 1879 in Elizabethville, Dauphin Co, PA.
      358   ii.   Laura J Buffington, born 20 Jul 1881 in Elizabethville, Dauphin Co, PA.
      359   iii.   Mabel E Buffington, born 20 Dec 1883 in Elizabethville, Dauphin Co, PA.
      360   iv.   Meta Buffington, born 15 Dec 1887 in Elizabethville, Dauphin Co, PA.
      361   v.   Bertie Buffington, born 10 Aug 1890 in Elizabethville, Dauphin Co, PA.
      362   vi.   Alice P Buffington, born 23 Nov 1892 in Elizabethville, Dauphin Co, PA; died 1963.
      363   vii.   Eldred Leroy Buffington, born 25 Jul 1897 in Elizabethville, Dauphin Co, PA; died 06 May 1961.
      364   viii.   Ethel M Buffington, born 06 Nov 1898 in Elizabethville, Dauphin Co, PA; died Sep 1979 in Harrisburg, PA.
+   365   ix.   Roland McKinley Buffington, born 18 Jun 1901 in Elizabethville, Dauphin Co, PA; died 14 Jul 1987 in Melbourne, Brevard, Florida.

184. Emma Bertha[7] Eisenhauer (Samuel P[6] Eisenhower, Frederick[5] Eisenhauer, Hans Peter[4], Hans Nicholas[3], Hans Peter[2], Hans[1]) was born 23 Jul 1876 in Millersburg, PA, and died 1941. She married **George Luther Strole** 07 Feb 1900. He was born 06 Nov 1872 in New Hope, VA, and died 12 Nov 1963 in Navarre, KS.

Children of Emma Eisenhauer and George Strole are:

      366   i.   Mabel[8] Strole, born Dec 1900.
      367   ii.   Dean E Strole, born 29 Jun 1902; died 06 Feb 1972. He married Mildred Elizabeth Wilson.
      368   iii.   Dale Strole, born 02 Nov 1903.
      369   iv.   Paul L. Strole, born 1906; died 1990.
      370   v.   Elmer Strole, born 1909.
      371   vi.   Freda Strole, born 1910.

Generation No. 6

188. Mary[8] Hampton (Hannah[7] Mikel, David H.[6], Maria Barbara[5] Eisenhauer, Hans Peter[4], Hans Nicholas[3], Hans Peter[2], Hans[1]) was born in , Wilkes, North Carolina. She married **John Brown** in , Wilkes, North Carolina. He was born in , Wilkes, North Carolina.

Children of Mary Hampton and John Brown are:

      372   i.   Rebecca[9] Brown, born in ,,North Carolina.
      373   ii.   Arminda Brown, born in , Wilkes, North Carolina.

374	iii.	Micajah Brown, born in , Wilkes, North Carolina.
375	iv.	Delphia Brown, born in ,Wilkes, North Carolina.
376	v.	Martha Brown, born in ,Wilkes, North Carolina.

190. Noah[8] Hampton (Hannah[7] Mikel, David H.[6], Maria Barbara[5] Eisenhauer, Hans Peter[4], Hans Nicholas[3], Hans Peter[2], Hans[1]) was born in , Wilkes, North Carolina. He married **Nancy E. Welborn** 06 Oct 1845 in ,Wilkes, North Carolina. She was born in North Carolina.

Children of Noah Hampton and Nancy Welborn are:
| 377 | i. | Martha[9] Hampton, born in North Carolina. |
| 378 | ii. | Mary Hampton. |

191. John[8] Hampton (Hannah[7] Mikel, David H.[6], Maria Barbara[5] Eisenhauer, Hans Peter[4], Hans Nicholas[3], Hans Peter[2], Hans[1]) was born in , Wilkes, North Carolina, and died in , Wilkes, North Carolina. He married **Lucretia Speaks** 20 Jan 1848 in , Wilkes, North Carolina. She was born in , Iredell, North Carolina.

Children of John Hampton and Lucretia Speaks are:
379	i.	Mary[9] Hampton, born in , Iredell, North Carolina.
380	ii.	James Hampton, born in North Carolina.
381	iii.	Nancy Hampton, born in North Carolina.

192. Rufus[8] Hampton (Hannah[7] Mikel, David H.[6], Maria Barbara[5] Eisenhauer, Hans Peter[4], Hans Nicholas[3], Hans Peter[2], Hans[1]) was born in , Wilkes, North Carolina, and died in , Johnson, Missouri. He married **Sarah Ann Gregory** 30 Oct 1854 in ,Wilkes, North Carolina. She was born in , Wilkes, North Carolina.

Children of Rufus Hampton and Sarah Gregory are:
382	i.	Rufus[9] Hampton, born in Missouri.
383	ii.	Franklin Hampton, born in Missouri.
384	iii.	Peter Hampton, born in Missouri.
385	iv.	James Hampton, born in Missouri.
+ 386	v.	William Silas Hampton, born 28 Feb 1857 in Pittsville, Johnson, Missouri; died 11 Mar 1924 in Rush Springs, Grady, Oklahoma.

198. David[8] Hampton (Hannah[7] Mikel, David H.[6], Maria Barbara[5] Eisenhauer, Hans Peter[4], Hans Nicholas[3], Hans Peter[2], Hans[1]) was born 22 Jul 1822 in , Wilkes, North Carolina, and died 16 Sep 1904 in , Johnson, Missouri. He married **(1) Elizabeth Daniels** in , Ashe, North Carolina. She was born in , Ashe, North Carolina, and died in Tennessee. He married **(2) Sarah Bailey** 05 May 1859 in ,Washington, Tennessee. She was born in North Carolina.

Children of David Hampton and Elizabeth Daniels are:
387	i.	Mary A.[9] Hampton, born in North Carolina.
388	ii.	Elbert Micagah Hampton, born in North Carolina. He married Sarah Jane.
+ 389	iii.	John W. Hampton, born in North Carolina.
390	iv.	William R. Hampton, born 08 Aug 1847 in , Wilkes, North Carolina; died 31 Mar 1900.
+ 391	v.	Noah Edward Hampton, born 02 May 1855 in Tennessee; died 24 May 1931.
392	vi.	Sarah Jane Hampton, born 08 Aug 1858 in Tennessee; died 11 Dec 1950.

Children of David Hampton and Sarah Bailey are:
| 393 | i. | David Robert[9] Hampton, born Sep 1860 in Tennessee. |
| 394 | ii. | Harriet Caroline Hampton, born 28 Feb 1862 in Johnson City, Washington, Tennessee; died 07 Oct 1952 in Independence, Jackson, Missouri. |

199. Silas[8] Hampton (Hannah[7] Mikel, David H.[6], Maria Barbara[5] Eisenhauer, Hans Peter[4], Hans Nicholas[3], Hans Peter[2], Hans[1]) was born 20 Jun 1832 in , Wilkes, North Carolina, and died 27 Oct 1911 in

Tekamah, Burt, Nebraska. He married **Mary Brown** 11 Jun 1851 in , Wilkes, North Carolina. She was born 13 Oct 1829 in , Wilkes , North Carolina, and died 02 Feb 1911 in , Johnson, Missouri.

Children of Silas Hampton and Mary Brown are:

395	i.	M. Henry E.[9] Hampton, born in North Carolina.
396	ii.	Lorenzo Hampton, born in ,,North Carolina.
397	iii.	Gritie Hampton, born in North Carolina.
398	iv.	Gabriel Morgan Hampton, born 1857 in ,,North Carolina.
399	v.	Alfred Hampton, born 1859 in ,,North Carolina.
400	vi.	Reta Hampton, born 05 Sep 1871 in ,Johnson, Missouri; died 01 Oct 1945 in ,Lafayette, Missouri. She married Sam White Stephenson 08 Feb 1899 in ,Lafayette, Missouri.

200. Romlour Agustus[8] Hampton (Hannah[7] Mikel, David H.[6], Maria Barbara[5] Eisenhauer, Hans Peter[4], Hans Nicholas[3], Hans Peter[2], Hans[1]) was born 24 May 1839 in Wilkes, North Carolina, and died 25 Oct 1908 in Johnson, Missouri. He married **Nancy A. Wagoner**. She was born 1842 in Kentucky, and died Aft. 1880.

Children of Romlour Hampton and Nancy Wagoner are:

401	i.	John[9] Hampton, born Abt. 1860.
402	ii.	Joseph Hampton, born Abt. 1860.
403	iii.	James P. Hampton, born 1862 in Missouri.
404	iv.	Mary I. Hampton, born 1864 in Missouri.
405	v.	Albert M. Hampton, born 1868 in Missouri.
406	vi.	Fannie M. Hampton, born 1871 in Missouri.
407	vii.	Nallie S. Hampton, born 1873 in Missouri.
408	viii.	Ella L. Hampton, born 1876 in Missouri.

201. Samuel[8] Mikel (John S.[7], David H.[6], Maria Barbara[5] Eisenhauer, Hans Peter[4], Hans Nicholas[3], Hans Peter[2], Hans[1]) was born in , Schuyler, Missouri. He married **Lavina Scholl** in Newton, Harvey, Kansas, daughter of James Scholl and Eliza Claywell. She was born in Illinois.

Children of Samuel Mikel and Lavina Scholl are:

409	i.	Millie[9] Mikel, born in ,,Illinois.
410	ii.	Lucy Mikel, born in ,,Missouri.
411	iii.	Jimmie Mikel, born in Illinois.
412	iv.	Perry Scholl, born in Illinois.

202. John S.[8] Mikel (John S.[7], David H.[6], Maria Barbara[5] Eisenhauer, Hans Peter[4], Hans Nicholas[3], Hans Peter[2], Hans[1]) was born in Kentucky, and died Aft. 1860. He married **Mary Ann Scholl** 02 Sep 1843 in ,Adair, Missouri. She was born in Illinois, and died Aft. 1870.

Children of John Mikel and Mary Scholl are:

413	i.	Samuel[9] Mikel, born 1845 in ,Schuyler., Missouri.
414	ii.	Polly A. Mikel, born 1848 in ,Schuyler, Missouri.
415	iii.	William Mikel, born 1849 in ,Schuyler, Missouri; died 1860.
416	iv.	Linda Mikel, born 1851 in ,Schuyler, Missouri.
417	v.	P. Boone Mikel, born 1852 in ,Schuyler, Missouri.
418	vi.	Margaret Mikel, born 1856 in ,Schuyler, Missouri.
419	vii.	Wesley Mikel, born 1856 in ,Schuyler, Missouri.
420	viii.	Noah Mikel, born 1859 in ,Schuyler, Missouri.
421	ix.	Aaron D. Mikel, born 1861 in ,,Missouri.
422	x.	Martha Mikel, born 1862 in ,,Missouri.

204. Whitaker W.[8] Mikel (John S.[7], David H.[6], Maria Barbara[5] Eisenhauer, Hans Peter[4], Hans Nicholas[3], Hans Peter[2], Hans[1]) was born in Kentucky. He married **(1) Patsy** in Missouri>. He married **(2) Martha Bragg** 16 Apr 1835 in ,Morgan, Illinois. She was born in Kentucky. He married **(3) Lottie Boyer** 14 Aug 1882 in LaPlata, Macon, Missouri.

Children of Whitaker Mikel and Martha Bragg are:
+ 423   i.   Noah W.[9] Mikel, born in Missouri.
  424   ii.   Eliza Mikel, born in ,,Missouri.
  425   iii.   John C. Mikel, born in ,,Missouri; died 12 Nov 1927 in ,Missourinterey, California.
+ 426   iv.   James T. Mikel, born 13 Sep 1850 in Missouri; died 31 Mar 1899.

205. Hugh Frank[8] Mikel (John S.[7], David H.[6], Maria Barbara[5] Eisenhauer, Hans Peter[4], Hans Nicholas[3], Hans Peter[2], Hans[1]) was born 09 Mar 1807 in , Rowan, North Carolina, and died 06 Jun 1884 in Polk Township, Adair, Missouri. He married **Charity Ann Scholl** in ,Morgan, Illinois, daughter of Peter Scholl and Mary Boone. She was born 16 Aug 1809 in , Clark, Kentucky, and died 23 Sep 1888 in , Adair, Missouri.

Children of Hugh Mikel and Charity Scholl are:
+ 427   i.   James Purvis[9] Mikel, born in <Macon Missouri>; died 22 Oct 1864.
+ 428   ii.   William L. Mikel, born in ,Mogan, Illinois; died 06 May 1860 in ,Adair, Missouri.
  429   iii.   Polly Ellen Mikel, born in , Adair, Missouri.
+ 430   iv.   Charles W. Mikel, born in ,Macon, Missouri; died in ,Sedgwick, Kansas.
+ 431   v.   Edward B. Mikel, born 1826 in ,Morgan, Illinois.
+ 432   vi.   John Noah Mikel, born 11 Sep 1830 in , Morgan, Illinois; died in , Adair, Missouri.
+ 433   vii.   George M. Mikel, born 1833 in , Morgan, Illinois; died 03 Apr 1876.
  434   viii.   Samuel Mikel, born 1834 in ,Of Macon, Missouri.
+ 435   ix.   David J. Mikel, born 12 Apr 1836 in ,Morgan, Illinois; died 07 Jul 1923.
+ 436   x.   Joseph P. Mikel, born 30 Mar 1837 in ,Morgan, Illinois; died 15 Oct 1872.
  437   xi.   Ellen J. Mikel, born 1846 in ,Of Schuyler, Missouri.
  438   xii.   Emily J. Mikel, born 1848 in ,Schuyler, Missouri; died 02 Jan 1866 in Winchester, Scott, Illinois.

207. William Silas[8] Mikel (John S.[7], David H.[6], Maria Barbara[5] Eisenhauer, Hans Peter[4], Hans Nicholas[3], Hans Peter[2], Hans[1]) was born 09 Jan 1833 in Wilkesboro, Wilkes, North Carolina, and died 28 Feb 1903 in Leavenworth, Leavenworth, Kansas. He married **(1) Nancy J. Stephenson** 23 May 1858 in , Schuyler, Missouri. She was born 09 Jan 1835 in ,of Adair, Missouri, and died 08 Apr 1866 in Warrensburg, Johnson, Missouri. He married **(2) Liltra Ann Wade** 14 Mar 1869 in Holden, Johnson, Missouri. She was born 03 Dec 1841 in Warrensburg, Johnson, Missouri, and died 01 Jan 1870 in Warrensburg, Johnson, Missouri. He married **(3) Catherine Hayes** 06 Apr 1871 in Warrensburg, Johnson, Missouri. She was born in New York.

Child of William Mikel and Nancy Stephenson is:
  439   i.   Laura[9] Mikel, born in Warrensburg, Johnson, Missouri.

Child of William Mikel and Liltra Wade is:
+ 440   i.   Walter Sherman[9] Mikel, born 13 Dec 1869 in Warrensburg, Johnson, Missouri; died 01 Jul 1934 in Farmington, San Juan, New Mexico.

Children of William Mikel and Catherine Hayes are:
  441   i.   Lela Clifton[9] Mikel, born in Warrensburg, Johnson, Missouri; died 24 Apr 1910.
  442   ii.   Marshall Mikel, born in Warrensburg, Johnson, Missouri.
  443   iii.   Fred Lane Mikel, born 04 Nov 1876 in ,Johnson, Missouri; died 17 Nov 1925. He married Zula Hale Mikel; born 20 Nov 1880.
  444   iv.   Zula Hale Mikel, born 20 Nov 1880. She married (1) Fred Lane Mikel; born 04 Nov 1876 in ,Johnson, Missouri; died 17 Nov 1925. She married (2) Asbell. She married (3) O. Dowd.

210. Mary Jane[8] Mikel (John S.[7], David H.[6], Maria Barbara[5] Eisenhauer, Hans Peter[4], Hans Nicholas[3], Hans Peter[2], Hans[1]) was born 01 May 1841 in Greentop, Schuyler, Missouri, and died 10 Jul 1923. She married **Robert N. Toler** 14 Jan 1866 in ,Adair, Missouri. He was born 13 Sep 1834 in ,,Illinois, and died 03 Aug 1902.

Children of Mary Mikel and Robert Toler are:
  445   i.   Edgar F.[9] Toler, born 1867 in Missouri.
  446   ii.   William L. Toler, born 1873 in ,,Missouri.

212. Lucy[8] **Minton** (Sarah[7] Mikel, David H.[6], Maria Barbara[5] Eisenhauer, Hans Peter[4], Hans Nicholas[3], Hans Peter[2], Hans[1]) was born 08 Feb 1832 in ,,North Carolina, and died Aft. 1865. She married **Edward B. Mikel** 28 Jun 1846 in ,Schuyler, Missouri, son of Hugh Mikel and Charity Scholl. He was born 1826 in ,Morgan, Illinois.

Children of Lucy Minton and Edward Mikel are:

	447	i.	Alfred[9] Mikel.
	448	ii.	Mikel.
+	449	iii.	Hugh D. Mikel, born 07 Dec 1847 in Missouri; died 01 Jan 1917.
+	450	iv.	Sarah F. Mikel, born Oct 1849 in ,Adair, Missouri; died 04 Oct 1923.
	451	v.	Martha J. Mikel, born 1855 in ,,Missouri. She married James Edwards 13 Nov 1877 in Independence, Missourintogomery, Kansas.
	452	vi.	Lewis Mikel, born 1858 in ,,Missouri.
+	453	vii.	Lucy Adeline Mikel, born 19 Jan 1864 in Green, Schuyler, Missouri; died 07 Sep 1949 in Perry, Noble, Oklahoma.

213. Martha Elizabeth[8] **Minton** (Sarah[7] Mikel, David H.[6], Maria Barbara[5] Eisenhauer, Hans Peter[4], Hans Nicholas[3], Hans Peter[2], Hans[1]) was born 21 Dec 1837 in ,,Kentucky, and died 25 Dec 1924 in Chanute, Kansas. She married **Lorenzo Dow Crapson**. He was born 18 Feb 1832 in ,,Pennsylvania, and died 02 Mar 1908 in Odense, Kansas.

Child of Martha Minton and Lorenzo Crapson is:

	454	i.	Amy[9] Crapson, born 22 Apr 1860 in Greentop, Missouri; died 06 Oct 1952 in Cherryvale, Kansas.

216. Betheny Louisa[8] **Mikel** (David Hugh[7], David H.[6], Maria Barbara[5] Eisenhauer, Hans Peter[4], Hans Nicholas[3], Hans Peter[2], Hans[1]) was born 03 Feb 1840 in ,,Tennessee, and died 14 Jan 1912. She married **(1) James Purvis Mikel**, son of Hugh Mikel and Charity Scholl. He was born in <Macon Missouri>, and died 22 Oct 1864. She married **(2) William Clark** 25 Dec 1864 in ,Schuyler , Missouri. He was born in Indiana. She married **(3) Theophilus Roberson** 22 Feb 1879 in ,Adair , Missouri. He was born in Iowa>.

Child of Betheny Mikel and James Mikel is:

+	455	i.	Levander L.[9] Mikel, born 27 May 1863 in , Schuyler, Missouri; died 19 May 1949 in Kirksville, Adair, Missouri.

Child of Betheny Mikel and William Clark is:

	456	i.	Charles A.[9] Clark, born in ,,Missouri.

Child of Betheny Mikel and Theophilus Roberson is:

	457	i.	J. A.[9] Roberson.

217. David Hugh[8] **Mikel** (David Hugh[7], David H.[6], Maria Barbara[5] Eisenhauer, Hans Peter[4], Hans Nicholas[3], Hans Peter[2], Hans[1]) was born 13 Aug 1841 in , Perry, Tennessee, and died in Missouri. He married **Sarah B. ?** in Greentop, Schuyler, Missouri. She was born in Ohio.

Children of David Mikel and Sarah ? are:

	458	i.	G. W.[9] Mikel, born in Missouri.
	459	ii.	W. A. Mikel, born in Missouri.

222. Henry[8] **Myers** (Lucinda[7] Mikel, David H.[6], Maria Barbara[5] Eisenhauer, Hans Peter[4], Hans Nicholas[3], Hans Peter[2], Hans[1]) was born 07 Nov 1830 in ,Wilkes , North Carolina, and died 08 May 1914. He married **Lucinda**. She was born 27 Feb 1834 in ,Perry , Ohio, and died 06 Sep 1902.

Child of Henry Myers and Lucinda is:

460   i.   Sarah[9] Myers, born 1859 in ,,Missouri.

227. James King[8] Mikel (Moses Loren[7], David H.[6], Maria Barbara[5] Eisenhauer, Hans Peter[4], Hans Nicholas[3], Hans Peter[2], Hans[1]) was born in ,Wilkes, North Carolina. He married **Angeline ?**. She was born in Virginia.

Children of James Mikel and Angeline ? are:
    461   i.   Theodore[9] Mikel, born in ,,North Carolina.
    462   ii.   Emmar Mikel, born in ,,North Carolina.

230. Charles Milton[8] Mikel (Moses Loren[7], David H.[6], Maria Barbara[5] Eisenhauer, Hans Peter[4], Hans Nicholas[3], Hans Peter[2], Hans[1]) was born 07 Feb 1855 in Moravian Falls, Wilkes, North Carolina, and died 17 Dec 1936 in Everett, Snohomish, Washington. He married **Elizabeth Lurena Osborn** 28 Mar 1879 in Solitude, Ashe, North Carolina. She was born Jan 1858 in Solitude, Ashe, North Carolina, and died 02 Jul 1914 in Brewster, Okanogan, Washington.

Children of Charles Mikel and Elizabeth Osborn are:
    463   i.   James Harvey[9] Mikel, born 19 Dec 1879 in Solitude, Ashe, North Carolina; died 29 May 1881 in Ruby Hill, Eureka, Nevada.
+   464   ii.   Arthur Milton Mikel, born 01 Jun 1882 in Ruby Hill, Eureka , Nevada; died 17 Jan 1959 in Chewelah, Stevens , Washington.
    465   iii.   John L. Mikel, born Feb 1884 in California; died in Washington.
+   466   iv.   Fred Caswell Mikel, born 23 Jul 1886 in Solitude, Ashe, North Carolina; died 30 Nov 1961 in Pateros, Okanogan, Washington.
+   467   v.   Joseph A Mikel, born 17 Apr 1888 in Green Cove, Washington, Virginia; died Dec 1974 in Seattle, King , Washington.
    468   vi.   Myrtie Bell Mikel, born Jan 1890 in Green Cove, Washington, Virginia; died Feb 1977 in ,,Washington.
    469   vii.   Margaret Alvira Mikel, born 09 Mar 1892 in Green Cove, Washington, Virginia; died 23 Feb 1980 in Seattle, King , Washington.
    470   viii.   Carl V Mikel, born Feb 1895 in Green Cove, Washington, Virginia. He married ? ?.

232. Mary[8] Brown (Rebecca[7] Mikel, David H.[6], Maria Barbara[5] Eisenhauer, Hans Peter[4], Hans Nicholas[3], Hans Peter[2], Hans[1]) was born in , Wilkes, North Carolina. She married **Joshua Senter Stanberry** 06 Sep 1858 in , Ashe, n.c.. He was born in Ashe, North Carolina>.

Children of Mary Brown and Joshua Stanberry are:
    471   i.   William E.[9] Stanberry.
    472   ii.   Sarah A. Stanberry.
    473   iii.   Harrison David Stanberry.
    474   iv.   Virginia Stanberry.
    475   v.   Arthur Stanberry.
    476   vi.   Emmet Stanberry.
    477   vii.   Gordie Stanberry.
    478   viii.   John Stanberry.
    479   ix.   ? Stanberry.
    480   x.   ? Stanberry.
    481   xi.   Nancy Stanberry, born 01 Jul 1864 in , Watauga, North Carolina>; died 1941.

234. John W.[8] Brown (Rebecca[7] Mikel, David H.[6], Maria Barbara[5] Eisenhauer, Hans Peter[4], Hans Nicholas[3], Hans Peter[2], Hans[1]) was born in , Wilkes, North Carolina. He married **Nancy C ?**. She was born in North Carolina.

Children of John Brown and Nancy ? are:
    482   i.   Lula J.[9] Brown, born in North Carolina.
    483   ii.   Cintha M. Brown, born in North Carolina.
    484   iii.   Mary B. Brown, born in North Carolina.
    485   iv.   Addie L. Brown, born in North Carolina.

236. Joseph^8 Brown (Rebecca^7 Mikel, David H.^{6}, Maria Barbara^5 Eisenhauer, Hans Peter^4, Hans Nicholas^3, Hans Peter^2, Hans^1) was born in , Wilkes, North Carolina. He married **Frankie Ashley**. She was born in North Carolina.

Children of Joseph Brown and Frankie Ashley are:
  486   i.   William M.^{9} Brown, born in North Carolina.
  487   ii. Roy M. Brown, born in North Carolina.

243. David A.^{8} Brown (Rebecca^7 Mikel, David H.^{6}, Maria Barbara^5 Eisenhauer, Hans Peter^4, Hans Nicholas^3, Hans Peter^2, Hans^1) was born in North Carolina. He married **Mary Jane Trivitte** in Boone, Watauga, North Carolina. She was born in North Carolina.

Child of David Brown and Mary Trivitte is:
+ 488   i.   Samuel Smith^9 Brown, born 20 Aug 1879 in Rutland, Watauga, North Carolina; died 06 Apr 1965 in Titusville, Brevard, Florida.

310. Harry I^8 Bentzel (Elizabeth Rebecca^7 Pyke, Catherine^6 Eisenhower, Frederick^5 Eisenhauer, Hans Peter^4, Hans Nicholas^3, Hans Peter^2, Hans^1) was born 1891 in Abilene, Dickinson Co, KS. He married **Lena Margaret Dalton**. She was born 11 Dec 1893.

Child of Harry Bentzel and Lena Dalton is:
  489   i.   Gerald Benton^9 Bentsel, born 04 Feb 1923.

312. Martha Rebecca^8 Witter (Mary Ann^7 Eisenhauer, Jacob Frederick^6, Frederick^5, Hans Peter^4, Hans Nicholas^3, Hans Peter^2, Hans^1) was born 27 Sep 1871 in Millersburg, PA, and died 20 Aug 1955 in Upland, CA. She married **Joseph Harvey Gish**. He was born 20 Sep 1875 in Liverpool, PA, and died Sep 1967 in Upland, CA.

Child of Martha Witter and Joseph Gish is:
  490   i.   Evelyn W^9 Gish, born 16 Jan 1912 in Abilene, Dickinson Co, KS; died 15 Dec 2001 in PA. She married Paul Edward Book; born 03 Mar 1919 in Custer Co, OK; died 21 Dec 1998 in Waynesboro, PA.

325. Lillian Elizabeth^8 Haldeman (Catherine Ann^7 Eisenhauer, Jacob Frederick^6, Frederick^5, Hans Peter^4, Hans Nicholas^3, Hans Peter^2, Hans^1) was born 27 Aug 1878. She married **Samuel W Brehm**. He was born in Palmyra, PA.

Children of Lillian Haldeman and Samuel Brehm are:
  491   i.   Zena Leroy^9 Brehm, born 07 Jan 1903.
  492   ii.   Eldred H Brehm, born 28 Nov 1904.
  493   iii. Irma Aurelia Brehm.
  494   iv.   Faithe Marie Brehm.

328. Katherine Ann^8 Haldeman (Catherine Ann^7 Eisenhauer, Jacob Frederick^6, Frederick^5, Hans Peter^4, Hans Nicholas^3, Hans Peter^2, Hans^1) was born 20 Jul 1883 in Hope, KS, and died 28 Nov 1959 in Abilene, Dickinson Co, KS. She married **Abraham Lincoln Epler** 05 Nov 1902 in Hope, KS. He was born Jun 1876 in Hummelstown, PA, and died 16 Jun 1923 in Gladwin, MI.

Children of Katherine Haldeman and Abraham Epler are:
  495   i.   Ruel Milton^9 Epler, born 14 Mar 1904; died 03 Feb 1977 in Wichita, KS.
  496   ii.   Martha Irene Epler, born 12 May 1906 in Whitehouse, OH; died 08 Oct 1924 in Detroit, KS.
  497   iii. Grant Barton Epler, born 29 May 1907; died 18 Jun 1988 in Lapeer, MI.
  498   iv.   Russell Emerson Epler, born 09 Jun 1909 in Canton, KS; died 20 Apr 1985 in Rochester, MI.
  499   v.   Blanche Pearl Epler, born 20 May 1918 in Gladwin, MI; died 24 Nov 2003 in KS. She married m

Scheideman.

500   vi.   ? Epler. She married Voiland Engle; born 10 Sep 1922.

501   vii.   Grace Lilian Epler, died Aft. 1985. She married m Campbell.

502   viii.   Paul Mark Epler, died Aft. 1985.

330. John Henry[8] **Haldeman** (Catherine Ann[7] Eisenhauer, Jacob Frederick[6], Frederick[5], Hans Peter[4], Hans Nicholas[3], Hans Peter[2], Hans[1]) was born 09 Jun 1886 in Hope, KS, and died 12 Dec 1969. He married **Viola C Rock** 11 Apr 1909 in Hope, KS. She was born 24 Feb 1889 in Illinois, and died 24 Jul 1976 in Abilene, Dickinson Co, KS.

Child of John Haldeman and Viola Rock is:

503   i.   Veri C[9] Haldeman, born 29 Jun 1911; died 01 Sep 1923 in Abilene, Dickinson Co, KS.

332. Harry Milton[8] **Haldeman** (Catherine Ann[7] Eisenhauer, Jacob Frederick[6], Frederick[5], Hans Peter[4], Hans Nicholas[3], Hans Peter[2], Hans[1]) was born 22 Apr 1889 in KS, and died 04 Jul 1968 in Hillsboro, KS. He married **Ollie B Rock** 29 Nov 1911. She was born 04 Nov 1890, and died 10 Feb 1981 in Topeka, KS.

Child of Harry Haldeman and Ollie Rock is:

504   i.   Eunic O[9] Haldeman, born 1913 in KS; died 1953. She married ? Nincehelser.

347. Arthur Bradford[8] **Eisenhower** (David Jacob[7] Eisenhauer, Jacob Frederick[6], Frederick[5], Hans Peter[4], Hans Nicholas[3], Hans Peter[2], Hans[1]) was born 11 Nov 1886 in Hope, Dickinson, Kansas, and died 26 Jan 1958. He married **(1) Alida B ?**. She was born 17 Feb 1889. He married **(2) Louis Sondra Grieb** 03 Sep 1926.

Child of Arthur Eisenhower and Alida ? is:

+ 505   i.   Katherine[9] Eisenhower, born 02 Jul 1914.

349. Dwight David[8] **Eisenhower** (David Jacob[7] Eisenhauer, Jacob Frederick[6], Frederick[5], Hans Peter[4], Hans Nicholas[3], Hans Peter[2], Hans[1]) was born 14 Oct 1890 in Denison, Grayson, Texas, and died 28 Mar 1969 in Washington, District Of, Columbia. He married **Mary Geneva Doud** 01 Jul 1916 in Denver, Denver, Colorado, daughter of John Doud and Elivera Carlson. She was born 14 Nov 1896 in Boone, Boone, Iowa, and died 31 Oct 1979 in Washington, D.C..

Children of Dwight Eisenhower and Mary Doud are:

+ 506   i.   John Sheldon Doud[9] Eisenhower, born 1923.

507   ii.   Doud Dwight Eisenhower, born 24 Sep 1917 in San Antonio, Bexar, Texas; died 02 Jan 1921 in Camp Meade, Maryland.

350. Roy Jacob[8] **Eisenhower** (David Jacob[7] Eisenhauer, Jacob Frederick[6], Frederick[5], Hans Peter[4], Hans Nicholas[3], Hans Peter[2], Hans[1]) was born 09 Aug 1892 in Abilene, Kansas, Kansas, and died 17 Jun 1942. He married **Edna Alice Shade** 18 Nov 1917 in Ellsworth, Ellsworth, Kansas. She was born 13 Sep 1891 in Ellis City, Ellis, Kansas, and died 26 Jun 1989 in Denver, Denver, Colorado.

Children of Roy Eisenhower and Edna Shade are:

508   i.   Patricia[9] Eisenhower, born 1918.

509   ii.   Peggy J Eisenhower, born 1923.

510   iii.   Lloyd E Eisenhower, born 1925.

511   iv.   Roy J Eisenhower, born Abt. 1930.

354. Mary Rebecca[8] **Eisenhower** (Ira A[7], Jacob Frederick[6] Eisenhauer, Frederick[5], Hans Peter[4], Hans Nicholas[3], Hans Peter[2], Hans[1]) was born Oct 1886, and died 29 May 1937 in Topeka, KS. She married **Jacob M Brandt**. He was born 02 Jul 1881 in Detroit, KS.

Children of Mary Eisenhower and Jacob Brandt are:

512	i.	Preston L[9] Brandt, born 07 Jan 1909; died 11 Apr 1977 in San Antonio, Bexar, Texas.
513	ii.	Orville E Brandt, born 28 Feb 1917.
514	iii.	Victor O Brandt, born 10 Sep 1920; died 16 Nov 1999.

365. Roland McKinley[8] Buffington (Mary Ann[7] Eisenhauer, Samuel P[6] Eisenhower, Frederick[5] Eisenhauer, Hans Peter[4], Hans Nicholas[3], Hans Peter[2], Hans[1]) was born 18 Jun 1901 in Elizabethville, Dauphin Co, PA, and died 14 Jul 1987 in Melbourne, Brevard, Florida. He married **Blanche Emmeta Kitzmiller** 08 Dec 1923 in Harrisburg, PA. She was born 12 Jan 1904 in Harrisburg, PA.

Children of Roland Buffington and Blanche Kitzmiller are:

+	515	i.	Dorothy Pauline[9] Buffington, born 05 Nov 1925 in Harrisburg, PA; died 18 Jan 1998 in Camp Hill, PA.
	516	ii.	Roland R Buffington, born 1929 in Harrisburg, PA.

Generation No. 7

386. William Silas[9] Hampton (Rufus[8], Hannah[7] Mikel, David H.[6], Maria Barbara[5] Eisenhauer, Hans Peter[4], Hans Nicholas[3], Hans Peter[2], Hans[1]) was born 28 Feb 1857 in Pittsville, Johnson, Missouri, and died 11 Mar 1924 in Rush Springs, Grady, Oklahoma. He married **Mary Francis Elizabeth Shore** 12 Oct 1883 in Holden, Lafayette, Missouri. She was born 28 Sep 1861 in ,Lafayette, Missouri, and died 17 Oct 1942 in Centerview, Johnson, Missouri.

Child of William Hampton and Mary Shore is:

517	i.	Clarence Sidney[10] Hampton, born 09 Sep 1884 in ,Johnson, Missouri; died 30 Mar 1942 in South Gate, Los Angeles, California. He married Eliza Catherine Jennings 28 Nov 1906 in Warrensburg, Johnson, Missouri; born 28 Jan 1890 in Odessa, Lafayette, Missouri; died 26 Sep 1985 in Redding, Shasta, California.

389. John W.[9] Hampton (David[8], Hannah[7] Mikel, David H.[6], Maria Barbara[5] Eisenhauer, Hans Peter[4], Hans Nicholas[3], Hans Peter[2], Hans[1]) was born in North Carolina. He married **Elizabeth ?**. She was born in North Carolina.

Children of John Hampton and Elizabeth ? are:

518	i.	William H.[10] Hampton, born in Kentucky.
519	ii.	Leslie Hampton, born in Kentucky.
520	iii.	Nunet B. Hampton, born in Kentucky.
521	iv.	Leucey J. Hampton, born in North Carolina.
522	v.	Ornie T. Hampton, born in Kentucky.

391. Noah Edward[9] Hampton (David[8], Hannah[7] Mikel, David H.[6], Maria Barbara[5] Eisenhauer, Hans Peter[4], Hans Nicholas[3], Hans Peter[2], Hans[1]) was born 02 May 1855 in Tennessee, and died 24 May 1931. He married **Jennie ?**. She was born in Missouri.

Children of Noah Hampton and Jennie ? are:

523	i.	Elma[10] Hampton, born in Kansas.
524	ii.	Arther Hampton, born in Missouri.

423. Noah W.[9] Mikel (Whitaker W.[8], John S.[7], David H.[6], Maria Barbara[5] Eisenhauer, Hans Peter[4], Hans Nicholas[3], Hans Peter[2], Hans[1]) was born in Missouri. He married **Barbara Isabelle Thrush** 1867. She was born 04 May 1847 in , Lee, Iowa, and died 24 Mar 1942 in LaPlata, Macon, Missouri.

Child of Noah Mikel and Barbara Thrush is:

525	i.	Mary Frances[10] Mikel, born in Missouri. She married Elijah Clem 05 Dec 1883 in , Adair, Missouri.

426. James T.[9] Mikel (Whitaker W.[8], John S.[7], David H.[6], Maria Barbara[5] Eisenhauer, Hans Peter[4], Hans Nicholas[3], Hans Peter[2], Hans[1]) was born 13 Sep 1850 in Missouri, and died 31 Mar 1899. He married **Amy W.**

Head 23 Oct 1881 in ,Adair, Missouri. She was born 20 Jun 1865, and died 19 Jun 1896.

Children of James Mikel and Amy Head are:

526	i.	W. M.[10] Mikel.
527	ii.	Mikel.
528	iii.	Mikel.
529	iv.	Mikel.
530	v.	John H. Mikel, born 1882; died 1950. He married Alice; born 1881; died 1951.
+ 531	vi.	James T. Mikel, born 31 Aug 1884 in , Macon, Missouri; died 02 Mar 1943 in Kirksville, Adair, Missouri.
532	vii.	William H. Mikel, born 08 Mar 1888; died 25 Jan 1946.

427.   James Purvis[9] Mikel (Hugh Frank[8], John S.[7], David H.[6], Maria Barbara[5] Eisenhauer, Hans Peter[4], Hans Nicholas[3], Hans Peter[2], Hans[1]) was born in <Macon Missouri>, and died 22 Oct 1864. He married **Betheny Louisa Mikel**, daughter of David Mikel and Margaret Swinney. She was born 03 Feb 1840 in ,,Tennessee, and died 14 Jan 1912.

Child is listed above under (216) Betheny Louisa Mikel.

428.   William L.[9] Mikel (Hugh Frank[8], John S.[7], David H.[6], Maria Barbara[5] Eisenhauer, Hans Peter[4], Hans Nicholas[3], Hans Peter[2], Hans[1]) was born in ,Mogan, Illinois, and died 06 May 1860 in ,Adair, Missouri. He married **Sarah Ann Knight** 1850 in ,Adair, Missouri. She was born Dec 1834 in ,Morgan, Ohio.

Children of William Mikel and Sarah Knight are:

533	i.	Angeline[10] Mikel, born in Va.
534	ii.	Joseph Mikel, born 1851 in Adair, Missouri.
+ 535	iii.	Henry Samuel Mikel, born 14 Oct 1851 in Adair, Missouri; died 24 Feb 1915 in Adair, Missouri.
536	iv.	John Mikel, born Oct 1856 in Adair, Missouri; died 12 Nov 1927 in Carmel, Monterey, California.
+ 537	v.	Mary Frances Mikel, born Mar 1859 in ,Greenup, Missouri; died 23 Mar 1945 in Carmel, Monterey, California.

430.   Charles W.[9] Mikel (Hugh Frank[8], John S.[7], David H.[6], Maria Barbara[5] Eisenhauer, Hans Peter[4], Hans Nicholas[3], Hans Peter[2], Hans[1]) was born in ,Macon, Missouri, and died in ,Sedgwick, Kansas. He married **Lucinda Elizabeth Stewart** 15 Mar 1869 in Lancaster, Schuyler, Missouri. She was born 06 Dec 1850 in Greenup, Greenup, Kentucky, and died 19 Aug 1926 in Denver, Denver, Colorado.

Children of Charles Mikel and Lucinda Stewart are:

538	i.	Charles Homer[10] Mikel, born in Kansas.
+ 539	ii.	Ida Belle Mikel, born 25 Dec 1869 in , Adair, Missouri; died 25 Oct 1931 in Lancaster , Schuyler, Missouri.
+ 540	iii.	Lydia Lottie Mikel, born 12 Jun 1872 in Greentop, Schuyler, Missouri; died 04 Dec 1920 in Bayfield, LaPlata, Colorado.

431.   Edward B.[9] Mikel (Hugh Frank[8], John S.[7], David H.[6], Maria Barbara[5] Eisenhauer, Hans Peter[4], Hans Nicholas[3], Hans Peter[2], Hans[1]) was born 1826 in ,Morgan, Illinois. He married **(1) Martha J. Hobs**.   He married **(2) Lucy Minton** 28 Jun 1846 in ,Schuyler, Missouri, daughter of Shadrack Minton and Sarah Mikel. She was born 08 Feb 1832 in ,,North Carolina, and died Aft. 1865.

Children are listed above under (212) Lucy Minton.

432.   John Noah[9] Mikel (Hugh Frank[8], John S.[7], David H.[6], Maria Barbara[5] Eisenhauer, Hans Peter[4], Hans Nicholas[3], Hans Peter[2], Hans[1]) was born 11 Sep 1830 in , Morgan, Illinois, and died in , Adair, Missouri. He married **(1) Melissa Dobbs**.   He married **(2) Missouri Edwards** 31 Jul 1853 in ,Schuyler, Missouri. She was born in Indiana, and died 25 Nov 1881 in , Adair, Missouri.

Children of John Mikel and Missouri Edwards are:

541	i.	William Albert[10] Mikel, born in ,Adair, Missouri; died Oct 1892.

542	ii.	Mary Alice Mikel, born in ,Adair, Missouri.
543	iii.	Cornelia H. Mikel, born in ,Adair, Missouri.
544	iv.	Barnum B. Mikel, born 28 Jan 1858 in ,Jackson, Missouri; died 31 Dec 1927 in Kansas City, Kansas.

543   iii.   Cornelia H. Mikel, born in ,Adair, Missouri.

542   ii.   Mary Alice Mikel, born in ,Adair, Missouri.
543   iii.   Cornelia H. Mikel, born in ,Adair, Missouri.
544   iv.   Barnum B. Mikel, born 28 Jan 1858 in ,Jackson, Missouri; died 31 Dec 1927 in Kansas City, Kansas.
545   v.   Sarah Jane Mikel, born 02 Mar 1860 in ,Adair, Missouri; died 06 Sep 1935 in ,Adair, Missouri.
546   vi.   Eliza Ellen Mikel, born 06 Mar 1862 in ,Adair, Missouri; died 20 Sep 1929 in Clinton Indiana.
547   vii.   Dora Bell Mikel, born 11 Oct 1863 in Polk Township, Adair, Missouri; died 15 Oct 1929 in Connelsville, Adair, Missouri.
548   viii.   Elizabeth Mikel, born 09 May 1867 in ,Adair, Missouri; died 14 Sep 1937 in Terra Haute, Vico, Indiana.
549   ix.   Charles Edward Mikel, born 1871 in ,Kansas.
+ 550   x.   George Washington Mikel, born 19 Jul 1874 in ,Adair, Missouri; died 22 Dec 1958.
551   xi.   Grace Mikel, born 13 Mar 1875 in ,Adair, Missouri; died 01 Feb 1955 in Kirksville, Adair, Missouri.
552   xii.   John Noah Mikel, born 25 Dec 1878 in ,Adair, Missouri; died Aug 1960.
553   xiii.   Anna M. Mikel, born 04 Nov 1879 in ,Adair, Missouri.
554   xiv.   Jesse Boone Mikel, born 1881 in ,Adair, Missouri; died 1898.

433. George M.[9] Mikel (Hugh Frank[8], John S.[7], David H.[6], Maria Barbara[5] Eisenhauer, Hans Peter[4], Hans Nicholas[3], Hans Peter[2], Hans[1]) was born 1833 in , Morgan, Illinois, and died 03 Apr 1876. He married **Susan E. Furnish** 03 Apr 1868 in , Adair, Missouri. She was born Jan 1850 in , Adair, Missouri, and died 24 Jun 1915.

Children of George Mikel and Susan Furnish are:
555   i.   Emma[10] Mikel, born in ,Adair, Missouri.
+ 556   ii.   Charity Ann Mikel, born in ,Adair, Missouri.
557   iii.   Nettie J. Mikel, born in ,Adair, Missouri. She married David M. Gregory 10 Feb 1889 in ,Adair, Missouri; born in Missouri.
+ 558   iv.   Reitty Belle Mikel, born 05 Aug 1874 in ,Adair, Missouri; died 09 May 1951.

435. David J.[9] Mikel (Hugh Frank[8], John S.[7], David H.[6], Maria Barbara[5] Eisenhauer, Hans Peter[4], Hans Nicholas[3], Hans Peter[2], Hans[1]) was born 12 Apr 1836 in ,Morgan, Illinois, and died 07 Jul 1923. He married **Lucinda E. Sutton**. She was born 16 Sep 1839 in ,,Illinois, and died 08 Dec 1917.

Children of David Mikel and Lucinda Sutton are:
559   i.   Charlie Frank[10] Mikel, born in , Adair, Missouri.
+ 560   ii.   George William Mikel, born 09 Sep 1867 in ,Of Adair, Missouri; died 07 Nov 1918 in ,Adair , Missouri, Ft. Madison Cemetery..
561   iii.   Frank Mikel, born 1871 in , Of Adair, Missouri>.
562   iv.   Warren C. Mikel, born 25 Mar 1872 in ,Of Adair, Missouri; died 11 Oct 1934. He married Mollie; born 07 Nov 1877; died 12 Apr 1949.
563   v.   Emaline Lena Mikel, born 19 Dec 1875 in , Of Adair, Missouri>; died May 1952 in Greentop, Schuyler, Missouri. She married James Oliver Towles 26 Sep 1900 in ,Adair , Missouri.
564   vi.   Mary E. Mikel, born 15 Aug 1877 in ,Adair , Missouri; died 12 Aug 1957 in Greentop, Schuyler , Missouri.
565   vii.   Milton S. Mikel, born 31 Mar 1879 in ,Of Adair, Missouri; died 22 Oct 1885 in ,Adair, Missouri.

436. Joseph P.[9] Mikel (Hugh Frank[8], John S.[7], David H.[6], Maria Barbara[5] Eisenhauer, Hans Peter[4], Hans Nicholas[3], Hans Peter[2], Hans[1]) was born 30 Mar 1837 in ,Morgan, Illinois, and died 15 Oct 1872. He married **(1) Uri Metcalf.** He married **(2) Sarah E. Cullop** 03 Apr 1863 in , Adair, Missouri. She was born 07 Dec 1847 in Missouri, and died 21 Jan 1928.

Children of Joseph Mikel and Sarah Cullop are:
566   i.   Louise Lewellen[10] Mikel, born in Missouri.
567   ii.   James Mikel, born in Missouri.
+ 568   iii.   Margaret Mikel, born 05 May 1865 in , Adair, Missouri; died 16 Sep 1961 in , Adair, Missouri.

440. Walter Sherman[9] Mikel (William Silas[8], John S.[7], David H.[6], Maria Barbara[5] Eisenhauer, Hans Peter[4], Hans Nicholas[3], Hans Peter[2], Hans[1]) was born 13 Dec 1869 in Warrensburg, Johnson, Missouri, and died 01 Jul 1934 in Farmington, San Juan, New Mexico. He married **Lydia Lottie Mikel** 13 Jan 1892 in

Pueblo, Pueblo, Colorado, daughter of Charles Mikel and Lucinda Stewart. She was born 12 Jun 1872 in Greentop, Schuyler, Missouri, and died 04 Dec 1920 in Bayfield, LaPlata, Colorado.

Children of Walter Mikel and Lydia Mikel are:

	569	i.	Walter S[10] Mikel, born 1903. He married ? ?.
	570	ii.	Florence Eva Mikel, born 12 May 1892 in Hooper, Alamosa, Colorado; died 15 Jun 1949 in San Anselmo, Marin, California. She married Joseph McEwen Walters 01 Jun 1910; born 31 Dec 1884 in Beaver, Beaver, Utah; died 24 Oct 1954 in Redway, Humbolt, California.
+	571	iii.	Gladys Melvina Mikel, born 23 Dec 1893 in Dukin, Saguache, Colorado; died 15 Jun 1921 in Mancos, Montezuma, Colorado.
	572	iv.	Marquerette Marie Mikel, born 08 Apr 1906 in Mancos, Montezuma, Colorado; died 29 Mar 1972.
	573	v.	Homer W Mikel, born 15 Dec 1912 in Mancos, Montezuma, Colorado.

449. Hugh D.[9] Mikel (Edward B.[9], Hugh Frank[8], John S.[7], David H.[6], Maria Barbara[5] Eisenhauer, Hans Peter[4], Hans Nicholas[3], Hans Peter[2], Hans[1]) was born 07 Dec 1847 in Missouri, and died 01 Jan 1917. He married **Amanda Jane Lowe** 22 Jan 1868 in ,Adair, Missouri. She was born 10 May 1851 in ,,Iowa, and died 01 Nov 1918.

Children of Hugh Mikel and Amanda Lowe are:

	574	i.	Howley B.[10] Mikel.
	575	ii.	Willard L. Mikel.
	576	iii.	Sally J. Mikel.
	577	iv.	George Evert Mikel.
+	578	v.	Generva E. Mikel, born 26 Jun 1871 in , Adair, Missouri; died 07 Mar 1906.

450. Sarah F.[9] Mikel (Edward B.[9], Hugh Frank[8], John S.[7], David H.[6], Maria Barbara[5] Eisenhauer, Hans Peter[4], Hans Nicholas[3], Hans Peter[2], Hans[1]) was born Oct 1849 in ,Adair, Missouri, and died 04 Oct 1923. She married **James W. Reid** 21 Dec 1870 in Independence, Montgomery, Kansas. He was born 1845 in Pekin, Tazewell , Illinois.

Children of Sarah Mikel and James Reid are:

579	i.	?[10] Reid, died in Infant.
580	ii.	Joseph H. Reid, born 1873 in Independence, Missourintogomery , Kansas.

453. Lucy Adeline[9] Mikel (Edward B.[9], Hugh Frank[8], John S.[7], David H.[6], Maria Barbara[5] Eisenhauer, Hans Peter[4], Hans Nicholas[3], Hans Peter[2], Hans[1]) was born 19 Jan 1864 in Green, Schuyler, Missouri, and died 07 Sep 1949 in Perry, Noble, Oklahoma. She married **Enos Enoch Berger** 24 Aug 1881 in Independence, Montgomery , Kansas. He was born 23 Apr 1856 in St. Charles, Madison, Iowa, and died 12 Dec 1933 in Perry, Noble, Oklahoma.

Children of Lucy Mikel and Enos Berger are:

581	i.	?[10] ?.
582	ii.	Berger.
583	iii.	? ?.
584	iv.	Zella Jane Berger, born 05 Aug 1882 in Independence, Montgomery, Kansas; died 27 May 1961.
585	v.	Clara Elizabeth Berger, born 26 Jul 1885 in Elk City, Elk, Kansas; died 01 Oct 1953 in Walnut Creek, Contra Costa, California.
586	vi.	George Edward Berger, born 10 Jun 1888 in Elk City, Elk, Kansas; died 25 Aug 1954.
587	vii.	Susan Frances Berger, born 03 Oct 1890 in Elk City, Elk, Kansas.
588	viii.	Hester Lyons Berger, born 05 Apr 1893 in Stillwater, Payne, Oklahoma.
589	ix.	Lucy Hazel Berger, born 07 May 1902 in Perry, Noble, Ok Ty; died 11 Dec 1910.

455. Levander L.[9] Mikel (James Purvis[9], Hugh Frank[8], John S.[7], David H.[6], Maria Barbara[5] Eisenhauer, Hans Peter[4], Hans Nicholas[3], Hans Peter[2], Hans[1]) was born 27 May 1863 in , Schuyler, Missouri, and died 19 May 1949 in Kirksville, Adair, Missouri. He married **(1) Mary E. Kimberly**. She was born 10 Aug 1864 in , Defiance, Ohio, and died 26 Nov 1941 in Pure Air, Adair, Missouri. He married **(2) America Susie Miller** 18 Dec 1884 in ,Adair , Missouri. She was born 01 Feb 1866, and died 30 Dec 1918.

Children of Levander Mikel and America Miller are:

+ 590   i.   Oda F.[10] Mikel.
   591   ii.   Mikel.
   592   iii.   Casper Mikel.
   593   iv.   Jesse William Mikel, born 11 Oct 1885 in ,Schuyler , Missouri; died 21 Feb 1968 in Kirksville, Adair , Missouri. He married Mella B. Burgin 06 Oct 1910 in Kirksville, Adair , Missouri; born 1888; died 19 Apr 1967.
   594   v.   Posie H. Mikel, born 12 Dec 1889; died 11 Aug 1891.
   595   vi.   Harry Mikel, born 23 Mar 1894 in ,Adair , Missouri; died 27 May 1986 in Queen City, Schuyler , Missouri. He married Nira Pearce 23 Apr 1920 in Macon, Macon , Missouri; born 01 Aug 1895; died 10 Nov 1972.
   596   vii.   Charles O. Mikel, born 07 Dec 1896. He married Edith A.; born 05 Dec 1902.
   597   viii.   John D. Mikel, born 15 Dec 1901 in , Adair, Missouri; died 16 Nov 1987 in Kirksville, Adair, Missouri. He married Ida Olga Drefs 23 Nov 1939 in Chicago, Cook , Illinois; born 03 Dec 1905 in Engadine, Mackinac , Michigan; died 28 Jun 1986 in Kirksville, Adair, Missouri.

464. Arthur Milton[9] Mikel (Charles Milton[8], Moses Loren[7], David H.[6], Maria Barbara[5] Eisenhauer, Hans Peter[4], Hans Nicholas[3], Hans Peter[2], Hans[1]) was born 01 Jun 1882 in Ruby Hill, Eureka , Nevada, and died 17 Jan 1959 in Chewelah, Stevens , Washington. He married **(1) Ada Belle Moretz** 17 Sep 1910 in ,Watauga , North Carolina. She was born 12 Oct 1885 in Missouriretz Mill, Watauga , North Carolina, and died 30 Apr 1916 in Brewster, Okanogan , Washington. He married **(2) Zena Fern Robbins** 08 Aug 1917 in ,,Washington. She died 1981 in Wenatchee, Chelan, Washington.

Children of Arthur Mikel and Ada Moretz are:
   598   i.   Mikel[10], born 07 Jul 1911 in Brewster, Okanogan, Washington; died 07 Jul 1911 in Brewster, Okanogan, Washington.
   599   ii.   Elwyn Arthur Mikel, born 10 Apr 1913 in Brewster, Okanogan , Washington; died 10 Jan 1980 in Spokane, Spokane, Washingtion.

466. Fred Caswell[9] Mikel (Charles Milton[8], Moses Loren[7], David H.[6], Maria Barbara[5] Eisenhauer, Hans Peter[4], Hans Nicholas[3], Hans Peter[2], Hans[1]) was born 23 Jul 1886 in Solitude, Ashe, North Carolina, and died 30 Nov 1961 in Pateros, Okanogan, Washington. He married **Mabel May Johnson** 03 Mar 1915 in Spokane, Spokane, Washington. She was born in Joplin Missouri.

Children of Fred Mikel and Mabel Johnson are:
   600   i.   Jean Lurena[10] Mikel, died 02 Feb 1996 in California.
   601   ii.   Richard Mikel, born 30 Dec 1920; died 12 Jul 1972 in Spokane, Spokane, Washingtion.
   602   iii.   Kenneth Mikel, born 25 Jan 1923 in ,,Washington; died Feb 1985 in ,King , Washington.

467. Joseph A[9] Mikel (Charles Milton[8], Moses Loren[7], David H.[6], Maria Barbara[5] Eisenhauer, Hans Peter[4], Hans Nicholas[3], Hans Peter[2], Hans[1]) was born 17 Apr 1888 in Green Cove, Washington, Virginia, and died Dec 1974 in Seattle, King , Washington. He married **? ?**.

Child of Joseph Mikel and ? ? is:
   603   i.   Wallace Stanley[10] Mikel, born 12 Aug 1913 in Brewster, Okanogan , Washington; died 24 Mar 1998 in Vancouver, Clark, Washington.

488. Samuel Smith[9] Brown (David A.[8], Rebecca[7] Mikel, David H.[6], Maria Barbara[5] Eisenhauer, Hans Peter[4], Hans Nicholas[3], Hans Peter[2], Hans[1]) was born 20 Aug 1879 in Rutland, Watauga, North Carolina, and died 06 Apr 1965 in Titusville, Brevard, Florida. He married **Martha Ella Welch** 06 Feb 1904 in North Carolina. She was born 18 Nov 1887 in Matney, Watauga , North Carolina, and died Jul 1960 in Titusville, Brevard, Florida.

Children of Samuel Brown and Martha Welch are:
   604   i.   Fred E.[10] Brown, born 05 Feb 1905 in Matney, Watauga , North Carolina; died 1966.
   605   ii.   Ira W. Brown, born 26 Jan 1907 in Matney, Watauga, North Carolina; died 1936.

606	iii.	Howard Brown, born 1909.
607	iv.	Emil Brown, born 1911.
608	v.	Winfred Tate Brown, born 27 Jun 1914 in Matney, Watauga , North Carolina; died 09 Apr 1973.
609	vi.	Linville Lee Brown, born 27 Apr 1916 in North Carolina.
610	vii.	Settie Brown, born 1919.
611	viii.	Horace Charles Brown, born 06 Jan 1923 in Titusville, Brevard, Florida; died 1966.

505. Katherine[9] Eisenhower (Arthur Bradford[8], David Jacob[7] Eisenhauer, Jacob Frederick[6], Frederick[5], Hans Peter[4], Hans Nicholas[3], Hans Peter[2], Hans[1]) was born 02 Jul 1914. She married **Berton Roueche** 28 Oct 1936. He was born 16 Apr 1910.

Child of Katherine Eisenhower and Berton Roueche is:
| 612 | i. | Arthur Bradford[10] Roueche, born 16 Nov 1942. |

506. John Sheldon Doud[9] Eisenhower (Dwight David[8], David Jacob[7] Eisenhauer, Jacob Frederick[6], Frederick[5], Hans Peter[4], Hans Nicholas[3], Hans Peter[2], Hans[1]) was born 1923. He married **Barbara Jean Thompson** Jul 1947. She was born Abt. 1925.

Children of John Eisenhower and Barbara Thompson are:
+	613	i.	Dwight David[10] Eisenhower, born 31 Mar 1948.
	614	ii.	Barbara Anne Eisenhower, born 30 May 1949.
	615	iii.	Susan Elaine Eisenhower, born 31 Dec 1951.
	616	iv.	Mary Jean Eisenhower, born 21 Dec 1955.

515. Dorothy Pauline[9] Buffington (Roland McKinley[8], Mary Ann[7] Eisenhauer, Samuel P[6] Eisenhower, Frederick[5] Eisenhauer, Hans Peter[4], Hans Nicholas[3], Hans Peter[2], Hans[1]) was born 05 Nov 1925 in Harrisburg, PA, and died 18 Jan 1998 in Camp Hill, PA. She married **Kenneth Richard Moyer**. He was born 01 Aug 1926, and died 13 Nov 1987.

Children of Dorothy Buffington and Kenneth Moyer are:
617	i.	Living[10] Moyer, born Abt. 1950.
618	ii.	Living Moyer, born Abt. 1952.
619	iii.	Living Moyer, born Abt. 1954.

Generation No. 8

531. James T.[10] Mikel (James T.[9], Whitaker W.[8], John S.[7], David H.[6], Maria Barbara[5] Eisenhauer, Hans Peter[4], Hans Nicholas[3], Hans Peter[2], Hans[1]) was born 31 Aug 1884 in , Macon, Missouri, and died 02 Mar 1943 in Kirksville, Adair, Missouri. He married **(1) Alta May Lyddon**. He married **(2) Flora ?** 10 Dec 1896 in ,Mason, Illinois.

Child of James Mikel and Alta Lyddon is:
| 620 | i. | Cleo Edward[11] Mikel, born 23 Apr 1908 in ,Adair, Missouri; died 05 Jan 1995 in Aurora, Colorado. |

Child of James Mikel and Flora ? is:
| 621 | i. | Mikel[11]. |

535. Henry Samuel[10] Mikel (William L.[9], Hugh Frank[8], John S.[7], David H.[6], Maria Barbara[5] Eisenhauer, Hans Peter[4], Hans Nicholas[3], Hans Peter[2], Hans[1]) was born 14 Oct 1851 in Adair, Missouri, and died 24 Feb 1915 in Adair, Missouri. He married **(1) Liddia Wood**. He married **(2) Mary Isabelle Gregory** 13 Sep 1876 in , Schuyler, Missouri. She was born 18 Jan 1858 in , Schuyler, Missouri, and died 24 Feb 1924.

Children of Henry Mikel and Liddia Wood are:
| 622 | i. | ?[11] ?. |
| 623 | ii. | ? ?. |

624   iii.   ? ?.

Children of Henry Mikel and Mary Gregory are:
- 625   i.   Warren[11] Mikel, died 06 Mar 1892.
- 626   ii.   James F. Mikel, born Dec 1877 in ,,Missouri.
- 627   iii.   Genie M. Mikel, born 11 Feb 1881; died 17 Aug 1881.
- 628   iv.   William M. Mikel, born 15 Jul 1882 in ,,Missouri; died 02 Aug 1905.
- 629   v.   Mikel, born 27 May 1886 in Greentop, Salt River Township, Schuyler, Missouri; died 27 May 1886 in Greentop, Salt River Township, Schuyler, Missouri.
- 630   vi.   Eva Adelma Mikel, born 27 May 1886 in Greentop, Salt River Township, Schuyler, Missouri; died 09 Nov 1979 in Kirksville, Adair, Missouri. She married (1) Anthony Epperson; born 11 Aug 1874 in Lancaster, Schuyler, Missouri; died 09 Apr 1960. She married (2) William M. Newcomer 03 Jan 1907 in , Adair, Missouri; born 11 Nov 1870 in , Adair, Missouri; died 31 Jul 1946 in Kirksville, Adair, Missouri.
- 631   vii.   Nettie Mikel, born Mar 1893 in ,,Missouri. She married Harrison C. Ruddell Jan 1912; born 08 Sep 1889 in Carthage, Hancock, Illinois; died Nov 1947 in Kirksville, Adair , Missouri.

537. Mary Frances[10] Mikel (William L.[9], Hugh Frank[8], John S.[7], David H.[6], Maria Barbara[5] Eisenhauer, Hans Peter[4], Hans Nicholas[3], Hans Peter[2], Hans[1]) was born Mar 1859 in ,Greenup, Missouri, and died 23 Mar 1945 in Carmel, Monterey, California. She married **John Thomas Stewart** 21 May 1876 in ,Schuyler, Missouri. He was born Sep 1848 in Greenup, Greenup, Kentucky.

Children of Mary Mikel and John Stewart are:
- + 632   i.   Walter C.[11] Stewart, born in ,,Missouri.
- 633   ii.   Ole W. Stewart, born Jan 1879 in ,,Missouri.

539. Ida Belle[10] Mikel (Charles W.[9], Hugh Frank[8], John S.[7], David H.[6], Maria Barbara[5] Eisenhauer, Hans Peter[4], Hans Nicholas[3], Hans Peter[2], Hans[1]) was born 25 Dec 1869 in , Adair, Missouri, and died 25 Oct 1931 in Lancaster , Schuyler, Missouri. She married **John Morgan Whitacre** 16 Sep 1888 in Lancaster, Schuyler, Missouri. He was born 18 Apr 1864 in , Schuyler, Missouri, and died 07 Oct 1946 in Lancaster, Schuyler, Missouri.

Children of Ida Mikel and John Whitacre are:
- + 634   i.   Charles Newton[11] Whitacre, born 15 Jun 1889 in Lancaster, Schuyler, Missouri; died 23 May 1953 in Bloomfield, Davis, Iowa.
- + 635   ii.   Chester Oral Whitacre, born 30 Nov 1890 in Lancaster, Schuyler, Missouri; died 23 Mar 1963 in Burlington, Des Moines, Iowa.
- + 636   iii.   John Leslie Whitacre, born 26 Aug 1892 in Lancaster, Schuyler, Missouri; died 04 Jun 1964 in Centerville, Iowa.
- + 637   iv.   Alta Effie Whitacre, born 19 Sep 1894 in Lancaster, Schuyler, Missouri; died 24 Sep 1972 in Kirksville, Adair, Missouri.
- + 638   v.   Minnie Estella Whitacre, born 01 Mar 1896 in Lancaster, Schuyler, Missouri; died 28 Feb 1973 in Burlington, Des Moines, Iowa.
- + 639   vi.   Essie Elizabeth Whitacre, born 09 Mar 1898 in Lancaster, Schuyler, Missouri; died 12 Jun 1931 in Kirksville, Adair, Missouri.
- 640   vii.   Opal Lydia Whitacre, born 20 Apr 1900 in Lancaster, Schuyler, Missouri; died 20 Feb 1991 in Queen City, Schuyler, Missouri. She married Edwin Raymond Hitch 24 Jun 1923 in Bloomfield, Davis, Iowa; born 30 Jun 1901 in Covington, Campbell, Kentucky; died 27 Jan 1962 in Lancaster, Schuyler, Missouri.
- 641   viii.   Vernon Jewell Whitacre, born 15 Jun 1902 in Lancaster, Schuyler, Missouri; died 01 Nov 1981 in Schenectady, Schenectady, New York.
- + 642   ix.   Kenneth Omer Whitacre, born 27 Feb 1905 in Lancaster, Schuyler, Missouri; died 21 Feb 1976 in Kirksville, Adair, Missouri.
- + 643   x.   Olen Aubry Whitacre, born 18 Apr 1906 in Lancaster, Schuyler, Missouri; died 27 Dec 1993 in Bakersfield, Kern, California.
- 644   xi.   Ida Berniece Whitacre, born 17 Dec 1909 in Lancaster, Schuyler, Missouri; died 22 Nov 1988 in Lancaster, Schuyler, Missouri. She married (1) Wayne Laverne Butts; born 22 Dec 1908 in ,Schuyler, Missouri; died 16 Dec 1991 in Kirksville, Adair, Missouri. She married (2) ? ?. She married (3) Wayne Laverne Butts Feb 1983; born 22 Dec 1908 in ,Schuyler, Missouri; died 16 Dec 1991 in Kirksville, Adair, Missouri.

+   645   xii.   Naomi Vernadean Whitacre, born 09 Dec 1912 in Lancaster, Schuyler, Missouri; died 27 Sep 1995 in Warrenton, Warren, Missouri.

540. Lydia Lottie[10] Mikel (Charles W.[9], Hugh Frank[8], John S.[7], David H.[6], Maria Barbara[5] Eisenhauer, Hans Peter[4], Hans Nicholas[3], Hans Peter[2], Hans[1]) was born 12 Jun 1872 in Greentop, Schuyler, Missouri, and died 04 Dec 1920 in Bayfield, LaPlata, Colorado. She married **Walter Sherman Mikel** 13 Jan 1892 in Pueblo, Pueblo, Colorado, son of William Mikel and Liltra Wade. He was born 13 Dec 1869 in Warrensburg, Johnson, Missouri, and died 01 Jul 1934 in Farmington, San Juan, New Mexico.

Children are listed above under (440) Walter Sherman Mikel.

550. George Washington[10] Mikel (John Noah[9], Hugh Frank[8], John S.[7], David H.[6], Maria Barbara[5] Eisenhauer, Hans Peter[4], Hans Nicholas[3], Hans Peter[2], Hans[1]) was born 19 Jul 1874 in ,Adair, Missouri, and died 22 Dec 1958. He married **Louisa Jane Mercer** 04 Apr 1897 in ,Adair, Missouri. She was born 25 Mar 1878 in ,Illinois, and died 29 Mar 1943 in LaPlata Cemetery, Macon, Missouri.

Children of George Mikel and Louisa Mercer are:
646   i.   Lousia[11] Mikel, born 1897.
647   ii.   Ada Ethel Mikel, born 23 May 1900.
648   iii.   Chester Paul Mikel, born 16 Sep 1904.
649   iv.   Dorcas E Mikel, born 1909.
650   v.   Evan L Mikel, born 1912.
651   vi.   Leslie L Mikel, born 1914.
652   vii.   Traverse Mikel, born 1916.
653   viii. Clora Alice Mikel, born 21 Apr 1917 in ,Macon, Missouri; died 15 Nov 1994 in Kirksville, Adair, Missouri.
654   ix.   Merle A Mikel, born 1920; died Bef. 1943.

556. Charity Ann[10] Mikel (George M.[9], Hugh Frank[8], John S.[7], David H.[6], Maria Barbara[5] Eisenhauer, Hans Peter[4], Hans Nicholas[3], Hans Peter[2], Hans[1]) was born in ,Adair, Missouri. She married **Albert Adams** 31 Jan 1887 in , Adair, Missouri. He died Dec 1921 in Greentop, Schuyler, Missouri.

Child of Charity Mikel and Albert Adams is:
+   655   i.   Everett Pearl[11] Adams, born 03 Jul 1887 in Greentop, Schuyler, Missouri; died 11 Aug 1942 in Greentop, Schuyler, Missouri.

558. Reitty Belle[10] Mikel (George M.[9], Hugh Frank[8], John S.[7], David H.[6], Maria Barbara[5] Eisenhauer, Hans Peter[4], Hans Nicholas[3], Hans Peter[2], Hans[1]) was born 05 Aug 1874 in ,Adair, Missouri, and died 09 May 1951. She married **Nathan C. Bledsoe** 13 Feb 1889 in , Adair, Missouri. He was born 15 Apr 1859 in ,,Arkansas, and died 09 Aug 1934.

Children of Reitty Mikel and Nathan Bledsoe are:
656   i.   Nora Mae[11] Bledsoe, born 29 May 1890 in ,Schuyler., Missouri; died 12 Jun 1938.
657   ii.   Ethel L. Bledsoe, born 13 Jun 1894; died 22 Jan 1965. She married Allen D. Lowe 22 Mar 1916 in Greentop, Schuyler, Missouri; born 26 Mar 1894; died 14 Jun 1960.
658   iii.   Leslie N. Bledsoe, born 24 May 1903 in Missouri; died 15 Apr 1977 in Missouri. He married Louise H. B. Hutchison 28 Jul 1929 in Macon, Macon, Missouri; born 02 May 1905; died 23 Aug 1972.

560. George William[10] Mikel (David J.[9], Hugh Frank[8], John S.[7], David H.[6], Maria Barbara[5] Eisenhauer, Hans Peter[4], Hans Nicholas[3], Hans Peter[2], Hans[1]) was born 09 Sep 1867 in ,Of Adair, Missouri, and died 07 Nov 1918 in ,Adair , Missouri, Ft. Madison Cemetery.. He married **May E. Towles** 18 Nov 1894 in ,Adair , Missouri.

Children of George Mikel and May Towles are:
659   i.   Beulah[11] Mikel.
660   ii.   Myrtle Mikel.
661   iii.   Ruth Mikel.

662   iv.   Eugene Mikel, born 13 Sep 1896; died 02 Feb 1897.

568. Margaret[10] Mikel (Joseph P.[9], Hugh Frank[8], John S.[7], David H.[6], Maria Barbara[5] Eisenhauer, Hans Peter[4], Hans Nicholas[3], Hans Peter[2], Hans[1]) was born 05 May 1865 in , Adair, Missouri, and died 16 Sep 1961 in , Adair, Missouri. She married **(1) James B. Dye** 24 Dec 1882. He was born 13 Mar 1857 in Illinois, and died 16 Jul 1936. She married **(2) Finis Gregory** 31 Dec 1893 in ,Adair , Missouri.

Child of Margaret Mikel and James Dye is:
663   i.   Alvie[11] Dye, born 31 Mar 1887; died 26 Jun 1974.

571. Gladys Melvina[10] Mikel (Walter Sherman[9], William Silas[8], John S.[7], David H.[6], Maria Barbara[5] Eisenhauer, Hans Peter[4], Hans Nicholas[3], Hans Peter[2], Hans[1]) was born 23 Dec 1893 in Dukin, Saguache, Colorado, and died 15 Jun 1921 in Mancos, Montezuma, Colorado. She married **Mark Willden** 29 Aug 1912 in Cortez, Montezuma, Colorado. He was born 16 Mar 1891 in Mancos, Montezuma, Colorado, and died 24 Aug 1977 in Durango, LaPlata, Colorado.

Children of Gladys Mikel and Mark Willden are:
664   i.   Leona Gladys[11] Willden, born 26 Jul 1914 in Mancos, Montezuma, Colorado; died 20 Jul 1960 in Naturita, San Miguel, Colorado.
665   ii.   Esther Corilla Willden, born 11 Oct 1915 in Mancos, Montezuma, Colorado; died 23 Jun 1987 in Provo, Utah, Utah.
666   iii.   Don Edward Willden, born 15 Oct 1916 in Mancos, Montezuma, Colorado; died 17 Dec 1997 in Lovell, Wyoming.
667   iv.   Elmer Sherman Willden, born 17 Feb 1918 in Mancos, Montezuma, Colorado; died 30 Oct 1974 in Colorado Springs, El Paso, Colorado.

578. Generva E.[10] Mikel (Hugh D.[10], Edward B.[9], Hugh Frank[8], John S.[7], David H.[6], Maria Barbara[5] Eisenhauer, Hans Peter[4], Hans Nicholas[3], Hans Peter[2], Hans[1]) was born 26 Jun 1871 in , Adair, Missouri, and died 07 Mar 1906. She married **William M. Newcomer** 13 Dec 1891 in ,Adair, Missouri. He was born 11 Nov 1870 in , Adair, Missouri, and died 31 Jul 1946 in Kirksville, Adair, Missouri.

Children of Generva Mikel and William Newcomer are:
668   i.   Georgie F.[11] Newcomer, died 03 Sep 1905.
669   ii.   Minnie E. Newcomer, born 14 May 1894 in n/Greentop, Schuyler, Missouri; died 17 Jan 1983 in Kirksville, Adair, Missouri. She married John H. Thompson; born 12 Mar 1892; died 04 Sep 1978.
670   iii.   Grace L. Newcomer, born 31 Dec 1895 in n/Greentop, Schuyler, Missouri; died 12 Sep 1975 in Rockford, Winnebago, Illinois.
671   iv.   Nellie Mae Newcomer, born 11 May 1898 in Greentop, Schuyler, Missouri; died 05 Aug 1984 in Kirksville, Adair, Missouri. She married Herman Victor Craig; born 09 Sep 1892 in Greentop, Schuyler, Missouri; died 07 Jul 1976 in Greentop, Schuyler, Missouri.
+   672   v.   Oscar Newcomer, born 15 Nov 1901 in n/Greentop, Schuyler, Missouri; died 26 Mar 1983 in Kirksville, Adair, Missouri.
673   vi.   Ethel L. Newcomer, born 26 May 1905 in Kirksville, Adair, Missouri; died 24 Sep 1991 in Kirksville, Adair, Missouri. She married William S. Thompson 26 Oct 1941 in Greentop, Schuyler, Missouri; born 28 Sep 1900 in Youngstown, Adair(?), Missouri; died 20 Dec 1956 in Kirksville, Adair, Missouri.

590. Oda F.[10] Mikel (Levander L.[10], James Purvis[9], Hugh Frank[8], John S.[7], David H.[6], Maria Barbara[5] Eisenhauer, Hans Peter[4], Hans Nicholas[3], Hans Peter[2], Hans[1]) She married **Clarence W. Gregory**. He was born 06 Feb 1888 in Iowa, and died 30 Mar 1968 in Kirksville, Adair, Missouri.

Children of Oda Mikel and Clarence Gregory are:
674   i.   Loreta[11] Gregory.
675   ii.   Henry Lee Gregory, born 13 Nov 1923 in Greentop, Schuyler, Missouri; died 02 Mar 1968 in , Adair, Missouri.

613. Dwight David[10] Eisenhower (John Sheldon Doud[9], Dwight David[8], David Jacob[7] Eisenhauer, Jacob

Frederick[6], Frederick[5], Hans Peter[4], Hans Nicholas[3], Hans Peter[2], Hans[1]) was born 31 Mar 1948. He married **Julie Nixon** 28 Dec 1968. She was born 05 Jul 1948.

Children of Dwight Eisenhower and Julie Nixon are:

    676   i.   Jennie[11] Eisenhower.
    677   ii.   Alex Eisenhower.
    678   iii. Melanie Eisenhower.

Generation No. 9

632. Walter C.[11] Stewart (Mary Frances[10] Mikel, William L.[9], Hugh Frank[8], John S.[7], David H.[6], Maria Barbara[5] Eisenhauer, Hans Peter[4], Hans Nicholas[3], Hans Peter[2], Hans[1]) was born in ,,Missouri.

Children of Walter C. Stewart are:

    679   i.   ?[12] Stewart.
    680   ii.   ? Stewart.

634. Charles Newton[11] Whitacre (Ida Belle[10] Mikel, Charles W.[9], Hugh Frank[8], John S.[7], David H.[6], Maria Barbara[5] Eisenhauer, Hans Peter[4], Hans Nicholas[3], Hans Peter[2], Hans[1]) was born 15 Jun 1889 in Lancaster, Schuyler, Missouri, and died 23 May 1953 in Bloomfield, Davis, Iowa. He married **Clara Ada White** 08 Mar 1913. She was born 20 Nov 1895 in Iowa, and died 19 Aug 1989 in Bloomfield, Davis, Iowa.

Children of Charles Whitacre and Clara White are:

 + 681   i.   Glen N.[12] Whitacre, born 08 Jan 1914 in Missouri; died 18 Oct 2003 in Bloomfield, Davis, Iowa.
 + 682   ii.   Hugh W. Whitacre, born 21 Apr 1915 in , Schuyler, Missouri; died 20 Feb 2001 in Springfield, Greene, Missouri.
 + 683   iii. Omer Charles Whitacre, born 27 Sep 1916 in Missouri; died 21 Oct 1987 in Bloomfield, Davis, Iowa.
    684   iv. Estel L. Whitacre, born 04 Jun 1918 in Iowa; died Sep 1986 in Missouri>.
    685   v.   Joan A Whitacre, born 1919. He married Sarah J. Harper; born in Iowa>; died in <Bloomfield, Davis, Iowa>.
 + 686   vi. Ray M Whitacre, born 1922.
 + 687   vii. Ella L. Whitacre, born 1923 in Missouri; died in Bloomfield, Davis, Iowa.

635. Chester Oral[11] Whitacre (Ida Belle[10] Mikel, Charles W.[9], Hugh Frank[8], John S.[7], David H.[6], Maria Barbara[5] Eisenhauer, Hans Peter[4], Hans Nicholas[3], Hans Peter[2], Hans[1]) was born 30 Nov 1890 in Lancaster, Schuyler, Missouri, and died 23 Mar 1963 in Burlington, Des Moines, Iowa. He married **Alta Nina McMains** 25 Feb 1914 in Bloomfield, Davis, Iowa. She was born 02 Jan 1895 in ,Davis, Iowa, and died 15 May 1971 in Burlington, Des Moines, Iowa.

Children of Chester Whitacre and Alta McMains are:

    688   i.   Harold O.[12] Whitacre, born in Lancaster, Schuyler, Missouri; died 24 Mar 1955 in Muscatine, Muscatine, Iowa.
    689   ii.   Carroll D. Whitacre, died Dec 1942.
 + 690   iii. Geneva B. Whitacre, born 16 Feb 1918 in ,Davis, Iowa; died 10 Aug 2001 in Burlington, Des Moines, Iowa.

636. John Leslie[11] Whitacre (Ida Belle[10] Mikel, Charles W.[9], Hugh Frank[8], John S.[7], David H.[6], Maria Barbara[5] Eisenhauer, Hans Peter[4], Hans Nicholas[3], Hans Peter[2], Hans[1]) was born 26 Aug 1892 in Lancaster, Schuyler, Missouri, and died 04 Jun 1964 in Centerville, Iowa. He married **(2) ? ?**.

Children of John Leslie Whitacre are:

 + 691   i.   ?[12] Whitacre.
    692   ii.   ? Whitacre. She married Charles Gillispie; born 20 Jul 1920; died 22 Apr 1988.
    693   iii. Ralph Whitacre.
    694   iv. Lowell Whitacre.

637. Alta Effie[11] Whitacre (Ida Belle[10] Mikel, Charles W.[9], Hugh Frank[8], John S.[7], David H.[6], Maria Barbara[5] Eisenhauer, Hans Peter[4], Hans Nicholas[3], Hans Peter[2], Hans[1]) was born 19 Sep 1894 in Lancaster, Schuyler, Missouri, and died 24 Sep 1972 in Kirksville, Adair, Missouri. She married **Eugene Aeschliman** 24 Dec 1914 in Lancaster, Schuyler, Missouri. He was born 30 May 1893 in Darby, Schuyler, Missouri, and died 24 Mar 1974 in Kirksville, Adair, Missouri.

Children of Alta Whitacre and Eugene Aeschliman are:

695	i.	Emogene[12] Aeschliman, born 14 Feb 1916.
696	ii.	Lucille Aeschliman, born 31 Oct 1917. She married Paul Leroy Beeler; born 23 Jan 1916 in Lancaster, Schuyler, Missouri; died 12 Oct 1997 in Lancaster, Schuyler, Missouri.
697	iii.	Essie Mildred Aeschliman, born 16 May 1925 in Lancaster, Schuyler, Missouri; died 18 Jun 1925 in Liberty Township, Schuyler, Missouri.
698	iv.	Opal Hildred Aeschliman, born 16 May 1925.

638. Minnie Estella[11] Whitacre (Ida Belle[10] Mikel, Charles W.[9], Hugh Frank[8], John S.[7], David H.[6], Maria Barbara[5] Eisenhauer, Hans Peter[4], Hans Nicholas[3], Hans Peter[2], Hans[1]) was born 01 Mar 1896 in Lancaster, Schuyler, Missouri, and died 28 Feb 1973 in Burlington, Des Moines, Iowa. She married **Paul Austin Tomey** 29 Aug 1914 in Lancaster, Schuyler, Missouri. He was born 16 Feb 1893 in Bloomfield, Davis, Iowa, and died 02 May 1963 in Burlington, Des Moines, Iowa.

Children of Minnie Whitacre and Paul Tomey are:

+	699	i.	Max H[12] Tomey, born 1921.
	700	ii.	Pauline Annette Tomey, born 02 Mar 1916 in Bloomfield, Davis, Iowa; died 06 Oct 1988 in Morning Sun, Louisa, Iowa. She married (1) Frank Niemann; born 08 Jan 1894; died Apr 1982 in Burlington, Des Moines, Iowa. She married (2) Edward Alfred Scott 17 Sep 1949 in Quincy, Adams, Illinois; born 14 Jul 1902 in Rome, Henry, Iowa; died 23 Jun 1984 in Mt. Pleasant, Henry, Iowa.
+	701	iii.	Jack Phillip Tomey, born 03 Sep 1918 in Des Moines, Polk, Iowa; died 22 Jun 1996 in Sunnyvale, Santa Clara, California.
+	702	iv.	Eugene Stewart Tomey, born 07 Oct 1923 in Boone, Boone, Iowa; died 14 Aug 2001 in Burlington, Des Moines, Iowa.
+	703	v.	Rex Whitacre Tomey, born 04 Dec 1924 in Boone, Boone, Iowa; died 21 May 2001 in Moline, Rock Island, Illinois.
+	704	vi.	William Joseph Tomey, born 22 Jul 1929 in Kirksville, Adair, Missouri; died 02 Oct 1994 in Anaheim, Orange, California.

639. Essie Elizabeth[11] Whitacre (Ida Belle[10] Mikel, Charles W.[9], Hugh Frank[8], John S.[7], David H.[6], Maria Barbara[5] Eisenhauer, Hans Peter[4], Hans Nicholas[3], Hans Peter[2], Hans[1]) was born 09 Mar 1898 in Lancaster, Schuyler, Missouri, and died 12 Jun 1931 in Kirksville, Adair, Missouri. She married **Edward Webster Grist** 29 Jul 1920 in Missouri. He was born 26 Mar 1898 in Lancaster, Schuyler, Missouri.

Child of Essie Whitacre and Edward Grist is:

| 705 | i. | ?[12] ?. |

642. Kenneth Omer[11] Whitacre (Ida Belle[10] Mikel, Charles W.[9], Hugh Frank[8], John S.[7], David H.[6], Maria Barbara[5] Eisenhauer, Hans Peter[4], Hans Nicholas[3], Hans Peter[2], Hans[1]) was born 27 Feb 1905 in Lancaster, Schuyler, Missouri, and died 21 Feb 1976 in Kirksville, Adair, Missouri. He married **Georgia Lee Hulen** 20 Jun 1926 in Lancaster, Schuyler, Missouri. She was born 31 Jan 1908 in Lancaster, Schuyler, Missouri, and died 19 Jun 1988 in Kirksville, Adair, Missouri.

Child of Kenneth Whitacre and Georgia Hulen is:

| 706 | i. | John George[12] Whitacre, born 06 Nov 1925 in Lancaster, Schuyler, Missouri; died 08 Nov 1925 in Lancaster, Schuyler, Missouri. |

643. Olen Aubry[11] Whitacre (Ida Belle[10] Mikel, Charles W.[9], Hugh Frank[8], John S.[7], David H.[6], Maria Barbara[5] Eisenhauer, Hans Peter[4], Hans Nicholas[3], Hans Peter[2], Hans[1]) was born 18 Apr 1906 in Lancaster, Schuyler, Missouri, and died 27 Dec 1993 in Bakersfield, Kern, California. He married **(1) ? ?**. He married **(2) Zelma L. Followwill**. She was born 22 Nov 1914 in Iowa, and died 28 Jan 1998 in Bakersfield, Kern,

California.

Child of Olen Whitacre and Zelma Followwill is:
     707   i.   Richard Allen[12] Whitacre, died 06 Mar 1929 in Seymour, Wayne, Iowa.

645. Naomi Vernadean[11] Whitacre (Ida Belle[10] Mikel, Charles W.[9], Hugh Frank[8], John S.[7], David H.[6], Maria Barbara[5] Eisenhauer, Hans Peter[4], Hans Nicholas[3], Hans Peter[2], Hans[1]) was born 09 Dec 1912 in Lancaster, Schuyler, Missouri, and died 27 Sep 1995 in Warrenton, Warren, Missouri. She married **Harry Bradley** 02 Nov 1933. He was born 15 Mar 1912 in ,,Missouri, and died Oct 1986 in Warrenton, Warren, Missouri.

Child of Naomi Whitacre and Harry Bradley is:
+   708   i.   John L.[12] Bradley, born in Missouri>; died in Missouri>.

655. Everett Pearl[11] Adams (Charity Ann[10] Mikel, George M.[9], Hugh Frank[8], John S.[7], David H.[6], Maria Barbara[5] Eisenhauer, Hans Peter[4], Hans Nicholas[3], Hans Peter[2], Hans[1]) was born 03 Jul 1887 in Greentop, Schuyler, Missouri, and died 11 Aug 1942 in Greentop, Schuyler, Missouri.

Children of Everett Pearl Adams are:
     709   i.   ?[12] Adams.
     710   ii.   ? Adams.
     711   iii.   ? Adams.

672. Oscar[11] Newcomer (Generva E.[11] Mikel, Hugh D.[10], Edward B.[9], Hugh Frank[8], John S.[7], David H.[6], Maria Barbara[5] Eisenhauer, Hans Peter[4], Hans Nicholas[3], Hans Peter[2], Hans[1]) was born 15 Nov 1901 in n/Greentop, Schuyler, Missouri, and died 26 Mar 1983 in Kirksville, Adair, Missouri. He married **Ethel Evelyn Dudgeon** 07 Apr 1928 in Greentop, Schuyler, Missouri. She was born 14 Jan 1908 in Connelsville, Adair, Missouri, and died 05 Apr 1983 in Kirksville, Adair, Missouri.

Children of Oscar Newcomer and Ethel Dudgeon are:
     712   i.   ?[12] Newcomer.
     713   ii.   ? Newcomer.
     714   iii.   Larena Jane Newcomer, born 04 Jan 1935; died 27 Jan 1935.

Generation No. 10

681. Glen N.[12] Whitacre (Charles Newton[11], Ida Belle[10] Mikel, Charles W.[9], Hugh Frank[8], John S.[7], David H.[6], Maria Barbara[5] Eisenhauer, Hans Peter[4], Hans Nicholas[3], Hans Peter[2], Hans[1]) was born 08 Jan 1914 in Missouri, and died 18 Oct 2003 in Bloomfield, Davis, Iowa. He married **Lorene I. Spurgeon**. She was born in Missouri, and died 13 Mar 2000 in Bloomfield, Davis, Iowa.

Children of Glen Whitacre and Lorene Spurgeon are:
+   715   i.   ?[13] Whitacre.
     716   ii.   Melody Whitacre, died Deceased.
+   717   iii.   ? Whitacre.

682. Hugh W.[12] Whitacre (Charles Newton[11], Ida Belle[10] Mikel, Charles W.[9], Hugh Frank[8], John S.[7], David H.[6], Maria Barbara[5] Eisenhauer, Hans Peter[4], Hans Nicholas[3], Hans Peter[2], Hans[1]) was born 21 Apr 1915 in , Schuyler, Missouri, and died 20 Feb 2001 in Springfield, Greene, Missouri. He married **Bertha J. Casteel** 06 Sep 1939 in Unionville, Missouri. She was born 24 Sep 1921 in Iowa>, and died 02 Mar 1996 in <Bloomfield, Davis, Iowa>.

Children of Hugh Whitacre and Bertha Casteel are:
+   718   i.   Bonnie Beth[13] Whitacre.
+   719   ii.   Jane Whitacre.

683. Omer Charles[12] **Whitacre** (Charles Newton[11], Ida Belle[10] Mikel, Charles W.[9], Hugh Frank[8], John S.[7], David H.[6], Maria Barbara[5] Eisenhauer, Hans Peter[4], Hans Nicholas[3], Hans Peter[2], Hans[1]) was born 27 Sep 1916 in Missouri, and died 21 Oct 1987 in Bloomfield, Davis, Iowa. He married **Mary Maurine Spilman** 19 Mar 1939 in Bloomfield, Davis, Iowa. She was born 19 Feb 1920 in Bloomfield, Davis, Iowa, and died 08 Nov 2002 in Bloomfield, Davis, Iowa.

Children of Omer Whitacre and Mary Spilman are:

| | 720 | i. | Kay[13] Whitacre. She married m Brunk. |
| + | 721 | ii. | Ken Whitacre. |

686. Ray M[12] **Whitacre** (Charles Newton[11], Ida Belle[10] Mikel, Charles W.[9], Hugh Frank[8], John S.[7], David H.[6], Maria Barbara[5] Eisenhauer, Hans Peter[4], Hans Nicholas[3], Hans Peter[2], Hans[1]) was born 1922. He married **Doris Sullivan**. She was born in <Bloomfield, Davis, Iowa>, and died in <Bloomfield, Davis, Iowa>.

Children of Ray Whitacre and Doris Sullivan are:

	722	i.	?[13] Whitacre.
	723	ii.	? Whitacre.
+	724	iii.	? Whitacre.

687. Ella L.[12] **Whitacre** (Charles Newton[11], Ida Belle[10] Mikel, Charles W.[9], Hugh Frank[8], John S.[7], David H.[6], Maria Barbara[5] Eisenhauer, Hans Peter[4], Hans Nicholas[3], Hans Peter[2], Hans[1]) was born 1923 in Missouri, and died in Bloomfield, Davis, Iowa. She married **Lowell A. Spurgeon**. He was born 27 Jul 1899 in Missouri, and died 01 Mar 1963 in Missouri.

Child of Ella Whitacre and Lowell Spurgeon is:

| + | 725 | i. | ?[13] Spurgeon. |

690. Geneva B.[12] **Whitacre** (Chester Oral[11], Ida Belle[10] Mikel, Charles W.[9], Hugh Frank[8], John S.[7], David H.[6], Maria Barbara[5] Eisenhauer, Hans Peter[4], Hans Nicholas[3], Hans Peter[2], Hans[1]) was born 16 Feb 1918 in ,Davis, Iowa, and died 10 Aug 2001 in Burlington, Des Moines, Iowa. She married **(1) Carl Dick Poole** Nov 1942. He died 1945. She married **(2) Robert B Stewart** 21 Jul 1948.

Children of Geneva Whitacre and Robert Stewart are:

+	726	i.	Linda[13] Stewart.
	727	ii.	John Stewart.
	728	iii.	Dale Stewart.
	729	iv.	David Stewart.

691. ?[12] **Whitacre** (John Leslie[11], Ida Belle[10] Mikel, Charles W.[9], Hugh Frank[8], John S.[7], David H.[6], Maria Barbara[5] Eisenhauer, Hans Peter[4], Hans Nicholas[3], Hans Peter[2], Hans[1]) She married **Gary Kerby**. He was born 04 Aug 1916, and died 04 Nov 1976.

Children of ? Whitacre and Gary Kerby are:

	730	i.	?[13] Kerby.
	731	ii.	? Kerby. She married ? ?.
+	732	iii.	? Kerby.
	733	iv.	? Kerby.
	734	v.	Eddie Kerby, born 02 Nov 1940; died 14 Nov 1958.
	735	vi.	Judy Kerby, born 19 Apr 1943; died Jul 1943.

699. Max H[12] **Tomey** (Minnie Estella[11] Whitacre, Ida Belle[10] Mikel, Charles W.[9], Hugh Frank[8], John S.[7], David H.[6], Maria Barbara[5] Eisenhauer, Hans Peter[4], Hans Nicholas[3], Hans Peter[2], Hans[1]) was born 1921. He married **(1) Virginia Arlene Lingle**. She was born 07 Nov 1921 in Iowa, and died Apr 1985 in Ottumwa, Wapello, Iowa. He married **(2) Thelma Laverne Hall**. She was born 20 Jan 1923 in Louisville, Jefferson,

Kentucky, and died 25 Mar 1988 in Burlington, Des Moines, Iowa. He married **(3) ? ?.**

Child of Max Tomey and Virginia Lingle is:
+   736   i.   ?[13] ?.

Children of Max Tomey and Thelma Hall are:
     737   i.   Max Allen[13] Tomey, born 18 Dec 1957 in Wiesbaden, Germany; died 22 Jan 1958 in Wiesbaden,
                        Germany.
     738   ii.   Jeffrey Keith Tomey, born 09 Sep 1959 in Dayton, Greene, Ohio; died 17 Feb 1969 in Burlington, Des
                        Moines, Iowa.

701. Jack Phillip[12] Tomey (Minnie Estella[11] Whitacre, Ida Belle[10] Mikel, Charles W.[9], Hugh Frank[8], John S.[7], David H.[6], Maria Barbara[5] Eisenhauer, Hans Peter[4], Hans Nicholas[3], Hans Peter[2], Hans[1]) was born 03 Sep 1918 in Des Moines, Polk, Iowa, and died 22 Jun 1996 in Sunnyvale, Santa Clara, California. He married **(1) Donna ?.**   He married **(2) ? ?.**

Children of Jack Tomey and Donna ? are:
     739   i.   Jack W[13] Tomey.
     740   ii.   Michael Tomey.
     741   iii. Karen Tomey. She married m Mayfield.
     742   iv.   Laurann Tomey. She married m Holm.

Children of Jack Tomey and ? ? are:
     743   i.   ?[13] ?.
     744   ii.   ? ?.

702. Eugene Stewart[12] Tomey (Minnie Estella[11] Whitacre, Ida Belle[10] Mikel, Charles W.[9], Hugh Frank[8], John S.[7], David H.[6], Maria Barbara[5] Eisenhauer, Hans Peter[4], Hans Nicholas[3], Hans Peter[2], Hans[1]) was born 07 Oct 1923 in Boone, Boone, Iowa, and died 14 Aug 2001 in Burlington, Des Moines, Iowa. He married **(1) ? ?.** He married **(2) Jeanne Anne Boschen** 22 Nov 1945 in Burlington, Des Moines, Iowa. She was born 14 Sep 1920 in Republic of Santo Domingo, West Indies, and died 20 May 1982 in Burlington, Des Moines, Iowa.

Children of Eugene Tomey and Jeanne Boschen are:
     745   i.   ?[13] ?.
     746   ii.   Eugene Stewart Tomey, born 06 Dec 1946 in Burlington, Des Moines, Iowa; died 10 Dec 1963 in
                        Burlington, Des Moines, Iowa.

703. Rex Whitacre[12] Tomey (Minnie Estella[11] Whitacre, Ida Belle[10] Mikel, Charles W.[9], Hugh Frank[8], John S.[7], David H.[6], Maria Barbara[5] Eisenhauer, Hans Peter[4], Hans Nicholas[3], Hans Peter[2], Hans[1]) was born 04 Dec 1924 in Boone, Boone, Iowa, and died 21 May 2001 in Moline, Rock Island, Illinois. He married **(1) Joyce Eleanor Pohren** 08 May 1946 in Burlington, Des Moines, Iowa. She was born 01 Dec 1925 in Oskaloosa, Mahaska, Iowa, and died Dec 1973 in Burlington, Des Moines, Iowa. He married **(2) Helen Lahr** 09 Feb 1956 in St. Paul, MN.

Child of Rex Tomey and Joyce Pohren is:
     747   i.   John[13] Tomey, born 22 Sep 1953 in Burlington, Des Moines, Iowa; died 22 Sep 1953 in Burlington,
                        Des Moines, Iowa.

Children of Rex Tomey and Helen Lahr are:
     748   i.   Mitchell[13] Tomey.
     749   ii.   Chreryl Tomey. She married m Jones.
     750   iii. Kristen Tomey. She married ? ?.
     751   iv.   Lisa Tomey. She married m Haynes.

704. William Joseph[12] Tomey (Minnie Estella[11] Whitacre, Ida Belle[10] Mikel, Charles W.[9], Hugh Frank[8], John S.[7], David H.[6], Maria Barbara[5] Eisenhauer, Hans Peter[4], Hans Nicholas[3], Hans Peter[2], Hans[1]) was born 22 Jul 1929 in Kirksville, Adair, Missouri, and died 02 Oct 1994 in Anaheim, Orange, California. He married **? ?**.

Children of William Tomey and ? ? are:
   752   i.   ?[13] ?. She married ? ?.
   753   ii.   ? ?.

708. John L.[12] Bradley (Naomi Vernadean[11] Whitacre, Ida Belle[10] Mikel, Charles W.[9], Hugh Frank[8], John S.[7], David H.[6], Maria Barbara[5] Eisenhauer, Hans Peter[4], Hans Nicholas[3], Hans Peter[2], Hans[1]) was born in Missouri>, and died in Missouri>.

Child of John L. Bradley is:
   754   i.   ?[13] ?.

Generation No. 11

715. ?[13] Whitacre (Glen N.[12], Charles Newton[11], Ida Belle[10] Mikel, Charles W.[9], Hugh Frank[8], John S.[7], David H.[6], Maria Barbara[5] Eisenhauer, Hans Peter[4], Hans Nicholas[3], Hans Peter[2], Hans[1])

Children of ? Whitacre are:
   755   i.   ?[14] Whitacre.
   756   ii.   ? Whitacre.
   757   iii.   ? Whitacre.

717. ?[13] Whitacre (Glen N.[12], Charles Newton[11], Ida Belle[10] Mikel, Charles W.[9], Hugh Frank[8], John S.[7], David H.[6], Maria Barbara[5] Eisenhauer, Hans Peter[4], Hans Nicholas[3], Hans Peter[2], Hans[1]) He married **? ?**.

Children of ? Whitacre and ? ? are:
   758   i.   ?[14] Whitacre.
   759   ii.   ? Whitacre.
   760   iii.   ? Whitacre.

718. Bonnie Beth[13] Whitacre (Hugh W.[12], Charles Newton[11], Ida Belle[10] Mikel, Charles W.[9], Hugh Frank[8], John S.[7], David H.[6], Maria Barbara[5] Eisenhauer, Hans Peter[4], Hans Nicholas[3], Hans Peter[2], Hans[1]) She married **m Hudson**.

Children of Bonnie Whitacre and m Hudson are:
   761   i.   ?[14] Hudson.
   762   ii.   ? Hudson.

719. Jane[13] Whitacre (Hugh W.[12], Charles Newton[11], Ida Belle[10] Mikel, Charles W.[9], Hugh Frank[8], John S.[7], David H.[6], Maria Barbara[5] Eisenhauer, Hans Peter[4], Hans Nicholas[3], Hans Peter[2], Hans[1]) She married **m Carr**.

Children of Jane Whitacre and m Carr are:
    763   i.   ?[14] Carr.
+ 764   ii.   ? Carr.
    765   iii.   ? Carr.
    766   iv.   ? Carr.
    767   v.   ? Carr.

721. Ken[13] Whitacre (Omer Charles[12], Charles Newton[11], Ida Belle[10] Mikel, Charles W.[9], Hugh Frank[8], John S.[7], David H.[6], Maria Barbara[5] Eisenhauer, Hans Peter[4], Hans Nicholas[3], Hans Peter[2], Hans[1])

Child of Ken Whitacre is:

    768   i.   ?[14] Whitacre.

724. ?[13] Whitacre (Ray M[12], Charles Newton[11], Ida Belle[10] Mikel, Charles W.[9], Hugh Frank[8], John S.[7], David H.[6], Maria Barbara[5] Eisenhauer, Hans Peter[4], Hans Nicholas[3], Hans Peter[2], Hans[1])

Children of ? Whitacre are:

    769   i.   ?[14] Whitacre.
    770   ii.   ? Whitacre.

725. ?[13] Spurgeon (Ella L.[12] Whitacre, Charles Newton[11], Ida Belle[10] Mikel, Charles W.[9], Hugh Frank[8], John S.[7], David H.[6], Maria Barbara[5] Eisenhauer, Hans Peter[4], Hans Nicholas[3], Hans Peter[2], Hans[1])

Children of ? Spurgeon are:

    771   i.   ?[14] Spurgeon.
    772   ii.   Shari Spurgeon, born 01 Aug 1964 in <Bloomfield, Davis, Iowa>; died 28 Jul 2001 in Iowa City, Johnson , Iowa.

726. Linda[13] Stewart (Geneva B.[12] Whitacre, Chester Oral[11], Ida Belle[10] Mikel, Charles W.[9], Hugh Frank[8], John S.[7], David H.[6], Maria Barbara[5] Eisenhauer, Hans Peter[4], Hans Nicholas[3], Hans Peter[2], Hans[1]) She married **m Davies**.

Children of Linda Stewart and m Davies are:

    773   i.   Robert[14] Davies.
    774   ii.   John Davies.

732. ?[13] Kerby (?[12] Whitacre, John Leslie[11], Ida Belle[10] Mikel, Charles W.[9], Hugh Frank[8], John S.[7], David H.[6], Maria Barbara[5] Eisenhauer, Hans Peter[4], Hans Nicholas[3], Hans Peter[2], Hans[1])

Child of ? Kerby is:

    775   i.   ?[14] Kerby.

736. ?[13] ? (Max H[12] Tomey, Minnie Estella[11] Whitacre, Ida Belle[10] Mikel, Charles W.[9], Hugh Frank[8], John S.[7], David H.[6], Maria Barbara[5] Eisenhauer, Hans Peter[4], Hans Nicholas[3], Hans Peter[2], Hans[1]) He married **Kathleen Nancy Adams**. She was born 15 Jan 1944 in El Sobrante, Contra Costa, California, and died 16 Dec 1997 in San Pablo, Contra Costa , California.

Children of ? ? and Kathleen Adams are:

+   776   i.   ?[14] ?.
    777   ii.   ? ?.

Generation No. 12

764. ?[14] Carr (Jane[13] Whitacre, Hugh W.[12], Charles Newton[11], Ida Belle[10] Mikel, Charles W.[9], Hugh Frank[8], John S.[7], David H.[6], Maria Barbara[5] Eisenhauer, Hans Peter[4], Hans Nicholas[3], Hans Peter[2], Hans[1]) She married **? ?**.

Child of ? Carr and ? ? is:

    778   i.   ?[15] ?.

776. ?[14] ? (?[13], Max H[12] Tomey, Minnie Estella[11] Whitacre, Ida Belle[10] Mikel, Charles W.[9], Hugh Frank[8], John S.[7], David H.[6], Maria Barbara[5] Eisenhauer, Hans Peter[4], Hans Nicholas[3], Hans Peter[2], Hans[1]) She married **? ?**.

Child of ? ? and ? ? is:
        779   i.   ?^{15} ?.

Above left is Isaac Jacob Matter (1794-1866 picture is circa 1860) a first cousin of Heinrich Matter, great -grandfather of the president. Isaac lived near Elizabethville. His first wife was Anna Maria (Umholtz) (1801-1825). Her gravestone (photograph by the author) is pictured at lower right. She is buried at St. John's Church near Berrysburg. Isaac then married Hannah Lenker (1806-1884) (above right) and the family emigrated to Illinois. The pictures of Isaac and Hannah are courtesy of www.bibleviews.com/Matter.

Descendants of Johannes Adams Matter

Generation No. 1

1. Johannes Adams[1] Matter was born 24 Jan 1731/32 in Altdorf, Alace-Lorraine Germany, and died 26 May 1802 in Upper Paxton Twp, Dauphine Co. Penn.. He married **Anna Barbara Arnhold**.

Children of Johannes Matter and Anna Arnhold are:

+	2	i.	John Michael[2] Matter, born 03 Oct 1763 in Lancaster Co, PA; died 12 Feb 1852 in Dauphin Co, PA.
+	3	ii.	Johannes Matter, born 17 Aug 1759 in New Holland, Lancaster Co, PA; died 30 Jun 1832 in Lykens Valley, Dauphin Co, PA.

Generation No. 2

2. John Michael[2] Matter (Johannes Adams[1]) was born 03 Oct 1763 in Lancaster Co, PA, and died 12 Feb 1852 in Dauphin Co, PA. He married **Anna Maria Romberger** in Probably, Dauphin County, Pa, daughter of Balthaser Romberger and Anna Traut. She was born 12 Jun 1771 in Lancaster Co, PA, and died 18 Mar 1866 in Dauphin Co, PA.

Children of John Matter and Anna Romberger are:

+	4	i.	Johannes[3] Matter, born 04 Jul 1788 in Dauphin, Pa; died 16 Feb 1816 in Dauphin Co., PA.
+	5	ii.	Anna Maria Matter, born 21 Jan 1790; died 29 Jan 1871.
+	6	iii.	Johann Michael Matter, born 29 Mar 1791 in Dauphin, Pa; died 11 Feb 1838 in Dauphin, Pa.
+	7	iv.	Johann George Matter, born 16 Feb 1793 in , Dauphin, Pa.
+	8	v.	Balthasar Matter, born 07 Jul 1795 in , Dauphin, Pa; died 21 Dec 1871 in , Dauphin, Pa.
+	9	vi.	Heinrich Matter, born 26 Dec 1796 in Elizabethville, PA; died 01 Oct 1868 in Lykens, PA.
	10	vii.	Anna Catherina Matter, born 14 Feb 1798 in , Dauphin, Pa.
	11	viii.	Georgianna Matter, born 14 Feb 1798 in Dauphin Co., PA.
	12	ix.	Elisabeth Matter, born 16 May 1799 in Dauphin Co., PA; died 16 Nov 1837 in Gratz, Lykens Twp., Dauphin Co., PA.
	13	x.	Anna Catharina Matter, born 07 Oct 1800 in Mifflin Twp, Dauphin Co., PA; died 13 Aug 1852 in Jefferson Twp., Dauphin Co., PA.
+	14	xi.	Catherine Matter, born 07 Oct 1800 in , Dauphin, Pa.
	15	xii.	Sophia Matter, born 07 Oct 1800 in Mifflin Twp, Dauphin Co., PA.
	16	xiii.	Jonas Matter, born 18 Apr 1802 in , Dauphin, Pa.
	17	xiv.	George Daniel Matter, born 03 Nov 1803 in Dauphin Co., PA; died 01 Oct 1873 in Beaver Twp., Jefferson Co., PA.
+	18	xv.	Michael Matter, born Abt. 1805; died 1838.
+	19	xvi.	Johann Solomon Matter, born 03 Mar 1806 in Mifflin Township, Dauphin, Pa; died 13 May 1877 in , Dauphin, Pa.
	20	xvii.	Infant Matter, born 05 Oct 1807 in Dauphin Co., PA; died Oct 1807 in Dauphin Co., PA.
	21	xviii.	Eva Matter, born 16 Jan 1810 in , Dauphin, Pa; died Abt. 1850.
	22	xix.	Adam Matter, born 01 Apr 1812 in , Dauphin, Pa; died 14 Sep 1889 in Rosecrans, Clinton Co., PA.
	23	xx.	Jacob Matter, born 02 Jul 1813 in , Dauphin, Pa; died 12 Feb 1875 in Dauphin Co., PA.
	24	xxi.	Regina Matter, born 25 Sep 1815 in Dauphin Co., PA; died Bef. 1852. She married Joseph Rowe.
	25	xxii.	Susanna Matter, born 25 Sep 1815 in , Dauphin, Pa; died 12 Aug 1903 in Gratz, Lykens Twp., Dauphin Co., PA.

3. Johannes[2] Matter (Johannes Adams[1]) was born 17 Aug 1759 in New Holland, Lancaster Co, PA, and died 30 Jun 1832 in Lykens Valley, Dauphin Co, PA. He married **Elizabeth Bergner**. She was born 16 Apr 1762 in Lykens Valley, Dauphin Co, PA, and died 18 Dec 1832 in Lykens Valley, Dauphin Co, PA.

Children of Johannes Matter and Elizabeth Bergner are:

26	i.	Catherine[3] Matter, born in PA; died in PA.
27	ii.	Christian Matter, born in PA; died in PA.
28	iii.	Elizabeth Matter, born in PA; died in PA.

29	iv.	Julia Matter, born in PA; died in Illinois.
30	v.	Margaret Matter, born in PA; died in PA.
31	vi.	Peter Matter, born in PA; died in PA.
32	vii.	Susan Matter, born in PA; died in PA.
+ 33	viii.	Jacob Matter, born 07 Feb 1790 in PA; died 22 Feb 1824 in Dauphin Co, PA.
+ 34	ix.	Isaac Jacob Matter, born 18 Sep 1794 in Mifflin Twp, Dauphin Co, PA; died 23 Jul 1866 in Stephenson Co, IL.
+ 35	x.	William Matter, born 08 Dec 1809 in PA; died 14 Apr 1905 in Stephenson Co, IL.

Generation No. 3

4. Johannes[3] Matter (John Michael[2], Johannes Adams[1]) was born 04 Jul 1788 in Dauphin, Pa, and died 16 Feb 1816 in Dauphin Co., PA. He married **Anna Maria Paul**. She was born 01 Jul 1789 in Dauphin Co., PA, and died 18 Mar 1866 in Dauphin Co., PA.

Children of Johannes Matter and Anna Paul are:

36	i.	Anna Maria[4] Matter, born 23 Oct 1810 in , Dauphin, Pa.
37	ii.	Elisabeth Matter, born 22 Jul 1812 in Dauphin Co., PA.
+ 38	iii.	Simon Matter, born 07 Oct 1813 in , Dauphin, Pa; died 03 Jun 1895 in Dauphin Co., PA.
39	iv.	Benjamin Matter, born 15 May 1815 in , Dauphin, Pa.

5. Anna Maria[3] Matter (John Michael[2], Johannes Adams[1]) was born 21 Jan 1790, and died 29 Jan 1871. She married **Peter Minnich** 21 Feb 1808 in Mifflin Twp., Dauphin Co., PA. He was born 11 Sep 1785 in Upper Paxton Twp., Dauphin Co., PA, and died 25 Sep 1855 in Washington Twp., Dauphin Co., PA.

Children of Anna Matter and Peter Minnich are:

40	i.	Peter[4] Minnich, born 19 Feb 1808 in Dauphin Co., PA.
41	ii.	Johannes Minnich, born 24 May 1809 in Mifflin Twp., Dauphin Co., PA; died 22 Jun 1894.
42	iii.	Daniel Minnich, born 24 Sep 1811 in Mifflin Twp., Dauphin Co., PA.
+ 43	iv.	Elizabeth Minnich, born 29 Dec 1813 in Mifflin Twp., Dauphin Co., PA; died 1882 in Dauphin Co., PA.
+ 44	v.	Michael Minnich, born Abt. 1814; died 10 Mar 1891 in Dauphin Co., PA.
+ 45	vi.	Catherine Minnich, born 24 Nov 1815 in Mifflin Twp., Dauphin Co., PA; died 28 Oct 1893.
+ 46	vii.	Sarah Minnich, born 17 Dec 1817 in Mifflin Twp., Dauphin Co., PA; died 10 May 1890 in Dauphin Co., PA.
47	viii.	Child Minnich, born 1819 in Mifflin Twp., Dauphin Co., PA.

6. Johann Michael[3] Matter (John Michael[2], Johannes Adams[1]) was born 29 Mar 1791 in Dauphin, Pa, and died 11 Feb 1838 in Dauphin, Pa. He married **(1) Anna Catherina Cooper** 25 Sep 1814 in Dauphin, Pa. She was born 17 Oct 1792 in Dauphin, Pa, and died 07 Nov 1824 in Dauphin, Pa. He married **(2) Margaret Rebecca Kiehner** 29 Mar 1825 in Mifflin Twp., Dauphin Co., PA. She was born 17 Mar 1805 in Dauphin Co., PA, and died 07 May 1854 in Dauphin Co., PA.

Children of Johann Matter and Anna Cooper are:

48	i.	David[4] Matter, born 13 Jun 1815 in , Dauphin, Pa; died 10 Jun 1871 in Dauphin Co., PA. He married Catharina Bomberger; born 11 Nov 1816; died 17 Jul 1889 in Dauphin Co., PA.
+ 49	ii.	Christopher Matter, born 29 May 1816 in Dauphin Co., PA; died 12 Oct 1843 in Lancaster Co., PA.
50	iii.	Margaret Matter, born 16 Aug 1817 in , Dauphin, Pa.
+ 51	iv.	Levi Matter, born 24 Nov 1820 in Dauphin, Pa; died 06 Dec 1895 in Washington Twp., Dauphin Co., PA.
52	v.	Christianna Matter, born 30 Jul 1823 in Dauphin Co., PA; died 20 Dec 1892 in Dauphin Co., PA.
53	vi.	Anna Matter, born Abt. 1824 in Dauphin Co., PA.

Children of Johann Matter and Margaret Kiehner are:

54	i.	Katharina Anna[4] Matter, born 09 Dec 1825 in Dauphin Co., PA.
55	ii.	Charles Matter, born 02 Dec 1826 in Dauphin Co., PA.
56	iii.	James Matter, born 14 Dec 1827 in Dauphin Co., PA.
57	iv.	Martin Matter, born 25 Jan 1829 in Dauphin Co., PA.

58	v.	Sarah Matter, born 03 Feb 1830 in Dauphin Co., PA.
59	vi.	Cunrath Matter, born 19 Mar 1831 in Dauphin Co., PA; died 18 Feb 1896 in Brodhead, Green Co., WI.
60	vii.	Elisabeth Matter, born 05 May 1832 in Dauphin Co., PA.
61	viii.	Reuben Matter, born 01 Aug 1833 in Dauphin Co., PA.
62	ix.	Lavina Magdalena Matter, born 22 Nov 1834 in Dauphin Co., PA.
63	x.	Mary Matter, born 01 May 1838 in Dauphin Co., PA.
64	xi.	Lewis Matter, born 06 Feb 1837; died 1902. He married Rebecca Hoffman; born 04 Nov 1838; died 30 Mar 1926.

7. Johann George[3] Matter (John Michael[2], Johannes Adams[1]) was born 16 Feb 1793 in , Dauphin, Pa. He married **Susanna Catharine Reigle**. She was born 17 Mar 1771.

Children of Johann Matter and Susanna Reigle are:

65	i.	Leah[4] Matter, born 22 May 1817 in Mifflin Twp, Dauphin Co., PA.
66	ii.	Joseph Matter, born 23 Aug 1818 in Mifflin Twp, Dauphin Co., PA.
67	iii.	Delila Matter, born 09 Feb 1825 in Mifflin Twp, Dauphin Co., PA.
68	iv.	Jonathon Matter, born 07 Aug 1826 in Mifflin Twp, Dauphin Co., PA.
69	v.	Elisabeth Matter, born 23 Feb 1832 in Mifflin Twp, Dauphin Co., PA.
70	vi.	Sara Matter, born 08 Jan 1833 in Mifflin Twp, Dauphin Co., PA.

8. Balthasar[3] Matter (John Michael[2], Johannes Adams[1]) was born 07 Jul 1795 in , Dauphin, Pa, and died 21 Dec 1871 in , Dauphin, Pa. He married **Catherine Ritzman** in No Data, Probably, Dauphin County, Pa. She was born 12 Feb 1797 in Dauphin Co., PA, and died 17 Oct 1864 in Gratz, Lykens Twp., Dauphin Co., PA.

Children of Balthasar Matter and Catherine Ritzman are:

71	i.	Emanuel[4] Matter.
72	ii.	Michael Matter, born 26 Apr 1818 in Mifflin Township, Dauphin, Pa. He married Anna Maria ?.
73	iii.	Susanna Matter, born 12 Jun 1819 in Mifflin Township, Dauphin, Pa.
74	iv.	Elizabeth Matter, born 15 Apr 1821 in Lykens Valley, Dauphin Co., PA; died 26 Sep 1852 in Lykens Valley, Dauphin Co., PA.
75	v.	Benneville Matter, born 25 Nov 1823 in Gratz, Lykens Twp., Dauphin Co., PA; died 28 Feb 1899 in , Dauphin, Pa. He married Veronica Snyder 1845 in No Data, Probably, Dauphin County, Pa; born 05 Dec 1822 in Halifax, Dauphin, Pa.
76	vi.	Leonard Motter, born 08 Mar 1826 in Dauphin Co., PA; died 17 Jul 1896 in Ogle Co., IL.
77	vii.	Abraham Matter, born 03 Jun 1828 in Lykens Twp., Dauphin Co., PA; died 23 May 1895 in Adeline, Maryland Twp., Ogle Co., IL.
78	viii.	Sarah Ann Matter, born 17 Jan 1833 in Dauphin Co., PA; died 12 Sep 1851 in Gratz, Lykens Twp., Dauphin Co., PA.
79	ix.	Edward Matter, born 1836 in Dauphin Co., PA; died 1881 in Dauphin Co., PA.

9. Heinrich[3] Matter (John Michael[2], Johannes Adams[1]) was born 26 Dec 1796 in Elizabethville, PA, and died 01 Oct 1868 in Lykens, PA. He married **Anna Marie Deitrich** in PA, daughter of Jacob Deitrich. She was born 15 Mar 1803 in Lykens, Dauphin, PA, and died 11 Nov 1865 in Lykens, Dauphin, PA.

Children of Heinrich Matter and Anna Deitrich are:

+	80	i.	Elisabeth[4] Matter, born 06 Feb 1820 in Dauphin Co., PA; died 09 Feb 1891 in Dauphin Co., PA.
	81	ii.	Thomas Matter, born 20 Apr 1821 in Dauphin Co., PA. He married (1) Margaretha ?; born 22 Jul 1831 in Dauphin Co., PA; died 09 Jul 1863 in Pennsylvania. He married (2) Lovina ?; born 28 Aug 1840 in Pennsylvania; died 25 Feb 1892 in Dauphin Co., PA.
+	82	iii.	Catharina Matter, born 29 Jan 1823 in Dauphin Co., PA; died 13 Mar 1915 in Dauphin Co., PA.
+	83	iv.	Margareta Rebecca Matter, born 18 Mar 1825 in Mifflin Twp, Dauphin, PA; died 22 Jun 1890 in Abilene, Dickinson Co , Kansas.
	84	v.	Nicholas Matter, born 07 Dec 1826 in Dauphin Co., PA; died 23 Jun 1865. He married Mathilda Lebo; born 31 May 1827 in Dauphin Co., PA; died 27 Aug 1917.
	85	vi.	Sarah Matter, born 1830. She married George R. Williard.
+	86	vii.	George Washington Matter, born 16 Jan 1832 in Elizabethville, Dauphin Co., PA; died 26 Sep 1878 in Dauphin Co., PA.
	87	viii.	Moses Matter, born 1834 in Elizabethville, Dauphin Co., PA; died 1836 in Elizabethville, Dauphin Co., PA.
	88	ix.	Mary Ann Matter, born 25 May 1841 in Elizabethville, Dauphin Co., PA; died 09 Feb 1904.

14. Catherine[3] Matter (John Michael[2], Johannes Adams[1]) was born 07 Oct 1800 in , Dauphin, Pa. She married **Johannes Ritzman.** He was born Abt. 1815.

Child of Catherine Matter and Johannes Ritzman is:

+ 89   i.   Anna Maria[4] Ritzman, born Abt. 1840.

18. Michael[3] Matter (John Michael[2], Johannes Adams[1]) was born Abt. 1805, and died 1838. He married **Catherine Kupper.** She was born Abt. 1805.

Child of Michael Matter and Catherine Kupper is:

+ 90   i.   Christopher[4] Matter, born Abt. 1830.

19. Johann Solomon[3] Matter (John Michael[2], Johannes Adams[1]) was born 03 Mar 1806 in Mifflin Township, Dauphin, Pa, and died 13 May 1877 in , Dauphin, Pa. He married **Isabella Row** in No Data, Probably, Dauphin County, Pa. She was born 30 Apr 1810 in , Dauphin, Pa, and died 27 Jan 1857 in , Dauphin, Pa.

Children of Johann Matter and Isabella Row are:

91   i.   Daniel[4] Matter, born 31 Jan 1831 in , Dauphin, Pa.
92   ii.   Susanna Matter, born 24 Jun 1851 in , Dauphin, Pa.
93   iii.   Solomon Matter, born 02 Aug 1854 in , Dauphin, Pa.

33. Jacob[3] Matter (Johannes[2], Johannes Adams[1]) was born 07 Feb 1790 in PA, and died 22 Feb 1824 in Dauphin Co, PA. He married **Sarah Fisher.** She was born 02 Feb 1789 in Dauphin Co, PA, and died 01 Jul 1838.

Child of Jacob Matter and Sarah Fisher is:

+ 94   i.   Joseph[4] Matter, born 05 May 1814; died 16 May 1857 in Lykens, Dauphin Co, PA.

34. Isaac Jacob[3] Matter (Johannes[2], Johannes Adams[1]) was born 18 Sep 1794 in Mifflin Twp, Dauphin Co, PA, and died 23 Jul 1866 in Stephenson Co, IL. He married **(1) Anna Maria Umholtz** 29 Jul 1820. She was born 11 Nov 1801 in PA, and died 24 Apr 1825 in Dauphin Co, PA. He married **(2) Hannah Lenker** 1827 in Millersburg, PA. She was born 14 May 1806, and died 08 Jun 1884 in Stephenson Co, IL.

Children of Isaac Matter and Anna Umholtz are:

95   i.   Jonathan[4] Matter, born 26 Apr 1822 in Dauphin Co, PA; died 21 Nov 1919 in Freeport, Stephenson Co., IL.
96   ii.   Moses Matter, born 13 Dec 1823.

Children of Isaac Matter and Hannah Lenker are:

+ 97   i.   William Henry[4] Matter, born 20 Mar 1836 in PA; died 07 Jan 1915 in Freeport, Stephenson Co, IL.
+ 98   ii.   Mary Anna Matter, born 12 Jul 1828 in Dauphin Co, PA; died 01 May 1898 in Stephenson Co, IL.
+ 99   iii.   Joseph Matter, born 11 Sep 1829 in Dauphin Co, PA; died 20 Apr 1903 in Freeport, Stephenson Co, IL.
   100   iv.   Catherine Matter, born 06 Dec 1831 in Dauphin Co, PA; died 02 Jun 1894 in Freeport, Stephenson Co, IL. She married Paul Warren Rockey 05 Jun 1856 in Freeport, Stephenson Co, IL; born 07 Mar 1831 in Clinton Co, PA.
   101   v.   Aaron Matter, born 12 Jul 1834 in PA; died 10 Aug 1855 in PA.
   102   vi.   Susan Emily Matter, born 27 Apr 1838 in PA; died 16 Apr 1910 in Jewell, Jewell Co., KS. She married Charles E Plowman 27 Feb 1868 in Stephenson Co, IL; born 09 Jun 1834 in York Co, PA.
   103   vii.   Lydia Jane Matter, born 05 Dec 1839 in PA; died 13 Apr 1904 in Buffalo Twp., Jewell Co., KS. She married William H Cameron; born 31 Dec 1839.
   104   viii.   Elizabeth Matter, born Abt. 1841. She married m Worick.
+ 105   ix.   David J Matter, born 1842; died 1919.
   106   x.   Sarah Matter, born 20 Sep 1843. She married m Folgate.

35. William³ Matter (Johannes², Johannes Adams¹) was born 08 Dec 1809 in PA, and died 14 Apr 1905 in Stephenson Co, IL. He married **Lena Troutman**. She was born 31 Mar 1814 in Northumberland Co, PA, and died 29 Mar 1899 in Stephenson Co, IL.

Children of William Matter and Lena Troutman are:

107	i.	Elizabeth⁴ Matter. She married m Fehr.
108	ii.	Moses Matter.
109	iii.	Jonathan Matter.
110	iv.	Leah Matter. She married m Tool.
111	v.	Susan Matter. She married m Fehr.
112	vi.	Conrad Matter.
113	vii.	Gideon Matter.
114	viii.	Sarah Matter. She married m Lambert.
115	ix.	James Matter.

Generation No. 4

38. Simon⁴ Matter (Johannes³, John Michael², Johannes Adams¹) was born 07 Oct 1813 in , Dauphin, Pa, and died 03 Jun 1895 in Dauphin Co., PA. He married **Sarah Swab** in No Data, Probably, Dauphin County, Pa. She was born in , Dauphin, Pa.

Children of Simon Matter and Sarah Swab are:

+	116	i.	Daniel⁵ Matter, born 1843 in , Dauphin, Pa.
	117	ii.	Sarah Matter, born 10 Jun 1852 in , Dauphin, Pa.
	118	iii.	Leah Jane Matter, born 19 Aug 1856 in , Dauphin, Pa.
	119	iv.	Amanda Matter, born 20 Jul 1860 in , Dauphin, Pa.
	120	v.	Ellen Elizabeth Matter, born 20 Oct 1864 in , Dauphin, Pa.

43. Elizabeth⁴ Minnich (Anna Maria³ Matter, John Michael², Johannes Adams¹) was born 29 Dec 1813 in Mifflin Twp., Dauphin Co., PA, and died 1882 in Dauphin Co., PA. She married **Johannes Travitz**. He was born 12 Jul 1810 in Jackson Twp., Dauphin Co., PA, and died 01 Mar 1880 in Jackson Twp., Dauphin Co., PA.

Child of Elizabeth Minnich and Johannes Travitz is:

| + | 121 | i. | Simon⁵ Travitz, born 10 May 1843 in Jackson Twp., Dauphin Co., PA; died 29 Jun 1917 in Jackson Twp., Dauphin Co., PA. |

44. Michael⁴ Minnich (Anna Maria³ Matter, John Michael², Johannes Adams¹) was born Abt. 1814, and died 10 Mar 1891 in Dauphin Co., PA. He married **Ruth Ann Kern**. She was born 16 Oct 1812 in Jackson Twp., Dauphin Co., PA, and died 16 Dec 1890 in Dauphin Co., PA.

Children of Michael Minnich and Ruth Kern are:

	122	i.	Jeremiah⁵ Minnich, born 03 Jul 1834 in Jackson Twp., Dauphin Co., PA; died 26 Mar 1857 in Dauphin Co., PA.
+	123	ii.	Josiah Minnich, born 02 Sep 1836 in Armstrong Valley, Jackson Twp., Dauphin Co., PA; died 02 Jan 1908 in Lykens Twp., Dauphin Co., PA.
+	124	iii.	Cyrus Minnich, born 05 Mar 1839; died 26 Jun 1900 in PA.
+	125	iv.	Uriah Minnich, born 12 Sep 1842 in Lykens Twp., Dauphin Co., PA; died 06 May 1901 in Lykens Twp., Dauphin Co., PA.
	126	v.	Elias Minnich, born 1844 in Jackson Twp., Dauphin Co., PA.
	127	vi.	Catherine Minnich, born 20 Mar 1850 in Jackson Twp., Dauphin Co., PA; died 21 Feb 1928. She married Cyrus Miller; born 09 May 1850; died 26 Nov 1922.
	128	vii.	Sarah Ann Minnich, born 1853 in Jackson Twp., Dauphin Co., PA.
	129	viii.	Mary Jane Minnich, born 30 Sep 1856 in Jackson Twp., Dauphin Co., PA; died 07 Mar 1857 in Jackson Twp., Dauphin Co., PA.

45. Catherine[4] Minnich (Anna Maria[3] Matter, John Michael[2], Johannes Adams[1]) was born 24 Nov 1815 in Mifflin Twp., Dauphin Co., PA, and died 28 Oct 1893. She married **Jacob Hoover**. He was born Abt. 1811 in Mifflin Twp., Dauphin Co., PA.

Children of Catherine Minnich and Jacob Hoover are:

	130	i.	Elizabeth[5] Hoover, born in Dauphin Co., PA.
	131	ii.	Ella Hoover, born in Dauphin Co., PA.
	132	iii.	Jacob Hoover, born in Dauphin Co., PA.
+	133	iv.	Solomon Hoover, born in Dauphin Co., PA.
	134	v.	Lloyd Hoover, born in Dauphin Co., PA.
+	135	vi.	Alfred Hoover, born 1840 in Dauphin Co., PA; died 1902.

46. Sarah[4] Minnich (Anna Maria[3] Matter, John Michael[2], Johannes Adams[1]) was born 17 Dec 1817 in Mifflin Twp., Dauphin Co., PA, and died 10 May 1890 in Dauphin Co., PA. She married **Jacob Gipple**. He was born 16 Jan 1815 in Pennsylvania, and died 23 Sep 1882 in Dauphin Co., PA.

Children of Sarah Minnich and Jacob Gipple are:

136	i.	Mary Ann[5] Gipple-I, born Sep 1838 in Dauphin Co., PA.
137	ii.	Eliza Gipple, born Abt. 1839 in Dauphin Co., PA.
138	iii.	Elizabeth Gipple, born 1840 in Dauphin Co., PA.
139	iv.	Lydia Ann Gipple, born Jul 1841 in Dauphin Co., PA.
140	v.	Mary Ann Gipple-Ii, born 1846 in Dauphin Co., PA.
141	vi.	Samuel H. Gipple, born Jun 1848 in Lykens Twp., Dauphin Co., PA; died 1920.
142	vii.	Aaron Gipple, born Oct 1850 in Dauphin Co., PA; died 1920.
143	viii.	Jacob J. Gipple, born Nov 1853 in Dauphin Co., PA; died 1927.
144	ix.	Joseph Gipple, born 28 Jul 1857 in Dauphin Co., PA.
145	x.	James A. Gipple, born Aug 1859 in Dauphin Co., PA; died 1920.

49. Christopher[4] Matter (Johann Michael[3], John Michael[2], Johannes Adams[1]) was born 29 May 1816 in Dauphin Co., PA, and died 12 Oct 1843 in Lancaster Co., PA. He married **Catherine Lenker** Abt. 1838. She was born 04 Oct 1820 in Dauphin Co., PA, and died 16 Jul 1891 in Dauphin Co., PA.

Children of Christopher Matter and Catherine Lenker are:

146	i.	John L.[5] Matter, born 08 Feb 1839 in Elizabethville, Dauphin Co., PA; died 31 Aug 1901 in Pennsylvania. He married Harriet L. Martz 31 Oct 1865 in Berrysburg, Daupnin Co., PA.
147	ii.	Michael Matter, born 28 Apr 1842 in Dauphin Co., PA; died 04 Dec 1912 in Hillsboro, Highland Co., OH. He married (1) Sarah Ann Keen 03 Oct 1865 in Dauphin Co., PA; born 17 Oct 1849 in Washington Twp., Dauphin Co., PA; died 07 Dec 1907 in Elizabethville, Dauphin Co., PA. He married (2) Mary Justice 20 Feb 1911 in Hillsboro, Highland Co., OH; born 20 Jan 1868 in Hillsboro, Highland Co., OH.
148	iii.	Christian Matter, born 09 May 1844 in Mifflin Twp, Dauphin Co., PA; died 31 Aug 1906 in Fisherville, Dauphin Co., PA.

51. Levi[4] Matter (Johann Michael[3], John Michael[2], Johannes Adams[1]) was born 24 Nov 1820 in Dauphin, Pa, and died 06 Dec 1895 in Washington Twp., Dauphin Co., PA. He married **Esther Dupendorf** in No Data, Probably, Dauphin County, Pa. She was born 11 Nov 1819 in Dauphin, Pa, and died 08 Jan 1904 in Dauphin, Pa.

Children of Levi Matter and Esther Dupendorf are:

| + | 149 | i. | Daniel D[5] Matter, born 11 Feb 1852 in , Dauphin, Pa; died 15 Jan 1934 in , Dauphin, Pa. |
| + | 150 | ii. | Sarah Ellen Matter, born 04 Mar 1855 in , Dauphin, Pa. |

80. Elisabeth[4] Matter (Heinrich[3], John Michael[2], Johannes Adams[1]) was born 06 Feb 1820 in Dauphin Co., PA, and died 09 Feb 1891 in Dauphin Co., PA. She married **(1) David Sheesley** Abt. 1838 in Dauphin Co., PA. He was born 14 Feb 1813, and died 23 Aug 1845. She married **(2) George Gilbert** Aft. 1845. He was born 31 Dec 1813 in PA, and died 10 Nov 1869. She married **(3) Philip Bowman** Aft. 1850.

Children of Elisabeth Matter and David Sheesley are:

 151 i. Rebecca⁵ Sheesley, born 16 Mar 1839 in Dauphin Co., PA; died 22 Jan 1870 in Dauphin Co., PA.
+ 152 ii. Sarah Etta Sheesley, born Aug 1840; died 24 Jun 1903 in Maple Grove Cemetery, Elizabethville, PA.
 153 iii. Anna Sheesley, born 02 Jan 1843; died 04 Jun 1843.

Children of Elisabeth Matter and George Gilbert are:

 154 i. Alfred⁵ Gilbert, born Sep 1849 in PA. He married Elizabeth ?.
 155 ii. Salome Gilbert, born Abt. 1854.
 156 iii. George W Gilbert, born Oct 1855. He married Ellen R ?.
+ 157 iv. Minerva Gilbert, born 03 Aug 1851 in Washington Twp, Dauphin Co, PA; died 05 Apr 1914.

82. Catharina⁴ Matter (Heinrich³, John Michael², Johannes Adams¹) was born 29 Jan 1823 in Dauphin Co., PA, and died 13 Mar 1915 in Dauphin Co., PA. She married **Phillip Wilbert**. He was born 29 Oct 1821, and died 02 Nov 1893 in Dauphin Co., PA.

Children of Catharina Matter and Phillip Wilbert are:

 158 i. Sarah Jane⁵ Wilbert, born 12 Jan 1848; died 23 Aug 1926. She married Daniel A. Miller 1870; born 1845; died 1901.
 159 ii. May Wilbert, born 17 Apr 1852; died 24 Dec 1857 in Dauphin Co., PA.
+ 160 iii. Lydia A. Wilbert, born 14 Mar 1854 in Dauphin County, PA; died 20 Oct 1930.
 161 iv. John H. Wilbert, born 21 Jun 1855 in Dauphin Co., PA; died 25 Dec 1857 in Dauphin Co., PA.
 162 v. Emeline Wilbert, born 04 May 1859 in Dauphin Co., PA; died 07 Aug 1861 in Dauphin Co., PA.
 163 vi. Amanda E. Wilbert, born 1861 in Dauphin Co., PA; died 03 Feb 1942 in Dauphin Co., PA. She married Wellington Klinger 08 Jul 1880 in Lykens Valley, Dauphin Co., PA; born 18 Mar 1858; died 1936.
 164 vii. Clara R. Wilbert, born 07 Oct 1863; died 06 Apr 1928. She married Alfred Bechtel 25 Feb 1882 in Dauphin Co., PA; born 03 Feb 1859; died 31 Dec 1924.
 165 viii. Mary Wilbert, born Abt. 1865 in Dauphin County, PA.

83. Margareta Rebecca⁴ Matter (Heinrich³, John Michael², Johannes Adams¹) was born 18 Mar 1825 in Mifflin Twp, Dauphin, PA, and died 22 Jun 1890 in Abilene, Dickinson Co , Kansas. She married **Jacob Frederick Eisenhauer** 25 Feb 1847 in Dauphin , Pennsylvania, son of Frederick Eisenhauer and Barbara Miller. He was born 19 Sep 1826 in Elizabethville, Washington Twp., Dauphin Co., PA, and died 20 May 1906 in Abilene, Dickinson Co , Kansas.

Children of Margareta Matter and Jacob Eisenhauer are:

 166 i. John H.⁵ Eisenhauer, born 07 Mar 1848 in Elizabethville, Dauphin Co PA; died 10 Apr 1857 in Elizabethville, Dauphin Co PA.
+ 167 ii. Mary Ann Eisenhauer, born 02 Sep 1849 in Elizabethville, Dauphin, Pennsylvania; died 27 Apr 1893 in Abilene, Dickinson, Kansas.
+ 168 iii. Catherine Ann Eisenhauer, born 19 Mar 1851 in Elizabethville, Dauphin, Pennsylvania; died 03 Apr 1924 in Ramona, Marion, Kansas.
 169 iv. Jacob F. Eisenhauer, born 03 Sep 1852 in Elizabethville, Dauphin Co PA; died 02 Oct 1852 in Elizabethville, Dauphin Co PA.
 170 v. Samuel F. Eisenhauer, born 30 Sep 1853 in Elizabethville, Dauphin Co PA; died 11 Jun 1854 in Elizabethville, Dauphin Co PA.
+ 171 vi. Susanna Eisenhauer, born 29 Oct 1854 in Elizabethville, Dauphin, Pennsylvania; died 14 Jun 1932 in York, PA.
 172 vii. Peter A. Eisenhauer, born 27 Nov 1855 in Elizabethville, Dauphin Co PA; died 04 Aug 1856 in Elizabethville, Dauphin Co PA.
 173 viii. Lydia A. Eisenhauer, born 27 Aug 1857 in Elizabethville, Dauphin Co PA; died 15 Nov 1874 in Elizabethville, Dauphin Co PA.
 174 ix. Emma Jane Eisenhauer, born 03 Dec 1859 in Elizabethville, Dauphin Co PA; died 08 May 1860 in Elizabethville, Dauphin Co PA.
+ 175 x. Amanda Hannah Eisenhauer, born 11 Dec 1861 in Elizabethville, Dauphin Co PA; died 25 Aug 1951 in Abilene, Dickinson Co, KS.
+ 176 xi. David Jacob Eisenhauer, born 23 Sep 1863 in Elizabethville, Dauphin, Pennsylvania; died 10 Mar 1942 in Abilene, Dickinson, Kansas.
 177 xii. Dr Abraham Lincoln Eisenhauer, born 22 Jul 1865 in Elizabethville, Dauphin Co PA; died 23 Dec 1944 in Upland, CA. He married Anna Long 1886; born 1865.

178	xiii.	Clinton Eisenhauer, born 30 Jul 1867 in Elizabethville, Dauphin Co, PA; died 10 Aug 1867 in Elizabethville, Dauphin Co, PA.
+ 179	xiv.	Ira A Eisenhower, born 30 Jul 1867 in Elizabethville, Dauphin, Pa; died 28 Mar 1943 in Los Angeles, CA.

86. George Washington[4] Matter (Heinrich[3], John Michael[2], Johannes Adams[1]) was born 16 Jan 1832 in Elizabethville, Dauphin Co., PA, and died 26 Sep 1878 in Dauphin Co., PA. He married **Margaret Cumbler** 08 Sep 1857 in Washington Twp., Dauphin Co., PA. She was born 22 Jul 1829, and died 30 Aug 1898 in Washington Twp., Dauphin Co., PA.

Children of George Matter and Margaret Cumbler are:
180	i.	Infant A[5] Matter, born 16 May 1858; died 1858.
181	ii.	Infant B Matter, born 16 May 1858; died 1858.
182	iii.	Caleb Wheeler Matter, born 21 Jul 1859; died 20 Jan 1862.
183	iv.	Andrew G Curton Matter, born 20 Jan 1861 in Dauphin Co, PA; died 25 Sep 1939 in Colony, Anderson, KS. He married Leona Margery Proctor; born 21 Jan 1865 in Minera, Mason County, Kentucky; died 30 Dec 1928 in Colony, Anderson, KS.
184	v.	Theodore Nathaniel Matter, born 05 May 1864 in Elizabethville, Dauphin Co, PA; died 19 Apr 1920 in Comfort, Kendall County, Texas. He married Sophia Roemer 22 Dec 1889 in Comfort, Kendall County, Texas; born 21 Mar 1871 in Comfort, Kendall County, Texas; died 08 Mar 1931 in Comfort, Kendall County, Texas.
185	vi.	Isabella Amelia Matter, born 12 Jan 1865 in Elizabethville, Dauphin Co, PA; died 06 Oct 1947 in Chicago, IL. She married F E Roach 28 Jan 1896 in San Antonio, TX; born Abt. 1861.
186	vii.	Mary Ellen Matter, born 05 Apr 1867; died 30 Jan 1953 in San Antonio, Bexar County, Texas. She married (1) Richard S Lambert 24 Apr 1888 in San Antonio, TX; born Abt. 1863. She married (2) Cecil Jacob Gerhard 20 Feb 1892 in San Antonio, TX; born Abt. 1863.
187	viii.	Clinton Jodus Matter, born 17 May 1870; died 05 Sep 1871.
188	ix.	Hannah Elizabeth Matter, born 30 Oct 1873; died 07 Nov 1959 in San Antonio, Bexar County, Texas. She married John A Wharton 16 Jun 1908; died Dec 1939.

89. Anna Maria[4] Ritzman (Catherine[3] Matter, John Michael[2], Johannes Adams[1]) was born Abt. 1840. She married **Christopher Gipple**. He was born Abt. 1840.

Children of Anna Ritzman and Christopher Gipple are:
+ 189	i.	Christian[5] Gipple, born Abt. 1865.
190	ii.	Samuel Gipple.
191	iii.	Catherine Gipple.
192	iv.	Sarah Gipple.
193	v.	Elizabeth Gipple. She married John Bender.
194	vi.	Susan Gipple.
+ 195	vii.	Mary Rebecca Gipple.
196	viii.	Leah Gipple.

90. Christopher[4] Matter (Michael[3], John Michael[2], Johannes Adams[1]) was born Abt. 1830. He married **Catherine Lenker**. She was born Abt. 1830.

Child of Christopher Matter and Catherine Lenker is:
+ 197	i.	Michael[5] Matter, born Abt. 1855.

94. Joseph[4] Matter (Jacob[3], Johannes[2], Johannes Adams[1]) was born 05 May 1814, and died 16 May 1857 in Lykens, Dauphin Co, PA. He married **Anna Mary Yerges**. She was born 22 Sep 1815 in Clarks Valley, Dauphin Co, PA, and died 25 Oct 1893 in Lykens, Dauphin Co, PA.

Children of Joseph Matter and Anna Yerges are:
198	i.	Oliver[5] Matter, died Mar 1862.
199	ii.	Emanuel Matter, born 1830; died 1863 in Lykens, Dauphin Co, PA.
+ 200	iii.	Anna Maria Matter, born 26 Feb 1836; died 20 Dec 1890 in Lykens, Dauphin, Pennsylvania.
201	iv.	John Matter, born 1839; died 1868.

202	v.	Henry Matter, born 1843.
203	vi.	Joseph Matter, born 1844.
204	vii.	Benjamin Matter, born 1845.
205	viii.	Jacob Matter, born 13 Jun 1845.
206	ix.	William Matter, born 03 Apr 1848.
207	x.	Ann Elizabeth Matter, born 28 Aug 1850.
208	xi.	Amos Matter, born 1852.
209	xii.	Benjamin Franklin Matter, born 03 Nov 1852.

97. William Henry[4] Matter (Isaac Jacob[3], Johannes[2], Johannes Adams[1]) was born 20 Mar 1836 in PA, and died 07 Jan 1915 in Freeport, Stephenson Co, IL. He married **Hannah Meyer**. She was born 28 Jan 1841 in Dauphin Co, PA, and died 07 Aug 1912 in Freeport, Stephenson Co, IL.

Children of William Matter and Hannah Meyer are:
210	i.	Adda Louella[5] Matter, born 15 Oct 1864.
211	ii.	Emma Iona Matter, born 23 Nov 1866.
212	iii.	Isaac Newton Matter, born 28 Jul 1870.
213	iv.	Cora Ann Matter, born 11 Mar 1877.
214	v.	Estella Hannah Matter, born 16 Dec 1879.

98. Mary Anna[4] Matter (Isaac Jacob[3], Johannes[2], Johannes Adams[1]) was born 12 Jul 1828 in Dauphin Co, PA, and died 01 May 1898 in Stephenson Co, IL. She married **James Folgate**. He was born 22 Jun 1830 in Centre Co, PA, and died 17 Apr 1905 in Stephenson Co, IL.

Children of Mary Matter and James Folgate are:
215	i.	Jonathon[5] Folgate, born 04 Jun 1851 in Stephenson Co, IL; died 07 Jun 1913. He married Malinda Leid 17 Mar 1878; born 1860 in Stephenson Co, IL.
216	ii.	Isaac James Folgate, born 02 Nov 1855 in Stephenson Co, IL; died 08 Feb 1940. He married Elizabeth Hannah Maye 09 Jan 1881; born 1862 in Stephenson Co, IL.
217	iii.	Uriah Theodore Folgate, born 16 Aug 1857 in Stephenson Co, IL; died 19 Oct 1933 in Stephenson Co, IL. He married Emme Yama Raeger; born 06 Nov 1863 in Stephenson Co, IL.
218	iv.	William Grant Folgate, born 21 May 1864 in Stephenson Co, IL; died 28 Jun 1948. He married Jennie Eleanor Mitchell 11 Dec 1890; born 1872.

99. Joseph[4] Matter (Isaac Jacob[3], Johannes[2], Johannes Adams[1]) was born 11 Sep 1829 in Dauphin Co, PA, and died 20 Apr 1903 in Freeport, Stephenson Co, IL. He married **Caroline Shaw** 15 Mar 1859 in Stephenson Co, IL. She was born 20 Jun 1829 in Centre Co, PA.

Children of Joseph Matter and Caroline Shaw are:
219	i.	Ida Alice[5] Matter, born 11 Dec 1859.
220	ii.	Laura A Matter, born 01 Mar 1861.
221	iii.	William Isaac Matter, born 19 Mar 1864.
222	iv.	Arthur Guy Matter, born 30 Oct 1867.
223	v.	Robert Elmer Matter, born 20 Aug 1869.
224	vi.	Orson Eugene Matter, born 02 Jan 1872.
225	vii.	Elias Elsworth Matter, born 01 Jan 1874.
226	viii.	Mabel Irene Matter, born 04 Dec 1876.

105. David J[4] Matter (Isaac Jacob[3], Johannes[2], Johannes Adams[1]) was born 1842, and died 1919. He married **Christina Elsesser**.

Child of David Matter and Christina Elsesser is:
| + | 227 | i. | Hannah Lorena[5] Matter, born 1869; died 1948. |

Generation No. 5

116. Daniel[5] Matter (Simon[4], Johannes[3], John Michael[2], Johannes Adams[1]) was born 1843 in , Dauphin,

Pa. He married **Lovina Miller** in No Data, Probably, Dauphin County, Pa. She was born in , Dauphin, Pa.

Children of Daniel Matter and Lovina Miller are:

228	i.	Henry[6] Matter, born 1870 in , Dauphin, Pa; died 1934 in Pa.
229	ii.	John Elias Matter, born 02 Oct 1873 in , Dauphin, Pa.
230	iii.	Isaac Walter Matter, born 14 Oct 1875 in , Dauphin, Pa.
231	iv.	William Elmer Matter, born 02 Mar 1879 in , Dauphin, Pa.

121. Simon[5] Travitz (Elizabeth[4] Minnich, Anna Maria[3] Matter, John Michael[2], Johannes Adams[1]) was born 10 May 1843 in Jackson Twp., Dauphin Co., PA, and died 29 Jun 1917 in Jackson Twp., Dauphin Co., PA. He married **Elizabeth Grimm**.

Child of Simon Travitz and Elizabeth Grimm is:

+ 232   i.   Katie L.[6] Travitz, born 06 Dec 1885 in Jackson Twp., Dauphin Co., PA; died 24 Dec 1955 in Detroit, Wayne Co., MI.

123. Josiah[5] Minnich (Michael[4], Anna Maria[3] Matter, John Michael[2], Johannes Adams[1]) was born 02 Sep 1836 in Armstrong Valley, Jackson Twp., Dauphin Co., PA, and died 02 Jan 1908 in Lykens Twp., Dauphin Co., PA. He married **(1) Elizabeth Deibler**. She was born Abt. 1840 in Jackson Twp., Dauphin Co., PA, and died 08 Jun 1874. He married **(2) Rebecca Johns** 25 Apr 1869 in Dauphin Co., PA. She was born Abt. 1848 in Jackson Twp., Dauphin Co., PA, and died 03 Jun 1885. He married **(3) Ellen Amanda Maurer** 18 Nov 1885 in Lykens Twp., Dauphin Co., PA. She was born 07 Oct 1855 in Locustdale, Schuylkill Co., PA, and died 23 Oct 1940 in William Penn, Shaft, Schuylkill Co., PA.

Children of Josiah Minnich and Rebecca Johns are:

+ 233   i.   Amos F.[6] Minnich, born 27 Nov 1869 in Jackson Twp., Dauphin Co., PA.
  234   ii.   Joseph Osceloa Minnich, born 17 Sep 1871 in Jackson Twp., Dauphin Co., PA; died 19 Sep 1898 in Jackson Twp., Dauphin Co., PA.
  235   iii. John W. Minnich, born 07 Apr 1873 in Jackson Twp., Dauphin Co., PA; died 10 Apr 1875 in Jackson Twp., Dauphin Co., PA.
+ 236   iv.   Claude E. Minnich, born 18 Mar 1875 in Jackson Twp., Dauphin Co., PA; died 1962 in Albany, Albany Co., NY.
  237   v.   Lorena Esther Edith Minnich, born 10 Dec 1879 in Jackson Twp., Dauphin Co., PA; died 22 Apr 1881 in Jackson Twp., Dauphin Co., PA.
+ 238   vi.   Edward Austin Minnich, born 12 Feb 1877 in Jackson Twp., Dauphin Co., PA; died 09 Oct 1958 in Harrisburg, Dauphin Co., PA.

Children of Josiah Minnich and Ellen Maurer are:

  239   i.   Sarah Irene[6] Minnich, born 23 Jul 1886 in Lykens Twp., Dauphin Co., PA; died 09 Mar 1974 in Dauphin Co., PA. She married Daniel C. Messner 09 May 1916; born Abt. 1882 in Lykens Twp., Dauphin Co., PA; died Abt. 1965 in Dauphin Co., PA.
+ 240   ii.   Carrie Elizabeth Minnich, born 18 Mar 1889 in Lykens Twp., Dauphin Co., PA; died 14 May 1971 in Kingston, Luzerne Co., PA.
  241   iii. Robert E. Minnich, born 29 May 1891 in Lykens Twp., Dauphin Co., PA; died 22 Oct 1918 in Lykens Twp., Dauphin Co., PA.
+ 242   iv.   Leona M. Minnich, born 27 Jul 1894 in Lykens Twp., Dauphin Co., PA; died 10 Aug 1973 in Shenandoah, Schuylkill Co., PA.

124. Cyrus[5] Minnich (Michael[4], Anna Maria[3] Matter, John Michael[2], Johannes Adams[1]) was born 05 Mar 1839, and died 26 Jun 1900 in PA. He married **Caroline McCulley**. She was born 04 Aug 1849, and died 05 Mar 1913 in PA.

Children of Cyrus Minnich and Caroline McCulley are:

  243   i.   Daughter[6] Minnich, born 24 Jan 1867 in Armstrong Valley, Jackson Twp., Dauphin Co., PA; died 07 Feb 1867 in Armstrong Valley, Jackson Twp., Dauphin Co., PA.
  244   ii.   Clement Elias Minnich, born 25 Dec 1867 in Armstrong Valley, Jackson Twp., Dauphin Co., PA; died 19 Dec 1943.
  245   iii. Catherine Agnes Minnich, born 10 Oct 1869 in Armstrong Valley, Jackson Twp., Dauphin Co., PA;

died 01 Mar 1934.

    246   iv.   Amos N. Minnich, born 11 May 1871 in Armstrong Valley, Jackson Twp., Dauphin Co., PA; died 07 May 1872 in Armstrong Valley, Jackson Twp., Dauphin Co., PA.

+ 247   v.   Aaron Frank Minnich, born 18 Aug 1873 in Armstrong Valley, Jackson Twp., Dauphin Co., PA; died 22 Dec 1937 in Tower City, Schuylkill Co., PA.

    248   vi.   Sara Alice Minnich, born 06 Oct 1875 in Armstrong Valley, Jackson Twp., Dauphin Co., PA; died 23 May 1962.

    249   vii.   Daughter Minnich, born 08 Jan 1878 in Armstrong Valley, Jackson Twp., Dauphin Co., PA; died 11 Jan 1878 in Armstrong Valley, Jackson Twp., Dauphin Co., PA.

    250   viii.   Charles Calvin Minnich, born 18 Jul 1879 in Armstrong Valley, Jackson Twp., Dauphin Co., PA; died 09 Feb 1946.

    251   ix.   Emma Jane Minnich, born 28 Sep 1882 in Armstrong Valley, Jackson Twp., Dauphin Co., PA; died 19 Feb 1952.

    252   x.   Irvin Elmer Minnich, born 31 Oct 1884 in Armstrong Valley, Jackson Twp., Dauphin Co., PA; died 15 Oct 1957.

    253   xi.   John A. Minnich, born 05 Aug 1886 in Armstrong Valley, Jackson Twp., Dauphin Co., PA; died 09 Feb 1894.

    254   xii.   Clara Edna Minnich, born 12 Apr 1889 in Armstrong Valley, Jackson Twp., Dauphin Co., PA; died 25 Jul 1925.

    255   xiii.   Harry Robert Minnich, born 09 Aug 1893 in Armstrong Valley, Jackson Twp., Dauphin Co., PA; died 21 Oct 1937.

125. Uriah⁵ Minnich (Michael⁴, Anna Maria³ Matter, John Michael², Johannes Adams¹) was born 12 Sep 1842 in Lykens Twp., Dauphin Co., PA, and died 06 May 1901 in Lykens Twp., Dauphin Co., PA. He married **Lusanna Ann Schoffstall** 1864 in Lykens Twp., Dauphin Co., PA. She was born Abt. 1846 in Washington Twp., Dauphin Co., PA.

Children of Uriah Minnich and Lusanna Schoffstall are:

+ 256   i.   Charlotta Lucreta⁶ Minnich, born Abt. 1862 in Washington Twp., Dauphin Co., PA.

+ 257   ii.   Martha J. Minnich, born 1864 in Washington Twp., Dauphin Co., PA; died 1927 in Lykens Twp., Dauphin Co., PA.

+ 258   iii.   James Minnich, born 1865 in Washington Twp., Dauphin Co., PA; died 06 Jul 1940 in Lykens Twp., Dauphin Co., PA.

+ 259   iv.   William Minnich, born 1867 in Washington Twp., Dauphin Co., PA.

+ 260   v.   Ira Oscar Minnich, born 03 Sep 1870 in Washington Twp., Dauphin Co., PA; died in Lykens Twp., Dauphin Co., PA.

+ 261   vi.   Mary Terressa Minnich, born 08 Dec 1871 in Dauphin Co., PA; died 1918.

    262   vii.   John Henry Minnich, born 23 Jun 1873 in Wiconisco, Dauphin Co., PA; died 29 Sep 1874 in Wiconisco, Dauphin Co., PA.

    263   viii.   Horace Penroe Minnich, born 23 Mar 1875 in Dauphin Co., PA; died 09 Jan 1895.

+ 264   ix.   Cardella Helen Minnich, born 21 Jun 1883 in Wiconisco, Dauphin Co., PA; died 1929 in Wiconisco, Dauphin Co., PA.

+ 265   x.   Clarence Minnich, born Abt. 1888 in Wiconisco, Dauphin Co., PA; died 1965.

133. Solomon⁵ Hoover (Catherine⁴ Minnich, Anna Maria³ Matter, John Michael², Johannes Adams¹) was born in Dauphin Co., PA. He married **?**.

Children of Solomon Hoover and ? are:

    266   i.   Jacob⁶ Hoover.

    267   ii.   Lloyd Hoover.

135. Alfred⁵ Hoover (Catherine⁴ Minnich, Anna Maria³ Matter, John Michael², Johannes Adams¹) was born 1840 in Dauphin Co., PA, and died 1902. He married **Mary Deibler**.

Children of Alfred Hoover and Mary Deibler are:

    268   i.   Ellen⁶ Hoover. She married John Umholtz.

    269   ii.   Charles Hoover.

+ 270   iii.   William Hoover, born 1864; died 1922.

149. Daniel D⁵ Matter (Levi⁴, Johann Michael³, John Michael², Johannes Adams¹) was born 11 Feb 1852 in , Dauphin, Pa, and died 15 Jan 1934 in , Dauphin, Pa. He married **Emma Jane Susanna Lark** in No Data, Probably, Dauphin County, Pa. She was born 15 Oct 1856 in , Dauphin, Pa, and died 17 Aug 1937 in , Dauphin, Pa.

Children of Daniel Matter and Emma Lark are:
271	i.	Carrie Minerva⁶ Matter, born 02 Sep 1874 in , Dauphin, Pa.
272	ii.	Aaron Franklin Matter, born 13 Dec 1878 in , Dauphin, Pa.

150. Sarah Ellen⁵ Matter (Levi⁴, Johann Michael³, John Michael², Johannes Adams¹) was born 04 Mar 1855 in , Dauphin, Pa. She married **Amos Koppenhoffer** Abt. 1877 in No Data, Probably, Dauphin County, Pa. He was born in , Dauphin, Pa.

Child of Sarah Matter and Amos Koppenhoffer is:
273	i.	Cora Agnes⁶ Koppenhoffer, born 12 Jan 1880 in , Dauphin, Pa.

152. Sarah Etta⁵ Sheesley (Elisabeth⁴ Matter, Heinrich³, John Michael², Johannes Adams¹) was born Aug 1840, and died 24 Jun 1903 in Maple Grove Cemetery, Elizabethville, PA. She married **Michael R Keiper**. He was born 05 Oct 1839 in Washington Twp, Dauphin Co, PA.

Child of Sarah Sheesley and Michael Keiper is:
274	i.	Katie S⁶ Keiper, born 03 Jul 1864 in Washington Twp, Dauphin Co, PA; died 07 Nov 1958 in Elizabethville, Dauphin Co, PA. She married Albert Morris Romberger; born 27 Jan 1863 in Lower Mahanoy Twp, Northumberland Co, PA; died 13 Apr 1948 in Elizabethville, Dauphin Co, PA.

157. Minerva⁵ Gilbert (Elisabeth⁴ Matter, Heinrich³, John Michael², Johannes Adams¹) was born 03 Aug 1851 in Washington Twp, Dauphin Co, PA, and died 05 Apr 1914. She married **George A Harner**. He was born 30 Oct 1848 in PA, and died 18 Jan 1924.

Child of Minerva Gilbert and George Harner is:
275	i.	Carrie E⁶ Harner, born 1873 in PA; died 07 May 1966. She married Harvey D Romberger; born 1871 in PA; died 1948.

160. Lydia A.⁵ Wilbert (Catharina⁴ Matter, Heinrich³, John Michael², Johannes Adams¹) was born 14 Mar 1854 in Dauphin County, PA, and died 20 Oct 1930. She married **John Calvin Lentz**. He was born 11 Feb 1851 in Jackson Township, Dauphin County, PA, and died 05 Jun 1895.

Children of Lydia Wilbert and John Lentz are:
	276	i.	John Philip⁶ Lentz, born 22 Nov 1872; died 30 Sep 1941.
	277	ii.	Annie Louise Lentz, born 20 Jun 1874.
	278	iii.	Katie E. Lentz, born 08 Mar 1879; died 05 Dec 1915.
	279	iv.	James Edwin Lentz, born 08 Mar 1879; died 31 May 1946.
	280	v.	Edwin Lentz, born 1881.
	281	vi.	Raymond Andrew Lentz, born 21 Oct 1881; died 02 Jul 1916.
+	282	vii.	Charles Warren Lentz, born 02 Dec 1884 in Dauphin County, PA; died 12 Aug 1968 in Millersburg, Dauphin County, PA.
	283	viii.	Daniel C. Lentz, born 12 Feb 1887; died 20 Oct 1914.
	284	ix.	Henry H. Lentz, born 31 Mar 1889.
	285	x.	Allen C. Lentz, born 10 Dec 1890.
	286	xi.	Joseph Harry Lentz, born 28 Sep 1892; died 26 Jan 1945.

167. Mary Ann⁵ Eisenhauer (Margareta Rebecca⁴ Matter, Heinrich³, John Michael², Johannes Adams¹) was born 02 Sep 1849 in Elizabethville, Dauphin, Pennsylvania, and died 27 Apr 1893 in Abilene, Dickinson, Kansas. She married **John J Witter**. He was born Jul 1840 in Prussia, and died 1918 in Abilene, Dickinson Co, KS.

Children of Mary Eisenhauer and John Witter are:

+   287   i.   Martha Rebecca[6] Witter, born 27 Sep 1871 in Millersburg, PA; died 20 Aug 1955 in Upland, CA.
     288   ii.   Harry Witter, born 1873 in PA.
     289   iii.   Amanda Witter, born 1877 in PA; died Nov 1883 in KS.
     290   iv.   Bessie Witter, born 19 Sep 1880; died 28 Sep 1883 in Abilene, Dickinson Co, KS.
     291   v.   Sadie Witter, born 01 Jan 1883 in Enterprise, KS; died 14 Jun 1982 in Abilene, Dickinson Co, KS. She married Lewis Steckley 27 May 1958 in Navarre, KS; died 16 Sep 1977.
     292   vi.   Susie A Witter, born 28 Jan 1885 in Enterprise, KS; died 23 Jul 1956 in Modesto, CA. She married Noah B Martin Abt. 1924 in CA.
     293   vii.   Johnnie Witter, born 18 Oct 1887 in Abilene, Dickinson Co, KS; died 06 Feb 1888 in Abilene, Dickinson Co, KS.
     294   viii.   Mamie Stella Witter, born 25 Nov 1888 in KS; died 29 Sep 1969 in KS.
     295   ix.   Ray I Witter, born 19 Jan 1891 in Enterprise, KS; died 26 Jan 1967 in Abilene, Dickinson Co, KS. He married Ruth V Book 18 Feb 1914; born 29 Dec 1894; died 02 Nov 1980 in Mechanicburg, PA.

168. Catherine Ann[5] Eisenhauer (Margareta Rebecca[4] Matter, Heinrich[3], John Michael[2], Johannes Adams[1]) was born 19 Mar 1851 in Elizabethville, Dauphin, Pennsylvania, and died 03 Apr 1924 in Ramona, Marion, Kansas. She married **Samuel B. Haldeman**. He was born 11 Jan 1846 in Bainsbridge, PA, and died 21 Oct 1928 in Abilene, Dickinson Co, KS.

Children of Catherine Eisenhauer and Samuel Haldeman are:

     296   i.   Hattie Jane[6] Haldeman, born 19 Jun 1872; died 1883.
     297   ii.   Mary Rebecca Haldeman, born 1874.
     298   iii.   Lydia Ann Haldeman, born 1875.
     299   iv.   John Thaddeus Haldeman, born 1876; died 1901.
+   300   v.   Lillian Elizabeth Haldeman, born 27 Aug 1878.
     301   vi.   Jesse Ira Haldeman, born 1879 in PA.
     302   vii.   Abraham Lincoln Haldeman, born 02 Feb 1882; died 1883.
+   303   viii.   Katherine Ann Haldeman, born 20 Jul 1883 in Hope, KS; died 28 Nov 1959 in Abilene, Dickinson Co, KS.
     304   ix.   Samuel Walter Haldeman, born 17 Dec 1884 in Hope, KS; died 23 Feb 1949 in Topeka, KS. He married Grace Johnson 15 Aug 1909.
+   305   x.   John Henry Haldeman, born 09 Jun 1886 in Hope, KS; died 12 Dec 1969.
     306   xi.   Milo Edward Haldeman, born Dec 1887.
+   307   xii.   Harry Milton Haldeman, born 22 Apr 1889 in KS; died 04 Jul 1968 in Hillsboro, KS.
     308   xiii.   Ora Blanche Haldeman, born Aug 1892 in KS. She married m Button.
     309   xiv.   Delilah Haldeman, born 1895 in KS. She married m Book.

171. Susanna[5] Eisenhauer (Margareta Rebecca[4] Matter, Heinrich[3], John Michael[2], Johannes Adams[1]) was born 29 Oct 1854 in Elizabethville, Dauphin, Pennsylvania, and died 14 Jun 1932 in York, PA. She married **Aaron Wetzel**. He was born 1849, and died 03 Jul 1947 in York, PA.

Children of Susanna Eisenhauer and Aaron Wetzel are:

     310   i.   Harper[6] Wetzel, born 1872; died 1873.
     311   ii.   Janny R. Wetzel, born 1874; died 1881.
     312   iii.   Franklin Jacob Wetzel, born 1876; died 1940.
     313   iv.   Sarah A. Wetzel, born 1878.
     314   v.   Raymond Wetzel, born 1880; died 1905.
     315   vi.   Minnie M. Wetzel, born 1883.
     316   vii.   Otto Robert Wetzel, born 1885.
     317   viii.   Grace Pearl Wetzel, born 1888.
     318   ix.   Della Mae Wetzel, born 1890; died 1902.
     319   x.   Vernon Wetzel, born 1894; died 1913.

175. Amanda Hannah[5] Eisenhauer (Margareta Rebecca[4] Matter, Heinrich[3], John Michael[2], Johannes Adams[1]) was born 11 Dec 1861 in Elizabethville, Dauphin Co, PA, and died 25 Aug 1951 in Abilene, Dickinson Co, KS. She married **Christian O Musser**. He was born 10 Nov 1863 in Mt. Joy, PA, and died 14 Apr 1950 in Abilene, Dickinson Co, KS.

Children of Amanda Eisenhauer and Christian Musser are:

320   i.   Beulah E[6] Musser, born 11 Jun 1887 in Abilene, Dickinson Co, KS; died 28 Nov 1945 in KS. She married Abram E Brechbill 1931; born 15 Nov 1881 in Abilene, Dickinson Co, KS; died 07 Aug 1964 in Abilene, Dickinson Co, KS.

321   ii.   Florence Musser, born 19 Mar 1895 in KS; died Apr 1969 in KS. She married A Ray Etherington.

176. David Jacob[5] Eisenhauer (Margareta Rebecca[4] Matter, Heinrich[3], John Michael[2], Johannes Adams[1]) was born 23 Sep 1863 in Elizabethville, Dauphin, Pennsylvania, and died 10 Mar 1942 in Abilene, Dickinson, Kansas. He married **Ida Elizabeth Stover** 23 Sep 1885 in Hope, Dickinson, Kansas, daughter of Simon Stover and Elizabeth Link. She was born 01 May 1862 in Mt. Sidney, VA, and died 11 Sep 1946 in Abilene, Dickinson Co, Kansas.

Children of David Eisenhauer and Ida Stover are:

+ 322   i.   Arthur Bradford[6] Eisenhower, born 11 Nov 1886 in Hope, Dickinson, Kansas; died 26 Jan 1958.

323   ii.   Edgar Newton Eisenhower, born 19 Jan 1889 in Hope, Dickinson, Kansas; died 12 Jul 1971 in Tacoma, Pierce, Washington.

+ 324   iii.   Dwight David Eisenhower, born 14 Oct 1890 in Denison, Grayson, Texas; died 28 Mar 1969 in Washington, District Of, Columbia.

+ 325   iv.   Roy Jacob Eisenhower, born 09 Aug 1892 in Abilene, Kansas, Kansas; died 17 Jun 1942.

326   v.   Paul Dawson A. Eisenhower, born 12 May 1894 in Abilene, Dickinson, Kansas; died 16 Mar 1895.

327   vi.   Earl Dewey Eisenhower, born 01 Feb 1898 in Abilene, Dickinson, Kansas; died 18 Dec 1968 in Scottsdale, Maricopa, Arizona. He married Kathryn McIntyre Snyder 29 Apr 1933 in Connellsville, Pennsylvania; born 15 Aug 1909 in Charleroi, Washington, Pennsylvania; died Sep 1986 in Scottsdale, Maricopa, Arizona.

328   vii.   Milton Stover Eisenhower, born 15 Sep 1899 in Abilene, Dickinson, Kansas; died 02 May 1985 in Baltimore, Maryland. He married Helen Elsie Eakin 12 Oct 1927 in Washington, District Of, Columbia; born 14 Aug 1904 in Manhattan, Riley, Kansas; died 10 Jul 1954.

179. Ira A[5] Eisenhower (Margareta Rebecca[4] Matter, Heinrich[3], John Michael[2], Johannes Adams[1]) was born 30 Jul 1867 in Elizabethville, Dauphin, Pa, and died 28 Mar 1943 in Los Angeles, CA. He married **Katherine E Dayhoff** 08 Sep 1885 in Abilene, KS. She was born 02 Sep 1865 in PA, and died 30 Dec 1930 in Shawnee Co, KS.

Children of Ira Eisenhower and Katherine Dayhoff are:

+ 329   i.   Mary Rebecca[6] Eisenhower, born Oct 1886; died 29 May 1937 in Topeka, KS.

330   ii.   Simon L Eisenhower, born 03 Dec 1895 in Abilene, Dickinson Co, KS; died 03 Dec 1895 in Abilene, Dickinson Co, KS.

331   iii.   Clinton Eisenhower, born Aft. 1895; died 1943.

189. Christian[5] Gipple (Anna Maria[4] Ritzman, Catherine[3] Matter, John Michael[2], Johannes Adams[1]) was born Abt. 1865. He married **Julie Ann Knorr**. She was born 1865.

Children of Christian Gipple and Julie Knorr are:

+ 332   i.   Aaron Otto[6] Gipple, born Abt. 1890.

333   ii.   Harry Wilson Gipple.

334   iii.   Martha Mabel Gipple.

335   iv.   Verna Mary Gipple.

195. Mary Rebecca[5] Gipple (Anna Maria[4] Ritzman, Catherine[3] Matter, John Michael[2], Johannes Adams[1]) She married **Aaron D Knorr**. He was born 1857.

Child of Mary Gipple and Aaron Knorr is:

+ 336   i.   Susan Alice[6] Knorr.

197. Michael[5] Matter (Christopher[4], Michael[3], John Michael[2], Johannes Adams[1]) was born Abt. 1855. He married **Sarah Anne Keen**. She was born Abt. 1855.

Child of Michael Matter and Sarah Keen is:

+ 337   i. Clara Ida Adeline[6] Matter, born Abt. 1880; died 09 Jun 1955 in Tower City, Schuylkill Co., PA.

200. Anna Maria[5] Matter (Joseph[4], Jacob[3], Johannes[2], Johannes Adams[1]) was born 26 Feb 1836, and died 20 Dec 1890 in Lykens, Dauphin, Pennsylvania. She married **Ludwig Stuppy** 1856 in Dauphin, Pennsylvania. He was born 15 Sep 1834 in Hutschenhausen, Mekleburg, Germany, and died 08 Sep 1887 in Dauphin, Pennsylvania.

Child of Anna Matter and Ludwig Stuppy is:

+ 338   i. Maria Theresa[6] Stuppy, born 1857 in Lykens, Dauphin, Pennsylvania; died 05 Jan 1890 in Lykens, Dauphin, Pennsylvania.

227. Hannah Lorena[5] Matter (David J[4], Isaac Jacob[3], Johannes[2], Johannes Adams[1]) was born 1869, and died 1948. She married **John Sidney Haines**.

Child of Hannah Matter and John Haines is:

+ 339   i. Percival J[6] Haines, born 1899; died 1990.

Generation No. 6

232. Katie L.[6] Travitz (Simon[5], Elizabeth[4] Minnich, Anna Maria[3] Matter, John Michael[2], Johannes Adams[1]) was born 06 Dec 1885 in Jackson Twp., Dauphin Co., PA, and died 24 Dec 1955 in Detroit, Wayne Co., MI. She married **Charles A. Machamer** 1903 in Pennsylvania. He was born in Dauphin Co., PA.

Child of Katie Travitz and Charles Machamer is:

340   i. Charlotte M.[7] Machamer, born 23 Aug 1904 in Jackson Twp., Dauphin Co., PA. She married Horace E. Ray.

233. Amos F.[6] Minnich (Josiah[5], Michael[4], Anna Maria[3] Matter, John Michael[2], Johannes Adams[1]) was born 27 Nov 1869 in Jackson Twp., Dauphin Co., PA. He married **Iva Cardella Schreffler** 22 Dec 1897 in Curtin, Schuylkill Co., PA. She was born Abt. 1876 in Curtin, Schuylkill Co., PA.

Children of Amos Minnich and Iva Schreffler are:

341   i. Mary[7] Minnich. She married Ralph Kratzer.
342   ii. Ethel E. Minnich, born 04 Oct 1907.
343   iii. Daughter Minnich.
344   iv. Stanley Minnich, born 05 Aug 1904.

236. Claude E.[6] Minnich (Josiah[5], Michael[4], Anna Maria[3] Matter, John Michael[2], Johannes Adams[1]) was born 18 Mar 1875 in Jackson Twp., Dauphin Co., PA, and died 1962 in Albany, Albany Co., NY. He married **Bertha O. Williams**. She was born 1877 in Wiconisco, Dauphin Co., PA, and died 02 Mar 1967 in Albany, Albany Co., NY.

Children of Claude Minnich and Bertha Williams are:

345   i. Robert[7] Minnich, born Abt. 1901.
346   ii. Lola Minnich, born in Williamstown, Dauphin Co., PA. She married ? Kramer.
347   iii. Millie Minnich, born in Dauphin Co., PA. She married ? Miller.
348   iv. Sara Minnich. She married ? MacFarlane.
349   v. Betty Minnich, born in Factoryville, PA. She married ? Christ.

238. Edward Austin[6] Minnich (Josiah[5], Michael[4], Anna Maria[3] Matter, John Michael[2], Johannes Adams[1]) was born 12 Feb 1877 in Jackson Twp., Dauphin Co., PA, and died 09 Oct 1958 in Harrisburg, Dauphin Co., PA. He married **Ardella Catherine Witmer** 1895. She was born 08 Dec 1879 in Gratz, Lykens

Twp., Dauphin Co., PA, and died 31 Dec 1977 in Dauphin Co., PA.

Children of Edward Minnich and Ardella Witmer are:

350	i.	Ellen Irene[7] Minnich, born 13 Jun 1895 in Wiconisco, Dauphin Co., PA; died 27 Jul 1979. She married Willis E. Dietrich; born Abt. 1891 in Dauphin Co., PA.
351	ii.	Mary Rebecca Minnich, born 29 Oct 1897 in Wiconisco, Dauphin Co., PA. She married Clarence Theodore Enders 12 May 1917 in Lykens Twp., Dauphin Co., PA; born 29 May 1896 in Lykens Twp., Dauphin Co., PA.
352	iii.	Ruby Royal Minnich, born 14 Oct 1899 in Wiconisco, Dauphin Co., PA. She married Sherman Rowe; born Abt. 1895 in Lykens Twp., Dauphin Co., PA.
353	iv.	Edward Eugene Minnich, born 03 Sep 1901 in Wiconisco, Dauphin Co., PA. He married Dorothy E. Cordy.
+ 354	v.	Laura E. Minnich, born 07 Jun 1903; died Abt. 1985.
355	vi.	John F. Minnich, born 24 Aug 1906 in Dauphin Co., PA. He married Florence P. Cooper 1925 in Hagerstown, Washington Co., MD.
356	vii.	Harry D. Minnich, born 24 Jan 1909 in Dauphin Co., PA; died 16 Dec 1989 in Dauphin Co., PA. He married Esther M. Bowman.
357	viii.	Marlin L. Minnich, born 17 Jun 1911 in Dauphin Co., PA; died 03 Jul 1990 in Dauphin Co., PA. He married Rayetta Robinson.
358	ix.	Margaret I. Minnich, born 13 Aug 1917 in Dauphin Co., PA. She married Henry W. Ibbserson.

240. Carrie Elizabeth[6] Minnich (Josiah[5], Michael[4], Anna Maria[3] Matter, John Michael[2], Johannes Adams[1]) was born 18 Mar 1889 in Lykens Twp., Dauphin Co., PA, and died 14 May 1971 in Kingston, Luzerne Co., PA. She married **George Raymond C. Lebo** 19 Mar 1910 in Harrisburg, Dauphin Co., PA. He was born 23 Oct 1889 in Lykens Twp., Dauphin Co., PA, and died 07 Dec 1956 in Shenandoah, Schuylkill Co., PA.

Children of Carrie Minnich and George Lebo are:

359	i.	Elsie[7] Lebo, born 18 Sep 1910 in Lykens Twp., Dauphin Co., PA. She married Nelson C. W. Stauffer 14 Oct 1933 in Elmira, Chemung Co., NY.
360	ii.	Dorothy Lebo, born 06 Feb 1912 in Lykens Twp., Dauphin Co., PA. She married William Miller.
361	iii.	Carl C. Lebo, born 19 Nov 1913 in Lykens Twp., Dauphin Co., PA. He married Anna Melusky 19 Jun 1935 in Shenandoah, Schuylkill Co., PA.
362	iv.	Robert H. Lebo, born 06 Oct 1915 in Schuylkill Co., PA. He married Margaret Anderson Jun 1937 in Shenandoah, Schuylkill Co., PA.

242. Leona M.[6] Minnich (Josiah[5], Michael[4], Anna Maria[3] Matter, John Michael[2], Johannes Adams[1]) was born 27 Jul 1894 in Lykens Twp., Dauphin Co., PA, and died 10 Aug 1973 in Shenandoah, Schuylkill Co., PA. She married **(1) Roy Jones** 07 Apr 1917. He was born Abt. 1890 in Lykens Twp., Dauphin Co., PA, and died 1938. She married **(2) Howard Frost** Aft. 1939. He was born Abt. 1890 in Lykens Twp., Dauphin Co., PA, and died 1989 in Schuylkill Co., PA.

Child of Leona Minnich and Roy Jones is:

363	i.	Leroy[7] Jones.

247. Aaron Frank[6] Minnich (Cyrus[5], Michael[4], Anna Maria[3] Matter, John Michael[2], Johannes Adams[1]) was born 18 Aug 1873 in Armstrong Valley, Jackson Twp., Dauphin Co., PA, and died 22 Dec 1937 in Tower City, Schuylkill Co., PA. He married **Clara Ida Adeline Matter** 20 Apr 1898, daughter of Michael Matter and Sarah Keen. She was born Abt. 1880, and died 09 Jun 1955 in Tower City, Schuylkill Co., PA.

Children of Aaron Minnich and Clara Matter are:

364	i.	Myrtle Irene[7] Minnich, born 24 Sep 1898 in Tower City, Schuylkill Co., PA; died 11 Apr 1967 in Tower City, Schuykilii Co., PA. She married Walter E. Brown 22 Jun 1918 in Tower City, Schuylkill Co., PA.
365	ii.	Harold Leroy Minnich, born 27 Jan 1901 in Tower City, Schuylkill Co., PA; died 13 Oct 1944 in Tower City, Schuykilii Co., PA. He married Beatrice Shomper 01 Dec 1920 in Williamstown, Dauphin Co., PA.
366	iii.	Erma Estella Minnich, born 28 Oct 1902 in Tower City, Schuylkill Co., PA; died 20 Mar 1987. She married Edward J. Coles 16 Nov 1921.

367	iv.	Sarah Caroline Minnich, born 10 Nov 1903 in Tower City, Schuylkill Co., PA; died 18 Jun 1960 in Tower City, Schuykilii Co., PA. She married (1) Clarence Yohe Oct 1925. She married (2) Morris L. Neumeister 21 Jun 1930 in Pottsville, Schuylkill Co., PA.
368	v.	William Grant Minnich, born 06 Jun 1905 in Tower City, Schuylkill Co., PA; died 23 Jan 1970 in Tower City, Schuykilii Co., PA. He married Ruth L. Bechtel 12 Mar 1927 in Tower City, Schuylkill Co., PA.
369	vi.	Anna Elizabeth Minnich, born 16 May 1907 in Tower City, Schuylkill Co., PA; died 29 Jan 1988 in Tower City, Schuykilii Co., PA.
370	vii.	Marlin Oswald Minnich, born 08 Jun 1909 in Tower City, Schuylkill Co., PA; died 02 Jul 1981 in Orwin, Schuylkill Co., PA. He married Vesta A. Carl Apr 1935 in Tower City, Schuylkill Co., PA.
+ 371	viii.	Arthur Franklin Minnich, born 09 Sep 1911 in Tower City, Schuylkill Co., PA; died 14 Apr 1991 in Tower City, Schuylkill Co., PA.
372	ix.	Son Minnich, born 16 Mar 1913 in Tower City, Schuylkill Co., PA; died 27 Apr 1913 in Tower City, Schuylkill Co., PA.
+ 373	x.	Mary Frances Minnich, born 26 May 1914 in Tower City, Schuylkill Co., PA; died 05 Jun 1976 in Tower City, Schuykilii Co., PA.
374	xi.	Russell Leo Minnich, born 08 Jun 1916 in Tower City, Schuylkill Co., PA; died 15 Jun 1916 in Tower City, Schuylkill Co., PA.
375	xii.	Lynn Arlington Minnich, born 13 Oct 1918 in Tower City, Schuylkill Co., PA; died 18 Sep 1963 in Williamstown, Dauphin Co., PA. He married Margaret T. Perseponko 06 Feb 1943 in Williamstown, Dauphin Co., PA.
376	xiii.	Donald Mark Minnich, born 08 Dec 1920 in Tower City, Schuylkill Co., PA; died 02 Jan 1923 in Tower City, Schuylkill Co., PA.
377	xiv.	Robert David Minnich, born 03 Jun 1922 in Tower City, Schuylkill Co., PA; died 23 Jun 1922 in Tower City, Schuylkill Co., PA.

256. Charlotta Lucreta[6] Minnich (Uriah[5], Michael[4], Anna Maria[3] Matter, John Michael[2], Johannes Adams[1]) was born Abt. 1862 in Washington Twp., Dauphin Co., PA. She married **Charles N. Coles** Jan 1900 in Lykens Twp., Dauphin Co., PA. He was born Abt. 1858.

Child of Charlotta Minnich and Charles Coles is:

378	i.	Mark Stanley[7] Coles, born 18 Aug 1901 in Dauphin Co., PA; died 1950 in Pennsylvania. He married Ruth A. Deibler.

257. Martha J.[6] Minnich (Uriah[5], Michael[4], Anna Maria[3] Matter, John Michael[2], Johannes Adams[1]) was born 1864 in Washington Twp., Dauphin Co., PA, and died 1927 in Lykens Twp., Dauphin Co., PA. She married **William Morris**. He was born Abt. 1860 in Washington Twp., Dauphin Co., PA.

Children of Martha Minnich and William Morris are:

379	i.	Arthur[7] Morris, born Abt. 1886 in Washington Twp., Dauphin Co., PA. He married Mary Holloway.
380	ii.	William Morris, Jr, born Abt. 1888 in Washington Twp., Dauphin Co., PA. He married Ruth Steely.
381	iii.	Estella M. Morris, born 24 Mar 1898 in Washington Twp., Dauphin Co., PA; died 01 Jul 1981 in Lykens Twp., Dauphin Co., PA. She married William Stroup 15 Aug 1915; born Abt. 1895.
382	iv.	Raymond Morris, born Abt. 1892 in Washington Twp., Dauphin Co., PA. He married Anna Beale.

258. James[6] Minnich (Uriah[5], Michael[4], Anna Maria[3] Matter, John Michael[2], Johannes Adams[1]) was born 1865 in Washington Twp., Dauphin Co., PA, and died 06 Jul 1940 in Lykens Twp., Dauphin Co., PA. He married **Viola Harmon**. She was born Abt. 1869 in Dauphin Co., PA.

Children of James Minnich and Viola Harmon are:

383	i.	Martha Rebecca[7] Minnich, born 1887 in Washington Twp., Dauphin Co., PA; died 08 Nov 1918 in Pennsylvania. She married George Coles.
384	ii.	Lucy Minnich, born 29 Dec 1889 in Washington Twp., Dauphin Co., PA; died 18 Feb 1965 in Philadelphia, Philadelphia Co., PA. She married Robert Collins.

259. William[6] Minnich (Uriah[5], Michael[4], Anna Maria[3] Matter, John Michael[2], Johannes Adams[1]) was born 1867 in Washington Twp., Dauphin Co., PA. He married **(1) Mary Salada**. She was born Abt. 1871 in Washington Twp., Dauphin Co., PA. He married **(2) Sally Tovy**. She was born Abt. 1871 in Dauphin Co., PA.

Child of William Minnich and Mary Salada is:

385   i.   Hallet[7] Minnich, born Abt. 1893 in Washington Twp., Dauphin Co., PA.

260. Ira Oscar[6] Minnich (Uriah[5], Michael[4], Anna Maria[3] Matter, John Michael[2], Johannes Adams[1]) was born 03 Sep 1870 in Washington Twp., Dauphin Co., PA, and died in Lykens Twp., Dauphin Co., PA. He married **Kate Schaffner**. She was born 01 Feb 1876 in Lykens Twp., Dauphin Co., PA, and died 14 Oct 1927 in Lykens Twp., Dauphin Co., PA.

Children of Ira Minnich and Kate Schaffner are:

386   i.   Mervin[7] Minnich, born Abt. 1896 in Lykens Twp., Dauphin Co., PA; died in Lykens Twp., Dauphin Co., PA.

387   ii. Claude Minnich, born Abt. 1898 in Lykens Twp., Dauphin Co., PA; died in Lykens Twp., Dauphin Co., PA.

388   iii. Louis Minnich, born Abt. 1900 in Lykens Twp., Dauphin Co., PA; died in Lykens Twp., Dauphin Co., PA. He married Catherine ?.

389   iv. Florence Minnich, born Abt. 1902 in Lykens Twp., Dauphin Co., PA; died in Lykens Twp., Dauphin Co., PA.

261. Mary Terressa[6] Minnich (Uriah[5], Michael[4], Anna Maria[3] Matter, John Michael[2], Johannes Adams[1]) was born 08 Dec 1871 in Dauphin Co., PA, and died 1918. She married **William Reddinger**. He was born Abt. 1867.

Children of Mary Minnich and William Reddinger are:

390   i.   Charlotte Cardella[7] Reddinger, born Abt. 1893. She married Joseph Kelly.

391   ii. Daniel Reddinger, born Abt. 1895. He married Beulah Hossler.

264. Cardella Helen[6] Minnich (Uriah[5], Michael[4], Anna Maria[3] Matter, John Michael[2], Johannes Adams[1]) was born 21 Jun 1883 in Wiconisco, Dauphin Co., PA, and died 1929 in Wiconisco, Dauphin Co., PA. She married **William Abel Werner**. He was born 02 Jan 1885 in Lykens Twp., Dauphin Co., PA, and died in Wiconisco, Dauphin Co., PA.

Children of Cardella Minnich and William Werner are:

392   i.   Melva[7] Werner, born 18 Aug 1914 in Lykens Twp., Dauphin Co., PA.

393   ii. Mark Eugene Werner, born 02 Sep 1923 in Mechanicsburg, Cumberland Co., PA; died 21 Apr 1982 in Lewisberry, York Co., PA.

394   iii. Harold E. Werner, born 26 Jul 1929 in Mechanicsburg, Cumberland Co., PA.

265. Clarence[6] Minnich (Uriah[5], Michael[4], Anna Maria[3] Matter, John Michael[2], Johannes Adams[1]) was born Abt. 1888 in Wiconisco, Dauphin Co., PA, and died 1965. He married **Myra Soloman**. She was born Abt. 1892 in Dauphin Co., PA.

Children of Clarence Minnich and Myra Soloman are:

395   i.   Jeremiah[7] Minnich.

396   ii. Maurice Minnich, born 10 Mar 1914 in Dauphin Co., PA.

270. William[6] Hoover (Alfred[5], Catherine[4] Minnich, Anna Maria[3] Matter, John Michael[2], Johannes Adams[1]) was born 1864, and died 1922. He married **Anna Romberger**.

Children of William Hoover and Anna Romberger are:

397   i.   Sallie[7] Hoover. She married John Hilbert.

398   ii. Mary Hoover. She married Charles Rebuck.

399   iii. Mark Hoover. He married Ruth Zimmerman.

400   iv. Henry Hoover. He married Florence Yeartz.

282. Charles Warren[6] Lentz (Lydia A.[5] Wilbert, Catharina[4] Matter, Heinrich[3], John Michael[2], Johannes Adams[1]) was born 02 Dec 1884 in Dauphin County, PA, and died 12 Aug 1968 in Millersburg, Dauphin County, PA. He married **Minnie Mae Riegle**. She was born 27 Jun 1889 in Mifflin Township, Dauphin County, PA, and died 17 Sep 1967 in Millersburg, Dauphin County, PA.

Children of Charles Lentz and Minnie Riegle are:

401	i.	LIVING[7]. He married (1) LIVING. He married (2) LIVING.
402	ii.	Clair Riegle Lentz, born 04 Sep 1910; died 17 Sep 1975 in Goldsboro, NC. He married LIVING.
403	iii.	Richard Riegle Lentz, born 16 Sep 1912; died 01 Feb 1951. He married (1) LIVING. He married (2) LIVING.
+ 404	iv.	Eugene Clinton Lentz, born 01 Mar 1915 in Pennsylvania; died 11 Feb 1945 in MIA World War II Philippines.
405	v.	Robert Calvin Lentz, born 19 Nov 1917; died 01 Jul 1997 in Baltimore, MD. He married LIVING.
406	vi.	William Benjamin Lentz, born 14 May 1920; died 18 Sep 1977 in Millersburg, Dauphin County, PA. He married LIVING.
407	vii.	Paul Jacob Lentz, born 20 Sep 1922; died 03 Nov 1994 in Leeds, MA. He married LIVING.

287. Martha Rebecca[6] Witter (Mary Ann[5] Eisenhauer, Margareta Rebecca[4] Matter, Heinrich[3], John Michael[2], Johannes Adams[1]) was born 27 Sep 1871 in Millersburg, PA, and died 20 Aug 1955 in Upland, CA. She married **Joseph Harvey Gish**. He was born 20 Sep 1875 in Liverpool, PA, and died Sep 1967 in Upland, CA.

Child of Martha Witter and Joseph Gish is:

408	i.	Evelyn W[7] Gish, born 16 Jan 1912 in Abilene, Dickinson Co, KS; died 15 Dec 2001 in PA. She married Paul Edward Book; born 03 Mar 1919 in Custer Co, OK; died 21 Dec 1998 in Waynesboro, PA.

300. Lillian Elizabeth[6] Haldeman (Catherine Ann[5] Eisenhauer, Margareta Rebecca[4] Matter, Heinrich[3], John Michael[2], Johannes Adams[1]) was born 27 Aug 1878. She married **Samuel W Brehm**. He was born in Palmyra, PA.

Children of Lillian Haldeman and Samuel Brehm are:

409	i.	Zena Leroy[7] Brehm, born 07 Jan 1903.
410	ii.	Eldred H Brehm, born 28 Nov 1904.
411	iii.	Irma Aurelia Brehm.
412	iv.	Faithe Marie Brehm.

303. Katherine Ann[6] Haldeman (Catherine Ann[5] Eisenhauer, Margareta Rebecca[4] Matter, Heinrich[3], John Michael[2], Johannes Adams[1]) was born 20 Jul 1883 in Hope, KS, and died 28 Nov 1959 in Abilene, Dickinson Co, KS. She married **Abraham Lincoln Epler** 05 Nov 1902 in Hope, KS. He was born Jun 1876 in Hummelstown, PA, and died 16 Jun 1923 in Gladwin, MI.

Children of Katherine Haldeman and Abraham Epler are:

413	i.	Ruel Milton[7] Epler, born 14 Mar 1904; died 03 Feb 1977 in Wichita, KS.
414	ii.	Martha Irene Epler, born 12 May 1906 in Whitehouse, OH; died 08 Oct 1924 in Detroit, KS.
415	iii.	Grant Barton Epler, born 29 May 1907; died 18 Jun 1988 in Lapeer, MI.
416	iv.	Russell Emerson Epler, born 09 Jun 1909 in Canton, KS; died 20 Apr 1985 in Rochester, MI.
417	v.	Blanche Pearl Epler, born 20 May 1918 in Gladwin, MI; died 24 Nov 2003 in KS. She married m Scheideman.
418	vi.	? Epler. She married Voiland Engle; born 10 Sep 1922.
419	vii.	Grace Lilian Epler, died Aft. 1985. She married m Campbell.
420	viii.	Paul Mark Epler, died Aft. 1985.

305. John Henry[6] Haldeman (Catherine Ann[5] Eisenhauer, Margareta Rebecca[4] Matter, Heinrich[3], John Michael[2], Johannes Adams[1]) was born 09 Jun 1886 in Hope, KS, and died 12 Dec 1969. He married **Viola C Rock** 11 Apr 1909 in Hope, KS. She was born 24 Feb 1889 in Illinois, and died 24 Jul 1976 in Abilene, Dickinson Co, KS.

Child of John Haldeman and Viola Rock is:

421   i.   Veri C[7] Haldeman, born 29 Jun 1911; died 01 Sep 1923 in Abilene, Dickinson Co, KS.

307. Harry Milton[6] Haldeman (Catherine Ann[5] Eisenhauer, Margareta Rebecca[4] Matter, Heinrich[3], John Michael[2], Johannes Adams[1]) was born 22 Apr 1889 in KS, and died 04 Jul 1968 in Hillsboro, KS. He married **Ollie B Rock** 29 Nov 1911. She was born 04 Nov 1890, and died 10 Feb 1981 in Topeka, KS.

Child of Harry Haldeman and Ollie Rock is:

422   i.   Eunic O[7] Haldeman, born 1913 in KS; died 1953. She married ? Nincehelser.

322. Arthur Bradford[6] Eisenhower (David Jacob[5] Eisenhauer, Margareta Rebecca[4] Matter, Heinrich[3], John Michael[2], Johannes Adams[1]) was born 11 Nov 1886 in Hope, Dickinson, Kansas, and died 26 Jan 1958. He married **(1) Alida B ?**. She was born 17 Feb 1889. He married **(2) Louis Sondra Grieb** 03 Sep 1926.

Child of Arthur Eisenhower and Alida ? is:

+   423   i.   Katherine[7] Eisenhower, born 02 Jul 1914.

324. Dwight David[6] Eisenhower (David Jacob[5] Eisenhauer, Margareta Rebecca[4] Matter, Heinrich[3], John Michael[2], Johannes Adams[1]) was born 14 Oct 1890 in Denison, Grayson, Texas, and died 28 Mar 1969 in Washington, District Of, Columbia. He married **Mary Geneva Doud** 01 Jul 1916 in Denver, Denver, Colorado, daughter of John Doud and Elivera Carlson. She was born 14 Nov 1896 in Boone, Boone, Iowa, and died 31 Oct 1979 in Washington, D.C..

Children of Dwight Eisenhower and Mary Doud are:

+   424   i.   John Sheldon Doud[7] Eisenhower, born 1923.

425   ii.   Doud Dwight Eisenhower, born 24 Sep 1917 in San Antonio, Bexar, Texas; died 02 Jan 1921 in Camp Meade, Maryland.

325. Roy Jacob[6] Eisenhower (David Jacob[5] Eisenhauer, Margareta Rebecca[4] Matter, Heinrich[3], John Michael[2], Johannes Adams[1]) was born 09 Aug 1892 in Abilene, Kansas, Kansas, and died 17 Jun 1942. He married **Edna Alice Shade** 18 Nov 1917 in Ellsworth, Ellsworth, Kansas. She was born 13 Sep 1891 in Ellis City, Ellis, Kansas, and died 26 Jun 1989 in Denver, Denver, Colorado.

Children of Roy Eisenhower and Edna Shade are:

426   i.   Patricia[7] Eisenhower, born 1918.

427   ii.   Peggy J Eisenhower, born 1923.

428   iii.   Lloyd E Eisenhower, born 1925.

429   iv.   Roy J Eisenhower, born Abt. 1930.

329. Mary Rebecca[6] Eisenhower (Ira A[5], Margareta Rebecca[4] Matter, Heinrich[3], John Michael[2], Johannes Adams[1]) was born Oct 1886, and died 29 May 1937 in Topeka, KS. She married **Jacob M Brandt**. He was born 02 Jul 1881 in Detroit, KS.

Children of Mary Eisenhower and Jacob Brandt are:

430   i.   Preston L[7] Brandt, born 07 Jan 1909; died 11 Apr 1977 in San Antonio, Bexar, Texas.

431   ii.   Orville E Brandt, born 28 Feb 1917.

432   iii.   Victor O Brandt, born 10 Sep 1920; died 16 Nov 1999.

332. Aaron Otto[6] Gipple (Christian[5], Anna Maria[4] Ritzman, Catherine[3] Matter, John Michael[2], Johannes Adams[1]) was born Abt. 1890.

Child of Aaron Otto Gipple is:

+   433   i.   Gerald[7] Gipple, born Abt. 1915.

336. Susan Alice[6] Knorr (Mary Rebecca[5] Gipple, Anna Maria[4] Ritzman, Catherine[3] Matter, John Michael[2], Johannes Adams[1]) She married **Christopher John Olsen Almlee**.

Child of Susan Knorr and Christopher Almlee is:
+   434   i.   Bernice Mildred[7] Almlee.

337. Clara Ida Adeline[6] Matter (Michael[5], Christopher[4], Michael[3], John Michael[2], Johannes Adams[1]) was born Abt. 1880, and died 09 Jun 1955 in Tower City, Schuylkill Co., PA. She married **Aaron Frank Minnich** 20 Apr 1898, son of Cyrus Minnich and Caroline McCulley. He was born 18 Aug 1873 in Armstrong Valley, Jackson Twp., Dauphin Co., PA, and died 22 Dec 1937 in Tower City, Schuylkill Co., PA.

Children are listed above under (247) Aaron Frank Minnich.

338. Maria Theresa[6] Stuppy (Anna Maria[5] Matter, Joseph[4], Jacob[3], Johannes[2], Johannes Adams[1]) was born 1857 in Lykens, Dauphin, Pennsylvania, and died 05 Jan 1890 in Lykens, Dauphin, Pennsylvania. She married **Jacob Sitlinger** 29 Jun 1878 in Zion Luthern Church. He was born Abt. 1855 in Lykens, Dauphin, Pennsylvania, and died 07 Nov 1917.

Children of Maria Stuppy and Jacob Sitlinger are:
      435   i.   Dorothy Delilah[7] Sitlinger, born 11 Sep 1880 in Lykens, Dauphin, Pennsylvania.
      436   ii. Claude Albert Sitlinger, born 25 Mar 1882 in Lykens, Dauphin, Pennsylvania.
+   437   iii. Ray Edwin Sitlinger, born 03 Jul 1884 in Lykens, Dauphin, Pennsylvania; died 14 Jul 1957.

339. Percival J[6] Haines (Hannah Lorena[5] Matter, David J[4], Isaac Jacob[3], Johannes[2], Johannes Adams[1]) was born 1899, and died 1990. He married **Emma Schrock**.

Child of Percival Haines and Emma Schrock is:
      438   i.   Leland M[7] Haines, born 1936.

Generation No. 7

354. Laura E.[7] Minnich (Edward Austin[6], Josiah[5], Michael[4], Anna Maria[3] Matter, John Michael[2], Johannes Adams[1]) was born 07 Jun 1903, and died Abt. 1985. She married **Harry Harper Hepler**. He was born 26 Jan 1904, and died Abt. 1985.

Children of Laura Minnich and Harry Hepler are:
      439   i.   Lorraine[8] Hepler, born 24 Oct 1923 in Dauphin Co., PA. She married ? Harner.
      440   ii. Harry Harper Hepler, born 18 Jun 1927 in Dauphin Co., PA. He married Hilda Davis; born Abt. 1928.
+   441   iii. Glenn Hepler, born 28 Jul 1928 in Dauphin Co., PA.
+   442   iv. Jack Arland Hepler, born 03 Feb 1931 in Dauphin Co., PA.
      443   v.   Kenneth Hepler, born 29 Apr 1933 in Dauphin Co., PA. He married Geraldine Hentz.
      444   vi. Beverly Jane Hepler, born 01 Sep 1936 in Dauphin Co., PA. She married James Snyder.

371. Arthur Franklin[7] Minnich (Aaron Frank[6], Cyrus[5], Michael[4], Anna Maria[3] Matter, John Michael[2], Johannes Adams[1]) was born 09 Sep 1911 in Tower City, Schuylkill Co., PA, and died 14 Apr 1991 in Tower City, Schuylkill Co., PA. He married **Mary Elizabeth Molko** 05 Oct 1935 in Lykens Twp., Dauphin Co., PA. She was born Abt. 1905.

Child of Arthur Minnich and Mary Molko is:
+   445   i.   John Arthur[8] Minnich, born Abt. 1930.

373. Mary Frances[7] Minnich (Aaron Frank[6], Cyrus[5], Michael[4], Anna Maria[3] Matter, John Michael[2], Johannes Adams[1]) was born 26 May 1914 in Tower City, Schuylkill Co., PA, and died 05 Jun 1976 in Tower

City, Schuykilii Co., PA. She married **Edwin Frosten Knorr** 14 Aug 1937 in Tower City, PA. He was born 26 May 1914 in Tower City, PA, and died 01 Dec 1978 in Tower City, PA.

Children of Mary Minnich and Edwin Knorr are:
+ 446   i.   Edwin Frances[8] Knorr, born Abt. 1940.
   447   ii.   Karen Kay Knorr, born Abt. 1940. She married Darrell E Shoop Abt. 1955; born Abt. 1930.

404. Eugene Clinton[7] Lentz (Charles Warren[6], Lydia A.[5] Wilbert, Catharina[4] Matter, Heinrich[3], John Michael[2], Johannes Adams[1]) was born 01 Mar 1915 in Pennsylvania, and died 11 Feb 1945 in MIA World War II Philippines. He married **Marie Lanigan** 23 Dec 1938. She died 1989.

Child of Eugene Lentz and Marie Lanigan is:
+ 448   i.   Living[8].

423. Katherine[7] Eisenhower (Arthur Bradford[6], David Jacob[5] Eisenhauer, Margareta Rebecca[4] Matter, Heinrich[3], John Michael[2], Johannes Adams[1]) was born 02 Jul 1914. She married **Berton Roueche** 28 Oct 1936. He was born 16 Apr 1910.

Child of Katherine Eisenhower and Berton Roueche is:
   449   i.   Arthur Bradford[8] Roueche, born 16 Nov 1942.

424. John Sheldon Doud[7] Eisenhower (Dwight David[6], David Jacob[5] Eisenhauer, Margareta Rebecca[4] Matter, Heinrich[3], John Michael[2], Johannes Adams[1]) was born 1923. He married **Barbara Jean Thompson** Jul 1947. She was born Abt. 1925.

Children of John Eisenhower and Barbara Thompson are:
+ 450   i.   Dwight David[8] Eisenhower, born 31 Mar 1948.
   451   ii.   Barbara Anne Eisenhower, born 30 May 1949.
   452   iii.   Susan Elaine Eisenhower, born 31 Dec 1951.
   453   iv.   Mary Jean Eisenhower, born 21 Dec 1955.

433. Gerald[7] Gipple (Aaron Otto[6], Christian[5], Anna Maria[4] Ritzman, Catherine[3] Matter, John Michael[2], Johannes Adams[1]) was born Abt. 1915.

Child of Gerald Gipple is:
   454   i.   Carol[8] Gipple, born Abt. 1940.

434. Bernice Mildred[7] Almlee (Susan Alice[6] Knorr, Mary Rebecca[5] Gipple, Anna Maria[4] Ritzman, Catherine[3] Matter, John Michael[2], Johannes Adams[1])

Child of Bernice Mildred Almlee is:
+ 455   i.   Nancy Jane[8] Foy.

437. Ray Edwin[7] Sitlinger (Maria Theresa[6] Stuppy, Anna Maria[5] Matter, Joseph[4], Jacob[3], Johannes[2], Johannes Adams[1]) was born 03 Jul 1884 in Lykens, Dauphin, Pennsylvania, and died 14 Jul 1957. He married **Amelia Rachel Sierer** 22 Jul 1903. She was born 01 Aug 1883 in Pennsylvania, and died 26 Jan 1969.

Children of Ray Sitlinger and Amelia Sierer are:
   456   i.   Jacob Charles[8] Sitlinger, born 12 Oct 1903; died 03 Aug 1993.
+ 457   ii.   Edward LeRoy Aaron Sitlinger, born 05 Mar 1905 in Pennsylvania, USA; died 19 Feb 1981 in Pennsylvania, USA.
   458   iii.   Harold Thurston Sitlinger, born 08 Jan 1907; died 17 Nov 1910.
   459   iv.   Lester Ray Sitlinger, born 01 Nov 1908; died 18 Oct 1953.
   460   v.   Kathleen Mildred Sitlinger, born 28 Mar 1911; died 15 Apr 1994.
   461   vi.   Cora Gertrude Sitlinger, born 16 Apr 1914; died 1990.

441. Glenn[8] Hepler (Laura E.[7] Minnich, Edward Austin[6], Josiah[5], Michael[4], Anna Maria[3] Matter, John Michael[2], Johannes Adams[1]) was born 28 Jul 1928 in Dauphin Co., PA. He married **Lois Laudenslager**.

Child of Glenn Hepler and Lois Laudenslager is:

    462   i.   Timothy[9] Hepler. He married Connie Williams; born in Elizabethville, Dauphin Co., PA.

442. Jack Arland[8] Hepler (Laura E.[7] Minnich, Edward Austin[6], Josiah[5], Michael[4], Anna Maria[3] Matter, John Michael[2], Johannes Adams[1]) was born 03 Feb 1931 in Dauphin Co., PA. He married **Irene Sitlinger**.

Children of Jack Hepler and Irene Sitlinger are:

    463   i.   Debbie[9] Hepler, born in Gratz, Lykens Twp., Dauphin Co., PA.
    464   ii.   Stan Hepler, born in Gratz, Lykens Twp., Dauphin Co., PA.
    465   iii.   Robert Hepler, born in Gratz, Lykens Twp., Dauphin Co., PA.
    466   iv.   William Hepler, born in Gratz, Lykens Twp., Dauphin Co., PA.

445. John Arthur[8] Minnich (Arthur Franklin[7], Aaron Frank[6], Cyrus[5], Michael[4], Anna Maria[3] Matter, John Michael[2], Johannes Adams[1]) was born Abt. 1930. He married **Yvonne Bohner**. She was born Abt. 1930.

Child of John Minnich and Yvonne Bohner is:

    467   i.   Debra Louise[9] Minnich, born 18 Jun 1958 in Lykens, PA. She married James Kandybowski 18 Jun 1977; born 29 Jul 1955 in Lykens, PA.

446. Edwin Frances[8] Knorr (Mary Frances[7] Minnich, Aaron Frank[6], Cyrus[5], Michael[4], Anna Maria[3] Matter, John Michael[2], Johannes Adams[1]) was born Abt. 1940. He married **Joan Mardell Schaeffer** Abt. 1955. She was born Abt. 1940.

Children of Edwin Knorr and Joan Schaeffer are:

    468   i.   Vicki[9] Knorr, born Abt. 1965; died Abt. 1965.
    469   ii.   Cindy Lee Knorr, born Abt. 1967.
    470   iii.   Edwin Frances Knorr, born Abt. 1969. He married Anita Heather Steward; born Abt. 1970.

448. Living[8] (Eugene Clinton[7] Lentz, Charles Warren[6], Lydia A.[5] Wilbert, Catharina[4] Matter, Heinrich[3], John Michael[2], Johannes Adams[1])

Children of Living are:

    471   i.   Living[9].
    472   ii.   Living.
+ 473   iii.   Living.
    474   iv.   Living.
    475   v.   Living.

450. Dwight David[8] Eisenhower (John Sheldon Doud[7], Dwight David[6], David Jacob[5] Eisenhauer, Margareta Rebecca[4] Matter, Heinrich[3], John Michael[2], Johannes Adams[1]) was born 31 Mar 1948. He married **Julie Nixon** 28 Dec 1968. She was born 05 Jul 1948.

Children of Dwight Eisenhower and Julie Nixon are:

    476   i.   Jennie[9] Eisenhower.
    477   ii.   Alex Eisenhower.
    478   iii.   Melanie Eisenhower.

455. Nancy Jane[8] Foy (Bernice Mildred[7] Almlee, Susan Alice[6] Knorr, Mary Rebecca[5] Gipple, Anna

Maria[4] Ritzman, Catherine[3] Matter, John Michael[2], Johannes Adams[1])

Child of Nancy Jane Foy is:
  479   i.   Jenelle[9] Benson.

457. Edward LeRoy Aaron[8] Sitlinger (Ray Edwin[7], Maria Theresa[6] Stuppy, Anna Maria[5] Matter, Joseph[4], Jacob[3], Johannes[2], Johannes Adams[1]) was born 05 Mar 1905 in Pennsylvania, USA, and died 19 Feb 1981 in Pennsylvania, USA. He married **(1) m Swigert**.   He married **(2) Mary Michalko** Abt. 1940 in Hagerstown, Maryland. She was born 31 Jan 1913 in Wiconisco, Dauphin, Pennsylvania, and died 05 Jun 1997 in Lewisburg, Union, Pennsylvania.

Children of Edward Sitlinger and Mary Michalko are:
  + 480   i.   Living[9] Sitlinger.
  + 481   ii.   Living Sitlinger.
  + 482   iii.   Living Sitlinger.
  + 483   iv.   Living Sitlinger.

Generation No. 9

473. Living[9] (Living[8], Eugene Clinton[7] Lentz, Charles Warren[6], Lydia A.[5] Wilbert, Catharina[4] Matter, Heinrich[3], John Michael[2], Johannes Adams[1]) She married **Living**.

Children of Living and Living are:
  484   i.   Living[10].
  485   ii.   Living.
  486   iii.   Living.
  487   iv.   Living.

480. Living[9] Sitlinger (Edward LeRoy Aaron[8], Ray Edwin[7], Maria Theresa[6] Stuppy, Anna Maria[5] Matter, Joseph[4], Jacob[3], Johannes[2], Johannes Adams[1]) She married **Living Benning**.

Children of Living Sitlinger and Living Benning are:
  + 488   i.   Living[10] Benning.
  + 489   ii.   Living Benning.
  + 490   iii.   Living Benning.
  + 491   iv.   Living Benning.
  + 492   v.   Living Benning.
  + 493   vi.   Living Benning.

481. Living[9] Sitlinger (Edward LeRoy Aaron[8], Ray Edwin[7], Maria Theresa[6] Stuppy, Anna Maria[5] Matter, Joseph[4], Jacob[3], Johannes[2], Johannes Adams[1]) She married **James Peffer**. He was born 04 Mar 1930 in Maryland, USA, and died 24 May 1977 in Cumberland, Pennsylvania, USA.

Children of Living Sitlinger and James Peffer are:
  494   i.   Living[10] Peffer.
  495   ii.   Living Peffer.
  496   iii.   Living Peffer.

482. Living[9] Sitlinger (Edward LeRoy Aaron[8], Ray Edwin[7], Maria Theresa[6] Stuppy, Anna Maria[5] Matter, Joseph[4], Jacob[3], Johannes[2], Johannes Adams[1]) She married **Living Lau**.

Child of Living Sitlinger and Living Lau is:
  497   i.   Living[10] Lau.

483. Living[9] Sitlinger (Edward LeRoy Aaron[8], Ray Edwin[7], Maria Theresa[6] Stuppy, Anna Maria[5] Matter,

Joseph[4], Jacob[3], Johannes[2], Johannes Adams[1]) He married **(1) Living**.   He married **(2) Living wife**.

Children of Living Sitlinger and Living are:
    498   i.   Living[10] Sitlinger.
    499   ii. Living Sitlinger.

Children of Living Sitlinger and Living wife are:
    500   i.   Living[10] Sitlinger.
    501   ii. Living Sitlinger.

Generation No. 10

   488. Living[10] Benning (Living[9] Sitlinger, Edward LeRoy Aaron[8], Ray Edwin[7], Maria Theresa[6] Stuppy, Anna Maria[5] Matter, Joseph[4], Jacob[3], Johannes[2], Johannes Adams[1]) She married **Living Alley**.

Children of Living Benning and Living Alley are:
    502   i.   Living[11] Alley.
    503   ii. Living Alley.
    504   iii. Living Alley.

   489. Living[10] Benning (Living[9] Sitlinger, Edward LeRoy Aaron[8], Ray Edwin[7], Maria Theresa[6] Stuppy, Anna Maria[5] Matter, Joseph[4], Jacob[3], Johannes[2], Johannes Adams[1]) She married **(1) Living Faust**.   She married **(2) Living Haller**.

Children of Living Benning and Living Faust are:
    505   i.   Living[11] Faust.
    506   ii. Living Faust.

   490. Living[10] Benning (Living[9] Sitlinger, Edward LeRoy Aaron[8], Ray Edwin[7], Maria Theresa[6] Stuppy, Anna Maria[5] Matter, Joseph[4], Jacob[3], Johannes[2], Johannes Adams[1]) He married **Living Taylor**.

Children of Living Benning and Living Taylor are:
    507   i.   Living[11] Benning.
    508   ii. Living Benning.

   491. Living[10] Benning (Living[9] Sitlinger, Edward LeRoy Aaron[8], Ray Edwin[7], Maria Theresa[6] Stuppy, Anna Maria[5] Matter, Joseph[4], Jacob[3], Johannes[2], Johannes Adams[1]) He married **Living**.

Children of Living Benning and Living are:
    509   i.   Living[11] Benning.
    510   ii. Living Benning.

   492. Living[10] Benning (Living[9] Sitlinger, Edward LeRoy Aaron[8], Ray Edwin[7], Maria Theresa[6] Stuppy, Anna Maria[5] Matter, Joseph[4], Jacob[3], Johannes[2], Johannes Adams[1]) He married **Living Keen**.

Children of Living Benning and Living Keen are:
    511   i.   Living[11] Benning.
    512   ii. Living Benning.

   493. Living[10] Benning (Living[9] Sitlinger, Edward LeRoy Aaron[8], Ray Edwin[7], Maria Theresa[6] Stuppy, Anna Maria[5] Matter, Joseph[4], Jacob[3], Johannes[2], Johannes Adams[1]) He married **Living Yerger**.

Child of Living Benning and Living Yerger is:
    513   i.   Living[11] Benning.

Balthaser Romberger was the 3rd great grandfather of the president. There are many other Balthaser Rombergers, however. Pictured at left is "Baltzer" Romberger (1778-1859) buried at St. John's Church Cemetery in Berrysburg. He was a 2nd great granduncle of the president.

Balthaser W Romberger (1825-1905) was the 1st cousin once removed of the president. He was the son of "Baltzer" and is also buried at St. John's.

Balthaser H Romberger (1843-1903) was the son of George J Romberger and was a second cousin twice removed of the president. He is also buried at St. John's.

(photos by the author)

George Romberger (1807-1873) and wife Mary (Hopple) Romberger (1809-1873) are buried at St. John's Church Cemetery near Berrysburg, PA. George was a 1st cousin 3 times removed of the president. He was also the father of Balthaser H Romberger from the previous page. (all photos by the author).

Descendants of Johann Bartholomus Romberger

Generation No. 1

1. Johann Bartholomus¹ Romberger was born 04 May 1716 in Franconia, Bavaria, and died 25 Sep 1800 in Lebanon, Lebanoh Co., PA. He married **(1) Elizabeth Matter** Abt. 1739, daughter of Richard Mather. She was born Abt. 1720 in England, and died Bef. 1753. He married **(2) Anna Sabrina Haas** 31 Mar 1761 in New Holland, Lancaster Co., PA. She was born in Alberthausen, Hessen, and died in Lancaster Co., PA.

Children of Johann Romberger and Elizabeth Matter are:

+	2	i.	Balthaser² Romberger, born 1736 in Franconia, Bavaria; died 1838 in Mifflin Twp, Dauphin Co, PA.
+	3	ii.	Adam Romberger, born 1740 in Franconia, Bavaria; died Nov 1800 in Anneville, Lebanon Co., PA.
+	4	iii.	Maria Eva Romberger, born 1740 in Franconia, Bavaria.

Children of Johann Romberger and Anna Haas are:

	5	i.	Maria Catherine² Romberger, born 19 Feb 1763 in New Holland, Lancaster Co., PA.
	6	ii.	Maria Magdalena Romberger, born 04 Dec 1764 in New Holland, Lancaster Co., PA.
+	7	iii.	Johannes Romberger, born 27 Feb 1767 in New Holland, Lancaster Co., PA.
	8	iv.	George Bartholomus Romberger, born 02 Aug 1768 in Lancaster Co., PA.

Generation No. 2

2. Balthaser² Romberger (Johann Bartholomus¹) was born 1736 in Franconia, Bavaria, and died 1838 in Mifflin Twp, Dauphin Co, PA. He married **(1) Anna Maria Traut** Abt. 1770 in Lebanon Co., PA. She was born 1753, and died Bef. 1797 in Mifflin Twp, Dauphin Co., PA. He married **(2) Susannah Lehman** 15 Jun 1798 in Harrisburg, Dauphin Co., PA. She was born Abt. 1770.

Children of Balthaser Romberger and Anna Traut are:

+	9	i.	Anna Maria³ Romberger, born 12 Jun 1771 in Lancaster Co, PA; died 18 Mar 1866 in Dauphin Co, PA.
+	10	ii.	Heinrich Romberger, born 12 Jul 1773 in New Holland, Lancaster Co, PA; died Bef. 31 Jan 1822.
+	11	iii.	Adam Romberger, born 03 Jun 1775 in Hew Holland, Lancaster Co., PA; died 17 Aug 1868 in Uniontown (Pillow), Dauphin Co., PA.
+	12	iv.	Anna Catharina Romberger, born 19 Mar 1777 in New Holland, Lancaster Co., PA; died 03 Jul 1851 in Wiconisco, Dauphin Co., PA.
+	13	v.	Balthaser Romberger, born 28 Dec 1778 in New Holland, Earl Twp., Lancaster Co., PA; died 16 Jun 1839 in Mifflin Twp, Dauphin Co., PA.
+	14	vi.	Johannes Romberger, born 29 Nov 1783 in Lancaster Co., PA; died 1840 in Porter Twp., Dauphin Co., PA.

Children of Balthaser Romberger and Susannah Lehman are:

+	15	i.	Susannah³ Romberger, born 16 Apr 1799 in Upper Paxton Twp., Dauphin Co., PA; died 23 Feb 1857.
+	16	ii.	Samuel Romberger, born 19 May 1803 in Upper Paxton Twp., Dauphin Co., PA.
+	17	iii.	Jacob Romberger, born 19 Jun 1806 in Upper Paxton Twp., Dauphin Co., PA; died 20 Nov 1864 in Wiconisco, Dauphin Co., PA.
+	18	iv.	Joseph Romberger, born 07 Nov 1811 in Upper Paxton Twp., Dauphin Co., PA; died 20 Jan 1890 in Gratz, Lykens Twp., Dauphin Co., PA.

3. Adam² Romberger (Johann Bartholomus¹) was born 1740 in Franconia, Bavaria, and died Nov 1800 in Anneville, Lebanon Co., PA. He married **Esther Cray** 04 Jul 1765 in Earl Twp., Lancaster Co., PA.

Children of Adam Romberger and Esther Cray are:

	19	i.	Anna Maria³ Romberger, born 15 May 1768 in Lancaster Co., PA.
+	20	ii.	Adam Romberger, born 24 Jun 1770 in Lancaster Co., PA; died 19 Mar 1832 in Franklin Twp., Huntington Co., PA.

+	21	iii.	Margaretta Mary Romberger, born 04 Jun 1772 in Lancaster Co., PA.
+	22	iv.	Johannes Romberger, born 27 Dec 1774 in Lancaster Co., PA.
+	23	v.	George Bartholomew Romberger, born 10 Nov 1776 in Lancaster Co., PA.
+	24	vi.	Eva Romberger, born 11 Feb 1779 in Lancaster Co., PA.
	25	vii.	Elizabeth Romberger, born 06 Oct 1781 in Lancaster Co., PA.
+	26	viii.	Jacob Romberger, born 28 Jan 1784 in Lancaster Co., PA.

4. Maria Eva² Romberger (Johann Bartholomus¹) was born 1740 in Franconia, Bavaria. She married **Peter Cray** 29 Sep 1765 in New Holland, Lancaster Co., PA. He was born Abt. 1740.

Children of Maria Romberger and Peter Cray are:
| | 27 | i. | Catharina³ Cray, born 13 Aug 1766 in Lancaster Co., PA. |
| | 28 | ii. | John P. Cray, born 1771. |

7. Johannes² Romberger (Johann Bartholomus¹) was born 27 Feb 1767 in New Holland, Lancaster Co., PA. He married **Susanna Schneider**. She was born Abt. 1768.

Children of Johannes Romberger and Susanna Schneider are:
| | 29 | i. | Barbara³ Romberger, born 1800. |
| | 30 | ii. | Elisabeth Romberger, born 1806. |

Generation No. 3

9. Anna Maria³ Romberger (Balthaser², Johann Bartholomus¹) was born 12 Jun 1771 in Lancaster Co, PA, and died 18 Mar 1866 in Dauphin Co, PA. She married **John Michael Matter** in Probably, Dauphin County, Pa, son of Johannes Matter and Anna Arnhold. He was born 03 Oct 1763 in Lancaster Co, PA, and died 12 Feb 1852 in Dauphin Co, PA.

Children of Anna Romberger and John Matter are:
+	31	i.	Johannes⁴ Matter, born 04 Jul 1788 in Dauphin, Pa; died 16 Feb 1816 in Dauphin Co., PA.
+	32	ii.	Anna Maria Matter, born 21 Jan 1790; died 29 Jan 1871.
+	33	iii.	Johann Michael Matter, born 29 Mar 1791 in Dauphin, Pa; died 11 Feb 1838 in Dauphin, Pa.
+	34	iv.	Johann George Matter, born 16 Feb 1793 in , Dauphin, Pa.
+	35	v.	Balthasar Matter, born 07 Jul 1795 in , Dauphin, Pa; died 21 Dec 1871 in , Dauphin, Pa.
+	36	vi.	Heinrich Matter, born 26 Dec 1796 in Elizabethville, PA; died 01 Oct 1868 in Lykens, PA.
	37	vii.	Anna Catherina Matter, born 14 Feb 1798 in , Dauphin, Pa.
	38	viii.	Georgianna Matter, born 14 Feb 1798 in Dauphin Co., PA.
	39	ix.	Elisabeth Matter, born 16 May 1799 in Dauphin Co., PA; died 16 Nov 1837 in Gratz, Lykens Twp., Dauphin Co., PA.
	40	x.	Anna Catharina Matter, born 07 Oct 1800 in Mifflin Twp, Dauphin Co., PA; died 13 Aug 1852 in Jefferson Twp., Dauphin Co., PA.
+	41	xi.	Catherine Matter, born 07 Oct 1800 in , Dauphin, Pa.
	42	xii.	Sophia Matter, born 07 Oct 1800 in Mifflin Twp, Dauphin Co., PA.
	43	xiii.	Jonas Matter, born 18 Apr 1802 in , Dauphin, Pa.
	44	xiv.	George Daniel Matter, born 03 Nov 1803 in Dauphin Co., PA; died 01 Oct 1873 in Beaver Twp., Jefferson Co., PA.
+	45	xv.	Michael Matter, born Abt. 1805; died 1838.
+	46	xvi.	Johann Solomon Matter, born 03 Mar 1806 in Mifflin Township, Dauphin, Pa; died 13 May 1877 in , Dauphin, Pa.
	47	xvii.	Infant Matter, born 05 Oct 1807 in Dauphin Co., PA; died Oct 1807 in Dauphin Co., PA.
	48	xviii.	Eva Matter, born 16 Jan 1810 in , Dauphin, Pa; died Abt. 1850.
	49	xix.	Adam Matter, born 01 Apr 1812 in , Dauphin, Pa; died 14 Sep 1889 in Rosecrans, Clinton Co., PA.
	50	xx.	Jacob Matter, born 02 Jul 1813 in , Dauphin, Pa; died 12 Feb 1875 in Dauphin Co., PA.
	51	xxi.	Regina Matter, born 25 Sep 1815 in Dauphin Co., PA; died Bef. 1852. She married Joseph Rowe.
	52	xxii.	Susanna Matter, born 25 Sep 1815 in , Dauphin, Pa; died 12 Aug 1903 in Gratz, Lykens Twp., Dauphin Co., PA.

10. Heinrich³ Romberger (Balthaser², Johann Bartholomus¹) was born 12 Jul 1773 in New Holland,

Lancaster Co, PA, and died Bef. 31 Jan 1822. He married **Elizabeth Hoffman** Bef. 1798. She was born Abt. 1777.

Child of Heinrich Romberger and Elizabeth Hoffman is:

53   i.   Elizabeth[4] Romberger, born 12 Dec 1798 in Upper Paxton Twp, Dauphin Co, PA; died WFT Est. 1833-1896.

11. Adam[3] Romberger (Balthaser[2], Johann Bartholomus[1]) was born 03 Jun 1775 in Hew Holland, Lancaster Co., PA, and died 17 Aug 1868 in Uniontown (Pillow), Dauphin Co., PA. He married **(1) Anna Maria Werner** Abt. 1794. He married **(2) Anna Catharina Paul** Abt. 1808. She was born 14 Apr 1788 in Dauphin Co., PA, and died 09 May 1862 in Dauphin Co., PA.

Children of Adam Romberger and Anna Werner are:

	54	i.	Eva Margaret[4] Romberger, born 10 May 1795 in Lykens Twp., Dauphin Co., PA.
	55	ii.	Anna Maria Romberger, born 15 Aug 1796 in Lykens Twp., Dauphin Co., PA.
	56	iii.	Susanna Romberger, born 02 Sep 1797 in Lykens Twp., Dauphin Co., PA. She married Jonathan Jacobs.
	57	iv.	Catharina Romberger, born 02 Sep 1798 in Dauphin Co., PA. She married Jacob Weaver.
+	58	v.	Elisabeth Romberger, born 02 May 1800.
+	59	vi.	John Romberger, born 24 Oct 1802 in PA; died 29 May 1891.
+	60	vii.	Sarah Salome Romberger, born 15 Jan 1804 in Lykens Twp., Dauphin Co., PA; died 1887.
	61	viii.	Barbara Romberger, born 03 May 1805 in Lykens Twp., Dauphin Co., PA.
	62	ix.	Jonas Romberger, born 1806 in Lykens Twp., Dauphin Co., PA.

Children of Adam Romberger and Anna Paul are:

	63	i.	Christina[4] Romberger, born 06 Jun 1809 in Berrysburg, Dauphin Co., PA; died 02 Feb 1849 in Pennsylvania.
+	64	ii.	Eva Romberger, born 28 Jun 1810 in Upper Paxton Twp., Dauphin Co., PA; died Sep 1876.
	65	iii.	Nancy Romberger, born 11 Sep 1811 in Upper Paxton Twp., Dauphin Co., PA; died 11 Feb 1891 in Northumberland Co., PA.
+	66	iv.	Lydia Ann Romberger, born 11 May 1813 in Upper Paxton Twp., Dauphin Co., PA.
	67	v.	Julianna Romberger, born 24 Aug 1814 in Dauphin Co., PA; died 31 Mar 1876.
+	68	vi.	Daniel Romberger, born 19 Feb 1816 in Lykens Twp., Dauphin Co., PA; died 29 Jul 1882 in Berrysburg, Dauphin Co., PA.
	69	vii.	Polly Romberger, born 1818 in Dauphin Co., PA.
	70	viii.	Isaac Romberger, born 26 Jun 1821 in Dauphin Co., PA; died 26 Sep 1912 in Dauphin Co., PA. He married Lydia Michael; born 14 Dec 1827; died 17 Jun 1870 in Dauphin Co., PA.
+	71	ix.	Hannah Romberger, born 30 Aug 1819 in PA; died 08 Oct 1893.

12. Anna Catharina[3] Romberger (Balthaser[2], Johann Bartholomus[1]) was born 19 Mar 1777 in New Holland, Lancaster Co., PA, and died 03 Jul 1851 in Wiconisco, Dauphin Co., PA. She married **John George Matter**. He was born 16 Jan 1771 in Dauphin Co., PA, and died 11 Oct 1855 in Dauphin Co., PA.

Children of Anna Romberger and John Matter are:

+	72	i.	Sarah[4] Matter.
	73	ii.	Michael Matter, born 12 Apr 1794 in Berrysburg, Mifflin Twp., Dauphin Co., PA; died 14 Jan 1880 in Dauphin Co., PA. He married Sarah Crum Abt. 1816; born 04 Mar 1799 in Frederick, Frederick Co., MD; died 10 Jun 1875 in Dauphin Co., PA.
	74	iii.	Johannes Matter, born 25 Oct 1795 in Mifflin Twp., Dauphin Co., PA; died Unknown in Ashland Co., OH.
	75	iv.	Joseph M. Matter, born 16 May 1797 in Mifflin Twp, Dauphin Co., PA; died 1842 in Dauphin Co., PA. He married (1) Susanna Ritzman; born 27 Feb 1799 in Dauphin Co., PA; died 22 Oct 1821 in Pennsylvania. He married (2) Catherina Schupp; born 12 Mar 1804 in Dauphin Co., PA; died 19 Aug 1879 in Adair Co., MO.
	76	v.	George Matter, born 11 Oct 1798 in Mifflin Twp, Dauphin Co., PA; died Unknown in Henry Co., OH.
	77	vi.	Anna Catharine Matter, born 04 Feb 1801 in Mifflin Twp, Dauphin Co, PA; died Bef. 1838.
	78	vii.	Daniel Matter, born 04 Feb 1801 in Mifflin Twp, Dauphin Co., PA.
	79	viii.	Anna Maria Matter, born 04 Feb 1803 in Mifflin Twp, Dauphin Co., PA; died Bef. 1855.
	80	ix.	Balthaser Matter, born 04 Feb 1805 in Mifflin Twp, Dauphin Co., PA; died 1880 in Ashland Co., OH.

81	x.	Elisabeth Matter, born 21 Aug 1807 in Mifflin Twp, Dauphin Co., PA. She married (1) John Weiss. She married (2) Henry Miller.
82	xi.	Salome Matter, born 15 Jul 1810 in Mifflin Twp, Dauphin Co., PA. She married Samuel Hibner.
83	xii.	Jacob Matter, born 14 Nov 1814 in Mifflin Twp, Dauphin Co., PA; died 24 Jul 1816 in Mifflin Twp, Dauphin Co., PA.
84	xiii.	Hannah Matter, born 26 Nov 1817 in Mifflin Twp, Dauphin Co., PA; died 28 Nov 1880 in Dauphin Co., PA.
85	xiv.	Susanna Matter, born 04 May 1820 in Mifflin Twp, Dauphin Co., PA; died 20 Mar 1882.

13. Balthaser[3] Romberger (Balthaser[2], Johann Bartholomus[1]) was born 28 Dec 1778 in New Holland, Earl Twp., Lancaster Co., PA, and died 16 Jun 1839 in Mifflin Twp, Dauphin Co., PA. He married **Elizabeth Sierer** 25 Dec 1802 in Dauphin Co., PA. She was born 15 Nov 1782 in Lancaster Co., PA, and died 02 Feb 1858 in Dauphin Co., PA.

Children of Balthaser Romberger and Elizabeth Sierer are:

	86	i.	Anna Mary[4] Romberger, born 12 Oct 1803 in Lebanob Co., PA; died 29 Nov 1871 in Mifflin Twp, Dauphin Co., PA. She married Daniel Matter; born 25 Sep 1800 in Dauphin Co., PA; died 03 Jun 1881 in Dauphin Co., PA.
	87	ii.	Anna Catharina Romberger, born 01 Oct 1805 in Upper Paxton Twp., Dauphin Co., PA; died 11 Aug 1856 in Dauphin Co., PA. She married John Philip Matter Bef. 1824; born 27 Apr 1796 in Dauphin Co., PA; died 20 Jan 1873 in Dauphin Co., PA.
+	88	iii.	George John Romberger, born 12 Nov 1807 in Upper Paxton Twp., Dauphin Co., PA; died 05 Jan 1873 in Berrysburg, Dauphin Co., PA.
+	89	iv.	Daniel Romberger, born 13 Mar 1810 in Upper Paxton Twp., Dauphin Co., PA; died 16 Jun 1833 in Mifflin Twp, Dauphin Co., PA.
	90	v.	Elizabeth Romberger, born 24 May 1812 in Lykens Valley, Dauphin Co., PA; died 16 Aug 1854 in Mifflin Twp, Dauphin Co., PA. She married Jacob Hoy; born 26 Mar 1808; died 19 Jun 1889 in Mifflin Twp, Dauphin Co., PA.
+	91	vi.	Susanna Romberger, born 30 Nov 1814 in Dauphin Co., PA; died 09 Dec 1845 in Mifflin Twp, Dauphin Co., PA.
+	92	vii.	Rebecca Romberger, born 17 Sep 1816 in Mifflin Twp, Dauphin Co., PA; died 29 Apr 1904 in Berrysburg, Mifflin Twp., Dauphin Co., PA.
	93	viii.	Hannah Romberger, born 11 Nov 1818 in Washington Twp., Dauphin Co., PA; died 29 Apr 1904 in Berrysburg, Mifflin Twp., Dauphin Co., PA. She married Jacob Woodside; born 13 Jun 1813 in Upper Paxton Twp., Dauphin Co., PA; died 02 Nov 1852 in Upper Paxton Twp., Dauphin Co., PA.
	94	ix.	Bengohan Romberger, born 17 Jan 1821 in Mifflin Twp, Dauphin Co., PA; died 29 Feb 1904 in Dauphin Co., PA. He married (1) Amelia Fisher 1842 in Washington Twp., Dauphin Co., PA; born 20 Aug 1822 in Mifflin Twp, Dauphin Co., PA. He married (2) Hannah Schreffler 02 Apr 1876 in Northumberland, Northumberland Co., PA; born 05 Jan 1837 in Northumberland Co., PA; died 03 Sep 1914 in Dauphin Co., PA.
	95	x.	David Romberger, born 12 Sep 1823 in Mifflin Twp, Dauphin Co., PA; died 11 May 1887 in Dauphin Co., PA. He married Anna Mary Schwab; born 21 Nov 1828; died 06 Oct 1903 in Dauphin Co., PA.
+	96	xi.	Balthaser W. Romberger, born 07 Dec 1825 in Mifflin Twp, Dauphin Co., PA; died 03 Nov 1905.

14. Johannes[3] Romberger (Balthaser[2], Johann Bartholomus[1]) was born 29 Nov 1783 in Lancaster Co., PA, and died 1840 in Porter Twp., Dauphin Co., PA. He married **Eva Hand**.

Children of Johannes Romberger and Eva Hand are:

| 97 | i. | Catherine[4] Romberger, born Abt. 1828; died 1913. |
| 98 | ii. | Daniel D. Romberger, born Abt. 1832. |

15. Susannah[3] Romberger (Balthaser[2], Johann Bartholomus[1]) was born 16 Apr 1799 in Upper Paxton Twp., Dauphin Co., PA, and died 23 Feb 1857. She married **Joseph Workman**. He was born 03 Dec 1795 in Lykens Twp., Dauphin Co., PA, and died 23 May 1857 in Pennsylvania.

Children of Susannah Romberger and Joseph Workman are:

	99	i.	Jacob[4] Workman.
	100	ii.	John Workman.
	101	iii.	Nancy Workman. She married (1) ? Sassman. She married (2) ? Singer.
+	102	iv.	Elizabeth Workman, born 16 Jul 1828 in Lykens Twp., Dauphin Co., PA; died 13 Feb 1907 in

Shamokin, Northumberland Co., PA.

103	v.	Henry Workman, born 23 Sep 1832; died 01 Sep 1897 in Shamokin, Northumberland Co., PA.
+ 104	vi.	Joseph R. Workman, born Abt. 1820.
+ 105	vii.	Catherine Workman, born 17 May 1838 in Pennsylvania; died 10 Feb 1877 in Schuylkill Co., PA.

16. Samuel[3] Romberger (Balthaser[2], Johann Bartholomus[1]) was born 19 May 1803 in Upper Paxton Twp., Dauphin Co., PA. He married **Elizabert Brown** Abt. 1834. She died Bef. 1850.

Children of Samuel Romberger and Elizabert Brown are:

106	i.	John[4] Romberger, born 1835.
107	ii.	Mary Romberger, born 06 Oct 1838 in Berrysburg, Mifflin Twp., Dauphin Co., PA; died 01 Nov 1936 in West Branch, Potter Co., PA. She married Augustus George Walborn 06 Aug 1858 in Lykens Valley, Dauphin Co., PA; born 02 Nov 1835 in Lykens Valley, Dauphin Co., PA; died 08 Feb 1903 in West Branch, Potter Co., PA.
108	iii.	Susanna Romberger, born 1841.
109	iv.	Christian Romberger, born 1845.
110	v.	Simon Romberger, born 1846.

17. Jacob[3] Romberger (Balthaser[2], Johann Bartholomus[1]) was born 19 Jun 1806 in Upper Paxton Twp., Dauphin Co., PA, and died 20 Nov 1864 in Wiconisco, Dauphin Co., PA. He married **Margaret R. Conrad** Abt. 1830. She was born 06 Jan 1810 in Pennsylvania, and died 03 Jun 1878 in Wiconisco, Dauphin Co., PA.

Children of Jacob Romberger and Margaret Conrad are:

111	i.	Sarah Conrad[4] Romberger, born 28 Nov 1828 in Lykens Valley, Dauphin Co., PA; died 21 Feb 1918 in Shamokin, Northumberland Co., PA.
112	ii.	Edward Romberger, born 1831 in Wiconisco, Dauphin Co., PA; died in Lehighton, Carbon Co., PA. He married Catherine E. Weiser.
113	iii.	William Romberger, born 1833 in Lykens Valley, Dauphin Co., PA; died 20 Nov 1862. He married Sarah J. Kocher.
114	iv.	Caroline C. Romberger, born 20 Oct 1833 in Lykens Valley, Dauphin Co., PA; died 01 Nov 1861 in Richfield, Juniata Co., PA. She married Jacob Haines.
115	v.	Josiah Romberger, born 20 Jan 1836 in Lykens Valley, Dauphin Co., PA; died 24 Jul 1884. He married Elizabeth Feaser.
116	vi.	Jacob J. Romberger, born 27 Jan 1840 in Lykens Valley, Dauphin Co., PA. He married Catherine ?.
117	vii.	Henry F. Romberger, born 05 Jun 1842 in Lykens Valley, Dauphin Co., PA.
118	viii.	Amanda Romberger, born 05 Jun 1842 in Lykens Valley, Dauphin Co., PA.
119	ix.	Emanuel Romberger, born 1847 in Wiconisco, Dauphin Co., PA. He married Lavina Lightner 26 Apr 1868 in Berrysburg, Daupnin Co., PA; born Abt. 1848.
120	x.	Mary Romberger, born 07 May 1849 in Lykens Valley, Dauphin Co., PA; died 1943 in Steelton, Dauphin Co., PA.

18. Joseph[3] Romberger (Balthaser[2], Johann Bartholomus[1]) was born 07 Nov 1811 in Upper Paxton Twp., Dauphin Co., PA, and died 20 Jan 1890 in Gratz, Lykens Twp., Dauphin Co., PA. He married **Rosanna Coleman** Abt. 1831. She was born 20 May 1810, and died 19 Dec 1884.

Children of Joseph Romberger and Rosanna Coleman are:

121	i.	John B.[4] Romberger, born 1832. He married Elizabeth ?.
122	ii.	Catherine Romberger, born 1835. She married Josiah ?.
123	iii.	Joseph D. Romberger, born 1893; died 02 Aug 1926.
124	iv.	Daniel Romberger, born 17 Mar 1840; died 17 Sep 1860 in Gratz, Lykens Twp., Dauphin Co., PA.
125	v.	Anna M. Romberger, born 1844. She married ? Waltz.
126	vi.	Sarah Romberger, born 1846. She married ? Bowman.
127	vii.	Hanna Lydia Romberger, born 1849. She married ? Ruhl.
128	viii.	Susanna Romberger, born 1854. She married John Moser.
129	ix.	Jonathon Romberger, born 1860.

20. Adam[3] Romberger (Adam[2], Johann Bartholomus[1]) was born 24 Jun 1770 in Lancaster Co., PA, and died 19 Mar 1832 in Franklin Twp., Huntington Co., PA. He married **Mary Ann Kaforth**. She was born Abt.

1771, and died 09 Mar 1859.

Children of Adam Romberger and Mary Kaforth are:
130	i.	Reuben[4] Romberger.
131	ii.	Levi A. Romberger, born 1796.
132	iii.	Elizabeth Romberger, born 1798.
133	iv.	Daniel Romberger, born 1800.
134	v.	Mary Romberger, born 1802.
135	vi.	Jacob Romberger, born 1808.
136	vii.	Fanny Romberger, born 1810.
137	viii.	William F. Romberger, born 1816.

21. Margaretta Mary[3] Romberger (Adam[2], Johann Bartholomus[1]) was born 04 Jun 1772 in Lancaster Co., PA. She married **John Rau**. He was born Abt. 1770.

Children of Margaretta Romberger and John Rau are:
138	i.	John[4] Rau,Jr.
139	ii.	Eve Rau.

22. Johannes[3] Romberger (Adam[2], Johann Bartholomus[1]) was born 27 Dec 1774 in Lancaster Co., PA. He married **Elizabeth Ellenberger**. She was born Abt. 1775.

Children of Johannes Romberger and Elizabeth Ellenberger are:
+	140	i.	Jacob[4] Romberger, born 1800.
+	141	ii.	Catherine Romberger, born 1801.
	142	iii.	Nancy Romberger, born 1805.
	143	iv.	Elizabeth Romberger, born 1808.
+	144	v.	John Romberger, born 1811.
+	145	vi.	Sarah Romberger, born 1811.
	146	vii.	Fanny Romberger, born 1815.
	147	viii.	Margaretha Romberger, born 1817.
+	148	ix.	Samuel Romberger, born 1818.
	149	x.	Mary Romberger, born 1819.

23. George Bartholomew[3] Romberger (Adam[2], Johann Bartholomus[1]) was born 10 Nov 1776 in Lancaster Co., PA. He married **Catherine Rider**. She was born Abt. 1777.

Children of George Romberger and Catherine Rider are:
	150	i.	Mary[4] Romberger.
	151	ii.	Margaret Romberger.
+	152	iii.	John Romberger, born 1805.
	153	iv.	Elisabeth Romberger, born 1808.
+	154	v.	George Romberger, born 1813.

24. Eva[3] Romberger (Adam[2], Johann Bartholomus[1]) was born 11 Feb 1779 in Lancaster Co., PA. She married **Joseph Krieder**. He was born Abt. 1778.

Children of Eva Romberger and Joseph Krieder are:
155	i.	Henry[4] Krieder, born 1803.
156	ii.	Elizabeth Krieder, born 1806.
157	iii.	John Krieder, born 1809.
158	iv.	Joseph Krieder, born 1813.
159	v.	Mary Krieder, born 1814.
160	vi.	Lydia Krieder, born 1816.
161	vii.	Esther Krieder, born 1818.

26. Jacob[3] Romberger (Adam[2], Johann Bartholomus[1]) was born 28 Jan 1784 in Lancaster Co., PA. He married **Elizabeth Funk**. She was born Abt. 1785.

Children of Jacob Romberger and Elizabeth Funk are:

+	162	i. George B.[4] Romberger, born 26 Apr 1807.
	163	ii. John Romberger, born 1808.
	164	iii. Adam Romberger, born 1810.
+	165	iv. Mary Romberger, born 1812.
+	166	v. Margaret Romberger, born 1814.
+	167	vi. Eva Romberger, born 1816.
	168	vii. Ararh Romberger, born 1818.
+	169	viii. Martin Romberger, born 1820.
+	170	ix. Betsy Romberger, born 1822.
+	171	x. Esther Romberger, born 1824.
	172	xi. Michael Romberger, born 1826.
	173	xii. Gilbert Romberger, born 1827.
	174	xiii. Barbara Romberger, born 1830.
	175	xiv. Cyrus Romberger, born 1834.

Generation No. 4

31. Johannes[4] Matter (Anna Maria[3] Romberger, Balthaser[2], Johann Bartholomus[1]) was born 04 Jul 1788 in Dauphin, Pa, and died 16 Feb 1816 in Dauphin Co., PA. He married **Anna Maria Paul**. She was born 01 Jul 1789 in Dauphin Co., PA, and died 18 Mar 1866 in Dauphin Co., PA.

Children of Johannes Matter and Anna Paul are:

	176	i. Anna Maria[5] Matter, born 23 Oct 1810 in , Dauphin, Pa.
	177	ii. Elisabeth Matter, born 22 Jul 1812 in Dauphin Co., PA.
+	178	iii. Simon Matter, born 07 Oct 1813 in , Dauphin, Pa; died 03 Jun 1895 in Dauphin Co., PA.
	179	iv. Benjamin Matter, born 15 May 1815 in , Dauphin, Pa.

32. Anna Maria[4] Matter (Anna Maria[3] Romberger, Balthaser[2], Johann Bartholomus[1]) was born 21 Jan 1790, and died 29 Jan 1871. She married **Peter Minnich** 21 Feb 1808 in Mifflin Twp., Dauphin Co., PA. He was born 11 Sep 1785 in Upper Paxton Twp., Dauphin Co., PA, and died 25 Sep 1855 in Washington Twp., Dauphin Co., PA.

Children of Anna Matter and Peter Minnich are:

	180	i. Peter[5] Minnich, born 19 Feb 1808 in Dauphin Co., PA.
	181	ii. Johannes Minnich, born 24 May 1809 in Mifflin Twp., Dauphin Co., PA; died 22 Jun 1894.
	182	iii. Daniel Minnich, born 24 Sep 1811 in Mifflin Twp., Dauphin Co., PA.
+	183	iv. Elizabeth Minnich, born 29 Dec 1813 in Mifflin Twp., Dauphin Co., PA; died 1882 in Dauphin Co., PA.
+	184	v. Michael Minnich, born Abt. 1814; died 10 Mar 1891 in Dauphin Co., PA.
+	185	vi. Catherine Minnich, born 24 Nov 1815 in Mifflin Twp., Dauphin Co., PA; died 28 Oct 1893.
+	186	vii. Sarah Minnich, born 17 Dec 1817 in Mifflin Twp., Dauphin Co., PA; died 10 May 1890 in Dauphin Co., PA.
	187	viii. Child Minnich, born 1819 in Mifflin Twp., Dauphin Co., PA.

33. Johann Michael[4] Matter (Anna Maria[3] Romberger, Balthaser[2], Johann Bartholomus[1]) was born 29 Mar 1791 in Dauphin, Pa, and died 11 Feb 1838 in Dauphin, Pa. He married **(1) Anna Catherina Cooper** 25 Sep 1814 in Dauphin, Pa. She was born 17 Oct 1792 in Dauphin, Pa, and died 07 Nov 1824 in Dauphin, Pa. He married **(2) Margaret Rebecca Kiehner** 29 Mar 1825 in Mifflin Twp., Dauphin Co., PA. She was born 17 Mar 1805 in Dauphin Co., PA, and died 07 May 1854 in Dauphin Co., PA.

Children of Johann Matter and Anna Cooper are:

	188	i. David[5] Matter, born 13 Jun 1815 in , Dauphin, Pa; died 10 Jun 1871 in Dauphin Co., PA. He married Catharina Bomberger; born 11 Nov 1816; died 17 Jul 1889 in Dauphin Co., PA.
+	189	ii. Christopher Matter, born 29 May 1816 in Dauphin Co., PA; died 12 Oct 1843 in Lancaster Co., PA.
	190	iii. Margaret Matter, born 16 Aug 1817 in , Dauphin, Pa.
+	191	iv. Levi Matter, born 24 Nov 1820 in Dauphin, Pa; died 06 Dec 1895 in Washington Twp., Dauphin Co.,

PA.

| 192 | v. | Christianna Matter, born 30 Jul 1823 in Dauphin Co., PA; died 20 Dec 1892 in Dauphin Co., PA. |
| 193 | vi. | Anna Matter, born Abt. 1824 in Dauphin Co., PA. |

Children of Johann Matter and Margaret Kiehner are:

194	i.	Katharina Anna[5] Matter, born 09 Dec 1825 in Dauphin Co., PA.
195	ii.	Charles Matter, born 02 Dec 1826 in Dauphin Co., PA.
196	iii.	James Matter, born 14 Dec 1827 in Dauphin Co., PA.
197	iv.	Martin Matter, born 25 Jan 1829 in Dauphin Co., PA.
198	v.	Sarah Matter, born 03 Feb 1830 in Dauphin Co., PA.
199	vi.	Cunrath Matter, born 19 Mar 1831 in Dauphin Co., PA; died 18 Feb 1896 in Brodhead, Green Co., WI.
200	vii.	Elisabeth Matter, born 05 May 1832 in Dauphin Co., PA.
201	viii.	Reuben Matter, born 01 Aug 1833 in Dauphin Co., PA.
202	ix.	Lavina Magdalena Matter, born 22 Nov 1834 in Dauphin Co., PA.
203	x.	Mary Matter, born 01 May 1838 in Dauphin Co., PA.
204	xi.	Lewis Matter, born 06 Feb 1837; died 1902. He married Rebecca Hoffman; born 04 Nov 1838; died 30 Mar 1926.

34. Johann George[4] Matter (Anna Maria[3] Romberger, Balthaser[2], Johann Bartholomus[1]) was born 16 Feb 1793 in , Dauphin, Pa. He married **Susanna Catharine Reigle**. She was born 17 Mar 1771.

Children of Johann Matter and Susanna Reigle are:

205	i.	Leah[5] Matter, born 22 May 1817 in Mifflin Twp, Dauphin Co., PA.
206	ii.	Joseph Matter, born 23 Aug 1818 in Mifflin Twp, Dauphin Co., PA.
207	iii.	Delila Matter, born 09 Feb 1825 in Mifflin Twp, Dauphin Co., PA.
208	iv.	Jonathon Matter, born 07 Aug 1826 in Mifflin Twp, Dauphin Co., PA.
209	v.	Elisabeth Matter, born 23 Feb 1832 in Mifflin Twp, Dauphin Co., PA.
210	vi.	Sara Matter, born 08 Jan 1833 in Mifflin Twp, Dauphin Co., PA.

35. Balthasar[4] Matter (Anna Maria[3] Romberger, Balthaser[2], Johann Bartholomus[1]) was born 07 Jul 1795 in , Dauphin, Pa, and died 21 Dec 1871 in , Dauphin, Pa. He married **Catherine Ritzman** in No Data, Probably, Dauphin County, Pa. She was born 12 Feb 1797 in Dauphin Co., PA, and died 17 Oct 1864 in Gratz, Lykens Twp., Dauphin Co., PA.

Children of Balthasar Matter and Catherine Ritzman are:

211	i.	Emanuel[5] Matter.
212	ii.	Michael Matter, born 26 Apr 1818 in Mifflin Township, Dauphin, Pa. He married Anna Maria ?.
213	iii.	Susanna Matter, born 12 Jun 1819 in Mifflin Township, Dauphin, Pa.
214	iv.	Elizabeth Matter, born 15 Apr 1821 in Lykens Valley, Dauphin Co., PA; died 26 Sep 1852 in Lykens Valley, Dauphin Co., PA.
215	v.	Benneville Matter, born 25 Nov 1823 in Gratz, Lykens Twp., Dauphin Co., PA; died 28 Feb 1899 in , Dauphin, Pa. He married Veronica Snyder 1845 in No Data, Probably, Dauphin County, Pa; born 05 Dec 1822 in Halifax, Dauphin, Pa.
216	vi.	Leonard Motter, born 08 Mar 1826 in Dauphin Co., PA; died 17 Jul 1896 in Ogle Co., IL.
217	vii.	Abraham Matter, born 03 Jun 1828 in Lykens Twp., Dauphin Co., PA; died 23 May 1895 in Adeline, Maryland Twp., Ogle Co., IL.
218	viii.	Sarah Ann Matter, born 17 Jan 1833 in Dauphin Co., PA; died 12 Sep 1851 in Gratz, Lykens Twp., Dauphin Co., PA.
219	ix.	Edward Matter, born 1836 in Dauphin Co., PA; died 1881 in Dauphin Co., PA.

36. Heinrich[4] Matter (Anna Maria[3] Romberger, Balthaser[2], Johann Bartholomus[1]) was born 26 Dec 1796 in Elizabethville, PA, and died 01 Oct 1868 in Lykens, PA. He married **Anna Marie Deitrich** in PA, daughter of Jacob Deitrich. She was born 15 Mar 1803 in Lykens, Dauphin, PA, and died 11 Nov 1865 in Lykens, Dauphin, PA.

Children of Heinrich Matter and Anna Deitrich are:

| + | 220 | i. | Elisabeth[5] Matter, born 06 Feb 1820 in Dauphin Co., PA; died 09 Feb 1891 in Dauphin Co., PA. |
| | 221 | ii. | Thomas Matter, born 20 Apr 1821 in Dauphin Co., PA. He married (1) Margaretha ?; born 22 Jul 1831 |

in Dauphin Co., PA; died 09 Jul 1863 in Pennsylvania. He married (2) Lovina ?; born 28 Aug 1840 in Pennsylvania; died 25 Feb 1892 in Dauphin Co., PA.

+ 222 iii. Catharina Matter, born 29 Jan 1823 in Dauphin Co., PA; died 13 Mar 1915 in Dauphin Co., PA.

+ 223 iv. Margareta Rebecca Matter, born 18 Mar 1825 in Mifflin Twp, Dauphin, PA; died 22 Jun 1890 in Abilene, Dickinson Co , Kansas.

 224 v. Nicholas Matter, born 07 Dec 1826 in Dauphin Co., PA; died 23 Jun 1865. He married Mathilda Lebo; born 31 May 1827 in Dauphin Co., PA; died 27 Aug 1917.

 225 vi. Sarah Matter, born 1830. She married George R. Williard.

+ 226 vii. George Washington Matter, born 16 Jan 1832 in Elizabethville, Dauphin Co., PA; died 26 Sep 1878 in Dauphin Co., PA.

 227 viii. Moses Matter, born 1834 in Elizabethville, Dauphin Co., PA; died 1836 in Elizabethville, Dauphin Co., PA.

 228 ix. Mary Ann Matter, born 25 May 1841 in Elizabethville, Dauphin Co., PA; died 09 Feb 1904.

41. Catherine⁴ Matter (Anna Maria³ Romberger, Balthaser², Johann Bartholomus¹) was born 07 Oct 1800 in , Dauphin, Pa. She married **Johannes Ritzman**. He was born Abt. 1815.

Child of Catherine Matter and Johannes Ritzman is:

+ 229 i. Anna Maria⁵ Ritzman, born Abt. 1840.

45. Michael⁴ Matter (Anna Maria³ Romberger, Balthaser², Johann Bartholomus¹) was born Abt. 1805, and died 1838. He married **Catherine Kupper**. She was born Abt. 1805.

Child of Michael Matter and Catherine Kupper is:

+ 230 i. Christopher⁵ Matter, born Abt. 1830.

46. Johann Solomon⁴ Matter (Anna Maria³ Romberger, Balthaser², Johann Bartholomus¹) was born 03 Mar 1806 in Mifflin Township, Dauphin, Pa, and died 13 May 1877 in , Dauphin, Pa. He married **Isabella Row** in No Data, Probably, Dauphin County, Pa. She was born 30 Apr 1810 in , Dauphin, Pa, and died 27 Jan 1857 in , Dauphin, Pa.

Children of Johann Matter and Isabella Row are:

 231 i. Daniel⁵ Matter, born 31 Jan 1831 in , Dauphin, Pa.

 232 ii. Susanna Matter, born 24 Jun 1851 in , Dauphin, Pa.

 233 iii. Solomon Matter, born 02 Aug 1854 in , Dauphin, Pa.

58. Elisabeth⁴ Romberger (Adam³, Balthaser², Johann Bartholomus¹) was born 02 May 1800. She married **Solomon Buffington**. He was born 29 Jan 1795 in St. Peter's Hoffman's Union Ch., Lykens Twn. Dauphin Co..

Children of Elisabeth Romberger and Solomon Buffington are:

 234 i. Solomon⁵ Buffington, born 30 Oct 1819; died 01 Jan 1878. He married Rebecca Margaret; born Abt. 1820; died in Y.

 235 ii. Susanna Buffington, born 23 Apr 1821.

 236 iii. Benjamin Buffington, born 21 Jan 1823. He married Catharine Hoke.

+ 237 iv. Elisabeth Buffington, born 21 Aug 1824; died Feb 1897 in PA.

+ 238 v. Josiah Buffington, born 16 Jan 1826 in Upper Paxton Twp; died 11 Jun 1900.

 239 vi. Jacob Buffington, born 05 Sep 1828.

 240 vii. Cornelius Buffington, born 07 Sep 1830.

59. John⁴ Romberger (Adam³, Balthaser², Johann Bartholomus¹) was born 24 Oct 1802 in PA, and died 29 May 1891. He married **Hannah Hoffman** 02 Jan 1827 in Lykens Twp., Dauphin Co., PA. She was born 10 Aug 1807, and died 14 Aug 1858.

Children of John Romberger and Hannah Hoffman are:

 241 i. Wilhelm⁵ Romberger, born 30 Dec 1827 in Dauphin Co., PA.

 242 ii. Elisabeth Romberger, born 15 May 1829.

243	iii.	Sara Romberger, born 15 Sep 1830.
244	iv.	Henry Romberger, born 1832.
245	v.	Amos Romberger, born 1834.
246	vi.	Mary Ann Romberger, born 1836.
247	vii.	Jacob Romberger, born 1839.

60. Sarah Salome[4] Romberger (Adam[3], Balthaser[2], Johann Bartholomus[1]) was born 15 Jan 1804 in Lykens Twp., Dauphin Co., PA, and died 1887. She married **Heinrich Rickert**. He was born 30 Mar 1802 in Lykens Twp., Dauphin Co., PA, and died 08 Dec 1864 in Dauphin Co., PA.

Children of Sarah Romberger and Heinrich Rickert are:

+	248	i.	Elizabeth[5] Rickert, born Dec 1822 in Lykens Twp., Dauphin Co., PA; died Aft. 1900 in Wiconisco Twp., Dauphin Co. PA.
	249	ii.	Hannah Rickert, born 11 Jun 1824 in Dauphin Co., PA; died 24 Jul 1849 in Dauphin Co., PA. She married Benjamin Reigel.
	250	iii.	William Henry Rickert, born 1825 in Dauphin Co., PA; died Bef. 1860 in Dauphin Co., PA. He married Annie Haines; born Abt. 1825 in Pennsylvania.
	251	iv.	Mary Rickert, born 15 Mar 1827 in Dauphin Co., PA; died 30 Sep 1847 in Dauphin Co., PA. She married John Marckley; born Abt. 1825 in Dauphin Co., PA.
+	252	v.	John Rickert, born 04 Jan 1829 in Powell's Valley, Dauphin Co., PA; died 31 Jul 1910 in Hampton Roads, VA.
	253	vi.	Rebecca Rickert, born 1838 in Dauphin Co., PA; died in Lykens Twp., Dauphin Co., PA. She married Jonathan Batdorf; born Abt. 1835 in Dauphin Co., PA.
	254	vii.	Lucetta Rickert, born 30 Jan 1840 in Dauphin Co., PA; died 22 Apr 1867 in Dauphin Co., PA. She married Jonas H. Batdorf 03 May 1857 in Dauphin Co., PA; born 24 Jul 1846 in Dauphin Co., PA; died 18 Jun 1890.
	255	viii.	Jonas H. Rickert, born 24 Jul 1846 in Lykens Twp., Dauphin Co., PA; died 18 Jun 1890 in Dauphin Co., PA.
+	256	ix.	Sarah Rickert, born Abt. 1836 in Dauphin Co., PA; died Abt. 1864.

64. Eva[4] Romberger (Adam[3], Balthaser[2], Johann Bartholomus[1]) was born 28 Jun 1810 in Upper Paxton Twp., Dauphin Co., PA, and died Sep 1876. She married **(1) Daniel Romberger** Bef. 1827, son of Balthaser Romberger and Elizabeth Sierer. He was born 13 Mar 1810 in Upper Paxton Twp., Dauphin Co., PA, and died 16 Jun 1833 in Mifflin Twp, Dauphin Co., PA. She married **(2) Jacob D. Hoffman** Abt. 1836. He was born 1812.

Children of Eva Romberger and Daniel Romberger are:

257	i.	Luther[5] Romberger.
258	ii.	Susan Romberger.
259	iii.	Gilbert Romberger, born 19 Jan 1829 in Dauphin Co., PA; died 10 Mar 1894 in Berrysburg, Mifflin Twp., Dauphin Co., PA.

Children of Eva Romberger and Jacob Hoffman are:

260	i.	Isaac[5] Hoffman.
261	ii.	Adam Hoffman.
262	iii.	George Hoffman, died 1888.
263	iv.	Ada Hoffman. She married M. Wilson McAlarney.
264	v.	Elmira Hoffman. She married Joseph C. McAlarney.
265	vi.	Rebecca Hoffman.
266	vii.	Sarah Hoffman.
267	viii.	Child Hoffman.

66. Lydia Ann[4] Romberger (Adam[3], Balthaser[2], Johann Bartholomus[1]) was born 11 May 1813 in Upper Paxton Twp., Dauphin Co., PA. She married **John Paffenberger**.

Children of Lydia Romberger and John Paffenberger are:

	268	i.	Amanda[5] Paffenberger, born 11 Apr 1844 in Dauphin Co., PA; died 25 May 1862 in Dauphin Co., PA.
+	269	ii.	Adam R. Paffenberger, born 1852 in Klingerstown, Schuylkill Co., PA; died Unknown.

68. Daniel⁴ Romberger (Adam³, Balthaser², Johann Bartholomus¹) was born 19 Feb 1816 in Lykens Twp., Dauphin Co., PA, and died 29 Jul 1882 in Berrysburg, Dauphin Co., PA. He married **Hannah Bergstresser**. She was born 26 Sep 1818, and died 13 Feb 1889 in Elizabethville, Dauphin Co, PA.

Children of Daniel Romberger and Hannah Bergstresser are:

270	i.	Adam⁵ Romberger, born 21 Aug 1839 in Gratz, PA; died 29 Jan 1904. He married Mary A Bohner.
271	ii.	Edward Romberger, born 30 Jul 1841.
272	iii.	Cyrus Romberger, born 14 Jul 1843.
273	iv.	Samuel B Romberger, born 09 Aug 1845.
+ 274	v.	Josiah Romberger, born 09 Oct 1847.
275	vi.	John Ambrose Romberger, born 21 Apr 1850.
276	vii.	Howard Henry Romberger, born 12 Jul 1852.
277	viii.	Alfred D Romberger, born 09 Oct 1854.

71. Hannah⁴ Romberger (Adam³, Balthaser², Johann Bartholomus¹) was born 30 Aug 1819 in PA, and died 08 Oct 1893. She married **Harry Wiest**. He was born 22 Nov 1817, and died 26 Oct 1867.

Children of Hannah Romberger and Harry Wiest are:

278	i.	Rebecca⁵ Wiest, born 27 Aug 1840; died 21 May 1842.
+ 279	ii.	Samuel L. Wiest, born 10 May 1844 in Hickory Corners, Northumberland Co., PA; died 10 Feb 1924 in Pennsylvania.
280	iii.	Jacob Wiest, born 06 Apr 1857 in Pillow, Dauphin Co., PA; died 20 Apr 1859 in Pillow, Dauphin Co., PA.
+ 281	iv.	Henry Wiest, born Unknown; died Unknown in Bernville, Penna..
+ 282	v.	Oliver Wiest, born 1855; died 1936.

72. Sarah⁴ Matter (Anna Catharina³ Romberger, Balthaser², Johann Bartholomus¹) She married **Samuel Witmer**.

Children of Sarah Matter and Samuel Witmer are:

283	i.	Catharine⁵ Witmer.
284	ii.	Josiah Witmer.
285	iii.	Jonas Witmer.
286	iv.	Sarah Witmer.

88. George John⁴ Romberger (Balthaser³, Balthaser², Johann Bartholomus¹) was born 12 Nov 1807 in Upper Paxton Twp., Dauphin Co., PA, and died 05 Jan 1873 in Berrysburg, Dauphin Co., PA. He married **Mary Hopple**. She was born 29 Apr 1807, and died 15 Mar 1873 in Berrysburg, Dauphin Co., PA.

Children of George Romberger and Mary Hopple are:

287	i.	Jonas⁵ Romberger, born 09 Sep 1830 in Pennsylvania; died 13 Jun 1906.
+ 288	ii.	John G Romberger, born 21 Sep 1833 in Pennsylvania; died 25 Feb 1885.
289	iii.	Hannah Romberger, born 15 Dec 1834 in Pennsylvania; died 07 Aug 1911. She married Edward E Koppenhaver 01 May 1859 in St. John's, Berrysburg, PA; born 22 Jan 1830; died 15 Oct 1907.
+ 290	iv.	George H Romberger, born 19 Oct 1838 in Pennsylvania; died 06 Apr 1907.
291	v.	Mary Romberger, born Abt. 1839.
292	vi.	Leah H Romberger, born 20 Sep 1840 in Pennsylvania; died 10 Nov 1911. She married Isaac Moyer 16 May 1861; born 24 Dec 1840 in Pennsylvania; died 20 Sep 1866.
+ 293	vii.	Balthaser H Romberger, born Feb 1843 in Pennsylvania; died 1903.
294	viii.	Sarah Romberger, born Abt. 1844.
295	ix.	Henry Romberger, born Abt. 1848.
296	x.	Conrad Romberger, born 25 Aug 1850; died 06 Sep 1852.
297	xi.	Susan Romberger, born Abt. 1851.
298	xii.	Samuel Romberger, born Abt. 1853.

89. Daniel⁴ Romberger (Balthaser³, Balthaser², Johann Bartholomus¹) was born 13 Mar 1810 in Upper

Paxton Twp., Dauphin Co., PA, and died 16 Jun 1833 in Mifflin Twp, Dauphin Co., PA. He married **Eva Romberger** Bef. 1827, daughter of Adam Romberger and Anna Paul. She was born 28 Jun 1810 in Upper Paxton Twp., Dauphin Co., PA, and died Sep 1876.

Children are listed above under (64) Eva Romberger.

91. Susanna[4] Romberger (Balthaser[3], Balthaser[2], Johann Bartholomus[1]) was born 30 Nov 1814 in Dauphin Co., PA, and died 09 Dec 1845 in Mifflin Twp, Dauphin Co., PA. She married **John Bordner**. He was born 1812, and died 1869.

Children of Susanna Romberger and John Bordner are:
299	i.	Elizabeth Bordner[5] Bordner, born 1836. She married John Hempel.
300	ii.	John W. Bordner, born Abt. 1840 in Upper Paxton Twp., Dauphin Co., PA.
301	iii.	William Henry Harrison Bordner, born 1842 in Dauphin Co., PA; died 1907.

92. Rebecca[4] Romberger (Balthaser[3], Balthaser[2], Johann Bartholomus[1]) was born 17 Sep 1816 in Mifflin Twp, Dauphin Co., PA, and died 29 Apr 1904 in Berrysburg, Mifflin Twp., Dauphin Co., PA. She married **Jeremiah Harner**. He was born 19 Dec 1813, and died 04 Mar 1868.

Child of Rebecca Romberger and Jeremiah Harner is:
302	i.	Sophia[5] Harner, born 03 Nov 1838; died 12 Jun 1858. She married Solomon Enterline; born 1837; died 1879.

96. Balthaser W.[4] Romberger (Balthaser[3], Balthaser[2], Johann Bartholomus[1]) was born 07 Dec 1825 in Mifflin Twp, Dauphin Co., PA, and died 03 Nov 1905. He married **(1) Sarah Orndorf** 1850. She was born 01 Nov 1826 in Pennsylvania, and died 27 Feb 1852 in Berrysburg, Mifflin Twp., Dauphin Co., PA. He married **(2) Helena Wagner** 10 Jul 1856 in Philadelphia, PA. She was born 03 Aug 1828, and died 02 Oct 1914 in Elizabethville, Dauphin Co., PA.

Child of Balthaser Romberger and Sarah Orndorf is:
303	i.	Henry Marshall[5] Romberger. He married Florence Smith.

Children of Balthaser Romberger and Helena Wagner are:
304	i.	Clara Louise[5] Romberger, born 1857 in Dauphin Co., PA; died 05 Oct 1895 in Water Valley, MS.
305	ii.	Charles E. Romberger, born 1859 in Dauphin Co., PA. He married ? Smith.

102. Elizabeth[4] Workman (Susannah[3] Romberger, Balthaser[2], Johann Bartholomus[1]) was born 16 Jul 1828 in Lykens Twp., Dauphin Co., PA, and died 13 Feb 1907 in Shamokin, Northumberland Co., PA. She married **Isaac Allison Smink** 04 Jun 1848 in Wiconisco, Dauphin Co., PA. He was born 22 Feb 1828 in East Hanover Twp., Lehigh Co., PA, and died 21 Oct 1906 in Shamokin, Northumberland Co., PA.

Children of Elizabeth Workman and Isaac Smink are:
306	i.	Sidney Ann[5] Smink, born 12 Apr 1849 in Wiconisco, Dauphin Co., PA; died 18 Apr 1931. She married Isaac Kerlin 29 Nov 1868 in Shamokin, Northumberland Co., PA; born 13 Aug 1846; died 05 Aug 1922.
+ 307	ii.	Sara A. E. Smink, born 09 Dec 1850 in Wiconisco, Dauphin Co., PA; died 02 Mar 1909 in Shamokin, Northumberland Co., PA.
308	iii.	John William Henry Smink, born 03 Sep 1852 in Wiconisco, Dauphin Co., PA; died 07 Apr 1853 in Wiconisco, Dauphin Co., PA.
309	iv.	Frank Alfred Smink, born 08 Mar 1854 in Wiconisco, Dauphin Co., PA; died 11 Feb 1915.
310	v.	Joseph Werkman Smink, born 27 Mar 1856; died 13 Apr 1920. He married Sarah Adams; born 14 Jul 1852; died 19 Oct 1927.
311	vi.	Julia Ann Smink, born 20 Jul 1857 in Wiconisco, Dauphin Co., PA; died 02 Oct 1931 in Shamokin, Northumberland Co., PA. She married John Franklin Stout 18 Dec 1875; born 1858 in Shamokin, Northumberland Co., PA; died 14 May 1935 in Shamokin, Northumberland Co., PA.
312	vii.	Anna Elizabeth Gisels Smink, born 04 May 1859 in Wiconisco, Dauphin Co., PA; died 14 Mar 1862 in Wiconisco, Dauphin Co., PA.

313	viii.	Elmer E. Smink, born 24 Feb 1862 in Wiconisco, Dauphin Co., PA. He married Gertrude Gothie.
314	ix.	Harry Abraham Lincoln Smink, born 07 May 1865 in Shamokin, Northumberland Co., PA; died 08 Apr 1925. He married Julia Prescott 05 Apr 1887.
315	x.	Minnie A. Smink, born 17 Feb 1867 in Shamokin, Northumberland Co., PA; died 17 Apr 1943 in Upper Augusta Twp., Northumberland Co., PA. She married Frank S. Kauffman 1879; born 1857; died 1881 in Shamokin, Northumberland Co., PA.
316	xi.	Carrie Estelle Smink, born 13 Oct 1869 in Shamokin, Northumberland Co., PA; died 01 Oct 1881 in Shamokin, Northumberland Co., PA.
317	xii.	Isaac Wilson Smink, born 14 Jun 1873 in Shamokin, Northumberland Co., PA; died 06 Nov 1880 in Shamokin, Northumberland Co., PA.

104. Joseph R.[4] Workman (Susannah[3] Romberger, Balthaser[2], Johann Bartholomus[1]) was born Abt. 1820. He married **Catherina ?**.

Children of Joseph Workman and Catherina ? are:

318	i.	Levina[5] Workman.
319	ii.	Israel Workman.
320	iii.	Joseph Workman.
321	iv.	Edward Workman. He married Mary Whited.
322	v.	John Workman. He married Catherine ?.
323	vi.	Levi Workman. He married Elizabeth Keiser 29 Jul 1865; born 20 Jan 1848 in Wiconisco, Dauphin Co., PA; died 01 Oct 1896.
324	vii.	Kitty Workman.
325	viii.	Hariet Workman.
326	ix.	Sarah Workman, born Jan 1841 in Williams Valley, Dauphin Co., PA; died 25 Sep 1920.

105. Catherine[4] Workman (Susannah[3] Romberger, Balthaser[2], Johann Bartholomus[1]) was born 17 May 1838 in Pennsylvania, and died 10 Feb 1877 in Schuylkill Co., PA. She married **Andrew Guise Hensel**. He was born 20 Feb 1831 in Pennsylvania, and died 14 Dec 1908 in Wiconisco, Dauphin Co., PA.

Children of Catherine Workman and Andrew Hensel are:

327	i.	Howard[5] Hensel.
328	ii.	Joseph Hensel.
329	iii.	Ira Hensel.
330	iv.	John Hensel.
331	v.	Emma Hensel.
332	vi.	Anna Hensel.
333	vii.	Lillie Hensel.

140. Jacob[4] Romberger (Johannes[3], Adam[2], Johann Bartholomus[1]) was born 1800. He married **?**.

Children of Jacob Romberger and ? are:

| 334 | i. | Elizabeth[5] Romberger, born Abt. 1830. |
| 335 | ii. | John A. Romberger, born 1833. |

141. Catherine[4] Romberger (Johannes[3], Adam[2], Johann Bartholomus[1]) was born 1801. She married **Abraham Houser**.

Children of Catherine Romberger and Abraham Houser are:

336	i.	Nancy[5] Houser, born 1831.
337	ii.	Margaretha Houser, born 1834.
338	iii.	Catherine Houser, born 1837.
339	iv.	Samuel Houser, born 1844.

144. John[4] Romberger (Johannes[3], Adam[2], Johann Bartholomus[1]) was born 1811. He married **(1) Elizabeth Leathers** Abt. 1835. He married **(2) Elisabeth Erhart** Abt. 1845.

Children of John Romberger and Elizabeth Leathers are:
340	i.	Jacob[5] Romberger, born 1836.
341	ii.	Anna Mary Romberger, born 1838.
342	iii.	Elisabeth Romberger, born 1840.
343	iv.	Franklin Romberger.

Children of John Romberger and Elisabeth Erhart are:
344	i.	Lavina[5] Romberger, born 1846.
345	ii.	Catherine Romberger, born 1848.
346	iii.	Alice J. Romberger, born 1855.
347	iv.	William Romberger, born 1861.
348	v.	John S. Romberger, born 1865.

145. Sarah[4] Romberger (Johannes[3], Adam[2], Johann Bartholomus[1]) was born 1811. She married **Conrad Fye**.

Children of Sarah Romberger and Conrad Fye are:
349	i.	Elisabeth[5] Fye, born 1835.
350	ii.	John C. Fye, born 1836.
351	iii.	Josiah Fye, born 1838.
352	iv.	Benjamin Fye, born 1841.
353	v.	Daniel Fye, born 1843.
354	vi.	David Fye, born 1845.
355	vii.	Lewis T. Fye, born 1848.
356	viii.	Sarah A. Fye, born 1850.
357	ix.	Jeremiah Fye, born 1852.
358	x.	Jerome A. Fye, born 1856.

148. Samuel[4] Romberger (Johannes[3], Adam[2], Johann Bartholomus[1]) was born 1818. He married **Catherine McKinney**. She was born Abt. 1820.

Children of Samuel Romberger and Catherine McKinney are:
359	i.	Martha E.[5] Romberger.
360	ii.	Joseph Romberger, born 1842.
361	iii.	John W. Romberger, born 1844.

152. John[4] Romberger (George Bartholomew[3], Adam[2], Johann Bartholomus[1]) was born 1805. He married **Elisabeth Row**.

Children of John Romberger and Elisabeth Row are:
362	i.	Isaac[5] Romberger, born 1829.
363	ii.	Catherine Romberger, born 1836.
364	iii.	Joseph Romberger, born 1838.
365	iv.	David Romberger, born 1842.
366	v.	Mary Romberger, born 1845.
367	vi.	John G. Romberger, born 1846.
368	vii.	Miriam Romberger, born 1848.

154. George[4] Romberger (George Bartholomew[3], Adam[2], Johann Bartholomus[1]) was born 1813. He married **Margaret Leathers**.

Children of George Romberger and Margaret Leathers are:
369	i.	George[5] Romberger.
370	ii.	Samuel Romberger.
371	iii.	Mary C. Romberger.
372	iv.	Oliver S. Romberger, born 1840.
373	v.	John H. Romberger, born 1846.

162. George B.⁴ Romberger (Jacob³, Adam², Johann Bartholomus¹) was born 26 Apr 1807. He married **?
Sellers**.

Children of George Romberger and ? Sellers are:
374	i.	Joseph⁵ Romberger, born 1830.
375	ii.	Balsar Romberger, born 1831.
376	iii.	Mary A. Romberger, born 1835.
377	iv.	George Washington Romberger, born 20 Apr 1837.
378	v.	Thaddeus Romberger, born 1839.
379	vi.	Regis Romberger, born 1841.
380	vii.	Sarah Romberger, born 1849.

165. Mary⁴ Romberger (Jacob³, Adam², Johann Bartholomus¹) was born 1812. She married **Moses
Dickson**.

Children of Mary Romberger and Moses Dickson are:
381	i.	George⁵ Dickson.
382	ii.	Samuel Dickson.
383	iii.	John A. Dickson.
384	iv.	Elizabeth Dickson.
385	v.	William Dickson.
386	vi.	Barbara Dickson.
387	vii.	Benjamin Dickson.

166. Margaret⁴ Romberger (Jacob³, Adam², Johann Bartholomus¹) was born 1814. She married **Cyrus
Chronister**. He was born Abt. 1813.

Children of Margaret Romberger and Cyrus Chronister are:
388	i.	Samuel⁵ Chronister, born 1836.
389	ii.	Jacob Chronister, born 1838.
390	iii.	Eliza Chronister, born 1841.
391	iv.	Elisabeth Chronister, born 1844.

167. Eva⁴ Romberger (Jacob³, Adam², Johann Bartholomus¹) was born 1816. She married **David Gates**.
He was born Abt. 1815.

Children of Eva Romberger and David Gates are:
392	i.	Cyrus⁵ Gates, born 1846.
393	ii.	Andrew Gates, born 1847.
394	iii.	Miles Gates, born 1848.
395	iv.	Mary Gates, born 1851.

169. Martin⁴ Romberger (Jacob³, Adam², Johann Bartholomus¹) was born 1820. He married **Elisabeth
Ross**.

Children of Martin Romberger and Elisabeth Ross are:
396	i.	Ellen⁵ Romberger.
397	ii.	Susan Romberger, born 1843.
398	iii.	John G. Romberger, born 1848.
399	iv.	Benner Romberger, born 1850.
400	v.	James Romberger, born 1856.
401	vi.	Jane Romberger, born 1856.

170. Betsy⁴ Romberger (Jacob³, Adam², Johann Bartholomus¹) was born 1822. She married **John Fox**.
He was born Abt. 1820.

Child of Betsy Romberger and John Fox is:
402   i.   Laura[5] Fox.

171. Esther[4] Romberger (Jacob[3], Adam[2], Johann Bartholomus[1]) was born 1824. She married **Joseph Grazier**.

Children of Esther Romberger and Joseph Grazier are:
403   i.   Martha[5] Grazier, born 1846.
404   ii.   Wilson Grazier, born 1848.
405   iii.   Jacob Grazier, born 1851.
406   iv.   Barbara Grazier, born 1851.
407   v.   Anna Grazier, born 1854.
408   vi.   Mary Grazier, born 1857.
409   vii.   Theodore Grazier, born 1860.
410   viii. Elisabeth Grazier, born 1861.
411   ix.   Elmer Grazier, born 1863.
412   x.   Oscar Grazier, born 1873.

Generation No. 5

178. Simon[5] Matter (Johannes[4], Anna Maria[3] Romberger, Balthaser[2], Johann Bartholomus[1]) was born 07 Oct 1813 in , Dauphin, Pa, and died 03 Jun 1895 in Dauphin Co., PA. He married **Sarah Swab** in No Data, Probably, Dauphin County, Pa. She was born in , Dauphin, Pa.

Children of Simon Matter and Sarah Swab are:
+ 413   i.   Daniel[6] Matter, born 1843 in , Dauphin, Pa.
    414   ii.   Sarah Matter, born 10 Jun 1852 in , Dauphin, Pa.
    415   iii.   Leah Jane Matter, born 19 Aug 1856 in , Dauphin, Pa.
    416   iv.   Amanda Matter, born 20 Jul 1860 in , Dauphin, Pa.
    417   v.   Ellen Elizabeth Matter, born 20 Oct 1864 in , Dauphin, Pa.

183. Elizabeth[5] Minnich (Anna Maria[4] Matter, Anna Maria[3] Romberger, Balthaser[2], Johann Bartholomus[1]) was born 29 Dec 1813 in Mifflin Twp., Dauphin Co., PA, and died 1882 in Dauphin Co., PA. She married **Johannes Travitz**. He was born 12 Jul 1810 in Jackson Twp., Dauphin Co., PA, and died 01 Mar 1880 in Jackson Twp., Dauphin Co., PA.

Child of Elizabeth Minnich and Johannes Travitz is:
+ 418   i.   Simon[6] Travitz, born 10 May 1843 in Jackson Twp., Dauphin Co., PA; died 29 Jun 1917 in Jackson Twp., Dauphin Co., PA.

184. Michael[5] Minnich (Anna Maria[4] Matter, Anna Maria[3] Romberger, Balthaser[2], Johann Bartholomus[1]) was born Abt. 1814, and died 10 Mar 1891 in Dauphin Co., PA. He married **Ruth Ann Kern**. She was born 16 Oct 1812 in Jackson Twp., Dauphin Co., PA, and died 16 Dec 1890 in Dauphin Co., PA.

Children of Michael Minnich and Ruth Kern are:
    419   i.   Jeremiah[6] Minnich, born 03 Jul 1834 in Jackson Twp., Dauphin Co., PA; died 26 Mar 1857 in Dauphin Co., PA.
+ 420   ii.   Josiah Minnich, born 02 Sep 1836 in Armstrong Valley, Jackson Twp., Dauphin Co., PA; died 02 Jan 1908 in Lykens Twp., Dauphin Co., PA.
+ 421   iii.   Cyrus Minnich, born 05 Mar 1839; died 26 Jun 1900 in PA.
+ 422   iv.   Uriah Minnich, born 12 Sep 1842 in Lykens Twp., Dauphin Co., PA; died 06 May 1901 in Lykens Twp., Dauphin Co., PA.
    423   v.   Elias Minnich, born 1844 in Jackson Twp., Dauphin Co., PA.
    424   vi.   Catherine Minnich, born 20 Mar 1850 in Jackson Twp., Dauphin Co., PA; died 21 Feb 1928. She married Cyrus Miller; born 09 May 1850; died 26 Nov 1922.
    425   vii.   Sarah Ann Minnich, born 1853 in Jackson Twp., Dauphin Co., PA.
    426   viii. Mary Jane Minnich, born 30 Sep 1856 in Jackson Twp., Dauphin Co., PA; died 07 Mar 1857 in

185. Catherine[5] Minnich (Anna Maria[4] Matter, Anna Maria[3] Romberger, Balthaser[2], Johann Bartholomus[1]) was born 24 Nov 1815 in Mifflin Twp., Dauphin Co., PA, and died 28 Oct 1893. She married **Jacob Hoover**. He was born Abt. 1811 in Mifflin Twp., Dauphin Co., PA.

Children of Catherine Minnich and Jacob Hoover are:

	427	i.	Elizabeth[6] Hoover, born in Dauphin Co., PA.
	428	ii.	Ella Hoover, born in Dauphin Co., PA.
	429	iii.	Jacob Hoover, born in Dauphin Co., PA.
+	430	iv.	Solomon Hoover, born in Dauphin Co., PA.
	431	v.	Lloyd Hoover, born in Dauphin Co., PA.
+	432	vi.	Alfred Hoover, born 1840 in Dauphin Co., PA; died 1902.

186. Sarah[5] Minnich (Anna Maria[4] Matter, Anna Maria[3] Romberger, Balthaser[2], Johann Bartholomus[1]) was born 17 Dec 1817 in Mifflin Twp., Dauphin Co., PA, and died 10 May 1890 in Dauphin Co., PA. She married **Jacob Gipple**. He was born 16 Jan 1815 in Pennsylvania, and died 23 Sep 1882 in Dauphin Co., PA.

Children of Sarah Minnich and Jacob Gipple are:

433	i.	Mary Ann[6] Gipple-I, born Sep 1838 in Dauphin Co., PA.
434	ii.	Eliza Gipple, born Abt. 1839 in Dauphin Co., PA.
435	iii.	Elizabeth Gipple, born 1840 in Dauphin Co., PA.
436	iv.	Lydia Ann Gipple, born Jul 1841 in Dauphin Co., PA.
437	v.	Mary Ann Gipple-Ii, born 1846 in Dauphin Co., PA.
438	vi.	Samuel H. Gipple, born Jun 1848 in Lykens Twp., Dauphin Co., PA; died 1920.
439	vii.	Aaron Gipple, born Oct 1850 in Dauphin Co., PA; died 1920.
440	viii.	Jacob J. Gipple, born Nov 1853 in Dauphin Co., PA; died 1927.
441	ix.	Joseph Gipple, born 28 Jul 1857 in Dauphin Co., PA.
442	x.	James A. Gipple, born Aug 1859 in Dauphin Co., PA; died 1920.

189. Christopher[5] Matter (Johann Michael[4], Anna Maria[3] Romberger, Balthaser[2], Johann Bartholomus[1]) was born 29 May 1816 in Dauphin Co., PA, and died 12 Oct 1843 in Lancaster Co., PA. He married **Catherine Lenker** Abt. 1838. She was born 04 Oct 1820 in Dauphin Co., PA, and died 16 Jul 1891 in Dauphin Co., PA.

Children of Christopher Matter and Catherine Lenker are:

443	i.	John L.[6] Matter, born 08 Feb 1839 in Elizabethville, Dauphin Co., PA; died 31 Aug 1901 in Pennsylvania. He married Harriet L. Martz 31 Oct 1865 in Berrysburg, Daupnin Co., PA.
444	ii.	Michael Matter, born 28 Apr 1842 in Dauphin Co., PA; died 04 Dec 1912 in Hillsboro, Highland Co., OH. He married (1) Sarah Ann Keen 03 Oct 1865 in Dauphin Co., PA; born 17 Oct 1849 in Washington Twp., Dauphin Co., PA; died 07 Dec 1907 in Elizabethville, Dauphin Co., PA. He married (2) Mary Justice 20 Feb 1911 in Hillsboro, Highland Co., OH; born 20 Jan 1868 in Hillsboro, Highland Co., OH.
445	iii.	Christian Matter, born 09 May 1844 in Mifflin Twp, Dauphin Co., PA; died 31 Aug 1906 in Fisherville, Dauphin Co., PA.

191. Levi[5] Matter (Johann Michael[4], Anna Maria[3] Romberger, Balthaser[2], Johann Bartholomus[1]) was born 24 Nov 1820 in Dauphin, Pa, and died 06 Dec 1895 in Washington Twp., Dauphin Co., PA. He married **Esther Dupendorf** in No Data, Probably, Dauphin County, Pa. She was born 11 Nov 1819 in Dauphin, Pa, and died 08 Jan 1904 in Dauphin, Pa.

Children of Levi Matter and Esther Dupendorf are:

+	446	i.	Daniel D[6] Matter, born 11 Feb 1852 in , Dauphin, Pa; died 15 Jan 1934 in , Dauphin, Pa.
+	447	ii.	Sarah Ellen Matter, born 04 Mar 1855 in , Dauphin, Pa.

220. Elisabeth[5] Matter (Heinrich[4], Anna Maria[3] Romberger, Balthaser[2], Johann Bartholomus[1]) was born 06 Feb 1820 in Dauphin Co., PA, and died 09 Feb 1891 in Dauphin Co., PA. She married **(1) David Sheesley**

Abt. 1838 in Dauphin Co., PA. He was born 14 Feb 1813, and died 23 Aug 1845. She married **(2) George Gilbert** Aft. 1845. He was born 31 Dec 1813 in PA, and died 10 Nov 1869. She married **(3) Philip Bowman** Aft. 1850.

Children of Elisabeth Matter and David Sheesley are:

	448	i.	Rebecca[6] Sheesley, born 16 Mar 1839 in Dauphin Co., PA; died 22 Jan 1870 in Dauphin Co., PA.
+	449	ii.	Sarah Etta Sheesley, born Aug 1840; died 24 Jun 1903 in Maple Grove Cemetery, Elizabethville, PA.
	450	iii.	Anna Sheesley, born 02 Jan 1843; died 04 Jun 1843.

Children of Elisabeth Matter and George Gilbert are:

	451	i.	Alfred[6] Gilbert, born Sep 1849 in PA. He married Elizabeth ?.
	452	ii.	Salome Gilbert, born Abt. 1854.
	453	iii.	George W Gilbert, born Oct 1855. He married Ellen R ?.
+	454	iv.	Minerva Gilbert, born 03 Aug 1851 in Washington Twp, Dauphin Co, PA; died 05 Apr 1914.

222. Catharina[5] Matter (Heinrich[4], Anna Maria[3] Romberger, Balthaser[2], Johann Bartholomus[1]) was born 29 Jan 1823 in Dauphin Co., PA, and died 13 Mar 1915 in Dauphin Co., PA. She married **Phillip Wilbert**. He was born 29 Oct 1821, and died 02 Nov 1893 in Dauphin Co., PA.

Children of Catharina Matter and Phillip Wilbert are:

	455	i.	Sarah Jane[6] Wilbert, born 12 Jan 1848; died 23 Aug 1926. She married Daniel A. Miller 1870; born 1845; died 1901.
	456	ii.	May Wilbert, born 17 Apr 1852; died 24 Dec 1857 in Dauphin Co., PA.
+	457	iii.	Lydia A. Wilbert, born 14 Mar 1854 in Dauphin County, PA; died 20 Oct 1930.
	458	iv.	John H. Wilbert, born 21 Jun 1855 in Dauphin Co., PA; died 25 Dec 1857 in Dauphin Co., PA.
	459	v.	Emeline Wilbert, born 04 May 1859 in Dauphin Co., PA; died 07 Aug 1861 in Dauphin Co., PA.
	460	vi.	Amanda E. Wilbert, born 1861 in Dauphin Co., PA; died 03 Feb 1942 in Dauphin Co., PA. She married Wellington Klinger 08 Jul 1880 in Lykens Valley, Dauphin Co., PA; born 18 Mar 1858; died 1936.
	461	vii.	Clara R. Wilbert, born 07 Oct 1863; died 06 Apr 1928. She married Alfred Bechtel 25 Feb 1882 in Dauphin Co., PA; born 03 Feb 1859; died 31 Dec 1924.
	462	viii.	Mary Wilbert, born Abt. 1865 in Dauphin County, PA.

223. Margareta Rebecca[5] Matter (Heinrich[4], Anna Maria[3] Romberger, Balthaser[2], Johann Bartholomus[1]) was born 18 Mar 1825 in Mifflin Twp, Dauphin, PA, and died 22 Jun 1890 in Abilene, Dickinson Co , Kansas. She married **Jacob Frederick Eisenhauer** 25 Feb 1847 in Dauphin , Pennsylvania, son of Frederick Eisenhauer and Barbara Miller. He was born 19 Sep 1826 in Elizabethville, Washington Twp., Dauphin Co., PA, and died 20 May 1906 in Abilene, Dickinson Co , Kansas.

Children of Margareta Matter and Jacob Eisenhauer are:

	463	i.	John H.[6] Eisenhauer, born 07 Mar 1848 in Elizabethville, Dauphin Co, PA; died 10 Apr 1857 in Elizabethville, Dauphin Co, PA.
+	464	ii.	Mary Ann Eisenhauer, born 02 Sep 1849 in Elizabethville, Dauphin, Pennsylvania; died 27 Apr 1893 in Abilene, Dickinson, Kansas.
+	465	iii.	Catherine Ann Eisenhauer, born 19 Mar 1851 in Elizabethville, Dauphin, Pennsylvania; died 03 Apr 1924 in Ramona, Marion, Kansas.
	466	iv.	Jacob F. Eisenhauer, born 03 Sep 1852 in Elizabethville, Dauphin Co, PA; died 02 Oct 1852 in Elizabethville, Dauphin Co, PA.
	467	v.	Samuel F. Eisenhauer, born 30 Sep 1853 in Elizabethville, Dauphin Co, PA; died 11 Jun 1854 in Elizabethville, Dauphin Co, PA.
+	468	vi.	Susanna Eisenhauer, born 29 Oct 1854 in Elizabethville, Dauphin, Pennsylvania; died 14 Jun 1932 in York, PA.
	469	vii.	Peter A. Eisenhauer, born 27 Nov 1855 in Elizabethville, Dauphin Co, PA; died 04 Aug 1856 in Elizabethville, Dauphin Co, PA.
	470	viii.	Lydia A. Eisenhauer, born 27 Aug 1857 in Elizabethville, Dauphin Co, PA; died 15 Nov 1874 in Elizabethville, Dauphin Co, PA.
	471	ix.	Emma Jane Eisenhauer, born 03 Dec 1859 in Elizabethville, Dauphin Co, PA; died 08 May 1860 in Elizabethville, Dauphin Co, PA.
+	472	x.	Amanda Hannah Eisenhauer, born 11 Dec 1861 in Elizabethville, Dauphin Co, PA; died 25 Aug 1951

in Abilene, Dickinson Co, KS.

+ 473   xi.   David Jacob Eisenhauer, born 23 Sep 1863 in Elizabethville, Dauphin, Pennsylvania; died 10 Mar 1942 in Abilene, Dickinson, Kansas.

474   xii.   Dr Abraham Lincoln Eisenhauer, born 22 Jul 1865 in Elizabethville, Dauphin Co, PA; died 23 Dec 1944 in Upland, CA. He married Anna Long 1886; born 1865.

475   xiii.   Clinton Eisenhauer, born 30 Jul 1867 in Elizabethville, Dauphin Co, PA; died 10 Aug 1867 in Elizabethville, Dauphin Co, PA.

+ 476   xiv.   Ira A Eisenhower, born 30 Jul 1867 in Elizabethville, Dauphin, Pa; died 28 Mar 1943 in Los Angeles, CA.

226. George Washington[5] Matter (Heinrich[4], Anna Maria[3] Romberger, Balthaser[2], Johann Bartholomus[1]) was born 16 Jan 1832 in Elizabethville, Dauphin Co., PA, and died 26 Sep 1878 in Dauphin Co., PA. He married **Margaret Cumbler** 08 Sep 1857 in Washington Twp., Dauphin Co., PA. She was born 22 Jul 1829, and died 30 Aug 1898 in Washington Twp., Dauphin Co., PA.

Children of George Matter and Margaret Cumbler are:

477   i.   Infant A[6] Matter, born 16 May 1858; died 1858.

478   ii.   Infant B Matter, born 16 May 1858; died 1858.

479   iii.   Caleb Wheeler Matter, born 21 Jul 1859; died 20 Jan 1862.

480   iv.   Andrew G Curton Matter, born 20 Jan 1861 in Dauphin Co, PA; died 25 Sep 1939 in Colony, Anderson, KS. He married Leona Margery Proctor; born 21 Jan 1865 in Minera, Mason County, Kentucky; died 30 Dec 1928 in Colony, Anderson, KS.

481   v.   Theodore Nathaniel Matter, born 05 May 1864 in Elizabethville, Dauphin Co, PA; died 19 Apr 1920 in Comfort, Kendall County, Texas. He married Sophia Roemer 22 Dec 1889 in Comfort, Kendall County, Texas; born 21 Mar 1871 in Comfort, Kendall County, Texas; died 08 Mar 1931 in Comfort, Kendall County, Texas.

482   vi.   Isabella Amelia Matter, born 12 Jan 1865 in Elizabethville, Dauphin Co, PA; died 06 Oct 1947 in Chicago, IL. She married F E Roach 28 Jan 1896 in San Antonio, TX; born Abt. 1861.

483   vii.   Mary Ellen Matter, born 05 Apr 1867; died 30 Jan 1953 in San Antonio, Bexar County, Texas. She married (1) Richard S Lambert 24 Apr 1888 in San Antonio, TX; born Abt. 1863. She married (2) Cecil Jacob Gerhard 20 Feb 1892 in San Antonio, TX; born Abt. 1863.

484   viii.   Clinton Jodus Matter, born 17 May 1870; died 05 Sep 1871.

485   ix.   Hannah Elizabeth Matter, born 30 Oct 1873; died 07 Nov 1959 in San Antonio, Bexar County, Texas. She married John A Wharton 16 Jun 1908; died Dec 1939.

229. Anna Maria[5] Ritzman (Catherine[4] Matter, Anna Maria[3] Romberger, Balthaser[2], Johann Bartholomus[1]) was born Abt. 1840. She married **Christopher Gipple**. He was born Abt. 1840.

Children of Anna Ritzman and Christopher Gipple are:

+ 486   i.   Christian[6] Gipple, born Abt. 1865.

487   ii.   Samuel Gipple.

488   iii.   Catherine Gipple.

489   iv.   Sarah Gipple.

490   v.   Elizabeth Gipple. She married John Bender.

491   vi.   Susan Gipple.

+ 492   vii.   Mary Rebecca Gipple.

493   viii.   Leah Gipple.

230. Christopher[5] Matter (Michael[4], Anna Maria[3] Romberger, Balthaser[2], Johann Bartholomus[1]) was born Abt. 1830. He married **Catherine Lenker**. She was born Abt. 1830.

Child of Christopher Matter and Catherine Lenker is:

+ 494   i.   Michael[6] Matter, born Abt. 1855.

237. Elisabeth[5] Buffington (Elisabeth[4] Romberger, Adam[3], Balthaser[2], Johann Bartholomus[1]) was born 21 Aug 1824, and died Feb 1897 in PA. She married **Isaac Schupp**. He was born 12 Jan 1820, and died 03 Jan 1876 in PA.

Children of Elisabeth Buffington and Isaac Schupp are:

495   i.   Sarah[6] Schupp, born 1847 in Millersburg, Dauphin Co, PA; died 1918 in Tyrone, PA.. She married Samuel B. Boyer; died Abt. 1904.

496   ii.   John H. Schupp, born 27 Mar 1848 in Millersburg, Dauphin Co, PA; died 1912 in Harrisburg, PA. He married Mary C. Timmons 21 Feb 1888 in Millersburg, Dauphin Co, PA; died in Y.

497   iii. Nathaniel P. Schupp, born 1853 in Millersburg, Dauphin Co, PA; died in PA. He married Lucinda Cabery; died in Y.

238. Josiah[5] Buffington (Elisabeth[4] Romberger, Adam[3], Balthaser[2], Johann Bartholomus[1]) was born 16 Jan 1826 in Upper Paxton Twp, and died 11 Jun 1900. He married **Susan Yeager** 18 Oct 1848. She was born 14 Dec 1826, and died 19 Apr 1912.

Child of Josiah Buffington and Susan Yeager is:

498   i.   Isaiah T.[6] Buffington, died in Y.

248. Elizabeth[5] Rickert (Sarah Salome[4] Romberger, Adam[3], Balthaser[2], Johann Bartholomus[1]) was born Dec 1822 in Lykens Twp., Dauphin Co., PA, and died Aft. 1900 in Wiconisco Twp., Dauphin Co. PA. She married **Daniel Shomper** in Dauphin Co., PA. He was born Abt. 1820 in Pennsylvania, and died Bef. 1870 in Wiconisco Twp., Dauphin Co. PA.

Children of Elizabeth Rickert and Daniel Shomper are:

499   i.   Lawrence[6] Shomper, born Abt. 1853 in Wiconisco Twp., Dauphin Co. PA.

500   ii.   John Adam Shomper, born Abt. 1855 in Wiconisco Twp., Dauphin Co. PA.

501   iii. Catherine R. Shomper, born Abt. 1862 in Wiconisco Twp., Dauphin Co. PA.

252. John[5] Rickert (Sarah Salome[4] Romberger, Adam[3], Balthaser[2], Johann Bartholomus[1]) was born 04 Jan 1829 in Powell's Valley, Dauphin Co., PA, and died 31 Jul 1910 in Hampton Roads, VA. He married **Sarah A. Palmer** 31 Jul 1853 in Lykens Twp., Dauphin Co., PA. She was born Abt. 1828 in Dauphin Co., PA.

Children of John Rickert and Sarah Palmer are:

502   i.   Benjamin F.[6] Rickert, born Abt. 1854 in Dauphin Co., PA.

503   ii.   Ann J. Rickert, born Abt. 1856 in Dauphin Co., PA.

504   iii. John H. Rickert, born Abt. 1857 in Dauphin Co., PA. He married ?.

505   iv.   Salome E. R Ickert, born 1860 in Dauphin Co., PA.

506   v.   George M . Rickert, born 1862 in Dauphin Co., PA.

507   vi.   James M. Rickert, born 1866 in Dauphin Co., PA.

256. Sarah[5] Rickert (Sarah Salome[4] Romberger, Adam[3], Balthaser[2], Johann Bartholomus[1]) was born Abt. 1836 in Dauphin Co., PA, and died Abt. 1864. She married **Daniel Merkel Wiest** Abt. 1856. He was born 07 Mar 1822 in Klingerstown, Schuylkill Co.,PA, and died 16 Sep 1901 in Klingerstown, Schuylkill Co.,PA.

Children of Sarah Rickert and Daniel Wiest are:

508   i.   Jefferson[6] Wiest, born Abt. 1856.

509   ii.   Lusianna Wiest, born Abt. 1858.

510   iii. Catharine Wiest, born Abt. 1860.

511   iv.   David Wiest, born Abt. 1862.

512   v.   Daughter Wiest, born Abt. 1864.

+   513   vi.   Jefferson Wiest, born 06 Jul 1855 in Klingerstown, Schuylkill Co.,PA; died 1893 in San Antonio, TX.

514   vii. Luisianna Wiest, born 27 Sep 1856 in Klingerstown, Schuylkill Co.,PA; died Unknown in Cincinnati, OH. She married ? Hewes; born Unknown; died Unknown.

515   viii. Catherine Wiest, born Abt. 1857 in Klingerstown, Schuylkill Co.,PA; died 1920 in San Antonio, TX.

516   ix.   David Wiest, born 30 Jun 1858 in Klingerstown, Schuylkill Co.,PA; died Unknown in Danville, IL.

517   x.   Daughter Wiest, born Unknown; died Unknown in Williamstown, Dauphin Co., PA. She married ?; born Unknown; died Unknown in Williamstown, Dauphin Co., PA.

269. Adam R.[5] Paffenberger (Lydia Ann[4] Romberger, Adam[3], Balthaser[2], Johann Bartholomus[1]) was born 1852 in Klingerstown, Schuylkill Co., PA, and died Unknown. He married **(1) Ella Amanda Wiest**. She was born 20 Feb 1853, and died 24 Dec 1888 in Klingerstown, PA. He married (2) **Ella Amanda Wiest**. She was born 20 Feb 1853 in Klingerstown, Schuylkill Co., PA, and died 24 Dec 1888 in Klingerstown, Schuylkill Co., PA.

Children of Adam Paffenberger and Ella Wiest are:

- \+ 518 i. Alvin Joseph Adam[6] Poffenberger, born 12 Jan 1872 in Klingerstown, Schuylkill Co., PA; died 26 May 1931 in Portland, Multnomah, OR.
- 519 ii. Daniel Lloyd Paffenberger, born 09 Aug 1873 in Klingerstown, Schuylkill Co., PA; died 17 May 1932 in Pennsylvania.
- 520 iii. Jennie Isabelle Paffenberger, born 02 Jul 1880 in Klingerstown, Schuylkill Co., PA; died 31 Oct 1957. She married (1) John Shaffer; born Abt. 1880. She married (2) John Schaffer; born Unknown; died Unknown.

274. Josiah[5] Romberger (Daniel[4], Adam[3], Balthaser[2], Johann Bartholomus[1]) was born 09 Oct 1847. He married **Sarah Matter**. She was born 10 Jul 1852.

Children of Josiah Romberger and Sarah Matter are:

- 521 i. Harvey D[6] Romberger, born 1871 in PA; died 1948. He married Carrie E Harner; born 1873 in PA; died 07 May 1966.
- 522 ii. Charles E Romberger, born 08 Jan 1873.

279. Samuel L.[5] Wiest (Hannah[4] Romberger, Adam[3], Balthaser[2], Johann Bartholomus[1]) was born 10 May 1844 in Hickory Corners, Northumberland Co., PA, and died 10 Feb 1924 in Pennsylvania. He married **Elizabeth E. Orwig** 19 Jul 1866 in Pillow, Jordan Twp., Northumberland Co., PA. She was born Abt. 1846 in Pillow, Dauphin Co., PA, and died Unknown.

Children of Samuel Wiest and Elizabeth Orwig are:

- \+ 523 i. Laurence Orwig[6] Wiest, born 14 Jun 1867 in Philadelphia, PA.
- \+ 524 ii. Warren Orwig Wiest, born 20 Oct 1868 in Philadelphia, PA.
- 525 iii. Ella May Wiest, born 06 Nov 1871 in Easton, Northampton Co., PA. She married Vincent Stanford.
- 526 iv. Grace Wiest, born 18 Apr 1877 in Mahanoy City, Schuylkill Co., PA. She married B. H. McCoy.
- 527 v. Maude Wiest, born 12 Feb 1879; died 18 Nov 1909.
- 528 vi. Ruth Wiest, born 28 Mar 1887; died 11 Aug 1890.

281. Henry[5] Wiest (Hannah[4] Romberger, Adam[3], Balthaser[2], Johann Bartholomus[1]) was born Unknown, and died Unknown in Bernville, Penna.. He married **?**.

Child of Henry Wiest and ? is:
- 529 i. Charles[6] Wiest.

282. Oliver[5] Wiest (Hannah[4] Romberger, Adam[3], Balthaser[2], Johann Bartholomus[1]) was born 1855, and died 1936. He married **Lydia A Lenker** in Pennsylvania. She was born 1860, and died 1953.

Children of Oliver Wiest and Lydia Lenker are:

- 530 i. Lovetta[6] Wiest, born in Pillow, Dauphin Co., PA.
- 531 ii. Hattie Wiest, born in Pillow, Dauphin Co., PA. She married William Knorr; born in Harrisburg, Dauphin Co., PA.
- \+ 532 iii. Charles A. Wiest, born in Pillow, Jordan Twp., Northumberland Co., PA; died 1947.
- 533 iv. Lily Wiest, born in Pennsylvania.

288. John G[5] Romberger (George John[4], Balthaser[3], Balthaser[2], Johann Bartholomus[1]) was born 21 Sep 1833 in Pennsylvania, and died 25 Feb 1885. He married **Hannah Clark**. She was born 10 Nov 1842 in Pennsylvania, and died 27 Feb 1922.

Children of John Romberger and Hannah Clark are:

- 534 i. Mary Elizabeth[6] Romberger, born 10 Nov 1863 in Pennsylvania; died 14 Nov 1872 in Pennsylvania.

535	ii.	William Romberger, born 12 Jan 1865 in Pennsylvania; died 11 Jun 1876 in Pennsylvania.
536	iii.	Emma C Romberger, born Abt. 1866.
537	iv.	David Romberger, born 04 Mar 1868.
538	v.	George Franklin Romberger, born 03 Nov 1869.
539	vi.	Jennie Romberger, born 19 Jul 1871.
540	vii.	Sallie Romberger, born 30 Jan 1873.
541	viii.	John Romberger, born 10 Aug 1874.
542	ix.	Samuel Oscar Romberger, born 13 Feb 1877; died 19 Aug 1877.
543	x.	Charles Romberger, born 14 Nov 1878.

290. George H[5] Romberger (George John[4], Balthaser[3], Balthaser[2], Johann Bartholomus[1]) was born 19 Oct 1838 in Pennsylvania, and died 06 Apr 1907. He married **Elizabeth Bressler**. She was born 20 May 1854 in Pennsylvania, and died 20 Mar 1920.

Children of George Romberger and Elizabeth Bressler are:
544	i.	Jonas Allen[6] Romberger, born 19 May 1877.
545	ii.	Daniel Romberger, born 10 Jan 1879.
546	iii.	James M Romberger, born 21 Aug 1880; died 14 Nov 1894.
547	iv.	Maggie Romberger, born Jan 1887.
548	v.	Hannah Romberger, born Aug 1888.

293. Balthaser H[5] Romberger (George John[4], Balthaser[3], Balthaser[2], Johann Bartholomus[1]) was born Feb 1843 in Pennsylvania, and died 1903. He married **Hannah Deibler** May 1870. She was born May 1848 in Pennsylvania, and died 1930.

Children of Balthaser Romberger and Hannah Deibler are:
549	i.	Mary Agatha[6] Romberger, born 21 Feb 1871; died 05 Feb 1873.
550	ii.	Sarah Elizabeth Romberger, born 31 Aug 1872.
551	iii.	Aaron Dewilla Romberger, born 26 Oct 1875; died 30 Oct 1879.
552	iv.	Henry Ammon Romberger, born 29 Jun 1877; died 29 Jun 1918.
553	v.	James W Romberger, born May 1880.
554	vi.	Darin Eugene Romberger, born 27 May 1880; died 1960. He married Mary Ellen Paul; born 1883; died 1953.
555	vii.	Hannah R Romberger, born Aug 1888.

307. Sara A. E.[5] Smink (Elizabeth[4] Workman, Susannah[3] Romberger, Balthaser[2], Johann Bartholomus[1]) was born 09 Dec 1850 in Wiconisco, Dauphin Co., PA, and died 02 Mar 1909 in Shamokin, Northumberland Co., PA. She married **James E. McKay** 11 Oct 1874 in Shamokin, Northumberland Co., PA. He was born 25 Nov 1846, and died 16 Jan 1900.

Children of Sara Smink and James McKay are:
| 556 | i. | Bessie[6] McKay, born 12 Dec 1869; died 21 Aug 1937 in Shamokin, Northumberland Co., PA. She married Samuel Lesher; born 1873; died 26 Oct 1932 in Shamokin, Northumberland Co., PA. |
| 557 | ii. | Jennie E. McKay, born 21 Aug 1882 in Northumberland Co., PA; died 26 Oct 1967 in Shamokin, Northumberland Co., PA. She married Samuel H. Miller; born 19 Apr 1883; died 16 May 1962 in Shamokin, Northumberland Co., PA. |

Generation No. 6

413. Daniel[6] Matter (Simon[5], Johannes[4], Anna Maria[3] Romberger, Balthaser[2], Johann Bartholomus[1]) was born 1843 in , Dauphin, Pa. He married **Lovina Miller** in No Data, Probably, Dauphin County, Pa. She was born in , Dauphin, Pa.

Children of Daniel Matter and Lovina Miller are:
558	i.	Henry[7] Matter, born 1870 in , Dauphin, Pa; died 1934 in Pa.
559	ii.	John Elias Matter, born 02 Oct 1873 in , Dauphin, Pa.
560	iii.	Isaac Walter Matter, born 14 Oct 1875 in , Dauphin, Pa.
561	iv.	William Elmer Matter, born 02 Mar 1879 in , Dauphin, Pa.

418. Simon[6] Travitz (Elizabeth[5] Minnich, Anna Maria[4] Matter, Anna Maria[3] Romberger, Balthaser[2], Johann Bartholomus[1]) was born 10 May 1843 in Jackson Twp., Dauphin Co., PA, and died 29 Jun 1917 in Jackson Twp., Dauphin Co., PA. He married **Elizabeth Grimm**.

Child of Simon Travitz and Elizabeth Grimm is:

+ 562   i.   Katie L.[7] Travitz, born 06 Dec 1885 in Jackson Twp., Dauphin Co., PA; died 24 Dec 1955 in Detroit, Wayne Co., MI.

420. Josiah[6] Minnich (Michael[5], Anna Maria[4] Matter, Anna Maria[3] Romberger, Balthaser[2], Johann Bartholomus[1]) was born 02 Sep 1836 in Armstrong Valley, Jackson Twp., Dauphin Co., PA, and died 02 Jan 1908 in Lykens Twp., Dauphin Co., PA. He married **(1) Elizabeth Deibler**. She was born Abt. 1840 in Jackson Twp., Dauphin Co., PA, and died 08 Jun 1874. He married **(2) Rebecca Johns** 25 Apr 1869 in Dauphin Co., PA. She was born Abt. 1848 in Jackson Twp., Dauphin Co., PA, and died 03 Jun 1885. He married **(3) Ellen Amanda Maurer** 18 Nov 1885 in Lykens Twp., Dauphin Co., PA. She was born 07 Oct 1855 in Locustdale, Schuylkill Co., PA, and died 23 Oct 1940 in William Penn, Shaft, Schuylkill Co., PA.

Children of Josiah Minnich and Rebecca Johns are:

+ 563   i.   Amos F.[7] Minnich, born 27 Nov 1869 in Jackson Twp., Dauphin Co., PA.
   564   ii.   Joseph Osceloa Minnich, born 17 Sep 1871 in Jackson Twp., Dauphin Co., PA; died 19 Sep 1898 in Jackson Twp., Dauphin Co., PA.
   565   iii.   John W. Minnich, born 07 Apr 1873 in Jackson Twp., Dauphin Co., PA; died 10 Apr 1875 in Jackson Twp., Dauphin Co., PA.
+ 566   iv.   Claude E. Minnich, born 18 Mar 1875 in Jackson Twp., Dauphin Co., PA; died 1962 in Albany, Albany Co., NY.
   567   v.   Lorena Esther Edith Minnich, born 10 Dec 1879 in Jackson Twp., Dauphin Co., PA; died 22 Apr 1881 in Jackson Twp., Dauphin Co., PA.
+ 568   vi.   Edward Austin Minnich, born 12 Feb 1877 in Jackson Twp., Dauphin Co., PA; died 09 Oct 1958 in Harrisburg, Dauphin Co., PA.

Children of Josiah Minnich and Ellen Maurer are:

   569   i.   Sarah Irene[7] Minnich, born 23 Jul 1886 in Lykens Twp., Dauphin Co., PA; died 09 Mar 1974 in Dauphin Co., PA. She married Daniel C. Messner 09 May 1916; born Abt. 1882 in Lykens Twp., Dauphin Co., PA; died Abt. 1965 in Dauphin Co., PA.
+ 570   ii.   Carrie Elizabeth Minnich, born 18 Mar 1889 in Lykens Twp., Dauphin Co., PA; died 14 May 1971 in Kingston, Luzerne Co., PA.
   571   iii.   Robert E. Minnich, born 29 May 1891 in Lykens Twp., Dauphin Co., PA; died 22 Oct 1918 in Lykens Twp., Dauphin Co., PA.
+ 572   iv.   Leona M. Minnich, born 27 Jul 1894 in Lykens Twp., Dauphin Co., PA; died 10 Aug 1973 in Shenandoah, Schuylkill Co., PA.

421. Cyrus[6] Minnich (Michael[5], Anna Maria[4] Matter, Anna Maria[3] Romberger, Balthaser[2], Johann Bartholomus[1]) was born 05 Mar 1839, and died 26 Jun 1900 in PA. He married **Caroline McCulley**. She was born 04 Aug 1849, and died 05 Mar 1913 in PA.

Children of Cyrus Minnich and Caroline McCulley are:

   573   i.   Daughter[7] Minnich, born 24 Jan 1867 in Armstrong Valley, Jackson Twp., Dauphin Co., PA; died 07 Feb 1867 in Armstrong Valley, Jackson Twp., Dauphin Co., PA.
   574   ii.   Clement Elias Minnich, born 25 Dec 1867 in Armstrong Valley, Jackson Twp., Dauphin Co., PA; died 19 Dec 1943.
   575   iii.   Catherine Agnes Minnich, born 10 Oct 1869 in Armstrong Valley, Jackson Twp., Dauphin Co., PA; died 01 Mar 1934.
   576   iv.   Amos N. Minnich, born 11 May 1871 in Armstrong Valley, Jackson Twp., Dauphin Co., PA; died 07 May 1872 in Armstrong Valley, Jackson Twp., Dauphin Co., PA.
+ 577   v.   Aaron Frank Minnich, born 18 Aug 1873 in Armstrong Valley, Jackson Twp., Dauphin Co., PA; died 22 Dec 1937 in Tower City, Schuylkill Co., PA.
   578   vi.   Sara Alice Minnich, born 06 Oct 1875 in Armstrong Valley, Jackson Twp., Dauphin Co., PA; died 23 May 1962.

579	vii.	Daughter Minnich, born 08 Jan 1878 in Armstrong Valley, Jackson Twp., Dauphin Co., PA; died 11 Jan 1878 in Armstrong Valley, Jackson Twp., Dauphin Co., PA.
580	viii.	Charles Calvin Minnich, born 18 Jul 1879 in Armstrong Valley, Jackson Twp., Dauphin Co., PA; died 09 Feb 1946.
581	ix.	Emma Jane Minnich, born 28 Sep 1882 in Armstrong Valley, Jackson Twp., Dauphin Co., PA; died 19 Feb 1952.
582	x.	Irvin Elmer Minnich, born 31 Oct 1884 in Armstrong Valley, Jackson Twp., Dauphin Co., PA; died 15 Oct 1957.
583	xi.	John A. Minnich, born 05 Aug 1886 in Armstrong Valley, Jackson Twp., Dauphin Co., PA; died 09 Feb 1894.
584	xii.	Clara Edna Minnich, born 12 Apr 1889 in Armstrong Valley, Jackson Twp., Dauphin Co., PA; died 25 Jul 1925.
585	xiii.	Harry Robert Minnich, born 09 Aug 1893 in Armstrong Valley, Jackson Twp., Dauphin Co., PA; died 21 Oct 1937.

422. Uriah[6] Minnich (Michael[5], Anna Maria[4] Matter, Anna Maria[3] Romberger, Balthaser[2], Johann Bartholomus[1]) was born 12 Sep 1842 in Lykens Twp., Dauphin Co., PA, and died 06 May 1901 in Lykens Twp., Dauphin Co., PA. He married **Lusanna Ann Schoffstall** 1864 in Lykens Twp., Dauphin Co., PA. She was born Abt. 1846 in Washington Twp., Dauphin Co., PA.

Children of Uriah Minnich and Lusanna Schoffstall are:

+	586	i.	Charlotta Lucreta[7] Minnich, born Abt. 1862 in Washington Twp., Dauphin Co., PA.
+	587	ii.	Martha J. Minnich, born 1864 in Washington Twp., Dauphin Co., PA; died 1927 in Lykens Twp., Dauphin Co., PA.
+	588	iii.	James Minnich, born 1865 in Washington Twp., Dauphin Co., PA; died 06 Jul 1940 in Lykens Twp., Dauphin Co., PA.
+	589	iv.	William Minnich, born 1867 in Washington Twp., Dauphin Co., PA.
+	590	v.	Ira Oscar Minnich, born 03 Sep 1870 in Washington Twp., Dauphin Co., PA; died in Lykens Twp., Dauphin Co., PA.
+	591	vi.	Mary Terressa Minnich, born 08 Dec 1871 in Dauphin Co., PA; died 1918.
	592	vii.	John Henry Minnich, born 23 Jun 1873 in Wiconisco, Dauphin Co., PA; died 29 Sep 1874 in Wiconisco, Dauphin Co., PA.
	593	viii.	Horace Penroe Minnich, born 23 Mar 1875 in Dauphin Co., PA; died 09 Jan 1895.
+	594	ix.	Cardella Helen Minnich, born 21 Jun 1883 in Wiconisco, Dauphin Co., PA; died 1929 in Wiconisco, Dauphin Co., PA.
+	595	x.	Clarence Minnich, born Abt. 1888 in Wiconisco, Dauphin Co., PA; died 1965.

430. Solomon[6] Hoover (Catherine[5] Minnich, Anna Maria[4] Matter, Anna Maria[3] Romberger, Balthaser[2], Johann Bartholomus[1]) was born in Dauphin Co., PA. He married **?**.

Children of Solomon Hoover and ? are:

596	i.	Jacob[7] Hoover.
597	ii.	Lloyd Hoover.

432. Alfred[6] Hoover (Catherine[5] Minnich, Anna Maria[4] Matter, Anna Maria[3] Romberger, Balthaser[2], Johann Bartholomus[1]) was born 1840 in Dauphin Co., PA, and died 1902. He married **Mary Deibler**.

Children of Alfred Hoover and Mary Deibler are:

598	i.	Ellen[7] Hoover. She married John Umholtz.
599	ii.	Charles Hoover.
+	600	iii.	William Hoover, born 1864; died 1922.

446. Daniel D[6] Matter (Levi[5], Johann Michael[4], Anna Maria[3] Romberger, Balthaser[2], Johann Bartholomus[1]) was born 11 Feb 1852 in , Dauphin, Pa, and died 15 Jan 1934 in , Dauphin, Pa. He married **Emma Jane Susanna Lark** in No Data, Probably, Dauphin County, Pa. She was born 15 Oct 1856 in , Dauphin, Pa, and died 17 Aug 1937 in , Dauphin, Pa.

Children of Daniel Matter and Emma Lark are:

601   i.   Carrie Minerva[7] Matter, born 02 Sep 1874 in , Dauphin, Pa.

602   ii.   Aaron Franklin Matter, born 13 Dec 1878 in , Dauphin, Pa.

447. Sarah Ellen[6] Matter (Levi[5], Johann Michael[4], Anna Maria[3] Romberger, Balthaser[2], Johann Bartholomus[1]) was born 04 Mar 1855 in , Dauphin, Pa. She married **Amos Koppenhoffer** Abt. 1877 in No Data, Probably, Dauphin County, Pa. He was born in , Dauphin, Pa.

Child of Sarah Matter and Amos Koppenhoffer is:

603   i.   Cora Agnes[7] Koppenhoffer, born 12 Jan 1880 in , Dauphin, Pa.

449. Sarah Etta[6] Sheesley (Elisabeth[5] Matter, Heinrich[4], Anna Maria[3] Romberger, Balthaser[2], Johann Bartholomus[1]) was born Aug 1840, and died 24 Jun 1903 in Maple Grove Cemetery, Elizabethville, PA. She married **Michael R Keiper**. He was born 05 Oct 1839 in Washington Twp, Dauphin Co, PA.

Child of Sarah Sheesley and Michael Keiper is:

604   i.   Katie S[7] Keiper, born 03 Jul 1864 in Washington Twp, Dauphin Co, PA; died 07 Nov 1958 in Elizabethville, Dauphin Co, PA. She married Albert Morris Romberger; born 27 Jan 1863 in Lower Mahanoy Twp, Northumberland Co, PA; died 13 Apr 1948 in Elizabethville, Dauphin Co, PA.

454. Minerva[6] Gilbert (Elisabeth[5] Matter, Heinrich[4], Anna Maria[3] Romberger, Balthaser[2], Johann Bartholomus[1]) was born 03 Aug 1851 in Washington Twp, Dauphin Co, PA, and died 05 Apr 1914. She married **George A Harner**. He was born 30 Oct 1848 in PA, and died 18 Jan 1924.

Child of Minerva Gilbert and George Harner is:

605   i.   Carrie E[7] Harner, born 1873 in PA; died 07 May 1966. She married Harvey D Romberger; born 1871 in PA; died 1948.

457. Lydia A.[6] Wilbert (Catharina[5] Matter, Heinrich[4], Anna Maria[3] Romberger, Balthaser[2], Johann Bartholomus[1]) was born 14 Mar 1854 in Dauphin County, PA, and died 20 Oct 1930. She married **John Calvin Lentz**. He was born 11 Feb 1851 in Jackson Township, Dauphin County, PA, and died 05 Jun 1895.

Children of Lydia Wilbert and John Lentz are:

606   i.   John Philip[7] Lentz, born 22 Nov 1872; died 30 Sep 1941.

607   ii.   Annie Louise Lentz, born 20 Jun 1874.

608   iii.   Katie E. Lentz, born 08 Mar 1879; died 05 Dec 1915.

609   iv.   James Edwin Lentz, born 08 Mar 1879; died 31 May 1946.

610   v.   Edwin Lentz, born 1881.

611   vi.   Raymond Andrew Lentz, born 21 Oct 1881; died 02 Jul 1916.

\+ 612   vii.   Charles Warren Lentz, born 02 Dec 1884 in Dauphin County, PA; died 12 Aug 1968 in Millersburg, Dauphin County, PA.

613   viii.   Daniel C. Lentz, born 12 Feb 1887; died 20 Oct 1914.

614   ix.   Henry H. Lentz, born 31 Mar 1889.

615   x.   Allen C. Lentz, born 10 Dec 1890.

616   xi.   Joseph Harry Lentz, born 28 Sep 1892; died 26 Jan 1945.

464. Mary Ann[6] Eisenhauer (Margareta Rebecca[5] Matter, Heinrich[4], Anna Maria[3] Romberger, Balthaser[2], Johann Bartholomus[1]) was born 02 Sep 1849 in Elizabethville, Dauphin, Pennsylvania, and died 27 Apr 1893 in Abilene, Dickinson, Kansas. She married **John J Witter**. He was born Jul 1840 in Prussia, and died 1918 in Abilene, Dickinson Co, KS.

Children of Mary Eisenhauer and John Witter are:

\+ 617   i.   Martha Rebecca[7] Witter, born 27 Sep 1871 in Millersburg, PA; died 20 Aug 1955 in Upland, CA.

618   ii.   Harry Witter, born 1873 in PA.

619   iii.   Amanda Witter, born 1877 in PA; died Nov 1883 in KS.

620   iv.   Bessie Witter, born 19 Sep 1880; died 28 Sep 1883 in Abilene, Dickinson Co, KS.

621   v.   Sadie Witter, born 01 Jan 1883 in Enterprise, KS; died 14 Jun 1982 in Abilene, Dickinson Co, KS.

She married Lewis Steckley 27 May 1958 in Navarre, KS; died 16 Sep 1977.

622   vi.   Susie A Witter, born 28 Jan 1885 in Enterprise, KS; died 23 Jul 1956 in Modesto, CA. She married Noah B Martin Abt. 1924 in CA.

623   vii.   Johnnie Witter, born 18 Oct 1887 in Abilene, Dickinson Co, KS; died 06 Feb 1888 in Abilene, Dickinson Co, KS.

624   viii.   Mamie Stella Witter, born 25 Nov 1888 in KS; died 29 Sep 1969 in KS.

625   ix.   Ray I Witter, born 19 Jan 1891 in Enterprise, KS; died 26 Jan 1967 in Abilene, Dickinson Co, KS. He married Ruth V Book 18 Feb 1914; born 29 Dec 1894; died 02 Nov 1980 in Mechanicburg, PA.

465. Catherine Ann[6] Eisenhauer (Margareta Rebecca[5] Matter, Heinrich[4], Anna Maria[3] Romberger, Balthaser[2], Johann Bartholomus[1]) was born 19 Mar 1851 in Elizabethville, Dauphin, Pennsylvania, and died 03 Apr 1924 in Ramona, Marion, Kansas. She married **Samuel B. Haldeman**. He was born 11 Jan 1846 in Bainsbridge, PA, and died 21 Oct 1928 in Abilene, Dickinson Co, KS.

Children of Catherine Eisenhauer and Samuel Haldeman are:

626   i.   Hattie Jane[7] Haldeman, born 19 Jun 1872; died 1883.

627   ii.   Mary Rebecca Haldeman, born 1874.

628   iii.   Lydia Ann Haldeman, born 1875.

629   iv.   John Thaddeus Haldeman, born 1876; died 1901.

+ 630   v.   Lillian Elizabeth Haldeman, born 27 Aug 1878.

631   vi.   Jesse Ira Haldeman, born 1879 in PA.

632   vii.   Abraham Lincoln Haldeman, born 02 Feb 1882; died 1883.

+ 633   viii.   Katherine Ann Haldeman, born 20 Jul 1883 in Hope, KS; died 28 Nov 1959 in Abilene, Dickinson Co, KS.

634   ix.   Samuel Walter Haldeman, born 17 Dec 1884 in Hope, KS; died 23 Feb 1949 in Topeka, KS. He married Grace Johnson 15 Aug 1909.

+ 635   x.   John Henry Haldeman, born 09 Jun 1886 in Hope, KS; died 12 Dec 1969.

636   xi.   Milo Edward Haldeman, born Dec 1887.

+ 637   xii.   Harry Milton Haldeman, born 22 Apr 1889 in KS; died 04 Jul 1968 in Hillsboro, KS.

638   xiii.   Ora Blanche Haldeman, born Aug 1892 in KS. She married m Button.

639   xiv.   Delilah Haldeman, born 1895 in KS. She married m Book.

468. Susanna[6] Eisenhauer (Margareta Rebecca[5] Matter, Heinrich[4], Anna Maria[3] Romberger, Balthaser[2], Johann Bartholomus[1]) was born 29 Oct 1854 in Elizabethville, Dauphin, Pennsylvania, and died 14 Jun 1932 in York, PA. She married **Aaron Wetzel**. He was born 1849, and died 03 Jul 1947 in York, PA.

Children of Susanna Eisenhauer and Aaron Wetzel are:

640   i.   Harper[7] Wetzel, born 1872; died 1873.

641   ii.   Janny R. Wetzel, born 1874; died 1881.

642   iii.   Franklin Jacob Wetzel, born 1876; died 1940.

643   iv.   Sarah A. Wetzel, born 1878.

644   v.   Raymond Wetzel, born 1880; died 1905.

645   vi.   Minnie M. Wetzel, born 1883.

646   vii.   Otto Robert Wetzel, born 1885.

647   viii.   Grace Pearl Wetzel, born 1888.

648   ix.   Della Mae Wetzel, born 1890; died 1902.

649   x.   Vernon Wetzel, born 1894; died 1913.

472. Amanda Hannah[6] Eisenhauer (Margareta Rebecca[5] Matter, Heinrich[4], Anna Maria[3] Romberger, Balthaser[2], Johann Bartholomus[1]) was born 11 Dec 1861 in Elizabethville, Dauphin Co, PA, and died 25 Aug 1951 in Abilene, Dickinson Co, KS. She married **Christian O Musser**. He was born 10 Nov 1863 in Mt. Joy, PA, and died 14 Apr 1950 in Abilene, Dickinson Co, KS.

Children of Amanda Eisenhauer and Christian Musser are:

650   i.   Beulah E[7] Musser, born 11 Jun 1887 in Abilene, Dickinson Co, KS; died 28 Nov 1945 in KS. She married Abram E Brechbill 1931; born 15 Nov 1881 in Abilene, Dickinson Co, KS; died 07 Aug 1964 in Abilene, Dickinson Co, KS.

651   ii.   Florence Musser, born 19 Mar 1895 in KS; died Apr 1969 in KS. She married A Ray Etherington.

473. David Jacob⁶ Eisenhauer (Margareta Rebecca⁵ Matter, Heinrich⁴, Anna Maria³ Romberger, Balthaser², Johann Bartholomus¹) was born 23 Sep 1863 in Elizabethville, Dauphin, Pennsylvania, and died 10 Mar 1942 in Abilene, Dickinson, Kansas. He married **Ida Elizabeth Stover** 23 Sep 1885 in Hope, Dickinson, Kansas, daughter of Simon Stover and Elizabeth Link. She was born 01 May 1862 in Mt. Sidney, VA, and died 11 Sep 1946 in Abilene, Dickinson Co , Kansas.

Children of David Eisenhauer and Ida Stover are:
+ 652   i.   Arthur Bradford⁷ Eisenhower, born 11 Nov 1886 in Hope, Dickinson, Kansas; died 26 Jan 1958.
   653   ii.   Edgar Newton Eisenhower, born 19 Jan 1889 in Hope, Dickinson, Kansas; died 12 Jul 1971 in Tacoma, Pierce, Washington.
+ 654   iii.   Dwight David Eisenhower, born 14 Oct 1890 in Denison, Grayson, Texas; died 28 Mar 1969 in Washington, District Of, Columbia.
+ 655   iv.   Roy Jacob Eisenhower, born 09 Aug 1892 in Abilene, Kansas, Kansas; died 17 Jun 1942.
   656   v.   Paul Dawson A. Eisenhower, born 12 May 1894 in Abilene, Dickinson, Kansas; died 16 Mar 1895.
   657   vi.   Earl Dewey Eisenhower, born 01 Feb 1898 in Abilene, Dickinson, Kansas; died 18 Dec 1968 in Scottsdale, Maricopa, Arizona. He married Kathryn McIntyre Snyder 29 Apr 1933 in Connellsville, Pennsylvania; born 15 Aug 1909 in Charleroi, Washington, Pennsylvania; died Sep 1986 in Scottsdale, Maricopa, Arizona.
   658   vii.   Milton Stover Eisenhower, born 15 Sep 1899 in Abilene, Dickinson, Kansas; died 02 May 1985 in Baltimore, Maryland. He married Helen Elsie Eakin 12 Oct 1927 in Washington, District Of, Columbia; born 14 Aug 1904 in Manhattan, Riley, Kansas; died 10 Jul 1954.

476. Ira A⁶ Eisenhower (Margareta Rebecca⁵ Matter, Heinrich⁴, Anna Maria³ Romberger, Balthaser², Johann Bartholomus¹) was born 30 Jul 1867 in Elizabethville, Dauphin, Pa, and died 28 Mar 1943 in Los Angeles, CA. He married **Katherine E Dayhoff** 08 Sep 1885 in Abilene, KS. She was born 02 Sep 1865 in PA, and died 30 Dec 1930 in Shawnee Co, KS.

Children of Ira Eisenhower and Katherine Dayhoff are:
+ 659   i.   Mary Rebecca⁷ Eisenhower, born Oct 1886; died 29 May 1937 in Topeka, KS.
   660   ii.   Simon L Eisenhower, born 03 Dec 1895 in Abilene, Dickinson Co, KS; died 03 Dec 1895 in Abilene, Dickinson Co, KS.
   661   iii.   Clinton Eisenhower, born Aft. 1895; died 1943.

486. Christian⁶ Gipple (Anna Maria⁵ Ritzman, Catherine⁴ Matter, Anna Maria³ Romberger, Balthaser², Johann Bartholomus¹) was born Abt. 1865. He married **Julie Ann Knorr**. She was born 1865.

Children of Christian Gipple and Julie Knorr are:
+ 662   i.   Aaron Otto⁷ Gipple, born Abt. 1890.
   663   ii.   Harry Wilson Gipple.
   664   iii.   Martha Mabel Gipple.
   665   iv.   Verna Mary Gipple.

492. Mary Rebecca⁶ Gipple (Anna Maria⁵ Ritzman, Catherine⁴ Matter, Anna Maria³ Romberger, Balthaser², Johann Bartholomus¹) She married **Aaron D Knorr**. He was born 1857.

Child of Mary Gipple and Aaron Knorr is:
+ 666   i.   Susan Alice⁷ Knorr.

494. Michael⁶ Matter (Christopher⁵, Michael⁴, Anna Maria³ Romberger, Balthaser², Johann Bartholomus¹) was born Abt. 1855. He married **Sarah Anne Keen**. She was born Abt. 1855.

Child of Michael Matter and Sarah Keen is:
+ 667   i.   Clara Ida Adeline⁷ Matter, born Abt. 1880; died 09 Jun 1955 in Tower City, Schuylkill Co., PA.

513. Jefferson⁶ Wiest (Sarah⁵ Rickert, Sarah Salome⁴ Romberger, Adam³, Balthaser², Johann

Bartholomus[1]) was born 06 Jul 1855 in Klingerstown, Schuylkill Co.,PA, and died 1893 in San Antonio, TX. He married **(1) Emma Jane Rickert** Abt. 1878. She was born Unknown in Williamstown, Dauphin Co., PA, and died Unknown. He married **(2) Mary Poteicher** Aft. 1882.

Children of Jefferson Wiest and Emma Rickert are:

    668   i.   William[7] Wiest, born Abt. 1879 in Klingerstown, Schuylkill Co., PA; died Unknown.

    669   ii.   Pauline Minerva Wiest, born 15 Jun 1881 in Klingerstown, Schuylkill Co., PA.

Children of Jefferson Wiest and Mary Poteicher are:

    670   i.   Sally[7] Wiest, born in Klingerstown, Schuylkill Co., PA. She married Isaac Bowman.

    671   ii.   Edward Wiest.

    672   iii.   Harry Wiest, died 1950 in Philadelphia, PA.

518. Alvin Joseph Adam[6] Poffenberger (Adam R.[5] Paffenberger, Lydia Ann[4] Romberger, Adam[3], Balthaser[2], Johann Bartholomus[1]) was born 12 Jan 1872 in Klingerstown, Schuylkill Co., PA, and died 26 May 1931 in Portland, Multnomah, OR. He married **Ida Celara Maurer** 28 Dec 1892 in Kalama, Cowlitz Co., WA. She was born 18 Feb 1875 in Klingerstown, Schuylkill Co., PA, and died 27 Nov 1941 in Chinook, Pacific Co., WA.

Children of Alvin Poffenberger and Ida Maurer are:

    673   i.   Roy Alvin[7] Poffenberger, born 1893 in Stella, Cowlitz Co., WA. He married Anna ?.

+ 674   ii.   Flora Jennie May Poffenberger, born 1895 in Stella, Cowlitz Co., WA; died 14 Dec 1918 in Portland Multnomah, OR.

+ 675   iii.   Roby Earl Poffenberger, born 26 Nov 1896 in Stella, Cowlitz Co., WA; died 30 Aug 1971 in Portland Multnomah, OR.

    676   iv.   Hattie L Poffenberger, born 1905 in Portland Multnomah, OR. She married John Schuler.

523. Laurence Orwig[6] Wiest (Samuel L.[5], Hannah[4] Romberger, Adam[3], Balthaser[2], Johann Bartholomus[1]) was born 14 Jun 1867 in Philadelphia, PA. He married **Millie J. ?**.

Children of Laurence Wiest and Millie ? are:

    677   i.   Clayton L.[7] Wiest, born 29 Jul 1891; died 28 Apr 1892.

    678   ii.   Charles W. Wiest, born 19 Mar 1895; died 21 Jan 1903.

524. Warren Orwig[6] Wiest (Samuel L.[5], Hannah[4] Romberger, Adam[3], Balthaser[2], Johann Bartholomus[1]) was born 20 Oct 1868 in Philadelphia, PA.

Children of Warren Orwig Wiest are:

    679   i.   Paul[7] Wiest.

    680   ii.   Russell Wiest.

    681   iii.   Margaret Wiest.

    682   iv.   George Wiest.

    683   v.   Corinne Wiest.

532. Charles A.[6] Wiest (Oliver[5], Hannah[4] Romberger, Adam[3], Balthaser[2], Johann Bartholomus[1]) was born in Pillow, Jordan Twp., Northumberland Co., PA, and died 1947. He married **(1) Mamie Zerb**. He married **(2) Mamie ?**.

Child of Charles Wiest and Mamie Zerb is:

    684   i.   Loyetta[7] Wiest, born in Pillow, Dauphin Co., PA. She married Robert Spotts 21 Oct 1933 in Clearfield, Clearfield Co., PA; born Unknown in Dalmatia RD, Lower Mahanoy Twp., Northumberland Co., PA.

Generation No. 7

562. Katie L.[7] Travitz (Simon[6], Elizabeth[5] Minnich, Anna Maria[4] Matter, Anna Maria[3] Romberger, Balthaser[2], Johann Bartholomus[1]) was born 06 Dec 1885 in Jackson Twp., Dauphin Co., PA, and died 24 Dec 1955 in Detroit, Wayne Co., MI. She married **Charles A. Machamer** 1903 in Pennsylvania. He was born in Dauphin Co., PA.

Child of Katie Travitz and Charles Machamer is:

685   i.   Charlotte M.[8] Machamer, born 23 Aug 1904 in Jackson Twp., Dauphin Co., PA. She married Horace E. Ray.

563. Amos F.[7] Minnich (Josiah[6], Michael[5], Anna Maria[4] Matter, Anna Maria[3] Romberger, Balthaser[2], Johann Bartholomus[1]) was born 27 Nov 1869 in Jackson Twp., Dauphin Co., PA. He married **Iva Cardella Schreffler** 22 Dec 1897 in Curtin, Schuylkill Co., PA. She was born Abt. 1876 in Curtin, Schuylkill Co., PA.

Children of Amos Minnich and Iva Schreffler are:

686   i.   Mary[8] Minnich. She married Ralph Kratzer.
687   ii.   Ethel E. Minnich, born 04 Oct 1907.
688   iii.   Daughter Minnich.
689   iv.   Stanley Minnich, born 05 Aug 1904.

566. Claude E.[7] Minnich (Josiah[6], Michael[5], Anna Maria[4] Matter, Anna Maria[3] Romberger, Balthaser[2], Johann Bartholomus[1]) was born 18 Mar 1875 in Jackson Twp., Dauphin Co., PA, and died 1962 in Albany, Albany Co., NY. He married **Bertha O. Williams**. She was born 1877 in Wiconisco, Dauphin Co., PA, and died 02 Mar 1967 in Albany, Albany Co., NY.

Children of Claude Minnich and Bertha Williams are:

690   i.   Robert[8] Minnich, born Abt. 1901.
691   ii.   Lola Minnich, born in Williamstown, Dauphin Co., PA. She married ? Kramer.
692   iii.   Millie Minnich, born in Dauphin Co., PA. She married ? Miller.
693   iv.   Sara Minnich. She married ? MacFarlane.
694   v.   Betty Minnich, born in Factoryville, PA. She married ? Christ.

568. Edward Austin[7] Minnich (Josiah[6], Michael[5], Anna Maria[4] Matter, Anna Maria[3] Romberger, Balthaser[2], Johann Bartholomus[1]) was born 12 Feb 1877 in Jackson Twp., Dauphin Co., PA, and died 09 Oct 1958 in Harrisburg, Dauphin Co., PA. He married **Ardella Catherine Witmer** 1895. She was born 08 Dec 1879 in Gratz, Lykens Twp., Dauphin Co., PA, and died 31 Dec 1977 in Dauphin Co., PA.

Children of Edward Minnich and Ardella Witmer are:

695   i.   Ellen Irene[8] Minnich, born 13 Jun 1895 in Wiconisco, Dauphin Co., PA; died 27 Jul 1979. She married Willis E. Dietrich; born Abt. 1891 in Dauphin Co., PA.
696   ii.   Mary Rebecca Minnich, born 29 Oct 1897 in Wiconisco, Dauphin Co., PA. She married Clarence Theodore Enders 12 May 1917 in Lykens Twp., Dauphin Co., PA; born 29 May 1896 in Lykens Twp., Dauphin Co., PA.
697   iii.   Ruby Royal Minnich, born 14 Oct 1899 in Wiconisco, Dauphin Co., PA. She married Sherman Rowe; born Abt. 1895 in Lykens Twp., Dauphin Co., PA.
698   iv.   Edward Eugene Minnich, born 03 Sep 1901 in Wiconisco, Dauphin Co., PA. He married Dorothy E. Cordy.
+   699   v.   Laura E. Minnich, born 07 Jun 1903; died Abt. 1985.
700   vi.   John F. Minnich, born 24 Aug 1906 in Dauphin Co., PA. He married Florence P. Cooper 1925 in Hagerstown, Washington Co., MD.
701   vii.   Harry D. Minnich, born 24 Jan 1909 in Dauphin Co., PA; died 16 Dec 1989 in Dauphin Co., PA. He married Esther M. Bowman.
702   viii.   Marlin L. Minnich, born 17 Jun 1911 in Dauphin Co., PA; died 03 Jul 1990 in Dauphin Co., PA. He married Rayetta Robinson.
703   ix.   Margaret I. Minnich, born 13 Aug 1917 in Dauphin Co., PA. She married Henry W. Ibbserson.

570. Carrie Elizabeth[7] Minnich (Josiah[6], Michael[5], Anna Maria[4] Matter, Anna Maria[3] Romberger, Balthaser[2], Johann Bartholomus[1]) was born 18 Mar 1889 in Lykens Twp., Dauphin Co., PA, and died 14 May

1971 in Kingston, Luzerne Co., PA. She married **George Raymond C. Lebo** 19 Mar 1910 in Harrisburg, Dauphin Co., PA. He was born 23 Oct 1889 in Lykens Twp., Dauphin Co., PA, and died 07 Dec 1956 in Shenandoah, Schuylkill Co., PA.

Children of Carrie Minnich and George Lebo are:

704   i.   Elsie[8] Lebo, born 18 Sep 1910 in Lykens Twp., Dauphin Co., PA. She married Nelson C. W. Stauffer 14 Oct 1933 in Elmira, Chemung Co., NY.

705   ii.   Dorothy Lebo, born 06 Feb 1912 in Lykens Twp., Dauphin Co., PA. She married William Miller.

706   iii.   Carl C. Lebo, born 19 Nov 1913 in Lykens Twp., Dauphin Co., PA. He married Anna Melusky 19 Jun 1935 in Shenandoah, Schuylkill Co., PA.

707   iv.   Robert H. Lebo, born 06 Oct 1915 in Schuylkill Co., PA. He married Margaret Anderson Jun 1937 in Shenandoah, Schuylkill Co., PA.

572. Leona M.[7] Minnich (Josiah[6], Michael[5], Anna Maria[4] Matter, Anna Maria[3] Romberger, Balthaser[2], Johann Bartholomus[1]) was born 27 Jul 1894 in Lykens Twp., Dauphin Co., PA, and died 10 Aug 1973 in Shenandoah, Schuylkill Co., PA. She married **(1) Roy Jones** 07 Apr 1917. He was born Abt. 1890 in Lykens Twp., Dauphin Co., PA, and died 1938. She married **(2) Howard Frost** Aft. 1939. He was born Abt. 1890 in Lykens Twp., Dauphin Co., PA, and died 1989 in Schuylkill Co., PA.

Child of Leona Minnich and Roy Jones is:

708   i.   Leroy[8] Jones.

577. Aaron Frank[7] Minnich (Cyrus[6], Michael[5], Anna Maria[4] Matter, Anna Maria[3] Romberger, Balthaser[2], Johann Bartholomus[1]) was born 18 Aug 1873 in Armstrong Valley, Jackson Twp., Dauphin Co., PA, and died 22 Dec 1937 in Tower City, Schuylkill Co., PA. He married **Clara Ida Adeline Matter** 20 Apr 1898, daughter of Michael Matter and Sarah Keen. She was born Abt. 1880, and died 09 Jun 1955 in Tower City, Schuylkill Co., PA.

Children of Aaron Minnich and Clara Matter are:

709   i.   Myrtle Irene[8] Minnich, born 24 Sep 1898 in Tower City, Schuylkill Co., PA; died 11 Apr 1967 in Tower City, Schuykilii Co., PA. She married Walter E. Brown 22 Jun 1918 in Tower City, Schuylkill Co., PA.

710   ii.   Harold Leroy Minnich, born 27 Jan 1901 in Tower City, Schuylkill Co., PA; died 13 Oct 1944 in Tower City, Schuykilii Co., PA. He married Beatrice Shomper 01 Dec 1920 in Williamstown, Dauphin Co., PA.

711   iii.   Erma Estella Minnich, born 28 Oct 1902 in Tower City, Schuylkill Co., PA; died 20 Mar 1987. She married Edward J. Coles 16 Nov 1921.

712   iv.   Sarah Caroline Minnich, born 10 Nov 1903 in Tower City, Schuylkill Co., PA; died 18 Jun 1960 in Tower City, Schuykilii Co., PA. She married (1) Clarence Yohe Oct 1925. She married (2) Morris L. Neumeister 21 Jun 1930 in Pottsville, Schuylkill Co., PA.

713   v.   William Grant Minnich, born 06 Jun 1905 in Tower City, Schuylkill Co., PA; died 23 Jan 1970 in Tower City, Schuykilii Co., PA. He married Ruth L. Bechtel 12 Mar 1927 in Tower City, Schuylkill Co., PA.

714   vi.   Anna Elizabeth Minnich, born 16 May 1907 in Tower City, Schuylkill Co., PA; died 29 Jan 1988 in Tower City, Schuykilii Co., PA.

715   vii.   Marlin Oswald Minnich, born 08 Jun 1909 in Tower City, Schuylkill Co., PA; died 02 Jul 1981 in Orwin, Schuylkill Co., PA. He married Vesta A. Carl Apr 1935 in Tower City, Schuylkill Co., PA.

+ 716   viii.   Arthur Franklin Minnich, born 09 Sep 1911 in Tower City, Schuylkill Co., PA; died 14 Apr 1991 in Tower City, Schuylkill Co., PA.

717   ix.   Son Minnich, born 16 Mar 1913 in Tower City, Schuylkill Co., PA; died 27 Apr 1913 in Tower City, Schuylkill Co., PA.

+ 718   x.   Mary Frances Minnich, born 26 May 1914 in Tower City, Schuylkill Co., PA; died 05 Jun 1976 in Tower City, Schuykilii Co., PA.

719   xi.   Russell Leo Minnich, born 08 Jun 1916 in Tower City, Schuylkill Co., PA; died 15 Jun 1916 in Tower City, Schuylkill Co., PA.

720   xii.   Lynn Arlington Minnich, born 13 Oct 1918 in Tower City, Schuylkill Co., PA; died 18 Sep 1963 in Williamstown, Dauphin Co., PA. He married Margaret T. Perseponko 06 Feb 1943 in Williamstown, Dauphin Co., PA.

721   xiii.   Donald Mark Minnich, born 08 Dec 1920 in Tower City, Schuylkill Co., PA; died 02 Jan 1923 in Tower City, Schuylkill Co., PA.

722 xiv. Robert David Minnich, born 03 Jun 1922 in Tower City, Schuylkill Co., PA; died 23 Jun 1922 in Tower City, Schuylkill Co., PA.

586. Charlotta Lucreta[7] Minnich (Uriah[6], Michael[5], Anna Maria[4] Matter, Anna Maria[3] Romberger, Balthaser[2], Johann Bartholomus[1]) was born Abt. 1862 in Washington Twp., Dauphin Co., PA. She married **Charles N. Coles** Jan 1900 in Lykens Twp., Dauphin Co., PA. He was born Abt. 1858.

Child of Charlotta Minnich and Charles Coles is:
723 i. Mark Stanley[8] Coles, born 18 Aug 1901 in Dauphin Co., PA; died 1950 in Pennsylvania. He married Ruth A. Deibler.

587. Martha J.[7] Minnich (Uriah[6], Michael[5], Anna Maria[4] Matter, Anna Maria[3] Romberger, Balthaser[2], Johann Bartholomus[1]) was born 1864 in Washington Twp., Dauphin Co., PA, and died 1927 in Lykens Twp., Dauphin Co., PA. She married **William Morris**. He was born Abt. 1860 in Washington Twp., Dauphin Co., PA.

Children of Martha Minnich and William Morris are:
724 i. Arthur[8] Morris, born Abt. 1886 in Washington Twp., Dauphin Co., PA. He married Mary Holloway.
725 ii. William Morris, Jr, born Abt. 1888 in Washington Twp., Dauphin Co., PA. He married Ruth Steely.
726 iii. Estella M. Morris, born 24 Mar 1898 in Washington Twp., Dauphin Co., PA; died 01 Jul 1981 in Lykens Twp., Dauphin Co., PA. She married William Stroup 15 Aug 1915; born Abt. 1895.
727 iv. Raymond Morris, born Abt. 1892 in Washington Twp., Dauphin Co., PA. He married Anna Beale.

588. James[7] Minnich (Uriah[6], Michael[5], Anna Maria[4] Matter, Anna Maria[3] Romberger, Balthaser[2], Johann Bartholomus[1]) was born 1865 in Washington Twp., Dauphin Co., PA, and died 06 Jul 1940 in Lykens Twp., Dauphin Co., PA. He married **Viola Harmon**. She was born Abt. 1869 in Dauphin Co., PA.

Children of James Minnich and Viola Harmon are:
728 i. Martha Rebecca[8] Minnich, born 1887 in Washington Twp., Dauphin Co., PA; died 08 Nov 1918 in Pennsylvania. She married George Coles.
729 ii. Lucy Minnich, born 29 Dec 1889 in Washington Twp., Dauphin Co., PA; died 18 Feb 1965 in Philadelphia, Philadelphia Co., PA. She married Robert Collins.

589. William[7] Minnich (Uriah[6], Michael[5], Anna Maria[4] Matter, Anna Maria[3] Romberger, Balthaser[2], Johann Bartholomus[1]) was born 1867 in Washington Twp., Dauphin Co., PA. He married **(1) Mary Salada**. She was born Abt. 1871 in Washington Twp., Dauphin Co., PA. He married **(2) Sally Tovy**. She was born Abt. 1871 in Dauphin Co., PA.

Child of William Minnich and Mary Salada is:
730 i. Hallet[8] Minnich, born Abt. 1893 in Washington Twp., Dauphin Co., PA.

590. Ira Oscar[7] Minnich (Uriah[6], Michael[5], Anna Maria[4] Matter, Anna Maria[3] Romberger, Balthaser[2], Johann Bartholomus[1]) was born 03 Sep 1870 in Washington Twp., Dauphin Co., PA, and died in Lykens Twp., Dauphin Co., PA. He married **Kate Schaffner**. She was born 01 Feb 1876 in Lykens Twp., Dauphin Co., PA, and died 14 Oct 1927 in Lykens Twp., Dauphin Co., PA.

Children of Ira Minnich and Kate Schaffner are:
731 i. Mervin[8] Minnich, born Abt. 1896 in Lykens Twp., Dauphin Co., PA; died in Lykens Twp., Dauphin Co., PA.
732 ii. Claude Minnich, born Abt. 1898 in Lykens Twp., Dauphin Co., PA; died in Lykens Twp., Dauphin Co., PA.
733 iii. Louis Minnich, born Abt. 1900 in Lykens Twp., Dauphin Co., PA; died in Lykens Twp., Dauphin Co., PA. He married Catherine ?.
734 iv. Florence Minnich, born Abt. 1902 in Lykens Twp., Dauphin Co., PA; died in Lykens Twp., Dauphin Co., PA.

591. Mary Terressa[7] Minnich (Uriah[6], Michael[5], Anna Maria[4] Matter, Anna Maria[3] Romberger, Balthaser[2], Johann Bartholomus[1]) was born 08 Dec 1871 in Dauphin Co., PA, and died 1918. She married **William Reddinger**. He was born Abt. 1867.

Children of Mary Minnich and William Reddinger are:
735   i.   Charlotte Cardella[8] Reddinger, born Abt. 1893. She married Joseph Kelly.
736   ii.   Daniel Reddinger, born Abt. 1895. He married Beulah Hossler.

594. Cardella Helen[7] Minnich (Uriah[6], Michael[5], Anna Maria[4] Matter, Anna Maria[3] Romberger, Balthaser[2], Johann Bartholomus[1]) was born 21 Jun 1883 in Wiconisco, Dauphin Co., PA, and died 1929 in Wiconisco, Dauphin Co., PA. She married **William Abel Werner**. He was born 02 Jan 1885 in Lykens Twp., Dauphin Co., PA, and died in Wiconisco, Dauphin Co., PA.

Children of Cardella Minnich and William Werner are:
737   i.   Melva[8] Werner, born 18 Aug 1914 in Lykens Twp., Dauphin Co., PA.
738   ii.   Mark Eugene Werner, born 02 Sep 1923 in Mechanicsburg, Cumberland Co., PA; died 21 Apr 1982 in Lewisberry, York Co., PA.
739   iii.   Harold E. Werner, born 26 Jul 1929 in Mechanicsburg, Cumberland Co., PA.

595. Clarence[7] Minnich (Uriah[6], Michael[5], Anna Maria[4] Matter, Anna Maria[3] Romberger, Balthaser[2], Johann Bartholomus[1]) was born Abt. 1888 in Wiconisco, Dauphin Co., PA, and died 1965. He married **Myra Soloman**. She was born Abt. 1892 in Dauphin Co., PA.

Children of Clarence Minnich and Myra Soloman are:
740   i.   Jeremiah[8] Minnich.
741   ii.   Maurice Minnich, born 10 Mar 1914 in Dauphin Co., PA.

600. William[7] Hoover (Alfred[6], Catherine[5] Minnich, Anna Maria[4] Matter, Anna Maria[3] Romberger, Balthaser[2], Johann Bartholomus[1]) was born 1864, and died 1922. He married **Anna Romberger**.

Children of William Hoover and Anna Romberger are:
742   i.   Sallie[8] Hoover. She married John Hilbert.
743   ii.   Mary Hoover. She married Charles Rebuck.
744   iii.   Mark Hoover. He married Ruth Zimmerman.
745   iv.   Henry Hoover. He married Florence Yeartz.

612. Charles Warren[7] Lentz (Lydia A.[6] Wilbert, Catharina[5] Matter, Heinrich[4], Anna Maria[3] Romberger, Balthaser[2], Johann Bartholomus[1]) was born 02 Dec 1884 in Dauphin County, PA, and died 12 Aug 1968 in Millersburg, Dauphin County, PA. He married **Minnie Mae Riegle**. She was born 27 Jun 1889 in Mifflin Township, Dauphin County, PA, and died 17 Sep 1967 in Millersburg, Dauphin County, PA.

Children of Charles Lentz and Minnie Riegle are:
746   i.   LIVING[8]. He married (1) LIVING. He married (2) LIVING.
747   ii.   Clair Riegle Lentz, born 04 Sep 1910; died 17 Sep 1975 in Goldsboro, NC. He married LIVING.
748   iii.   Richard Riegle Lentz, born 16 Sep 1912; died 01 Feb 1951. He married (1) LIVING. He married (2) LIVING.
+   749   iv.   Eugene Clinton Lentz, born 01 Mar 1915 in Pennsylvania; died 11 Feb 1945 in MIA World War II Philippines.
750   v.   Robert Calvin Lentz, born 19 Nov 1917; died 01 Jul 1997 in Baltimore, MD. He married LIVING.
751   vi.   William Benjamin Lentz, born 14 May 1920; died 18 Sep 1977 in Millersburg, Dauphin County, PA. He married LIVING.
752   vii.   Paul Jacob Lentz, born 20 Sep 1922; died 03 Nov 1994 in Leeds, MA. He married LIVING.

617. Martha Rebecca[7] Witter (Mary Ann[6] Eisenhauer, Margareta Rebecca[5] Matter, Heinrich[4], Anna Maria[3] Romberger, Balthaser[2], Johann Bartholomus[1]) was born 27 Sep 1871 in Millersburg, PA, and died 20

Aug 1955 in Upland, CA. She married **Joseph Harvey Gish**. He was born 20 Sep 1875 in Liverpool, PA, and died Sep 1967 in Upland, CA.

Child of Martha Witter and Joseph Gish is:
    753   i.   Evelyn W[8] Gish, born 16 Jan 1912 in Abilene, Dickinson Co, KS; died 15 Dec 2001 in PA. She married Paul Edward Book; born 03 Mar 1919 in Custer Co, OK; died 21 Dec 1998 in Waynesboro, PA.

630. Lillian Elizabeth[7] Haldeman (Catherine Ann[6] Eisenhauer, Margareta Rebecca[5] Matter, Heinrich[4], Anna Maria[3] Romberger, Balthaser[2], Johann Bartholomus[1]) was born 27 Aug 1878. She married **Samuel W Brehm**. He was born in Palmyra, PA.

Children of Lillian Haldeman and Samuel Brehm are:
    754   i.   Zena Leroy[8] Brehm, born 07 Jan 1903.
    755   ii.   Eldred H Brehm, born 28 Nov 1904.
    756   iii. Irma Aurelia Brehm.
    757   iv. Faithe Marie Brehm.

633. Katherine Ann[7] Haldeman (Catherine Ann[6] Eisenhauer, Margareta Rebecca[5] Matter, Heinrich[4], Anna Maria[3] Romberger, Balthaser[2], Johann Bartholomus[1]) was born 20 Jul 1883 in Hope, KS, and died 28 Nov 1959 in Abilene, Dickinson Co, KS. She married **Abraham Lincoln Epler** 05 Nov 1902 in Hope, KS. He was born Jun 1876 in Hummelstown, PA, and died 16 Jun 1923 in Gladwin, MI.

Children of Katherine Haldeman and Abraham Epler are:
    758   i.   Ruel Milton[8] Epler, born 14 Mar 1904; died 03 Feb 1977 in Wichita, KS.
    759   ii.   Martha Irene Epler, born 12 May 1906 in Whitehouse, OH; died 08 Oct 1924 in Detroit, KS.
    760   iii. Grant Barton Epler, born 29 May 1907; died 18 Jun 1988 in Lapeer, MI.
    761   iv. Russell Emerson Epler, born 09 Jun 1909 in Canton, KS; died 20 Apr 1985 in Rochester, MI.
    762   v.   Blanche Pearl Epler, born 20 May 1918 in Gladwin, MI; died 24 Nov 2003 in KS. She married m Scheideman.
    763   vi. ? Epler. She married Voiland Engle; born 10 Sep 1922.
    764   vii. Grace Lilian Epler, died Aft. 1985. She married m Campbell.
    765 viii. Paul Mark Epler, died Aft. 1985.

635. John Henry[7] Haldeman (Catherine Ann[6] Eisenhauer, Margareta Rebecca[5] Matter, Heinrich[4], Anna Maria[3] Romberger, Balthaser[2], Johann Bartholomus[1]) was born 09 Jun 1886 in Hope, KS, and died 12 Dec 1969. He married **Viola C Rock** 11 Apr 1909 in Hope, KS. She was born 24 Feb 1889 in Illinois, and died 24 Jul 1976 in Abilene, Dickinson Co, KS.

Child of John Haldeman and Viola Rock is:
    766   i.   Veri C[8] Haldeman, born 29 Jun 1911; died 01 Sep 1923 in Abilene, Dickinson Co, KS.

637. Harry Milton[7] Haldeman (Catherine Ann[6] Eisenhauer, Margareta Rebecca[5] Matter, Heinrich[4], Anna Maria[3] Romberger, Balthaser[2], Johann Bartholomus[1]) was born 22 Apr 1889 in KS, and died 04 Jul 1968 in Hillsboro, KS. He married **Ollie B Rock** 29 Nov 1911. She was born 04 Nov 1890, and died 10 Feb 1981 in Topeka, KS.

Child of Harry Haldeman and Ollie Rock is:
    767   i.   Eunic O[8] Haldeman, born 1913 in KS; died 1953. She married ? Nincehelser.

652. Arthur Bradford[7] Eisenhower (David Jacob[6] Eisenhauer, Margareta Rebecca[5] Matter, Heinrich[4], Anna Maria[3] Romberger, Balthaser[2], Johann Bartholomus[1]) was born 11 Nov 1886 in Hope, Dickinson, Kansas, and died 26 Jan 1958. He married **(1) Alida B ?**. She was born 17 Feb 1889. He married **(2) Louis Sondra Grieb** 03 Sep 1926.

Child of Arthur Eisenhower and Alida ? is:

+ 768 i. Katherine[8] Eisenhower, born 02 Jul 1914.

654. Dwight David[7] Eisenhower (David Jacob[6] Eisenhauer, Margareta Rebecca[5] Matter, Heinrich[4], Anna Maria[3] Romberger, Balthaser[2], Johann Bartholomus[1]) was born 14 Oct 1890 in Denison, Grayson, Texas, and died 28 Mar 1969 in Washington, District Of, Columbia. He married **Mary Geneva Doud** 01 Jul 1916 in Denver, Denver, Colorado, daughter of John Doud and Elivera Carlson. She was born 14 Nov 1896 in Boone, Boone, Iowa, and died 31 Oct 1979 in Washington, D.C..

Children of Dwight Eisenhower and Mary Doud are:
+ 769 i. John Sheldon Doud[8] Eisenhower, born 1923.
 770 ii. Doud Dwight Eisenhower, born 24 Sep 1917 in San Antonio, Bexar, Texas; died 02 Jan 1921 in Camp Meade, Maryland.

655. Roy Jacob[7] Eisenhower (David Jacob[6] Eisenhauer, Margareta Rebecca[5] Matter, Heinrich[4], Anna Maria[3] Romberger, Balthaser[2], Johann Bartholomus[1]) was born 09 Aug 1892 in Abilene, Kansas, Kansas, and died 17 Jun 1942. He married **Edna Alice Shade** 18 Nov 1917 in Ellsworth, Ellsworth, Kansas. She was born 13 Sep 1891 in Ellis City, Ellis, Kansas, and died 26 Jun 1989 in Denver, Denver, Colorado.

Children of Roy Eisenhower and Edna Shade are:
 771 i. Patricia[8] Eisenhower, born 1918.
 772 ii. Peggy J Eisenhower, born 1923.
 773 iii. Lloyd E Eisenhower, born 1925.
 774 iv. Roy J Eisenhower, born Abt. 1930.

659. Mary Rebecca[7] Eisenhower (Ira A[6], Margareta Rebecca[5] Matter, Heinrich[4], Anna Maria[3] Romberger, Balthaser[2], Johann Bartholomus[1]) was born Oct 1886, and died 29 May 1937 in Topeka, KS. She married **Jacob M Brandt**. He was born 02 Jul 1881 in Detroit, KS.

Children of Mary Eisenhower and Jacob Brandt are:
 775 i. Preston L[8] Brandt, born 07 Jan 1909; died 11 Apr 1977 in San Antonio, Bexar, Texas.
 776 ii. Orville E Brandt, born 28 Feb 1917.
 777 iii. Victor O Brandt, born 10 Sep 1920; died 16 Nov 1999.

662. Aaron Otto[7] Gipple (Christian[6], Anna Maria[5] Ritzman, Catherine[4] Matter, Anna Maria[3] Romberger, Balthaser[2], Johann Bartholomus[1]) was born Abt. 1890.

Child of Aaron Otto Gipple is:
+ 778 i. Gerald[8] Gipple, born Abt. 1915.

666. Susan Alice[7] Knorr (Mary Rebecca[6] Gipple, Anna Maria[5] Ritzman, Catherine[4] Matter, Anna Maria[3] Romberger, Balthaser[2], Johann Bartholomus[1]) She married **Christopher John Olsen Almlee**.

Child of Susan Knorr and Christopher Almlee is:
+ 779 i. Bernice Mildred[8] Almlee.

667. Clara Ida Adeline[7] Matter (Michael[6], Christopher[5], Michael[4], Anna Maria[3] Romberger, Balthaser[2], Johann Bartholomus[1]) was born Abt. 1880, and died 09 Jun 1955 in Tower City, Schuylkill Co., PA. She married **Aaron Frank Minnich** 20 Apr 1898, son of Cyrus Minnich and Caroline McCulley. He was born 18 Aug 1873 in Armstrong Valley, Jackson Twp., Dauphin Co., PA, and died 22 Dec 1937 in Tower City, Schuylkill Co., PA.

Children are listed above under (577) Aaron Frank Minnich.

674. Flora Jennie May[7] Poffenberger (Alvin Joseph Adam[6], Adam R.[5] Paffenberger, Lydia Ann[4]

Romberger, Adam[3], Balthaser[2], Johann Bartholomus[1]) was born 1895 in Stella, Cowlitz Co., WA, and died 14 Dec 1918 in Portland Multnomah, OR. She married **F.J. Hissey** Abt. 1917 in Portland, Multnomah Co., OR. He was born Abt. 1890.

Child of Flora Poffenberger and F.J. Hissey is:

    780   i.   Infant Daughter[8] ?, born 1918 in Portland Multnomah, OR; died 1918 in Portland Multnomah, OR.

675. **Roby Earl[7] Poffenberger** (Alvin Joseph Adam[6], Adam R.[5] Paffenberger, Lydia Ann[4] Romberger, Adam[3], Balthaser[2], Johann Bartholomus[1]) was born 26 Nov 1896 in Stella, Cowlitz Co., WA, and died 30 Aug 1971 in Portland Multnomah, OR. He married **Hazel Margreta Carlson** 17 Sep 1921. She was born 26 Jun 1900 in Skamokawa, Wahkaikum Co., WA, and died 13 Oct 1976 in Portland Multnomah, OR.

Child of Roby Poffenberger and Hazel Carlson is:

+   781   i.   June Madeline[8] Poffenberger, born 08 Dec 1925 in Portland Multnomah, OR.

Generation No. 8

699. **Laura E.[8] Minnich** (Edward Austin[7], Josiah[6], Michael[5], Anna Maria[4] Matter, Anna Maria[3] Romberger, Balthaser[2], Johann Bartholomus[1]) was born 07 Jun 1903, and died Abt. 1985. She married **Harry Harper Hepler**. He was born 26 Jan 1904, and died Abt. 1985.

Children of Laura Minnich and Harry Hepler are:

    782   i.   Lorraine[9] Hepler, born 24 Oct 1923 in Dauphin Co., PA. She married ? Harner.
    783   ii.   Harry Harper Hepler, born 18 Jun 1927 in Dauphin Co., PA. He married Hilda Davis; born Abt. 1928.
+   784   iii.   Glenn Hepler, born 28 Jul 1928 in Dauphin Co., PA.
+   785   iv.   Jack Arland Hepler, born 03 Feb 1931 in Dauphin Co., PA.
    786   v.   Kenneth Hepler, born 29 Apr 1933 in Dauphin Co., PA. He married Geraldine Hentz.
    787   vi.   Beverly Jane Hepler, born 01 Sep 1936 in Dauphin Co., PA. She married James Snyder.

716. **Arthur Franklin[8] Minnich** (Aaron Frank[7], Cyrus[6], Michael[5], Anna Maria[4] Matter, Anna Maria[3] Romberger, Balthaser[2], Johann Bartholomus[1]) was born 09 Sep 1911 in Tower City, Schuylkill Co., PA, and died 14 Apr 1991 in Tower City, Schuylkill Co., PA. He married **Mary Elizabeth Molko** 05 Oct 1935 in Lykens Twp., Dauphin Co., PA. She was born Abt. 1905.

Child of Arthur Minnich and Mary Molko is:

+   788   i.   John Arthur[9] Minnich, born Abt. 1930.

718. **Mary Frances[8] Minnich** (Aaron Frank[7], Cyrus[6], Michael[5], Anna Maria[4] Matter, Anna Maria[3] Romberger, Balthaser[2], Johann Bartholomus[1]) was born 26 May 1914 in Tower City, Schuylkill Co., PA, and died 05 Jun 1976 in Tower City, Schuykilii Co., PA. She married **Edwin Frosten Knorr** 14 Aug 1937 in Tower City, PA. He was born 26 May 1914 in Tower City, PA, and died 01 Dec 1978 in Tower City, PA.

Children of Mary Minnich and Edwin Knorr are:

+   789   i.   Edwin Frances[9] Knorr, born Abt. 1940.
    790   ii.   Karen Kay Knorr, born Abt. 1940. She married Darrell E Shoop Abt. 1955; born Abt. 1930.

749. **Eugene Clinton[8] Lentz** (Charles Warren[7], Lydia A.[6] Wilbert, Catharina[5] Matter, Heinrich[4], Anna Maria[3] Romberger, Balthaser[2], Johann Bartholomus[1]) was born 01 Mar 1915 in Pennsylvania, and died 11 Feb 1945 in MIA World War II Philippines. He married **Marie Lanigan** 23 Dec 1938. She died 1989.

Child of Eugene Lentz and Marie Lanigan is:

+   791   i.   Living[9].

768. **Katherine[8] Eisenhower** (Arthur Bradford[7], David Jacob[6] Eisenhauer, Margareta Rebecca[5] Matter,

Heinrich[4], Anna Maria[3] Romberger, Balthaser[2], Johann Bartholomus[1]) was born 02 Jul 1914. She married **Berton Roueche** 28 Oct 1936. He was born 16 Apr 1910.

Child of Katherine Eisenhower and Berton Roueche is:
    792   i.   Arthur Bradford[9] Roueche, born 16 Nov 1942.

    769. John Sheldon Doud[8] Eisenhower (Dwight David[7], David Jacob[6] Eisenhauer, Margareta Rebecca[5] Matter, Heinrich[4], Anna Maria[3] Romberger, Balthaser[2], Johann Bartholomus[1]) was born 1923. He married **Barbara Jean Thompson** Jul 1947. She was born Abt. 1925.

Children of John Eisenhower and Barbara Thompson are:
+ 793   i.   Dwight David[9] Eisenhower, born 31 Mar 1948.
    794   ii. Barbara Anne Eisenhower, born 30 May 1949.
    795   iii. Susan Elaine Eisenhower, born 31 Dec 1951.
    796   iv. Mary Jean Eisenhower, born 21 Dec 1955.

    778. Gerald[8] Gipple (Aaron Otto[7], Christian[6], Anna Maria[5] Ritzman, Catherine[4] Matter, Anna Maria[3] Romberger, Balthaser[2], Johann Bartholomus[1]) was born Abt. 1915.

Child of Gerald Gipple is:
    797   i.   Carol[9] Gipple, born Abt. 1940.

    779. Bernice Mildred[8] Almlee (Susan Alice[7] Knorr, Mary Rebecca[6] Gipple, Anna Maria[5] Ritzman, Catherine[4] Matter, Anna Maria[3] Romberger, Balthaser[2], Johann Bartholomus[1])

Child of Bernice Mildred Almlee is:
+ 798   i.   Nancy Jane[9] Foy.

    781. June Madeline[8] Poffenberger (Roby Earl[7], Alvin Joseph Adam[6], Adam R.[5] Paffenberger, Lydia Ann[4] Romberger, Adam[3], Balthaser[2], Johann Bartholomus[1]) was born 08 Dec 1925 in Portland Multnomah, OR. She married **Gunner Nilsson** 02 Jul 1950. He was born 02 Apr 1908 in Halsingborg, Sweden.

Child of June Poffenberger and Gunner Nilsson is:
    799   i.   Lisa Britt[9] Nilsson, born 1957 in Oregon.

Generation No. 9

    784. Glenn[9] Hepler (Laura E.[8] Minnich, Edward Austin[7], Josiah[6], Michael[5], Anna Maria[4] Matter, Anna Maria[3] Romberger, Balthaser[2], Johann Bartholomus[1]) was born 28 Jul 1928 in Dauphin Co., PA. He married **Lois Laudenslager**.

Child of Glenn Hepler and Lois Laudenslager is:
    800   i.   Timothy[10] Hepler. He married Connie Williams; born in Elizabethville, Dauphin Co., PA.

    785. Jack Arland[9] Hepler (Laura E.[8] Minnich, Edward Austin[7], Josiah[6], Michael[5], Anna Maria[4] Matter, Anna Maria[3] Romberger, Balthaser[2], Johann Bartholomus[1]) was born 03 Feb 1931 in Dauphin Co., PA. He married **Irene Sitlinger**.

Children of Jack Hepler and Irene Sitlinger are:
    801   i.   Debbie[10] Hepler, born in Gratz, Lykens Twp., Dauphin Co., PA.
    802   ii. Stan Hepler, born in Gratz, Lykens Twp., Dauphin Co., PA.
    803   iii. Robert Hepler, born in Gratz, Lykens Twp., Dauphin Co., PA.
    804   iv. William Hepler, born in Gratz, Lykens Twp., Dauphin Co., PA.

788. John Arthur[9] **Minnich** (Arthur Franklin[8], Aaron Frank[7], Cyrus[6], Michael[5], Anna Maria[4] Matter, Anna Maria[3] Romberger, Balthaser[2], Johann Bartholomus[1]) was born Abt. 1930. He married **Yvonne Bohner**. She was born Abt. 1930.

Child of John Minnich and Yvonne Bohner is:

    805   i.   Debra Louise[10] Minnich, born 18 Jun 1958 in Lykens, PA. She married James Kandybowski 18 Jun 1977; born 29 Jul 1955 in Lykens, PA.

789. Edwin Frances[9] **Knorr** (Mary Frances[8] Minnich, Aaron Frank[7], Cyrus[6], Michael[5], Anna Maria[4] Matter, Anna Maria[3] Romberger, Balthaser[2], Johann Bartholomus[1]) was born Abt. 1940. He married **Joan Mardell Schaeffer** Abt. 1955. She was born Abt. 1940.

Children of Edwin Knorr and Joan Schaeffer are:

    806   i.   Vicki[10] Knorr, born Abt. 1965; died Abt. 1965.
    807   ii.   Cindy Lee Knorr, born Abt. 1967.
    808   iii. Edwin Frances Knorr, born Abt. 1969. He married Anita Heather Steward; born Abt. 1970.

791. Living[9] (Eugene Clinton[8] Lentz, Charles Warren[7], Lydia A.[6] Wilbert, Catharina[5] Matter, Heinrich[4], Anna Maria[3] Romberger, Balthaser[2], Johann Bartholomus[1])

Children of Living are:

    809   i.   Living[10].
    810   ii.   Living.
+   811   iii. Living.
    812   iv. Living.
    813   v.   Living.

793. Dwight David[9] **Eisenhower** (John Sheldon Doud[8], Dwight David[7], David Jacob[6] Eisenhauer, Margareta Rebecca[5] Matter, Heinrich[4], Anna Maria[3] Romberger, Balthaser[2], Johann Bartholomus[1]) was born 31 Mar 1948. He married **Julie Nixon** 28 Dec 1968. She was born 05 Jul 1948.

Children of Dwight Eisenhower and Julie Nixon are:

    814   i.   Jennie[10] Eisenhower.
    815   ii.   Alex Eisenhower.
    816   iii. Melanie Eisenhower.

798. Nancy Jane[9] **Foy** (Bernice Mildred[8] Almlee, Susan Alice[7] Knorr, Mary Rebecca[6] Gipple, Anna Maria[5] Ritzman, Catherine[4] Matter, Anna Maria[3] Romberger, Balthaser[2], Johann Bartholomus[1])

Child of Nancy Jane Foy is:

    817   i.   Jenelle[10] Benson.

Generation No. 10

811. Living[10] (Living[9], Eugene Clinton[8] Lentz, Charles Warren[7], Lydia A.[6] Wilbert, Catharina[5] Matter, Heinrich[4], Anna Maria[3] Romberger, Balthaser[2], Johann Bartholomus[1]) She married **Living**.

Children of Living and Living are:

    818   i.   Living[11].
    819   ii.   Living.
    820   iii. Living.
    821   iv. Living.

Descendants of John Jacob Miller

Generation No. 1

1. John Jacob² Miller (Jacob¹ Mueller) was born 24 Sep 1728 in Germany, and died 02 Mar 1767 in Pa.

Children of John Jacob Miller are:
+   2   i.   John³ Miller, born Abt. 1755 in Pa; died 04 Mar 1788 in Pa.
     3   ii.   David Miller, born Abt. 1758 in Pa.
+   4   iii.   Abraham Miller, born 1761 in Somerset, Pa; died 24 Apr 1834 in Brothersvalley T, Somerset, Pa.

Generation No. 2

2. John³ Miller (John Jacob², Jacob¹ Mueller) was born Abt. 1755 in Pa, and died 04 Mar 1788 in Pa. He married **Susanna Raysor** in Pa. She was born Abt. 1759.

Children of John Miller and Susanna Raysor are:
     5   i.   Anna⁴ Miller, born Abt. 1781 in Pa.
     6   ii.   Jacob Miller, born Abt. 1783 in Pa.
     7   iii.   John Miller, born Abt. 1785 in Pa.
     8   iv.   Elizabeth Miller, born Abt. 1787 in Pa.
+   9   v.   Barbara Miller, born 27 May 1789 in Elizabethville, Dauphin, Pa; died 01 Jan 1862 in Millersburg, Dauphin, Pa.

4. Abraham³ Miller (John Jacob², Jacob¹ Mueller) was born 1761 in Somerset, Pa, and died 24 Apr 1834 in Brothersvalley T, Somerset, Pa. He married **Anna Maria Troutman** Abt. 1817 in Brothersvalley Twp., Somerset Co., PA. She was born 08 Sep 1783 in Greenwich Twp, Berks, Pa, and died 05 Nov 1869 in Somerset County, Pa.

Children of Abraham Miller and Anna Troutman are:
+   10   i.   Lydia⁴ Miller, born 22 Sep 1817 in Brothersvalley Twp., Somerset Co., PA; died 24 Jan 1904 in Brothersvalley Twp., Somerset Co., PA.
+   11   ii.   Anna Miller, born 29 Aug 1820 in Brothersvalley Twp., Somerset Co., PA; died 24 Aug 1891 in Brothersvalley Twp., Somerset Co., PA.
+   12   iii.   Daniel Miller, born 05 Oct 1822 in Brothersvalley Twp., Somerset Co., PA; died 26 Nov 1910 in Brooklyn Twp., Lee Co., IL.
+   13   iv.   Jonathan A. Miller, born 13 Mar 1825 in Brothersvalley Twp., Somerset Co., PA; died 25 Aug 1900 in Brothersvalley Twp., Somerset Co., PA.
     14   v.   Michael Miller, born Abt. 1829 in Brothersvalley Twp., Somerset Co., PA.

Generation No. 3

9. Barbara⁴ Miller (John³, John Jacob², Jacob¹ Mueller) was born 27 May 1789 in Elizabethville, Dauphin, Pa, and died 01 Jan 1862 in Millersburg, Dauphin, Pa. She married **Frederick Eisenhauer** 1816 in Linglestown, Dauphin, Pa, son of Hans Eisenhauer and Anna Dissinger. He was born 15 Jul 1794 in Linglestown, Dauphin, Pennsylvania, and died 13 Mar 1884 in Belle Springs, Dickinson, Kansas.

Children of Barbara Miller and Frederick Eisenhauer are:
+   15   i.   Polly⁵ Eisenhauer, born 13 Aug 1817 in Elizabethville, Dauphin, Pennsylvania; died 09 Dec 1863.
+   16   ii.   Anna Eisenhauer, born 25 Aug 1819 in Elizabethville, Dauphin, Pennsylvania; died 26 Dec 1849 in Elizabethville, Dauphin, Pennsylvania.
     17   iii.   John David Eisenhauer, born 23 Jun 1821 in Elizabethville, Dauphin, Pennsylvania; died 13 Dec 1840 in Dauphin Co, PA.
+   18   iv.   Catherine Eisenhower, born 11 Jul 1824 in Elizabethville, Dauphin Co, PA; died 07 Nov 1907 in Abilene, Dickinson, Kansas.

+ 19   v.   Jacob Frederick Eisenhauer, born 19 Sep 1826 in Elizabethville, Washington Twp., Dauphin Co., PA; died 20 May 1906 in Abilene, Dickinson Co , Kansas.

+ 20   vi. Samuel P Eisenhower, born 04 Feb 1831 in Elizabethville, Dauphin, Pennsylvania.

10. Lydia⁴ Miller (Abraham³, John Jacob², Jacob¹ Mueller) was born 22 Sep 1817 in Brothersvalley Twp., Somerset Co., PA, and died 24 Jan 1904 in Brothersvalley Twp., Somerset Co., PA. She married **Perry P Walker** 01 Dec 1838 in Brothersvalley Twp., Somerset Co., PA. He was born 23 Jan 1817 in Brothersvalley Twp., Somerset Co., PA, and died 18 Jun 1896 in Brothersvalley Twp., Somerset Co., PA.

Child of Lydia Miller and Perry Walker is:
21   i.   Charles⁵ Walker, born Abt. 1849 in Somerset Twp., Somerset Co., PA.

11. Anna⁴ Miller (Abraham³, John Jacob², Jacob¹ Mueller) was born 29 Aug 1820 in Brothersvalley Twp., Somerset Co., PA, and died 24 Aug 1891 in Brothersvalley Twp., Somerset Co., PA. She married **Noah Stoner** Abt. 1846 in Brothersvalley Twp., Somerset Co., PA. He was born 02 Sep 1815 in Somerst Co., PA, and died 20 Mar 1886 in Brothersvalley Twp., Somerset Co., PA.

Children of Anna Miller and Noah Stoner are:
22   i.   Sara⁵ Stoner, born 06 Mar 1847 in Stoneycreek Twp., Somerset Co., PA; died 11 May 1916 in Brothersvalley Twp., Somerset Co., PA.
23   ii.   William J Stoner, born Abt. 1853 in Stoneycreek Twp., Somerset Co., PA.
24   iii. Ellen Stoner, born Abt. 1855 in Stoneycreek Twp., Somerset Co., PA.
25   iv.   Emma Stoner, born Abt. 1860 in Stoneycreek Twp., Somerset Co., PA.
26   v.   Charles Stoner, born Abt. 1864 in Stoneycreek Twp., Somerset Co., PA.

12. Daniel⁴ Miller (Abraham³, John Jacob², Jacob¹ Mueller) was born 05 Oct 1822 in Brothersvalley Twp., Somerset Co., PA, and died 26 Nov 1910 in Brooklyn Twp., Lee Co., IL. He married **(1) Elizabeth Lewis** 1844 in Summit Twp., Somerset Co., PA. She was born Abt. 1823 in Somerset Co., PA, and died Abt. 1846 in Summit Twp., Somerset Co., PA. He married **(2) Leah Gittinger** 02 Aug 1849 in Baughman Twp., Wayne Co., OH. She was born 03 Jan 1831 in Earl Twp., Lancaster Co., PA, and died 19 Jun 1899 in Brooklyn Twp., Lee Co., IL.

Child of Daniel Miller and Elizabeth Lewis is:
27   i.   Ephriam⁵ Miller, born 24 Oct 1845 in Summit Twp., Somerset Co., PA; died Bef. 1904.

Children of Daniel Miller and Leah Gittinger are:
28   i.   Sarah Jane⁵ Miller, born 04 Apr 1850 in Baughman Twp., Wayne Co., OH; died Abt. 1912 in Earlville, LaSalle Co., IL.
29   ii.   Milo Turner Miller, born 04 Jul 1851 in Baughman Twp., Wayne Co., OH; died 21 Oct 1938 in Jerome, ID.
30   iii. Lewis Scott Miller, born 08 Jan 1853 in Canal Fulton, Stark Co., OH; died 20 Nov 1932 in Fort Collins, Larimer C., CO.
31   iv.   Franklin Miller, born 27 Oct 1855 in Brooklyn Twp., Lee Co., IL; died in Berwyn, Custer Co., NE.
32   v.   David Miller, born 10 Oct 1857 in Brooklyn Twp., Lee Co., IL; died 14 Feb 1924 in Fort Collins, Larimer Co., CO.
33   vi.   Mary E Miller, born 03 Apr 1859 in Brooklyn Twp., Lee Co., IL; died 03 May 1955 in Fort Collins, Larimer Co., CO.
34   vii. William Miller, born 06 Oct 1861 in Brooklyn Twp., Lee Co., IL; died 27 Jul 1947 in Twin Falls, Twin Falls Co., ID.
35   viii. John A Miller, born 29 Apr 1865 in Brooklyn Twp., Lee Co., IL; died Abt. 1963 in Los Angeles, Los Angeles, Co., CA.
36   ix.   Martha Miller, born 29 Apr 1865 in Brooklyn Twp., Lee Co., IL; died Aft. 1920 in Fort Collins, Larimer Co., CO.

13. Jonathan A.⁴ Miller (Abraham³, John Jacob², Jacob¹ Mueller) was born 13 Mar 1825 in Brothersvalley Twp., Somerset Co., PA, and died 25 Aug 1900 in Brothersvalley Twp., Somerset Co., PA. He married **Caroline Walker** 09 Jan 1848 in Brothersvalley Twp., Somerset Co., PA. She was born 06 May 1823 in Brothersvalley Twp., Somerset Co., PA, and died 07 Oct 1912 in Brothersvalley Twp., Somerset Co., PA.

Children of Jonathan Miller and Caroline Walker are:

37	i.	Willliam J[5] Miller, born 10 Feb 1848 in Brothersvalley Twp., Somerset Co., PA; died 10 Feb 1931 in Berlin Cemetery, Berlin, PA.
38	ii.	Ellen Miller, born 25 Feb 1861 in Brothersvalley Twp., Somerset Co., PA; died 02 May 1927 in Brothersvalley Twp., Somerset Co., PA.

Generation No. 4

15. Polly[5] Eisenhauer (Barbara[4] Miller, John[3], John Jacob[2], Jacob[1] Mueller) was born 13 Aug 1817 in Elizabethville, Dauphin, Pennsylvania, and died 09 Dec 1863. She married **Benjamin Miller**.

Children of Polly Eisenhauer and Benjamin Miller are:

39	i.	John[6] Miller, born 1837.
40	ii.	Susan Miller, born 1840.

16. Anna[5] Eisenhauer (Barbara[4] Miller, John[3], John Jacob[2], Jacob[1] Mueller) was born 25 Aug 1819 in Elizabethville, Dauphin, Pennsylvania, and died 26 Dec 1849 in Elizabethville, Dauphin, Pennsylvania. She married **Joseph Novinger** 1839 in ,Dauphin , Pennsylvania. He was born 08 Feb 1810 in Upper Paxton Twp, Dauphin Co, PA.

Children of Anna Eisenhauer and Joseph Novinger are:

41	i.	James[6] Novinger.
42	ii.	John D. Novinger, born 21 Dec 1840 in Dauphin Co, PA. He married Leah Jane Orndorff.
43	iii.	Samuel P. Novinger, born 11 Oct 1842. He married Catherine Shaffetall.
44	iv.	Mary Ann Novinger, born 1844. She married William Stauffer.
45	v.	Catherine Novinger, born 19 Jul 1846. She married Eubert Dufler.
46	vi.	Elizabeth Novinger, born 25 Aug 1848 in Dauphin Co, PA; died 06 Jun 1938. She married John Abraham Keifer.

18. Catherine[5] Eisenhower (Barbara[4] Miller, John[3], John Jacob[2], Jacob[1] Mueller) was born 11 Jul 1824 in Elizabethville, Dauphin Co, PA, and died 07 Nov 1907 in Abilene, Dickinson, Kansas. She married **Samuel Pyke** 30 Mar 1848 in Pennsylvania. He was born 06 Apr 1825 in York, PA, and died 26 May 1887 in Abilene, Dickinson Co, KS.

Children of Catherine Eisenhower and Samuel Pyke are:

+	47	i.	John David[6] Pyke, born 14 Jul 1849; died 1904.
+	48	ii.	Jacob Frederick Pyke, born 16 Oct 1851; died 1896.
	49	iii.	Susan Pyke, born 17 Jul 1853.
	50	iv.	Mary Ann Pyke, born 26 Mar 1855; died 1856.
+	51	v.	Sarah Catherine Pyke, born 29 Nov 1856; died 1930.
	52	vi.	Samuel Peter Pyke, born 23 Jul 1860; died 1880.
+	53	vii.	Anna Jane Pyke, born 22 May 1864.
+	54	viii.	Elizabeth Rebecca Pyke, born 09 Apr 1869 in Millersburg, PA; died 1895.

19. Jacob Frederick[5] Eisenhauer (Barbara[4] Miller, John[3], John Jacob[2], Jacob[1] Mueller) was born 19 Sep 1826 in Elizabethville, Washington Twp., Dauphin Co., PA, and died 20 May 1906 in Abilene, Dickinson Co , Kansas. He married **Margareta Rebecca Matter** 25 Feb 1847 in Dauphin , Pennsylvania, daughter of Heinrich Matter and Anna Deitrich. She was born 18 Mar 1825 in Mifflin Twp, Dauphin, PA, and died 22 Jun 1890 in Abilene, Dickinson Co , Kansas.

Children of Jacob Eisenhauer and Margareta Matter are:

	55	i.	John H.[6] Eisenhauer, born 07 Mar 1848 in Elizabethville, Dauphin Co, PA; died 10 Apr 1857 in Elizabethville, Dauphin Co, PA.
+	56	ii.	Mary Ann Eisenhauer, born 02 Sep 1849 in Elizabethville, Dauphin, Pennsylvania; died 27 Apr 1893

in Abilene, Dickinson, Kansas.

+ 57   iii. Catherine Ann Eisenhauer, born 19 Mar 1851 in Elizabethville, Dauphin, Pennsylvania; died 03 Apr 1924 in Ramona, Marion, Kansas.

58   iv. Jacob F. Eisenhauer, born 03 Sep 1852 in Elizabethville, Dauphin Co, PA; died 02 Oct 1852 in Elizabethville, Dauphin Co, PA.

59   v. Samuel F. Eisenhauer, born 30 Sep 1853 in Elizabethville, Dauphin Co, PA; died 11 Jun 1854 in Elizabethville, Dauphin Co, PA.

+ 60   vi. Susanna Eisenhauer, born 29 Oct 1854 in Elizabethville, Dauphin, Pennsylvania; died 14 Jun 1932 in York, PA.

61   vii. Peter A. Eisenhauer, born 27 Nov 1855 in Elizabethville, Dauphin Co, PA; died 04 Aug 1856 in Elizabethville, Dauphin Co, PA.

62   viii. Lydia A. Eisenhauer, born 27 Aug 1857 in Elizabethville, Dauphin Co, PA; died 15 Nov 1874 in Elizabethville, Dauphin Co, PA.

63   ix. Emma Jane Eisenhauer, born 03 Dec 1859 in Elizabethville, Dauphin Co, PA; died 08 May 1860 in Elizabethville, Dauphin Co, PA.

+ 64   x. Amanda Hannah Eisenhauer, born 11 Dec 1861 in Elizabethville, Dauphin Co, PA; died 25 Aug 1951 in Abilene, Dickinson Co, KS.

+ 65   xi. David Jacob Eisenhauer, born 23 Sep 1863 in Elizabethville, Dauphin, Pennsylvania; died 10 Mar 1942 in Abilene, Dickinson, Kansas.

66   xii. Dr Abraham Lincoln Eisenhauer, born 22 Jul 1865 in Elizabethville, Dauphin Co, PA; died 23 Dec 1944 in Upland, CA. He married Anna Long 1886; born 1865.

67   xiii. Clinton Eisenhauer, born 30 Jul 1867 in Elizabethville, Dauphin Co, PA; died 10 Aug 1867 in Elizabethville, Dauphin Co, PA.

+ 68   xiv. Ira A Eisenhower, born 30 Jul 1867 in Elizabethville, Dauphin, Pa; died 28 Mar 1943 in Los Angeles, CA.

20. Samuel P[5] Eisenhower (Barbara[4] Miller, John[3], John Jacob[2], Jacob[1] Mueller) was born 04 Feb 1831 in Elizabethville, Dauphin, Pennsylvania. He married **(1) Lydia Orndorff**. He married **(2) Mary Ann Orndorff** 21 Oct 1855 in ,,Pennsylvania. She was born 1839, and died 1932.

Children of Samuel Eisenhower and Mary Orndorff are:

69   i. William Henry[6] Eisenhauer, born 1858; died 1926. He married Alice Hoover.

70   ii. Eisenhauer, born 1859; died 1859.

+ 71   iii. Mary Ann Eisenhauer, born 1860 in Elizabethville, Dauphin Co, PA; died 1918.

72   iv. Leah Jane Eisenhauer, born 1864; died 1865.

73   v. Elizabeth Eisenhauer, born 1868; died 1875.

74   vi. Sarah Ellen Eisenhauer, born 1873; died 1942. She married Abram Book.

75   vii. John Franklin Eisenhauer, born 1874. He married Mabel Blanche Beasler.

+ 76   viii. Emma Bertha Eisenhauer, born 23 Jul 1876 in Millersburg, PA; died 1941.

77   ix. James Monroe Eisenhauer, born 1878; died 1941. He married Josephine Gastbend.

78   x. Simon Peter Eisenhauer, born 1880. He married Edythe Rager.

Generation No. 5

47. John David[6] Pyke (Catherine[5] Eisenhower, Barbara[4] Miller, John[3], John Jacob[2], Jacob[1] Mueller) was born 14 Jul 1849, and died 1904. He married **Anna Lesher**. She was born 1846, and died 1904.

Children of John Pyke and Anna Lesher are:

79   i. Abraham Solomon[7] Pyke, born 1873; died 1954.

80   ii. William Franklin Pyke, born 1875; died 1964.

81   iii. Isaac Lesher Pyke, born 1878; died 1962.

82   iv. John Albert Pyke, born 1879; died 1968.

83   v. Rhoda Leah Pyke, born 1881; died 1920.

84   vi. Franklin Milton Pyke, born 1883; died 1967.

85   vii. Samuel Wesley Pyke, born 1888; died 1963.

86   viii. Ernest James Pyke, born 1894; died 1970.

48. Jacob Frederick[6] Pyke (Catherine[5] Eisenhower, Barbara[4] Miller, John[3], John Jacob[2], Jacob[1] Mueller) was born 16 Oct 1851, and died 1896. He married **Susan Jane Bowers**. She was born 1848, and died Aft. 1880.

Children of Jacob Pyke and Susan Bowers are:

87	i.	Anna C^7 Pyke, born 1873.
88	ii.	Lilly M Pyke, born 1874.
89	iii.	Harry M Pyke, born 1876.
90	iv.	Catherine E Pyke, born 1879.
91	v.	Samuel Frederick Pyke, born 1882; died 1965.
92	vi.	Elizabeth Pyke, born 1883.
93	vii.	Cora Pyke, born 1885.
94	viii.	Susan Pyke, born 1889; died 1904.
95	ix.	Jacob Herb Pyke, born 1894; died 1982.

51. Sarah Catherine^6 Pyke (Catherine^5 Eisenhower, Barbara^4 Miller, John^3, John Jacob^2, Jacob^1 Mueller) was born 29 Nov 1856, and died 1930. She married **John Henry Romberger**. He was born 1857, and died 1930.

Children of Sarah Pyke and John Romberger are:

96	i.	Charles Oscar^7 Romberger, born 1887; died 1980.
97	ii.	James Frank Romberger, born 1888; died 1950.
98	iii.	Mary Elizabeth Romberger, born 1889; died 1949.
99	iv.	Mabel Catherine Romberger, born 1890; died 1946.
100	v.	Thomas Pyke Romberger, born 1894; died 1968.

53. Anna Jane^6 Pyke (Catherine^5 Eisenhower, Barbara^4 Miller, John^3, John Jacob^2, Jacob^1 Mueller) was born 22 May 1864. She married **Alfred Henry Fair**. He was born 30 Dec 1863 in Pennsylvania, and died 21 Sep 1929.

Children of Anna Pyke and Alfred Fair are:

101	i.	Alice^7 Fair, born Bef. 1888.
102	ii.	Mabel Fair, born 1888.
103	iii.	Maude Fair, born 1890.
104	iv.	George Fair, born 07 Jun 1894.

54. Elizabeth Rebecca^6 Pyke (Catherine^5 Eisenhower, Barbara^4 Miller, John^3, John Jacob^2, Jacob^1 Mueller) was born 09 Apr 1869 in Millersburg, PA, and died 1895. She married **William Harvey Bentzel**. He was born 24 Aug 1864, and died 23 Dec 1892.

Children of Elizabeth Pyke and William Bentzel are:

+	105	i.	Harry I^7 Bentzel, born 1891 in Abilene, Dickinson Co, KS.
	106	ii.	Ida Viola Rosabel Bentzel, born Abt. 1893.

56. Mary Ann^6 Eisenhauer (Jacob Frederick^5, Barbara^4 Miller, John^3, John Jacob^2, Jacob^1 Mueller) was born 02 Sep 1849 in Elizabethville, Dauphin, Pennsylvania, and died 27 Apr 1893 in Abilene, Dickinson, Kansas. She married **John J Witter**. He was born Jul 1840 in Prussia, and died 1918 in Abilene, Dickinson Co, KS.

Children of Mary Eisenhauer and John Witter are:

+	107	i.	Martha Rebecca^7 Witter, born 27 Sep 1871 in Millersburg, PA; died 20 Aug 1955 in Upland, CA.
	108	ii.	Harry Witter, born 1873 in PA.
	109	iii.	Amanda Witter, born 1877 in PA; died Nov 1883 in KS.
	110	iv.	Bessie Witter, born 19 Sep 1880; died 28 Sep 1883 in Abilene, Dickinson Co, KS.
	111	v.	Sadie Witter, born 01 Jan 1883 in Enterprise, KS; died 14 Jun 1982 in Abilene, Dickinson Co, KS. She married Lewis Steckley 27 May 1958 in Navarre, KS; died 16 Sep 1977.
	112	vi.	Susie A Witter, born 28 Jan 1885 in Enterprise, KS; died 23 Jul 1956 in Modesto, CA. She married Noah B Martin Abt. 1924 in CA.
	113	vii.	Johnnie Witter, born 18 Oct 1887 in Abilene, Dickinson Co, KS; died 06 Feb 1888 in Abilene, Dickinson Co, KS.
	114	viii.	Mamie Stella Witter, born 25 Nov 1888 in KS; died 29 Sep 1969 in KS.

115   ix.   Ray I Witter, born 19 Jan 1891 in Enterprise, KS; died 26 Jan 1967 in Abilene, Dickinson Co, KS. He married Ruth V Book 18 Feb 1914; born 29 Dec 1894; died 02 Nov 1980 in Mechanicburg, PA.

57. Catherine Ann[6] Eisenhauer (Jacob Frederick[5], Barbara[4] Miller, John[3], John Jacob[2], Jacob[1] Mueller) was born 19 Mar 1851 in Elizabethville, Dauphin, Pennsylvania, and died 03 Apr 1924 in Ramona, Marion, Kansas. She married **Samuel B. Haldeman.** He was born 11 Jan 1846 in Bainsbridge, PA, and died 21 Oct 1928 in Abilene, Dickinson Co, KS.

Children of Catherine Eisenhauer and Samuel Haldeman are:

    116   i.   Hattie Jane[7] Haldeman, born 19 Jun 1872; died 1883.
    117   ii.   Mary Rebecca Haldeman, born 1874.
    118   iii.   Lydia Ann Haldeman, born 1875.
    119   iv.   John Thaddeus Haldeman, born 1876; died 1901.
+ 120   v.   Lillian Elizabeth Haldeman, born 27 Aug 1878.
    121   vi.   Jesse Ira Haldeman, born 1879 in PA.
    122   vii.   Abraham Lincoln Haldeman, born 02 Feb 1882; died 1883.
+ 123   viii.   Katherine Ann Haldeman, born 20 Jul 1883 in Hope, KS; died 28 Nov 1959 in Abilene, Dickinson Co, KS.
    124   ix.   Samuel Walter Haldeman, born 17 Dec 1884 in Hope, KS; died 23 Feb 1949 in Topeka, KS. He married Grace Johnson 15 Aug 1909.
+ 125   x.   John Henry Haldeman, born 09 Jun 1886 in Hope, KS; died 12 Dec 1969.
    126   xi.   Milo Edward Haldeman, born Dec 1887.
+ 127   xii.   Harry Milton Haldeman, born 22 Apr 1889 in KS; died 04 Jul 1968 in Hillsboro, KS.
    128   xiii.   Ora Blanche Haldeman, born Aug 1892 in KS. She married m Button.
    129   xiv.   Delilah Haldeman, born 1895 in KS. She married m Book.

60. Susanna[6] Eisenhauer (Jacob Frederick[5], Barbara[4] Miller, John[3], John Jacob[2], Jacob[1] Mueller) was born 29 Oct 1854 in Elizabethville, Dauphin, Pennsylvania, and died 14 Jun 1932 in York, PA. She married **Aaron Wetzel.** He was born 1849, and died 03 Jul 1947 in York, PA.

Children of Susanna Eisenhauer and Aaron Wetzel are:

    130   i.   Harper[7] Wetzel, born 1872; died 1873.
    131   ii.   Janny R. Wetzel, born 1874; died 1881.
    132   iii.   Franklin Jacob Wetzel, born 1876; died 1940.
    133   iv.   Sarah A. Wetzel, born 1878.
    134   v.   Raymond Wetzel, born 1880; died 1905.
    135   vi.   Minnie M. Wetzel, born 1883.
    136   vii.   Otto Robert Wetzel, born 1885.
    137   viii.   Grace Pearl Wetzel, born 1888.
    138   ix.   Della Mae Wetzel, born 1890; died 1902.
    139   x.   Vernon Wetzel, born 1894; died 1913.

64. Amanda Hannah[6] Eisenhauer (Jacob Frederick[5], Barbara[4] Miller, John[3], John Jacob[2], Jacob[1] Mueller) was born 11 Dec 1861 in Elizabethville, Dauphin Co, PA, and died 25 Aug 1951 in Abilene, Dickinson Co, KS. She married **Christian O Musser.** He was born 10 Nov 1863 in Mt. Joy, PA, and died 14 Apr 1950 in Abilene, Dickinson Co, KS.

Children of Amanda Eisenhauer and Christian Musser are:

    140   i.   Beulah E[7] Musser, born 11 Jun 1887 in Abilene, Dickinson Co, KS; died 28 Nov 1945 in KS. She married Abram E Brechbill 1931; born 15 Nov 1881 in Abilene, Dickinson Co, KS; died 07 Aug 1964 in Abilene, Dickinson Co, KS.
    141   ii.   Florence Musser, born 19 Mar 1895 in KS; died Apr 1969 in KS. She married A Ray Etherington.

65. David Jacob[6] Eisenhauer (Jacob Frederick[5], Barbara[4] Miller, John[3], John Jacob[2], Jacob[1] Mueller) was born 23 Sep 1863 in Elizabethville, Dauphin, Pennsylvania, and died 10 Mar 1942 in Abilene, Dickinson, Kansas. He married **Ida Elizabeth Stover** 23 Sep 1885 in Hope, Dickinson, Kansas, daughter of Simon Stover and Elizabeth Link. She was born 01 May 1862 in Mt. Sidney, VA, and died 11 Sep 1946 in Abilene, Dickinson Co , Kansas.

Children of David Eisenhauer and Ida Stover are:

+ 142   i.   Arthur Bradford[7] Eisenhower, born 11 Nov 1886 in Hope, Dickinson, Kansas; died 26 Jan 1958.
143   ii.   Edgar Newton Eisenhower, born 19 Jan 1889 in Hope, Dickinson, Kansas; died 12 Jul 1971 in Tacoma, Pierce, Washington.
+ 144   iii.   Dwight David Eisenhower, born 14 Oct 1890 in Denison, Grayson, Texas; died 28 Mar 1969 in Washington, District Of, Columbia.
+ 145   iv.   Roy Jacob Eisenhower, born 09 Aug 1892 in Abilene, Kansas, Kansas; died 17 Jun 1942.
146   v.   Paul Dawson A. Eisenhower, born 12 May 1894 in Abilene, Dickinson, Kansas; died 16 Mar 1895.
147   vi.   Earl Dewey Eisenhower, born 01 Feb 1898 in Abilene, Dickinson, Kansas; died 18 Dec 1968 in Scottsdale, Maricopa, Arizona. He married Kathryn McIntyre Snyder 29 Apr 1933 in Connellsville, Pennsylvania; born 15 Aug 1909 in Charleroi, Washington, Pennsylvania; died Sep 1986 in Scottsdale, Maricopa, Arizona.
148   vii.   Milton Stover Eisenhower, born 15 Sep 1899 in Abilene, Dickinson, Kansas; died 02 May 1985 in Baltimore, Maryland. He married Helen Elsie Eakin 12 Oct 1927 in Washington, District Of, Columbia; born 14 Aug 1904 in Manhattan, Riley, Kansas; died 10 Jul 1954.

68. Ira A[6] Eisenhower (Jacob Frederick[5] Eisenhauer, Barbara[4] Miller, John[3], John Jacob[2], Jacob[1] Mueller) was born 30 Jul 1867 in Elizabethville, Dauphin, Pa, and died 28 Mar 1943 in Los Angeles, CA. He married **Katherine E Dayhoff** 08 Sep 1885 in Abilene, KS. She was born 02 Sep 1865 in PA, and died 30 Dec 1930 in Shawnee Co, KS.

Children of Ira Eisenhower and Katherine Dayhoff are:

+ 149   i.   Mary Rebecca[7] Eisenhower, born Oct 1886; died 29 May 1937 in Topeka, KS.
150   ii.   Simon L Eisenhower, born 03 Dec 1895 in Abilene, Dickinson Co, KS; died 03 Dec 1895 in Abilene, Dickinson Co, KS.
151   iii.   Clinton Eisenhower, born Aft. 1895; died 1943.

71. Mary Ann[6] Eisenhauer (Samuel P[5] Eisenhower, Barbara[4] Miller, John[3], John Jacob[2], Jacob[1] Mueller) was born 1860 in Elizabethville, Dauphin Co, PA, and died 1918. She married **Alfred Peter Buffington** 1878, son of John Buffington and Elizabeth Fight. He was born 1856 in Elizabethville, Dauphin Co, PA, and died 1902.

Children of Mary Eisenhauer and Alfred Buffington are:

152   i.   Annie E[7] Buffington, born 29 Aug 1879 in Elizabethville, Dauphin Co, PA.
153   ii.   Laura J Buffington, born 20 Jul 1881 in Elizabethville, Dauphin Co, PA.
154   iii.   Mabel E Buffington, born 20 Dec 1883 in Elizabethville, Dauphin Co, PA.
155   iv.   Meta Buffington, born 15 Dec 1887 in Elizabethville, Dauphin Co, PA.
156   v.   Bertie Buffington, born 10 Aug 1890 in Elizabethville, Dauphin Co, PA.
157   vi.   Alice P Buffington, born 23 Nov 1892 in Elizabethville, Dauphin Co, PA; died 1963.
158   vii.   Eldred Leroy Buffington, born 25 Jul 1897 in Elizabethville, Dauphin Co, PA; died 06 May 1961.
159   viii.   Ethel M Buffington, born 06 Nov 1898 in Elizabethville, Dauphin Co, PA; died Sep 1979 in Harrisburg, PA.
+ 160   ix.   Roland McKinley Buffington, born 18 Jun 1901 in Elizabethville, Dauphin Co, PA; died 14 Jul 1987 in Melbourne, Brevard, Florida.

76. Emma Bertha[6] Eisenhauer (Samuel P[5] Eisenhower, Barbara[4] Miller, John[3], John Jacob[2], Jacob[1] Mueller) was born 23 Jul 1876 in Millersburg, PA, and died 1941. She married **George Luther Strole** 07 Feb 1900. He was born 06 Nov 1872 in New Hope, VA, and died 12 Nov 1963 in Navarre, KS.

Children of Emma Eisenhauer and George Strole are:

161   i.   Mabel[7] Strole, born Dec 1900.
162   ii.   Dean E Strole, born 29 Jun 1902; died 06 Feb 1972. He married Mildred Elizabeth Wilson.
163   iii.   Dale Strole, born 02 Nov 1903.
164   iv.   Paul L. Strole, born 1906; died 1990.
165   v.   Elmer Strole, born 1909.
166   vi.   Freda Strole, born 1910.

105. Harry I⁷ Bentzel (Elizabeth Rebecca⁶ Pyke, Catherine⁵ Eisenhower, Barbara⁴ Miller, John³, John Jacob², Jacob¹ Mueller) was born 1891 in Abilene, Dickinson Co, KS. He married **Lena Margaret Dalton**. She was born 11 Dec 1893.

Child of Harry Bentzel and Lena Dalton is:

    167   i.   Gerald Benton⁸ Bentsel, born 04 Feb 1923.

107. Martha Rebecca⁷ Witter (Mary Ann⁶ Eisenhauer, Jacob Frederick⁵, Barbara⁴ Miller, John³, John Jacob², Jacob¹ Mueller) was born 27 Sep 1871 in Millersburg, PA, and died 20 Aug 1955 in Upland, CA. She married **Joseph Harvey Gish**. He was born 20 Sep 1875 in Liverpool, PA, and died Sep 1967 in Upland, CA.

Child of Martha Witter and Joseph Gish is:

    168   i.   Evelyn W⁸ Gish, born 16 Jan 1912 in Abilene, Dickinson Co, KS; died 15 Dec 2001 in PA. She married Paul Edward Book; born 03 Mar 1919 in Custer Co, OK; died 21 Dec 1998 in Waynesboro, PA.

120. Lillian Elizabeth⁷ Haldeman (Catherine Ann⁶ Eisenhauer, Jacob Frederick⁵, Barbara⁴ Miller, John³, John Jacob², Jacob¹ Mueller) was born 27 Aug 1878. She married **Samuel W Brehm**. He was born in Palmyra, PA.

Children of Lillian Haldeman and Samuel Brehm are:

    169   i.   Zena Leroy⁸ Brehm, born 07 Jan 1903.
    170   ii.   Eldred H Brehm, born 28 Nov 1904.
    171   iii.   Irma Aurelia Brehm.
    172   iv.   Faithe Marie Brehm.

123. Katherine Ann⁷ Haldeman (Catherine Ann⁶ Eisenhauer, Jacob Frederick⁵, Barbara⁴ Miller, John³, John Jacob², Jacob¹ Mueller) was born 20 Jul 1883 in Hope, KS, and died 28 Nov 1959 in Abilene, Dickinson Co, KS. She married **Abraham Lincoln Epler** 05 Nov 1902 in Hope, KS. He was born Jun 1876 in Hummelstown, PA, and died 16 Jun 1923 in Gladwin, MI.

Children of Katherine Haldeman and Abraham Epler are:

    173   i.   Ruel Milton⁸ Epler, born 14 Mar 1904; died 03 Feb 1977 in Wichita, KS.
    174   ii.   Martha Irene Epler, born 12 May 1906 in Whitehouse, OH; died 08 Oct 1924 in Detroit, KS.
    175   iii.   Grant Barton Epler, born 29 May 1907; died 18 Jun 1988 in Lapeer, MI.
    176   iv.   Russell Emerson Epler, born 09 Jun 1909 in Canton, KS; died 20 Apr 1985 in Rochester, MI.
    177   v.   Blanche Pearl Epler, born 20 May 1918 in Gladwin, MI; died 24 Nov 2003 in KS. She married m Scheideman.
    178   vi.   ? Epler. She married Voiland Engle; born 10 Sep 1922.
    179   vii.   Grace Lilian Epler, died Aft. 1985. She married m Campbell.
    180   viii.   Paul Mark Epler, died Aft. 1985.

125. John Henry⁷ Haldeman (Catherine Ann⁶ Eisenhauer, Jacob Frederick⁵, Barbara⁴ Miller, John³, John Jacob², Jacob¹ Mueller) was born 09 Jun 1886 in Hope, KS, and died 12 Dec 1969. He married **Viola C Rock** 11 Apr 1909 in Hope, KS. She was born 24 Feb 1889 in Illinois, and died 24 Jul 1976 in Abilene, Dickinson Co, KS.

Child of John Haldeman and Viola Rock is:

    181   i.   Veri C⁸ Haldeman, born 29 Jun 1911; died 01 Sep 1923 in Abilene, Dickinson Co, KS.

127. Harry Milton⁷ Haldeman (Catherine Ann⁶ Eisenhauer, Jacob Frederick⁵, Barbara⁴ Miller, John³, John Jacob², Jacob¹ Mueller) was born 22 Apr 1889 in KS, and died 04 Jul 1968 in Hillsboro, KS. He married **Ollie B Rock** 29 Nov 1911. She was born 04 Nov 1890, and died 10 Feb 1981 in Topeka, KS.

Child of Harry Haldeman and Ollie Rock is:
182   i. Eunic O[8] Haldeman, born 1913 in KS; died 1953. She married ? Nincehelser.

142. Arthur Bradford[7] Eisenhower (David Jacob[6] Eisenhauer, Jacob Frederick[5], Barbara[4] Miller, John[3], John Jacob[2], Jacob[1] Mueller) was born 11 Nov 1886 in Hope, Dickinson, Kansas, and died 26 Jan 1958. He married **(1) Alida B ?**. She was born 17 Feb 1889. He married **(2) Louis Sondra Grieb** 03 Sep 1926.

Child of Arthur Eisenhower and Alida ? is:
+   183   i. Katherine[8] Eisenhower, born 02 Jul 1914.

144. Dwight David[7] Eisenhower (David Jacob[6] Eisenhauer, Jacob Frederick[5], Barbara[4] Miller, John[3], John Jacob[2], Jacob[1] Mueller) was born 14 Oct 1890 in Denison, Grayson, Texas, and died 28 Mar 1969 in Washington, District Of, Columbia. He married **Mary Geneva Doud** 01 Jul 1916 in Denver, Denver, Colorado, daughter of John Doud and Elivera Carlson. She was born 14 Nov 1896 in Boone, Boone, Iowa, and died 31 Oct 1979 in Washington, D.C..

Children of Dwight Eisenhower and Mary Doud are:
+   184   i. John Sheldon Doud[8] Eisenhower, born 1923.
    185   ii. Doud Dwight Eisenhower, born 24 Sep 1917 in San Antonio, Bexar, Texas; died 02 Jan 1921 in Camp Meade, Maryland.

145. Roy Jacob[7] Eisenhower (David Jacob[6] Eisenhauer, Jacob Frederick[5], Barbara[4] Miller, John[3], John Jacob[2], Jacob[1] Mueller) was born 09 Aug 1892 in Abilene, Kansas, Kansas, and died 17 Jun 1942. He married **Edna Alice Shade** 18 Nov 1917 in Ellsworth, Ellsworth, Kansas. She was born 13 Sep 1891 in Ellis City, Ellis, Kansas, and died 26 Jun 1989 in Denver, Denver, Colorado.

Children of Roy Eisenhower and Edna Shade are:
    186   i. Patricia[8] Eisenhower, born 1918.
    187   ii. Peggy J Eisenhower, born 1923.
    188   iii. Lloyd E Eisenhower, born 1925.
    189   iv. Roy J Eisenhower, born Abt. 1930.

149. Mary Rebecca[7] Eisenhower (Ira A[6], Jacob Frederick[5] Eisenhauer, Barbara[4] Miller, John[3], John Jacob[2], Jacob[1] Mueller) was born Oct 1886, and died 29 May 1937 in Topeka, KS. She married **Jacob M Brandt**. He was born 02 Jul 1881 in Detroit, KS.

Children of Mary Eisenhower and Jacob Brandt are:
    190   i. Preston L[8] Brandt, born 07 Jan 1909; died 11 Apr 1977 in San Antonio, Bexar, Texas.
    191   ii. Orville E Brandt, born 28 Feb 1917.
    192   iii. Victor O Brandt, born 10 Sep 1920; died 16 Nov 1999.

160. Roland McKinley[7] Buffington (Mary Ann[6] Eisenhauer, Samuel P[5] Eisenhower, Barbara[4] Miller, John[3], John Jacob[2], Jacob[1] Mueller) was born 18 Jun 1901 in Elizabethville, Dauphin Co, PA, and died 14 Jul 1987 in Melbourne, Brevard, Florida. He married **Blanche Emmeta Kitzmiller** 08 Dec 1923 in Harrisburg, PA. She was born 12 Jan 1904 in Harrisburg, PA.

Children of Roland Buffington and Blanche Kitzmiller are:
+   193   i. Dorothy Pauline[8] Buffington, born 05 Nov 1925 in Harrisburg, PA; died 18 Jan 1998 in Camp Hill, PA.
    194   ii. Roland R Buffington, born 1929 in Harrisburg, PA.

Generation No. 7

183. Katherine[8] Eisenhower (Arthur Bradford[7], David Jacob[6] Eisenhauer, Jacob Frederick[5], Barbara[4] Miller, John[3], John Jacob[2], Jacob[1] Mueller) was born 02 Jul 1914. She married **Berton Roueche** 28 Oct 1936.

He was born 16 Apr 1910.

Child of Katherine Eisenhower and Berton Roueche is:
    195   i.   Arthur Bradford[9] Roueche, born 16 Nov 1942.

184. John Sheldon Doud[8] Eisenhower (Dwight David[7], David Jacob[6] Eisenhauer, Jacob Frederick[5], Barbara[4] Miller, John[3], John Jacob[2], Jacob[1] Mueller) was born 1923. He married **Barbara Jean Thompson** Jul 1947. She was born Abt. 1925.

Children of John Eisenhower and Barbara Thompson are:
+   196   i.   Dwight David[9] Eisenhower, born 31 Mar 1948.
    197   ii. Barbara Anne Eisenhower, born 30 May 1949.
    198   iii. Susan Elaine Eisenhower, born 31 Dec 1951.
    199   iv. Mary Jean Eisenhower, born 21 Dec 1955.

193. Dorothy Pauline[8] Buffington (Roland McKinley[7], Mary Ann[6] Eisenhauer, Samuel P[5] Eisenhower, Barbara[4] Miller, John[3], John Jacob[2], Jacob[1] Mueller) was born 05 Nov 1925 in Harrisburg, PA, and died 18 Jan 1998 in Camp Hill, PA. She married **Kenneth Richard Moyer**. He was born 01 Aug 1926, and died 13 Nov 1987.

Children of Dorothy Buffington and Kenneth Moyer are:
    200   i.   Living[9] Moyer, born Abt. 1950.
    201   ii. Living Moyer, born Abt. 1952.
    202   iii. Living Moyer, born Abt. 1954.

Generation No. 8

196. Dwight David[9] Eisenhower (John Sheldon Doud[8], Dwight David[7], David Jacob[6] Eisenhauer, Jacob Frederick[5], Barbara[4] Miller, John[3], John Jacob[2], Jacob[1] Mueller) was born 31 Mar 1948. He married **Julie Nixon** 28 Dec 1968. She was born 05 Jul 1948.

Children of Dwight Eisenhower and Julie Nixon are:
    203   i.   Jennie[10] Eisenhower.
    204   ii. Alex Eisenhower.
    205   iii. Melanie Eisenhower.

Descendants of George Michael Boone

Generation No. 1

1. George Michael³ Boone (George², George¹) was born 19 Mar 1665/66 in Stoke, Exeter, Devonshire, England, and died 07 Aug 1744 in Exeter Township, Berks, Pennsylvania. He married **Mary Maugridge** 16 Aug 1689 in Stoke, Canon, Devonshire, England, daughter of John Maugridge and Mary Milton. She was born 23 Dec 1668 in Bradninch, Exeter, Devonshire, England, and died 02 Feb 1739/40 in Exeter, Berks, Pennsylvania.

Children of George Boone and Mary Maugridge are:

	2	i.	George⁴ Boone, born 24 Jul 1690 in Bradninch, Exeter, Devonshire, England; died 20 Nov 1753 in Exeter, Berks, Pennsylvania. He married Debrah Howell 17 Sep 1713 in Abington, Philadelphia, Pennsylvania, Pennsylvania.
+	3	ii.	Sarah Boone, born 29 Feb 1691/92 in Bradninch, Exeter, Devonshire, England; died 20 Nov 1743 in Virginia.
	4	iii.	Mary Boone, born 26 Sep 1694 in Bradninch, Devon, Eng; died 20 May 1696 in Bradninch, Exeter, Devonshire, England.
+	5	iv.	Squire Boone, born 25 Nov 1696 in Bradninch, Exeter, Devonshire, England; died 02 Jan 1765 in Salisbury, Rowan, North Carolina.
	6	v.	Mary Boone, born 23 Sep 1699 in Stoak, Exeter, Devonshire, England; died 16 Jan 1774 in Reading, Berks, Pennsylvania. She married John Webb 13 Sep 1720 in Berks , Pennsylvania.
	7	vi.	John Boone, born 14 Jan 1701/02 in Bradninch, Exeter, Devonshire, England; died 10 Oct 1785 in Bradninch, Exeter, Devonshire, England.
	8	vii.	Joseph Boone, born 05 Apr 1704 in Stoak, Exeter, Devonshire, England; died 30 Jan 1776 in Reading, Berks, Pennsylvania. He married (1) Mary ?. He married (2) Catherine 30 Jan 1776 in Exeter Township, Berks , Pn.
+	9	viii.	Benjamin Boone, born 16 Jul 1706 in Bradninch, Exeter, Devonshire, England; died 17 Oct 1762 in ,Exeter, Berks, Pennsylvania.
	10	ix.	James Boone, born 18 Jul 1709 in Stoak, Exeter, Devonshire, England; died 01 Sep 1785 in Exeter Township, Berks, Pennsylvania. He married (1) Mary Foulke 26 May 1735 in Exter, Berks, Pennsylvania. He married (2) Anne Griffith 20 Oct 1757 in Pennsylvania.
	11	x.	Samuel Boone, born 07 Jul 1711 in Stoak, Exeter, Devonshire, England; died 06 Aug 1745 in Reading, Berks, Pennsylvania. He married Elizabeth Cassel 29 Oct 1734 in Philadelphia, Philadelphia, Pennsylvania.

Generation No. 2

3. Sarah⁴ Boone (George Michael³, George², George¹) was born 29 Feb 1691/92 in Bradninch, Exeter, Devonshire, England, and died 20 Nov 1743 in Virginia. She married **Jacob Stover** 15 Mar 1714/15 in Christ Church, Philadelphia, Philadelphia, Pennsylvania, son of Christian Stover and ? Stover. He was born in Switzerland, and died 24 Jun 1741 in , Orange, Virginia.

Children of Sarah Boone and Jacob Stover are:

	12	i.	?⁵ Stover, born in North Carolina>. She married ? ?.
	13	ii.	Jacob Stover, born in Christ Church, Philadelphia, Pennsylvania; died in South Carolina>. He married (1) Elizabeth Ruffner in Stoverstown, Shenandoah, Virginia. He married (2) Catherine ?.
	14	iii.	Barbara Stover, born in Philadelphia Pennsylvania; died in Massanutten, Augusta. She married (1) Martin Kauffman in Lancaster, Pennsylvania. She married (2) Martin Nissly. She married (3) John Lionberger in Augusta , Virginia.
+	15	iv.	Abraham Stover, born in Oley Township, Berks, Pennsylvania.

5. Squire⁴ Boone (George Michael³, George², George¹) was born 25 Nov 1696 in Bradninch, Exeter, Devonshire, England, and died 02 Jan 1765 in Salisbury, Rowan, North Carolina. He married **Sarah Morgan** 27 Jul 1720 in Owyne, Berks, Pennsylvania. She was born in Exeter, Berks, Pennsylvania, and died 01 Jan 1777 in ,Rowan, North Carolina.

Children of Squire Boone and Sarah Morgan are:

16		i.	Nathaniel[5] Boone, born in Exeter, Berks, Pennsylvania.
+	17	ii.	Sarah Cassandra Boone, born 18 Jun 1724 in New Britian Township, Bucks, Pennsylvania; died in ,Madison, Kentucky.
+	18	iii.	Israel Boone, born 20 May 1726 in Chalfont, New Britain Township, Bucks, Pennsylvania; died 26 Jun 1756 in Mocksville, Rowan, North Carolina.
+	19	iv.	Samuel Boone, born 20 May 1728 in Near Chalfont, New Britain Township, Berks, Pennsylvania; died in Athens, Fayette, Kentucky.
	20	v.	Jonathan Boone, born 17 Dec 1730 in New Britain Township, Bucks, Pennsylvania; died in Winchester, Randolph, Indiana. He married (1) Elizabeth Dagley. He married (2) Mary Carter in ,North Carolina. He married (3) Mary Callaway.
	21	vi.	Elizabeth Boone, born 16 Feb 1731/32 in Exeter Twp., Berks, Pennsylvania; died 25 Feb 1818 in ,Fayette, Kentucky. She married William Grant 1751 in Yadkinville, Surr, North Carolina.
+	22	vii.	Daniel Boone, born 27 Oct 1734 in Exeter Township, Berks, Pennsylvania; died 26 Sep 1820 in Teuque Creek, St. Charles, Missouri.
+	23	viii.	Mary Boone, born 14 Nov 1736 in Exeter Township, Philadelphia, Berks, Pennsylvania; died 06 Jul 1819 in ,Rowan, North Carolina.
+	24	ix.	George Boone, born 13 Jan 1738/39 in Exeter, Berks, Pennsylvania; died 11 Nov 1820 in Richmond, Shelby, Kentucky.
+	25	x.	Edward Boone, born 30 Nov 1740 in Exeter, Berks , Pennsylvania; died 06 Oct 1780 in Blue Lick, Clark, Kentucky.
+	26	xi.	Squire Boone II, born 16 Oct 1744 in Exeter Township, Berks, Pennsylvania; died 15 Aug 1815 in Buck Creek, Corydon, Harrison, Indiana.
+	27	xii.	Hannah Boone, born 22 Aug 1746 in Exeter Twp., Berks, Pennsylvania; died 09 Apr 1828 in Tompkinville, Missourinroe, Kentucky.

9. Benjamin[4] Boone (George Michael[3], George[2], George[1]) was born 16 Jul 1706 in Bradninch, Exeter, Devonshire, England, and died 17 Oct 1762 in ,Exeter, Berks, Pennsylvania. He married **Ann Farmer** 28 Sep 1726 in Abington, Bucks, Pennsylvania. She was born in Saffron, Walden, England.

Child of Benjamin Boone and Ann Farmer is:

+	28	i.	John[5] Boone, born in Exeter Township, Berks, Pennsylvania.

Generation No. 3

15. Abraham[5] Stover (Sarah[4] Boone, George Michael[3], George[2], George[1]) was born in Oley Township, Berks, Pennsylvania. He married **Sarah ?**. She was born in <Oley Township, Berks, Pennsylvania>.

Children of Abraham Stover and Sarah ? are:

29		i.	Jeremiah[6] Stover, born in Virginia; died in Wilkesco North Carolina. He married Mary ?.
30		ii.	Henry Stover, born 1741 in Franklin , Virginia; died 1798 in Franklin , Virginia. He married Anna Kline.
+	31	iii.	Daniel Stover, born 1750 in Augusta , Virginia; died 1826 in ,Augusta, Virginia.

17. Sarah Cassandra[5] Boone (Squire[4], George Michael[3], George[2], George[1]) was born 18 Jun 1724 in New Britian Township, Bucks, Pennsylvania, and died in ,Madison, Kentucky. She married **John D. Wilcoxson** 29 May 1742 in ,Rowan, North Carolina. He was born 06 Sep 1720 in , Berks, Pennsylvania, and died 03 Feb 1782 in Bryan's Station, Fayette, Kentucky.

Children of Sarah Boone and John Wilcoxson are:

32	i.	Rachel[6] Wilcoxson, born in Femme, Osage Missouri; died in Femme, Osage, Missouri. She married William Bryant.
33	ii.	George Wilcoxson, born in , Berks, Pennsylvania.
34	iii.	Elizabeth Willcoxson, born in , Madison, Kentucky>; died in , Madison, Kentucky.
35	iv.	Elizabeth Wilcoxson, born in Yadkin Valley, Rowan, North Carolina; died in , Kentucky.
36	v.	David Wilcoxson, born 22 Oct 1742 in , Berks, Pennsylvania>; died 25 Feb 1834 in , Giles, Tennessee.
37	vi.	John Wilcoxson, born 1744 in Berks , Pa; died 1835 in Howard , Missouri.
38	vii.	Nancy Wilcoxson, born 17 Mar 1744/45 in ,Berks, Pennsylvania; died 30 Oct 1790 in , Wilkes,

		Pennsylvania.
39	viii.	Isaac Wilcoxson, born 1753 in , Rowan, North Carolina; died Bef. 10 Oct 1783 in , Rowan, North Carolina.
40	ix.	Isreal Wilcoxson, born 1757 in , Rowan, North Carolina; died 1780 in Bryan's Station, Fayette, Kentucky.
41	x.	William Wilcoxson, born 1762 in Rowan , Va; died 1828 in Barren , Kentucky.
42	xi.	Sarah Wilcoxson, born 1764 in , Rowan, North Carolina.

18.   Israel⁵ Boone (Squire⁴, George Michael³, George², George¹) was born 20 May 1726 in Chalfont, New Britain Township, Bucks, Pennsylvania, and died 26 Jun 1756 in Mocksville, Rowan, North Carolina.   He married **Mary Scrogin Wharton** 13 Dec 1747 in , Lancaster, Pennsylvania.

Child of Israel Boone and Mary Wharton is:

+ 43	i.	Elizabeth⁶ Boone.

19.   Samuel⁵ Boone (Squire⁴, George Michael³, George², George¹) was born 20 May 1728 in Near Chalfont, New Britain Township, Berks, Pennsylvania, and died in Athens, Fayette, Kentucky.   He married **Sarah Day** in , Berks, Pennsylvania.   She was born in , Berks, Pennsylvania, and died in Missouri.

Children of Samuel Boone and Sarah Day are:

44	i.	Samuel⁶ Boone, born 21 Mar 1758 in Yadkin River, North Carolina.
+ 45	ii.	Squire Boone Sr., born 13 Oct 1760 in Yadkin District, Rowan, North Carolina; died 28 Jun 1817 in Elkton, Todd, Kentucky.

22.   Daniel⁵ Boone (Squire⁴, George Michael³, George², George¹) was born 27 Oct 1734 in Exeter Township, Berks, Pennsylvania, and died 26 Sep 1820 in Teuque Creek, St. Charles, Missouri.   He married **Rebecca Bryan** 14 Aug 1756 in Yadkin River Valley, Rowan, North Carolina.   She was born 07 Feb 1738/39 in Winchester, Frederick, Virginia, and died 18 Mar 1813 in Marthasville, Warren, Missouri.

Children of Daniel Boone and Rebecca Bryan are:

46	i.	James⁶ Boone, born 05 Mar 1757 in Bear Creek, Yadkin, North Carolina; died 10 Oct 1773 in Powell Valley, Virginia.
47	ii.	Israel Boone, born 25 Jan 1759 in Bear Creek, Yadkin, North Carolina; died 19 Sep 1782 in Blue Lick Kentucky.
+ 48	iii.	Susannah Boone, born 11 Feb 1760 in Yadkin River Country, Rowan, North Carolina; died 19 Oct 1800 in St. Charles, Missouri.
+ 49	iv.	Jemima Boone, born 04 Oct 1762 in Culpepper, Virginia; died 30 Aug 1829 in Marthasville, Warren, Missouri.
+ 50	v.	Lavina Boone, born 23 Mar 1766 in Sugar Creek, North Carolina; died 06 Apr 1802 in ,Clark, Kentucky.
+ 51	vi.	Rebecca Boone, born 26 May 1768 in Yadkin River Country, Rowan, North Carolina; died 14 Jul 1805 in Boonesborough, Kentucky.
+ 52	vii.	Daniel Morgan Boone, born 23 Dec 1769 in Wilkesboro, Yadkin, North Carolina; died 13 Jul 1839 in Cholera, Westport, Missouri.
+ 53	viii.	Jesse Bryan Boone, born 23 May 1773 in Yadkin Valley, Rowan, North Carolina; died 22 Dec 1820 in St. Louis, St. Louis, Missouri.
54	ix.	William Bryan Boone, born 29 Jan 1775 in Castle's Woods, Clinch River, Virginia; died Jul 1775 in Castle's Woods, Clinch River, Virginia.
+ 55	x.	Nathan Boone, born 03 Feb 1781 in Cross Plains, Rowan , North Carolina; died 16 Oct 1856 in ,Green, Missouri.

23.   Mary⁵ Boone (Squire⁴, George Michael³, George², George¹) was born 14 Nov 1736 in Exeter Township, Philadelphia, Berks, Pennsylvania, and died 06 Jul 1819 in ,Rowan, North Carolina.   She married **(1) Peter Scholl**.   He was born 15 Sep 1754 in Shenandoah Valley, Page, Virginia, and died 11 Sep 1821 in Stoner Fork, Clark, Kentucky.   She married **(2) William Bryan Sr.** in , Rowan, North Carolina.   He was born 06 Mar 1732/33 in Winchester, Frederick, Virginia, and died 07 May 1780 in Bryan's Station, Fayette, Kentucky.   She married **(3) Charles Smith**.

Children of Mary Boone and William Bryan are:

+ 56   i.   Sarah[6] Bryan, born in North Carolina>; died in , Fayette, Kentucky.
+ 57   ii. Samuel Bryan, born 06 May 1756 in , Rowan, North Carolina; died 04 Mar 1837 in Indianapolis, Marion, Indiana.
+ 58   iii. Daniel Boone Bryan, born 10 Feb 1758 in , Rowan, North Carolina; died 28 Feb 1845 in ,Fayette, Kentucky.
   59   iv. William Bryan, born 07 Dec 1760 in , Rowan, North Carolina; died 07 May 1780 in Bryan's Station, Fayette, Kentucky.
   60   v.   Phoebe Bryan, born 24 Jan 1763 in Rowan , North Carolina; died Apr 1785 in Green , Kenucky. She married James Forbush; born in , Rowan, North Carolina; died in , Green, Kentucky.
   61   vi. Hannah Bryan, born 10 Jan 1765 in , Rowan, North Carolina. She married (1) John Westrope. She married (2) John Wicoff.
   62   vii. John Bryan, born 06 Feb 1768 in , Rowan, North Carolina; died in Bryan's Station, Fayette, Kentucky.
   63   viii. Abner Bryan, born 21 Nov 1772 in , Rowan, North Carolina; died Apr 1780.
   64   ix. Elizabeth Bryan, born 16 Nov 1774 in , Rowan, North Carolina. She married Joseph DeHart.
   65   x.   Mary Bryan, born 07 Jan 1777 in , Rowan, North Carolina. She married (1) John VanHoose Sr.. She married (2) Joseph Ingels.

24. George[5] Boone (Squire[4], George Michael[3], George[2], George[1]) was born 13 Jan 1738/39 in Exeter, Berks, Pennsylvania, and died 11 Nov 1820 in Richmond, Shelby, Kentucky. He married **Nancy Ann Linville** 28 Nov 1764 in Oley, Berks, Pennsylvania. She was born 1744 in Exeter Berks, Pennsylvania, and died 28 Mar 1814 in Shelbyville, Shelby, Kentucky.

Children of George Boone and Nancy Linville are:

+ 66   i.   John Linville[6] Boone, born in Bear Creek, Rowan, North Carolina; died in ,Calloway, Missouri.
   67   ii. Ellender Boone, born in , Rowan, North Carolina; died 17 Jul 1799. She married David Wilcox.
   68   iii. George Boone, born in North Carolina; died 1831 in ,Shelby, Kentucky.
   69   iv. Sarah Boone. She married ? ?.
   70   v.   Nester Boone.
+ 71   vi. Elizabeth Boone, born 21 Jul 1765 in Yadkin River, Rowan, North Carolina.
+ 72   vii. William Linville Boone, born 22 Feb 1768 in North Carolina; died 13 Apr 1847 in ,Shelby, Kentucky.
+ 73   viii. Mary Boone, born 02 Apr 1776; died 14 Sep 1831.
   74   ix. Susannah Boone, born 22 Apr 1778; died 16 Oct 1804. She married William Hern 08 Apr 1795.
+ 75   x.   Samuel Boone, born 15 Jan 1782 in Kentucky; died 19 Sep 1869 in ,Calloway, Missouri.

25. Edward[5] Boone (Squire[4], George Michael[3], George[2], George[1]) was born 30 Nov 1740 in Exeter, Berks , Pennsylvania, and died 06 Oct 1780 in Blue Lick, Clark, Kentucky. He married **Martha Bryan** 1758 in Yadkin River, Rowan , North Carolina. She was born 19 Mar 1736/37 in Winchester, Frederick, Virginia, and died 23 Jun 1793 in Blue Lick, Clark, Kentucky.

Children of Edward Boone and Martha Bryan are:

+ 76   i.   Banton[6] Boone.
+ 77   ii. Joseph Boone Sr., born in Yadkin District, Rowan, North Carolina; died in Shelbyville, Shelby, Indiana.
+ 78   iii. Charity Boone, born 11 Oct 1758 in Yadkin District, Rowan, North Carolina; died 07 Apr 1853 in Perry, Pike, Illinois.
+ 79   iv. Jane Boone, born 18 Sep 1762 in ,Rowan, North Carolina; died 01 Dec 1812 in Feliciana Parish, Louisiana.
+ 80   v.   Mary M. Boone, born 05 Dec 1764 in , Rowan, North Carolina; died 28 Sep 1825 in Stoner Creek, Clark, Kentucky.
   81   vi. George Boone, born 19 Nov 1765 in ,North Carolina. He married Martha Hazelrigg 09 Jul 1793 in ,Clark, Kentucky.
+ 82   vii. Sarah Boone, born 06 Mar 1771 in Yadkin District, Rowan, North Carolina; died 18 Jul 1866 in Dry Valley, Putnam, Tennessee.

26. Squire[5] Boone II (Squire[4], George Michael[3], George[2], George[1]) was born 16 Oct 1744 in Exeter Township, Berks, Pennsylvania, and died 15 Aug 1815 in Buck Creek, Corydon, Harrison, Indiana. He married **(1) Bryan** in <New Britian, Or Exeter Berks, Pennsylvania>. He married **(2) Jane Van Cleve** 08 Aug 1765 in , Rowan, North Carolina. She was born 16 Oct 1749 in New Brunswick, Middlesex, New Jersey, and died 10

Mar 1829 in Otter Creek, Meade/Hardin, Kentucky.

Children of Squire Boone and Jane Van Cleve are:

83	i.	Johnathon[6] Boone, born 30 Aug 1766 in Yadkin, Rowan, North Carolina; died 18 Mar 1837 in Alton, Crawford, Indiana.
+ 84	ii.	Moses Boone, born 23 Feb 1769 in Yadkin River, Rowan, North Carolina; died 08 Mar 1852 in Manhattan, Putnam, Indiana.
85	iii.	Isaiah Boone, born 17 Nov 1772 in Yadkin, Rowan, North Carolina; died Aft. 1846 in Mauckport Indiana.
86	iv.	Sarah Boone, born 26 Sep 1774 in Yadkin, Rowan , North Carolina; died 26 Jun 1846 in , Boone, Missouri.
87	v.	Enoch Morgan Boone, born 16 Oct 1777 in Ft. Boonesborough, Meade, Kentucky; died 08 Feb 1862 in Garnetsville, Meade, Kentucky.

27. Hannah[5] Boone (Squire[4], George Michael[3], George[2], George[1]) was born 22 Aug 1746 in Exeter Twp., Berks, Pennsylvania, and died 09 Apr 1828 in Tompkinville, Missourinroe, Kentucky. She married **(1) John Stewart** 14 Feb 1765 in ,Rowan, North Carolina. She married **(2) Richard Pennington** 15 May 1777 in Salisbury, Rowan, North Carolina.

Child of Hannah Boone and Richard Pennington is:

88	i.	Daniel[6] Pennington.

28. John[5] Boone (Benjamin[4], George Michael[3], George[2], George[1]) was born in Exeter Township, Berks, Pennsylvania. He married **Rebecca Bryan**. She was born in North Carolina.

Child of John Boone and Rebecca Bryan is:

+ 89	i.	John Bryan[6] Boone, born in Hunting Creek, Rowan, North Carolina.

Generation No. 4

31. Daniel[6] Stover (Abraham[5], Sarah[4] Boone, George Michael[3], George[2], George[1]) was born 1750 in Augusta , Virginia, and died 1826 in ,Augusta, Virginia.

Child of Daniel Stover is:

+ 90	i.	Daniel[7] Stover, born Abt. 1780 in Augusta Co, VA; died 18 Jan 1862 in Augusta Co, VA.

43. Elizabeth[6] Boone (Israel[5], Squire[4], George Michael[3], George[2], George[1]) She married **John Power**.

Child of Elizabeth Boone and John Power is:

+ 91	i.	Mary[7] Power, born 10 Nov 1773 in ,Rowan, North Carolina.

45. Squire[6] Boone Sr. (Samuel[5], Squire[4], George Michael[3], George[2], George[1]) was born 13 Oct 1760 in Yadkin District, Rowan, North Carolina, and died 28 Jun 1817 in Elkton, Todd, Kentucky. He married **(1) Mourning Grubbs**. She was born in <Fincastle, Lee, Kentucky>, and died in <St. Charles Missouri>. He married **(2) Anna Grubbs** 01 Sep 1784 in ,Fayette, Kentucky. She was born 23 Jun 1766 in , Albemarle, Virginia>, and died 26 Aug 1843 in Elkton, Todd, Kentucky.

Children of Squire Boone and Anna Grubbs are:

92	i.	Boone[7], born in , Fayette, Kentucky; died in , Fayette, Kentucky.
93	ii.	Boone, born in , Fayette, Kentucky; died in , Fayette, Kentucky.
94	iii.	Thomas Boone, born 24 Dec 1785 in , Fayette, Kentucky; died 22 Sep 1855 in Winchester, Scott, Illinois.
95	iv.	Susannah Boone, born 28 Jan 1787 in ,Fayette, Kentucky; died Aft. 18 Feb 1817.
96	v.	Lucy Boone, born 15 Oct 1792 in ,Fayette, Kentucky; died 18 Oct 1822.
97	vi.	Cynthia Ann Boone, born 11 May 1795 in , Fayette, Kentucky; died 17 Mar 1887 in ,Montgomery, Illinois.

98	vii.	Samuel Boone, born 02 Sep 1797 in ,Fayette, Kentucky; died 28 May 1835 in Kentucky.
99	viii.	Squire H. Boone, born 02 Sep 1797 in ,Fayette, Kentucky; died 06 Jul 1836 in ,Todd, Kentucky. He married Emily New.
100	ix.	Ira Boone, born 17 Dec 1799 in ,Fayette, Kentucky; died 06 Aug 1849 in Elkton, Todd, Kentucky.
101	x.	Isaiah H. Boone, born 07 Mar 1802 in ,Fayette, Kentucky; died 23 Nov 1835.
102	xi.	Diedema Boone, born 11 Aug 1804 in , Fayette, Kentucky; died 14 Sep 1824 in ,Todd.
103	xii.	Higgason Grubbs Boone, born 08 Oct 1806 in ,Fayette, Kentucky; died 08 Mar 1885 in Elkton, Todd, Kentucky.
104	xiii.	Levi Day Boone, born 08 Dec 1808 in Lexington, Fayette, Kentucky; died 24 Jan 1882 in Chicago, Cook, Illinois. He married Nancy Boone.
+ 105	xiv.	Hayden Boone, born 07 Jun 1810 in , St Charles, Missouri; died 23 Jan 1857 in , Warren, Missouri.
106	xv.	Nancy Boone, born 24 Dec 1811 in ,Fayette, Kentucky.
107	xvi.	Polly Boone, born 27 Jan 1814 in ,Fayette, Kentucky; died 28 Oct 1822 in ,Todd, Kentucky.

48. Susannah[6] Boone (Daniel[5], Squire[4], George Michael[3], George[2], George[1]) was born 11 Feb 1760 in Yadkin River Country, Rowan, North Carolina, and died 19 Oct 1800 in St. Charles, Missouri. She married **William Hays Sr.** Mar 1775 in ,Rowan, North Carolina. He was born 13 Dec 1754 in North Carolina, and died 13 Dec 1804 in Missouri.

Children of Susannah Boone and William Hays are:

+ 108	i.	Susannah A.[7] Hays.
109	ii.	Daniel Hays.
110	iii.	Greenup Hays.
111	iv.	Mahala Hays. She married ? ?.
112	v.	Delinda Hays.
113	vi.	Elizabeth Hays, born 1776; died 1828. She married Isaac Van Bibber.
114	vii.	Jemima Hayes, born 1778. She married James Davis.
+ 115	viii.	William Hays, born 1780; died 1845.
116	ix.	Jesse Hays, born Bef. 1817.

49. Jemima[6] Boone (Daniel[5], Squire[4], George Michael[3], George[2], George[1]) was born 04 Oct 1762 in Culpepper, Virginia, and died 30 Aug 1829 in Marthasville, Warren, Missouri. She married **John Flanders Callaway** 1777 in Boonesborough, Kentucky. He was born 09 Dec 1752 in Albermarle , Virginia, and died 22 Feb 1829 in ,Montgomery, Missouri.

Children of Jemima Boone and John Callaway are:

117	i.	Daniel Boone[7] Callaway.
118	ii.	Sarah Callaway.
119	iii.	Tabatha Callaway.
120	iv.	Minerva Callaway.
+ 121	v.	Frances Callaway.
+ 122	vi.	James Callaway, born 1781; died 07 Mar 1815 in Loutre Creek.
+ 123	vii.	Susannah Callaway, born 04 Jan 1791; died 25 Dec 1876.
+ 124	viii.	Elizabeth Callaway, born 15 Feb 1797 in Boone's Station, Fayette, Kentucky; died 01 Jun 1867 in ,Warren, Missouri.

50. Lavina[6] Boone (Daniel[5], Squire[4], George Michael[3], George[2], George[1]) was born 23 Mar 1766 in Sugar Creek, North Carolina, and died 06 Apr 1802 in ,Clark, Kentucky. She married **Joseph Scholl Sr.** 1785 in Kentucky. He was born Jan 1755 in ,Rowan, North Carolina, and died 15 Jan 1833 in ,Clark, Kentucky.

Children of Lavina Boone and Joseph Scholl are:

125	i.	Jesse Boone[7] Scholl. He married ? ?.
126	ii.	Marcia Scholl. She married James Holliday 31 Mar 1808.
127	iii.	Leah Scholl. She married John Newman 25 Dec 1814.
128	iv.	Joseph Scholl. He married (1) ? ?. He married (2) ? ?.
129	v.	Daniel Boone Scholl.
130	vi.	Celia Scholl.
131	vii.	Marcus Scholl. He married Betsey Martin 22 Jun 1821.
+ 132	viii.	Septimus Scholl, born 1789; died 1849.

51. Rebecca[6] **Boone** (Daniel[5], Squire[4], George Michael[3], George[2], George[1]) was born 26 May 1768 in Yadkin River Country, Rowan, North Carolina, and died 14 Jul 1805 in Boonesborough, Kentucky. She married **Philip Goe** 1788 in ,,Kentucky. He was born 23 Dec 1769 in Pennsylvania, and died Mar 1805 in ,Nicholas, Kentucky.

Children of Rebecca Boone and Philip Goe are:

133	i.	Daniel B.[7] Goe.
134	ii.	Nathan B. Goe.
135	iii.	Noble Goe.
136	iv.	Tarleton Goe.
137	v.	Nelly Goe.
138	vi.	Dorcas Goe. He married ? ?.
139	vii.	William Goe, died in bef 1868.

52. Daniel Morgan[6] **Boone** (Daniel[5], Squire[4], George Michael[3], George[2], George[1]) was born 23 Dec 1769 in Wilkesboro, Yadkin, North Carolina, and died 13 Jul 1839 in Cholera, Westport, Missouri. He married **Sarah Griffin Lewis** 02 Mar 1800 in St. Charles, Missouri. She was born 20 Jan 1786 in Rocky Springs, Goochland, Virginia, and died 19 Jun 1850 in ,Jackson, Missouri.

Children of Daniel Boone and Sarah Lewis are:

	140	i.	Milton L.[7] Boone.
	141	ii.	Morgan Boone. He married (1) Disa Stewart. He married (2) Mary Ann Randolph.
	142	iii.	John W. Boone.
	143	iv.	Nathan Boone.
	144	v.	Daniel Boone.
	145	vi.	Edward H. Boone.
	146	vii.	Elizabeth Levica Boone. She married Jesse White.
	147	viii.	Alonzo Havington Boone. He married Elizabeth Stewart 17 Dec 1840.
	148	ix.	James Boone. He married Lorinda Corbo.
	149	x.	Napoleon Boone.
+	150	xi.	Lindsey Boone, born 22 Oct 1811 in , St Charles, Missouri; died Feb 1834 in Missouri.
	151	xii.	Cassandra Boone, born 03 Nov 1821 in , Gasconde, Missouri; died 20 May 1845 in Missouri. She married Crosby.

53. Jesse Bryan[6] **Boone** (Daniel[5], Squire[4], George Michael[3], George[2], George[1]) was born 23 May 1773 in Yadkin Valley, Rowan, North Carolina, and died 22 Dec 1820 in St. Louis, St. Louis, Missouri. He married **Chloe Van Bibber** Sep 1790 in Boonesboro, Madison, Kentucky. She was born 13 Aug 1772 in ,Botetourt, Virginia, and died Aug 1822 in ,Calloway, Missouri.

Children of Jesse Boone and Chloe Van Bibber are:

	152	i.	Van D.[7] Boone.
	153	ii.	James M. Boone.
	154	iii.	Alonzo Boone.
	155	iv.	Madison Boone. He married ? ?.
	156	v.	Jeremiah Boone, born 1793.
	157	vi.	Harriet Boone, born 1794.
+	158	vii.	Alphonso Boone Sr., born 07 Nov 1796 in , Madison, Kentucky; died 01 Feb 1850 in Long's Bar California.
+	159	viii.	Minerva S. Boone, born 1799; died 1850.
+	160	ix.	Panthea Grant Boone, born 20 Sep 1801 in Maysville, Greenup, Kentucky; died 23 Sep 1880 in Napa , Napa, California.
+	161	x.	Albert Gallatin Boone, born 17 Apr 1806 in Massachusetts; died 14 Jul 1884 in Denver, Denver, Colorado.
	162	xi.	Emily Boone, born 1811.
+	163	xii.	Van Daniel Boone, born 29 Apr 1814 in ,Howard, Missouri; died 04 Mar 1871 in Boone, Pueblo, Colorado.

55. Nathan[6] Boone (Daniel[5], Squire[4], George Michael[3], George[2], George[1]) was born 03 Feb 1781 in Cross Plains, Rowan , North Carolina, and died 16 Oct 1856 in ,Green, Missouri. He married **Olive Van Bibber** 26 Sep 1799 in Point Pleasant, Virginia. She was born 13 Apr 1783 in ,Greenbrier, Virginia, and died 12 Nov 1858 in ,Green, Missouri.

Children of Nathan Boone and Olive Van Bibber are:

164	i.	Delinda[7] Boone. She married James Craig 29 Apr 1819.
165	ii.	James Boone. He married ? ?.
166	iii.	John Coburn Boone.
167	iv.	Jemima Boone. She married ? ?.
168	v.	Melcina Boone.
169	vi.	Nancy Boone.
170	vii.	Benjamin Howard Boone.
171	viii.	Levica Boone.
172	ix.	Melvian Boone.
173	x.	Susan Boone. She married ? ?.
174	xi.	Olive Boone. She married ? ?.
175	xii.	Sarah Boone. She married ? ?.
176	xiii.	Mahala Boone. She married ? ?.
177	xiv.	Melba Boone.
178	xv.	Mary Boone, born 1822; died 1915.

56. Sarah[6] Bryan (Mary[5] Boone, Squire[4], George Michael[3], George[2], George[1]) was born in North Carolina>, and died in , Fayette, Kentucky. She married **(1) William Chinn**. She married **(2) Sr. Grimes James** 22 Mar 1787 in , Fayette, Kentucky. He was born in North Carolina, and died in , Fayette, Kentucky.

Children of Sarah Bryan and William Chinn are:

179	i.	Sarah[7] Chinn. She married ? ?.
180	ii.	William Chinn.
181	iii.	Nancy B. Chinn, died 1856. She married ? ?.
182	iv.	John F. Chinn.
183	v.	Alfred S. Chinn, died in River Raisin.
184	vi.	Rhoda D. Chinn. She married ? ?.
185	vii.	Elizabeth Chinn. She married ? ?.
186	viii.	Franklin B. Chinn, born 1800.
187	ix.	Morgan B. Chinn, born 1801; died 1870.

Children of Sarah Bryan and Sr. James are:

188	i.	Elizabeth[7] Grimes.
189	ii.	John Grimes, died Bef. 05 Jun 1828.
190	iii.	Mary 'Polly' Grimes.
191	iv.	Nancy Grimes, born 1788; died 07 May 1836.
192	v.	Phebe Bryan Grimes, born 04 Mar 1795 in , Fayette, Kentucky; died 31 Mar 1862 in , Lawrence, Alabama.
193	vi.	Grimes James, born 1796 in Fayette, Kentucky; died 08 Apr 1873.
194	vii.	Sarah Grimes, born 1799.
195	viii.	Parmelia Grimes, born 1801.
196	ix.	Melinda Grimes, born 20 Dec 1802 in Fayette, Kentucky; died 09 Feb 1867 in Lee, Mississippi.
197	x.	Caroline Grimes, born Jun 1806 in Fayette, Kentucky; died 22 Jul 1876 in Fayette, Kentucky.

57. Samuel[6] Bryan (Mary[5] Boone, Squire[4], George Michael[3], George[2], George[1]) was born 06 May 1756 in , Rowan, North Carolina, and died 04 Mar 1837 in Indianapolis, Marion, Indiana. He married **Mary Hunt** 05 Oct 1775 in , Rowan, North Carolina. She was born in Of Rowan, North Carolina.

Children of Samuel Bryan and Mary Hunt are:

198	i.	Samuel[7] Bryan.
199	ii.	Phoebe Bryan, born 06 Sep 1778; died Apr 1781.
200	iii.	William Bryan, born 22 Jan 1780; died 1830.
201	iv.	Abner Bryan, born 1783 in Tennessee; died 1783.

202	v.	Thomas Bryan, born 20 Mar 1787.
203	vi.	Mary Bryan, born 05 May 1789; died 20 Jun 1890.
204	vii.	Daniel Bryan, born 05 Mar 1791; died Feb 1804.

58. Daniel Boone^6 Bryan (Mary^5 Boone, Squire^4, George Michael^3, George^2, George^1) was born 10 Feb 1758 in , Rowan, North Carolina, and died 28 Feb 1845 in ,Fayette, Kentucky. He married **Elizabeth Turner**.

Children of Daniel Bryan and Elizabeth Turner are:

205	i.	Joseph^7 Bryan, born in ,Rowan, North Carolina.
206	ii.	Elizabeth Bryan.
207	iii.	Phoebe Bryan.
208	iv.	Sallie Bryan.
209	v.	Samuel Bryan.
210	vi.	Daniel Bryan.
211	vii.	Louis Bryan.
212	viii.	Mary Bryan.
213	ix.	Thomas Bryan.
214	x.	William Turner Bryan, born 02 Dec 1787 in Fayette, Kentucky; died 28 Jul 1854 in Fayette, Kentucky.

66. John Linville^6 Boone (George^5, Squire^4, George Michael^3, George^2, George^1) was born in Bear Creek, Rowan, North Carolina, and died in ,Calloway, Missouri. He married **Mary Polly Morris**.

Children of John Boone and Mary Morris are:

	215	i.	George^7 Boone, born in ,,Missouri.
	216	ii.	Mary Boone, born in Missouri.
	217	iii.	Ervin Boone, born in Missouri.
	218	iv.	Orvy Boone.
+	219	v.	Elizabeth Boone, born in ,,Missouri.
	220	vi.	Joshua Morris Boone, born 1792 in ,Madison, Kentucky; died 11 Apr 1845 in ,Calloway, Missouri.
+	221	vii.	Nancy Linville Boone, born 30 Apr 1798 in , Shelby, Kentucky; died 09 Apr 1839 in , Montgomery, Missouri.
	222	viii.	Garland Boone, born 1802 in ,Madison, Kentucky. He married Martha Jane Patton 10 Aug 1841 in ,Warren, Missouri.
+	223	ix.	Delia Morris Boone, born 26 Jun 1807; died 1901.
	224	x.	Urbain Boone, born 1809 in Gallinton, Kentucky. He married Mary in Jackson , Iowa.
+	225	xi.	Alonzo Boone, born 26 May 1810 in Gallinton Kentucky; died 15 Apr 1876 in Cherokee Arizona.

71. Elizabeth^6 Boone (George^5, Squire^4, George Michael^3, George^2, George^1) was born 21 Jul 1765 in Yadkin River, Rowan, North Carolina. She married **Jesse Copher** 1792.

Children of Elizabeth Boone and Jesse Copher are:

	226	i.	Mary^7 Copher. She married ? ?.
	227	ii.	Phebe Copher.
	228	iii.	Udosha Copher. She married ? ?.
	229	iv.	Nancy Boone Copher, born 1782.
	230	v.	Thomas Copher, born 1784; died 1840.
	231	vi.	Jurusha Copher, born 1793; died 1859. She married Kirkly.
	232	vii.	Sarah Copher, born 1795; died 1859. She married Dooly.
	233	viii.	Samuel Boone Copher, born 1797; died 1879. He married Anna Maupin Turner.
	234	ix.	Hettie Boone Copher, born 1803; died 1842.
	235	x.	David Newton Copher, born 1805; died 1831.
+	236	xi.	Eleanor Copher, born 1806; died 1868.

72. William Linville^6 Boone (George^5, Squire^4, George Michael^3, George^2, George^1) was born 22 Feb 1768 in North Carolina, and died 13 Apr 1847 in ,Shelby, Kentucky. He married **(1) Ann Perry**.   He married **(2) Nancy Grubbs** 16 Aug 1789 in , Madison, Kentucky. She was born 08 Jun 1771 in Fincastle, Lee, Kentucky, and died 22 Mar 1835 in Fayette, Howard, Missouri.

Children of William Boone and Nancy Grubbs are:

+ 237   i.   Cassandra[7] Boone, died in Fayette, Howard, Missouri.
    238   ii.   Hampton Lynch Boone. He married Maria Louise Roberts.
    239   iii.   Matilda Boone, born in , Madison, Kentucky; died in Shelbyville Kentucky. She married William Wilson 01 Oct 1816 in , Shelby, Kentucky; died in Shelbyville Kentucky.
    240   iv.   Nestor Boone.
    241   v.   William Crawford Boone.
    242   vi.   Lucy Boone, born 1790 in , Madison, Kentucky; died in , Shelby, Kentucky. She married Andrew Tribble 24 Jun 1810 in , Shelby, Kentucky; born 02 Dec 1785.
+ 243   vii.   Mildred Boone, born 11 Dec 1795 in Madison, County , Kentucky; died 16 Nov 1852 in , Shelby, Kentucky.
    244   viii.   Cassandra Boone, born 1796 in , Madison, Kentucky; died in Fayette, Howard, Missouri. She married William Carson 1817 in , Howard, Missouri.

73. Mary[6] Boone (George[5], Squire[4], George Michael[3], George[2], George[1]) was born 02 Apr 1776, and died 14 Sep 1831. She married **Peter Burris Tribble** 08 Oct 1793.

Child of Mary Boone and Peter Tribble is:
    245   i.   Peter[7] Tribble, born 1812.

75. Samuel[6] Boone (George[5], Squire[4], George Michael[3], George[2], George[1]) was born 15 Jan 1782 in Kentucky, and died 19 Sep 1869 in ,Calloway, Missouri. He married **Anna Simpson** 1804.

Children of Samuel Boone and Anna Simpson are:
    246   i.   Mary A.[7] Boone.
    247   ii.   Maximilla Boone.
    248   iii.   Martha L. Boone.
    249   iv.   Samuel Tucker Boone.
    250   v.   Nestor Boone.
+ 251   vi.   Elizabeth C. Boone.
    252   vii.   Maxemille Boone.
+ 253   viii.   Jeptha Vining Boone, born 1806; died 1881.

76. Banton[6] Boone (Edward[5], Squire[4], George Michael[3], George[2], George[1]) He married **Elizabeth C. Boone** 26 Jun 1828, daughter of Samuel Boone and Anna Simpson.

Child of Banton Boone and Elizabeth Boone is:
    254   i.   Banton II[7] Boone.

77. Joseph[6] Boone Sr. (Edward[5], Squire[4], George Michael[3], George[2], George[1]) was born in Yadkin District, Rowan, North Carolina, and died in Shelbyville, Shelby, Indiana. He married **(1) Joseph Boone Fry** 17 Jan 1789. He married **(2) Rebecca Locke** 04 Jun 1794 in ,,Clark, Kentucky. He married **(3) Nancy** Nov 1843 in ,,Shelby, Indiana.

Children of Joseph Boone and Rebecca Locke are:
    255   i.   Boone[7].
    256   ii.   Boone.

78. Charity[6] Boone (Edward[5], Squire[4], George Michael[3], George[2], George[1]) was born 11 Oct 1758 in Yadkin District, Rowan, North Carolina, and died 07 Apr 1853 in Perry, Pike, Illinois. She married **Francis Elledge** 1778 in Yadkin River, Rowan, North Carolina. He was born 18 Feb 1749/50 in Yadkin District, Rowan, North Carolina, and died Aug 1827 in , Pike, Illinois.

Children of Charity Boone and Francis Elledge are:
+ 257   i.   Mary[7] Elledge, born 19 Sep 1777 in Kentucky; died Sep 1826 in Green River Kentucky.
+ 258   ii.   James Elledge, born 02 Oct 1779 in North Carolina; died 30 Oct 1847 in Lancaster, Grant, Wisconsin.

+	259	iii.	Benjamin Franklin Elledge, born 20 Jan 1782 in ,,Kentucky; died 31 Oct 1853 in Pike, Illinois.

+ 259   iii. Benjamin Franklin Elledge, born 20 Jan 1782 in ,,Kentucky; died 31 Oct 1853 in Pike, Illinois.

+ 260   iv. Leonard Boone Elledge, born 24 Dec 1783 in ,,Kentucky; died 04 Jun 1841 in Griggsville, Pike, Illinois.

+ 261   v. Martha Jane Elledge, born 24 Jul 1786 in ,Fayette/Clark, Kentucky; died 11 Aug 1846 in ,Macon/Adair, Missouri.

+ 262   vi. Nancy Elledge, born 04 Oct 1788 in ,,North Carolina; died 1861 in ,Sullivan, Indiana.

+ 263   vii. Edward Boone Elledge, born 30 Sep 1791 in Kentucky; died 12 Sep 1829 in , Morgan, Illinois.

+ 264   viii. Charity Sarah Elledge, born 04 May 1795 in Boone's Fort, Fayette, Kentucky; died 06 Oct 1878 in Winchester, Scott, Illinois.

     265   ix. William Elledge, born 06 Jun 1797 in ,,Kentucky; died 13 Nov 1830 in Jacksonville, Morgan, Illinois. He married Tabitha Bell.

     266   x. Jesse Bryan Elledge, born 12 Aug 1800; died 14 Feb 1875 in Winterset, Madison, Iowa. He married Elizabeth Phillips 02 Sep 1819 in ,Clark, Kentucky.

     267   xi. Jemina Elledge, born 19 Sep 1803 in ,,Kentucky; died 22 Jul 1900 in ,Madison, Iowa. She married Richard Beall 1818 in ,,Kentucky.

79. Jane[6] Boone (Edward[5], Squire[4], George Michael[3], George[2], George[1]) was born 18 Sep 1762 in ,Rowan, North Carolina, and died 01 Dec 1812 in Feliciana Parish, Louisiana. She married **John Morgan** 1785.

Children of Jane Boone and John Morgan are:

+ 268   i. Nancy[7] Morgan.

     269   ii. Martha Morgan. She married ? ?.

     270   iii. Mary Morgan. She married ? ?.

     271   iv. Elizabeth Morgan. She married ? ?.

     272   v. Sarah Morgan.

     273   vi. Daniel Morgan. He married (1) ? ?. He married (2) ? ?. He married (3) ? ?.

     274   vii. Charity Morgan. She married ? ?.

     275   viii. William Morgan. He married ? ?.

     276   ix. Hannah Morgan. She married ? ?.

     277   x. John Morgan, born 1783; died 1803.

     278   xi. George Morgan, born 1792.

     279   xii. Cyrus Morgan, born 1801; died 1802.

     280   xiii. Joseph Morgan, born 1801; died 1801.

80. Mary M.[6] Boone (Edward[5], Squire[4], George Michael[3], George[2], George[1]) was born 05 Dec 1764 in , Rowan, North Carolina, and died 28 Sep 1825 in Stoner Creek, Clark, Kentucky. She married **Peter Scholl** in Boone's Station Kentucky. He was born 15 Sep 1754 in Shenandoah Valley, Page, Virginia, and died 11 Sep 1821 in Stoner Fork, Clark, Kentucky.

Children of Mary Boone and Peter Scholl are:

     281   i. Edward B.[7] Scholl.

     282   ii. Martha Scholl, born in Boone's Station, Clark, Kentucky; died 10 Oct 1840. She married Horton Wells 12 Aug 1799 in , Clark, Kentucky.

     283   iii. Lydia Ann Scholl, born in Boone's Station, Clark, Kentucky. She married (1) Frazier. She married (2) Boone Hays 03 Jun 1807 in ,Clark , Kentucky; born 1783; died 1850 in Marysville, California.

+ 284   iv. Joseph Scholl, born in , Clark, Kentucky; died in Kentucky.

     285   v. Peter Morgan Scholl, born in ,Clark, Kentucky; died in ,Calloway, Missouri. He married Elizabeth Hulse 17 Mar 1823.

+ 286   vi. Dudley Scholl, born in ,Clark, Kentucky; died 14 Dec 1862 in Atchison, Atchison, Kansas.

     287   vii. Mary Scholl, born in ,Clark, Kentucky; died in ,,Missouri. She married Archibald Talbert Hite 24 Jul 1824 in ,Clark, Kentucky.

     288   viii. Louisa Scholl, born in , Clark, Kentucky. She married (1) Francis Key 22 Oct 1825 in ,Clark, Kentucky. She married (2) Thomas K. Norris 13 Mar 1835 in ,Pike, Illinois.

     289   ix. Peter Scholl.

+ 290   x. William Scholl, born 22 Sep 1784 in Boone's Station, Fayette, Kentucky; died 14 Aug 1846 in Macon, Adair, Missouri.

     291   xi. John Scholl, born 05 Apr 1787 in Boone's Station, Clark, Kentucky; died Jun 1868 in , Calloway, Missouri. He married Icenia Linah Jones 05 Jan 1815 in Fayette, Clark, Illinois.

+ 292   xii. Malinda Scholl, born 25 Aug 1791 in , Clark, Kentucky; died 13 Nov 1865 in Pleasant Vale, Pike, Illinois.

+ 293   xiii.   Jesse Bryan Scholl, born 30 Nov 1797 in , Clark, Kentucky; died 06 Feb 1858 in Winchester, Scott, Illinois.

+ 294   xiv.   Edward Boone Scholl, born 11 Oct 1801 in ,Clark, Kentucky; died 09 Mar 1862 in Griggsville, Pike, Illinois.

+ 295   xv.   Charity Ann Scholl, born 16 Aug 1809 in , Clark, Kentucky; died 23 Sep 1888 in , Adair, Missouri.

82. Sarah⁶ Boone (Edward⁵, Squire⁴, George Michael³, George², George¹) was born 06 Mar 1771 in Yadkin District, Rowan, North Carolina, and died 18 Jul 1866 in Dry Valley, Putnam, Tennessee. She married **William Hunter** 1787. He was born 10 Mar 1768 in ,Jaessamine, Kentucky, and died 1862 in ,White, Tennessee.

Children of Sarah Boone and William Hunter are:
    296   i.   Jepsee⁷ Hunter.
    297   ii.   Polly Hunter.
    298   iii.   William Hunter.
+ 299   iv.   Joseph Hunter.
    300   v.   Marcy Hunter.
+ 301   vi.   Mary Polly Hunter, born 11 Nov 1789 in Boone's Station, Clark, Kentucky; died 07 Oct 1878 in Sparta, White, Tennessee.
+ 302   vii.   Dudley Hunter, born 21 Nov 1794 in Tennessee; died 27 Oct 1862 in Dry Valley, Putnam, Tennessee.

84. Moses⁶ Boone (Squire⁵, Squire⁴, George Michael³, George², George¹) was born 23 Feb 1769 in Yadkin River, Rowan, North Carolina, and died 08 Mar 1852 in Manhattan, Putnam, Indiana. He married **Hannah Boone** 26 Dec 1786 in , Jefferson, Kentucky. She was born 06 Feb 1770 in , Frederick, Maryland, and died 08 Mar 1828.

Children of Moses Boone and Hannah Boone are:
    303   i.   Cassandra⁷ Boone, born in Indiana>.
    304   ii.   Samuel Boone, born in Indiana.
    305   iii.   Emmet Boone, born in , Shelby, Kentucky>.
    306   iv.   Warren Boone, born in Indiana.
    307   v.   Daniel Boone, born in , Shelby, Kentucky>.
    308   vi.   Nancy Boone, born in , Shelby, Kentucky>.
    309   vii.   Cassa Boone, born in , Shelby, Kentucky>.
    310   viii.   Sallie Boone, born in , Shelby, Kentucky>.
    311   ix.   Betty Boone, born in , Shelby, Kentucky>.
    312   x.   Jennie Boone, born in , Shelby, Kentucky>.
    313   xi.   Susan Boone, born in Indiana.
    314   xii.   Squire Boone, born 07 Jun 1794 in , Shelby, Kentucky>; died 05 Dec 1879 in , Boone, Iowa.
    315   xiii.   Robert Emmett Boone, born 01 Apr 1809 in , Harrison, Indiana.

89. John Bryan⁶ Boone (John⁵, Benjamin⁴, George Michael³, George², George¹) was born in Hunting Creek, Rowan, North Carolina. He married **Elizabeth Little** 21 Sep 1805 in , Wake, North Carolina. She was born in Huntington, Rowan, North Carolina, and died 03 Sep 1852.

Child of John Boone and Elizabeth Little is:
+ 316   i.   Andrew Jackson⁷ Boone, born 25 Sep 1823 in North Carolina; died in Missouri>.

Generation No. 5

90. Daniel⁷ Stover (Daniel⁶, Abraham⁵, Sarah⁴ Boone, George Michael³, George², George¹) was born Abt. 1780 in Augusta Co, VA, and died 18 Jan 1862 in Augusta Co, VA. He married **Mary Hannah** 30 Mar 1803 in Augusta Co, VA. She was born Abt. 1781 in Augusta Co, VA, and died Abt. 1852.

Child of Daniel Stover and Mary Hannah is:
+ 317   i.   Simon P⁸ Stover, born 28 Sep 1822 in Augusta Co, VA; died 11 Dec 1873 in Augusta Co, VA.

91. Mary[7] **Power** (Elizabeth[6] Boone, Israel[5], Squire[4], George Michael[3], George[2], George[1]) was born 10 Nov 1773 in ,Rowan, North Carolina. She married **David Bryan** 1791 in ,,Kentucky. He was born 29 Oct 1757 in ,Rowan, North Carolina, and died 20 Mar 1837 in Between Dutzow and Marthasville, Warren , Missouri.

Children of Mary Power and David Bryan are:

318	i.	Drucilla[8] Bryan, born in Marthasville, Warren, Missouri.
319	ii.	James Bryan, born 1792 in ,,,Kentucky; died 1835 in ,Warren, Missouri. He married Malinda Morgan 16 Apr 1818 in ,Warren, Missouri; born 1811 in , Warren , Missouri.; died 1839 in ,,Warren , Missouri..
+ 320	iii.	Morgan Bryan, born 20 Aug 1794 in ,Rowan, North Carolina; died 07 Aug 1857 in ,Warren, Missouri.
321	iv.	Elizabeth Bryan, born 1796 in Bryan's Station, Kentucky; died 1820.
322	v.	Mary Bryan, born 06 Dec 1798 in Bryan's Station, Kentucky; died 26 Mar 1867.
323	vi.	Willis Bryan, born 07 Nov 1801 in ,St Charles, Missouri; died 31 Aug 1867. He married Czarina Lamme; born 11 Feb 1805 in ,St Charles, Missouri; died 24 Oct 1836.
324	vii.	John Bryan, born 1803 in Marthasville, Warren, Missouri. He married Hulda Lamme 1835 in ,,North Carolina; born 1812 in ,Rowan, North Carolina.
325	viii.	Susan Bryan, born 1805 in Marthasville, Warren, Missouri.
326	ix.	Samuel Bryan, born 1809 in Marthasville, Warren, Missouri.
327	x.	William K. Bryan, born 1811 in Marthasville, Warren, Missouri.

105. Hayden[7] **Boone** (Squire[6], Samuel[5], Squire[4], George Michael[3], George[2], George[1]) was born 07 Jun 1810 in , St Charles, Missouri, and died 23 Jan 1857 in , Warren, Missouri. He married **Emaline Roberta Callaway** in , Montgomery, Missouri. She was born 07 Jun 1810 in , St Charles, Missouri, and died 23 Jan 1857 in Marthasville, Warren, Missouri.

Children of Hayden Boone and Emaline Callaway are:

328	i.	Martha Jane[8] Boone, born in Marthasville, Warren, Missouri; died 14 Jun 1870 in , Yolo, California.
329	ii.	Mary Elizabeth Boone, born 13 May 1826 in Missouri; died 26 Oct 1889 in Winters, Yolo, California.
330	iii.	James Orville Boone, born 02 Feb 1828 in Missouri; died 24 May 1902 in Benicia, Contra Costa, California.
331	iv.	Wellington Treeson Boone, born 31 Dec 1829 in Missouri; died 10 Oct 1882 in Alamo, Contra Costa, California.
332	v.	William T. Boone, born 1833 in , Missouri; died 1852.
333	vi.	John Calloway Boone, born 26 Nov 1834 in Missouri; died 18 May 1865 in Marthasville, Warren, Missouri.
334	vii.	Octavia Ann Boone, born 11 Aug 1836 in Marthasville, Warren, Missouri; died 04 Feb 1853 in Marthasville, Warren, Missouri.
335	viii.	Joel Hayden Boone, born 19 Jul 1839 in , Warren, Missouri; died 14 Apr 1887 in Danville, Contra Costa, California.
336	ix.	Sarah E. Boone, born 1840 in Missouri; died Oct 1869 in , Yolo, California.
337	x.	Cemer C. Boone, born 16 Aug 1844 in Missouri; died 30 Sep 1844 in Marthasville, Warren, Missouri.
338	xi.	Leonidas Lonnie Boone, born 11 May 1847 in , Warren, Missouri.

108. Susannah A.[7] **Hays** (Susannah[6] Boone, Daniel[5], Squire[4], George Michael[3], George[2], George[1]) She married **? ?**.

Child of Susannah Hays and ? ? is:

+ 339	i.	?[8] ?.

115. William[7] **Hays** (Susannah[6] Boone, Daniel[5], Squire[4], George Michael[3], George[2], George[1]) was born 1780, and died 1845. He married **Phoebe Stevens**.

Child of William Hays and Phoebe Stevens is:

+ 340	i.	Sarah W.[8] Hays, born 18 Jan 1819 in , St. Charles, Missouri; died 23 May 1889.

121. Frances[7] **Callaway** (Jemima[6] Boone, Daniel[5], Squire[4], George Michael[3], George[2], George[1]) She married **William T. Lamme**.

Children of Frances Callaway and William Lamme are:

341   i.   Czarina[8] Lamme, born 11 Feb 1805 in ,St Charles, Missouri; died 24 Oct 1836. She married Willis Bryan; born 07 Nov 1801 in ,St Charles, Missouri; died 31 Aug 1867.

342   ii.   Hulda Lamme, born 1812 in ,Rowan, North Carolina. She married John Bryan 1835 in ,,North Carolina; born 1803 in Marthasville, Warren, Missouri.

122. James[7] Callaway (Jemima[6] Boone, Daniel[5], Squire[4], George Michael[3], George[2], George[1]) was born 1781, and died 07 Mar 1815 in Loutre Creek. He married **Nancy Howell**.

Child of James Callaway and Nancy Howell is:

+   343   i.   Susan[8] Callaway, born 1828; died 1881.

123. Susannah[7] Callaway (Jemima[6] Boone, Daniel[5], Squire[4], George Michael[3], George[2], George[1]) was born 04 Jan 1791, and died 25 Dec 1876. She married **Thomas W. Howell** 10 Jul 1806. He was born 14 Mar 1783, and died 12 Sep 1869.

Child of Susannah Callaway and Thomas Howell is:

+   344   i.   Pizarro[8] Howell, born 28 Nov 1811; died 12 Sep 1881.

124. Elizabeth[7] Callaway (Jemima[6] Boone, Daniel[5], Squire[4], George Michael[3], George[2], George[1]) was born 15 Feb 1797 in Boone's Station, Fayette, Kentucky, and died 01 Jun 1867 in ,Warren, Missouri. She married **Morgan Bryan** 15 Feb 1815 in ,Warren, Missouri, son of David Bryan and Mary Power. He was born 20 Aug 1794 in ,Rowan, North Carolina, and died 07 Aug 1857 in ,Warren, Missouri.

Children of Elizabeth Callaway and Morgan Bryan are:

345   i.   Melcina Callaway[8] Bryan, born 18 Oct 1816 in ,Warren, Missouri; died 11 Dec 1893. She married Lynn Clever 30 Jan 1834.

346   ii.   Iciline Archibald Bryan, born 10 Jan 1832 in ,Warren, Missouri.

132. Septimus[7] Scholl (Lavina[6] Boone, Daniel[5], Squire[4], George Michael[3], George[2], George[1]) was born 1789, and died 1849. He married **Sallie Miller**.

Children of Septimus Scholl and Sallie Miller are:

347   i.   Daniel Boone[8] Scholl.

348   ii.   Nelson Scholl.

349   iii.   Joseph Scholl, died 1847.

350   iv.   Marcus Scholl. He married (1) ? ?. He married (2) Betsey Martin 22 Jun 1821.

351   v.   Cyrus Scholl, died 1868.

352   vi.   Elizabeth Scholl. She married ? ?.

353   vii.   Catherine Scholl, born 1820; died 1874. She married Rodney Martin Hinde.

150. Lindsey[7] Boone (Daniel Morgan[6], Daniel[5], Squire[4], George Michael[3], George[2], George[1]) was born 22 Oct 1811 in , St Charles, Missouri, and died Feb 1834 in Missouri. He married **Sarah Grooms** 14 Jan 1832 in , Jackson, Missouri. She was born in , Jackson, Missouri>.

Child of Lindsey Boone and Sarah Grooms is:

354   i.   Cassandra[8] Boone, born in , Jackson, Missouri>. She married Franklin Whitely 02 Aug 1850 in , DeKalb, Missouri.

158. Alphonso[7] Boone Sr. (Jesse Bryan[6], Daniel[5], Squire[4], George Michael[3], George[2], George[1]) was born 07 Nov 1796 in , Madison, Kentucky, and died 01 Feb 1850 in Long's Bar California. He married **Nancy Linville Boone** 21 Feb 1822 in Round Prairie, Callaway, Missouri, daughter of John Boone and Mary Morris. She was born 30 Apr 1798 in , Shelby, Kentucky, and died 09 Apr 1839 in , Montgomery, Missouri.

Children of Alphonso Boone and Nancy Boone are:

355	i.	Lucy[8] Boone.
356	ii.	James C. Boone, died in Idaho.
+ 357	iii.	Chloe Donnelly Boone, born 09 Dec 1822 in , Montgomery, Missouri; died 10 Feb 1909 in , Montgomery, Missouri.
+ 358	iv.	Jesse Van Bibber Boone, born 25 Jan 1824 in ,Montgomery, Missouri; died 24 Mar 1872 in Williamsville, Oegon.
+ 359	v.	Mary Elizabeth Boone, born 03 Apr 1825 in ,Montgomery, Missouri; died 04 Jun 1907 in Coquille, Coos, Oregon.
+ 360	vi.	George Luther Boone, born 06 Jun 1826 in ,Montgomery, Missouri; died 04 Dec 1910 in Medford, Jackson, Oregon.
+ 361	vii.	Joshua Morris Boone, born 30 Jul 1833 in , Montgomery, Missouri; died in , Benton, Oregon.
+ 362	viii.	Alphonso Daniel Boone, born 03 Jun 1837 in Jefferson City, Cole, Missouri; died 30 Mar 1915 in Sumner, Coos, Oregon.

159. Minerva S.[7] Boone (Jesse Bryan[6], Daniel[5], Squire[4], George Michael[3], George[2], George[1]) was born 1799, and died 1850. She married **Wynkoop Warner**.

Child of Minerva Boone and Wynkoop Warner is:

+ 363	i.	Thoedore Fulton[8] Warner, born 1818; died 1891.

160. Panthea Grant[7] Boone (Jesse Bryan[6], Daniel[5], Squire[4], George Michael[3], George[2], George[1]) was born 20 Sep 1801 in Maysville, Greenup, Kentucky, and died 23 Sep 1880 in Napa , Napa, California. She married **Lilburn Williams Boggs** in <Lexington, Fayette, Kentucky>. He was born 14 Dec 1796 in Lexington, Fayette, Kentucky, and died 14 Mar 1860 in Napa , Napa, California.

Children of Panthea Boone and Lilburn Boggs are:

364	i.	Thomas Oliver[8] Boggs, born in , Greenup, Kentucky>.
+ 365	ii.	William Montgomery Boggs, born 21 Oct 1826 in Missouri; died 22 Apr 1911 in Napa , Napa, California.
366	iii.	John Boggs, born 1832 in Independence, Jackson, Missouri.

161. Albert Gallatin[7] Boone (Jesse Bryan[6], Daniel[5], Squire[4], George Michael[3], George[2], George[1]) was born 17 Apr 1806 in Massachusetts, and died 14 Jul 1884 in Denver, Denver, Colorado. He married **(1) Catherine Pierson**. She was born in Massachusetts. He married **(2) Ann Reid Hamilton** 09 Jul 1829. She was born 25 Dec 1811 in , Agusta, Virginia, and died 21 Apr 1842. He married **(3) Zeralda Randall** 20 Jan 1845.

Children of Albert Boone and Ann Hamilton are:

367	i.	Boone[8], born 20 Apr 1830 in , Fayette, Kentucky; died 20 Apr 1830 in , Fayette, Kentucky.
368	ii.	William Ashley Boone, born 04 Jan 1832 in , Fayette, Kentucky.
369	iii.	John Hamilton Boone, born 06 Jan 1834 in , Rowan, North Carolina.
370	iv.	Margaret Ann Boone, born 01 Aug 1836 in , Fayette, Kentucky. She married Sidney S. Barnes 26 Mar 1863.
+ 371	v.	Eliza Yantis Boone, born 02 Jun 1838 in , Fayette, Kentucky.
+ 372	vi.	Agnes B. Boone, born 02 Dec 1840 in Missouri.

Children of Albert Boone and Zeralda Randall are:

373	i.	Minerva Warner[8] Boone. She married ? ?.
374	ii.	Martha Randall Boone.
375	iii.	Mollie Boggs Boone, born 02 Nov 1845. She married Benjamin Davies Spencer 15 Sep 1863.

163. Van Daniel[7] Boone (Jesse Bryan[6], Daniel[5], Squire[4], George Michael[3], George[2], George[1]) was born 29 Apr 1814 in ,Howard, Missouri, and died 04 Mar 1871 in Boone, Pueblo, Colorado. He married **Mary Ann Randall** 09 Jan 1845 in Westport, Missouri. She was born 07 Mar 1823 in London, Laurel, Kentucky, and died 18 Sep 1909 in Walsenburg, Huerfano, Colorado.

Children of Van Boone and Mary Randall are:

- \+ 376   i.   Albert Gallatin^8 Boone, born 25 Nov 1845 in ,Jackson, Missouri; died 22 Jun 1916 in Pagosa Springs, Archuleta, Colorado.
- \+ 377   ii.   Emma Henderson Boone, born 31 May 1848 in Westport, Jackson, Missouri; died 21 Aug 1925 in ,Pueblo, Colorado.
- 378   iii.   William Randall Boone, born 02 Nov 1850 in ,Jackson, Missouri; died Bef. 1925.
- 379   iv.   Zeralda Engleton Boone, born 24 Apr 1852 in ,Jackson, Missouri; died Feb 1918 in Callahan, Florida. She married Conrad Otto Unfug.
- \+ 380   v.   Harriet Baber Boone, born 11 Feb 1855 in ,Jackson, Missouri; died 22 Mar 1925 in Pueblo, Pueblo, Colorado.
- 381   vi.   Charles Randall Boone, born 31 Jan 1858 in Westport, Jackson, Missouri; died 12 Jan 1943.
- 382   vii.   Benjamin Franklin Boone, born 23 Aug 1863 in Boone, Pueblo, Colorado; died 03 Jan 1935.
- 383   viii.   Jesse Murray Boone, born 22 Mar 1866 in Boone, Pueblo, Colorado; died 25 Nov 1899 in ,Jackson, Missouri.

219. Elizabeth^7 Boone (John Linville^6, George^5, Squire^4, George Michael^3, George^2, George^1) was born in ,,Missouri. She married **John Hamblin** 18 Nov 1816 in Shelby , Kentucky.

Children of Elizabeth Boone and John Hamblin are:

- 384   i.   Emily^8 Hamblin.
- 385   ii.   Mary Hamblin. She married ? ?.
- 386   iii.   Elizabeth Hamblin.
- 387   iv.   Ann Hamblin.
- 388   v.   Delia Hamblin. She married ? ?.
- 389   vi.   Piercy Hamblin.
- 390   vii.   George Hamblin.
- 391   viii.   Orva Hamblin. She married ? ?.
- 392   ix.   Eliza Hamblin.
- 393   x.   Lucinda Hamblin.

221. Nancy Linville^7 Boone (John Linville^6, George^5, Squire^4, George Michael^3, George^2, George^1) was born 30 Apr 1798 in , Shelby, Kentucky, and died 09 Apr 1839 in , Montgomery, Missouri. She married **Alphonso Boone Sr.** 21 Feb 1822 in Round Prairie, Callaway, Missouri, son of Jesse Boone and Chloe Van Bibber. He was born 07 Nov 1796 in , Madison, Kentucky, and died 01 Feb 1850 in Long's Bar California.

Children are listed above under (158) Alphonso Boone Sr..

223. Delia Morris^7 Boone (John Linville^6, George^5, Squire^4, George Michael^3, George^2, George^1) was born 26 Jun 1807, and died 1901. She married **John May** 20 Feb 1834 in Calloway , Missouri.

Children of Delia Boone and John May are:

- 394   i.   Richard^8 May.
- 395   ii.   George May.
- 396   iii.   Hinton May.
- 397   iv.   Ira May.
- 398   v.   John May.
- 399   vi.   William May, born 1835; died 1905.

225. Alonzo^7 Boone (John Linville^6, George^5, Squire^4, George Michael^3, George^2, George^1) was born 26 May 1810 in Gallinton Kentucky, and died 15 Apr 1876 in Cherokee Arizona. He married **(1) Mary Jane Jackson** 02 Jan 1834. He married **(2) Hannah Dyers** 30 May 1841. He married **(3) Martha Jane Merchant** 28 Feb 1847.

Children of Alonzo Boone and Mary Jackson are:

- 400   i.   Mary Clarissa^8 Boone, born 27 Nov 1834; died 06 Sep 1839.
- \+ 401   ii.   Charlie Edgar Boone, born 15 Jul 1837; died 01 Oct 1912.

Children of Alonzo Boone and Hannah Dyers are:
   402   i.   Francis Marion[8] Boone, born 14 Jul 1842; died 14 Feb 1874.
   403   ii.   Mary Ann Elizabeth Boone, born 01 Aug 1843; died 14 Oct 1843.

Children of Alonzo Boone and Martha Merchant are:
   404   i.   Lillie Bell[8] Boone. She married Mathias Gargus.
   405   ii.   Sarah Jane Boone, born 02 Jan 1848; died 16 Sep 1874. She married Henry Tate.
+ 406   iii. Martha Susan Boone, born 09 Mar 1850 in ,Callaway, Missouri; died 16 Sep 1929.
   407   iv.   Hannah Ruth Boone, born 20 Jan 1854; died 17 Aug 1902. She married Warren Tate.
+ 408   v.   John William Alonzo Boone, born 14 Jun 1854 in , Callaway, Missouri; died 30 Oct 1933.
   409   vi.   Nancy L. Boone, born 18 Feb 1856.
+ 410   vii. Emma Josephine Boone, born 06 Oct 1857; died 06 Dec 1918.
   411   viii. George Morris Boone, born 16 Mar 1859; died Aug 1871.
+ 412   ix.   Delia Ellen Boone, born 11 Nov 1860 in ,Callaway, Missouri; died 21 Sep 1894.
+ 413   x.   Richard Bass Boone, born 23 Sep 1862; died Sep 1963.
+ 414   xi.   Samuel Lee Boone, born 11 Apr 1864; died 31 Mar 1929.
+ 415   xii. Arthur Tucker Boone, born 16 Jan 1866 in , Callaway, Missouri; died 31 Mar 1956.
+ 416   xiii. Annie Eliza Boone, born 22 Sep 1869; died 03 May 1963.

236. Eleanor[7] Copher (Elizabeth[6] Boone, George[5], Squire[4], George Michael[3], George[2], George[1]) was born 1806, and died 1868. She married **David McQuitty**.

Child of Eleanor Copher and David McQuitty is:
   417   i.   Almirinda[8] McQuitty, born 1831.

237. Cassandra[7] Boone (William Linville[6], George[5], Squire[4], George Michael[3], George[2], George[1]) died in Fayette, Howard, Missouri. She married **William Carson** in Kentucky.

Children of Cassandra Boone and William Carson are:
   418   i.   Claiborne J.[8] Carson.
   419   ii.   James Thomas Carson.
   420   iii. George Hampton Carson.
   421   iv.   Cassandra Carson.
   422   v.   Milly Carson.
   423   vi.   Frank Carson.

243. Mildred[7] Boone (William Linville[6], George[5], Squire[4], George Michael[3], George[2], George[1]) was born 11 Dec 1795 in Madison, County , Kentucky, and died 16 Nov 1852 in , Shelby, Kentucky. She married **William Carson** in Kentucky.

Child of Mildred Boone and William Carson is:
   424   i.   Adaline[8] Carson, born in Kentucky.

251. Elizabeth C.[7] Boone (Samuel[6], George[5], Squire[4], George Michael[3], George[2], George[1]) She married **(1) ? ?.** She married **(2) Banton Boone** 26 Jun 1828, son of Edward Boone and Martha Bryan.

Child is listed above under (76) Banton Boone.

253. Jeptha Vining[7] Boone (Samuel[6], George[5], Squire[4], George Michael[3], George[2], George[1]) was born 1806, and died 1881. He married **Catherine Graham**.

Children of Jeptha Boone and Catherine Graham are:
   425   i.   James[8] Boone.
   426   ii.   Robert G. Boone, born 1832.
   427   iii. Anna Boone, born 1835.
   428   iv.   Samuel Boone, born 1836.

429	v.	Isabellar Boone, born 1837.
430	vi.	Martha Boone, born 1843.
431	vii.	Catherine Boone, born 1848.
+ 432	viii.	Jeptha Vining Boone, born 1851; died 1940.

257. Mary[7] Elledge (Charity[6] Boone, Edward[5], Squire[4], George Michael[3], George[2], George[1]) was born 19 Sep 1777 in Kentucky, and died Sep 1826 in Green River Kentucky. She married **Robert Alcorn** in Kentucky. He was born in , Augusta, Virginia, and died 26 Aug 1831.

Children of Mary Elledge and Robert Alcorn are:

433	i.	Charity[8] Alcorn, born in , Madison, Kentucky.
434	ii.	John Alcorn, born 1799 in , Madison, Kentucky.
435	iii.	Cynthia Alcorn, born 1801 in , Madison, Kentucky.
436	iv.	Francis Alcorn, born 25 Aug 1803 in Kentucky>; died 1873.
437	v.	Fanny Alcorn, born 1813 in , Madison, Kentucky.

258. James[7] Elledge (Charity[6] Boone, Edward[5], Squire[4], George Michael[3], George[2], George[1]) was born 02 Oct 1779 in North Carolina, and died 30 Oct 1847 in Lancaster, Grant, Wisconsin. He married **Mary McCoy** 1818 in Tennessee.

Children of James Elledge and Mary McCoy are:

438	i.	Lucy[8] Elledge.
439	ii.	Adeline Elledge.
440	iii.	Matilda Elledge.
441	iv.	Banner Boone Elledge.
442	v.	Nathan Boone Elledge.

259. Benjamin Franklin[7] Elledge (Charity[6] Boone, Edward[5], Squire[4], George Michael[3], George[2], George[1]) was born 20 Jan 1782 in ,,Kentucky, and died 31 Oct 1853 in Pike, Illinois. He married **Catherine Reynolds** 10 Apr 1806 in Clark, Kentucky.

Children of Benjamin Elledge and Catherine Reynolds are:

443	i.	Harvey V.[8] Elledge.
444	ii.	Evelyn Boone Elledge.
445	iii.	Elledge.

260. Leonard Boone[7] Elledge (Charity[6] Boone, Edward[5], Squire[4], George Michael[3], George[2], George[1]) was born 24 Dec 1783 in ,,Kentucky, and died 04 Jun 1841 in Griggsville, Pike, Illinois. He married **(1) Rebecca**. He married **(2) Mary Mc Clain** 01 Feb 1802 in ,Adair, Kentucky.

Children of Leonard Elledge and Mary Mc Clain are:

+ 446	i.	Alexander Boone[8] Elledge.
447	ii.	Thomas Elledge, died 1826. He married Margaret; died 1826.
448	iii.	Uriah Elledge, born 21 Nov 1802 in Clark, Kentucky; died 12 Apr 1887 in Pike, Illinois. He married (1) Delia Ball Kellogg. He married (2) Catherine Scott 26 Mar 1825 in Morgan, Illinois; born 1806; died 1855.

261. Martha Jane[7] Elledge (Charity[6] Boone, Edward[5], Squire[4], George Michael[3], George[2], George[1]) was born 24 Jul 1786 in ,Fayette/Clark, Kentucky, and died 11 Aug 1846 in ,Macon/Adair, Missouri. She married **William Scholl** 15 May 1806 in , Jessamine, Kentucky, son of Peter Scholl and Mary Boone. He was born 22 Sep 1784 in Boone's Station, Fayette, Kentucky, and died 14 Aug 1846 in Macon, Adair, Missouri.

Children of Martha Elledge and William Scholl are:

449	i.	?[8] Scholl, born in ,,Illinois.
450	ii.	Elizabeth Scholl, born in Louisville, Jefferson, Kentucky; died 01 Feb 1872 in Portland, Multnomah, Oregon. She married Withers.

451	iii.	Julia Scholl.

451   iii.   Julia Scholl.
452   iv.   Dulceney Scholl, born 19 Feb 1806 in ,Jessamine, Kentucky; died 07 Dec 1863 in ,Sutter, California. She married John Caton Wadsworth; born in , Orange, New York.
453   v.   Delcina Scholl, born 19 Feb 1807 in Kentucky; died 07 Dec 1863 in California.
+ 454   vi.   Peter Morgan Scholl, born 20 Oct 1809 in ,Clark, Kentucky; died 23 Nov 1872 in Portland, Multnomah, Oregon.
+ 455   vii.   Elledge Scholl, born 28 Jan 1812 in ,Clark, Kentucky; died 08 Oct 1877 in Lancaster, Schuyler, Missouri.
+ 456   viii. William Boone Scholl, born 14 Apr 1813 in n/Louisville, Jefferson, Kentucky.
457   ix.   Charlotte Scholl, born 1815 in ,,Kentucky.
458   x.   Edward A. Scholl, born 1819 in Louisville, Jefferson, Kentucky.
459   xi.   Joseph B. Scholl, born 10 Apr 1821 in ,,Kentucky. He married Sarah G. Floyd 15 Mar 1846 in ,Adair, Missouri.
460   xii.   Levisa Scholl, born 1825 in Louisville, Jefferson, Kentucky; died 02 Feb 1867.
461   xiii. Telitha Scholl, born 1825 in Louisville, Jefferson, Kentucky; died in ,Pike, Illinois.

262. Nancy⁷ Elledge (Charity⁶ Boone, Edward⁵, Squire⁴, George Michael³, George², George¹) was born 04 Oct 1788 in ,,North Carolina, and died 1861 in ,Sullivan, Indiana. She married **(1) Norris**. She married **(2) Nathan Phillips**.

Children of Nancy Elledge and Norris are:
462   i.   Martha S.⁸ Elledge.
+ 463   ii.   Katherine Ann Norris.
464   iii.   Thomas K. Norris. He married (1) ? ?. He married (2) Louisa Scholl 13 Mar 1835 in ,Pike, Illinois; born in , Clark, Kentucky.
465   iv.   Sophia C. Elledge.

263. Edward Boone⁷ Elledge (Charity⁶ Boone, Edward⁵, Squire⁴, George Michael³, George², George¹) was born 30 Sep 1791 in Kentucky, and died 12 Sep 1829 in , Morgan, Illinois. He married **Malinda Scholl** 23 Aug 1812 in , Clark, Kentucky, daughter of Peter Scholl and Mary Boone. She was born 25 Aug 1791 in , Clark, Kentucky, and died 13 Nov 1865 in Pleasant Vale, Pike, Illinois.

Children of Edward Elledge and Malinda Scholl are:
466   i.   Levina⁸ Elledge.
467   ii.   Jemima Elledge.
468   iii.   Lydia Elledge.
469   iv.   James Boone Elledge.
470   v.   William Tilford Elledge.

264. Charity Sarah⁷ Elledge (Charity⁶ Boone, Edward⁵, Squire⁴, George Michael³, George², George¹) was born 04 May 1795 in Boone's Fort, Fayette, Kentucky, and died 06 Oct 1878 in Winchester, Scott, Illinois. She married **(1) Thomas Allen**. He was born in Kentucky>. She married **(2) Jesse Bryan Scholl** 01 Sep 1818 in , Bath, Kentucky, son of Peter Scholl and Mary Boone. He was born 30 Nov 1797 in , Clark, Kentucky, and died 06 Feb 1858 in Winchester, Scott, Illinois.

Children of Charity Elledge and Jesse Scholl are:
471   i.   Francis Marion⁸ Scholl, died in Winchester, Scott, Illinois. He married ? ?.
472   ii.   Lydia Scholl, died in <Decatur Illinois>. She married ? ?.
+ 473   iii.   James M. Scholl.
+ 474   iv.   Edward Boone Scholl, born 11 Sep 1826 in , Morgan, Illinois; died 28 Apr 1909.

268. Nancy⁷ Morgan (Jane⁶ Boone, Edward⁵, Squire⁴, George Michael³, George², George¹) She married **George Washington Thacker**.

Children of Nancy Morgan and George Thacker are:
475   i.   Jane L.⁸ Thacker, born 1824 in Louisiana. She married J. A. McMullen in Mississippi; died Bef. 1867.
476   ii.   Mary Thacker, born 1828. She married Daniel G. Grantham in Harrison, Texas.
477   iii.   William Washington Thacker, born 1831 in Mississippi. He married Margaret F. Hampton in Texas;

died 1928 in Texas.

478   iv.   James R. Thacker, born 1833 in Mississippi. He married Susannah Patton in Texas; died 1928 in Texas.

479   v.   Anne Elizabeth Thacker, born 1840 in Mississippi. She married George McDuffey Hendrix; died 1928 in Texas.

480   vi.   Sarah Thacker, born 1842 in Mississippi.

284. Joseph[7] Scholl (Mary M.[6] Boone, Edward[5], Squire[4], George Michael[3], George[2], George[1]) was born in , Clark, Kentucky, and died in Kentucky. He married **Malinda Muir** 23 Aug 1812 in , Clark, Kentucky.

Children of Joseph Scholl and Malinda Muir are:

481   i.   Joseph[8] Scholl.
482   ii.   Scholl.
483   iii.   Deward Scholl.
484   iv.   Isahi Scholl.
485   v.   Caroline Scholl.

286. Dudley[7] Scholl (Mary M.[6] Boone, Edward[5], Squire[4], George Michael[3], George[2], George[1]) was born in ,Clark, Kentucky, and died 14 Dec 1862 in Atchison, Atchison, Kansas. He married **Katherine Ann Norris** 24 Jul 1826 in ,Clark, Kentucky, daughter of Norris and Nancy Elledge.

Children of Dudley Scholl and Katherine Norris are:

486   i.   Julia Ann[8] Scholl. She married G. L. Miner 01 Jan 1837 in ,Pike, Illinois.
487   ii.   Martha E. Scholl. She married ? ?.
488   iii.   Charlotte F. Scholl. She married Henry Little 23 Mar 1843 in ,Pike, Illinois.
489   iv.   Scholl.
490   v.   William Wallace Scholl.
491   vi.   Josephine L. Scholl. She married ? ?.

290. William[7] Scholl (Mary M.[6] Boone, Edward[5], Squire[4], George Michael[3], George[2], George[1]) was born 22 Sep 1784 in Boone's Station, Fayette, Kentucky, and died 14 Aug 1846 in Macon, Adair, Missouri. He married **Martha Jane Elledge** 15 May 1806 in , Jessamine, Kentucky, daughter of Francis Elledge and Charity Boone. She was born 24 Jul 1786 in ,Fayette/Clark, Kentucky, and died 11 Aug 1846 in ,Macon/Adair, Missouri.

Children are listed above under (261) Martha Jane Elledge.

292. Malinda[7] Scholl (Mary M.[6] Boone, Edward[5], Squire[4], George Michael[3], George[2], George[1]) was born 25 Aug 1791 in , Clark, Kentucky, and died 13 Nov 1865 in Pleasant Vale, Pike, Illinois. She married **(1) Edward Boone Elledge** 23 Aug 1812 in , Clark, Kentucky, son of Francis Elledge and Charity Boone. He was born 30 Sep 1791 in Kentucky, and died 12 Sep 1829 in , Morgan, Illinois. She married **(2) Joseph Jackson** 1832 in ,,Kentucky.

Children are listed above under (263) Edward Boone Elledge.

Children of Malinda Scholl and Joseph Jackson are:

492   i.   Martha[8] Jackson.
493   ii.   Joseph S. Jackson.
494   iii.   Malinda Jackson.

293. Jesse Bryan[7] Scholl (Mary M.[6] Boone, Edward[5], Squire[4], George Michael[3], George[2], George[1]) was born 30 Nov 1797 in , Clark, Kentucky, and died 06 Feb 1858 in Winchester, Scott, Illinois. He married **Charity Sarah Elledge** 01 Sep 1818 in , Bath, Kentucky, daughter of Francis Elledge and Charity Boone. She was born 04 May 1795 in Boone's Fort, Fayette, Kentucky, and died 06 Oct 1878 in Winchester, Scott, Illinois.

Children are listed above under (264) Charity Sarah Elledge.

294. Edward Boone[7] **Scholl** (Mary M.[6] Boone, Edward[5], Squire[4], George Michael[3], George[2], George[1]) was born 11 Oct 1801 in ,Clark, Kentucky, and died 09 Mar 1862 in Griggsville, Pike, Illinois. He married **Susannah Bentley** 18 Jul 1826 in ,Scott, Illinois. She was born 08 Feb 1811.

Children of Edward Scholl and Susannah Bentley are:

495	i.	Scholl[8].
496	ii.	Scholl.
497	iii.	William P. Scholl.

295. Charity Ann[7] **Scholl** (Mary M.[6] Boone, Edward[5], Squire[4], George Michael[3], George[2], George[1]) was born 16 Aug 1809 in , Clark, Kentucky, and died 23 Sep 1888 in , Adair, Missouri. She married **Hugh Frank Mikel** in ,Morgan, Illinois, son of John Mikel and Sarah Whitacre. He was born 09 Mar 1807 in , Rowan, North Carolina, and died 06 Jun 1884 in Polk Township, Adair, Missouri.

Children of Charity Scholl and Hugh Mikel are:

+	498	i.	James Purvis[8] Mikel, born in <Macon Missouri>; died 22 Oct 1864.
+	499	ii.	William L. Mikel, born in ,Mogan, Illinois; died 06 May 1860 in ,Adair, Missouri.
	500	iii.	Polly Ellen Mikel, born in , Adair, Missouri.
+	501	iv.	Charles W. Mikel, born in ,Macon, Missouri; died in ,Sedgwick, Kansas.
+	502	v.	Edward B. Mikel, born 1826 in ,Morgan, Illinois.
+	503	vi.	John Noah Mikel, born 11 Sep 1830 in , Morgan, Illinois; died in , Adair, Missouri.
+	504	vii.	George M. Mikel, born 1833 in , Morgan, Illinois; died 03 Apr 1876.
	505	viii.	Samuel Mikel, born 1834 in ,Of Macon, Missouri.
+	506	ix.	David J. Mikel, born 12 Apr 1836 in ,Morgan, Illinois; died 07 Jul 1923.
+	507	x.	Joseph P. Mikel, born 30 Mar 1837 in ,Morgan, Illinois; died 15 Oct 1872.
	508	xi.	Ellen J. Mikel, born 1846 in ,Of Schuyler, Missouri.
	509	xii.	Emily J. Mikel, born 1848 in ,Schuyler, Missouri; died 02 Jan 1866 in Winchester, Scott, Illinois.

299. Joseph[7] **Hunter** (Sarah[6] Boone, Edward[5], Squire[4], George Michael[3], George[2], George[1]) He married **Mary Dickenson**.

Children of Joseph Hunter and Mary Dickenson are:

	510	i.	Polly[8] Hunter.
+	511	ii.	Elizabeth Hunter, died 05 Jul 1871 in , White, Tennessee.
	512	iii.	Sarah Hunter.
	513	iv.	Joseph Hunter.

301. Mary Polly[7] **Hunter** (Sarah[6] Boone, Edward[5], Squire[4], George Michael[3], George[2], George[1]) was born 11 Nov 1789 in Boone's Station, Clark, Kentucky, and died 07 Oct 1878 in Sparta, White, Tennessee. She married **James Hudgens** in , Clark, Kentucky. He was born 13 Mar 1787 in Rocky Springs, Goochland, Virginia, and died 08 Aug 1847 in Sparta, White, Tennessee.

Children of Mary Hunter and James Hudgens are:

	514	i.	Joseph[8] Hudgens.
+	515	ii.	William Hudgens, born 08 Feb 1813 in Tennessee; died 12 Aug 1882 in Tennessee.
+	516	iii.	Dudley Hampton Hudgens, born 25 May 1814 in , White, Tennessee; died 21 Jun 1878 in Sparta, White, Tennessee.
	517	iv.	Carl Hudgens, born 26 Feb 1816.
	518	v.	Shelby Hudgens, born 26 Feb 1816 in , White, Tennessee; died 01 Oct 1866 in , White, Tennessee. He married Mary Austin 07 Jun 1838 in Sparta, White, Tennessee; born in Lost Creek, White, Tennessee.
+	519	vi.	Hampton Hamilton Hudgens, born 28 Nov 1819 in ,,Tennessee; died 20 Dec 1896 in , White, Tennessee.
	520	vii.	John Hudgens, born 07 Sep 1821; died 05 Dec 1850.
	521	viii.	Sarah Sally Hudgens, born 07 Sep 1823; died 25 Jun 1833 in , White, Tennessee.
+	522	ix.	Catherine Hudgens, born 20 Nov 1825 in Sparta, White, Tennessee; died 02 Sep 1881 in Sparta, White, Tennessee.
+	523	x.	Crocket Hudgens, born 28 Jun 1827 in ,White, Tennessee; died 15 Aug 1900 in ,White, Tennessee.

302. Dudley[7] Hunter (Sarah[6] Boone, Edward[5], Squire[4], George Michael[3], George[2], George[1]) was born 21 Nov 1794 in Tennessee, and died 27 Oct 1862 in Dry Valley, Putnam, Tennessee. He married **(1) Henrietta Lancaster Officer**. He married **(2) Polly Clark**. He married **(3) Sallie Hunter** 14 Mar 1839 in White, daughter of Dudley Hunter and Polly Clark. She was born 16 Feb 1822. He married **(4) Amy Emma Gist Lowery** 17 Oct 1844 in White. She was born in Tennessee.

Child of Dudley Hunter and Henrietta Officer is:
+ 524   i.   Elizabeth[8] Hunter, born 15 Mar 1829 in ,White.

Children of Dudley Hunter and Polly Clark are:
+ 525   i.   Sallie[8] Hunter, born 16 Feb 1822.
+ 526   ii.   Joe Hunter, born 11 Apr 1824; died 12 Jul 1886.
   527   iii.   Polly Hunter, born 10 Nov 1826.

Children of Dudley Hunter and Sallie Hunter are:
+ 528   i.   Henry Ward Beecher[8] Hunter.
   529   ii.   Dudley Hunter, born 23 Jan 1840.
   530   iii.   Martha Ann Hunter, born 10 Apr 1841.
   531   iv.   Edward Boone Hunter, born 02 Jul 1842.
   532   v.   Mary Elizabeth Hunter, born 17 Apr 1845.
   533   vi.   Sarah Jane Hunter, born 23 Oct 1846.
   534   vii.   Pauline Margaret Hunter, born 07 Jul 1849.
   535   viii.   Amanda Jane Hunter, born 06 Jul 1851.
+ 536   ix.   Joseph Hall Hunter, born 04 Dec 1852; died 04 Sep 1924.
   537   x.   Caroline Frances Hunter, born 16 Apr 1856.
   538   xi.   Braxton Douglas Hunter, born 11 Feb 1860.
   539   xii.   Hugh Dudley Hunter, born 11 Jul 1862.

Children of Dudley Hunter and Amy Lowery are:
   540   i.   Daniel[8] Hunter, born 18 Aug 1845 in ,White; died 04 Mar 1854 in ,White.
   541   ii.   William Hunter, born 12 Nov 1846 in ,White; died Mar 1854 in ,White.
   542   iii.   Charles Hunter, born 13 Aug 1848 in ,White; died Mar 1854 in ,White.
   543   iv.   Barger Hunter, born 04 May 1850 in ,White; died Mar 1854 in ,White.
   544   v.   Rush Hunter, born 04 Mar 1854 in ,White; died 1940 in ,Putnam, Missouri. He married Hannah Brown 06 Sep 1877 in White.
   545   vi.   Mary H. Hunter, born 06 Jun 1856 in , White, Tennessee; died 11 Dec 1935 in , White, Tennessee. She married (1) Tom F. Moore. She married (2) Crocket Hudgens; born 28 Jun 1827 in ,White, Tennessee; died 15 Aug 1900 in ,White, Tennessee.
   546   vii.   Vance Hunter, born Aug 1860 in ,White.

316. Andrew Jackson[7] Boone (John Bryan[6], John[5], Benjamin[4], George Michael[3], George[2], George[1]) was born 25 Sep 1823 in North Carolina, and died in Missouri>. He married **Sarah Elizabeth Miller** 04 Jul 1838 in , Obion, Tennessee. She was born in , White, Tennessee.

Child of Andrew Boone and Sarah Miller is:
+ 547   i.   William Henry[8] Boone, born 02 Apr 1848 in Chillicothe, Livingston, Missouri; died 24 Jan 1924 in , Livingston, Missouri.

Generation No. 6

317. Simon P[8] Stover (Daniel[7], Daniel[6], Abraham[5], Sarah[4] Boone, George Michael[3], George[2], George[1]) was born 28 Sep 1822 in Augusta Co, VA, and died 11 Dec 1873 in Augusta Co, VA. He married **Elizabeth Ida Link** 31 Dec 1848 in Augusta Co, VA. She was born 19 Nov 1822 in Augusta Co, VA, and died 28 Mar 1867 in Augusta Co, VA.

Child of Simon Stover and Elizabeth Link is:

+ 548   i. Ida Elizabeth[9] Stover, born 01 May 1862 in Mt. Sidney, VA; died 11 Sep 1946 in Abilene, Dickinson Co , Kansas.

320. Morgan[8] Bryan (Mary[7] Power, Elizabeth[6] Boone, Israel[5], Squire[4], George Michael[3], George[2], George[1]) was born 20 Aug 1794 in ,Rowan, North Carolina, and died 07 Aug 1857 in ,Warren, Missouri. He married **Elizabeth Callaway** 15 Feb 1815 in ,Warren, Missouri, daughter of John Callaway and Jemima Boone. She was born 15 Feb 1797 in Boone's Station, Fayette, Kentucky, and died 01 Jun 1867 in ,Warren, Missouri.

Children are listed above under (124) Elizabeth Callaway.

339. ?[8] ? (Susannah A.[7] Hays, Susannah[6] Boone, Daniel[5], Squire[4], George Michael[3], George[2], George[1]) He married **? ?**.

Child of ? ? and ? ? is:
+ 549   i. ?[9] ?.

340. Sarah W.[8] Hays (William[7], Susannah[6] Boone, Daniel[5], Squire[4], George Michael[3], George[2], George[1]) was born 18 Jan 1819 in , St. Charles, Missouri, and died 23 May 1889. She married **Jefferson Bell Benson** 15 Mar 1838 in , Callaway, Missouri. He was born 06 Aug 1806 in Maryland, and died 13 Jun 1895.

Children of Sarah Hays and Jefferson Benson are:
  550   i.   Thomas W.[9] Benson, born 15 Feb 1839 in , Callaway, Missouri>.
  551   ii. Phoebe Benson, born 16 Feb 1840 in Bluffton, Montgomery, Missouri; died 07 Sep 1840 in Bluffton, Montgomery, Missouri.
  552   iii. James S. Benson, born 03 Aug 1842 in Bluffton, Montgomery, Missouri.
  553   iv. George Washington Benson, born 05 May 1844 in Bluffton, Montgomery, Missouri; died 23 Apr 1915.
+ 554   v.   Marquis De Lafayette Benson, born 13 Feb 1846 in Bluffton, Montgomery, Missouri; died 26 Aug 1931 in Bluffton, Montgomery, Missouri.
  555   vi. Taylor Benson, born 07 Oct 1847 in Bluffton, Montgomery, Missouri; died 23 Oct 1868 in Bluffton, Montgomery, Missouri.
  556   vii. Susan Ophelia Benson, born 20 Aug 1849 in Bluffton, Montgomery, Missouri; died 14 Jan 1940.
  557   viii. Verlinia Millington Benson, born 13 Mar 1855 in Bluffton, Montgomery, Missouri; died 13 Apr 1864.
  558   ix. John Wesley Benson, born 05 Jan 1859 in Bluffton, Montgomery, Missouri.

343. Susan[8] Callaway (James[7], Jemima[6] Boone, Daniel[5], Squire[4], George Michael[3], George[2], George[1]) was born 1828, and died 1881. She married **Solomon Shobe**.

Children of Susan Callaway and Solomon Shobe are:
  559   i.   Larkin Daniel[9] Shobe, born 1857 in Missouri; died 1937 in Missouri. He married Sarah Brubridge Summers.
+ 560   ii. Anna Bell Shobe, born 1860; died 1936.
+ 561   iii. Mary Virginia Shobe, born 1862; died 1951.
  562   iv. George Rodney Shobe, born 1865; died 1945. He married Lyda Mann.

344. Pizarro[8] Howell (Susannah[7] Callaway, Jemima[6] Boone, Daniel[5], Squire[4], George Michael[3], George[2], George[1]) was born 28 Nov 1811, and died 12 Sep 1881. He married **Maria Hoffman** 11 Jun 1840. She was born 17 Nov 1813, and died 28 May 1885.

Child of Pizarro Howell and Maria Hoffman is:
+ 563   i.   Coanza Burilla[9] Howell, born 17 Jun 1841; died 23 Oct 1922.

357. Chloe Donnelly[8] Boone (Alphonso[7], Jesse Bryan[6], Daniel[5], Squire[4], George Michael[3], George[2], George[1]) was born 09 Dec 1822 in , Montgomery, Missouri, and died 10 Feb 1909 in , Montgomery, Missouri. She married **George L. Curry** 14 Mar 1848 in Clackmas , Missouri.

Children of Chloe Boone and George Curry are:

564	i.	Mary Florence[9] Curry. She married ? ?.
565	ii.	Norwood Litton Curry, born in Oregon. He married Lily L.; born in Oregon.
566	iii.	Ratliffe Curry, born 1851.
567	iv.	Willie Lane Curry, born 1855.
568	v.	Ethel A. Curry, born 1859.
569	vi.	George L. Curry, born 1862; died Bef. 1870.

358. Jesse Van Bibber[8] Boone (Alphonso[7], Jesse Bryan[6], Daniel[5], Squire[4], George Michael[3], George[2], George[1]) was born 25 Jan 1824 in ,Montgomery, Missouri, and died 24 Mar 1872 in Williamsville, Oegon. He married **Elizabeth Fudge** 23 Sep 1851 in ,Polk, Oregon.

Children of Jesse Boone and Elizabeth Fudge are:

570	i.	Sonora[9] Boone. She married Vital Cimino 24 Jan 1860.
571	ii.	John Boone.
572	iii.	Mary Boone, born 1855. She married Henry C. Merwin 26 Feb 1871.
573	iv.	George L. Boone, born 1857; died 1865.
574	v.	Montgomery Boone, born 1857.
575	vi.	Alphonso Boone, born 1859.
576	vii.	Minerva Boone, born 1859; died 1865.
577	viii.	Van Daniel Boone, born 1864.

359. Mary Elizabeth[8] Boone (Alphonso[7], Jesse Bryan[6], Daniel[5], Squire[4], George Michael[3], George[2], George[1]) was born 03 Apr 1825 in ,Montgomery, Missouri, and died 04 Jun 1907 in Coquille, Coos, Oregon. She married **Thomas Cecil Norris** 01 Oct 1844 in Westport, Missouri.

Children of Mary Boone and Thomas Norris are:

578	i.	James Davis[9] Norris, born 08 Feb 1846 in Missouri; died 14 Feb 1846 in Missouri.
579	ii.	George William Norris, born 05 Dec 1847; died 25 Apr 1919 in Oregon City, Oregon.
580	iii.	Mary Caroline Norris, born 16 Sep 1850; died 25 Apr 1942 in Oregon. She married John Leston Barker 14 Sep 1871.
581	iv.	Louisa Sophia Norris, born 30 Apr 1855 in Marysville, Oregon; died 21 Mar 1922 in McKinley, Oregon. She married Lawson A. Lawhorn 17 Oct 1877 in Coos , Oregon.
582	v.	Virginia L. Norris, born 01 Aug 1864 in Roseburg, Oregon; died 18 Oct 1864 in Roseburg, Oregon.
583	vi.	Jesse Albert Norris, born 13 Oct 1868; died 16 Sep 1872 in Fairview, Oregon.
584	vii.	Thomas Cecil Norris, born 28 Apr 1869; died Sep 1931 in Alturas, California. He married Christina Harris 22 Dec 1886 in Coos , Oregon.

360. George Luther[8] Boone (Alphonso[7], Jesse Bryan[6], Daniel[5], Squire[4], George Michael[3], George[2], George[1]) was born 06 Jun 1826 in ,Montgomery, Missouri, and died 04 Dec 1910 in Medford, Jackson, Oregon. He married **Mourning Ann Young** 31 Mar 1852 in ,Benton, Oregon. She was born 15 Jun 1828 in Indiana, and died 19 Jan 1920.

Children of George Boone and Mourning Young are:

	585	i.	Theodore[9] Boone, born 29 Dec 1853 in Corvallis, Benton, Oregon; died 19 Jun 1884.
	586	ii.	Nancy Ellen Boone, born 18 Oct 1855 in Corvallis, Benton, Oregon; died May 1920.
	587	iii.	William Clay Boone, born 02 Feb 1858 in Philomath, Benton, Oregon; died 07 Jul 1936.
	588	iv.	Thomas Norris Boone, born 23 Nov 1859 in Philomath, Benton, Oregon; died 20 Jun 1942.
	589	v.	Chloe Jane Boone, born 23 Feb 1862 in Philomath, Benton, Oregon.
	590	vi.	Mary Florence Boone, born 16 Mar 1864 in Philomath, Benton, Oregon; died 09 Jul 1864 in Philomath, Benton, Oregon.
+	591	vii.	Emma Crusita Boone, born 13 Aug 1865 in Philomath, Benton, Oregon; died 09 Jun 1947 in Corvallis, Benton, Oregon.
	592	viii.	Jonathan May Boone, born 22 Jan 1868 in Philomath, Benton, Oregon; died 04 Jan 1907.
	593	ix.	George Alphonso Boone, born 11 Jan 1870 in Philomath, Benton, Oregon.
	594	x.	Albert Pope Boone, born 12 Jul 1872 in Yaquina, Lincoln, Oregon; died 24 Apr 1955.
	595	xi.	Ethel Boone, born 05 Dec 1874 in Yaquina, Lincoln, Oregon.
	596	xii.	Olive Boone, born 09 Dec 1877 in Yaquina, Lincoln, Oregon.
	597	xiii.	Daniel Armstrong Boone, born 17 May 1879 in Yaquina, Lincoln, Oregon; died Nov 1942.
	598	xiv.	Victor L. Boone, born 21 May 1881 in Yaquina, Lincoln, Oregon; died 11 Sep 1921.

361. Joshua Morris⁸ Boone (Alphonso⁷, Jesse Bryan⁶, Daniel⁵, Squire⁴, George Michael³, George², George¹) was born 30 Jul 1833 in , Montgomery, Missouri, and died in , Benton, Oregon. He married **Mary Lucinda Minkler** 13 Oct 1863 in ,Clackcames, Oregon. She was born in Missouri.

Children of Joshua Boone and Mary Minkler are:
599	i.	Clara⁹ Boone, born in Oregon.
600	ii.	Jacob Boone, born in Oregon.
601	iii.	Walter Boone, born in Oregon.
602	iv.	Adeline Boone, born in Oregon.
603	v.	Lincoln Boone, born in Oregon.

362. Alphonso Daniel⁸ Boone (Alphonso⁷, Jesse Bryan⁶, Daniel⁵, Squire⁴, George Michael³, George², George¹) was born 03 Jun 1837 in Jefferson City, Cole, Missouri, and died 30 Mar 1915 in Sumner, Coos, Oregon. He married **Leathea Nancy Barker** 21 Mar 1875 in Sumner, Coos, Oregon. She was born 22 Jan 1848 in , Jackson, Missouri, and died 29 Mar 1915 in Sumner, Coos, Oregon.

Children of Alphonso Boone and Leathea Barker are:
+	604	i.	Jesse Archie⁹ Boone, born 15 Jul 1876 in Sumner, Coos, Oregon; died 31 Oct 1924 in Sumner, Coos, Oregon.
+	605	ii.	Lulu Louise Boone, born 15 Jul 1878 in Sumner, Coos, Oregon; died 12 Jan 1944 in ,Coos, Oregon.
	606	iii.	James Lilburn Boone, born 20 Aug 1880 in Sumner, Coos, Oregon; died 22 May 1939 in Sumner, Coos, Oregon. He married ? ?.
	607	iv.	Mary Ethel Boone, born 20 May 1882 in ,Coos, Oregon. She married Lorenzo Dow Belieu 16 Apr 1908 in ,,Oregon; born 15 Feb 1882 in ,Coos, Oregon; died 05 Mar 1976 in Coos Bay, Coos, Oregon.
	608	v.	Harry Cleveland Boone, born 19 Nov 1884 in Sumner, Coos, Oregon; died 22 Oct 1966 in Sumner, Coos, Oregon. He married Ella L.; born 1883; died 1954.
+	609	vi.	Myrtle Leola Boone, born 17 Oct 1887 in ,Coos, Oregon.

363. Thoedore Fulton⁸ Warner (Minerva S.⁷ Boone, Jesse Bryan⁶, Daniel⁵, Squire⁴, George Michael³, George², George¹) was born 1818, and died 1891. He married **(1) Emily Hart Underhill**.

Child of Thoedore Warner and Emily Underhill is:
610	i.	Angela Sanford⁹ Warner, born 1844; died 1908. She married Marcus Newton Blakemore.

365. William Montgomery⁸ Boggs (Panthea Grant⁷ Boone, Jesse Bryan⁶, Daniel⁵, Squire⁴, George Michael³, George², George¹) was born 21 Oct 1826 in Missouri, and died 22 Apr 1911 in Napa , Napa, California. He married **Sonora Louisa Hicklin** 23 Mar 1846 in Pleasent Hill Cass, Missouri. She was born 05 Aug 1825 in Pleasant Hill, Cass, Missouri, and died 05 Mar 1902.

Children of William Boggs and Sonora Hicklin are:
	611	i.	Jefferson⁹ Boggs, born in , Sonoma, California.
	612	ii.	William D. Boggs, born in , Napa, California.
+	613	iii.	Lilburn W. Boggs, born in , Sonoma, California.
	614	iv.	Sterling Boggs, born in , Napa, California.
	615	v.	Angus Boggs, born in , Sonoma, California.
	616	vi.	Guadalupe Boggs, born in , Sonoma, California.
	617	vii.	Mary F. Boggs, born May 1856 in , Sonoma, California; died 28 Nov 1907.

371. Eliza Yantis⁸ Boone (Albert Gallatin⁷, Jesse Bryan⁶, Daniel⁵, Squire⁴, George Michael³, George², George¹) was born 02 Jun 1838 in , Fayette, Kentucky. She married **Henry William Jones** 02 Apr 1855 in , St Charles, Missouri. He was born in , St Charles, Missouri.

Children of Eliza Boone and Henry Jones are:
618	i.	Albert Boone⁹ Jones, born 15 Mar 1857 in , St Charles, Missouri.
619	ii.	James Hamilton Jones, born 18 Dec 1860 in , St Charles, Missouri.
620	iii.	Ann Reid Jones, born 15 Sep 1862 in , St Charles, Missouri.

621	iv.	Henry William Jones, born 08 Dec 1864 in , St Charles, Missouri.
622	v.	Frances Jones, born Feb 1867 in , St Charles, Missouri.
623	vi.	Mary Jones, born 14 Dec 1869 in , St Charles, Missouri.
624	vii.	Zeralda Jones, born 29 May 1872 in , St Charles, Missouri.
625	viii.	Margaret Jones, born 16 Sep 1874 in , St Charles, Missouri.

372. Agnes B.[8] Boone (Albert Gallatin[7], Jesse Bryan[6], Daniel[5], Squire[4], George Michael[3], George[2], George[1]) was born 02 Dec 1840 in Missouri. She married **Elmer Otis**. He was born in Ma.

Children of Agnes Boone and Elmer Otis are:
626	i.	Mary B.[9] Otis, born in Id.
627	ii.	Francis I. Otis, born in Or.
628	iii.	Martha M. S. Otis, born in Or.
629	iv.	Albert J. Otis, born in Or.
630	v.	Joseph F. Otis, born in Dak.
631	vi.	Margraet M. Otis, born in Dak.

376. Albert Gallatin[8] Boone (Van Daniel[7], Jesse Bryan[6], Daniel[5], Squire[4], George Michael[3], George[2], George[1]) was born 25 Nov 1845 in ,Jackson, Missouri, and died 22 Jun 1916 in Pagosa Springs, Archuleta, Colorado. He married **Susan Fosdick**.

Children of Albert Boone and Susan Fosdick are:
632	i.	Elsie B.[9] Boone.
633	ii.	Boone.
634	iii.	Fosdick Boone.
635	iv.	Mary Boone, born 1877; died 1878.
636	v.	Van Daniel Boone, born 1879.
637	vi.	David Boone, born 1880.
638	vii.	Henry A. Boone, born 1881.
639	viii.	Jesse M. Boone, born 1890.
640	ix.	Elliott Boone, born 1894.
641	x.	Esther Boone, born 1897; died 1984.

377. Emma Henderson[8] Boone (Van Daniel[7], Jesse Bryan[6], Daniel[5], Squire[4], George Michael[3], George[2], George[1]) was born 31 May 1848 in Westport, Jackson, Missouri, and died 21 Aug 1925 in ,Pueblo, Colorado. She married **Lewis Barnum** 04 Sep 1866 in , Boone, Colorado. He was born 1870, and died 1937.

Child of Emma Boone and Lewis Barnum is:
| 642 | i. | Mary[9] Barnum, born 1866; died 1893. |

380. Harriet Baber[8] Boone (Van Daniel[7], Jesse Bryan[6], Daniel[5], Squire[4], George Michael[3], George[2], George[1]) was born 11 Feb 1855 in ,Jackson, Missouri, and died 22 Mar 1925 in Pueblo, Pueblo, Colorado. She married **Theodore Robert Jones Sr.** 05 Oct 1876 in , Boone, Colorado, son of Henry William Jones. He was born 02 Sep 1847 in Fort Wayne, Allen, Indiana, and died 13 May 1927 in Los Angeles, Los Angeles, California.

Children of Harriet Boone and Theodore Jones are:
643	i.	Charlotte Stevens[9] Jones, born 24 Aug 1877 in Pueblo, Pueblo, Colorado; died 26 Nov 1878 in Pueblo, Pueblo, Colorado.
644	ii.	Theodore William Jones, born 04 Dec 1879 in Pueblo, Pueblo, Colorado.
645	iii.	Emma Barnum Jones, born 28 Dec 1882 in Pueblo, Pueblo, Colorado; died Feb 1944.
646	iv.	Price Davis Jones, born 30 Jan 1887 in Boone, Pueblo, Colorado.
647	v.	Helen Breckenridge Jones, born 07 Apr 1889 in Pueblo, Pueblo, Colorado; died 13 Jan 1891 in Pueblo, Pueblo, Colorado.
648	vi.	Penton Francisco Jones, born 17 Jul 1895 in Pueblo, Pueblo, Colorado; died 27 Nov 1978 in California.
649	vii.	Katherine Brackenridge Jones, born 04 Aug 1899 in Pueblo, Pueblo, Colorado; died Oct 1975 in California.

401. Charlie Edgar⁸ Boone (Alonzo⁷, John Linville⁶, George⁵, Squire⁴, George Michael³, George², George¹) was born 15 Jul 1837, and died 01 Oct 1912. He married **Annie Woodson Anderson**.

Children of Charlie Boone and Annie Anderson are:
650	i.	David Richard⁹ Boone, born 31 Jan 1877; died Jan 1955.
651	ii.	Mary Eleanor Boone, born 20 Jan 1878; died 13 Sep 1962.
652	iii.	Robert Henry Boone, born 26 Jun 1879; died 14 Jul 1952.
653	iv.	William Edgar Boone, born 13 Jul 1884; died 16 Aug 1932.

406. Martha Susan⁸ Boone (Alonzo⁷, John Linville⁶, George⁵, Squire⁴, George Michael³, George², George¹) was born 09 Mar 1850 in ,Callaway, Missouri, and died 16 Sep 1929. She married **James E. Kettle**. He was born in Indiana.

Children of Martha Boone and James Kettle are:
	654	i.	Elmer C.⁹ Kettle, born in Missouri; died 22 Mar 1914.
+	655	ii.	? ?.
	656	iii.	Eugene Kettle, born 08 Nov 1873 in , Audrain, Missouri; died 07 Jan 1960 in Missourintgonery City, Audrain, Missouri. He married ? ?.
	657	iv.	Edward Kettle, born 28 Nov 1875 in Missouri; died 10 May 1956. He married Ida Sailor.
	658	v.	Lottie Ethel Kettle, born 15 Nov 1880; died 10 Nov 1966.
+	659	vi.	Delia Onie Kettle, born 25 Feb 1884.
	660	vii.	Anna Belle Kettle, born 14 Sep 1884; died 08 Nov 1980.

408. John William Alonzo⁸ Boone (Alonzo⁷, John Linville⁶, George⁵, Squire⁴, George Michael³, George², George¹) was born 14 Jun 1854 in , Callaway, Missouri, and died 30 Oct 1933. He married **Nancy C. Kaloeck** 02 Dec 1879. She was born in Missouri.

Children of John Boone and Nancy Kaloeck are:
	661	i.	Martha S.⁹ Boone. She married ? ?.
	662	ii.	Ellen L. Boone. She married (1) ? ?. She married (2) ? ?. She married (3) ? ?.
	663	iii.	? ?. She married ? ?.
+	664	iv.	Alfred Obediah Boone, born 10 Jan 1881; died 11 Jan 1969.
+	665	v.	Minnie O. Boone, born 27 Feb 1882; died 23 Apr 1913.
	666	vi.	Bulah G. Boone, born 20 Aug 1883; died 24 Feb 1967. She married (1) William Archibald Young. She married (2) Julius Autenreith.
	667	vii.	Samuel Grover Boone, born 07 Jan 1887; died 19 May 1971. He married Cordie Windsor 26 May 1909 in Montgomery , Missouri.
	668	viii.	William R. Boone, born 09 Jan 1891; died 10 Nov 1935. He married (1) ? ?. He married (2) ? ?.
	669	ix.	Onie N. Boone, born 29 Nov 1894; died 28 Dec 1894.
	670	x.	Dollie Boone, born 09 Nov 1900; died 09 Nov 1900.

410. Emma Josephine⁸ Boone (Alonzo⁷, John Linville⁶, George⁵, Squire⁴, George Michael³, George², George¹) was born 06 Oct 1857, and died 06 Dec 1918. She married **Israel S. Kettle**.

Children of Emma Boone and Israel Kettle are:
671	i.	Roy Menefee⁹ Kettle, born 09 Apr 1890; died Aug 1971 in Vandiver Village, Audrain, Missouri.
672	ii.	Willie Kettle, born 23 Jan 1898; died 23 Jan 1898.

412. Delia Ellen⁸ Boone (Alonzo⁷, John Linville⁶, George⁵, Squire⁴, George Michael³, George², George¹) was born 11 Nov 1860 in ,Callaway, Missouri, and died 21 Sep 1894. She married **Eugene Albert Kettle**. He was born 08 Sep 1881.

Children of Delia Boone and Eugene Kettle are:
673	i.	Emme Eugene⁹ Kettle, born 08 Aug 1882.
674	ii.	Vergie Florence Kettle, born 15 Sep 1883; died 22 Jun 1958.

413. Richard Bass⁸ Boone (Alonzo⁷, John Linville⁶, George⁵, Squire⁴, George Michael³, George², George¹) was born 23 Sep 1862, and died Sep 1963. He married **(1) ? ?.**   He married **(2) Lucy Jane Tate.** She died 1919.

Children of Richard Boone and Lucy Tate are:
675	i.	?⁹ ?. He married ? ?.
676	ii.	? ?. She married ? ?.
677	iii.	? ?. She married ? ?.
678	iv.	? ?.
679	v.	? ?. She married ? ?.
680	vi.	? ?. He married ? ?.
681	vii.	? ?.
682	viii.	? ?. He married ? ?.
683	ix.	Mann Boone, died in Wwii.
684	x.	Leo Alonzo Boone, born 23 Oct 1899; died 10 Jul 1979. He married ? ?.

414. Samuel Lee⁸ Boone (Alonzo⁷, John Linville⁶, George⁵, Squire⁴, George Michael³, George², George¹) was born 11 Apr 1864, and died 31 Mar 1929. He married **Bell Tate.**

Child of Samuel Boone and Bell Tate is:
685	i.	?⁹ ?.

415. Arthur Tucker⁸ Boone (Alonzo⁷, John Linville⁶, George⁵, Squire⁴, George Michael³, George², George¹) was born 16 Jan 1866 in , Callaway, Missouri, and died 31 Mar 1956. He married **Anna Belle Penn** 25 Mar 1891.

Children of Arthur Boone and Anna Penn are:
686	i.	?⁹ ?.
687	ii.	? ?.
688	iii.	Nellie Blanch Boone, born 29 Mar 1892.

416. Annie Eliza⁸ Boone (Alonzo⁷, John Linville⁶, George⁵, Squire⁴, George Michael³, George², George¹) was born 22 Sep 1869, and died 03 May 1963. She married **Mathias Gargus** 06 Nov 1890 in Chamois, Missouri.

Children of Annie Boone and Mathias Gargus are:
689	i.	Martin Lee⁹ Gargus. He married ? ?.
690	ii.	Clarence Bell Gargus. He married ? ?.
691	iii.	John Alonzo Gargus. He married ? ?.
692	iv.	Mathias Lincoln Gargus. He married ? ?.
693	v.	Earl Gargus. He married ? ?.
694	vi.	Pearl Gargus. He married ? ?.
695	vii.	Ulysses Grant Gargus. He married ? ?.
696	viii.	Living Gargus. He married ? ?.

432. Jeptha Vining⁸ Boone (Jeptha Vining⁷, Samuel⁶, George⁵, Squire⁴, George Michael³, George², George¹) was born 1851, and died 1940. He married **Cathren.**

Children of Jeptha Boone and Cathren are:
697	i.	?⁹ ?. He married ? ?.
698	ii.	? ?.
699	iii.	? ?.
700	iv.	? ?.
701	v.	Lloyd Earl Boone, born 1888; died 1968. He married ? ?.
702	vi.	Lester L. Boone, born 1893; died 1986. He married ? ?.

446. Alexander Boone⁸ Elledge (Leonard Boone⁷, Charity⁶ Boone, Edward⁵, Squire⁴, George Michael³,

George[2], George[1]) He married **(1) Rebecca Beall**. She was born 1787, and died 1850. He married **(2) ? ?**.

Child of Alexander Elledge and Rebecca Beall is:
703   i.   Thomas P.[9] Elledge, died 1826.

454. Peter Morgan[8] Scholl (William[7], Mary M.[6] Boone, Edward[5], Squire[4], George Michael[3], George[2], George[1]) was born 20 Oct 1809 in ,Clark, Kentucky, and died 23 Nov 1872 in Portland, Multnomah, Oregon. He married **Elizabeth Cowhick** 14 Aug 1828 in ,Morgan, Illinois.

Children of Peter Scholl and Elizabeth Cowhick are:
704   i.   Lucy[9] Scholl.
705   ii.   George W. Scholl.
706   iii. Sarah H. Scholl.
707   iv.   William T. Scholl.
708   v.   Mary S. Scholl.
709   vi.   Peter Boone Scholl.

455. Elledge[8] Scholl (William[7], Mary M.[6] Boone, Edward[5], Squire[4], George Michael[3], George[2], George[1]) was born 28 Jan 1812 in ,Clark, Kentucky, and died 08 Oct 1877 in Lancaster, Schuyler, Missouri. He married **Amanda Cobb** 29 Dec 1842 in ,Adair, Missouri. She was born 03 Apr 1820 in Barbarsville, Knox, Kentucky, and died 01 Jan 1903 in Lancaster, Schuyler, Missouri.

Children of Elledge Scholl and Amanda Cobb are:
710   i.   ?[9] Scholl.
+ 711   ii.   Martha Jane Scholl, born 09 Oct 1843 in ,Adair/Macon, Missouri; died 12 Mar 1912 in Unionville, Putnam, Missouri.
+ 712   iii. Ambrose Scholl, born 15 Jul 1846 in , Adair, Missouri; died 18 Mar 1911 in Lancaster, Schuyler, Missouri.
   713   iv.   Frances Elizabeth Scholl, born 26 Nov 1849 in ,Adair, Missouri; died 31 Aug 1937. She married William F. Mitchell 12 Mar 1907.
+ 714   v.   Emily Anna Scholl, born 22 Dec 1851 in Lancaster, Schuyler, Missouri; died 22 May 1920 in Kirksville, Adair, Missouri.
   715   vi.   Mary Susan Scholl, born May 1856 in Lancaster, Schuyler, Missouri; died 17 Jan 1929 in Lancaster, Schuyler, Missouri.

456. William Boone[8] Scholl (William[7], Mary M.[6] Boone, Edward[5], Squire[4], George Michael[3], George[2], George[1]) was born 14 Apr 1813 in n/Louisville, Jefferson, Kentucky. He married **Elnore Shores** 20 Oct 1834 in ,Harrison, Indiana.

Children of William Scholl and Elnore Shores are:
716   i.   Hulda[9] Scholl.
717   ii.   Scholl.
718   iii. Elizabeth T. Scholl.
719   iv.   Mary Scholl.
720   v.   Susan A. Scholl.
721   vi.   Nancy E. Scholl.
722   vii. Tamar A. Scholl.

463. Katherine Ann[8] Norris (Nancy[7] Elledge, Charity[6] Boone, Edward[5], Squire[4], George Michael[3], George[2], George[1]) She married **Dudley Scholl** 24 Jul 1826 in ,Clark, Kentucky, son of Peter Scholl and Mary Boone. He was born in ,Clark, Kentucky, and died 14 Dec 1862 in Atchison, Atchison, Kansas.

Children are listed above under (286) Dudley Scholl.

473. James M.[8] Scholl (Jesse Bryan[7], Mary M.[6] Boone, Edward[5], Squire[4], George Michael[3], George[2], George[1]) He married **(1) Matilda Killebrew** 02 May 1844 in ,Scott, Illinois. She died 18 Aug 1850. He married **(2) Eliza B. Claywell** 04 Apr 1854.

Children of James Scholl and Eliza Claywell are:

+ 723   i.   Lavina[9] Scholl, born in Illinois.
   724   ii.   William A. Scholl.
   725   iii.   Scholl.
   726   iv.   John F. Scholl.

474. Edward Boone[8] Scholl (Jesse Bryan[7], Mary M.[6] Boone, Edward[5], Squire[4], George Michael[3], George[2], George[1]) was born 11 Sep 1826 in , Morgan, Illinois, and died 28 Apr 1909. He married **Lucy King** 07 Mar 1852 in , Scott, Illinois. She was born 01 Jun 1829 in Tennessee, and died 25 Nov 1899.

Children of Edward Scholl and Lucy King are:

   727   i.   Sarah E.[9] Scholl, born in Illinois.
   728   ii.   Emma Scholl, born in , Scott, Illinois. She married Abslom McGlasson 05 Dec 1880 in Winchester, Scott, Illinois; born in Illinois.
   729   iii.   Lydia C. Scholl, born in Illinois.
   730   iv.   John R. Scholl, born in , Scott, Illinois. He married (1) ? ?. He married (2) Emma J. McGlasson 06 Nov 1881 in ,Scott, Illinois.
   731   v.   Jesse B. Scholl, born in , Scott, Illinois. He married Sallie J. Milliken 05 Sep 1886.
+ 732   vi.   Scholl.
   733   vii.   James M. Scholl, born 11 Oct 1853 in , Scott, Illinois; died 05 Aug 1862.

498. James Purvis[8] Mikel (Charity Ann[7] Scholl, Mary M.[6] Boone, Edward[5], Squire[4], George Michael[3], George[2], George[1]) was born in <Macon Missouri>, and died 22 Oct 1864. He married **Betheny Louisa Mikel**, daughter of David Mikel and Margaret Swinney. She was born 03 Feb 1840 in ,,Tennessee, and died 14 Jan 1912.

Child of James Mikel and Betheny Mikel is:

+ 734   i.   Levander L.[9] Mikel, born 27 May 1863 in , Schuyler, Missouri; died 19 May 1949 in Kirksville, Adair, Missouri.

499. William L.[8] Mikel (Charity Ann[7] Scholl, Mary M.[6] Boone, Edward[5], Squire[4], George Michael[3], George[2], George[1]) was born in ,Mogan, Illinois, and died 06 May 1860 in ,Adair, Missouri. He married **Sarah Ann Knight** 1850 in ,Adair, Missouri. She was born Dec 1834 in ,Morgan, Ohio.

Children of William Mikel and Sarah Knight are:

   735   i.   Angeline[9] Mikel, born in Va.
   736   ii.   Joseph Mikel, born 1851 in Adair, Missouri.
+ 737   iii.   Henry Samuel Mikel, born 14 Oct 1851 in Adair, Missouri; died 24 Feb 1915 in Adair, Missouri.
   738   iv.   John Mikel, born Oct 1856 in Adair, Missouri; died 12 Nov 1927 in Carmel, Monterey, California.
+ 739   v.   Mary Frances Mikel, born Mar 1859 in ,Greenup, Missouri; died 23 Mar 1945 in Carmel, Monterey, California.

501. Charles W.[8] Mikel (Charity Ann[7] Scholl, Mary M.[6] Boone, Edward[5], Squire[4], George Michael[3], George[2], George[1]) was born in ,Macon, Missouri, and died in ,Sedgwick, Kansas. He married **Lucinda Elizabeth Stewart** 15 Mar 1869 in Lancaster, Schuyler, Missouri. She was born 06 Dec 1850 in Greenup, Greenup, Kentucky, and died 19 Aug 1926 in Denver, Denver, Colorado.

Children of Charles Mikel and Lucinda Stewart are:

   740   i.   Charles Homer[9] Mikel, born in Kansas.
+ 741   ii.   Ida Belle Mikel, born 25 Dec 1869 in , Adair, Missouri; died 25 Oct 1931 in Lancaster , Schuyler, Missouri.
+ 742   iii.   Lydia Lottie Mikel, born 12 Jun 1872 in Greentop, Schuyler, Missouri; died 04 Dec 1920 in Bayfield, LaPlata, Colorado.

502. Edward B.[8] Mikel (Charity Ann[7] Scholl, Mary M.[6] Boone, Edward[5], Squire[4], George Michael[3],

George[2], George[1]) was born 1826 in ,Morgan, Illinois. He married **(1) Martha J. Hobs**.   He married **(2) Lucy Minton** 28 Jun 1846 in ,Schuyler, Missouri, daughter of Shadrack Minton and Sarah Mikel. She was born 08 Feb 1832 in ,,North Carolina, and died Aft. 1865.

Children of Edward Mikel and Lucy Minton are:

	743	i.	Alfred[9] Mikel.
	744	ii.	Mikel.
+	745	iii.	Hugh D. Mikel, born 07 Dec 1847 in Missouri; died 01 Jan 1917.
+	746	iv.	Sarah F. Mikel, born Oct 1849 in ,Adair, Missouri; died 04 Oct 1923.
	747	v.	Martha J. Mikel, born 1855 in ,,Missouri. She married James Edwards 13 Nov 1877 in Independence, Missourintogomery, Kansas.
	748	vi.	Lewis Mikel, born 1858 in ,,Missouri.
+	749	vii.	Lucy Adeline Mikel, born 19 Jan 1864 in Green, Schuyler, Missouri; died 07 Sep 1949 in Perry, Noble, Oklahoma.

503. John Noah[8] Mikel (Charity Ann[7] Scholl, Mary M.[6] Boone, Edward[5], Squire[4], George Michael[3], George[2], George[1]) was born 11 Sep 1830 in , Morgan, Illinois, and died in , Adair, Missouri. He married **(1) Melissa Dobbs**.   He married **(2) Missouri Edwards** 31 Jul 1853 in ,Schuyler, Missouri. She was born in Indiana, and died 25 Nov 1881 in , Adair, Missouri.

Children of John Mikel and Missouri Edwards are:

	750	i.	William Albert[9] Mikel, born in ,Adair, Missouri; died Oct 1892.
	751	ii.	Mary Alice Mikel, born in ,Adair, Missouri.
	752	iii.	Cornelia H. Mikel, born in ,Adair, Missouri.
	753	iv.	Barnum B. Mikel, born 28 Jan 1858 in ,Jackson, Missouri; died 31 Dec 1927 in Kansas City, Kansas.
	754	v.	Sarah Jane Mikel, born 02 Mar 1860 in ,Adair, Missouri; died 06 Sep 1935 in ,Adair, Missouri.
	755	vi.	Eliza Ellen Mikel, born 06 Mar 1862 in ,Adair, Missouri; died 20 Sep 1929 in Clinton Indiana.
	756	vii.	Dora Bell Mikel, born 11 Oct 1863 in Polk Township, Adair, Missouri; died 15 Oct 1929 in Connelsville, Adair, Missouri.
	757	viii.	Elizabeth Mikel, born 09 May 1867 in ,Adair, Missouri; died 14 Sep 1937 in Terra Haute, Vico, Indiana.
	758	ix.	Charles Edward Mikel, born 1871 in ,Kansas.
+	759	x.	George Washington Mikel, born 19 Jul 1874 in ,Adair, Missouri; died 22 Dec 1958.
	760	xi.	Grace Mikel, born 13 Mar 1875 in ,Adair, Missouri; died 01 Feb 1955 in Kirksville, Adair, Missouri.
	761	xii.	John Noah Mikel, born 25 Dec 1878 in ,Adair, Missouri; died Aug 1960.
	762	xiii.	Anna M. Mikel, born 04 Nov 1879 in ,Adair, Missouri.
	763	xiv.	Jesse Boone Mikel, born 1881 in ,Adair, Missouri; died 1898.

504. George M.[8] Mikel (Charity Ann[7] Scholl, Mary M.[6] Boone, Edward[5], Squire[4], George Michael[3], George[2], George[1]) was born 1833 in , Morgan, Illinois, and died 03 Apr 1876. He married **Susan E. Furnish** 03 Apr 1868 in , Adair, Missouri. She was born Jan 1850 in , Adair, Missouri, and died 24 Jun 1915.

Children of George Mikel and Susan Furnish are:

	764	i.	Emma[9] Mikel, born in ,Adair, Missouri.
+	765	ii.	Charity Ann Mikel, born in ,Adair, Missouri.
	766	iii.	Nettie J. Mikel, born in ,Adair, Missouri. She married David M. Gregory 10 Feb 1889 in ,Adair, Missouri; born in Missouri.
+	767	iv.	Reitty Belle Mikel, born 05 Aug 1874 in ,Adair, Missouri; died 09 May 1951.

506. David J.[8] Mikel (Charity Ann[7] Scholl, Mary M.[6] Boone, Edward[5], Squire[4], George Michael[3], George[2], George[1]) was born 12 Apr 1836 in ,Morgan, Illinois, and died 07 Jul 1923. He married **Lucinda E. Sutton**. She was born 16 Sep 1839 in ,,Illinois, and died 08 Dec 1917.

Children of David Mikel and Lucinda Sutton are:

	768	i.	Charlie Frank[9] Mikel, born in , Adair, Missouri.
+	769	ii.	George William Mikel, born 09 Sep 1867 in ,Of Adair, Missouri; died 07 Nov 1918 in ,Adair , Missouri, Ft. Madison Cemetery..
	770	iii.	Frank Mikel, born 1871 in , Of Adair, Missouri>.
	771	iv.	Warren C. Mikel, born 25 Mar 1872 in ,Of Adair, Missouri; died 11 Oct 1934. He married Mollie;

born 07 Nov 1877; died 12 Apr 1949.

772   v.   Emaline Lena Mikel, born 19 Dec 1875 in , Of Adair, Missouri>; died May 1952 in Greentop, Schuyler, Missouri. She married James Oliver Towles 26 Sep 1900 in ,Adair , Missouri.

773   vi.   Mary E. Mikel, born 15 Aug 1877 in ,Adair , Missouri; died 12 Aug 1957 in Greentop, Schuyler , Missouri.

774   vii.   Milton S. Mikel, born 31 Mar 1879 in ,Of Adair, Missouri; died 22 Oct 1885 in ,Adair, Missouri.

507. Joseph P.[8] Mikel (Charity Ann[7] Scholl, Mary M.[6] Boone, Edward[5], Squire[4], George Michael[3], George[2], George[1]) was born 30 Mar 1837 in ,Morgan, Illinois, and died 15 Oct 1872. He married **(1) Uri Metcalf**. He married **(2) Sarah E. Cullop** 03 Apr 1863 in , Adair, Missouri. She was born 07 Dec 1847 in Missouri, and died 21 Jan 1928.

Children of Joseph Mikel and Sarah Cullop are:

775   i.   Louise Lewellen[9] Mikel, born in Missouri.

776   ii.   James Mikel, born in Missouri.

+ 777   iii.   Margaret Mikel, born 05 May 1865 in , Adair, Missouri; died 16 Sep 1961 in , Adair, Missouri.

511. Elizabeth[8] Hunter (Joseph[7], Sarah[6] Boone, Edward[5], Squire[4], George Michael[3], George[2], George[1]) died 05 Jul 1871 in , White, Tennessee. She married **(1) Solomon Harrison**. She married **(2) Mathew Wallace**.

Child of Elizabeth Hunter and Solomon Harrison is:

+ 778   i.   ?? ?.

Children of Elizabeth Hunter and Mathew Wallace are:

779   i.   John[9] Wallace.

780   ii.   Mary Wallace, born 1837.

781   iii.   Thomas Jefferson Wallace, born 1840; died 1912.

515. William[8] Hudgens (Mary Polly[7] Hunter, Sarah[6] Boone, Edward[5], Squire[4], George Michael[3], George[2], George[1]) was born 08 Feb 1813 in Tennessee, and died 12 Aug 1882 in Tennessee. He married **Syrena** 1835 in Tennessee. She was born 04 Apr 1810 in Tennessee, and died 26 Jan 1879 in Tennessee.

Children of William Hudgens and Syrena are:

782   i.   William H.[9] Hudgens, born in , White, Tennessee.

783   ii.   Shirley Hudgens.

+ 784   iii.   Edward Boone Hudgens, born in , White, Tennessee.

785   iv.   Taylor Hudgens, born in Tennessee. He married Frances; born in Tennessee.

786   v.   Lou Hudgens. She married ? ?.

787   vi.   Mary A. Hudgens. She married ? ?.

788   vii.   Sarah A. Hudgens. She married ? ?.

789   viii.   Malinda Hudgens. She married ? ?.

790   ix.   Dudley Hudgens, born in Tennessee.

+ 791   x.   Joseph Hudgens, born 25 Apr 1836 in Tennessee; died 31 May 1917 in Algood, Putnam, Tennessee.

792   xi.   Shelby Hudgens, born 1842.

+ 793   xii.   Rachael Hudgens, born 25 Apr 1846 in , White, Tennessee; died 22 Jun 1887 in , Putnam, Tennessee.

794   xiii.   Zachery Taylor Hudgens, born 16 Nov 1848 in Dry Valley, Putnam, Tennessee; died 20 Nov 1889 in Dry Valley, Putnam, Tennessee.

516. Dudley Hampton[8] Hudgens (Mary Polly[7] Hunter, Sarah[6] Boone, Edward[5], Squire[4], George Michael[3], George[2], George[1]) was born 25 May 1814 in , White, Tennessee, and died 21 Jun 1878 in Sparta, White, Tennessee. He married **(1) Elizabeth Austin**. She was born 16 Oct 1816 in Tennessee. He married **(2) Alice Lowery**.

Children of Dudley Hudgens and Elizabeth Austin are:

795   i.   Obe[9] Hudgens, born in Tennessee; died 19 Oct 1930 in , White, Tennessee.

+ 796   ii.   Amanda Hudgens, born 18 Sep 1839 in Tennessee; died 10 Jan 1875.

Children of Dudley Hudgens and Alice Lowery are:
797   i.   James⁹ Hudgens, born 11 Sep 1836 in Sparta, White, Tennessee; died 11 Sep 1868 in Sparta, White, Tennessee.
798   ii. Charles Hudgens, born 20 Nov 1848 in Sparta, White, Tennessee; died 03 Nov 1869 in Sparta, White, Tennessee.

519. Hampton Hamilton⁸ Hudgens (Mary Polly⁷ Hunter, Sarah⁶ Boone, Edward⁵, Squire⁴, George Michael³, George², George¹) was born 28 Nov 1819 in ,,Tennessee, and died 20 Dec 1896 in , White, Tennessee. He married **Eliza Waller** 20 Jan 1842 in Sparta, White, Tennessee. She was born 20 Aug 1824 in , White, Tennessee, and died 17 Jan 1905 in , White, Tennessee.

Children of Hampton Hudgens and Eliza Waller are:
+   799   i.   Charles⁹ Hudgens, born in , White, Tennessee.
+   800   ii.   James P. Hudgens, born in , White, Tennessee.
    801   iii. Kate Dourney Hudgens.
    802   iv.   Robert Hudgens.
    803   v.   Stanton Hudgens, born in , White, Tennessee.
    804   vi.   Amy Hudgens, born in , White, Tennessee.
    805   vii. Vance H. Hudgens, born 05 Jul 1845.
+   806   viii. Merrill Doyle Hudgens, born 24 Nov 1849 in Sparta, White, Tennessee; died 10 May 1920 in Quanah, Hardeman, Texas.
    807   ix.   Emma Hudgens, born 1851.
+   808   x.   Daniel Boone Hudgens, born 07 Feb 1856 in , White, Tennessee; died 30 May 1928 in , White, Tennessee.
    809   xi.   William S. Hudgens, born 1861.
    810   xii. Annie Hudgens, born 26 Sep 1863 in , White, Tennessee; died in , White, Tennessee.
    811   xiii. John Edward Hudgens, born 26 Sep 1863 in , White, Tennessee; died in , White, Tennessee.

522. Catherine⁸ Hudgens (Mary Polly⁷ Hunter, Sarah⁶ Boone, Edward⁵, Squire⁴, George Michael³, George², George¹) was born 20 Nov 1825 in Sparta, White, Tennessee, and died 02 Sep 1881 in Sparta, White, Tennessee. She married **(1) Marion Fisk**. He was born in Tennessee. She married **(2) D. Charles Lowry Sr.** 18 Jan 1844 in Tennessee. He was born 10 Mar 1810 in , White, Tennessee, and died 02 Sep 1884 in Sparta, White, Tennessee.

Child of Catherine Hudgens and Marion Fisk is:
    812   i.   Newton⁹ Fisk, born 20 May 1871 in Tennessee; died 04 Feb 1929 in , White, Tennessee.

Children of Catherine Hudgens and D. Lowry are:
    813   i.   Crocket⁹ Lowery, born in Hot Springs Arkansas; died in Hot Springs Arkansas.
+   814   ii.   Mary Lowry, born 12 Mar 1846 in Tennessee; died 18 Mar 1935 in Tennessee.
+   815   iii. D. Charles Lowery, born 24 Jan 1850 in Sparta, White, Tennessee; died 14 Aug 1889 in Sparta, White, Tennessee.

523. Crocket⁸ Hudgens (Mary Polly⁷ Hunter, Sarah⁶ Boone, Edward⁵, Squire⁴, George Michael³, George², George¹) was born 28 Jun 1827 in ,White, Tennessee, and died 15 Aug 1900 in ,White, Tennessee. He married **(1) Mary H. Hunter**, daughter of Dudley Hunter and Amy Lowery. She was born 06 Jun 1856 in , White, Tennessee, and died 11 Dec 1935 in , White, Tennessee. He married **(2) Lucinda Fisk** 17 Oct 1850 in , White, Tennessee. She was born 26 Jul 1833 in , White, Tennessee, and died 22 Oct 1888 in , White, Tennessee.

Children of Crocket Hudgens and Lucinda Fisk are:
    816   i.   Joseph⁹ Hudgens, born in , White, Tennessee.
    817   ii.   Charley Hudgens, born in , White, Tennessee.
    818   iii. Sally Hudgens, born in , White, Tennessee.
    819   iv.   Waman Hudgens, born in , White, Tennessee.
    820   v.   Martha Hudgens, born in , White, Tennessee.
    821   vi.   James Hudgens, born in , White, Tennessee.

+   822   vii.   Hampton P. Hudgens.

524. Elizabeth⁸ Hunter (Dudley⁷, Sarah⁶ Boone, Edward⁵, Squire⁴, George Michael³, George², George¹) was born 15 Mar 1829 in ,White. She married **James B. Lowery** 27 Nov 1845 in White. He was born 1828 in White.

Children of Elizabeth Hunter and James Lowery are:
   823   i.   Dudley⁹ Lowery, born 1846.
   824   ii.   Seth Lowery, born 1848.

525. Sallie⁸ Hunter (Dudley⁷, Sarah⁶ Boone, Edward⁵, Squire⁴, George Michael³, George², George¹) was born 16 Feb 1822. She married **Dudley Hunter** 14 Mar 1839 in White, son of William Hunter and Sarah Boone. He was born 21 Nov 1794 in Tennessee, and died 27 Oct 1862 in Dry Valley, Putnam, Tennessee.

Children are listed above under (302) Dudley Hunter.

526. Joe⁸ Hunter (Dudley⁷, Sarah⁶ Boone, Edward⁵, Squire⁴, George Michael³, George², George¹) was born 11 Apr 1824, and died 12 Jul 1886. He married **(1) Lettie Ison**. He married **(2) Miss ? Dowell**. He married **(3) Mary Martha Bohanon** 27 Nov 1845 in White. She died 07 Mar 1885.

Children of Joe Hunter and Mary Bohanon are:
   825   i.   Synda⁹ Hunter.
   826   ii.   Betty Hunter.
   827   iii. Amy Hunter. She married ? ?.
   828   iv.   Dudley Hunter. He married ? ?.
   829   v.   Wash Hunter.
   830   vi.   Joe Hunter.
+ 831   vii. John Hunter.
   832   viii. Cynthia Hunter. She married ? ?.
   833   ix.   Polly Hunter. She married ? ?.
+ 834   x.   Sarah Hunter, born 27 Feb 1848 in Tennessee; died 07 Jul 1895 in Dry Valley Tennessee.
+ 835   xi.   Crocket Hunter, born 03 Jun 1850 in White; died 21 Jun 1907.
+ 836   xii. Mary Hunter, born 1852 in White.
   837   xiii. Lucinda Hunter, born 1852.
   838   xiv. Eliza Hunter, born 1856.

528. Henry Ward Beecher⁸ Hunter (Dudley⁷, Sarah⁶ Boone, Edward⁵, Squire⁴, George Michael³, George², George¹) He married **? ?**.

Children of Henry Hunter and ? ? are:
   839   i.   Pauline⁹ Hunter. She married ? ?.
   840   ii.   Laura Hunter.
   841   iii. Marie Hunter.
   842   iv.   William Hunter.
   843   v.   Braxton Douglas Hunter, born 30 Jun 1810 in ,Missouricasin, North Carolina; died 20 Jul 1897. He married Frances ?; born in Tennessee.

536. Joseph Hall⁸ Hunter (Dudley⁷, Sarah⁶ Boone, Edward⁵, Squire⁴, George Michael³, George², George¹) was born 04 Dec 1852, and died 04 Sep 1924. He married **Libby Lou Bohannon** 22 Jul 1883 in Pleasant Bohannon's home. She was born 07 Feb 1862, and died 05 Jan 1947.

Children of Joseph Hunter and Libby Bohannon are:
+ 844   i.   Clarence Pleasant⁹ Hunter.
+ 845   ii.   Walter Benton Hunter.
+ 846   iii. Pleasant Braxton Hunter.
+ 847   iv.   Laura May Hunter.
+ 848   v.   Wilburn Henry Hunter, born 25 Jun 1887.

188

+ 849   vi.   Edward Boone Hunter, born 17 Sep 1889.
   850   vii.   Sally Allen Hunter, born 10 Aug 1892.

547. William Henry[8] Boone (Andrew Jackson[7], John Bryan[6], John[5], Benjamin[4], George Michael[3], George[2], George[1]) was born 02 Apr 1848 in Chillicothe, Livingston, Missouri, and died 24 Jan 1924 in , Livingston, Missouri. He married **Nancy Jane Turner** 15 Mar 1864 in <Chillicothe, Livingston, Missouri>. She was born 31 Jan 1845 in , Grundy, Missouri, and died 24 Jan 1924.

Children of William Boone and Nancy Turner are:

   851   i.   William Eugene[9] Boone, born 29 Jun 1865 in Chillicothe, Levingston, Missouri; died 15 Oct 1898.
   852   ii.   Mary Letitica Boone, born 24 Jun 1867 in Chillicothe, Livingston, Missouri; died 02 Feb 1906.
   853   iii.   Elzora F. Boone, born 30 Jul 1870 in Chillicothe, Livingston, Missouri.
   854   iv.   Lenora Boone, born 26 Mar 1872 in Chillicothe, Livingston, Missouri.
   855   v.   Leah Jane Boone, born 19 Sep 1874 in Chillicothe, Levingston, Missouri; died 14 Aug 1926 in Of, Livingston, Missouri. She married Orron Treat McLallen 20 Feb 1895 in , Livingston, Missouri; born 09 Jan 1866 in Breckenridge, Caldwell, Missouri; died 20 Jun 1944 in Chillicothe, Livingston, Missouri.
   856   vi.   Roy Clarence Boone, born 06 Dec 1876 in Chillicothe, Livingston, Missouri; died 05 Apr 1910.
   857   vii.   Estella Florence Boone, born 03 Jul 1879 in Chillicothe, Livingston, Missouri; died 29 Aug 1901.
   858   viii.   James Paschal Boone, born 29 Aug 1881 in Chillicothe, Levingston, Missouri; died 10 Aug 1933 in <Hickory Creek, Grundy, Missouri>. He married (1) Maude May Minnick 30 Apr 1905 in Missouri; born 04 Mar 1881 in , Grundy, Missouri. He married (2) Katherine Boone 11 Mar 1914 in , Grundy, Missouri; born 11 Mar 1894 in , Livingston, Missouri; died 01 Sep 1917.
   859   ix.   Ettie Emma Boone, born 24 Jun 1884 in Chillicothe, Livingston, Missouri.

Generation No. 7

548. Ida Elizabeth[9] Stover (Simon P[8], Daniel[7], Daniel[6], Abraham[5], Sarah[4] Boone, George Michael[3], George[2], George[1]) was born 01 May 1862 in Mt. Sidney, VA, and died 11 Sep 1946 in Abilene, Dickinson Co , Kansas. She married **David Jacob Eisenhauer** 23 Sep 1885 in Hope, Dickinson, Kansas, son of Jacob Eisenhauer and Margareta Matter. He was born 23 Sep 1863 in Elizabethville, Dauphin, Pennsylvania, and died 10 Mar 1942 in Abilene, Dickinson, Kansas.

Children of Ida Stover and David Eisenhauer are:

+ 860   i.   Arthur Bradford[10] Eisenhower, born 11 Nov 1886 in Hope, Dickinson, Kansas; died 26 Jan 1958.
   861   ii.   Edgar Newton Eisenhower, born 19 Jan 1889 in Hope, Dickinson, Kansas; died 12 Jul 1971 in Tacoma, Pierce, Washington.
+ 862   iii.   Dwight David Eisenhower, born 14 Oct 1890 in Denison, Grayson, Texas; died 28 Mar 1969 in Washington, District Of, Columbia.
+ 863   iv.   Roy Jacob Eisenhower, born 09 Aug 1892 in Abilene, Kansas, Kansas; died 17 Jun 1942.
   864   v.   Paul Dawson A. Eisenhower, born 12 May 1894 in Abilene, Dickinson, Kansas; died 16 Mar 1895.
   865   vi.   Earl Dewey Eisenhower, born 01 Feb 1898 in Abilene, Dickinson, Kansas; died 18 Dec 1968 in Scottsdale, Maricopa, Arizona. He married Kathryn McIntyre Snyder 29 Apr 1933 in Connellsville, Pennsylvania; born 15 Aug 1909 in Charleroi, Washington, Pennsylvania; died Sep 1986 in Scottsdale, Maricopa, Arizona.
   866   vii.   Milton Stover Eisenhower, born 15 Sep 1899 in Abilene, Dickinson, Kansas; died 02 May 1985 in Baltimore, Maryland. He married Helen Elsie Eakin 12 Oct 1927 in Washington, District Of, Columbia; born 14 Aug 1904 in Manhattan, Riley, Kansas; died 10 Jul 1954.

549. ?[9] ? (?[8], Susannah A.[7] Hays, Susannah[6] Boone, Daniel[5], Squire[4], George Michael[3], George[2], George[1]) He married **? ?**.

Child of ? ? and ? ? is:

+ 867   i.   ?[10] ?.

554. Marquis De Lafayette[9] Benson (Sarah W.[8] Hays, William[7], Susannah[6] Boone, Daniel[5], Squire[4], George Michael[3], George[2], George[1]) was born 13 Feb 1846 in Bluffton, Montgomery, Missouri, and died 26 Aug 1931 in Bluffton, Montgomery, Missouri. He married **Leanna Jane Moore** 07 Jan 1869 in Missouri. She was born 09 Apr 1845 in Missouri, and died 28 Feb 1914.

Children of Marquis Benson and Leanna Moore are:
    868   i.   Suella[10] Benson, born in Loutre Montgomery, Missouri.
    869   ii.   Preston Bell Benson, born 21 Oct 1872 in Americus, Montgomery, Missouri; died 05 Aug 1960.
    870   iii.   Mary Leona Benson, born 10 Dec 1875 in Loutre, Montgomery, Missouri; died 30 Jan 1974 in , Montgomery, Missouri.
+   871   iv.   Virgy Wheeler Benson, born 23 Dec 1878 in Loutre Montgomery, Missouri; died 06 Dec 1959.

560. Anna Bell[9] Shobe (Susan[8] Callaway, James[7], Jemima[6] Boone, Daniel[5], Squire[4], George Michael[3], George[2], George[1]) was born 1860, and died 1936. She married **John Hall Glenn**.

Children of Anna Shobe and John Glenn are:
    872   i.   ?[10] ?. He married ? ?.
    873   ii.   ? ?. He married ? ?.
    874   iii.   ? ?. He married ? ?.
    875   iv.   ? ?. He married ? ?.

561. Mary Virginia[9] Shobe (Susan[8] Callaway, James[7], Jemima[6] Boone, Daniel[5], Squire[4], George Michael[3], George[2], George[1]) was born 1862, and died 1951. She married **Sam M. Stevenson**.

Children of Mary Shobe and Sam Stevenson are:
    876   i.   ?[10] ?. She married (1) ? ?. She married (2) ? ?.
    877   ii.   ? ?. She married ? ?.

563. Coanza Burilla[9] Howell (Pizarro[8], Susannah[7] Callaway, Jemima[6] Boone, Daniel[5], Squire[4], George Michael[3], George[2], George[1]) was born 17 Jun 1841, and died 23 Oct 1922. She married **James Francis Stewart** 08 Sep 1859. He was born 28 Feb 1837, and died 25 Jun 1915.

Child of Coanza Howell and James Stewart is:
+   878   i.   Charles Ferney[10] Stewart, born 09 Apr 1865; died 04 Feb 1946.

591. Emma Crusita[9] Boone (George Luther[8], Alphonso[7], Jesse Bryan[6], Daniel[5], Squire[4], George Michael[3], George[2], George[1]) was born 13 Aug 1865 in Philomath, Benton, Oregon, and died 09 Jun 1947 in Corvallis, Benton, Oregon. She married **Lester Thomas Dobson** 02 Aug 1890 in Yaquina, Lincoln, Oregon. He was born 26 May 1862 in Deloit, Crawford, Iowa, and died 29 Dec 1900 in Yaquina, Lincoln, Oregon.

Child of Emma Boone and Lester Dobson is:
    879   i.   Myrtle Estelle[10] Dobson, born 17 Jul 1895 in Yaquina, Lincoln, Oregon; died 25 Apr 1962 in Portland, Tulmah , Oregon. She married Guy Lamond Raven 19 Feb 1928; born 17 Jun 1886 in Eden, Elgin, Ontario; died 18 Sep 1955 in Otis, Lincoln, Oregon.

604. Jesse Archie[9] Boone (Alphonso Daniel[8], Alphonso[7], Jesse Bryan[6], Daniel[5], Squire[4], George Michael[3], George[2], George[1]) was born 15 Jul 1876 in Sumner, Coos, Oregon, and died 31 Oct 1924 in Sumner, Coos, Oregon. He married **Estell Conger** 24 Jan 1905 in Coquille, Coos , Oregon.

Children of Jesse Boone and Estell Conger are:
    880   i.   ?[10] ?.
    881   ii.   ? ?.

605. Lulu Louise[9] Boone (Alphonso Daniel[8], Alphonso[7], Jesse Bryan[6], Daniel[5], Squire[4], George Michael[3], George[2], George[1]) was born 15 Jul 1878 in Sumner, Coos, Oregon, and died 12 Jan 1944 in ,Coos, Oregon. She married **Eric William Cardell** 17 Dec 1902 in Sumner, Coos, Oregon.

Children of Lulu Boone and Eric Cardell are:

882	i.	?[10] ?.
883	ii.	? ?. She married ? ?.
884	iii.	? ?. She married ? ?.

609. Myrtle Leola[9] Boone (Alphonso Daniel[8], Alphonso[7], Jesse Bryan[6], Daniel[5], Squire[4], George Michael[3], George[2], George[1]) was born 17 Oct 1887 in ,Coos, Oregon. She married **Nels Hamilton Hanson** 04 Jul 1909 in Sumner, Coos, Oregon.

Child of Myrtle Boone and Nels Hanson is:
| 885 | i. | ?[10] ?. |

613. Lilburn W.[9] Boggs (William Montgomery[8], Panthea Grant[7] Boone, Jesse Bryan[6], Daniel[5], Squire[4], George Michael[3], George[2], George[1]) was born in , Sonoma, California. He married **Virginia A.** in , Sonoma, California. She was born in Missouri.

Children of Lilburn Boggs and Virginia A. are:
886	i.	Wade Thomas[10] Boggs, born in California.
887	ii.	Chester A. Boggs, born in California.
888	iii.	Lilburn F. Boggs, born in California.
889	iv.	Virginia Boggs, born in California.
890	v.	Mary O. Boggs, born in California.
891	vi.	Edith Boone Boggs, born 25 Jul 1876 in California.

655. ?[9] ? (Martha Susan[8] Boone, Alonzo[7], John Linville[6], George[5], Squire[4], George Michael[3], George[2], George[1]) He married **? ?**.

Children of ? ? and ? ? are:
892	i.	?[10] ?.
893	ii.	? ?. He married ? ?.
894	iii.	? ?.

659. Delia Onie[9] Kettle (Martha Susan[8] Boone, Alonzo[7], John Linville[6], George[5], Squire[4], George Michael[3], George[2], George[1]) was born 25 Feb 1884. She married **Ward** 25 Feb 1884.

Child of Delia Kettle and Ward is:
| + | 895 | i. | Minnie Louise[10] Ward. |

664. Alfred Obediah[9] Boone (John William Alonzo[8], Alonzo[7], John Linville[6], George[5], Squire[4], George Michael[3], George[2], George[1]) was born 10 Jan 1881, and died 11 Jan 1969. He married **Maud Price Tate** 26 Nov 1902.

Children of Alfred Boone and Maud Tate are:
+	896	i.	?[10] ?.
+	897	ii.	? ?.
+	898	iii.	? ?.
+	899	iv.	Katie Gertrude Boone, born 18 Sep 1903 in Montgomery, Missouri; died 04 Dec 1976.
	900	v.	Harvey Lee Boone, born 18 Jun 1905; died 30 Nov 1966.
+	901	vi.	George Edwin Boone, born 28 May 1911 in , St. Charles, Missouri; died Dec 1973.
	902	vii.	Charles Burton Boone, born 20 Jul 1913; died 23 Nov 1913.

665. Minnie O.[9] Boone (John William Alonzo[8], Alonzo[7], John Linville[6], George[5], Squire[4], George Michael[3], George[2], George[1]) was born 27 Feb 1882, and died 23 Apr 1913. She married **Levi Young** 02 Aug 1902.

Children of Minnie Boone and Levi Young are:

+ 903   i.   ?[10] ?.
    904   ii.   ? ?.
    905   iii.   ? ?.
    906   iv.   ? ?.

711. Martha Jane[9] Scholl (Elledge[8], William[7], Mary M.[6] Boone, Edward[5], Squire[4], George Michael[3], George[2], George[1]) was born 09 Oct 1843 in ,Adair/Macon, Missouri, and died 12 Mar 1912 in Unionville, Putnam, Missouri. She married **Harbart Lancaster Weatherford** 14 Jul 1861 in Lancaster, Schuyler, Missouri. He was born 24 Oct 1839 in Lancaster, Schuyler, Missouri, and died 12 Apr 1914.

Children of Martha Scholl and Harbart Weatherford are:

    907   i.   Mary Effie[10] Weatherford, born 18 Jul 1863; died 12 Jan 1932. She married Ernest T. Williams; born 22 Aug 1864; died 04 Dec 1945.
    908   ii.   Franklin Ambrose Weatherford, born 13 Feb 1866; died 02 May 1920. He married Anna Belle Tatman; born 11 Dec 1871; died Jan 1947.
    909   iii.   Guy Ulysses Weatherford, born 01 Sep 1869; died 22 Aug 1917.
    910   iv.   Bertha J. Weatherford, born 03 Dec 1873; died 23 Sep 1945. She married Robert W. Crumpacker; born 01 Aug 1854; died 11 Dec 1949.
    911   v.   Winfred Lee Weatherford, born 03 Feb 1876; died 20 Jan 1943.
+ 912   vi.   Stella E. Weatherford, born 22 Feb 1878; died 20 Jul 1942.

712. Ambrose[9] Scholl (Elledge[8], William[7], Mary M.[6] Boone, Edward[5], Squire[4], George Michael[3], George[2], George[1]) was born 15 Jul 1846 in , Adair, Missouri, and died 18 Mar 1911 in Lancaster, Schuyler, Missouri. He married **(1) Emily Craig** 24 Oct 1869 in , Schuyler, Missouri.   He married **(2) Lucinda Elizabeth Stewart** 27 Sep 1873 in ,Adair, Missouri. She was born 06 Dec 1850 in Greenup, Greenup, Kentucky, and died 19 Aug 1926 in Denver, Denver, Colorado.

Children of Ambrose Scholl and Lucinda Stewart are:

    913   i.   Effie A.[10] Scholl, born 19 Apr 1875 in Lancaster, Schuyler, Missouri; died 28 Aug 1909. She married Anthony Epperson 27 Nov 1895 in Kirksville, Adair, Missouri; born 11 Aug 1874 in Lancaster, Schuyler, Missouri; died 09 Apr 1960.
    914   ii.   William Elledge Scholl, born 27 Apr 1877 in , Schuyler, Missouri; died Jan 1953. He married Emma Elizabeth Martin 08 Dec 1901 in ,Schuyler, Missouri; born 17 Dec 1881 in ,Schuyler, Missouri; died 02 Aug 1960 in Garden City, Kansas.
+ 915   iii.   Anna May Scholl, born 06 Jan 1879 in Lancaster, Schuyler, Missouri; died 19 Oct 1943 in Rapid City South Dakota.
+ 916   iv.   Elmer Joseph Scholl, born 21 Mar 1881 in ,Schuyler, Missouri; died 09 Sep 1956.
    917   v.   Herbert Edward Scholl, born 24 Sep 1883 in ,,Missouri; died 12 Sep 1959. He married Rose Kimbel.
+ 918   vi.   Mary Mural Scholl, born 04 Nov 1885 in Lancaster, Schuyler, Missouri; died 05 Apr 1923 in Centerville, Appanoose, Iowa.
    919   vii.   Harley Richard Scholl, born 02 Feb 1887 in Lancaster, Schuyler, Missouri; died 26 Nov 1949 in Phoenix, Maricopa, Arizona. He married ? ?.
    920   viii.   Lena Florence Scholl, born 06 May 1890 in Lancaster, Schuyler, Missouri; died 08 Nov 1971 in Denver, Denver, Colorado. She married ? ?.
    921   ix.   Jesse Albert Scholl, born 27 Apr 1892 in ,,Missouri; died 1949. He married ? ?.

714. Emily Anna[9] Scholl (Elledge[8], William[7], Mary M.[6] Boone, Edward[5], Squire[4], George Michael[3], George[2], George[1]) was born 22 Dec 1851 in Lancaster, Schuyler, Missouri, and died 22 May 1920 in Kirksville, Adair, Missouri. She married **J. Will Simmons**.

Child of Emily Scholl and J. Simmons is:
    922   i.   ?[10] ?.

723. Lavina[9] Scholl (James M.[8], Jesse Bryan[7], Mary M.[6] Boone, Edward[5], Squire[4], George Michael[3], George[2], George[1]) was born in Illinois. She married **Samuel Mikel** in Newton, Harvey, Kansas, son of John Mikel and Sarah Whitacre. He was born in , Schuyler, Missouri.

Children of Lavina Scholl and Samuel Mikel are:

923	i.	Millie[10] Mikel, born in ,,Illinois.
924	ii.	Lucy Mikel, born in ,,Missouri.
925	iii.	Jimmie Mikel, born in Illinois.
926	iv.	Perry Scholl, born in Illinois.

732. Scholl[9] (Edward Boone[8], Jesse Bryan[7], Mary M.[6] Boone, Edward[5], Squire[4], George Michael[3], George[2], George[1])

Child of Scholl is:

| 927 | i. | Orley[10] Scholl, born in Missouri. |

734. Levander L.[9] Mikel (James Purvis[8], Charity Ann[7] Scholl, Mary M.[6] Boone, Edward[5], Squire[4], George Michael[3], George[2], George[1]) was born 27 May 1863 in , Schuyler, Missouri, and died 19 May 1949 in Kirksville, Adair, Missouri. He married **(1) Mary E. Kimberly**. She was born 10 Aug 1864 in , Defiance, Ohio, and died 26 Nov 1941 in Pure Air, Adair, Missouri. He married **(2) America Susie Miller** 18 Dec 1884 in ,Adair , Missouri. She was born 01 Feb 1866, and died 30 Dec 1918.

Children of Levander Mikel and America Miller are:

+	928	i.	Oda F.[10] Mikel.
	929	ii.	Mikel.
	930	iii.	Casper Mikel.
	931	iv.	Jesse William Mikel, born 11 Oct 1885 in ,Schuyler , Missouri; died 21 Feb 1968 in Kirksville, Adair , Missouri. He married Mella B. Burgin 06 Oct 1910 in Kirksville, Adair , Missouri; born 1888; died 19 Apr 1967.
	932	v.	Posie H. Mikel, born 12 Dec 1889; died 11 Aug 1891.
	933	vi.	Harry Mikel, born 23 Mar 1894 in ,Adair , Missouri; died 27 May 1986 in Queen City, Schuyler , Missouri. He married Nira Pearce 23 Apr 1920 in Macon, Macon , Missouri; born 01 Aug 1895; died 10 Nov 1972.
	934	vii.	Charles O. Mikel, born 07 Dec 1896. He married Edith A.; born 05 Dec 1902.
	935	viii.	John D. Mikel, born 15 Dec 1901 in , Adair, Missouri; died 16 Nov 1987 in Kirksville, Adair, Missouri. He married Ida Olga Drefs 23 Nov 1939 in Chicago, Cook , Illinois; born 03 Dec 1905 in Engadine, Mackinac , Michigan; died 28 Jun 1986 in Kirksville, Adair, Missouri.

737. Henry Samuel[9] Mikel (William L.[8], Charity Ann[7] Scholl, Mary M.[6] Boone, Edward[5], Squire[4], George Michael[3], George[2], George[1]) was born 14 Oct 1851 in Adair, Missouri, and died 24 Feb 1915 in Adair, Missouri. He married **(1) Liddia Wood**. He married **(2) Mary Isabelle Gregory** 13 Sep 1876 in , Schuyler, Missouri. She was born 18 Jan 1858 in , Schuyler, Missouri, and died 24 Feb 1924.

Children of Henry Mikel and Liddia Wood are:

936	i.	?[10] ?.
937	ii.	? ?.
938	iii.	? ?.

Children of Henry Mikel and Mary Gregory are:

939	i.	Warren[10] Mikel, died 06 Mar 1892.
940	ii.	James F. Mikel, born Dec 1877 in ,,Missouri.
941	iii.	Genie M. Mikel, born 11 Feb 1881; died 17 Aug 1881.
942	iv.	William M. Mikel, born 15 Jul 1882 in ,,Missouri; died 02 Aug 1905.
943	v.	Mikel, born 27 May 1886 in Greentop, Salt River Township, Schuyler, Missouri; died 27 May 1886 in Greentop, Salt River Township, Schuyler, Missouri.
944	vi.	Eva Adelma Mikel, born 27 May 1886 in Greentop, Salt River Township, Schuyler, Missouri; died 09 Nov 1979 in Kirksville, Adair, Missouri. She married (1) Anthony Epperson; born 11 Aug 1874 in Lancaster, Schuyler, Missouri; died 09 Apr 1960. She married (2) William M. Newcomer 03 Jan 1907 in , Adair, Missouri; born 11 Nov 1870 in , Adair, Missouri; died 31 Jul 1946 in Kirksville, Adair, Missouri.
945	vii.	Nettie Mikel, born Mar 1893 in ,,Missouri. She married Harrison C. Ruddell Jan 1912; born 08 Sep 1889 in Carthage, Hancock, Illinois; died Nov 1947 in Kirksville, Adair , Missouri.

739. Mary Frances[9] Mikel (William L.[8], Charity Ann[7] Scholl, Mary M.[6] Boone, Edward[5], Squire[4], George Michael[3], George[2], George[1]) was born Mar 1859 in ,Greenup, Missouri, and died 23 Mar 1945 in Carmel, Monterey, California. She married **John Thomas Stewart** 21 May 1876 in ,Schuyler, Missouri. He was born Sep 1848 in Greenup, Greenup, Kentucky.

Children of Mary Mikel and John Stewart are:

+ 946   i.   Walter C.[10] Stewart, born in ,,Missouri.
   947   ii.   Ole W. Stewart, born Jan 1879 in ,,Missouri.

741. Ida Belle[9] Mikel (Charles W.[8], Charity Ann[7] Scholl, Mary M.[6] Boone, Edward[5], Squire[4], George Michael[3], George[2], George[1]) was born 25 Dec 1869 in , Adair, Missouri, and died 25 Oct 1931 in Lancaster , Schuyler, Missouri. She married **John Morgan Whitacre** 16 Sep 1888 in Lancaster, Schuyler, Missouri. He was born 18 Apr 1864 in , Schuyler, Missouri, and died 07 Oct 1946 in Lancaster, Schuyler, Missouri.

Children of Ida Mikel and John Whitacre are:

+ 948   i.   Charles Newton[10] Whitacre, born 15 Jun 1889 in Lancaster, Schuyler, Missouri; died 23 May 1953 in Bloomfield, Davis, Iowa.
+ 949   ii.   Chester Oral Whitacre, born 30 Nov 1890 in Lancaster, Schuyler, Missouri; died 23 Mar 1963 in Burlington, Des Moines, Iowa.
+ 950   iii.   John Leslie Whitacre, born 26 Aug 1892 in Lancaster, Schuyler, Missouri; died 04 Jun 1964 in Centerville, Iowa.
+ 951   iv.   Alta Effie Whitacre, born 19 Sep 1894 in Lancaster, Schuyler, Missouri; died 24 Sep 1972 in Kirksville, Adair, Missouri.
+ 952   v.   Minnie Estella Whitacre, born 01 Mar 1896 in Lancaster, Schuyler, Missouri; died 28 Feb 1973 in Burlington, Des Moines, Iowa.
+ 953   vi.   Essie Elizabeth Whitacre, born 09 Mar 1898 in Lancaster, Schuyler, Missouri; died 12 Jun 1931 in Kirksville, Adair, Missouri.
   954   vii.   Opal Lydia Whitacre, born 20 Apr 1900 in Lancaster, Schuyler, Missouri; died 20 Feb 1991 in Queen City, Schuyler, Missouri. She married Edwin Raymond Hitch 24 Jun 1923 in Bloomfield, Davis, Iowa; born 30 Jun 1901 in Covington, Campbell, Kentucky; died 27 Jan 1962 in Lancaster, Schuyler, Missouri.
   955   viii.   Vernon Jewell Whitacre, born 15 Jun 1902 in Lancaster, Schuyler, Missouri; died 01 Nov 1981 in Schenectady, Schenectady, New York.
+ 956   ix.   Kenneth Omer Whitacre, born 27 Feb 1905 in Lancaster, Schuyler, Missouri; died 21 Feb 1976 in Kirksville, Adair, Missouri.
+ 957   x.   Olen Aubry Whitacre, born 18 Apr 1906 in Lancaster, Schuyler, Missouri; died 27 Dec 1993 in Bakersfield, Kern, California.
   958   xi.   Ida Berniece Whitacre, born 17 Dec 1909 in Lancaster, Schuyler, Missouri; died 22 Nov 1988 in Lancaster, Schuyler, Missouri. She married (1) Wayne Laverne Butts; born 22 Dec 1908 in ,Schuyler, Missouri; died 16 Dec 1991 in Kirksville, Adair, Missouri. She married (2) ? ?. She married (3) Wayne Laverne Butts Feb 1983; born 22 Dec 1908 in ,Schuyler, Missouri; died 16 Dec 1991 in Kirksville, Adair, Missouri.
+ 959   xii.   Naomi Vernadean Whitacre, born 09 Dec 1912 in Lancaster, Schuyler, Missouri; died 27 Sep 1995 in Warrenton, Warren, Missouri.

742. Lydia Lottie[9] Mikel (Charles W.[8], Charity Ann[7] Scholl, Mary M.[6] Boone, Edward[5], Squire[4], George Michael[3], George[2], George[1]) was born 12 Jun 1872 in Greentop, Schuyler, Missouri, and died 04 Dec 1920 in Bayfield, LaPlata, Colorado. She married **Walter Sherman Mikel** 13 Jan 1892 in Pueblo, Pueblo, Colorado, son of William Mikel and Liltra Wade. He was born 13 Dec 1869 in Warrensburg, Johnson, Missouri, and died 01 Jul 1934 in Farmington, San Juan, New Mexico.

Children of Lydia Mikel and Walter Mikel are:

   960   i.   Walter S[10] Mikel, born 1903. He married ? ?.
   961   ii.   Florence Eva Mikel, born 12 May 1892 in Hooper, Alamosa, Colorado; died 15 Jun 1949 in San Anselmo, Marin, California. She married Joseph McEwen Walters 01 Jun 1910; born 31 Dec 1884 in Beaver, Beaver, Utah; died 24 Oct 1954 in Redway, Humbolt, California.
+ 962   iii.   Gladys Melvina Mikel, born 23 Dec 1893 in Dukin, Saguache, Colorado; died 15 Jun 1921 in Mancos, Montezuma, Colorado.
   963   iv.   Marquerette Marie Mikel, born 08 Apr 1906 in Mancos, Montezuma, Colorado; died 29 Mar 1972.

964   v.   Homer W Mikel, born 15 Dec 1912 in Mancos, Montezuma, Colorado.

745. Hugh D.[9] Mikel (Edward B.[8], Charity Ann[7] Scholl, Mary M.[6] Boone, Edward[5], Squire[4], George Michael[3], George[2], George[1]) was born 07 Dec 1847 in Missouri, and died 01 Jan 1917. He married **Amanda Jane Lowe** 22 Jan 1868 in ,Adair, Missouri. She was born 10 May 1851 in ,,Iowa, and died 01 Nov 1918.

Children of Hugh Mikel and Amanda Lowe are:

    965   i.   Howley B.[10] Mikel.
    966   ii.   Willard L. Mikel.
    967   iii.   Sally J. Mikel.
    968   iv.   George Evert Mikel.
+ 969   v.   Generva E. Mikel, born 26 Jun 1871 in , Adair, Missouri; died 07 Mar 1906.

746. Sarah F.[9] Mikel (Edward B.[8], Charity Ann[7] Scholl, Mary M.[6] Boone, Edward[5], Squire[4], George Michael[3], George[2], George[1]) was born Oct 1849 in ,Adair, Missouri, and died 04 Oct 1923. She married **James W. Reid** 21 Dec 1870 in Independence, Montgomery, Kansas. He was born 1845 in Pekin, Tazewell , Illinois.

Children of Sarah Mikel and James Reid are:

    970   i.   ?[10] Reid, died in Infant.
    971   ii.   Joseph H. Reid, born 1873 in Independence, Missourintogomery , Kansas.

749. Lucy Adeline[9] Mikel (Edward B.[8], Charity Ann[7] Scholl, Mary M.[6] Boone, Edward[5], Squire[4], George Michael[3], George[2], George[1]) was born 19 Jan 1864 in Green, Schuyler, Missouri, and died 07 Sep 1949 in Perry, Noble, Oklahoma. She married **Enos Enoch Berger** 24 Aug 1881 in Independence, Montgomery , Kansas. He was born 23 Apr 1856 in St. Charles, Madison, Iowa, and died 12 Dec 1933 in Perry, Noble, Oklahoma.

Children of Lucy Mikel and Enos Berger are:

    972   i.   ?[10] ?.
    973   ii.   Berger.
    974   iii.   ? ?.
    975   iv.   Zella Jane Berger, born 05 Aug 1882 in Independence, Montgomery, Kansas; died 27 May 1961.
    976   v.   Clara Elizabeth Berger, born 26 Jul 1885 in Elk City, Elk, Kansas; died 01 Oct 1953 in Walnut Creek, Contra Costa, California.
    977   vi.   George Edward Berger, born 10 Jun 1888 in Elk City, Elk, Kansas; died 25 Aug 1954.
    978   vii.   Susan Frances Berger, born 03 Oct 1890 in Elk City, Elk, Kansas.
    979   viii.   Hester Lyons Berger, born 05 Apr 1893 in Stillwater, Payne, Oklahoma.
    980   ix.   Lucy Hazel Berger, born 07 May 1902 in Perry, Noble, Ok Ty; died 11 Dec 1910.

759. George Washington[9] Mikel (John Noah[8], Charity Ann[7] Scholl, Mary M.[6] Boone, Edward[5], Squire[4], George Michael[3], George[2], George[1]) was born 19 Jul 1874 in ,Adair, Missouri, and died 22 Dec 1958. He married **Louisa Jane Mercer** 04 Apr 1897 in ,Adair, Missouri. She was born 25 Mar 1878 in ,Illinois, and died 29 Mar 1943 in LaPlata Cemetery, Macon, Missouri.

Children of George Mikel and Louisa Mercer are:

    981   i.   Lousia[10] Mikel, born 1897.
    982   ii.   Ada Ethel Mikel, born 23 May 1900.
    983   iii.   Chester Paul Mikel, born 16 Sep 1904.
    984   iv.   Dorcas E Mikel, born 1909.
    985   v.   Evan L Mikel, born 1912.
    986   vi.   Leslie L Mikel, born 1914.
    987   vii.   Traverse Mikel, born 1916.
    988   viii.   Clora Alice Mikel, born 21 Apr 1917 in ,Macon, Missouri; died 15 Nov 1994 in Kirksville, Adair, Missouri.
    989   ix.   Merle A Mikel, born 1920; died Bef. 1943.

765. Charity Ann[9] Mikel (George M.[8], Charity Ann[7] Scholl, Mary M.[6] Boone, Edward[5], Squire[4], George

Michael³, George², George¹) was born in ,Adair, Missouri. She married **Albert Adams** 31 Jan 1887 in , Adair, Missouri. He died Dec 1921 in Greentop, Schuyler, Missouri.

Child of Charity Mikel and Albert Adams is:
+ 990   i. Everett Pearl¹⁰ Adams, born 03 Jul 1887 in Greentop, Schuyler, Missouri; died 11 Aug 1942 in
                 Greentop, Schuyler, Missouri.

767. Reitty Belle⁹ Mikel (George M.⁸, Charity Ann⁷ Scholl, Mary M.⁶ Boone, Edward⁵, Squire⁴, George
Michael³, George², George¹) was born 05 Aug 1874 in ,Adair, Missouri, and died 09 May 1951. She married
Nathan C. Bledsoe 13 Feb 1889 in , Adair, Missouri. He was born 15 Apr 1859 in ,,Arkansas, and died 09
Aug 1934.

Children of Reitty Mikel and Nathan Bledsoe are:
     991   i. Nora Mae¹⁰ Bledsoe, born 29 May 1890 in ,Schuyler., Missouri; died 12 Jun 1938.
     992   ii. Ethel L. Bledsoe, born 13 Jun 1894; died 22 Jan 1965. She married Allen D. Lowe 22 Mar 1916 in
                   Greentop, Schuyler, Missouri; born 26 Mar 1894; died 14 Jun 1960.
     993   iii. Leslie N. Bledsoe, born 24 May 1903 in Missouri; died 15 Apr 1977 in Missouri. He married Louise
                   H. B. Hutchison 28 Jul 1929 in Macon, Macon, Missouri; born 02 May 1905; died 23 Aug 1972.

769. George William⁹ Mikel (David J.⁸, Charity Ann⁷ Scholl, Mary M.⁶ Boone, Edward⁵, Squire⁴, George
Michael³, George², George¹) was born 09 Sep 1867 in ,Of Adair, Missouri, and died 07 Nov 1918 in ,Adair ,
Missouri, Ft. Madison Cemetery.. He married **May E. Towles** 18 Nov 1894 in ,Adair , Missouri.

Children of George Mikel and May Towles are:
     994   i. Beulah¹⁰ Mikel.
     995   ii. Myrtle Mikel.
     996   iii. Ruth Mikel.
     997   iv. Eugene Mikel, born 13 Sep 1896; died 02 Feb 1897.

777. Margaret⁹ Mikel (Joseph P.⁸, Charity Ann⁷ Scholl, Mary M.⁶ Boone, Edward⁵, Squire⁴, George
Michael³, George², George¹) was born 05 May 1865 in , Adair, Missouri, and died 16 Sep 1961 in , Adair,
Missouri. She married **(1) James B. Dye** 24 Dec 1882. He was born 13 Mar 1857 in Illinois, and died 16 Jul
1936. She married **(2) Finis Gregory** 31 Dec 1893 in ,Adair , Missouri.

Child of Margaret Mikel and James Dye is:
     998   i. Alvie¹⁰ Dye, born 31 Mar 1887; died 26 Jun 1974.

778. ?⁹ ? (Elizabeth⁸ Hunter, Joseph⁷, Sarah⁶ Boone, Edward⁵, Squire⁴, George Michael³, George²,
George¹) She married **? ?**.

Child of ? ? and ? ? is:
+ 999   i. ?¹⁰ ?.

784. Edward Boone⁹ Hudgens (William⁸, Mary Polly⁷ Hunter, Sarah⁶ Boone, Edward⁵, Squire⁴, George
Michael³, George², George¹) was born in , White, Tennessee. He married **Ann ?**. She was born in Tennessee.

Child of Edward Hudgens and Ann ? is:
    1000   i. Robbard¹⁰ Hudgens, born in , White, Tennessee.

791. Joseph⁹ Hudgens (William⁸, Mary Polly⁷ Hunter, Sarah⁶ Boone, Edward⁵, Squire⁴, George Michael³,
George², George¹) was born 25 Apr 1836 in Tennessee, and died 31 May 1917 in Algood, Putnam, Tennessee.
He married **Caroline Williams** 11 Dec 1856. She was born 12 Mar 1835 in Dry Valley, Putnam, Tennessee,
and died 19 May 1899 in Dry Valley, Putnam, Tennessee.

Children of Joseph Hudgens and Caroline Williams are:

- 1001   i.   Charles L.[10] Hudgens, born 01 Jan 1858 in Dry Valley, Putnam, Tennessee; died 14 Jul 1932 in Dry Valley, Putnam, Tennessee. He married Lizzie; born in , Putnam, Tennessee.
- 1002   ii.   Mary Hudgens, born 25 Jan 1861 in , Putnam, Tennessee.
- 1003   iii.   Louverna Hudgens, born 20 Sep 1862 in Dry Valley, Putnam, Tennessee; died 18 Mar 1893 in Dry Valley, Putnam, Tennessee.
- 1004   iv.   Clumindia Hudgens, born 30 Jan 1867 in , Putnam, Tennessee.
- 1005   v.   John Hudgens, born 26 Nov 1868 in , Putnam, Tennessee.
- 1006   vi.   Joseph Hudgens, born 23 Jul 1870 in , White, Tennessee; died in Texas.
- 1007   vii.   Malinda Hudgens, born 04 Dec 1873 in Dry Valley, Putnam, Tennessee; died 24 Sep 1898 in Dry Valley, Putnam, Tennessee.
- + 1008   viii.   Byrd Murry Hudgens, born 28 Jul 1878 in Algood, Putnam, Tennessee; died 31 Oct 1951 in Cookeville, Putnam, Tennessee.

793. Rachael[9] Hudgens (William[8], Mary Polly[7] Hunter, Sarah[6] Boone, Edward[5], Squire[4], George Michael[3], George[2], George[1]) was born 25 Apr 1846 in , White, Tennessee, and died 22 Jun 1887 in , Putnam, Tennessee. She married **David Farley** 1865 in Tennessee.

Children of Rachael Hudgens and David Farley are:

- + 1009   i.   William[10] Farley.
- 1010   ii.   Malinda Farley.

796. Amanda[9] Hudgens (Dudley Hampton[8], Mary Polly[7] Hunter, Sarah[6] Boone, Edward[5], Squire[4], George Michael[3], George[2], George[1]) was born 18 Sep 1839 in Tennessee, and died 10 Jan 1875. She married **Lawsen Brown**. He was born in Tennessee.

Child of Amanda Hudgens and Lawsen Brown is:

- 1011   i.   John[10] Brown, born in Tennessee; died 11 Oct 1932 in , White, Tennessee.

799. Charles[9] Hudgens (Hampton Hamilton[8], Mary Polly[7] Hunter, Sarah[6] Boone, Edward[5], Squire[4], George Michael[3], George[2], George[1]) was born in , White, Tennessee. He married **Clarissa Jane Cope**. She was born in Tennessee.

Children of Charles Hudgens and Clarissa Cope are:

- 1012   i.   Jane[10] Hudgens, born in , White, Tennessee.
- 1013   ii.   Robert Hudgens, born in , White, Tennessee.
- 1014   iii.   Bell Hudgens, born in , White, Tennessee.
- 1015   iv.   Ellis Hudgens, born in , White, Tennessee.
- 1016   v.   Lizzie Hudgens, born in , White, Tennessee.
- 1017   vi.   Daisie Hugens, born in , White, Tennessee.

800. James P.[9] Hudgens (Hampton Hamilton[8], Mary Polly[7] Hunter, Sarah[6] Boone, Edward[5], Squire[4], George Michael[3], George[2], George[1]) was born in , White, Tennessee. He married **(1) Melvina Doyle Herd** 19 Nov 1865 in , White, Tennessee. She was born in , White, Tennessee. He married **(2) America Caroline Baker** 29 Oct 1896 in , White, Tennessee. She was born in , White, Tennessee.

Children of James Hudgens and Melvina Herd are:

- 1018   i.   Nicholas[10] Hudgens, born in , White, Tennessee.
- 1019   ii.   William M. Hudgens, born in , White, Tennessee.
- 1020   iii.   Ella B. Hudgens, born in , White, Tennessee.
- 1021   iv.   Mary E. Hudgens, born in , White, Tennessee.
- + 1022   v.   Laura Hudgens, born 20 Dec 1875 in , White, Tennessee; died 18 Feb 1964.

806. Merrill Doyle[9] Hudgens (Hampton Hamilton[8], Mary Polly[7] Hunter, Sarah[6] Boone, Edward[5], Squire[4], George Michael[3], George[2], George[1]) was born 24 Nov 1849 in Sparta, White, Tennessee, and died 10 May 1920 in Quanah, Hardeman, Texas. He married **Elvira Jeffrey** Sep 1877. She was born 20 Nov 1862 in Texas, and died 29 Oct 1922 in Staples, Guadalupe, Texas.

Children of Merrill Hudgens and Elvira Jeffrey are:
       1023   i.   Hudgens[10].
       1024   ii.   Hudgens.
       1025   iii. Elvin Hamilton Hudgens, born 20 Nov 1878 in Staples, Guadalupe, Texas; died 20 Jul 1879.
       1026   iv. Dennis Alvin Hudgens, born 03 Feb 1882 in Staples, Guadalupe, Texas; died 12 Oct 1955.
+   1027   v.   Ollie Lee Hudgens, born 07 Nov 1885 in Staples, Guadalupe, Texas; died 18 Mar 1931 in Las Vegas City, San Miguel, New Mexico.
+   1028   vi. James Rufus Hudgens, born 04 Dec 1892 in Staples, Guadalupe, Texas; died 28 Oct 1939.
       1029   vii. Glen Fox Hudgens, born 20 Jul 1906 in Staples, Guadalupe, Texas; died 20 Jun 1908.

808. Daniel Boone[9] Hudgens (Hampton Hamilton[8], Mary Polly[7] Hunter, Sarah[6] Boone, Edward[5], Squire[4], George Michael[3], George[2], George[1]) was born 07 Feb 1856 in , White, Tennessee, and died 30 May 1928 in , White, Tennessee. He married **Mary Catherine Gist** 08 Dec 1875. She was born 17 Sep 1855 in , White, Tennessee, and died 06 Oct 1932 in , White, Tennessee.

Children of Daniel Hudgens and Mary Gist are:
+   1030   i.   Henry Claude[10] Hudgens.
+   1031   ii.   Willie Hampton Hudgens.
       1032   iii. Allie Hudgens.
       1033   iv. Alvie Hudgens.
+   1034   v.   Maude Hudgens.
+   1035   vi. Lee Ernest Hudgens.
+   1036   vii. Roy Merrell Hudgens.
+   1037   viii. Clarence Hugh Hudgens, born 30 Sep 1877 in , White, Tennessee; died 10 Jul 1932.
+   1038   ix. John Everette Hudgens, born 28 Sep 1880 in , Guadalupe, Texas; died 23 Jul 1947 in El Paso, El Paso, Texas.
+   1039   x.   Lester Boone Hudgens, born 19 Aug 1893; died 31 Mar 1957.

814. Mary[9] Lowry (Catherine[8] Hudgens, Mary Polly[7] Hunter, Sarah[6] Boone, Edward[5], Squire[4], George Michael[3], George[2], George[1]) was born 12 Mar 1846 in Tennessee, and died 18 Mar 1935 in Tennessee. She married **Daniel W. Young.**

Children of Mary Lowry and Daniel Young are:
       1040   i.   ?[10] ?.
       1041   ii.   Daniel W. Young.
       1042   iii. Nannie Young, born 16 Apr 1867.
       1043   iv. Kate Young, born 28 Mar 1873.
       1044   v.   Mallie Young, born 28 Mar 1878.
       1045   vi. Maggie Young, born 13 Apr 1879.

815. D. Charles[9] Lowery (Catherine[8] Hudgens, Mary Polly[7] Hunter, Sarah[6] Boone, Edward[5], Squire[4], George Michael[3], George[2], George[1]) was born 24 Jan 1850 in Sparta, White, Tennessee, and died 14 Aug 1889 in Sparta, White, Tennessee. He married **Maggie Meredith** 18 Jan 1876 in , White, Tennessee. She was born in Texas.

Children of D. Lowery and Maggie Meredith are:
       1046   i.   Eli[10] Lowery, born in Tennessee.
       1047   ii.   Jimmie Lowery, born in Tennessee.

822. Hampton P.[9] Hudgens (Crocket[8], Mary Polly[7] Hunter, Sarah[6] Boone, Edward[5], Squire[4], George Michael[3], George[2], George[1]) He married **? ?.**

Children of Hampton Hudgens and ? ? are:
       1048   i.   ?[10] ?.
       1049   ii.   ? ?.

831. John⁹ Hunter (Joe⁸, Dudley⁷, Sarah⁶ Boone, Edward⁵, Squire⁴, George Michael³, George², George¹) He married **(1) ? ?**. He married **(2) ? ?**.

Child of John Hunter and ? ? is:
    1050   i.   ?¹⁰ ?.

Child of John Hunter and ? ? is:
    1051   i.   ?¹⁰ ?.

834. Sarah⁹ Hunter (Joe⁸, Dudley⁷, Sarah⁶ Boone, Edward⁵, Squire⁴, George Michael³, George², George¹) was born 27 Feb 1848 in Tennessee, and died 07 Jul 1895 in Dry Valley Tennessee. She married **Francis Marion Bullock** 24 Feb 1870 in Cedar Hill Community, Tennessee. He was born 23 Jan 1843 in Tennessee, and died 08 Mar 1917 in Dry Valley, Putnam, Tennessee.

Children of Sarah Hunter and Francis Bullock are:
+   1052   i.   Mary Ollie¹⁰ Bullock, born 11 Dec 1870 in Cedar Hill, Putnam, Tennessee; died 15 Feb 1924 in Tennessee.
+   1053   ii.   Martha Ann Bullock, born 15 Sep 1874 in Cedar Hill, Putnam, Tennessee; died 25 Sep 1941.
+   1054   iii. Eliza Naomi Bullock, born 15 Jan 1877 in Cedar Hill, Putnam, Tennessee; died 09 Jul 1973 in Cookeville, Putnam, Tennessee.
+   1055   iv. Joseph Bullock, born 11 Dec 1878 in Cedar Hill, Putnam, Tennessee; died 08 Jan 1954.
+   1056   v.   Ida Pauline Bullock, born 15 Oct 1881; died 26 Sep 1954.

835. Crocket⁹ Hunter (Joe⁸, Dudley⁷, Sarah⁶ Boone, Edward⁵, Squire⁴, George Michael³, George², George¹) was born 03 Jun 1850 in White, and died 21 Jun 1907. He married **Cydia McCormick**.

Child of Crocket Hunter and Cydia McCormick is:
    1057   i.   John W.¹⁰ Hunter, born 12 Aug 1886; died 21 May 1958. He married ? ?.

836. Mary⁹ Hunter (Joe⁸, Dudley⁷, Sarah⁶ Boone, Edward⁵, Squire⁴, George Michael³, George², George¹) was born 1852 in White.

Child of Mary Hunter is:
    1058   i.   ?¹⁰ ?.

844. Clarence Pleasant⁹ Hunter (Joseph Hall⁸, Dudley⁷, Sarah⁶ Boone, Edward⁵, Squire⁴, George Michael³, George², George¹) He married **? ?**.

Children of Clarence Hunter and ? ? are:
    1059   i.   ?¹⁰ ?.
    1060   ii.   ? ?.
    1061   iii. ? ?.
    1062   iv. ? ?.

845. Walter Benton⁹ Hunter (Joseph Hall⁸, Dudley⁷, Sarah⁶ Boone, Edward⁵, Squire⁴, George Michael³, George², George¹) He married **? ?**.

Children of Walter Hunter and ? ? are:
    1063   i.   ?¹⁰ ?.
    1064   ii.   ? ?.

846. Pleasant Braxton⁹ Hunter (Joseph Hall⁸, Dudley⁷, Sarah⁶ Boone, Edward⁵, Squire⁴, George Michael³, George², George¹) He married **? ?**.

Child of Pleasant Hunter and ? ? is:
    1065   i. ?[10] ?.

    847. Laura May[9] Hunter (Joseph Hall[8], Dudley[7], Sarah[6] Boone, Edward[5], Squire[4], George Michael[3], George[2], George[1]) She married **? ?**.

Child of Laura Hunter and ? ? is:
    1066   i. ?[10] ?.

    848. Wilburn Henry[9] Hunter (Joseph Hall[8], Dudley[7], Sarah[6] Boone, Edward[5], Squire[4], George Michael[3], George[2], George[1]) was born 25 Jun 1887. He married **? ?**.

Child of Wilburn Hunter and ? ? is:
    1067   i. ?[10] ?.

    849. Edward Boone[9] Hunter (Joseph Hall[8], Dudley[7], Sarah[6] Boone, Edward[5], Squire[4], George Michael[3], George[2], George[1]) was born 17 Sep 1889. He married **? ?**.

Children of Edward Hunter and ? ? are:
    1068   i. ?[10] ?.
    1069   ii. ? ?.
    1070   iii. ? ?.
    1071   iv. ? ?.
    1072   v. ? ?.

Generation No. 8

    860. Arthur Bradford[10] Eisenhower (Ida Elizabeth[9] Stover, Simon P[8], Daniel[7], Daniel[6], Abraham[5], Sarah[4] Boone, George Michael[3], George[2], George[1]) was born 11 Nov 1886 in Hope, Dickinson, Kansas, and died 26 Jan 1958. He married **(1) Alida B ?**. She was born 17 Feb 1889. He married **(2) Louis Sondra Grieb** 03 Sep 1926.

Child of Arthur Eisenhower and Alida ? is:
+   1073   i. Katherine[11] Eisenhower, born 02 Jul 1914.

    862. Dwight David[10] Eisenhower (Ida Elizabeth[9] Stover, Simon P[8], Daniel[7], Daniel[6], Abraham[5], Sarah[4] Boone, George Michael[3], George[2], George[1]) was born 14 Oct 1890 in Denison, Grayson, Texas, and died 28 Mar 1969 in Washington, District Of, Columbia. He married **Mary Geneva Doud** 01 Jul 1916 in Denver, Denver, Colorado, daughter of John Doud and Elivera Carlson. She was born 14 Nov 1896 in Boone, Boone, Iowa, and died 31 Oct 1979 in Washington, D.C..

Children of Dwight Eisenhower and Mary Doud are:
+   1074   i. John Sheldon Doud[11] Eisenhower, born 1923.
    1075   ii. Doud Dwight Eisenhower, born 24 Sep 1917 in San Antonio, Bexar, Texas; died 02 Jan 1921 in Camp Meade, Maryland.

    863. Roy Jacob[10] Eisenhower (Ida Elizabeth[9] Stover, Simon P[8], Daniel[7], Daniel[6], Abraham[5], Sarah[4] Boone, George Michael[3], George[2], George[1]) was born 09 Aug 1892 in Abilene, Kansas, Kansas, and died 17 Jun 1942. He married **Edna Alice Shade** 18 Nov 1917 in Ellsworth, Ellsworth, Kansas. She was born 13 Sep 1891 in Ellis City, Ellis, Kansas, and died 26 Jun 1989 in Denver, Denver, Colorado.

Children of Roy Eisenhower and Edna Shade are:
    1076   i. Patricia[11] Eisenhower, born 1918.

1077   ii.   Peggy J Eisenhower, born 1923.
1078   iii. Lloyd E Eisenhower, born 1925.
1079   iv. Roy J Eisenhower, born Abt. 1930.

867. ?[10] ? (?[9], ?[8], Susannah A.[7] Hays, Susannah[6] Boone, Daniel[5], Squire[4], George Michael[3], George[2], George[1]) He married **(1) ? ?.**   He married **(2) ? ?.**

Child of ? ? and ? ? is:
1080   i. ?[11] ?.

Child of ? ? and ? ? is:
1081   i. ?[11] ?.

871. Virgy Wheeler[10] Benson (Marquis De Lafayette[9], Sarah W.[8] Hays, William[7], Susannah[6] Boone, Daniel[5], Squire[4], George Michael[3], George[2], George[1]) was born 23 Dec 1878 in Loutre Montgomery, Missouri, and died 06 Dec 1959. She married **Charles F. Brown** 28 May 1914. He was born 08 Jul 1867 in Missouri, and died 20 Sep 1940.

Children of Virgy Benson and Charles Brown are:
1082   i. ?[11] ?. She married ? ?.
1083   ii. ? ?.

878. Charles Ferney[10] Stewart (Coanza Burilla[9] Howell, Pizarro[8], Susannah[7] Callaway, Jemima[6] Boone, Daniel[5], Squire[4], George Michael[3], George[2], George[1]) was born 09 Apr 1865, and died 04 Feb 1946. He married **Mary Virginia Morris** 21 Apr 1869. She was born 12 Oct 1869.

Child of Charles Stewart and Mary Morris is:
+   1084   i. Percey DeWitte[11] Stewart, born 25 Mar 1893.

895. Minnie Louise[10] Ward (Delia Onie[9] Kettle, Martha Susan[8] Boone, Alonzo[7], John Linville[6], George[5], Squire[4], George Michael[3], George[2], George[1]) She married **? ?.**

Child of Minnie Ward and ? ? is:
1085   i. ?[11] ?.

896. ?[10] ? (Alfred Obediah[9] Boone, John William Alonzo[8], Alonzo[7], John Linville[6], George[5], Squire[4], George Michael[3], George[2], George[1]) She married **? ?.**

Children of ? ? and ? ? are:
1086   i. ?[11] ?.
1087   ii. ? ?.
1088   iii. ? ?.

897. ?[10] ? (Alfred Obediah[9] Boone, John William Alonzo[8], Alonzo[7], John Linville[6], George[5], Squire[4], George Michael[3], George[2], George[1]) She married **? ?.**

Children of ? ? and ? ? are:
1089   i. ?[11] ?.
1090   ii. ? ?.
1091   iii. ? ?.
1092   iv. ? ?.
1093   v. ? ?.
1094   vi. ? ?.
1095   vii. ? ?.

898. ?^{10} ? (Alfred Obediah^9 Boone, John William Alonzo^8, Alonzo^7, John Linville^6, George^5, Squire^4, George Michael^3, George^2, George^1) She married **(1)** ? ?.   She married **(2)** ? ?.

Children of ? ? and ? ? are:
```
1096    i.    ?¹¹ ?.
1097    ii.   ? ?.
```

899. Katie Gertrude^{10} Boone (Alfred Obediah^9, John William Alonzo^8, Alonzo^7, John Linville^6, George^5, Squire^4, George Michael^3, George^2, George^1) was born 18 Sep 1903 in Montgomery, Missouri, and died 04 Dec 1976. She married **(1)** ? ?.   She married **(2)** ? ?.   She married **(3)** ? ?.

Children of Katie Boone and ? ? are:
```
1098    i.    ?¹¹ ?.
1099    ii.   ? ?.
```

Children of Katie Boone and ? ? are:
```
+  1100    i.     ?¹¹ ?.
   1101    ii.    ? ?.
   1102    iii.   ? ?.
   1103    iv.    ? ?.
```

901. George Edwin^{10} Boone (Alfred Obediah^9, John William Alonzo^8, Alonzo^7, John Linville^6, George^5, Squire^4, George Michael^3, George^2, George^1) was born 28 May 1911 in , St. Charles, Missouri, and died Dec 1973. He married **? ?.**

Children of George Boone and ? ? are:
```
1104    i.    ?¹¹ ?.
1105    ii.   ? ?.
1106    iii.  ? ?.
1107    iv.   ? ?.
1108    v.    ? ?.
```

903. ?^{10} ? (Minnie O.^{9} Boone, John William Alonzo^8, Alonzo^7, John Linville^6, George^5, Squire^4, George Michael^3, George^2, George^1) She married **(1)** ? ?.   She married **(2)** ? ?.   She married **(3)** ? ?.

Children of ? ? and ? ? are:
```
1109    i.    ?¹¹ ?.
1110    ii.   ? ?.
```

912. Stella E.^{10} Weatherford (Martha Jane^9 Scholl, Elledge^8, William^7, Mary M.^{6} Boone, Edward^5, Squire^4, George Michael^3, George^2, George^1) was born 22 Feb 1878, and died 20 Jul 1942. She married **John Thomas Robinson**. He was born 14 Nov 1875, and died 24 Jun 1929.

Child of Stella Weatherford and John Robinson is:
```
1111    i.    Virginia Evelyn¹¹ Robinson, born 29 Feb 1920; died 24 Sep 1920.
```

915. Anna May^{10} Scholl (Ambrose^9, Elledge^8, William^7, Mary M.^{6} Boone, Edward^5, Squire^4, George Michael^3, George^2, George^1) was born 06 Jan 1879 in Lancaster, Schuyler, Missouri, and died 19 Oct 1943 in Rapid City South Dakota. She married **Alva L. Ryan** 31 Mar 1897 in Lancaster, Schuyler, Missouri. He was born 27 Sep 1876 in Lancaster, Schuyler , Missouri, and died 06 Dec 1956 in Rapid City South Dakota.

Children of Anna Scholl and Alva Ryan are:
```
1112    i.    Ruth Marie¹¹ Ryan, born 11 Jan 1898 in Lancaster, Schuyler, Missouri; died 19 Feb 1985 in Pierre,
```

South Dakota.

1113	ii.	Elmer William Ryan, born 14 Dec 1899 in Lancaster, Schuyler, Missouri; died 05 Aug 1982 in Union City, California.
1114	iii.	Hattie Gwendolyn Ryan, born 18 Dec 1903; died 26 Dec 1903.
1115	iv.	Ryan, born 18 Jan 1904; died 26 Jan 1904.
1116	v.	Virginia Elizabeth Ryan, born 23 May 1910 in Pierre, South Dakota; died 12 Aug 1927 in Pierre, South Dakota.

916. Elmer Joseph[10] Scholl (Ambrose[9], Elledge[8], William[7], Mary M.[6] Boone, Edward[5], Squire[4], George Michael[3], George[2], George[1]) was born 21 Mar 1881 in ,Schuyler, Missouri, and died 09 Sep 1956. He married **(1) Esther ?**. He married **(2) Lula Burris** 18 May 1902 in Lancaster, Schuyler, Missouri.

Child of Elmer Scholl and Lula Burris is:

| 1117 | i. | Annie Mary[11] Scholl, born 07 Apr 1910 in , Schuyler, Missouri; died 24 Aug 1910 in Lancaster, Schuyler, Missouri. |

918. Mary Mural[10] Scholl (Ambrose[9], Elledge[8], William[7], Mary M.[6] Boone, Edward[5], Squire[4], George Michael[3], George[2], George[1]) was born 04 Nov 1885 in Lancaster, Schuyler, Missouri, and died 05 Apr 1923 in Centerville, Appanoose, Iowa. She married **William A. Turner** 27 Dec 1905 in ,Schuyler, Missouri. He was born 1876, and died 1948.

Children of Mary Scholl and William Turner are:

| 1118 | i. | ?[11] ?. |
| 1119 | ii. | ? ?. |

928. Oda F.[10] Mikel (Levander L.[9], James Purvis[8], Charity Ann[7] Scholl, Mary M.[6] Boone, Edward[5], Squire[4], George Michael[3], George[2], George[1]) She married **Clarence W. Gregory**. He was born 06 Feb 1888 in Iowa, and died 30 Mar 1968 in Kirksville, Adair, Missouri.

Children of Oda Mikel and Clarence Gregory are:

| 1120 | i. | Loreta[11] Gregory. |
| 1121 | ii. | Henry Lee Gregory, born 13 Nov 1923 in Greentop, Schuyler, Missouri; died 02 Mar 1968 in , Adair, Missouri. |

946. Walter C.[10] Stewart (Mary Frances[9] Mikel, William L.[8], Charity Ann[7] Scholl, Mary M.[6] Boone, Edward[5], Squire[4], George Michael[3], George[2], George[1]) was born in ,,Missouri.

Children of Walter C. Stewart are:

| 1122 | i. | ?[11] Stewart. |
| 1123 | ii. | ? Stewart. |

948. Charles Newton[10] Whitacre (Ida Belle[9] Mikel, Charles W.[8], Charity Ann[7] Scholl, Mary M.[6] Boone, Edward[5], Squire[4], George Michael[3], George[2], George[1]) was born 15 Jun 1889 in Lancaster, Schuyler, Missouri, and died 23 May 1953 in Bloomfield, Davis, Iowa. He married **Clara Ada White** 08 Mar 1913. She was born 20 Nov 1895 in Iowa, and died 19 Aug 1989 in Bloomfield, Davis, Iowa.

Children of Charles Whitacre and Clara White are:

+	1124	i.	Glen N.[11] Whitacre, born 08 Jan 1914 in Missouri; died 18 Oct 2003 in Bloomfield, Davis, Iowa.
+	1125	ii.	Hugh W. Whitacre, born 21 Apr 1915 in , Schuyler, Missouri; died 20 Feb 2001 in Springfield, Greene, Missouri.
+	1126	iii.	Omer Charles Whitacre, born 27 Sep 1916 in Missouri; died 21 Oct 1987 in Bloomfield, Davis, Iowa.
	1127	iv.	Estel L. Whitacre, born 04 Jun 1918 in Iowa; died Sep 1986 in Missouri>.
	1128	v.	Joan A Whitacre, born 1919. He married Sarah J. Harper; born in Iowa>; died in <Bloomfield, Davis, Iowa>.
+	1129	vi.	Ray M Whitacre, born 1922.
+	1130	vii.	Ella L. Whitacre, born 1923 in Missouri; died in Bloomfield, Davis, Iowa.

949. Chester Oral[10] **Whitacre** (Ida Belle[9] Mikel, Charles W.[8], Charity Ann[7] Scholl, Mary M.[6] Boone, Edward[5], Squire[4], George Michael[3], George[2], George[1]) was born 30 Nov 1890 in Lancaster, Schuyler, Missouri, and died 23 Mar 1963 in Burlington, Des Moines, Iowa. He married **Alta Nina McMains** 25 Feb 1914 in Bloomfield, Davis, Iowa. She was born 02 Jan 1895 in ,Davis, Iowa, and died 15 May 1971 in Burlington, Des Moines, Iowa.

Children of Chester Whitacre and Alta McMains are:

	1131	i.	Harold O.[11] Whitacre, born in Lancaster, Schuyler, Missouri; died 24 Mar 1955 in Muscatine, Muscatine, Iowa.
	1132	ii.	Carroll D. Whitacre, died Dec 1942.
+	1133	iii.	Geneva B. Whitacre, born 16 Feb 1918 in ,Davis, Iowa; died 10 Aug 2001 in Burlington, Des Moines, Iowa.

950. John Leslie[10] **Whitacre** (Ida Belle[9] Mikel, Charles W.[8], Charity Ann[7] Scholl, Mary M.[6] Boone, Edward[5], Squire[4], George Michael[3], George[2], George[1]) was born 26 Aug 1892 in Lancaster, Schuyler, Missouri, and died 04 Jun 1964 in Centerville, Iowa. He married **(2) ? ?.**

Children of John Leslie Whitacre are:

+	1134	i.	?[11] Whitacre.
	1135	ii.	? Whitacre. She married Charles Gillispie; born 20 Jul 1920; died 22 Apr 1988.
	1136	iii.	Ralph Whitacre.
	1137	iv.	Lowell Whitacre.

951. Alta Effie[10] **Whitacre** (Ida Belle[9] Mikel, Charles W.[8], Charity Ann[7] Scholl, Mary M.[6] Boone, Edward[5], Squire[4], George Michael[3], George[2], George[1]) was born 19 Sep 1894 in Lancaster, Schuyler, Missouri, and died 24 Sep 1972 in Kirksville, Adair, Missouri. She married **Eugene Aeschliman** 24 Dec 1914 in Lancaster, Schuyler, Missouri. He was born 30 May 1893 in Darby, Schuyler, Missouri, and died 24 Mar 1974 in Kirksville, Adair, Missouri.

Children of Alta Whitacre and Eugene Aeschliman are:

	1138	i.	Emogene[11] Aeschliman, born 14 Feb 1916.
	1139	ii.	Lucille Aeschliman, born 31 Oct 1917. She married Paul Leroy Beeler; born 23 Jan 1916 in Lancaster, Schuyler, Missouri; died 12 Oct 1997 in Lancaster, Schuyler, Missouri.
	1140	iii.	Essie Mildred Aeschliman, born 16 May 1925 in Lancaster, Schuyler, Missouri; died 18 Jun 1925 in Liberty Township, Schuyler, Missouri.
	1141	iv.	Opal Hildred Aeschliman, born 16 May 1925.

952. Minnie Estella[10] **Whitacre** (Ida Belle[9] Mikel, Charles W.[8], Charity Ann[7] Scholl, Mary M.[6] Boone, Edward[5], Squire[4], George Michael[3], George[2], George[1]) was born 01 Mar 1896 in Lancaster, Schuyler, Missouri, and died 28 Feb 1973 in Burlington, Des Moines, Iowa. She married **Paul Austin Tomey** 29 Aug 1914 in Lancaster, Schuyler, Missouri. He was born 16 Feb 1893 in Bloomfield, Davis, Iowa, and died 02 May 1963 in Burlington, Des Moines, Iowa.

Children of Minnie Whitacre and Paul Tomey are:

+	1142	i.	Max H[11] Tomey, born 1921.
	1143	ii.	Pauline Annette Tomey, born 02 Mar 1916 in Bloomfield, Davis, Iowa; died 06 Oct 1988 in Morning Sun, Louisa, Iowa. She married (1) Frank Niemann; born 08 Jan 1894; died Apr 1982 in Burlington, Des Moines, Iowa. She married (2) Edward Alfred Scott 17 Sep 1949 in Quincy, Adams, Illinois; born 14 Jul 1902 in Rome, Henry, Iowa; died 23 Jun 1984 in Mt. Pleasant, Henry, Iowa.
+	1144	iii.	Jack Phillip Tomey, born 03 Sep 1918 in Des Moines, Polk, Iowa; died 22 Jun 1996 in Sunnyvale, Santa Clara, California.
+	1145	iv.	Eugene Stewart Tomey, born 07 Oct 1923 in Boone, Boone, Iowa; died 14 Aug 2001 in Burlington, Des Moines, Iowa.
+	1146	v.	Rex Whitacre Tomey, born 04 Dec 1924 in Boone, Boone, Iowa; died 21 May 2001 in Moline, Rock Island, Illinois.
+	1147	vi.	William Joseph Tomey, born 22 Jul 1929 in Kirksville, Adair, Missouri; died 02 Oct 1994 in Anaheim,

Orange, California.

953. Essie Elizabeth[10] Whitacre (Ida Belle[9] Mikel, Charles W.[8], Charity Ann[7] Scholl, Mary M.[6] Boone, Edward[5], Squire[4], George Michael[3], George[2], George[1]) was born 09 Mar 1898 in Lancaster, Schuyler, Missouri, and died 12 Jun 1931 in Kirksville, Adair, Missouri. She married **Edward Webster Grist** 29 Jul 1920 in Missouri. He was born 26 Mar 1898 in Lancaster, Schuyler, Missouri.

Child of Essie Whitacre and Edward Grist is:
1148   i.   ?[11] ?.

956. Kenneth Omer[10] Whitacre (Ida Belle[9] Mikel, Charles W.[8], Charity Ann[7] Scholl, Mary M.[6] Boone, Edward[5], Squire[4], George Michael[3], George[2], George[1]) was born 27 Feb 1905 in Lancaster, Schuyler, Missouri, and died 21 Feb 1976 in Kirksville, Adair, Missouri. He married **Georgia Lee Hulen** 20 Jun 1926 in Lancaster, Schuyler, Missouri. She was born 31 Jan 1908 in Lancaster, Schuyler, Missouri, and died 19 Jun 1988 in Kirksville, Adair, Missouri.

Child of Kenneth Whitacre and Georgia Hulen is:
1149   i.   John George[11] Whitacre, born 06 Nov 1925 in Lancaster, Schuyler, Missouri; died 08 Nov 1925 in Lancaster, Schuyler, Missouri.

957. Olen Aubry[10] Whitacre (Ida Belle[9] Mikel, Charles W.[8], Charity Ann[7] Scholl, Mary M.[6] Boone, Edward[5], Squire[4], George Michael[3], George[2], George[1]) was born 18 Apr 1906 in Lancaster, Schuyler, Missouri, and died 27 Dec 1993 in Bakersfield, Kern, California. He married **(1) ? ?.** He married **(2) Zelma L. Followwill**. She was born 22 Nov 1914 in Iowa, and died 28 Jan 1998 in Bakersfield, Kern, California.

Child of Olen Whitacre and Zelma Followwill is:
1150   i.   Richard Allen[11] Whitacre, died 06 Mar 1929 in Seymour, Wayne, Iowa.

959. Naomi Vernadean[10] Whitacre (Ida Belle[9] Mikel, Charles W.[8], Charity Ann[7] Scholl, Mary M.[6] Boone, Edward[5], Squire[4], George Michael[3], George[2], George[1]) was born 09 Dec 1912 in Lancaster, Schuyler, Missouri, and died 27 Sep 1995 in Warrenton, Warren, Missouri. She married **Harry Bradley** 02 Nov 1933. He was born 15 Mar 1912 in ,,Missouri, and died Oct 1986 in Warrenton, Warren, Missouri.

Child of Naomi Whitacre and Harry Bradley is:
+   1151   i.   John L.[11] Bradley, born in Missouri>; died in Missouri>.

962. Gladys Melvina[10] Mikel (Lydia Lottie[9], Charles W.[8], Charity Ann[7] Scholl, Mary M.[6] Boone, Edward[5], Squire[4], George Michael[3], George[2], George[1]) was born 23 Dec 1893 in Dukin, Saguache, Colorado, and died 15 Jun 1921 in Mancos, Montezuma, Colorado. She married **Mark Willden** 29 Aug 1912 in Cortez, Montezuma, Colorado. He was born 16 Mar 1891 in Mancos, Montezuma, Colorado, and died 24 Aug 1977 in Durango, LaPlata, Colorado.

Children of Gladys Mikel and Mark Willden are:
1152   i.   Leona Gladys[11] Willden, born 26 Jul 1914 in Mancos, Montezuma, Colorado; died 20 Jul 1960 in Naturita, San Miguel, Colorado.
1153   ii.   Esther Corilla Willden, born 11 Oct 1915 in Mancos, Montezuma, Colorado; died 23 Jun 1987 in Provo, Utah, Utah.
1154   iii. Don Edward Willden, born 15 Oct 1916 in Mancos, Montezuma, Colorado; died 17 Dec 1997 in Lovell, Wyoming.
1155   iv.   Elmer Sherman Willden, born 17 Feb 1918 in Mancos, Montezuma, Colorado; died 30 Oct 1974 in Colorado Springs, El Paso, Colorado.

969. Generva E.[10] Mikel (Hugh D.[9], Edward B.[8], Charity Ann[7] Scholl, Mary M.[6] Boone, Edward[5], Squire[4], George Michael[3], George[2], George[1]) was born 26 Jun 1871 in , Adair, Missouri, and died 07 Mar 1906.

She married **William M. Newcomer** 13 Dec 1891 in ,Adair, Missouri. He was born 11 Nov 1870 in , Adair, Missouri, and died 31 Jul 1946 in Kirksville, Adair, Missouri.

Children of Generva Mikel and William Newcomer are:

    1156   i.   Georgie F.[11] Newcomer, died 03 Sep 1905.

    1157   ii.   Minnie E. Newcomer, born 14 May 1894 in n/Greentop, Schuyler, Missouri; died 17 Jan 1983 in Kirksville, Adair, Missouri. She married John H. Thompson; born 12 Mar 1892; died 04 Sep 1978.

    1158   iii.   Grace L. Newcomer, born 31 Dec 1895 in n/Greentop, Schuyler, Missouri; died 12 Sep 1975 in Rockford, Winnebago, Illinois.

    1159   iv.   Nellie Mae Newcomer, born 11 May 1898 in Greentop, Schuyler, Missouri; died 05 Aug 1984 in Kirksville, Adair, Missouri. She married Herman Victor Craig; born 09 Sep 1892 in Greentop, Schuyler, Missouri; died 07 Jul 1976 in Greentop, Schuyler, Missouri.

+   1160   v.   Oscar Newcomer, born 15 Nov 1901 in n/Greentop, Schuyler, Missouri; died 26 Mar 1983 in Kirksville, Adair, Missouri.

    1161   vi.   Ethel L. Newcomer, born 26 May 1905 in Kirksville, Adair, Missouri; died 24 Sep 1991 in Kirksville, Adair, Missouri. She married William S. Thompson 26 Oct 1941 in Greentop, Schuyler, Missouri; born 28 Sep 1900 in Youngstown, Adair(?), Missouri; died 20 Dec 1956 in Kirksville, Adair, Missouri.

990. Everett Pearl[10] Adams (Charity Ann[9] Mikel, George M.[8], Charity Ann[7] Scholl, Mary M.[6] Boone, Edward[5], Squire[4], George Michael[3], George[2], George[1]) was born 03 Jul 1887 in Greentop, Schuyler, Missouri, and died 11 Aug 1942 in Greentop, Schuyler, Missouri.

Children of Everett Pearl Adams are:

    1162   i.   ?[11] Adams.

    1163   ii.   ? Adams.

    1164   iii.   ? Adams.

999. ?[10] ? (?[9], Elizabeth[8] Hunter, Joseph[7], Sarah[6] Boone, Edward[5], Squire[4], George Michael[3], George[2], George[1]) She married **? ?**.

Child of ? ? and ? ? is:

+   1165   i.   ?[11] ?.

1008. Byrd Murry[10] Hudgens (Joseph[9], William[8], Mary Polly[7] Hunter, Sarah[6] Boone, Edward[5], Squire[4], George Michael[3], George[2], George[1]) was born 28 Jul 1878 in Algood, Putnam, Tennessee, and died 31 Oct 1951 in Cookeville, Putnam, Tennessee. He married **Eliza Naomi Bullock** 11 Oct 1903 in , Putnam, Tennessee, daughter of Francis Bullock and Sarah Hunter. She was born 15 Jan 1877 in Cedar Hill, Putnam, Tennessee, and died 09 Jul 1973 in Cookeville, Putnam, Tennessee.

Children of Byrd Hudgens and Eliza Bullock are:

    1166   i.   Willie Shelva[11] Hudgens, born 22 Aug 1904; died 03 Feb 1985 in Cookeville, Putnam, Tennessee.

+   1167   ii.   Edward Boone Hudgens Sr., born 18 Mar 1906 in Cookeville, Tennessee; died 31 Aug 1975 in Nashville, Tennessee.

    1168   iii.   Joseph Franklin Hudgens, born 18 Sep 1907; died 07 Mar 1986. He married (1) ? ?. He married (2) Dimple Loftis 24 Sep 1932 in Cookeville, Putnam, Tennessee; born 12 Aug 1902 in Cookeville, Putnam, Tennessee; died 30 Nov 1961 in Nashville, Tennessee.

    1169   iv.   Eva Pauline Hudgens, born 12 Oct 1908 in Algood, Putnam, Tennessee; died 07 Jan 1994 in Cookeville Tennessee.

1009. William[10] Farley (Rachael[9] Hudgens, William[8], Mary Polly[7] Hunter, Sarah[6] Boone, Edward[5], Squire[4], George Michael[3], George[2], George[1]) He married **? ?**.

Child of William Farley and ? ? is:

    1170   i.   ?[11] ?. She married ? ?.

1022. Laura[10] Hudgens (James P.[9], Hampton Hamilton[8], Mary Polly[7] Hunter, Sarah[6] Boone, Edward[5],

Squire[4], George Michael[3], George[2], George[1]) was born 20 Dec 1875 in , White, Tennessee, and died 18 Feb 1964. She married **Elkana Peek** 18 Dec 1904 in White. He was born 17 Oct 1869 in Putnam, and died 22 Sep 1946.

Children of Laura Hudgens and Elkana Peek are:
+   1171   i.   ?[11] ?.
    1172   ii.   Mertie Lee Peek, born 11 Sep 1906; died 24 Dec 1912.

1027.   Ollie Lee[10] Hudgens (Merrill Doyle[9], Hampton Hamilton[8], Mary Polly[7] Hunter, Sarah[6] Boone, Edward[5], Squire[4], George Michael[3], George[2], George[1]) was born 07 Nov 1885 in Staples, Guadalupe, Texas, and died 18 Mar 1931 in Las Vegas City, San Miguel, New Mexico. She married **John Wesley Houser** 02 Nov 1906 in Martindale, Guadalupe, Texas. He was born 12 Aug 1885 in Gatesville, Coryell, Texas, and died 17 Mar 1968 in Cockrell Hill, Dallas, Texas.

Children of Ollie Hudgens and John Houser are:
    1173   i.   ?[11] Houser, born in Hamilton, Hamilton, Texas; died in Hamilton, Hamilton, Texas.
    1174   ii.   ? Houser.
    1175   iii.   ? Houser.
    1176   iv.   ? Houser.
    1177   v.   Lilly Houser, born in Hamilton, Hamilton, Texas; died in Hamilton, Hamilton, Texas.
    1178   vi.   ? Houser.
    1179   vii.   ? Houser.
    1180   viii. ? Houser.
    1181   ix.   Wendell Irving Houser, born 11 Sep 1907 in Hamilton, Hamilton, Texas; died 28 May 1966.
    1182   x.   Martha Ellen Houser, born 11 Apr 1922 in Post, Garza, Texas; died 18 Mar 1937.
    1183   xi.   Laura Lee Houser, born 01 Dec 1924 in Tapoka, Lynn, Texas; died 18 Mar 1937.
    1184   xii.   Imogene Houser, born 06 Oct 1926 in Lovington, Lea, New Mexico; died 18 Mar 1937.

1028.   James Rufus[10] Hudgens (Merrill Doyle[9], Hampton Hamilton[8], Mary Polly[7] Hunter, Sarah[6] Boone, Edward[5], Squire[4], George Michael[3], George[2], George[1]) was born 04 Dec 1892 in Staples, Guadalupe, Texas, and died 28 Oct 1939. He married **? ?**.

Child of James Hudgens and ? ? is:
+   1185   i.   Annie Juanita[11] Hudgens, born 1912; died 1996.

1030.   Henry Claude[10] Hudgens (Daniel Boone[9], Hampton Hamilton[8], Mary Polly[7] Hunter, Sarah[6] Boone, Edward[5], Squire[4], George Michael[3], George[2], George[1]) He married **? ?**.

Child of Henry Hudgens and ? ? is:
    1186   i.   ?[11] ?.

1031.   Willie Hampton[10] Hudgens (Daniel Boone[9], Hampton Hamilton[8], Mary Polly[7] Hunter, Sarah[6] Boone, Edward[5], Squire[4], George Michael[3], George[2], George[1]) He married **? ?**.

Children of Willie Hudgens and ? ? are:
    1187   i.   ?[11] ?.
    1188   ii.   ? ?.
    1189   iii.   ? ?.
    1190   iv.   ? ?.
    1191   v.   ? ?.

1034.   Maude[10] Hudgens (Daniel Boone[9], Hampton Hamilton[8], Mary Polly[7] Hunter, Sarah[6] Boone, Edward[5], Squire[4], George Michael[3], George[2], George[1])

Children of Maude Hudgens are:
    1192   i.   ?[11] ?.

1193   ii.   ? ?.
1194   iii.   ? ?.

1035. Lee Ernest[10] Hudgens (Daniel Boone[9], Hampton Hamilton[8], Mary Polly[7] Hunter, Sarah[6] Boone, Edward[5], Squire[4], George Michael[3], George[2], George[1]) He married **? ?.**

Child of Lee Hudgens and ? ? is:
1195   i.   ?[11] ?.

1036. Roy Merrell[10] Hudgens (Daniel Boone[9], Hampton Hamilton[8], Mary Polly[7] Hunter, Sarah[6] Boone, Edward[5], Squire[4], George Michael[3], George[2], George[1]) He married **? ?.**

Children of Roy Hudgens and ? ? are:
1196   i.   ?[11] ?.
1197   ii.   ? ?.
1198   iii.   ? ?.
1199   iv.   ? ?.

1037. Clarence Hugh[10] Hudgens (Daniel Boone[9], Hampton Hamilton[8], Mary Polly[7] Hunter, Sarah[6] Boone, Edward[5], Squire[4], George Michael[3], George[2], George[1]) was born 30 Sep 1877 in , White, Tennessee, and died 10 Jul 1932. He married **?**.

Children of Clarence Hudgens and ? are:
1200   i.   ?[11] ?.
1201   ii.   ? ?.
1202   iii.   ? ?.
1203   iv.   ? ?.
1204   v.   ? ?.

1038. John Everette[10] Hudgens (Daniel Boone[9], Hampton Hamilton[8], Mary Polly[7] Hunter, Sarah[6] Boone, Edward[5], Squire[4], George Michael[3], George[2], George[1]) was born 28 Sep 1880 in , Guadelupe, Texas, and died 23 Jul 1947 in El Paso, El Paso, Texas. He married **Minnie Pearl Lewis** 18 Feb 1906. She was born 15 Mar 1887 in Doyle, White , Tennessee, and died in New Mexico.

Children of John Hudgens and Minnie Lewis are:
1205   i.   ?[11] ?.
1206   ii.   Karl Dennis Hudgens, born 19 Feb 1907 in Tennessee; died in El Paso, El Paso, Texas.
1207   iii.   Johnnie Pauline Hudgens, born 01 Jan 1914 in Tennessee; died in Arizona.
+ 1208   iv.   James Don Hudgens, born 01 Jun 1918 in Sparta, White, Tennessee; died 15 Jan 1971 in Hobbs, Lea, New Mexico.

1039. Lester Boone[10] Hudgens (Daniel Boone[9], Hampton Hamilton[8], Mary Polly[7] Hunter, Sarah[6] Boone, Edward[5], Squire[4], George Michael[3], George[2], George[1]) was born 19 Aug 1893, and died 31 Mar 1957. He married **? ?.**

Children of Lester Hudgens and ? ? are:
1209   i.   ?[11] ?.
1210   ii.   ? ?.
1211   iii.   ? ?.
1212   iv.   ? ?.
1213   v.   Hubert Maris Hudgens, born 07 Jun 1913 in Tennessee; died 20 Jun 1992 in Sparta, White, Tennessee.

1052. Mary Ollie[10] Bullock (Sarah[9] Hunter, Joe[8], Dudley[7], Sarah[6] Boone, Edward[5], Squire[4], George Michael[3], George[2], George[1]) was born 11 Dec 1870 in Cedar Hill, Putnam, Tennessee, and died 15 Feb 1924 in Tennessee. She married **George Pennington** 30 Oct 1898. He was born 06 Feb 1868, and died 04 Mar 1942.

Child of Mary Bullock and George Pennington is:

 1214   i.   Hubert[11] Pennington, born 11 Dec 1899; died 13 Oct 1960.

1053. Martha Ann[10] Bullock (Sarah[9] Hunter, Joe[8], Dudley[7], Sarah[6] Boone, Edward[5], Squire[4], George Michael[3], George[2], George[1]) was born 15 Sep 1874 in Cedar Hill, Putnam, Tennessee, and died 25 Sep 1941. She married **Bufford Finley Henry** in , Putnam, Tennessee. He was born 04 Nov 1872, and died 21 Oct 1926 in Pontiac, Oakland, Michigan.

Children of Martha Bullock and Bufford Henry are:
+ 1215   i.   Thomas Finley[11] Henry.
+ 1216   ii.   Living Henry.
   1217   iii.   Living Henry. He married ? ?.
+ 1218   iv.   Living Henry.
   1219   v.   Mary Hattie Henry, born 30 Oct 1896 in , Putnam, Tennessee; died 14 Feb 1942.
+ 1220   vi.   Frank Bullock Henry, born 18 Oct 1898 in , Putnam, Tennessee; died 03 Jan 1977 in , Putnam, Tennessee.
+ 1221   vii.   Sallie Bessie Henry, born 13 Apr 1901; died 10 Oct 1962.
   1222   viii.   Cordell Henry, born 18 Apr 1911; died 03 May 1922.

1054. Eliza Naomi[10] Bullock (Sarah[9] Hunter, Joe[8], Dudley[7], Sarah[6] Boone, Edward[5], Squire[4], George Michael[3], George[2], George[1]) was born 15 Jan 1877 in Cedar Hill, Putnam, Tennessee, and died 09 Jul 1973 in Cookeville, Putnam, Tennessee. She married **Byrd Murry Hudgens** 11 Oct 1903 in , Putnam, Tennessee, son of Joseph Hudgens and Caroline Williams. He was born 28 Jul 1878 in Algood, Putnam, Tennessee, and died 31 Oct 1951 in Cookeville, Putnam, Tennessee.

Children are listed above under (1008) Byrd Murry Hudgens.

1055. Joseph[10] Bullock (Sarah[9] Hunter, Joe[8], Dudley[7], Sarah[6] Boone, Edward[5], Squire[4], George Michael[3], George[2], George[1]) was born 11 Dec 1878 in Cedar Hill, Putnam, Tennessee, and died 08 Jan 1954. He married **Eva Johnson**. She was born 01 Jun 1878, and died 02 Feb 1967.

Children of Joseph Bullock and Eva Johnson are:
+ 1223   i.   ?[11] ?.
   1224   ii.   Mamie Lou Bullock, born 20 Nov 1899; died 23 Aug 1902.
+ 1225   iii.   Ida Myrtle Bullock, born 30 Dec 1901; died 26 Sep 1980.
+ 1226   iv.   Nannie Joe Bullock, born 04 Oct 1904; died 20 Dec 1980.
   1227   v.   Willie Ruth Bullock, born 03 Feb 1913; died 20 Sep 1964. She married ? ?.
   1228   vi.   Sarah Edith Bullock, born 09 Dec 1917; died 08 Apr 1972. She married ? ?.

1056. Ida Pauline[10] Bullock (Sarah[9] Hunter, Joe[8], Dudley[7], Sarah[6] Boone, Edward[5], Squire[4], George Michael[3], George[2], George[1]) was born 15 Oct 1881, and died 26 Sep 1954. She married **(1) Storm Hitchcock**. He was born 21 Aug 1882, and died 31 Aug 1923. She married **(2) John Dowell**. She married **(3) Birch Dowell**.

Children of Ida Bullock and Storm Hitchcock are:
+ 1229   i.   ?[11] ?.
   1230   ii.   ? ?.
+ 1231   iii.   ? ?.
+ 1232   iv.   Laura Mae Hitchcock, born 03 May 1911; died 03 Mar 1979.

Generation No. 9

1073. Katherine[11] Eisenhower (Arthur Bradford[10], Ida Elizabeth[9] Stover, Simon P[8], Daniel[7], Daniel[6], Abraham[5], Sarah[4] Boone, George Michael[3], George[2], George[1]) was born 02 Jul 1914. She married **Berton Roueche** 28 Oct 1936. He was born 16 Apr 1910.

Child of Katherine Eisenhower and Berton Roueche is:
    1233   i.   Arthur Bradford[12] Roueche, born 16 Nov 1942.

1074. John Sheldon Doud[11] Eisenhower (Dwight David[10], Ida Elizabeth[9] Stover, Simon P[8], Daniel[7], Daniel[6], Abraham[5], Sarah[4] Boone, George Michael[3], George[2], George[1]) was born 1923. He married **Barbara Jean Thompson** Jul 1947. She was born Abt. 1925.

Children of John Eisenhower and Barbara Thompson are:
+   1234   i.   Dwight David[12] Eisenhower, born 31 Mar 1948.
       1235   ii.   Barbara Anne Eisenhower, born 30 May 1949.
       1236   iii. Susan Elaine Eisenhower, born 31 Dec 1951.
       1237   iv. Mary Jean Eisenhower, born 21 Dec 1955.

1084. Percey DeWitte[11] Stewart (Charles Ferney[10], Coanza Burilla[9] Howell, Pizarro[8], Susannah[7] Callaway, Jemima[6] Boone, Daniel[5], Squire[4], George Michael[3], George[2], George[1]) was born 25 Mar 1893. He married **Mary Beulah Keithly** 18 Jun 1919. She was born 24 May, and died 20 Apr 1959.

Child of Percey Stewart and Mary Keithly is:
    1238   i.   ?[12] ?.

1100. ?[11] ? (Katie Gertrude[10] Boone, Alfred Obediah[9], John William Alonzo[8], Alonzo[7], John Linville[6], George[5], Squire[4], George Michael[3], George[2], George[1]) He married **? ?**.

Child of ? ? and ? ? is:
    1239   i.   ?[12] ?.

1124. Glen N.[11] Whitacre (Charles Newton[10], Ida Belle[9] Mikel, Charles W.[8], Charity Ann[7] Scholl, Mary M.[6] Boone, Edward[5], Squire[4], George Michael[3], George[2], George[1]) was born 08 Jan 1914 in Missouri, and died 18 Oct 2003 in Bloomfield, Davis, Iowa. He married **Lorene I. Spurgeon**. She was born in Missouri, and died 13 Mar 2000 in Bloomfield, Davis, Iowa.

Children of Glen Whitacre and Lorene Spurgeon are:
+   1240   i.   ?[12] Whitacre.
       1241   ii.   Melody Whitacre, died Deceased.
+   1242   iii. ? Whitacre.

1125. Hugh W.[11] Whitacre (Charles Newton[10], Ida Belle[9] Mikel, Charles W.[8], Charity Ann[7] Scholl, Mary M.[6] Boone, Edward[5], Squire[4], George Michael[3], George[2], George[1]) was born 21 Apr 1915 in , Schuyler, Missouri, and died 20 Feb 2001 in Springfield, Greene, Missouri. He married **Bertha J. Casteel** 06 Sep 1939 in Unionville, Missouri. She was born 24 Sep 1921 in Iowa>, and died 02 Mar 1996 in <Bloomfield, Davis, Iowa>.

Children of Hugh Whitacre and Bertha Casteel are:
+   1243   i.   Bonnie Beth[12] Whitacre.
+   1244   ii.   Jane Whitacre.

1126. Omer Charles[11] Whitacre (Charles Newton[10], Ida Belle[9] Mikel, Charles W.[8], Charity Ann[7] Scholl, Mary M.[6] Boone, Edward[5], Squire[4], George Michael[3], George[2], George[1]) was born 27 Sep 1916 in Missouri, and died 21 Oct 1987 in Bloomfield, Davis, Iowa. He married **Mary Maurine Spilman** 19 Mar 1939 in Bloomfield, Davis, Iowa. She was born 19 Feb 1920 in Bloomfield, Davis, Iowa, and died 08 Nov 2002 in Bloomfield, Davis, Iowa.

Children of Omer Whitacre and Mary Spilman are:
    1245   i.   Kay[12] Whitacre. She married m Brunk.

+   1246   ii.   Ken Whitacre.

1129. Ray M[11] **Whitacre** (Charles Newton[10], Ida Belle[9] Mikel, Charles W.[8], Charity Ann[7] Scholl, Mary M.[6] Boone, Edward[5], Squire[4], George Michael[3], George[2], George[1]) was born 1922. He married **Doris Sullivan**. She was born in <Bloomfield, Davis, Iowa>, and died in <Bloomfield, Davis, Iowa>.

Children of Ray Whitacre and Doris Sullivan are:
     1247   i.   ?[12] Whitacre.
     1248   ii.   ? Whitacre.
+   1249   iii.   ? Whitacre.

1130. Ella L.[11] **Whitacre** (Charles Newton[10], Ida Belle[9] Mikel, Charles W.[8], Charity Ann[7] Scholl, Mary M.[6] Boone, Edward[5], Squire[4], George Michael[3], George[2], George[1]) was born 1923 in Missouri, and died in Bloomfield, Davis, Iowa. She married **Lowell A. Spurgeon**. He was born 27 Jul 1899 in Missouri, and died 01 Mar 1963 in Missouri.

Child of Ella Whitacre and Lowell Spurgeon is:
+   1250   i.   ?[12] Spurgeon.

1133. Geneva B.[11] **Whitacre** (Chester Oral[10], Ida Belle[9] Mikel, Charles W.[8], Charity Ann[7] Scholl, Mary M.[6] Boone, Edward[5], Squire[4], George Michael[3], George[2], George[1]) was born 16 Feb 1918 in ,Davis, Iowa, and died 10 Aug 2001 in Burlington, Des Moines, Iowa. She married **(1) Carl Dick Poole** Nov 1942. He died 1945. She married **(2) Robert B Stewart** 21 Jul 1948.

Children of Geneva Whitacre and Robert Stewart are:
+   1251   i.   Linda[12] Stewart.
     1252   ii.   John Stewart.
     1253   iii.   Dale Stewart.
     1254   iv.   David Stewart.

1134. ?[11] **Whitacre** (John Leslie[10], Ida Belle[9] Mikel, Charles W.[8], Charity Ann[7] Scholl, Mary M.[6] Boone, Edward[5], Squire[4], George Michael[3], George[2], George[1]) She married **Gary Kerby**. He was born 04 Aug 1916, and died 04 Nov 1976.

Children of ? Whitacre and Gary Kerby are:
     1255   i.   ?[12] Kerby.
     1256   ii.   ? Kerby. She married ? ?.
+   1257   iii.   ? Kerby.
     1258   iv.   ? Kerby.
     1259   v.   Eddie Kerby, born 02 Nov 1940; died 14 Nov 1958.
     1260   vi.   Judy Kerby, born 19 Apr 1943; died Jul 1943.

1142. Max H[11] **Tomey** (Minnie Estella[10] Whitacre, Ida Belle[9] Mikel, Charles W.[8], Charity Ann[7] Scholl, Mary M.[6] Boone, Edward[5], Squire[4], George Michael[3], George[2], George[1]) was born 1921. He married **(1) Virginia Arlene Lingle**. She was born 07 Nov 1921 in Iowa, and died Apr 1985 in Ottumwa, Wapello, Iowa. He married **(2) Thelma Laverne Hall**. She was born 20 Jan 1923 in Louisville, Jefferson, Kentucky, and died 25 Mar 1988 in Burlington, Des Moines, Iowa. He married **(3) ? ?**.

Child of Max Tomey and Virginia Lingle is:
+   1261   i.   ?[12] ?.

Children of Max Tomey and Thelma Hall are:
     1262   i.   Max Allen[12] Tomey, born 18 Dec 1957 in Wiesbaden, Germany; died 22 Jan 1958 in Wiesbaden, Germany.
     1263   ii.   Jeffrey Keith Tomey, born 09 Sep 1959 in Dayton, Greene, Ohio; died 17 Feb 1969 in Burlington, Des

Moines, Iowa.

1144. Jack Phillip[11] Tomey (Minnie Estella[10] Whitacre, Ida Belle[9] Mikel, Charles W.[8], Charity Ann[7] Scholl, Mary M.[6] Boone, Edward[5], Squire[4], George Michael[3], George[2], George[1]) was born 03 Sep 1918 in Des Moines, Polk, Iowa, and died 22 Jun 1996 in Sunnyvale, Santa Clara, California. He married **(1) Donna ?**. He married **(2) ? ?**.

Children of Jack Tomey and Donna ? are:
  1264   i.   Jack W[12] Tomey.
  1265   ii.   Michael Tomey.
  1266   iii. Karen Tomey. She married m Mayfield.
  1267   iv.   Laurann Tomey. She married m Holm.

Children of Jack Tomey and ? ? are:
  1268   i.   ?[12] ?.
  1269   ii.   ? ?.

1145. Eugene Stewart[11] Tomey (Minnie Estella[10] Whitacre, Ida Belle[9] Mikel, Charles W.[8], Charity Ann[7] Scholl, Mary M.[6] Boone, Edward[5], Squire[4], George Michael[3], George[2], George[1]) was born 07 Oct 1923 in Boone, Boone, Iowa, and died 14 Aug 2001 in Burlington, Des Moines, Iowa. He married **(1) ? ?**.   He married **(2) Jeanne Anne Boschen** 22 Nov 1945 in Burlington, Des Moines, Iowa. She was born 14 Sep 1920 in Republic of Santo Domingo, West Indies, and died 20 May 1982 in Burlington, Des Moines, Iowa.

Children of Eugene Tomey and Jeanne Boschen are:
  1270   i.   ?[12] ?.
  1271   ii.   Eugene Stewart Tomey, born 06 Dec 1946 in Burlington, Des Moines, Iowa; died 10 Dec 1963 in Burlington, Des Moines, Iowa.

1146. Rex Whitacre[11] Tomey (Minnie Estella[10] Whitacre, Ida Belle[9] Mikel, Charles W.[8], Charity Ann[7] Scholl, Mary M.[6] Boone, Edward[5], Squire[4], George Michael[3], George[2], George[1]) was born 04 Dec 1924 in Boone, Boone, Iowa, and died 21 May 2001 in Moline, Rock Island, Illinois. He married **(1) Joyce Eleanor Pohren** 08 May 1946 in Burlington, Des Moines, Iowa. She was born 01 Dec 1925 in Oskaloosa, Mahaska, Iowa, and died Dec 1973 in Burlington, Des Moines, Iowa. He married **(2) Helen Lahr** 09 Feb 1956 in St. Paul, MN.

Child of Rex Tomey and Joyce Pohren is:
  1272   i.   John[12] Tomey, born 22 Sep 1953 in Burlington, Des Moines, Iowa; died 22 Sep 1953 in Burlington, Des Moines, Iowa.

Children of Rex Tomey and Helen Lahr are:
  1273   i.   Mitchell[12] Tomey.
  1274   ii.   Chreryl Tomey. She married m Jones.
  1275   iii. Kristen Tomey. She married ? ?.
  1276   iv.   Lisa Tomey. She married m Haynes.

1147. William Joseph[11] Tomey (Minnie Estella[10] Whitacre, Ida Belle[9] Mikel, Charles W.[8], Charity Ann[7] Scholl, Mary M.[6] Boone, Edward[5], Squire[4], George Michael[3], George[2], George[1]) was born 22 Jul 1929 in Kirksville, Adair, Missouri, and died 02 Oct 1994 in Anaheim, Orange, California. He married **? ?**.

Children of William Tomey and ? ? are:
  1277   i.   ?[12] ?. She married ? ?.
  1278   ii.   ? ?.

1151. John L.[11] Bradley (Naomi Vernadean[10] Whitacre, Ida Belle[9] Mikel, Charles W.[8], Charity Ann[7]

Scholl, Mary M.[6] Boone, Edward[5], Squire[4], George Michael[3], George[2], George[1]) was born in Missouri>, and died in Missouri>.

Child of John L. Bradley is:
    1279   i.   ?[12] ?.

1160. Oscar[11] Newcomer (Generva E.[10] Mikel, Hugh D.[9], Edward B.[8], Charity Ann[7] Scholl, Mary M.[6] Boone, Edward[5], Squire[4], George Michael[3], George[2], George[1]) was born 15 Nov 1901 in n/Greentop, Schuyler, Missouri, and died 26 Mar 1983 in Kirksville, Adair, Missouri. He married **Ethel Evelyn Dudgeon** 07 Apr 1928 in Greentop, Schuyler, Missouri. She was born 14 Jan 1908 in Connelsville, Adair, Missouri, and died 05 Apr 1983 in Kirksville, Adair, Missouri.

Children of Oscar Newcomer and Ethel Dudgeon are:
    1280   i.   ?[12] Newcomer.
    1281   ii.   ? Newcomer.
    1282   iii. Larena Jane Newcomer, born 04 Jan 1935; died 27 Jan 1935.

1165. ?[11] ? (?[10], ?[9], Elizabeth[8] Hunter, Joseph[7], Sarah[6] Boone, Edward[5], Squire[4], George Michael[3], George[2], George[1]) She married **? ?.**

Child of ? ? and ? ? is:
    1283   i.   ?[12] ?.

1167. Edward Boone[11] Hudgens Sr. (Byrd Murry[10], Joseph[9], William[8], Mary Polly[7] Hunter, Sarah[6] Boone, Edward[5], Squire[4], George Michael[3], George[2], George[1]) was born 18 Mar 1906 in Cookeville, Tennessee, and died 31 Aug 1975 in Nashville, Tennessee. He married **Janie Hammit Leake** 12 Jun 1929 in Collierville, Tennessee. She was born 04 Jan 1908 in Collierville, Tennessee, and died 07 Sep 1976 in Nashville, Tennessee.

Children of Edward Hudgens and Janie Leake are:
    1284   i.   ?[12] ?.
    1285   ii.   ? ?.

1171. ?[11] ? (Laura[10] Hudgens, James P.[9], Hampton Hamilton[8], Mary Polly[7] Hunter, Sarah[6] Boone, Edward[5], Squire[4], George Michael[3], George[2], George[1]) He married **? ?.**

Children of ? ? and ? ? are:
    1286   i.   ?[12] ?.
    1287   ii.   ? ?.

1185. Annie Juanita[11] Hudgens (James Rufus[10], Merrill Doyle[9], Hampton Hamilton[8], Mary Polly[7] Hunter, Sarah[6] Boone, Edward[5], Squire[4], George Michael[3], George[2], George[1]) was born 1912, and died 1996.

Child of Annie Juanita Hudgens is:
    1288   i.   ?[12] ?.

1208. James Don[11] Hudgens (John Everette[10], Daniel Boone[9], Hampton Hamilton[8], Mary Polly[7] Hunter, Sarah[6] Boone, Edward[5], Squire[4], George Michael[3], George[2], George[1]) was born 01 Jun 1918 in Sparta, White, Tennessee, and died 15 Jan 1971 in Hobbs, Lea, New Mexico. He married **Alice Evelyn Magrill** 06 Jan 1940. She was born 29 Jun 1917 in Longview, Gregg, Texas, and died 19 Jan 1982 in New Mexico.

Children of James Hudgens and Alice Magrill are:
    1289   i.   ?[12] ?.
    1290   ii.   ? ?.

1215. Thomas Finley[11] Henry (Martha Ann[10] Bullock, Sarah[9] Hunter, Joe[8], Dudley[7], Sarah[6] Boone, Edward[5], Squire[4], George Michael[3], George[2], George[1]) He married **? ?**.

Children of Thomas Henry and ? ? are:
1291   i.   ?[12] ?.
1292   ii. ? ?.
1293   iii. ? ?.

1216. Living[11] Henry (Martha Ann[10] Bullock, Sarah[9] Hunter, Joe[8], Dudley[7], Sarah[6] Boone, Edward[5], Squire[4], George Michael[3], George[2], George[1]) He married **? ?**.

Children of Living Henry and ? ? are:
1294   i.   ?[12] ?.
1295   ii. ? ?.

1218. Living[11] Henry (Martha Ann[10] Bullock, Sarah[9] Hunter, Joe[8], Dudley[7], Sarah[6] Boone, Edward[5], Squire[4], George Michael[3], George[2], George[1])

Children of Living Henry are:
1296   i.   ?[12] ?.
1297   ii. ? ?.

1220. Frank Bullock[11] Henry (Martha Ann[10] Bullock, Sarah[9] Hunter, Joe[8], Dudley[7], Sarah[6] Boone, Edward[5], Squire[4], George Michael[3], George[2], George[1]) was born 18 Oct 1898 in , Putnam, Tennessee, and died 03 Jan 1977 in , Putnam, Tennessee. He married **? ?**.

Children of Frank Henry and ? ? are:
1298   i.   ?[12] ?.
1299   ii. ? ?.
1300   iii. ? ?.
1301   iv. ? ?.
1302   v. ? ?.
1303   vi. ? ?.
1304   vii. Clarence Henry, born Jun 1921; died 15 Apr 1923.
1305   viii. Annie Rachel Henry, born Oct 1925; died 12 Jul 1926.

1221. Sallie Bessie[11] Henry (Martha Ann[10] Bullock, Sarah[9] Hunter, Joe[8], Dudley[7], Sarah[6] Boone, Edward[5], Squire[4], George Michael[3], George[2], George[1]) was born 13 Apr 1901, and died 10 Oct 1962. She married **? ?**.

Children of Sallie Henry and ? ? are:
1306   i.   ?[12] ?.
1307   ii. Hilda Jean Smith, born 1935; died 03 Dec 1963.

1223. ?[11] ? (Joseph[10] Bullock, Sarah[9] Hunter, Joe[8], Dudley[7], Sarah[6] Boone, Edward[5], Squire[4], George Michael[3], George[2], George[1]) She married **Ollie D. Alloway**. He was born 09 Mar 1913, and died 10 Jan 1945.

Children of ? ? and Ollie Alloway are:
1308   i.   William Thomas[12] Alloway.
1309   ii. ? ?.

1225. Ida Myrtle[11] Bullock (Joseph[10], Sarah[9] Hunter, Joe[8], Dudley[7], Sarah[6] Boone, Edward[5], Squire[4], George Michael[3], George[2], George[1]) was born 30 Dec 1901, and died 26 Sep 1980. She married **Walter Alex**

Terry. He died Bef. 1959.

Children of Ida Bullock and Walter Terry are:
    1310   i.   ?[12] ?.
    1311   ii.   ? ?.

    1226. Nannie Joe[11] **Bullock** (Joseph[10], Sarah[9] Hunter, Joe[8], Dudley[7], Sarah[6] Boone, Edward[5], Squire[4], George Michael[3], George[2], George[1]) was born 04 Oct 1904, and died 20 Dec 1980. She married **? ?**.

Child of Nannie Bullock and ? ? is:
    1312   i.   ?[12] ?.

    1229. ?[11] **?** (Ida Pauline[10] Bullock, Sarah[9] Hunter, Joe[8], Dudley[7], Sarah[6] Boone, Edward[5], Squire[4], George Michael[3], George[2], George[1]) She married **? ?**.

Child of ? ? and ? ? is:
    1313   i.   ?[12] ?.

    1231. ?[11] **?** (Ida Pauline[10] Bullock, Sarah[9] Hunter, Joe[8], Dudley[7], Sarah[6] Boone, Edward[5], Squire[4], George Michael[3], George[2], George[1]) She married **? ?**.

Children of ? ? and ? ? are:
    1314   i.   ?[12] ?.
    1315   ii.   ? ?.

    1232. Laura Mae[11] **Hitchcock** (Ida Pauline[10] Bullock, Sarah[9] Hunter, Joe[8], Dudley[7], Sarah[6] Boone, Edward[5], Squire[4], George Michael[3], George[2], George[1]) was born 03 May 1911, and died 03 Mar 1979. She married **? ?**.

Children of Laura Hitchcock and ? ? are:
    1316   i.   ?[12] ?.
    1317   ii.   ? ?.
    1318   iii.   Jackie Randolph, born 24 Mar 1932; died 22 Sep 1933.

Generation No. 10

    1234. Dwight David[12] **Eisenhower** (John Sheldon Doud[11], Dwight David[10], Ida Elizabeth[9] Stover, Simon P[8], Daniel[7], Daniel[6], Abraham[5], Sarah[4] Boone, George Michael[3], George[2], George[1]) was born 31 Mar 1948. He married **Julie Nixon** 28 Dec 1968. She was born 05 Jul 1948.

Children of Dwight Eisenhower and Julie Nixon are:
    1319   i.   Jennie[13] Eisenhower.
    1320   ii.   Alex Eisenhower.
    1321   iii.   Melanie Eisenhower.

    1240. ?[12] **Whitacre** (Glen N.[11], Charles Newton[10], Ida Belle[9] Mikel, Charles W.[8], Charity Ann[7] Scholl, Mary M.[6] Boone, Edward[5], Squire[4], George Michael[3], George[2], George[1])

Children of ? Whitacre are:
    1322   i.   ?[13] Whitacre.
    1323   ii.   ? Whitacre.
    1324   iii.   ? Whitacre.

    1242. ?[12] **Whitacre** (Glen N.[11], Charles Newton[10], Ida Belle[9] Mikel, Charles W.[8], Charity Ann[7] Scholl,

Mary M.[6] Boone, Edward[5], Squire[4], George Michael[3], George[2], George[1]) He married **? ?**.

Children of ? Whitacre and ? ? are:
1325   i.   ?[13] Whitacre.
1326   ii. ? Whitacre.
1327   iii. ? Whitacre.

1243. Bonnie Beth[12] Whitacre (Hugh W.[11], Charles Newton[10], Ida Belle[9] Mikel, Charles W.[8], Charity Ann[7] Scholl, Mary M.[6] Boone, Edward[5], Squire[4], George Michael[3], George[2], George[1]) She married **m Hudson**.

Children of Bonnie Whitacre and m Hudson are:
1328   i.   ?[13] Hudson.
1329   ii. ? Hudson.

1244. Jane[12] Whitacre (Hugh W.[11], Charles Newton[10], Ida Belle[9] Mikel, Charles W.[8], Charity Ann[7] Scholl, Mary M.[6] Boone, Edward[5], Squire[4], George Michael[3], George[2], George[1]) She married **m Carr**.

Children of Jane Whitacre and m Carr are:
       1330   i.   ?[13] Carr.
+   1331   ii. ? Carr.
       1332   iii. ? Carr.
       1333   iv. ? Carr.
       1334   v. ? Carr.

1246. Ken[12] Whitacre (Omer Charles[11], Charles Newton[10], Ida Belle[9] Mikel, Charles W.[8], Charity Ann[7] Scholl, Mary M.[6] Boone, Edward[5], Squire[4], George Michael[3], George[2], George[1])

Child of Ken Whitacre is:
1335   i.   ?[13] Whitacre.

1249. ?[12] Whitacre (Ray M[11], Charles Newton[10], Ida Belle[9] Mikel, Charles W.[8], Charity Ann[7] Scholl, Mary M.[6] Boone, Edward[5], Squire[4], George Michael[3], George[2], George[1])

Children of ? Whitacre are:
1336   i.   ?[13] Whitacre.
1337   ii. ? Whitacre.

1250. ?[12] Spurgeon (Ella L.[11] Whitacre, Charles Newton[10], Ida Belle[9] Mikel, Charles W.[8], Charity Ann[7] Scholl, Mary M.[6] Boone, Edward[5], Squire[4], George Michael[3], George[2], George[1])

Children of ? Spurgeon are:
1338   i.   ?[13] Spurgeon.
1339   ii. Shari Spurgeon, born 01 Aug 1964 in <Bloomfield, Davis, Iowa>; died 28 Jul 2001 in Iowa City, Johnson , Iowa.

1251. Linda[12] Stewart (Geneva B.[11] Whitacre, Chester Oral[10], Ida Belle[9] Mikel, Charles W.[8], Charity Ann[7] Scholl, Mary M.[6] Boone, Edward[5], Squire[4], George Michael[3], George[2], George[1]) She married **m Davies**.

Children of Linda Stewart and m Davies are:
1340   i.   Robert[13] Davies.
1341   ii. John Davies.

1257. ?[12] Kerby (?[11] Whitacre, John Leslie[10], Ida Belle[9] Mikel, Charles W.[8], Charity Ann[7] Scholl, Mary M.[6] Boone, Edward[5], Squire[4], George Michael[3], George[2], George[1])

Child of ? Kerby is:
     1342   i.   ?[13] Kerby.

1261. ?[12] ? (Max H[11] Tomey, Minnie Estella[10] Whitacre, Ida Belle[9] Mikel, Charles W.[8], Charity Ann[7] Scholl, Mary M.[6] Boone, Edward[5], Squire[4], George Michael[3], George[2], George[1]) He married **Kathleen Nancy Adams**. She was born 15 Jan 1944 in El Sobrante, Contra Costa, California, and died 16 Dec 1997 in San Pablo, Contra Costa , California.

Children of ? ? and Kathleen Adams are:
+   1343   i.   ?[13] ?.
     1344   ii. ? ?.

Generation No. 11

1331. ?[13] Carr (Jane[12] Whitacre, Hugh W.[11], Charles Newton[10], Ida Belle[9] Mikel, Charles W.[8], Charity Ann[7] Scholl, Mary M.[6] Boone, Edward[5], Squire[4], George Michael[3], George[2], George[1]) She married **? ?**.

Child of ? Carr and ? ? is:
     1345   i.   ?[14] ?.

1343. ?[13] ? (?[12], Max H[11] Tomey, Minnie Estella[10] Whitacre, Ida Belle[9] Mikel, Charles W.[8], Charity Ann[7] Scholl, Mary M.[6] Boone, Edward[5], Squire[4], George Michael[3], George[2], George[1]) She married **? ?**.

Child of ? ? and ? ? is:
     1346   i.   ?[14] ?.

Notes Regarding the Kinship Report

Following is a comprehensive listing of all individuals in the database who are related to Dwight D. Eisenhower. If an individual is related to the former president multiple ways, only the closest relationship is given.

Often, I receive questions about the "degrees of cousin-hood". People often find this numbering scheme confusing - especially when getting into the "degrees removed". Following is a guideline to help understand how closely related varying degrees of cousins are:

First Cousins - share identical grandparents. If you are a first cousin to someone, your father or mother is the brother or sister to the father or mother of your first cousin. (This one is easy!)

First Cousins Once Removed - The children of your first cousin are your first cousins once removed. Likewise, your are first cousins once removed to them - just removed in the opposite direction!

Second Cousins - share identical great-grandparents.

Third Cousins - share identical great great grandparents. By now you should be getting the idea.

Third Cousin Thrice Removed - As an example, this individual would be three generations earlier or younger than the third cousin of Dwight D. Eisenhower. Higgason Grubbs Boone is such a cousin to Dwight. Another way to look at it is Dwight's great great grandparents were also Higgason's 5th great grandparents.

Another question I am often asked - "If I am a 2nd cousin 5 times removed, how much of a 'blood relation' am I?"

A short answer to this question is - "Not much!". But seriously, think of it this way:

If you share one set of grandparents, then you are a 50% "blood relation". So, first cousins would be in this category. If you share one set of great-grandparents, then you are a 25% "blood relation". Each generation then is diluted by half. So, 3rd cousins would be 12.5%, fourth cousins 6.25%, fifth cousins 3.125%, etc. For each degree removed, then divide the number by 2. So, a third cousin thrice removed would be the equivalent of 12.5% divided by 8 - or about 1.6%.

Looking "up" the family tree is just as intersting. Each generation back, divide the degree of blood relations by 2. So, for instance, you are 50% related to each set of grandparents, 25% for great grandparents, etc. The most interesting thing to note about this - regardless of the last name of the grandparents, - you have an equivalent degree of relation. So, if the names of the great grandparants were Eisenhower, Stover, Boone, Romberger, Matter, Jones, Smith & Johnson - but your last name was Eisenhower - you would not be anymore an Eisenhower than you are any of the other names. The last name is passed through an unbroken paternal line. However, you are just as related to the multitude of "broken" maternal lines.

Name	Relationship with Dwight Eisenhower	Civil	Canon
?	Wife of the 2nd cousin twice removed		
?	Wife of the 3rd cousin once removed		
?	Wife of the 2nd cousin once removed		
?	Wife of the 2nd cousin 3 times removed		
?	Wife of the 6th cousin		
?	Husband of the 3rd cousin once removed		
?, ?	Wife of the half 3rd cousin 4 times removed		
?, ?	Husband of the half 1st cousin twice removed		
?, ?	Wife of the 6th cousin		
?, ?	Wife of the 6th cousin		
?, ?	6th cousin	XIV	7
?, ?	6th cousin once removed	XV	8
?, ?	6th cousin once removed	XV	8
?, ?	Husband of the 4th cousin twice removed		
?, ?	Husband of the 4th cousin twice removed		
?, ?	Wife of the half 3rd cousin 4 times removed		
?, ?	Husband of the 3rd great-grandaunt		
?, ?	Husband of the half 3rd cousin 6 times removed		
?, ?	Wife of the half 3rd cousin 5 times removed		
?, ?	Wife of the 4th cousin twice removed		
?, ?	Husband of the 4th cousin twice removed		
?, ?	Wife of the half 3rd cousin 4 times removed		
?, ?	Wife of the 5th cousin once removed		
?, ?	Half 3rd cousin 6 times removed	XIV	10
?, ?	Half 3rd cousin 6 times removed	XIV	10
?, ?	Husband of the half 3rd cousin 5 times removed		
?, ?	Half 3rd cousin 5 times removed	XIII	9
?, ?	Wife of the 6th cousin once removed		
?, ?	Wife of the 4th cousin twice removed		
?, ?	Half 3rd cousin twice removed	X	6
?, ?	Husband of the 3rd cousin 3 times removed		
?, ?	Husband of the 3rd cousin 3 times removed		
?, ?	Husband of the 3rd cousin 3 times removed		
?, ?	Husband of the 3rd cousin 3 times removed		
?, ?	Husband of the 3rd cousin 3 times removed		
?, ?	Wife of the half 3rd cousin once removed		
?, ?	Half 3rd cousin 3 times removed	XI	7
?, ?	Wife of the half 3rd cousin 3 times removed		
?, ?	Husband of the half 1st cousin twice removed		
?, ?	Wife of the 3rd cousin 3 times removed		
?, ?	Half 3rd cousin 3 times removed	XI	7
?, ?	Husband of the 3rd cousin 3 times removed		
?, ?	Half 3rd cousin 3 times removed	XI	7
?, ?	Husband of the 3rd cousin 3 times removed		
?, ?	Husband of the 3rd cousin 3 times removed		
?, ?	Husband of the 2nd cousin 4 times removed		
?, ?	Half 3rd cousin twice removed	X	6
?, ?	Husband of the 3rd cousin 3 times removed		
?, ?	Husband of the 3rd cousin 3 times removed		
?, ?	Husband of the 3rd cousin 3 times removed		
?, ?	Wife of the 3rd cousin 3 times removed		
?, ?	Husband of the 3rd cousin 3 times removed		
?, ?	Wife of the 3rd cousin 3 times removed		
?, ?	Wife of the 3rd cousin 3 times removed		
?, ?	Husband of the 3rd cousin 3 times removed		
?, ?	4th cousin twice removed	XII	7
?, ?	Husband of the 3rd cousin 3 times removed		
?, ?	Wife of the 3rd cousin 3 times removed		
?, ?	Wife of the 3rd cousin 3 times removed		
?, ?	Wife of the 3rd cousin 3 times removed		
?, ?	Wife of the 3rd cousin 3 times removed		
?, ?	Wife of the 3rd cousin 3 times removed		
?, ?	Wife of the 3rd cousin 3 times removed		
?, ?	Husband of the 3rd cousin 3 times removed		
?, ?	Husband of the 3rd cousin 3 times removed		
?, ?	Husband of the 3rd cousin 3 times removed		
?, ?	Husband of the 3rd cousin 3 times removed		
?, ?	Husband of the 3rd cousin 3 times removed		
?, ?	Half 3rd cousin 5 times removed	XIII	9

Name	Relationship with Dwight Eisenhower	Civil	Canon
?, ?	6th cousin twice removed	XVI	9
?, ?	Wife of the 4th cousin twice removed		
?, ?	6th cousin	XIV	7
?, ?	5th cousin once removed	XIII	7
?, ?	Wife of the 4th cousin twice removed		
?, ?	5th cousin once removed	XIII	7
?, ?	Wife of the 4th cousin twice removed		
?, ?	Husband of the 4th cousin twice removed		
?, ?	Husband of the 4th cousin twice removed		
?, ?	Husband of the 4th cousin twice removed		
?, ?	Husband of the 4th cousin twice removed		
?, ?	Husband of the 4th cousin twice removed		
?, ?	5th cousin once removed	XIII	7
?, ?	5th cousin once removed	XIII	7
?, ?	5th cousin once removed	XIII	7
?, ?	5th cousin once removed	XIII	7
?, ?	5th cousin once removed	XIII	7
?, ?	5th cousin once removed	XIII	7
?, ?	5th cousin once removed	XIII	7
?, ?	5th cousin once removed	XIII	7
?, ?	5th cousin once removed	XIII	7
?, ?	Wife of the 4th cousin twice removed		
?, ?	5th cousin once removed	XIII	7
?, ?	5th cousin once removed	XIII	7
?, ?	5th cousin once removed	XIII	7
?, ?	5th cousin once removed	XIII	7
?, ?	5th cousin once removed	XIII	7
?, ?	Husband of the 5th cousin once removed		
?, ?	Husband of the 5th cousin once removed		
?, ?	Husband of the 5th cousin once removed		
?, ?	Husband of the 5th cousin once removed		
?, ?	6th cousin	XIV	7
?, ?	Wife of the 5th cousin once removed		
?, ?	6th cousin	XIV	7
?, ?	Wife of the 4th cousin twice removed		
?, ?	Husband of the 5th cousin once removed		
?, ?	Wife of the 5th cousin once removed		
?, ?	Wife of the 5th cousin once removed		
?, ?	6th cousin	XIV	7
?, ?	Wife of the 5th cousin once removed		
?, ?	6th cousin	XIV	7
?, ?	Husband of the 5th cousin once removed		
?, ?	Husband of the 5th cousin once removed		
?, ?	Husband of the 5th cousin once removed		
?, ?	6th cousin	XIV	7
?, ?	Wife of the 5th cousin once removed		
?, ?	6th cousin	XIV	7
?, ?	6th cousin	XIV	7
?, ?	6th cousin	XIV	7
?, ?	6th cousin	XIV	7
?, ?	6th cousin	XIV	7
?, ?	6th cousin	XIV	7
?, ?	6th cousin	XIV	7
?, ?	Husband of the 5th cousin once removed		
?, ?	6th cousin	XIV	7
?, ?	6th cousin	XIV	7
?, ?	6th cousin	XIV	7
?, ?	6th cousin	XIV	7
?, ?	Wife of the 5th cousin once removed		
?, ?	6th cousin	XIV	7
?, ?	Wife of the 5th cousin once removed		
?, ?	Wife of the 5th cousin once removed		
?, ?	6th cousin	XIV	7
?, ?	6th cousin	XIV	7
?, ?	6th cousin	XIV	7
?, ?	6th cousin	XIV	7
?, ?	6th cousin	XIV	7
?, ?	6th cousin	XIV	7

Name	Relationship with Dwight Eisenhower	Civil	Canon
?, ?	6th cousin	XIV	7
?, ?	6th cousin	XIV	7
?, ?	6th cousin	XIV	7
?, ?	6th cousin	XIV	7
?, ?	Wife of the 5th cousin once removed		
?, ?	Wife of the 5th cousin once removed		
?, ?	Husband of the 5th cousin once removed		
?, ?	Husband of the 5th cousin once removed		
?, ?	Husband of the 5th cousin once removed		
?, ?	Husband of the 5th cousin once removed		
?, ?	Husband of the 5th cousin once removed		
?, ?	Wife of the 5th cousin once removed		
?, ?	Husband of the 5th cousin once removed		
?, ?	Husband of the 5th cousin once removed		
?, ?	Wife of the 5th cousin once removed		
?, ?	Husband of the 5th cousin once removed		
?, ?	Wife of the 5th cousin once removed		
?, ?	Wife of the 5th cousin once removed		
?, ?	Wife of the 5th cousin once removed		
?, ?	Wife of the 5th cousin once removed		
?, ?	Wife of the 5th cousin once removed		
?, ?	Wife of the 5th cousin once removed		
?, ?	Wife of the 5th cousin once removed		
?, ?	Wife of the 5th cousin once removed		
?, ?	Wife of the 5th cousin once removed		
?, ?	Wife of the 5th cousin once removed		
?, ?	Wife of the 5th cousin once removed		
?, ?	Wife of the 5th cousin once removed		
?, ?	Wife of the 6th cousin		
?, ?	6th cousin once removed	XV	8
?, ?	Wife of the 6th cousin		
?, ?	6th cousin once removed	XV	8
?, ?	6th cousin once removed	XV	8
?, ?	6th cousin once removed	XV	8
?, ?	6th cousin once removed	XV	8
?, ?	6th cousin once removed	XV	8
?, ?	6th cousin once removed	XV	8
?, ?	6th cousin once removed	XV	8
?, ?	Wife of the 6th cousin		
?, ?	6th cousin once removed	XV	8
?, ?	Wife of the 6th cousin		
?, ?	6th cousin once removed	XV	8
?, ?	6th cousin once removed	XV	8
?, ?	6th cousin once removed	XV	8
?, ?	6th cousin once removed	XV	8
?, ?	6th cousin once removed	XV	8
?, ?	6th cousin once removed	XV	8
?, ?	6th cousin once removed	XV	8
?, ?	Wife of the 6th cousin		
?, ?	6th cousin once removed	XV	8
?, ?	Wife of the 6th cousin		
?, ?	6th cousin once removed	XV	8
?, ?	6th cousin once removed	XV	8
?, ?	6th cousin once removed	XV	8
?, ?	6th cousin once removed	XV	8
?, ?	Wife of the 6th cousin		
?, ?	6th cousin once removed	XV	8
?, ?	Wife of the 5th cousin once removed		
?, ?	6th cousin	XIV	7
?, ?	6th cousin	XIV	7
?, ?	6th cousin	XIV	7
?, ?	6th cousin	XIV	7
?, ?	Wife of the 5th cousin once removed		
?, ?	6th cousin	XIV	7
?, ?	Wife of the 5th cousin once removed		
?, ?	6th cousin	XIV	7

Name	Relationship with Dwight Eisenhower	Civil	Canon
?, ?	6th cousin	XIV	7
?, ?	6th cousin	XIV	7
?, ?	6th cousin	XIV	7
?, ?	6th cousin	XIV	7
?, ?	Wife of the 5th cousin once removed		
?, ?	6th cousin	XIV	7
?, ?	6th cousin	XIV	7
?, ?	Wife of the 5th cousin once removed		
?, ?	6th cousin	XIV	7
?, ?	Husband of the 5th cousin once removed		
?, ?	6th cousin	XIV	7
?, ?	Husband of the 5th cousin once removed		
?, ?	Wife of the 6th cousin		
?, ?	6th cousin once removed	XV	8
?, ?	6th cousin once removed	XV	8
?, ?	6th cousin once removed	XV	8
?, ?	6th cousin once removed	XV	8
?, ?	Husband of the 6th cousin		
?, ?	6th cousin once removed	XV	8
?, ?	6th cousin once removed	XV	8
?, ?	Wife of the 6th cousin		
?, ?	6th cousin once removed	XV	8
?, ?	Wife of the 6th cousin		
?, ?	6th cousin once removed	XV	8
?, ?	Wife of the 6th cousin		
?, ?	Wife of the 6th cousin		
?, ?	Wife of the 6th cousin		
?, ?	Wife of the 6th cousin		
?, ?	Husband of the 6th cousin		
?, ?	Husband of the 6th cousin		
?, ?	Husband of the 6th cousin		
?, ?	Husband of the 6th cousin		
?, ?	Husband of the 6th cousin		
?, ?	Husband of the 6th cousin		
?, ?	6th cousin once removed	XV	8
?, ?	Wife of the 6th cousin		
?, ?	Husband of the 6th cousin		
?, ?	Husband of the 6th cousin		
?, ?	6th cousin once removed	XV	8
?, ?	6th cousin once removed	XV	8
?, ?	Husband of the 6th cousin		
?, ?	6th cousin once removed	XV	8
?, ?	6th cousin once removed	XV	8
?, ?	6th cousin once removed	XV	8
?, ?	Wife of the 6th cousin		
?, ?	6th cousin once removed	XV	8
?, ?	6th cousin once removed	XV	8
?, ?	6th cousin once removed	XV	8
?, ?	6th cousin once removed	XV	8
?, ?	Wife of the half 3rd cousin 4 times removed		
?, ?	6th cousin once removed	XV	8
?, ?	Husband of the 6th cousin		
?, ?	6th cousin once removed	XV	8
?, ?	6th cousin once removed	XV	8
?, ?	6th cousin once removed	XV	8
?, ?	Husband of the 6th cousin		
?, ?	6th cousin once removed	XV	8
?, ?	6th cousin once removed	XV	8
?, ?	6th cousin once removed	XV	8
?, ?	6th cousin once removed	XV	8
?, ?	6th cousin once removed	XV	8
?, ?	6th cousin once removed	XV	8
?, ?	Husband of the 6th cousin		
?, ?	6th cousin once removed	XV	8
?, ?	6th cousin once removed	XV	8
?, ?	Husband of the 6th cousin		
?, ?	Ex-husband of the 6th cousin		
?, ?	Ex-husband of the 6th cousin		
?, ?	Ex-husband of the 6th cousin		

Name	Relationship with Dwight Eisenhower	Civil	Canon
?, ?	6th cousin once removed	XV	8
?, ?	6th cousin once removed	XV	8
?, ?	6th cousin twice removed	XVI	9
?, ?	6th cousin twice removed	XVI	9
?, ?	6th cousin twice removed	XVI	9
?, ?	6th cousin twice removed	XVI	9
?, ?	6th cousin twice removed	XVI	9
?, ?	Wife of the 6th cousin once removed		
?, ?	Wife of the 6th cousin once removed		
?, ?	6th cousin twice removed	XVI	9
?, ?	6th cousin twice removed	XVI	9
?, ?	Husband of the 6th cousin once removed		
?, ?	Wife of the 6th cousin once removed		
?, ?	6th cousin twice removed	XVI	9
?, ?	6th cousin twice removed	XVI	9
?, ?	Wife of the 6th cousin once removed		
?, ?	6th cousin twice removed	XVI	9
?, ?	6th cousin twice removed	XVI	9
?, ?	6th cousin twice removed	XVI	9
?, ?	6th cousin twice removed	XVI	9
?, ?	6th cousin twice removed	XVI	9
?, ?	6th cousin twice removed	XVI	9
?, ?	Husband of the 6th cousin once removed		
?, ?	6th cousin twice removed	XVI	9
?, ?	Wife of the 6th cousin once removed		
?, ?	6th cousin twice removed	XVI	9
?, ?	6th cousin twice removed	XVI	9
?, ?	Wife of the 6th cousin once removed		
?, ?	6th cousin twice removed	XVI	9
?, ?	6th cousin twice removed	XVI	9
?, ?	6th cousin twice removed	XVI	9
?, ?	6th cousin twice removed	XVI	9
?, ?	Husband of the 6th cousin once removed		
?, ?	6th cousin twice removed	XVI	9
?, ?	Husband of the 6th cousin once removed		
?, ?	6th cousin twice removed	XVI	9
?, ?	Husband of the 6th cousin once removed		
?, ?	Husband of the 6th cousin once removed		
?, ?	6th cousin twice removed	XVI	9
?, ?	6th cousin twice removed	XVI	9
?, ?	Husband of the 6th cousin once removed		
?, ?	6th cousin twice removed	XVI	9
?, ?	Husband of the 6th cousin once removed		
?, ?	6th cousin twice removed	XVI	9
?, ?	6th cousin twice removed	XVI	9
?, ?	Husband of the 6th cousin once removed		
?, ?	6th cousin twice removed	XVI	9
?, ?	Husband of the 6th cousin once removed		
?, ?	6th cousin twice removed	XVI	9
?, ?	Half 3rd cousin 7 times removed	XV	11
?, ?	Wife of the half 3rd cousin twice removed		
?, ?	Wife of the half 3rd cousin once removed		
?, ?	6th cousin	XIV	7
?, ?	Half 3rd cousin 5 times removed	XIII	9
?, ?	Husband of the half 3rd cousin 5 times removed		
?, ?	Half 3rd cousin 5 times removed	XIII	9
?, ?	Half 3rd cousin 5 times removed	XIII	9
?, ?	Half 3rd cousin 5 times removed	XIII	9
?, ?	Half 3rd cousin 5 times removed	XIII	9
?, ?	7th great-grandmother	IX	9
?, ?	6th cousin once removed	XV	8
?, ?	7th great-grandmother	IX	9
?, ?	Wife of the half 3rd cousin 3 times removed		
?, ?	Husband of the half 3rd cousin 5 times removed		
?, ?	Husband of the 6th cousin		
?, ?	Husband of the half 3rd cousin 3 times removed		
?, ?	Half 3rd cousin 4 times removed	XII	8
?, ?	Half 3rd cousin 7 times removed	XV	11
?, ?	Husband of the half 3rd cousin 6 times removed		
?, Alida B	Sister-in-law		

Name	Relationship with Dwight Eisenhower	Civil	Canon
?, Angeline	Wife of the half 3rd cousin		
?, Ann	Wife of the 5th cousin once removed		
?, Anna	Wife of the 4th cousin		
?, Anna Maria	Wife of the 1st cousin twice removed		
?, Catherina	Wife of the half 1st cousin 3 times removed		
?, Catherine	Wife of the half 2nd cousin twice removed		
?, Catherine	Wife of the half 1st cousin 3 times removed		
?, Catherine	Wife of the 3rd great-granduncle		
?, Catherine	Wife of the half great-granduncle		
?, Donna	Wife of the half 3rd cousin 4 times removed		
?, Elizabeth	Wife of the half 1st cousin 3 times removed		
?, Elizabeth	Wife of the half 1st cousin once removed		
?, Elizabeth	Wife of the half 3rd cousin once removed		
?, Ellen R	Wife of the half 1st cousin once removed		
?, Esther	Wife of the 6th cousin		
?, Flora	Wife of the half 3rd cousin twice removed		
?, Frances	Wife of the 5th cousin once removed		
?, Infant Daughter	4th cousin once removed	XI	6
?, Jennie	Wife of the half 3rd cousin once removed		
?, Josiah	Husband of the half 1st cousin 3 times removed		
?, Lovina	Wife of the half granduncle		
?, Mamie	Wife of the 3rd cousin once removed		
?, Margaret	Wife of the 4th great-grandfather		
?, Margaretha	Wife of the half granduncle		
?, Mary	Wife of the 2nd great-granduncle		
?, Mary	Wife of the 4th great-granduncle		
?, Millie J.	Wife of the 3rd cousin once removed		
?, Nancy C	Wife of the half 3rd cousin		
?, Ruth	Wife of the 4th great-grandfather		
?, Sarah	3rd great-grandmother	V	5
?, Sarah B.	Wife of the half 3rd cousin		
A., Edith	Wife of the half 3rd cousin twice removed		
A., Virginia	Wife of the 5th cousin once removed		
Adams, ?	Half 3rd cousin 4 times removed	XII	8
Adams, ?	Half 3rd cousin 4 times removed	XII	8
Adams, ?	Half 3rd cousin 4 times removed	XII	8
Adams, Albert	Husband of the half 3rd cousin twice removed		
Adams, Everett Pearl	Half 3rd cousin 3 times removed	XI	7
Adams, Kathleen Nancy	Wife of the half 3rd cousin 5 times removed		
Adams, Sarah	Wife of the half 2nd cousin twice removed		
Aeschliman, Emogene	Half 3rd cousin 4 times removed	XII	8
Aeschliman, Essie Mildred	Half 3rd cousin 4 times removed	XII	8
Aeschliman, Eugene	Husband of the half 3rd cousin 3 times removed		
Aeschliman, Lucille	Half 3rd cousin 4 times removed	XII	8
Aeschliman, Opal Hildred	Half 3rd cousin 4 times removed	XII	8
Agleston, Barbara	Wife of the half 1st cousin twice removed		
Alcorn, Charity	4th cousin twice removed	XII	7
Alcorn, Cynthia	4th cousin twice removed	XII	7
Alcorn, Fanny	4th cousin twice removed	XII	7
Alcorn, Francis	4th cousin twice removed	XII	7
Alcorn, John	4th cousin twice removed	XII	7
Alcorn, Robert	Husband of the 3rd cousin 3 times removed		
Alice	Wife of the half 3rd cousin twice removed		
Allen, Adelaide	Half 3rd cousin	VIII	4
Allen, Allendal	Half 3rd cousin	VIII	4
Allen, Clarkston	Half 2nd cousin once removed	VII	4
Allen, David	Husband of the half 1st cousin twice removed		
Allen, Elizabeth	Half 2nd cousin once removed	VII	4
Allen, Felena	Half 2nd cousin once removed	VII	4
Allen, Hiram	Half 2nd cousin once removed	VII	4
Allen, Jesse	Husband of the half 1st cousin twice removed		
Allen, John	Half 2nd cousin once removed	VII	4
Allen, John	Half 3rd cousin	VIII	4
Allen, Synthia Ann	Half 2nd cousin once removed	VII	4
Allen, Thomas	Husband of the 3rd cousin 3 times removed		
Allen, Willburfarce	Half 2nd cousin once removed	VII	4
Alley, Living	4th cousin 5 times removed	XV	10
Alley, Living	Husband of the 4th cousin 4 times removed		
Alley, Living	4th cousin 5 times removed	XV	10
Alley, Living	4th cousin 5 times removed	XV	10
Alloway, Ollie D.	Husband of the 6th cousin once removed		

Name	Relationship with Dwight Eisenhower	Civil	Canon
Alloway, William Thomas	6th cousin twice removed	XVI	9
Almlee, Bernice Mildred	3rd cousin once removed	IX	5
Almlee, Christopher John Olsen	Husband of the 3rd cousin		
Alphonia	Wife of the half 2nd cousin once removed		
Anderson, Annie Woodson	Wife of the 4th cousin twice removed		
Anderson, Rachel	Wife of the half 2nd cousin once removed		
Arnhold, Anna Barbara	3rd great-grandmother	V	5
Asbell	Husband of the half 3rd cousin once removed		
Ashley, Ben	Husband of the half 3rd cousin		
Ashley, Frankie	Wife of the half 3rd cousin		
Austin, Elizabeth	Wife of the 4th cousin twice removed		
Austin, Mary	Wife of the 4th cousin twice removed		
Autenreith, Julius	Husband of the 5th cousin once removed		
Bailey, Sarah	Wife of the half 3rd cousin		
Baker, America Caroline	Wife of the 5th cousin once removed		
Barber, Elisha	Husband of the half 1st cousin twice removed		
Barker, John Leston	Husband of the 5th cousin once removed		
Barker, Leathea Nancy	Wife of the 4th cousin twice removed		
Barnes, Sidney S.	Husband of the 4th cousin twice removed		
Barnum, Lewis	Husband of the 4th cousin twice removed		
Barnum, Mary	5th cousin once removed	XIII	7
Barringer, Mary	Wife of the half 2nd cousin once removed		
Barringer, Susanna	Wife of the half 2nd cousin once removed		
Batdorf, Jonas H.	Husband of the 2nd cousin twice removed		
Batdorf, Jonathan	Husband of the 2nd cousin twice removed		
Beall, Rebecca	Wife of the 4th cousin twice removed		
Beall, Richard	Husband of the 3rd cousin 3 times removed		
Beasler, Mabel Blanche	Wife of the half 1st cousin once removed		
Bechtel, Alfred	Husband of the half 1st cousin once removed		
Bechtel, Ruth L.	Wife of the 3rd cousin once removed		
Beckenbach, Anne	Wife of the 4th great-grandfather		
Beeler, Paul Leroy	Husband of the half 3rd cousin 4 times removed		
Belieu, Lorenzo Dow	Husband of the 5th cousin once removed		
Bell, Tabitha	Wife of the 3rd cousin 3 times removed		
Bender, John	Husband of the 2nd cousin once removed		
Benning, Living	4th cousin 5 times removed	XV	10
Benning, Living	4th cousin 4 times removed	XIV	9
Benning, Living	Husband of the 4th cousin 3 times removed		
Benning, Living	4th cousin 4 times removed	XIV	9
Benning, Living	4th cousin 4 times removed	XIV	9
Benning, Living	4th cousin 4 times removed	XIV	9
Benning, Living	4th cousin 4 times removed	XIV	9
Benning, Living	4th cousin 4 times removed	XIV	9
Benning, Living	4th cousin 5 times removed	XV	10
Benning, Living	4th cousin 5 times removed	XV	10
Benning, Living	4th cousin 5 times removed	XV	10
Benning, Living	4th cousin 5 times removed	XV	10
Benning, Living	4th cousin 5 times removed	XV	10
Benning, Living	4th cousin 5 times removed	XV	10
Benson, George Washington	5th cousin once removed	XIII	7
Benson, James S.	5th cousin once removed	XIII	7
Benson, Jefferson Bell	Husband of the 4th cousin twice removed		
Benson, Jenelle	3rd cousin 3 times removed	XI	7
Benson, John Wesley	5th cousin once removed	XIII	7
Benson, Marquis De Lafayette	5th cousin once removed	XIII	7
Benson, Mary Leona	6th cousin	XIV	7
Benson, Phoebe	5th cousin once removed	XIII	7
Benson, Preston Bell	6th cousin	XIV	7
Benson, Suella	6th cousin	XIV	7
Benson, Susan Ophelia	5th cousin once removed	XIII	7
Benson, Taylor	5th cousin once removed	XIII	7
Benson, Thomas W.	5th cousin once removed	XIII	7
Benson, Verlinia Millington	5th cousin once removed	XIII	7
Benson, Virgy Wheeler	6th cousin	XIV	7
Bentley, Jane Preshill	Wife of the half 2nd cousin once removed		
Bentley, Susannah	Wife of the 3rd cousin 3 times removed		
Bentsel, Gerald Benton	Half 2nd cousin once removed	VII	4
Bentzel, Harry I	Half 2nd cousin	VI	3
Bentzel, Ida Viola Rosabel	Half 2nd cousin	VI	3
Bentzel, William Harvey	Husband of the half 1st cousin once removed		
Berger	Half 3rd cousin twice removed	X	6

Name	Relationship with Dwight Eisenhower	Civil	Canon
Berger, Clara Elizabeth	Half 3rd cousin twice removed	X	6
Berger, Enos Enoch	Husband of the half 3rd cousin once removed		
Berger, George Edward	Half 3rd cousin twice removed	X	6
Berger, Hester Lyons	Half 3rd cousin twice removed	X	6
Berger, Lucy Hazel	Half 3rd cousin twice removed	X	6
Berger, Susan Frances	Half 3rd cousin twice removed	X	6
Berger, Zella Jane	Half 3rd cousin twice removed	X	6
Bergner, Elizabeth	Wife of the 2nd great-granduncle		
Bergstresser, Hannah	Wife of the 1st cousin 3 times removed		
Betsy	Half 1st cousin 3 times removed	VII	5
Blakemore, Marcus Newton	Husband of the 5th cousin once removed		
Bledsoe, Ethel L.	Half 3rd cousin 3 times removed	XI	7
Bledsoe, Leslie N.	Half 3rd cousin 3 times removed	XI	7
Bledsoe, Nathan C.	Husband of the half 3rd cousin twice removed		
Bledsoe, Nora Mae	Half 3rd cousin 3 times removed	XI	7
Bludhart, Elizabeth	Half 2nd cousin once removed	VII	4
Bludhart, Jacob	Husband of the half 1st cousin twice removed		
Bludhart, Margaret	Half 2nd cousin once removed	VII	4
Boger, Leah	Wife of the half 2nd cousin once removed		
Boggs, Angus	5th cousin once removed	XIII	7
Boggs, Chester A.	6th cousin	XIV	7
Boggs, Edith Boone	6th cousin	XIV	7
Boggs, Guadalupe	5th cousin once removed	XIII	7
Boggs, Jefferson	5th cousin once removed	XIII	7
Boggs, John	4th cousin twice removed	XII	7
Boggs, Lilburn F.	6th cousin	XIV	7
Boggs, Lilburn W.	5th cousin once removed	XIII	7
Boggs, Lilburn Williams	Husband of the 3rd cousin 3 times removed		
Boggs, Mary F.	5th cousin once removed	XIII	7
Boggs, Mary O.	6th cousin	XIV	7
Boggs, Sterling	5th cousin once removed	XIII	7
Boggs, Thomas Oliver	4th cousin twice removed	XII	7
Boggs, Virginia	6th cousin	XIV	7
Boggs, Wade Thomas	6th cousin	XIV	7
Boggs, William D.	5th cousin once removed	XIII	7
Boggs, William Montgomery	4th cousin twice removed	XII	7
Bohannon, Libby Lou	Wife of the 4th cousin twice removed		
Bohanon, Mary Martha	Wife of the 4th cousin twice removed		
Bohner, Mary A	Wife of the 2nd cousin twice removed		
Bohner, Yvonne	Wife of the 3rd cousin twice removed		
Bomberger, Catharina	Wife of the 1st cousin twice removed		
Book, Abram	Husband of the half 1st cousin once removed		
Book, m	Husband of the 1st cousin		
Book, Paul Edward	Husband of the 1st cousin once removed		
Book, Ruth V	Wife of the 1st cousin		
Boone	3rd cousin 3 times removed	XI	7
Boone	3rd cousin 3 times removed	XI	7
Boone	3rd cousin 3 times removed	XI	7
Boone	5th cousin once removed	XIII	7
Boone	3rd cousin 3 times removed	XI	7
Boone	4th cousin twice removed	XII	7
Boone, Adeline	5th cousin once removed	XIII	7
Boone, Agnes B.	4th cousin twice removed	XII	7
Boone, Albert Gallatin	3rd cousin 3 times removed	XI	7
Boone, Albert Gallatin	4th cousin twice removed	XII	7
Boone, Albert Pope	5th cousin once removed	XIII	7
Boone, Alfred Obediah	5th cousin once removed	XIII	7
Boone, Alonzo	3rd cousin 3 times removed	XI	7
Boone, Alonzo	3rd cousin 3 times removed	XI	7
Boone, Alonzo Havington	3rd cousin 3 times removed	XI	7
Boone, Alphonso	5th cousin once removed	XIII	7
Boone, Alphonso Daniel	4th cousin twice removed	XII	7
Boone, Alphonso Sr.	3rd cousin 3 times removed	XI	7
Boone, Andrew Jackson	3rd cousin 3 times removed	XI	7
Boone, Anna	4th cousin twice removed	XII	7
Boone, Annie Eliza	4th cousin twice removed	XII	7
Boone, Arthur Tucker	4th cousin twice removed	XII	7
Boone, Banton	2nd cousin 4 times removed	X	7
Boone, Banton II	3rd cousin 3 times removed	XI	7
Boone, Benjamin	4th great-granduncle	VIII	7
Boone, Benjamin Franklin	4th cousin twice removed	XII	7

Name	Relationship with Dwight Eisenhower	Civil	Canon
Boone, Benjamin Howard	3rd cousin 3 times removed	XI	7
Boone, Betty	3rd cousin 3 times removed	XI	7
Boone, Bulah G.	5th cousin once removed	XIII	7
Boone, Cassa	3rd cousin 3 times removed	XI	7
Boone, Cassandra	3rd cousin 3 times removed	XI	7
Boone, Cassandra	4th cousin twice removed	XII	7
Boone, Cassandra	3rd cousin 3 times removed	XI	7
Boone, Cassandra	3rd cousin 3 times removed	XI	7
Boone, Cassandra	3rd cousin 3 times removed	XI	7
Boone, Catherine	4th cousin twice removed	XII	7
Boone, Cemer C.	4th cousin twice removed	XII	7
Boone, Charity	2nd cousin 4 times removed	X	7
Boone, Charles Burton	6th cousin	XIV	7
Boone, Charles Randall	4th cousin twice removed	XII	7
Boone, Charlie Edgar	4th cousin twice removed	XII	7
Boone, Chloe Donnelly	4th cousin twice removed	XII	7
Boone, Chloe Jane	5th cousin once removed	XIII	7
Boone, Clara	5th cousin once removed	XIII	7
Boone, Cynthia Ann	3rd cousin 3 times removed	XI	7
Boone, Daniel	3rd cousin 3 times removed	XI	7
Boone, Daniel	3rd cousin 3 times removed	XI	7
Boone, Daniel	1st cousin 5 times removed	IX	7
Boone, Daniel Armstrong	5th cousin once removed	XIII	7
Boone, Daniel Morgan	2nd cousin 4 times removed	X	7
Boone, David	5th cousin once removed	XIII	7
Boone, David Richard	5th cousin once removed	XIII	7
Boone, Delia Ellen	4th cousin twice removed	XII	7
Boone, Delia Morris	3rd cousin 3 times removed	XI	7
Boone, Delinda	3rd cousin 3 times removed	XI	7
Boone, Diedema	3rd cousin 3 times removed	XI	7
Boone, Dollie	5th cousin once removed	XIII	7
Boone, Edward	1st cousin 5 times removed	IX	7
Boone, Edward H.	3rd cousin 3 times removed	XI	7
Boone, Eliza Yantis	4th cousin twice removed	XII	7
Boone, Elizabeth	3rd cousin 3 times removed	XI	7
Boone, Elizabeth	2nd cousin 4 times removed	X	7
Boone, Elizabeth	1st cousin 5 times removed	IX	7
Boone, Elizabeth	2nd cousin 4 times removed	X	7
Boone, Elizabeth C.	3rd cousin 3 times removed	XI	7
Boone, Elizabeth Levica	3rd cousin 3 times removed	XI	7
Boone, Ellen L.	5th cousin once removed	XIII	7
Boone, Ellender	2nd cousin 4 times removed	X	7
Boone, Elliott	5th cousin once removed	XIII	7
Boone, Elsie B.	5th cousin once removed	XIII	7
Boone, Elzora F.	5th cousin once removed	XIII	7
Boone, Emily	3rd cousin 3 times removed	XI	7
Boone, Emma Crusita	5th cousin once removed	XIII	7
Boone, Emma Henderson	4th cousin twice removed	XII	7
Boone, Emma Josephine	4th cousin twice removed	XII	7
Boone, Emmet	3rd cousin 3 times removed	XI	7
Boone, Enoch Morgan	2nd cousin 4 times removed	X	7
Boone, Ervin	3rd cousin 3 times removed	XI	7
Boone, Estella Florence	5th cousin once removed	XIII	7
Boone, Esther	5th cousin once removed	XIII	7
Boone, Ethel	5th cousin once removed	XIII	7
Boone, Ettie Emma	5th cousin once removed	XIII	7
Boone, Fosdick	5th cousin once removed	XIII	7
Boone, Francis Marion	4th cousin twice removed	XII	7
Boone, Garland	3rd cousin 3 times removed	XI	7
Boone, George	2nd cousin 4 times removed	X	7
Boone, George	3rd cousin 3 times removed	XI	7
Boone, George	4th great-granduncle	VIII	7
Boone, George	1st cousin 5 times removed	IX	7
Boone, George	2nd cousin 4 times removed	X	7
Boone, George Alphonso	5th cousin once removed	XIII	7
Boone, George Edwin	6th cousin	XIV	7
Boone, George I	7th great-grandfather	IX	9
Boone, George II	6th great-grandfather	VIII	8
Boone, George L.	5th cousin once removed	XIII	7
Boone, George Luther	4th cousin twice removed	XII	7
Boone, George Michael	5th great-grandfather	VII	7

Name	Relationship with Dwight Eisenhower	Civil	Canon
Boone, George Morris	4th cousin twice removed	XII	7
Boone, Hampton Lynch	3rd cousin 3 times removed	XI	7
Boone, Hannah	1st cousin 5 times removed	IX	7
Boone, Hannah	Wife of the 2nd cousin 4 times removed		
Boone, Hannah Ruth	4th cousin twice removed	XII	7
Boone, Harriet	3rd cousin 3 times removed	XI	7
Boone, Harriet Baber	4th cousin twice removed	XII	7
Boone, Harry Cleveland	5th cousin once removed	XIII	7
Boone, Harvey Lee	6th cousin	XIV	7
Boone, Hayden	3rd cousin 3 times removed	XI	7
Boone, Henry	5th great-granduncle	IX	8
Boone, Henry A.	5th cousin once removed	XIII	7
Boone, Higgason Grubbs	3rd cousin 3 times removed	XI	7
Boone, Ira	3rd cousin 3 times removed	XI	7
Boone, Isabellar	4th cousin twice removed	XII	7
Boone, Isaiah	2nd cousin 4 times removed	X	7
Boone, Isaiah H.	3rd cousin 3 times removed	XI	7
Boone, Israel	1st cousin 5 times removed	IX	7
Boone, Israel	2nd cousin 4 times removed	X	7
Boone, Jacob	5th cousin once removed	XIII	7
Boone, James	3rd cousin 3 times removed	XI	7
Boone, James	3rd cousin 3 times removed	XI	7
Boone, James	4th cousin twice removed	XII	7
Boone, James	4th great-granduncle	VIII	7
Boone, James	2nd cousin 4 times removed	X	7
Boone, James C.	4th cousin twice removed	XII	7
Boone, James Lilburn	5th cousin once removed	XIII	7
Boone, James M.	3rd cousin 3 times removed	XI	7
Boone, James Orville	4th cousin twice removed	XII	7
Boone, James Paschal	5th cousin once removed	XIII	7
Boone, Jane	2nd cousin 4 times removed	X	7
Boone, Jemima	3rd cousin 3 times removed	XI	7
Boone, Jemima	2nd cousin 4 times removed	X	7
Boone, Jennie	3rd cousin 3 times removed	XI	7
Boone, Jeptha Vining	3rd cousin 3 times removed	XI	7
Boone, Jeptha Vining	4th cousin twice removed	XII	7
Boone, Jeremiah	3rd cousin 3 times removed	XI	7
Boone, Jesse Archie	5th cousin once removed	XIII	7
Boone, Jesse Bryan	2nd cousin 4 times removed	X	7
Boone, Jesse M.	5th cousin once removed	XIII	7
Boone, Jesse Murray	4th cousin twice removed	XII	7
Boone, Jesse Van Bibber	4th cousin twice removed	XII	7
Boone, Joel Hayden	4th cousin twice removed	XII	7
Boone, John	5th cousin once removed	XIII	7
Boone, John	1st cousin 5 times removed	IX	7
Boone, John	5th great-granduncle	IX	8
Boone, John	4th great-granduncle	VIII	7
Boone, John Bryan	2nd cousin 4 times removed	X	7
Boone, John Calloway	4th cousin twice removed	XII	7
Boone, John Coburn	3rd cousin 3 times removed	XI	7
Boone, John Hamilton	4th cousin twice removed	XII	7
Boone, John Linville	2nd cousin 4 times removed	X	7
Boone, John W.	3rd cousin 3 times removed	XI	7
Boone, John William Alonzo	4th cousin twice removed	XII	7
Boone, Johnathon	2nd cousin 4 times removed	X	7
Boone, Jonathan	1st cousin 5 times removed	IX	7
Boone, Jonathan May	5th cousin once removed	XIII	7
Boone, Joseph	4th great-granduncle	VIII	7
Boone, Joseph Sr.	2nd cousin 4 times removed	X	7
Boone, Joshua Morris	3rd cousin 3 times removed	XI	7
Boone, Joshua Morris	4th cousin twice removed	XII	7
Boone, Katherine	Wife of the 5th cousin once removed		
Boone, Katie Gertrude	6th cousin	XIV	7
Boone, Lavina	2nd cousin 4 times removed	X	7
Boone, Leah Jane	5th cousin once removed	XIII	7
Boone, Lenora	5th cousin once removed	XIII	7
Boone, Leo Alonzo	5th cousin once removed	XIII	7
Boone, Leonidas Lonnie	4th cousin twice removed	XII	7
Boone, Lester L.	5th cousin once removed	XIII	7
Boone, Levi Day	3rd cousin 3 times removed	XI	7
Boone, Levica	3rd cousin 3 times removed	XI	7

Name	Relationship with Dwight Eisenhower	Civil	Canon
Boone, Lillie Bell	4th cousin twice removed	XII	7
Boone, Lincoln	5th cousin once removed	XIII	7
Boone, Lindsey	3rd cousin 3 times removed	XI	7
Boone, Lloyd Earl	5th cousin once removed	XIII	7
Boone, Lucy	4th cousin twice removed	XII	7
Boone, Lucy	3rd cousin 3 times removed	XI	7
Boone, Lucy	3rd cousin 3 times removed	XI	7
Boone, Lulu Louise	5th cousin once removed	XIII	7
Boone, Madison	3rd cousin 3 times removed	XI	7
Boone, Mahala	3rd cousin 3 times removed	XI	7
Boone, Mann	5th cousin once removed	XIII	7
Boone, Margaret Ann	4th cousin twice removed	XII	7
Boone, Martha	4th cousin twice removed	XII	7
Boone, Martha Jane	4th cousin twice removed	XII	7
Boone, Martha L.	3rd cousin 3 times removed	XI	7
Boone, Martha Randall	4th cousin twice removed	XII	7
Boone, Martha S.	5th cousin once removed	XIII	7
Boone, Martha Susan	4th cousin twice removed	XII	7
Boone, Mary	3rd cousin 3 times removed	XI	7
Boone, Mary	4th great-grandaunt	VIII	7
Boone, Mary	4th great-grandaunt	VIII	7
Boone, Mary	1st cousin 5 times removed	IX	7
Boone, Mary	2nd cousin 4 times removed	X	7
Boone, Mary	3rd cousin 3 times removed	XI	7
Boone, Mary	5th cousin once removed	XIII	7
Boone, Mary	5th cousin once removed	XIII	7
Boone, Mary A.	3rd cousin 3 times removed	XI	7
Boone, Mary Ann Elizabeth	4th cousin twice removed	XII	7
Boone, Mary Clarissa	4th cousin twice removed	XII	7
Boone, Mary Eleanor	5th cousin once removed	XIII	7
Boone, Mary Elizabeth	4th cousin twice removed	XII	7
Boone, Mary Elizabeth	4th cousin twice removed	XII	7
Boone, Mary Ethel	5th cousin once removed	XIII	7
Boone, Mary Florence	5th cousin once removed	XIII	7
Boone, Mary Letitica	5th cousin once removed	XIII	7
Boone, Mary M.	2nd cousin 4 times removed	X	7
Boone, Matilda	3rd cousin 3 times removed	XI	7
Boone, Maxemille	3rd cousin 3 times removed	XI	7
Boone, Maximilla	3rd cousin 3 times removed	XI	7
Boone, Melba	3rd cousin 3 times removed	XI	7
Boone, Melcina	3rd cousin 3 times removed	XI	7
Boone, Melvian	3rd cousin 3 times removed	XI	7
Boone, Mildred	3rd cousin 3 times removed	XI	7
Boone, Milton L.	3rd cousin 3 times removed	XI	7
Boone, Minerva	5th cousin once removed	XIII	7
Boone, Minerva S.	3rd cousin 3 times removed	XI	7
Boone, Minerva Warner	4th cousin twice removed	XII	7
Boone, Minnie O.	5th cousin once removed	XIII	7
Boone, Mollie Boggs	4th cousin twice removed	XII	7
Boone, Montgomery	5th cousin once removed	XIII	7
Boone, Morgan	3rd cousin 3 times removed	XI	7
Boone, Moses	2nd cousin 4 times removed	X	7
Boone, Myrtle Leola	5th cousin once removed	XIII	7
Boone, Nancy	3rd cousin 3 times removed	XI	7
Boone, Nancy	Wife of the 3rd cousin 3 times removed		
Boone, Nancy	3rd cousin 3 times removed	XI	7
Boone, Nancy	3rd cousin 3 times removed	XI	7
Boone, Nancy Ellen	5th cousin once removed	XIII	7
Boone, Nancy L.	4th cousin twice removed	XII	7
Boone, Nancy Linville	3rd cousin 3 times removed	XI	7
Boone, Napoleon	3rd cousin 3 times removed	XI	7
Boone, Nathan	3rd cousin 3 times removed	XI	7
Boone, Nathan	2nd cousin 4 times removed	X	7
Boone, Nathaniel	1st cousin 5 times removed	IX	7
Boone, Nellie Blanch	5th cousin once removed	XIII	7
Boone, Nester	2nd cousin 4 times removed	X	7
Boone, Nestor	3rd cousin 3 times removed	XI	7
Boone, Nestor	3rd cousin 3 times removed	XI	7
Boone, Octavia Ann	4th cousin twice removed	XII	7
Boone, Olive	3rd cousin 3 times removed	XI	7
Boone, Olive	5th cousin once removed	XIII	7

Name	Relationship with Dwight Eisenhower	Civil	Canon
Boone, Onie N.	5th cousin once removed	XIII	7
Boone, Orvy	3rd cousin 3 times removed	XI	7
Boone, Panthea Grant	3rd cousin 3 times removed	XI	7
Boone, Percis	5th great-grandaunt	IX	8
Boone, Polly	3rd cousin 3 times removed	XI	7
Boone, Rebecca	2nd cousin 4 times removed	X	7
Boone, Richard Bass	4th cousin twice removed	XII	7
Boone, Robert Emmett	3rd cousin 3 times removed	XI	7
Boone, Robert G.	4th cousin twice removed	XII	7
Boone, Robert Henry	5th cousin once removed	XIII	7
Boone, Roy Clarence	5th cousin once removed	XIII	7
Boone, Sallie	3rd cousin 3 times removed	XI	7
Boone, Samuel	3rd cousin 3 times removed	XI	7
Boone, Samuel	4th great-granduncle	VIII	7
Boone, Samuel	1st cousin 5 times removed	IX	7
Boone, Samuel	2nd cousin 4 times removed	X	7
Boone, Samuel	2nd cousin 4 times removed	X	7
Boone, Samuel	3rd cousin 3 times removed	XI	7
Boone, Samuel	4th cousin twice removed	XII	7
Boone, Samuel Grover	5th cousin once removed	XIII	7
Boone, Samuel Lee	4th cousin twice removed	XII	7
Boone, Samuel Tucker	3rd cousin 3 times removed	XI	7
Boone, Sarah	3rd cousin 3 times removed	XI	7
Boone, Sarah	2nd cousin 4 times removed	X	7
Boone, Sarah	4th great-grandmother	VI	6
Boone, Sarah	2nd cousin 4 times removed	X	7
Boone, Sarah	2nd cousin 4 times removed	X	7
Boone, Sarah Cassandra	1st cousin 5 times removed	IX	7
Boone, Sarah E.	4th cousin twice removed	XII	7
Boone, Sarah Jane	4th cousin twice removed	XII	7
Boone, Sonora	5th cousin once removed	XIII	7
Boone, Squire	4th great-granduncle	VIII	7
Boone, Squire	3rd cousin 3 times removed	XI	7
Boone, Squire H.	3rd cousin 3 times removed	XI	7
Boone, Squire II	1st cousin 5 times removed	IX	7
Boone, Squire Sr.	2nd cousin 4 times removed	X	7
Boone, Susan	3rd cousin 3 times removed	XI	7
Boone, Susan	3rd cousin 3 times removed	XI	7
Boone, Susannah	2nd cousin 4 times removed	X	7
Boone, Susannah	2nd cousin 4 times removed	X	7
Boone, Susannah	3rd cousin 3 times removed	XI	7
Boone, Theodore	5th cousin once removed	XIII	7
Boone, Thomas	3rd cousin 3 times removed	XI	7
Boone, Thomas Norris	5th cousin once removed	XIII	7
Boone, Urbain	3rd cousin 3 times removed	XI	7
Boone, Van D.	3rd cousin 3 times removed	XI	7
Boone, Van Daniel	3rd cousin 3 times removed	XI	7
Boone, Van Daniel	5th cousin once removed	XIII	7
Boone, Van Daniel	5th cousin once removed	XIII	7
Boone, Victor L.	5th cousin once removed	XIII	7
Boone, Walter	5th cousin once removed	XIII	7
Boone, Warren	3rd cousin 3 times removed	XI	7
Boone, Wellington Treeson	4th cousin twice removed	XII	7
Boone, William Ashley	4th cousin twice removed	XII	7
Boone, William Bryan	2nd cousin 4 times removed	X	7
Boone, William Clay	5th cousin once removed	XIII	7
Boone, William Crawford	3rd cousin 3 times removed	XI	7
Boone, William Edgar	5th cousin once removed	XIII	7
Boone, William Eugene	5th cousin once removed	XIII	7
Boone, William Henry	4th cousin twice removed	XII	7
Boone, William Linville	2nd cousin 4 times removed	X	7
Boone, William R.	5th cousin once removed	XIII	7
Boone, William Randall	4th cousin twice removed	XII	7
Boone, William T.	4th cousin twice removed	XII	7
Boone, Zeralda Engleton	4th cousin twice removed	XII	7
Bordner, Elizabeth Bordner	2nd cousin twice removed	VIII	5
Bordner, John	Husband of the 1st cousin 3 times removed		
Bordner, John W.	2nd cousin twice removed	VIII	5
Bordner, William Henry Harrison	2nd cousin twice removed	VIII	5
Boschen, Jeanne Anne	Wife of the half 3rd cousin 4 times removed		
Bowers, Susan Jane	Wife of the half 1st cousin once removed		

Name	Relationship with Dwight Eisenhower	Civil	Canon
Bowman, ?	Husband of the half 1st cousin 3 times removed		
Bowman, Elizabeth	Wife of the half 3rd cousin		
Bowman, Isaac	Husband of the 4th cousin		
Bowman, Philip	Husband of the half grandaunt		
Boyer, Lottie	Wife of the half 3rd cousin		
Boyer, Samuel B.	Husband of the 3rd cousin once removed		
Bradley, Harry	Husband of the half 3rd cousin 3 times removed		
Bradley, John L.	Half 3rd cousin 4 times removed	XII	8
Bragg, Martha	Wife of the half 3rd cousin		
Brandt, Jacob M	Husband of the 1st cousin		
Brandt, Orville E	1st cousin once removed	V	3
Brandt, Preston L	1st cousin once removed	V	3
Brandt, Victor O	1st cousin once removed	V	3
Brechbill, Abram E	Husband of the 1st cousin		
Brehm, Eldred H	1st cousin once removed	V	3
Brehm, Faithe Marie	1st cousin once removed	V	3
Brehm, Irma Aurelia	1st cousin once removed	V	3
Brehm, Samuel W	Husband of the 1st cousin		
Brehm, Zena Leroy	1st cousin once removed	V	3
Bressler, Elizabeth	Wife of the 2nd cousin twice removed		
Brower, Elias	Husband of the half 3rd cousin		
Brown, Addie L.	Half 3rd cousin once removed	IX	5
Brown, Arminda	Half 3rd cousin once removed	IX	5
Brown, Benjamin F.	Half 3rd cousin	VIII	4
Brown, Charles F.	Husband of the 6th cousin		
Brown, Cintha M.	Half 3rd cousin once removed	IX	5
Brown, David A.	Half 3rd cousin	VIII	4
Brown, Delphia	Half 3rd cousin once removed	IX	5
Brown, Elizabert	Wife of the half 2nd great-granduncle		
Brown, Emil	Half 3rd cousin twice removed	X	6
Brown, Fred E.	Half 3rd cousin twice removed	X	6
Brown, Hannah	Wife of the 4th cousin twice removed		
Brown, Horace Charles	Half 3rd cousin twice removed	X	6
Brown, Howard	Half 3rd cousin twice removed	X	6
Brown, Ira W.	Half 3rd cousin twice removed	X	6
Brown, John	6th cousin	XIV	7
Brown, John	Husband of the half 3rd cousin		
Brown, John W.	Half 3rd cousin	VIII	4
Brown, Joseph	Half 3rd cousin	VIII	4
Brown, Julia	Half 3rd cousin	VIII	4
Brown, Laura E.	Half 3rd cousin	VIII	4
Brown, Lawsen	Husband of the 5th cousin once removed		
Brown, Linville Lee	Half 3rd cousin twice removed	X	6
Brown, Lucy	Half 3rd cousin	VIII	4
Brown, Lula J.	Half 3rd cousin once removed	IX	5
Brown, Maria	Half 3rd cousin	VIII	4
Brown, Martha	Half 3rd cousin once removed	IX	5
Brown, Martha	Half 3rd cousin	VIII	4
Brown, Martha E.	Wife of the half 3rd cousin		
Brown, Martishe R.	Half 3rd cousin	VIII	4
Brown, Mary	Half 3rd cousin	VIII	4
Brown, Mary	Wife of the half 3rd cousin		
Brown, Mary B.	Half 3rd cousin once removed	IX	5
Brown, Micajah	Half 3rd cousin once removed	IX	5
Brown, Rebecca	Half 3rd cousin once removed	IX	5
Brown, Roy M.	Half 3rd cousin once removed	IX	5
Brown, Samuel	Husband of the half 2nd cousin once removed		
Brown, Samuel Smith	Half 3rd cousin once removed	IX	5
Brown, Sarah	Half 3rd cousin	VIII	4
Brown, Settie	Half 3rd cousin twice removed	X	6
Brown, Walter E.	Husband of the 3rd cousin once removed		
Brown, William	Half 3rd cousin	VIII	4
Brown, William M.	Half 3rd cousin once removed	IX	5
Brown, Winfred Tate	Half 3rd cousin twice removed	X	6
Brunk, m	Husband of the half 3rd cousin 5 times removed		
Bryan	Wife of the 1st cousin 5 times removed		
Bryan, Abner	2nd cousin 4 times removed	X	7
Bryan, Abner	3rd cousin 3 times removed	XI	7
Bryan, Daniel	3rd cousin 3 times removed	XI	7
Bryan, Daniel	3rd cousin 3 times removed	XI	7
Bryan, Daniel Boone	2nd cousin 4 times removed	X	7

Name	Relationship with Dwight Eisenhower	Civil	Canon
Bryan, David	Husband of the 3rd cousin 3 times removed		
Bryan, Drucilla	4th cousin twice removed	XII	7
Bryan, Elizabeth	3rd cousin 3 times removed	XI	7
Bryan, Elizabeth	2nd cousin 4 times removed	X	7
Bryan, Elizabeth	4th cousin twice removed	XII	7
Bryan, Hannah	2nd cousin 4 times removed	X	7
Bryan, Iciline Archibald	4th cousin twice removed	XII	7
Bryan, James	4th cousin twice removed	XII	7
Bryan, John	2nd cousin 4 times removed	X	7
Bryan, John	4th cousin twice removed	XII	7
Bryan, Joseph	3rd cousin 3 times removed	XI	7
Bryan, Louis	3rd cousin 3 times removed	XI	7
Bryan, Martha	Wife of the 1st cousin 5 times removed		
Bryan, Mary	3rd cousin 3 times removed	XI	7
Bryan, Mary	2nd cousin 4 times removed	X	7
Bryan, Mary	3rd cousin 3 times removed	XI	7
Bryan, Mary	4th cousin twice removed	XII	7
Bryan, Melcina Callaway	4th cousin twice removed	XII	7
Bryan, Morgan	4th cousin twice removed	XII	7
Bryan, Phoebe	3rd cousin 3 times removed	XI	7
Bryan, Phoebe	2nd cousin 4 times removed	X	7
Bryan, Phoebe	3rd cousin 3 times removed	XI	7
Bryan, Rebecca	Wife of the 1st cousin 5 times removed		
Bryan, Rebecca	Wife of the 1st cousin 5 times removed		
Bryan, Sallie	3rd cousin 3 times removed	XI	7
Bryan, Samuel	3rd cousin 3 times removed	XI	7
Bryan, Samuel	3rd cousin 3 times removed	XI	7
Bryan, Samuel	2nd cousin 4 times removed	X	7
Bryan, Samuel	4th cousin twice removed	XII	7
Bryan, Sarah	2nd cousin 4 times removed	X	7
Bryan, Susan	4th cousin twice removed	XII	7
Bryan, Thomas	3rd cousin 3 times removed	XI	7
Bryan, Thomas	3rd cousin 3 times removed	XI	7
Bryan, William	2nd cousin 4 times removed	X	7
Bryan, William	3rd cousin 3 times removed	XI	7
Bryan, William K.	4th cousin twice removed	XII	7
Bryan, William Sr.	Husband of the 1st cousin 5 times removed		
Bryan, William Turner	3rd cousin 3 times removed	XI	7
Bryan, Willis	4th cousin twice removed	XII	7
Bryant, William	Husband of the 2nd cousin 4 times removed		
Buffington, Alfred Peter	Husband of the half 1st cousin once removed		
Buffington, Alice P	Half 2nd cousin	VI	3
Buffington, Annie E	Half 2nd cousin	VI	3
Buffington, Benjamin	2nd cousin twice removed	VIII	5
Buffington, Bertie	Half 2nd cousin	VI	3
Buffington, Cornelius	2nd cousin twice removed	VIII	5
Buffington, Dorothy Pauline	Half 2nd cousin once removed	VII	4
Buffington, Eldred Leroy	Half 2nd cousin	VI	3
Buffington, Elisabeth	2nd cousin twice removed	VIII	5
Buffington, Ethel M	Half 2nd cousin	VI	3
Buffington, Isaiah T.	3rd cousin once removed	IX	5
Buffington, Jacob	2nd cousin twice removed	VIII	5
Buffington, Josiah	2nd cousin twice removed	VIII	5
Buffington, Laura J	Half 2nd cousin	VI	3
Buffington, Mabel E	Half 2nd cousin	VI	3
Buffington, Meta	Half 2nd cousin	VI	3
Buffington, Roland McKinley	Half 2nd cousin	VI	3
Buffington, Roland R	Half 2nd cousin once removed	VII	4
Buffington, Solomon	Husband of the 1st cousin 3 times removed		
Buffington, Solomon	2nd cousin twice removed	VIII	5
Buffington, Susanna	2nd cousin twice removed	VIII	5
Bullock, Eliza Naomi	6th cousin	XIV	7
Bullock, Francis Marion	Husband of the 5th cousin once removed		
Bullock, Ida Myrtle	6th cousin once removed	XV	8
Bullock, Ida Pauline	6th cousin	XIV	7
Bullock, Joseph	6th cousin	XIV	7
Bullock, Mamie Lou	6th cousin once removed	XV	8
Bullock, Martha Ann	6th cousin	XIV	7
Bullock, Mary Ollie	6th cousin	XIV	7
Bullock, Nannie Joe	6th cousin once removed	XV	8
Bullock, Sarah Edith	6th cousin once removed	XV	8

Name	Relationship with Dwight Eisenhower	Civil	Canon
Bullock, Willie Ruth	6th cousin once removed	XV	8
Burgin, Mella B.	Wife of the half 3rd cousin twice removed		
Burkett, George Park	Husband of the half 3rd cousin		
Burris, Lula	Wife of the 6th cousin		
Button, m	Husband of the 1st cousin		
Butts, Wayne Laverne	Husband of the half 3rd cousin 3 times removed		
Cabery, Lucinda	Wife of the 3rd cousin once removed		
Callaway, Daniel Boone	3rd cousin 3 times removed	XI	7
Callaway, Elizabeth	3rd cousin 3 times removed	XI	7
Callaway, Emaline Roberta	Wife of the 3rd cousin 3 times removed		
Callaway, Frances	3rd cousin 3 times removed	XI	7
Callaway, James	3rd cousin 3 times removed	XI	7
Callaway, John Flanders	Husband of the 2nd cousin 4 times removed		
Callaway, Mary	Wife of the 1st cousin 5 times removed		
Callaway, Minerva	3rd cousin 3 times removed	XI	7
Callaway, Sarah	3rd cousin 3 times removed	XI	7
Callaway, Susan	4th cousin twice removed	XII	7
Callaway, Susannah	3rd cousin 3 times removed	XI	7
Callaway, Tabatha	3rd cousin 3 times removed	XI	7
Cameron, William H	Husband of the 2nd cousin twice removed		
Campbell, m	Husband of the 1st cousin once removed		
Camper, Francis	Husband of the half 1st cousin twice removed		
Cardell, Eric William	Husband of the 5th cousin once removed		
Carl	1st cousin twice removed	VI	4
Carl, Vesta A.	Wife of the 3rd cousin once removed		
Carlson, Elivera Mathilda	Mother-in-law		
Carlson, Hazel Margreta	Wife of the 4th cousin		
Carr, ?	Half 3rd cousin 6 times removed	XIV	10
Carr, ?	Half 3rd cousin 6 times removed	XIV	10
Carr, ?	Half 3rd cousin 6 times removed	XIV	10
Carr, ?	Half 3rd cousin 6 times removed	XIV	10
Carr, ?	Half 3rd cousin 6 times removed	XIV	10
Carr, m	Husband of the half 3rd cousin 5 times removed		
Carson, Adaline	4th cousin twice removed	XII	7
Carson, Cassandra	4th cousin twice removed	XII	7
Carson, Claiborne J.	4th cousin twice removed	XII	7
Carson, Frank	4th cousin twice removed	XII	7
Carson, George Hampton	4th cousin twice removed	XII	7
Carson, James Thomas	4th cousin twice removed	XII	7
Carson, Milly	4th cousin twice removed	XII	7
Carson, William	Husband of the 3rd cousin 3 times removed		
Carter, Mary	Ex-wife of the 1st cousin 5 times removed		
Cassel, Elizabeth	Wife of the 4th great-granduncle		
Casteel, Bertha J.	Wife of the half 3rd cousin 4 times removed		
Catherine	Wife of the 4th great-granduncle		
Catherine	Wife of the half 1st cousin twice removed		
Cathren	Wife of the 4th cousin twice removed		
Cenia	Wife of the 3rd cousin 3 times removed		
Chinn, Alfred S.	3rd cousin 3 times removed	XI	7
Chinn, Elizabeth	3rd cousin 3 times removed	XI	7
Chinn, Franklin B.	3rd cousin 3 times removed	XI	7
Chinn, John F.	3rd cousin 3 times removed	XI	7
Chinn, Morgan B.	3rd cousin 3 times removed	XI	7
Chinn, Nancy B.	3rd cousin 3 times removed	XI	7
Chinn, Rhoda D.	3rd cousin 3 times removed	XI	7
Chinn, Sarah	3rd cousin 3 times removed	XI	7
Chinn, William	Husband of the 2nd cousin 4 times removed		
Chinn, William	3rd cousin 3 times removed	XI	7
Christoph	1st cousin twice removed	VI	4
Chronister, Cyrus	Husband of the 2nd cousin 3 times removed		
Chronister, Elisabeth	3rd cousin twice removed	X	6
Chronister, Eliza	3rd cousin twice removed	X	6
Chronister, Jacob	3rd cousin twice removed	X	6
Chronister, Samuel	3rd cousin twice removed	X	6
Cimino, Vital	Husband of the 5th cousin once removed		
Clark, Charles A.	Half 3rd cousin once removed	IX	5
Clark, Hannah	Wife of the 2nd cousin twice removed		
Clark, Polly	Wife of the 3rd cousin 3 times removed		
Clark, William	Husband of the half 3rd cousin		
Claywell, Eliza B.	Wife of the 4th cousin twice removed		
Clem, Elijah	Husband of the half 3rd cousin twice removed		

Name	Relationship with Dwight Eisenhower	Civil	Canon
Clever, Lynn	Husband of the 4th cousin twice removed		
Cobb, Amanda	Wife of the 4th cousin twice removed		
Cobb, Olive Minerva	Wife of the half 3rd cousin		
Coleman, Rosanna	Wife of the half 2nd great-granduncle		
Coles, Edward J.	Husband of the 3rd cousin once removed		
Conger, Estell	Wife of the 5th cousin once removed		
Conrad	1st cousin twice removed	VI	4
Conrad, Margaret R.	Wife of the half 2nd great-granduncle		
Cooper, Anna Catherina	Wife of the great-granduncle		
Cope, Clarissa Jane	Wife of the 5th cousin once removed		
Copher, David Newton	3rd cousin 3 times removed	XI	7
Copher, Eleanor	3rd cousin 3 times removed	XI	7
Copher, Hettie Boone	3rd cousin 3 times removed	XI	7
Copher, Jesse	Husband of the 2nd cousin 4 times removed		
Copher, Jurusha	3rd cousin 3 times removed	XI	7
Copher, Mary	3rd cousin 3 times removed	XI	7
Copher, Nancy Boone	3rd cousin 3 times removed	XI	7
Copher, Phebe	3rd cousin 3 times removed	XI	7
Copher, Samuel Boone	3rd cousin 3 times removed	XI	7
Copher, Sarah	3rd cousin 3 times removed	XI	7
Copher, Thomas	3rd cousin 3 times removed	XI	7
Copher, Udosha	3rd cousin 3 times removed	XI	7
Corbo, Lorinda	Wife of the 3rd cousin 3 times removed		
Cowhick, Elizabeth	Wife of the 4th cousin twice removed		
Craig, Emily	Wife of the 5th cousin once removed		
Craig, Herman Victor	Husband of the half 3rd cousin 3 times removed		
Craig, James	Husband of the 3rd cousin 3 times removed		
Crapson, Amy	Half 3rd cousin once removed	IX	5
Crapson, Lorenzo Dow	Husband of the half 3rd cousin		
Cray, Catharina	1st cousin 4 times removed	VIII	6
Cray, Esther	Wife of the 3rd great-granduncle		
Cray, John P.	1st cousin 4 times removed	VIII	6
Cray, Peter	Husband of the 3rd great-grandaunt		
Croply, Elizabeth	Wife of the half 2nd cousin once removed		
Crosby	Husband of the 3rd cousin 3 times removed		
Crum, Sarah	Wife of the 1st cousin 3 times removed		
Crumpacker, Robert W.	Husband of the 6th cousin		
Cullop, Sarah E.	Wife of the half 3rd cousin once removed		
Cumbler, Margaret	Wife of the half granduncle		
Curry, Ethel A.	5th cousin once removed	XIII	7
Curry, George L.	Husband of the 4th cousin twice removed		
Curry, George L.	5th cousin once removed	XIII	7
Curry, Mary Florence	5th cousin once removed	XIII	7
Curry, Norwood Litton	5th cousin once removed	XIII	7
Curry, Ratliffe	5th cousin once removed	XIII	7
Curry, Willie Lane	5th cousin once removed	XIII	7
Dagley, Elizabeth	Wife of the 1st cousin 5 times removed		
Dalton, Lena Margaret	Wife of the half 2nd cousin		
Daniels, Elizabeth	Wife of the half 3rd cousin		
Davies, John	Half 3rd cousin 6 times removed	XIV	10
Davies, m	Husband of the half 3rd cousin 5 times removed		
Davies, Robert	Half 3rd cousin 6 times removed	XIV	10
Davis, James	Husband of the 3rd cousin 3 times removed		
Day, Jim	Husband of the half 3rd cousin		
Day, Sarah	Wife of the 1st cousin 5 times removed		
Dayhoff, Katherine E	Wife of the uncle		
DeHart, Joseph	Husband of the 2nd cousin 4 times removed		
Deibler, Hannah	Wife of the 2nd cousin twice removed		
Deibler, Mary	Wife of the 2nd cousin once removed		
Deitrich, Anna Marie	Wife of the great-grandfather		
Devitt, Anna	Wife of the half 2nd cousin once removed		
Dickenson, Mary	Wife of the 3rd cousin 3 times removed		
Dickson, Barbara	3rd cousin twice removed	X	6
Dickson, Benjamin	3rd cousin twice removed	X	6
Dickson, Elizabeth	3rd cousin twice removed	X	6
Dickson, George	3rd cousin twice removed	X	6
Dickson, John A.	3rd cousin twice removed	X	6
Dickson, Moses	Husband of the 2nd cousin 3 times removed		
Dickson, Samuel	3rd cousin twice removed	X	6
Dickson, William	3rd cousin twice removed	X	6
Dissinger, Anna Margaret	2nd great-grandmother	IV	4

Name	Relationship with Dwight Eisenhower	Civil	Canon
Dissinger, Peter	3rd great-grandfather	V	5
Dobbs, Melissa	Wife of the half 3rd cousin once removed		
Dobson, Lester Thomas	Husband of the 5th cousin once removed		
Dobson, Myrtle Estelle	6th cousin	XIV	7
Dooly	Husband of the 3rd cousin 3 times removed		
Doty, Lucinda	Wife of the half 1st cousin twice removed		
Doud, John Sheldon	Father-in-law		
Doud, Mary Geneva	Wife		
Dowd, O.	Husband of the half 3rd cousin once removed		
Dowell, ?	Wife of the 4th cousin twice removed		
Dowell, Birch	Husband of the 6th cousin		
Dowell, John	Husband of the 6th cousin		
Drefs, Ida Olga	Wife of the half 3rd cousin twice removed		
Dry, Caty	Wife of the half 2nd cousin once removed		
Dudgeon, Ethel Evelyn	Wife of the half 3rd cousin 3 times removed		
Dufler, Eubert	Husband of the half 1st cousin once removed		
Dupendorf, Esther	Wife of the 1st cousin twice removed		
Dye, Alvie	Half 3rd cousin 3 times removed	XI	7
Dye, James B.	Husband of the half 3rd cousin twice removed		
Dyers, Hannah	Wife of the 3rd cousin 3 times removed		
Eakin, Helen Elsie	Sister-in-law		
Edwards, James	Husband of the half 3rd cousin once removed		
Edwards, Missouri	Wife of the half 3rd cousin once removed		
Eisenhauer	5th great-grandmother	VII	7
Eisenhauer	Half 3rd cousin	VIII	4
Eisenhauer	Half 1st cousin once removed	V	3
Eisenhauer, ?	Half 3rd cousin	VIII	4
Eisenhauer, ?	Half 3rd cousin	VIII	4
Eisenhauer, Abraham	Half 2nd cousin once removed	VII	4
Eisenhauer, Abraham Lincoln	Uncle	III	2
Eisenhauer, Adeline	Half 3rd cousin	VIII	4
Eisenhauer, Agnes	Half 2nd cousin once removed	VII	4
Eisenhauer, Alexander	Half 2nd cousin once removed	VII	4
Eisenhauer, Alexander Caleb	Half 2nd cousin once removed	VII	4
Eisenhauer, Amanda Hannah	Aunt	III	2
Eisenhauer, Amanda Leah	Half 3rd cousin	VIII	4
Eisenhauer, Andrew	Half 2nd cousin once removed	VII	4
Eisenhauer, Ann	Great-grandaunt	V	4
Eisenhauer, Ann	Half 2nd cousin once removed	VII	4
Eisenhauer, Ann Eliza	Half 3rd cousin	VIII	4
Eisenhauer, Anna	Half 2nd cousin once removed	VII	4
Eisenhauer, Anna	Half grandaunt	IV	3
Eisenhauer, Anna Margaretha	3rd great-grandaunt	VII	6
Eisenhauer, Anna Margaretha	Half great-grandaunt	V	4
Eisenhauer, Anna Maria Elizabeth	Half great-grandaunt	V	4
Eisenhauer, Anna May	Half 1st cousin twice removed	VI	4
Eisenhauer, Barbara	Great-grandaunt	V	4
Eisenhauer, Barbara	Half 2nd cousin once removed	VII	4
Eisenhauer, Barbara S.	Half 3rd cousin	VIII	4
Eisenhauer, Catherine	Half 1st cousin twice removed	VI	4
Eisenhauer, Catherine	Great-grandaunt	V	4
Eisenhauer, Catherine	Half 1st cousin twice removed	VI	4
Eisenhauer, Catherine	Half 2nd cousin once removed	VII	4
Eisenhauer, Catherine	Half 2nd cousin once removed	VII	4
Eisenhauer, Catherine	Half 2nd cousin once removed	VII	4
Eisenhauer, Catherine Ann	Aunt	III	2
Eisenhauer, Caty	Half 2nd cousin once removed	VII	4
Eisenhauer, Christina	Great-grandaunt	V	4
Eisenhauer, Christine	Half 2nd cousin once removed	VII	4
Eisenhauer, Clinton	Uncle	III	2
Eisenhauer, Daniel	Half 2nd cousin once removed	VII	4
Eisenhauer, Daniel	Half 2nd cousin once removed	VII	4
Eisenhauer, Daniel Monroe	Half 3rd cousin	VIII	4
Eisenhauer, David G. W.	Half 3rd cousin	VIII	4
Eisenhauer, David Jacob	Father	I	1
Eisenhauer, Elijah J.	Half 3rd cousin	VIII	4
Eisenhauer, Eliza M.	Half 2nd cousin once removed	VII	4
Eisenhauer, Elizabeth	Half 1st cousin twice removed	VI	4
Eisenhauer, Elizabeth	Half 2nd cousin once removed	VII	4
Eisenhauer, Elizabeth	Half 2nd cousin once removed	VII	4
Eisenhauer, Elizabeth	Half 2nd cousin once removed	VII	4

Name	Relationship with Dwight Eisenhower	Civil	Canon
Eisenhauer, Elizabeth	Half 2nd cousin once removed	VII	4
Eisenhauer, Elizabeth	Half 1st cousin once removed	V	3
Eisenhauer, Elizabeth Catharina	3rd great-grandaunt	VII	6
Eisenhauer, Emma Bertha	Half 1st cousin once removed	V	3
Eisenhauer, Emma Jane	Aunt	III	2
Eisenhauer, Emma L.	Half 3rd cousin	VIII	4
Eisenhauer, Frank	Half 3rd cousin	VIII	4
Eisenhauer, Frederick	Great-grandfather	III	3
Eisenhauer, G. Adam	Half 2nd cousin once removed	VII	4
Eisenhauer, George Michael	Half 1st cousin twice removed	VI	4
Eisenhauer, George Michael	Half great-granduncle	V	4
Eisenhauer, George Michael	Half 2nd cousin once removed	VII	4
Eisenhauer, George W.	Half 2nd cousin once removed	VII	4
Eisenhauer, George W.	Half 1st cousin twice removed	VI	4
Eisenhauer, Hannah	Half 1st cousin twice removed	VI	4
Eisenhauer, Hans	Husband of the 5th great-grandmother		
Eisenhauer, Hans	5th great-grandfather	VII	7
Eisenhauer, Hans Nichol	Half 3rd great-granduncle	VII	6
Eisenhauer, Hans Nicholas	3rd great-grandfather	V	5
Eisenhauer, Hans Peter	4th great-grandfather	VI	6
Eisenhauer, Hans Peter	2nd great-grandfather	IV	4
Eisenhauer, Henry Michael	Half 2nd cousin once removed	VII	4
Eisenhauer, Isaac	Half 2nd cousin once removed	VII	4
Eisenhauer, Isabella	Half 2nd cousin once removed	VII	4
Eisenhauer, J. Jacob	Half 1st cousin twice removed	VI	4
Eisenhauer, Jacob	Half 1st cousin twice removed	VI	4
Eisenhauer, Jacob	Half 2nd cousin once removed	VII	4
Eisenhauer, Jacob	Half 2nd cousin once removed	VII	4
Eisenhauer, Jacob	Half 3rd cousin	VIII	4
Eisenhauer, Jacob Burns	Half 2nd cousin once removed	VII	4
Eisenhauer, Jacob Burns	Half 3rd cousin	VIII	4
Eisenhauer, Jacob F.	Uncle	III	2
Eisenhauer, Jacob Frederick	Grandfather	II	2
Eisenhauer, Jacob H.	Half 2nd cousin once removed	VII	4
Eisenhauer, James Co.	Half 3rd cousin	VIII	4
Eisenhauer, James H.	Half 3rd cousin	VIII	4
Eisenhauer, James Harvey	Half 2nd cousin once removed	VII	4
Eisenhauer, James Monroe	Half 1st cousin once removed	V	3
Eisenhauer, James V.	Half 2nd cousin once removed	VII	4
Eisenhauer, Jane Catherine	Half 2nd cousin once removed	VII	4
Eisenhauer, Johann Peter	Half 3rd great-granduncle	VII	6
Eisenhauer, Johanna	2nd great-grandaunt	VI	5
Eisenhauer, Johannes	2nd great-granduncle	VI	5
Eisenhauer, Johannes	Half 1st cousin twice removed	VI	4
Eisenhauer, Johannes	Half 1st cousin twice removed	VI	4
Eisenhauer, John	Half 3rd cousin	VIII	4
Eisenhauer, John	Half great-granduncle	V	4
Eisenhauer, John	Half 2nd cousin once removed	VII	4
Eisenhauer, John	Half 3rd cousin	VIII	4
Eisenhauer, John A.	Half 2nd cousin once removed	VII	4
Eisenhauer, John David	Half 1st cousin twice removed	VI	4
Eisenhauer, John David	Half granduncle	IV	3
Eisenhauer, John Edward	Half 3rd cousin	VIII	4
Eisenhauer, John Franklin	Half 1st cousin once removed	V	3
Eisenhauer, John Frederick	Half great-granduncle	V	4
Eisenhauer, John H.	Uncle	III	2
Eisenhauer, John J.	Half 2nd cousin once removed	VII	4
Eisenhauer, John J.	Half 3rd cousin	VIII	4
Eisenhauer, John Jacob	Great-granduncle	V	4
Eisenhauer, John Michael	Half 1st cousin twice removed	VI	4
Eisenhauer, John Nicholas	Half 1st cousin twice removed	VI	4
Eisenhauer, John Nicholas	Half great-granduncle	V	4
Eisenhauer, John Peter	Great-granduncle	V	4
Eisenhauer, John W.	Half 2nd cousin once removed	VII	4
Eisenhauer, Jonathan	Half 2nd cousin once removed	VII	4
Eisenhauer, Joseph	Half 1st cousin twice removed	VI	4
Eisenhauer, Joseph	Half 2nd cousin once removed	VII	4
Eisenhauer, Joseph J.	Half 2nd cousin once removed	VII	4
Eisenhauer, Leah Jane	Half 1st cousin once removed	V	3
Eisenhauer, Lucy Ellen	Half 3rd cousin	VIII	4
Eisenhauer, Lydia A.	Aunt	III	2

Name	Relationship with Dwight Eisenhower	Civil	Canon
Eisenhauer, Margaret	Great-grandaunt	V	4
Eisenhauer, Margaret	Half 2nd cousin once removed	VII	4
Eisenhauer, Margaret	Half 2nd cousin once removed	VII	4
Eisenhauer, Margaret	Half 2nd cousin once removed	VII	4
Eisenhauer, Margaret	Half 3rd cousin	VIII	4
Eisenhauer, Maria Barbara	Half great-grandaunt	V	4
Eisenhauer, Maria Magdalena	2nd great-grandaunt	VI	5
Eisenhauer, Maria Magdalena	Half great-grandaunt	V	4
Eisenhauer, Maria Magdalena	Half 1st cousin twice removed	VI	4
Eisenhauer, Maria Sara	3rd great-grandaunt	VII	6
Eisenhauer, Marie Elizabeth	Half 1st cousin twice removed	VI	4
Eisenhauer, Marie Elizabeth	Half 1st cousin twice removed	VI	4
Eisenhauer, Martin	Half 1st cousin twice removed	VI	4
Eisenhauer, Martin	2nd great-granduncle	VI	5
Eisenhauer, Martin	Half 2nd cousin once removed	VII	4
Eisenhauer, Mary	Half 2nd cousin once removed	VII	4
Eisenhauer, Mary	Half 1st cousin twice removed	VI	4
Eisenhauer, Mary	Half 2nd cousin once removed	VII	4
Eisenhauer, Mary	Half 2nd cousin once removed	VII	4
Eisenhauer, Mary	Half 2nd cousin once removed	VII	4
Eisenhauer, Mary A.	Half 3rd cousin	VIII	4
Eisenhauer, Mary Ann	Half 2nd cousin once removed	VII	4
Eisenhauer, Mary Ann	Aunt	III	2
Eisenhauer, Mary Ann	Half 1st cousin once removed	V	3
Eisenhauer, Matilda C.	Half 2nd cousin once removed	VII	4
Eisenhauer, Michael	Half 2nd cousin once removed	VII	4
Eisenhauer, Peter	Half great-granduncle	V	4
Eisenhauer, Peter	Half 1st cousin twice removed	VI	4
Eisenhauer, Peter	Half 1st cousin twice removed	VI	4
Eisenhauer, Peter	Half 2nd cousin once removed	VII	4
Eisenhauer, Peter A.	Uncle	III	2
Eisenhauer, Philipp	Half great-granduncle	V	4
Eisenhauer, Phillipina	Half 2nd cousin once removed	VII	4
Eisenhauer, Polly	Half grandaunt	IV	3
Eisenhauer, Polly	Half 3rd cousin	VIII	4
Eisenhauer, Rachel	Half 2nd cousin once removed	VII	4
Eisenhauer, Richard L.	Half 3rd cousin	VIII	4
Eisenhauer, Sally	Half 2nd cousin once removed	VII	4
Eisenhauer, Samuel	Half great-granduncle	V	4
Eisenhauer, Samuel F.	Uncle	III	2
Eisenhauer, Samuel L.	Half 2nd cousin once removed	VII	4
Eisenhauer, Sarah	Half 1st cousin twice removed	VI	4
Eisenhauer, Sarah	Half 2nd cousin once removed	VII	4
Eisenhauer, Sarah Ellen	Half 1st cousin once removed	V	3
Eisenhauer, Sarah Jane	Half 2nd cousin once removed	VII	4
Eisenhauer, Selina V.	Half 3rd cousin	VIII	4
Eisenhauer, Simon Peter	Half 1st cousin once removed	V	3
Eisenhauer, Susanna	Half 3rd cousin	VIII	4
Eisenhauer, Susanna	Aunt	III	2
Eisenhauer, Susannah	Half 1st cousin twice removed	VI	4
Eisenhauer, Susannah	Half 1st cousin twice removed	VI	4
Eisenhauer, Susannah	Half 2nd cousin once removed	VII	4
Eisenhauer, Timothy N.	Half 2nd cousin once removed	VII	4
Eisenhauer, Virginia F. E.	Half 3rd cousin	VIII	4
Eisenhauer, William Henry	Half 1st cousin once removed	V	3
Eisenhauer, William L.	Half 3rd cousin	VIII	4
Eisenhauer, William Mitchell	Half 2nd cousin once removed	VII	4
Eisenhower, Alex	Great-grandson	III	3
Eisenhower, Arthur Bradford	Brother	II	1
Eisenhower, Barbara Anne	Granddaughter	II	2
Eisenhower, Catherine	Half grandaunt	IV	3
Eisenhower, Clinton	1st cousin	IV	2
Eisenhower, Doud Dwight	Son of the wife		
Eisenhower, Dwight David	Self		0
Eisenhower, Dwight David	Grandson	II	2
Eisenhower, Earl Dewey	Brother	II	1
Eisenhower, Edgar Newton	Brother	II	1
Eisenhower, Ira A	Uncle	III	2
Eisenhower, Jennie	Great-granddaughter	III	3
Eisenhower, John Sheldon Doud	Son	I	1
Eisenhower, Katherine	Niece	III	2

Name	Relationship with Dwight Eisenhower	Civil	Canon
Eisenhower, Lloyd E	Nephew	III	2
Eisenhower, Martin	2nd great-granduncle	VI	5
Eisenhower, Mary Jean	Granddaughter	II	2
Eisenhower, Mary Rebecca	1st cousin	IV	2
Eisenhower, Melanie	Great-granddaughter	III	3
Eisenhower, Milton Stover	Brother	II	1
Eisenhower, Patricia	Niece	III	2
Eisenhower, Paul Dawson A.	Brother	II	1
Eisenhower, Peggy J	Niece	III	2
Eisenhower, Roy J	Nephew	III	2
Eisenhower, Roy Jacob	Brother	II	1
Eisenhower, Samuel P	Half granduncle	IV	3
Eisenhower, Simon L	1st cousin	IV	2
Eisenhower, Susan Elaine	Granddaughter	II	2
Elamanda	Wife of the 2nd cousin twice removed		
Elizabeth	Wife of the half 2nd cousin once removed		
Elizabeth	Wife of the half great-granduncle		
Elledge	4th cousin twice removed	XII	7
Elledge, Adeline	4th cousin twice removed	XII	7
Elledge, Alexander Boone	4th cousin twice removed	XII	7
Elledge, Banner Boone	4th cousin twice removed	XII	7
Elledge, Benjamin Franklin	3rd cousin 3 times removed	XI	7
Elledge, Charity Sarah	3rd cousin 3 times removed	XI	7
Elledge, Edward Boone	3rd cousin 3 times removed	XI	7
Elledge, Evelyn Boone	4th cousin twice removed	XII	7
Elledge, Francis	Husband of the 2nd cousin 4 times removed		
Elledge, Harvey V.	4th cousin twice removed	XII	7
Elledge, James	3rd cousin 3 times removed	XI	7
Elledge, James Boone	4th cousin twice removed	XII	7
Elledge, Jemima	4th cousin twice removed	XII	7
Elledge, Jemina	3rd cousin 3 times removed	XI	7
Elledge, Jesse Bryan	3rd cousin 3 times removed	XI	7
Elledge, Leonard Boone	3rd cousin 3 times removed	XI	7
Elledge, Levina	4th cousin twice removed	XII	7
Elledge, Lucy	4th cousin twice removed	XII	7
Elledge, Lydia	4th cousin twice removed	XII	7
Elledge, Martha Jane	3rd cousin 3 times removed	XI	7
Elledge, Martha S.	4th cousin twice removed	XII	7
Elledge, Mary	3rd cousin 3 times removed	XI	7
Elledge, Matilda	4th cousin twice removed	XII	7
Elledge, Nancy	3rd cousin 3 times removed	XI	7
Elledge, Nathan Boone	4th cousin twice removed	XII	7
Elledge, Sophia C.	4th cousin twice removed	XII	7
Elledge, Thomas	4th cousin twice removed	XII	7
Elledge, Thomas P.	5th cousin once removed	XIII	7
Elledge, Uriah	4th cousin twice removed	XII	7
Elledge, William	3rd cousin 3 times removed	XI	7
Elledge, William Tilford	4th cousin twice removed	XII	7
Ellenberger, Elizabeth	Wife of the 1st cousin 4 times removed		
Elsesser, Christina	Wife of the 2nd cousin twice removed		
Engle, Voiland	Husband of the 1st cousin once removed		
Enterline, Solomon	Husband of the 2nd cousin twice removed		
Epler, ?	1st cousin once removed	V	3
Epler, Abraham Lincoln	Husband of the 1st cousin		
Epler, Blanche Pearl	1st cousin once removed	V	3
Epler, Grace Lilian	1st cousin once removed	V	3
Epler, Grant Barton	1st cousin once removed	V	3
Epler, Martha Irene	1st cousin once removed	V	3
Epler, Paul Mark	1st cousin once removed	V	3
Epler, Ruel Milton	1st cousin once removed	V	3
Epler, Russell Emerson	1st cousin once removed	V	3
Epperson, Anthony	Husband of the half 3rd cousin 3 times removed		
Erhart, Elisabeth	Wife of the 2nd cousin 3 times removed		
Etherington, A Ray	Husband of the 1st cousin		
Eva	Wife of the half 1st cousin twice removed		
Fair, Alfred Henry	Husband of the half 1st cousin once removed		
Fair, Alice	Half 2nd cousin	VI	3
Fair, George	Half 2nd cousin	VI	3
Fair, Mabel	Half 2nd cousin	VI	3
Fair, Maude	Half 2nd cousin	VI	3
Fallace, Ann	7th great-grandmother	IX	9

Name	Relationship with Dwight Eisenhower	Civil	Canon
Farley, David	Husband of the 5th cousin once removed		
Farley, Malinda	6th cousin	XIV	7
Farley, William	6th cousin	XIV	7
Farmer, Ann	Wife of the 4th great-granduncle		
Faust, Living	Husband of the 4th cousin 4 times removed		
Faust, Living	4th cousin 5 times removed	XV	10
Faust, Living	4th cousin 5 times removed	XV	10
Feaser, Elizabeth	Wife of the half 1st cousin 3 times removed		
Fehr, m	Husband of the 2nd cousin twice removed		
Fehr, m	Husband of the 2nd cousin twice removed		
Fischer, Michael	Husband of the 2nd great-grandaunt		
Fisher, Amelia	Wife of the 1st cousin 3 times removed		
Fisher, Anna Maria	Wife of the half great-granduncle		
Fisher, Sarah	Wife of the 1st cousin 3 times removed		
Fisk, Lucinda	Wife of the 4th cousin twice removed		
Fisk, Marion	Husband of the 4th cousin twice removed		
Fisk, Newton	5th cousin once removed	XIII	7
Floyd, Sarah G.	Wife of the 4th cousin twice removed		
Folgate, Isaac James	3rd cousin once removed	IX	5
Folgate, James	Husband of the 2nd cousin twice removed		
Folgate, Jonathon	3rd cousin once removed	IX	5
Folgate, m	Husband of the 2nd cousin twice removed		
Folgate, Uriah Theodore	3rd cousin once removed	IX	5
Folgate, William Grant	3rd cousin once removed	IX	5
Followwill, Zelma L.	Ex-wife of the half 3rd cousin 3 times removed		
Forbush, James	Husband of the 2nd cousin 4 times removed		
Fosdick, Susan	Wife of the 4th cousin twice removed		
Foulke, Mary	Wife of the 4th great-granduncle		
Fox, John	Husband of the 2nd cousin 3 times removed		
Fox, Laura	3rd cousin twice removed	X	6
Fox, Mary Ann	Wife of the half 2nd cousin once removed		
Foy, Nancy Jane	3rd cousin twice removed	X	6
Frances	Wife of the 5th cousin once removed		
Frazier	Husband of the 3rd cousin 3 times removed		
Fry, Joseph Boone	Wife of the 2nd cousin 4 times removed		
Fudge, Elizabeth	Wife of the 4th cousin twice removed		
Funk, Elizabeth	Wife of the 1st cousin 4 times removed		
Furnish, Susan E.	Wife of the half 3rd cousin once removed		
Fye, Benjamin	3rd cousin twice removed	X	6
Fye, Conrad	Husband of the 2nd cousin 3 times removed		
Fye, Daniel	3rd cousin twice removed	X	6
Fye, David	3rd cousin twice removed	X	6
Fye, Elisabeth	3rd cousin twice removed	X	6
Fye, Jeremiah	3rd cousin twice removed	X	6
Fye, Jerome A.	3rd cousin twice removed	X	6
Fye, John C.	3rd cousin twice removed	X	6
Fye, Josiah	3rd cousin twice removed	X	6
Fye, Lewis T.	3rd cousin twice removed	X	6
Fye, Sarah A.	3rd cousin twice removed	X	6
Gallimore, Elizabeth	Wife of the half 2nd cousin once removed		
Gargus, Clarence Bell	5th cousin once removed	XIII	7
Gargus, Earl	5th cousin once removed	XIII	7
Gargus, John Alonzo	5th cousin once removed	XIII	7
Gargus, Living	5th cousin once removed	XIII	7
Gargus, Martin Lee	5th cousin once removed	XIII	7
Gargus, Mathias	Husband of the 4th cousin twice removed		
Gargus, Mathias Lincoln	5th cousin once removed	XIII	7
Gargus, Pearl	5th cousin once removed	XIII	7
Gargus, Ulysses Grant	5th cousin once removed	XIII	7
Gastbend, Josephine	Wife of the half 1st cousin once removed		
Gates, Andrew	3rd cousin twice removed	X	6
Gates, Cyrus	3rd cousin twice removed	X	6
Gates, David	Husband of the 2nd cousin 3 times removed		
Gates, Mary	3rd cousin twice removed	X	6
Gates, Miles	3rd cousin twice removed	X	6
Gearhart, Elizabeth M.	Wife of the half 1st cousin twice removed		
Gerhard, Cecil Jacob	Husband of the half 1st cousin once removed		
Gilbert, Alfred	Half 1st cousin once removed	V	3
Gilbert, Asa	Husband of the half 3rd cousin		
Gilbert, George	Husband of the half grandaunt		
Gilbert, George W	Half 1st cousin once removed	V	3

Name	Relationship with Dwight Eisenhower	Civil	Canon
Gilbert, Minerva	Half 1st cousin once removed	V	3
Gilbert, Salome	Half 1st cousin once removed	V	3
Gillispie, Charles	Husband of the half 3rd cousin 4 times removed		
Gipple, Aaron	2nd cousin once removed	VII	4
Gipple, Aaron Otto	3rd cousin	VIII	4
Gipple, Carol	3rd cousin twice removed	X	6
Gipple, Catherine	2nd cousin once removed	VII	4
Gipple, Christian	2nd cousin once removed	VII	4
Gipple, Christopher	Husband of the 1st cousin twice removed		
Gipple, Eliza	2nd cousin once removed	VII	4
Gipple, Elizabeth	2nd cousin once removed	VII	4
Gipple, Elizabeth	2nd cousin once removed	VII	4
Gipple, Gerald	3rd cousin once removed	IX	5
Gipple, Harry Wilson	3rd cousin	VIII	4
Gipple, Jacob	Husband of the 1st cousin twice removed		
Gipple, Jacob J.	2nd cousin once removed	VII	4
Gipple, James A.	2nd cousin once removed	VII	4
Gipple, Joseph	2nd cousin once removed	VII	4
Gipple, Leah	2nd cousin once removed	VII	4
Gipple, Lydia Ann	2nd cousin once removed	VII	4
Gipple, Martha Mabel	3rd cousin	VIII	4
Gipple, Mary Rebecca	2nd cousin once removed	VII	4
Gipple, Samuel	2nd cousin once removed	VII	4
Gipple, Samuel H.	2nd cousin once removed	VII	4
Gipple, Sarah	2nd cousin once removed	VII	4
Gipple, Susan	2nd cousin once removed	VII	4
Gipple, Verna Mary	3rd cousin	VIII	4
Gipple-I, Mary Ann	2nd cousin once removed	VII	4
Gipple-Ii, Mary Ann	2nd cousin once removed	VII	4
Gish, Evelyn W	1st cousin once removed	V	3
Gish, Joseph Harvey	Husband of the 1st cousin		
Gist, Mary Catherine	Wife of the 5th cousin once removed		
Glenn, John Hall	Husband of the 5th cousin once removed		
Goe, Daniel B.	3rd cousin 3 times removed	XI	7
Goe, Dorcas	3rd cousin 3 times removed	XI	7
Goe, Nathan B.	3rd cousin 3 times removed	XI	7
Goe, Nelly	3rd cousin 3 times removed	XI	7
Goe, Noble	3rd cousin 3 times removed	XI	7
Goe, Philip	Husband of the 2nd cousin 4 times removed		
Goe, Tarleton	3rd cousin 3 times removed	XI	7
Goe, William	3rd cousin 3 times removed	XI	7
Goode, Harvey L.	Husband of the half 2nd cousin once removed		
Goode, Julia Ann	Wife of the half 2nd cousin once removed		
Goodnite, Barbara	Wife of the half 2nd cousin once removed		
Goodrich, Francis	Wife of the half 2nd cousin once removed		
Gothie, Gertrude	Wife of the half 2nd cousin twice removed		
Graff, Elizabeth	Wife of the 2nd great-grandfather		
Graham, Catherine	Wife of the 3rd cousin 3 times removed		
Grant, William	Husband of the 1st cousin 5 times removed		
Grantham, Daniel G.	Husband of the 4th cousin twice removed		
Grazier, Anna	3rd cousin twice removed	X	6
Grazier, Barbara	3rd cousin twice removed	X	6
Grazier, Elisabeth	3rd cousin twice removed	X	6
Grazier, Elmer	3rd cousin twice removed	X	6
Grazier, Jacob	3rd cousin twice removed	X	6
Grazier, Joseph	Husband of the 2nd cousin 3 times removed		
Grazier, Martha	3rd cousin twice removed	X	6
Grazier, Mary	3rd cousin twice removed	X	6
Grazier, Oscar	3rd cousin twice removed	X	6
Grazier, Theodore	3rd cousin twice removed	X	6
Grazier, Wilson	3rd cousin twice removed	X	6
Gregory, Clarence W.	Husband of the half 3rd cousin twice removed		
Gregory, David M.	Husband of the half 3rd cousin twice removed		
Gregory, Finis	Husband of the half 3rd cousin twice removed		
Gregory, Henry Lee	Half 3rd cousin 3 times removed	XI	7
Gregory, Loreta	Half 3rd cousin 3 times removed	XI	7
Gregory, Mary Isabelle	Wife of the half 3rd cousin twice removed		
Gregory, Sarah Ann	Wife of the half 3rd cousin		
Grieb, Louis Sondra	Sister-in-law		
Griffith, Anne	Wife of the 4th great-granduncle		
Grimes, Caroline	3rd cousin 3 times removed	XI	7

Name	Relationship with Dwight Eisenhower	Civil	Canon
Grimes, Elizabeth	3rd cousin 3 times removed	XI	7
Grimes, John	3rd cousin 3 times removed	XI	7
Grimes, Mary 'Polly'	3rd cousin 3 times removed	XI	7
Grimes, Melinda	3rd cousin 3 times removed	XI	7
Grimes, Nancy	3rd cousin 3 times removed	XI	7
Grimes, Parmelia	3rd cousin 3 times removed	XI	7
Grimes, Phebe Bryan	3rd cousin 3 times removed	XI	7
Grimes, Sarah	3rd cousin 3 times removed	XI	7
Grimm, Elizabeth	Wife of the 2nd cousin once removed		
Grist, Edward Webster	Husband of the half 3rd cousin 3 times removed		
Grooms, Sarah	Wife of the 3rd cousin 3 times removed		
Grubbs, Anna	Wife of the 2nd cousin 4 times removed		
Grubbs, Mourning	Wife of the 2nd cousin 4 times removed		
Grubbs, Nancy	Wife of the 2nd cousin 4 times removed		
Guaen, Patrick	Husband of the half 2nd cousin once removed		
Haas, Anna Sabrina	Wife of the 4th great-grandfather		
Haines, Annie	Wife of the 2nd cousin twice removed		
Haines, Jacob	Husband of the half 1st cousin 3 times removed		
Haines, John Sidney	Husband of the 3rd cousin once removed		
Haines, Leland M	4th cousin once removed	XI	6
Haines, Percival J	4th cousin	X	5
Haldeman, Abraham Lincoln	1st cousin	IV	2
Haldeman, Delilah	1st cousin	IV	2
Haldeman, Eunic O	1st cousin once removed	V	3
Haldeman, Harry Milton	1st cousin	IV	2
Haldeman, Hattie Jane	1st cousin	IV	2
Haldeman, Jesse Ira	1st cousin	IV	2
Haldeman, John Henry	1st cousin	IV	2
Haldeman, John Thaddeus	1st cousin	IV	2
Haldeman, Katherine Ann	1st cousin	IV	2
Haldeman, Lillian Elizabeth	1st cousin	IV	2
Haldeman, Lydia Ann	1st cousin	IV	2
Haldeman, Mary Rebecca	1st cousin	IV	2
Haldeman, Milo Edward	1st cousin	IV	2
Haldeman, Ora Blanche	1st cousin	IV	2
Haldeman, Samuel B.	Husband of the aunt		
Haldeman, Samuel Walter	1st cousin	IV	2
Haldeman, Veri C	1st cousin once removed	V	3
Hall, Thelma Laverne	Wife of the half 3rd cousin 4 times removed		
Haller, Living	Husband of the 4th cousin 4 times removed		
Hamblin, Ann	4th cousin twice removed	XII	7
Hamblin, Delia	4th cousin twice removed	XII	7
Hamblin, Eliza	4th cousin twice removed	XII	7
Hamblin, Elizabeth	4th cousin twice removed	XII	7
Hamblin, Emily	4th cousin twice removed	XII	7
Hamblin, George	4th cousin twice removed	XII	7
Hamblin, John	Husband of the 3rd cousin 3 times removed		
Hamblin, Lucinda	4th cousin twice removed	XII	7
Hamblin, Mary	4th cousin twice removed	XII	7
Hamblin, Orva	4th cousin twice removed	XII	7
Hamblin, Piercy	4th cousin twice removed	XII	7
Hamilton, Ann Reid	Wife of the 3rd cousin 3 times removed		
Hamilton, Jane A.	Wife of the half 2nd cousin once removed		
Hamilton, W. H.	Husband of the half 3rd cousin		
Hampton	Half 3rd cousin	VIII	4
Hampton	Half 3rd cousin	VIII	4
Hampton	Half 3rd cousin	VIII	4
Hampton	Half 3rd cousin	VIII	4
Hampton, ?	Half 3rd cousin	VIII	4
Hampton, Albert M.	Half 3rd cousin once removed	IX	5
Hampton, Alfred	Half 3rd cousin once removed	IX	5
Hampton, Arther	Half 3rd cousin twice removed	X	6
Hampton, Clarence Sidney	Half 3rd cousin twice removed	X	6
Hampton, David	Half 3rd cousin	VIII	4
Hampton, David Robert	Half 3rd cousin once removed	IX	5
Hampton, Elbert Micagah	Half 3rd cousin once removed	IX	5
Hampton, Ella L.	Half 3rd cousin once removed	IX	5
Hampton, Elma	Half 3rd cousin twice removed	X	6
Hampton, Fannie M.	Half 3rd cousin once removed	IX	5
Hampton, Franklin	Half 3rd cousin once removed	IX	5
Hampton, Gabriel Morgan	Half 3rd cousin once removed	IX	5

Name	Relationship with Dwight Eisenhower	Civil	Canon
Hampton, Gritie	Half 3rd cousin once removed	IX	5
Hampton, Harriet Caroline	Half 3rd cousin once removed	IX	5
Hampton, James	Half 3rd cousin once removed	IX	5
Hampton, James	Half 3rd cousin once removed	IX	5
Hampton, James P.	Half 3rd cousin once removed	IX	5
Hampton, John	Half 3rd cousin	VIII	4
Hampton, John	Half 3rd cousin once removed	IX	5
Hampton, John W.	Half 3rd cousin once removed	IX	5
Hampton, Joseph	Half 3rd cousin once removed	IX	5
Hampton, Leslie	Half 3rd cousin twice removed	X	6
Hampton, Leucey J.	Half 3rd cousin twice removed	X	6
Hampton, Lorenzo	Half 3rd cousin	VIII	4
Hampton, Lorenzo	Half 3rd cousin once removed	IX	5
Hampton, M. Henry E.	Half 3rd cousin once removed	IX	5
Hampton, Margaret F.	Wife of the 4th cousin twice removed		
Hampton, Martha	Half 3rd cousin once removed	IX	5
Hampton, Mary	Half 3rd cousin	VIII	4
Hampton, Mary	Half 3rd cousin once removed	IX	5
Hampton, Mary	Half 3rd cousin once removed	IX	5
Hampton, Mary A.	Half 3rd cousin once removed	IX	5
Hampton, Mary I.	Half 3rd cousin once removed	IX	5
Hampton, Micajah I.	Husband of the half 2nd cousin once removed		
Hampton, Nallie S.	Half 3rd cousin once removed	IX	5
Hampton, Nancy	Half 3rd cousin once removed	IX	5
Hampton, Noah	Half 3rd cousin	VIII	4
Hampton, Noah Edward	Half 3rd cousin once removed	IX	5
Hampton, Nunet B.	Half 3rd cousin twice removed	X	6
Hampton, Ornie T.	Half 3rd cousin twice removed	X	6
Hampton, Peter	Half 3rd cousin once removed	IX	5
Hampton, Reta	Half 3rd cousin once removed	IX	5
Hampton, Romlour Agustus	Half 3rd cousin	VIII	4
Hampton, Rufus	Half 3rd cousin once removed	IX	5
Hampton, Rufus	Half 3rd cousin	VIII	4
Hampton, Sarah Jane	Half 3rd cousin once removed	IX	5
Hampton, Silas	Half 3rd cousin	VIII	4
Hampton, William H.	Half 3rd cousin twice removed	X	6
Hampton, William James	Half 3rd cousin	VIII	4
Hampton, William R.	Half 3rd cousin once removed	IX	5
Hampton, William Silas	Half 3rd cousin once removed	IX	5
Hand, Eva	Wife of the 2nd great-granduncle		
Hannah, Mary	Great-grandmother	III	3
Hanson, Nels Hamilton	Husband of the 5th cousin once removed		
Harner, Carrie E	Half 2nd cousin	VI	3
Harner, George A	Husband of the half 1st cousin once removed		
Harner, Jeremiah	Husband of the 1st cousin 3 times removed		
Harner, Sophia	2nd cousin twice removed	VIII	5
Harper, Sarah J.	Wife of the half 3rd cousin 4 times removed		
Harris, Christina	Wife of the 5th cousin once removed		
Harrison, Solomon	Husband of the 4th cousin twice removed		
Hayes, Catherine	Wife of the half 3rd cousin		
Hayes, Jemima	3rd cousin 3 times removed	XI	7
Haynes, m	Husband of the half 3rd cousin 5 times removed		
Hayr, Margaret	Wife of the half 2nd cousin once removed		
Hays, Boone	Husband of the 3rd cousin 3 times removed		
Hays, Daniel	3rd cousin 3 times removed	XI	7
Hays, Delinda	3rd cousin 3 times removed	XI	7
Hays, Elizabeth	3rd cousin 3 times removed	XI	7
Hays, Greenup	3rd cousin 3 times removed	XI	7
Hays, Jesse	3rd cousin 3 times removed	XI	7
Hays, Mahala	3rd cousin 3 times removed	XI	7
Hays, Sarah W.	4th cousin twice removed	XII	7
Hays, Susannah A.	3rd cousin 3 times removed	XI	7
Hays, William	3rd cousin 3 times removed	XI	7
Hays, William Sr.	Husband of the 2nd cousin 4 times removed		
Hazelrigg, Martha	Wife of the 2nd cousin 4 times removed		
Head, Amy W.	Wife of the half 3rd cousin once removed		
Hempel, John	Husband of the 2nd cousin twice removed		
Hendrix, George McDuffey	Husband of the 4th cousin twice removed		
Henry, Annie Rachel	6th cousin twice removed	XVI	9
Henry, Bufford Finley	Husband of the 6th cousin		
Henry, Clarence	6th cousin twice removed	XVI	9

Name	Relationship with Dwight Eisenhower	Civil	Canon
Henry, Cordell	6th cousin once removed	XV	8
Henry, Frank Bullock	6th cousin once removed	XV	8
Henry, Living	6th cousin once removed	XV	8
Henry, Living	6th cousin once removed	XV	8
Henry, Living	6th cousin once removed	XV	8
Henry, Mary Hattie	6th cousin once removed	XV	8
Henry, Sallie Bessie	6th cousin once removed	XV	8
Henry, Thomas Finley	6th cousin once removed	XV	8
Hensel, Andrew Guise	Husband of the half 1st cousin 3 times removed		
Hensel, Anna	Half 2nd cousin twice removed	VIII	5
Hensel, Emma	Half 2nd cousin twice removed	VIII	5
Hensel, Howard	Half 2nd cousin twice removed	VIII	5
Hensel, Ira	Half 2nd cousin twice removed	VIII	5
Hensel, John	Half 2nd cousin twice removed	VIII	5
Hensel, Joseph	Half 2nd cousin twice removed	VIII	5
Hensel, Lillie	Half 2nd cousin twice removed	VIII	5
Henson	Husband of the half 2nd cousin once removed		
Henton, George	Husband of the 5th great-grandaunt		
Herd, Melvina Doyle	Wife of the 5th cousin once removed		
Hern, William	Husband of the 2nd cousin 4 times removed		
Hewes, ?	Husband of the 3rd cousin once removed		
Hibner, Samuel	Husband of the 1st cousin 3 times removed		
Hicklin, Sonora Louisa	Wife of the 4th cousin twice removed		
Hilbert, John	Husband of the 3rd cousin once removed		
Hinde, Rodney Martin	Husband of the 4th cousin twice removed		
Hissey, F.J.	Husband of the 4th cousin		
Hitch, Edwin Raymond	Husband of the half 3rd cousin 3 times removed		
Hitchcock, Laura Mae	6th cousin once removed	XV	8
Hitchcock, Storm	Husband of the 6th cousin		
Hite, Archibald Talbert	Husband of the 3rd cousin 3 times removed		
Hobs, Martha J.	Wife of the half 3rd cousin once removed		
Hoffman, Ada	2nd cousin twice removed	VIII	5
Hoffman, Adam	2nd cousin twice removed	VIII	5
Hoffman, Child	2nd cousin twice removed	VIII	5
Hoffman, Elizabeth	Wife of the 2nd great-granduncle		
Hoffman, Elmira	2nd cousin twice removed	VIII	5
Hoffman, George	2nd cousin twice removed	VIII	5
Hoffman, Isaac	2nd cousin twice removed	VIII	5
Hoffman, Jacob D.	Husband of the 1st cousin 3 times removed		
Hoffman, Maria	Wife of the 4th cousin twice removed		
Hoffman, Rebecca	2nd cousin twice removed	VIII	5
Hoffman, Rebecca	Wife of the 1st cousin twice removed		
Hoffman, Sarah	2nd cousin twice removed	VIII	5
Hoke, Catharine	Wife of the 2nd cousin twice removed		
Holliday, James	Husband of the 3rd cousin 3 times removed		
Holm, m	Husband of the half 3rd cousin 5 times removed		
Hoover, Alfred	2nd cousin once removed	VII	4
Hoover, Alice	Wife of the half 1st cousin once removed		
Hoover, Charles	3rd cousin	VIII	4
Hoover, Elizabeth	2nd cousin once removed	VII	4
Hoover, Ella	2nd cousin once removed	VII	4
Hoover, Ellen	3rd cousin	VIII	4
Hoover, Henry	3rd cousin once removed	IX	5
Hoover, Jacob	2nd cousin once removed	VII	4
Hoover, Jacob	3rd cousin	VIII	4
Hoover, Jacob	Husband of the 1st cousin twice removed		
Hoover, Lloyd	2nd cousin once removed	VII	4
Hoover, Lloyd	3rd cousin	VIII	4
Hoover, Mark	3rd cousin once removed	IX	5
Hoover, Mary	3rd cousin once removed	IX	5
Hoover, Sallie	3rd cousin once removed	IX	5
Hoover, Solomon	2nd cousin once removed	VII	4
Hoover, William	3rd cousin	VIII	4
Hopple, Mary	Wife of the 1st cousin 3 times removed		
Houser, ?	6th cousin once removed	XV	8
Houser, ?	6th cousin once removed	XV	8
Houser, ?	6th cousin once removed	XV	8
Houser, ?	6th cousin once removed	XV	8
Houser, ?	6th cousin once removed	XV	8
Houser, ?	6th cousin once removed	XV	8
Houser, ?	6th cousin once removed	XV	8

Name	Relationship with Dwight Eisenhower	Civil	Canon
Houser, Abraham	Husband of the 2nd cousin 3 times removed		
Houser, Catherine	3rd cousin twice removed	X	6
Houser, Imogene	6th cousin once removed	XV	8
Houser, John Wesley	Husband of the 6th cousin		
Houser, Laura Lee	6th cousin once removed	XV	8
Houser, Lilly	6th cousin once removed	XV	8
Houser, Margaretha	3rd cousin twice removed	X	6
Houser, Martha Ellen	6th cousin once removed	XV	8
Houser, Nancy	3rd cousin twice removed	X	6
Houser, Samuel	3rd cousin twice removed	X	6
Houser, Wendell Irving	6th cousin once removed	XV	8
Howell, Coanza Burilla	5th cousin once removed	XIII	7
Howell, Debrah	Wife of the 4th great-granduncle		
Howell, Nancy	Wife of the 3rd cousin 3 times removed		
Howell, Pizarro	4th cousin twice removed	XII	7
Howell, Thomas W.	Husband of the 3rd cousin 3 times removed		
Hoy, Jacob	Husband of the 1st cousin 3 times removed		
Hudgens	6th cousin	XIV	7
Hudgens	6th cousin	XIV	7
Hudgens, Allie	6th cousin	XIV	7
Hudgens, Alvie	6th cousin	XIV	7
Hudgens, Amanda	5th cousin once removed	XIII	7
Hudgens, Amy	5th cousin once removed	XIII	7
Hudgens, Annie	5th cousin once removed	XIII	7
Hudgens, Annie Juanita	6th cousin once removed	XV	8
Hudgens, Bell	6th cousin	XIV	7
Hudgens, Byrd Murry	6th cousin	XIV	7
Hudgens, Carl	4th cousin twice removed	XII	7
Hudgens, Catherine	4th cousin twice removed	XII	7
Hudgens, Charles	5th cousin once removed	XIII	7
Hudgens, Charles	5th cousin once removed	XIII	7
Hudgens, Charles L.	6th cousin	XIV	7
Hudgens, Charley	5th cousin once removed	XIII	7
Hudgens, Clarence Hugh	6th cousin	XIV	7
Hudgens, Clumindia	6th cousin	XIV	7
Hudgens, Crocket	4th cousin twice removed	XII	7
Hudgens, Daniel Boone	5th cousin once removed	XIII	7
Hudgens, Dennis Alvin	6th cousin	XIV	7
Hudgens, Dudley	5th cousin once removed	XIII	7
Hudgens, Dudley Hampton	4th cousin twice removed	XII	7
Hudgens, Edward Boone	5th cousin once removed	XIII	7
Hudgens, Edward Boone Sr.	6th cousin once removed	XV	8
Hudgens, Ella B.	6th cousin	XIV	7
Hudgens, Ellis	6th cousin	XIV	7
Hudgens, Elvin Hamilton	6th cousin	XIV	7
Hudgens, Emma	5th cousin once removed	XIII	7
Hudgens, Eva Pauline	6th cousin once removed	XV	8
Hudgens, Glen Fox	6th cousin	XIV	7
Hudgens, Hampton Hamilton	4th cousin twice removed	XII	7
Hudgens, Hampton P.	5th cousin once removed	XIII	7
Hudgens, Henry Claude	6th cousin	XIV	7
Hudgens, Hubert Maris	6th cousin once removed	XV	8
Hudgens, James	5th cousin once removed	XIII	7
Hudgens, James	Husband of the 3rd cousin 3 times removed		
Hudgens, James	5th cousin once removed	XIII	7
Hudgens, James Don	6th cousin once removed	XV	8
Hudgens, James P.	5th cousin once removed	XIII	7
Hudgens, James Rufus	6th cousin	XIV	7
Hudgens, Jane	6th cousin	XIV	7
Hudgens, John	4th cousin twice removed	XII	7
Hudgens, John	6th cousin	XIV	7
Hudgens, John Edward	5th cousin once removed	XIII	7
Hudgens, John Everette	6th cousin	XIV	7
Hudgens, Johnnie Pauline	6th cousin once removed	XV	8
Hudgens, Joseph	5th cousin once removed	XIII	7
Hudgens, Joseph	4th cousin twice removed	XII	7
Hudgens, Joseph	5th cousin once removed	XIII	7
Hudgens, Joseph	6th cousin	XIV	7
Hudgens, Joseph Franklin	6th cousin once removed	XV	8
Hudgens, Karl Dennis	6th cousin once removed	XV	8
Hudgens, Kate Dourney	5th cousin once removed	XIII	7

Name	Relationship with Dwight Eisenhower	Civil	Canon
Hudgens, Laura	6th cousin	XIV	7
Hudgens, Lee Ernest	6th cousin	XIV	7
Hudgens, Lester Boone	6th cousin	XIV	7
Hudgens, Lizzie	6th cousin	XIV	7
Hudgens, Lou	5th cousin once removed	XIII	7
Hudgens, Louverna	6th cousin	XIV	7
Hudgens, Malinda	5th cousin once removed	XIII	7
Hudgens, Malinda	6th cousin	XIV	7
Hudgens, Martha	5th cousin once removed	XIII	7
Hudgens, Mary	6th cousin	XIV	7
Hudgens, Mary A.	5th cousin once removed	XIII	7
Hudgens, Mary E.	6th cousin	XIV	7
Hudgens, Maude	6th cousin	XIV	7
Hudgens, Merrill Doyle	5th cousin once removed	XIII	7
Hudgens, Nicholas	6th cousin	XIV	7
Hudgens, Obe	5th cousin once removed	XIII	7
Hudgens, Ollie Lee	6th cousin	XIV	7
Hudgens, Rachael	5th cousin once removed	XIII	7
Hudgens, Robbard	6th cousin	XIV	7
Hudgens, Robert	6th cousin	XIV	7
Hudgens, Robert	5th cousin once removed	XIII	7
Hudgens, Roy Merrell	6th cousin	XIV	7
Hudgens, Sally	5th cousin once removed	XIII	7
Hudgens, Sarah A.	5th cousin once removed	XIII	7
Hudgens, Sarah Sally	4th cousin twice removed	XII	7
Hudgens, Shelby	4th cousin twice removed	XII	7
Hudgens, Shelby	5th cousin once removed	XIII	7
Hudgens, Shirley	5th cousin once removed	XIII	7
Hudgens, Stanton	5th cousin once removed	XIII	7
Hudgens, Taylor	5th cousin once removed	XIII	7
Hudgens, Vance H.	5th cousin once removed	XIII	7
Hudgens, Waman	5th cousin once removed	XIII	7
Hudgens, William	4th cousin twice removed	XII	7
Hudgens, William H.	5th cousin once removed	XIII	7
Hudgens, William M.	6th cousin	XIV	7
Hudgens, William S.	5th cousin once removed	XIII	7
Hudgens, Willie Hampton	6th cousin	XIV	7
Hudgens, Willie Shelva	6th cousin once removed	XV	8
Hudgens, Zachery Taylor	5th cousin once removed	XIII	7
Hudson, ?	Half 3rd cousin 6 times removed	XIV	10
Hudson, ?	Half 3rd cousin 6 times removed	XIV	10
Hudson, m	Husband of the half 3rd cousin 5 times removed		
Hugens, Daisie	6th cousin	XIV	7
Hulen, Georgia Lee	Wife of the half 3rd cousin 3 times removed		
Hull	Wife of the half 2nd cousin once removed		
Hulse, Elizabeth	Wife of the 3rd cousin 3 times removed		
Hunsucker, Margaret	Wife of the half 2nd cousin once removed		
Hunt, Mary	Wife of the 2nd cousin 4 times removed		
Hunter, Amanda Jane	4th cousin twice removed	XII	7
Hunter, Amy	5th cousin once removed	XIII	7
Hunter, Barger	4th cousin twice removed	XII	7
Hunter, Betty	5th cousin once removed	XIII	7
Hunter, Braxton Douglas	5th cousin once removed	XIII	7
Hunter, Braxton Douglas	4th cousin twice removed	XII	7
Hunter, Caroline Frances	4th cousin twice removed	XII	7
Hunter, Charles	4th cousin twice removed	XII	7
Hunter, Clarence Pleasant	5th cousin once removed	XIII	7
Hunter, Crocket	5th cousin once removed	XIII	7
Hunter, Cynthia	5th cousin once removed	XIII	7
Hunter, Daniel	4th cousin twice removed	XII	7
Hunter, Dudley	5th cousin once removed	XIII	7
Hunter, Dudley	3rd cousin 3 times removed	XI	7
Hunter, Dudley	4th cousin twice removed	XII	7
Hunter, Edward Boone	4th cousin twice removed	XII	7
Hunter, Edward Boone	5th cousin once removed	XIII	7
Hunter, Eliza	5th cousin once removed	XIII	7
Hunter, Elizabeth	4th cousin twice removed	XII	7
Hunter, Elizabeth	4th cousin twice removed	XII	7
Hunter, Henry Ward Beecher	4th cousin twice removed	XII	7
Hunter, Hugh Dudley	4th cousin twice removed	XII	7
Hunter, Jepsee	3rd cousin 3 times removed	XI	7

Name	Relationship with Dwight Eisenhower	Civil	Canon
Hunter, Joe	5th cousin once removed	XIII	7
Hunter, Joe	4th cousin twice removed	XII	7
Hunter, John	5th cousin once removed	XIII	7
Hunter, John W.	6th cousin	XIV	7
Hunter, Joseph	4th cousin twice removed	XII	7
Hunter, Joseph	3rd cousin 3 times removed	XI	7
Hunter, Joseph Hall	4th cousin twice removed	XII	7
Hunter, Laura	5th cousin once removed	XIII	7
Hunter, Laura May	5th cousin once removed	XIII	7
Hunter, Lucinda	5th cousin once removed	XIII	7
Hunter, Marcy	3rd cousin 3 times removed	XI	7
Hunter, Marie	5th cousin once removed	XIII	7
Hunter, Martha Ann	4th cousin twice removed	XII	7
Hunter, Mary	5th cousin once removed	XIII	7
Hunter, Mary Elizabeth	4th cousin twice removed	XII	7
Hunter, Mary H.	4th cousin twice removed	XII	7
Hunter, Mary Polly	3rd cousin 3 times removed	XI	7
Hunter, Pauline	5th cousin once removed	XIII	7
Hunter, Pauline Margaret	4th cousin twice removed	XII	7
Hunter, Pleasant Braxton	5th cousin once removed	XIII	7
Hunter, Polly	3rd cousin 3 times removed	XI	7
Hunter, Polly	4th cousin twice removed	XII	7
Hunter, Polly	5th cousin once removed	XIII	7
Hunter, Polly	4th cousin twice removed	XII	7
Hunter, Rush	4th cousin twice removed	XII	7
Hunter, Sallie	4th cousin twice removed	XII	7
Hunter, Sally Allen	5th cousin once removed	XIII	7
Hunter, Sarah	4th cousin twice removed	XII	7
Hunter, Sarah	5th cousin once removed	XIII	7
Hunter, Sarah Jane	4th cousin twice removed	XII	7
Hunter, Synda	5th cousin once removed	XIII	7
Hunter, Vance	4th cousin twice removed	XII	7
Hunter, Walter Benton	5th cousin once removed	XIII	7
Hunter, Wash	5th cousin once removed	XIII	7
Hunter, Wilburn Henry	5th cousin once removed	XIII	7
Hunter, William	3rd cousin 3 times removed	XI	7
Hunter, William	5th cousin once removed	XIII	7
Hunter, William	Husband of the 2nd cousin 4 times removed		
Hunter, William	4th cousin twice removed	XII	7
Hutchison, Louise H. B.	Wife of the half 3rd cousin 3 times removed		
Ickert, Salome E. R	3rd cousin once removed	IX	5
Ike	Self		0
Ingels, Joseph	Husband of the 2nd cousin 4 times removed		
Ison, Lettie	Wife of the 4th cousin twice removed		
Jackson, Joseph	Husband of the 3rd cousin 3 times removed		
Jackson, Joseph S.	4th cousin twice removed	XII	7
Jackson, Malinda	4th cousin twice removed	XII	7
Jackson, Martha	4th cousin twice removed	XII	7
Jackson, Mary Jane	Wife of the 3rd cousin 3 times removed		
Jacobs, Jonathan	Husband of the 1st cousin 3 times removed		
James, Grimes	3rd cousin 3 times removed	XI	7
James, Sr. Grimes	Husband of the 2nd cousin 4 times removed		
Jane, Sarah	Wife of the half 3rd cousin once removed		
Jeff	3rd cousin 3 times removed	XI	7
Jeffrey, Elvira	Wife of the 5th cousin once removed		
Jennings, Eliza Catherine	Wife of the half 3rd cousin twice removed		
John	Husband of the 1st cousin twice removed		
Johnson, Eva	Wife of the 6th cousin		
Johnson, Grace	Wife of the 1st cousin		
Johnson, Kimber	Husband of the half 3rd cousin		
Johnson, Mabel May	Wife of the half 3rd cousin once removed		
Johnson, Myra	Wife of the half 3rd cousin		
Jones, Albert Boone	5th cousin once removed	XIII	7
Jones, Ann Reid	5th cousin once removed	XIII	7
Jones, Charlotte Stevens	5th cousin once removed	XIII	7
Jones, Emma Barnum	5th cousin once removed	XIII	7
Jones, Frances	5th cousin once removed	XIII	7
Jones, Helen Breckenridge	5th cousin once removed	XIII	7
Jones, Henry William	Husband of the 4th cousin twice removed		
Jones, Henry William	5th cousin once removed	XIII	7
Jones, Icenia Linah	Wife of the 3rd cousin 3 times removed		

Name	Relationship with Dwight Eisenhower	Civil	Canon
Jones, James Hamilton	5th cousin once removed	XIII	7
Jones, Katherine Brackenridge	5th cousin once removed	XIII	7
Jones, m	Husband of the half 3rd cousin 5 times removed		
Jones, Margaret	5th cousin once removed	XIII	7
Jones, Mary	5th cousin once removed	XIII	7
Jones, Penton Francisco	5th cousin once removed	XIII	7
Jones, Price Davis	5th cousin once removed	XIII	7
Jones, Theodore Robert Sr.	Husband of the 4th cousin twice removed		
Jones, Theodore William	5th cousin once removed	XIII	7
Jones, Zeralda	5th cousin once removed	XIII	7
Justice, Mary	Wife of the 2nd cousin once removed		
Kaforth, Mary Ann	Wife of the 1st cousin 4 times removed		
Kaloeck, Nancy C.	Wife of the 4th cousin twice removed		
Kandybowski, James	Husband of the 3rd cousin 3 times removed		
Katie	Wife of the 1st cousin 3 times removed		
Kauffman, Frank S.	Husband of the half 2nd cousin twice removed		
Kauffman, Martin	Husband of the 3rd great-grandaunt		
Keen, Living	Wife of the 4th cousin 4 times removed		
Keen, Sarah Ann	Wife of the 2nd cousin once removed		
Keen, Sarah Anne	Wife of the 2nd cousin once removed		
Keifer, John Abraham	Husband of the half 1st cousin once removed		
Keiper, Katie S	Half 2nd cousin	VI	3
Keiper, Michael R	Husband of the half 1st cousin once removed		
Keiser, Elizabeth	Wife of the half 2nd cousin twice removed		
Keithly, Mary Beulah	Wife of the 6th cousin once removed		
Kellogg, Delia Ball	Wife of the 4th cousin twice removed		
Kenup, Mary	Wife of the half 1st cousin twice removed		
Kerby, ?	Half 3rd cousin 6 times removed	XIV	10
Kerby, ?	Half 3rd cousin 5 times removed	XIII	9
Kerby, ?	Half 3rd cousin 5 times removed	XIII	9
Kerby, ?	Half 3rd cousin 5 times removed	XIII	9
Kerby, Eddie	Half 3rd cousin 5 times removed	XIII	9
Kerby, Gary	Husband of the half 3rd cousin 4 times removed		
Kerby, Judy	Half 3rd cousin 5 times removed	XIII	9
Kerlin, Isaac	Husband of the half 2nd cousin twice removed		
Kettle, Anna Belle	5th cousin once removed	XIII	7
Kettle, Delia Onie	5th cousin once removed	XIII	7
Kettle, Edward	5th cousin once removed	XIII	7
Kettle, Elmer C.	5th cousin once removed	XIII	7
Kettle, Emme Eugene	5th cousin once removed	XIII	7
Kettle, Eugene	5th cousin once removed	XIII	7
Kettle, Eugene Albert	Husband of the 4th cousin twice removed		
Kettle, Israel S.	Husband of the 4th cousin twice removed		
Kettle, James E.	Husband of the 4th cousin twice removed		
Kettle, Lottie Ethel	5th cousin once removed	XIII	7
Kettle, Roy Menefee	5th cousin once removed	XIII	7
Kettle, Vergie Florence	5th cousin once removed	XIII	7
Kettle, Willie	5th cousin once removed	XIII	7
Key, Francis	Husband of the 3rd cousin 3 times removed		
Kiehner, Margaret Rebecca	Wife of the great-granduncle		
Killebrew, Matilda	Wife of the 4th cousin twice removed		
Kimbel, Rose	Wife of the 6th cousin		
Kimberly, Mary E.	Wife of the half 3rd cousin once removed		
King, Lucy	Wife of the 4th cousin twice removed		
King, Nancy Catherine	Wife of the half 2nd cousin once removed		
Kirkly	Husband of the 3rd cousin 3 times removed		
Kitty	4th cousin twice removed	XII	7
Kitzmiller, Blanche Emmeta	Wife of the half 2nd cousin		
Kleinan, Hannah	Wife of the half great-granduncle		
Kline, Anna	Wife of the 2nd great-granduncle		
Klinger, Wellington	Husband of the half 1st cousin once removed		
Knepley, Conrad	Husband of the great-grandaunt		
Knepley, Jacob	1st cousin twice removed	VI	4
Knepley, Jefferson	1st cousin twice removed	VI	4
Knepley, Mary	1st cousin twice removed	VI	4
Knepley, William	1st cousin twice removed	VI	4
Knight, Sarah Ann	Wife of the half 3rd cousin once removed		
Knorr, Aaron D	Husband of the 2nd cousin once removed		
Knorr, Cindy Lee	3rd cousin 3 times removed	XI	7
Knorr, Edwin Frances	3rd cousin twice removed	X	6

Name	Relationship with Dwight Eisenhower	Civil	Canon
Knorr, Edwin Frances	3rd cousin 3 times removed	XI	7
Knorr, Edwin Frosten	Husband of the 3rd cousin once removed		
Knorr, Julie Ann	Wife of the 2nd cousin once removed		
Knorr, Karen Kay	3rd cousin twice removed	X	6
Knorr, Susan Alice	3rd cousin	VIII	4
Knorr, Vicki	3rd cousin 3 times removed	XI	7
Knorr, William	Husband of the 3rd cousin once removed		
Kocher, Sarah J.	Wife of the half 1st cousin 3 times removed		
Koppenhaver, Edward E	Husband of the 2nd cousin twice removed		
Koppenhoffer, Amos	Husband of the 2nd cousin once removed		
Koppenhoffer, Cora Agnes	3rd cousin	VIII	4
Krebs, Christine Maria	Wife of the half 1st cousin twice removed		
Krieder, Elizabeth	2nd cousin 3 times removed	IX	6
Krieder, Esther	2nd cousin 3 times removed	IX	6
Krieder, Henry	2nd cousin 3 times removed	IX	6
Krieder, John	2nd cousin 3 times removed	IX	6
Krieder, Joseph	Husband of the 1st cousin 4 times removed		
Krieder, Joseph	2nd cousin 3 times removed	IX	6
Krieder, Lydia	2nd cousin 3 times removed	IX	6
Krieder, Mary	2nd cousin 3 times removed	IX	6
Kupper	Wife of the great-granduncle		
Kupper, Catherine	Wife of the great-granduncle		
L., Ella	Wife of the 5th cousin once removed		
L., Lily	Wife of the 5th cousin once removed		
Lahr, Helen	Wife of the half 3rd cousin 4 times removed		
Lambert, m	Husband of the 2nd cousin twice removed		
Lambert, Richard S	Husband of the half 1st cousin once removed		
Lamme, Czarina	4th cousin twice removed	XII	7
Lamme, Hulda	4th cousin twice removed	XII	7
Lamme, William T.	Husband of the 3rd cousin 3 times removed		
Lanigan, Marie	Wife of the half 2nd cousin once removed		
Lantz, Esther	Wife of the half 1st cousin twice removed		
Lark, Emma Jane Susanna	Wife of the 2nd cousin once removed		
Lau, Living	Husband of the 4th cousin 3 times removed		
Lau, Living	4th cousin 4 times removed	XIV	9
Lawhorn, Lawson A.	Husband of the 5th cousin once removed		
Leake, Janie Hammit	Wife of the 6th cousin once removed		
Leathers, Elizabeth	Wife of the 2nd cousin 3 times removed		
Leathers, Margaret	Wife of the 2nd cousin 3 times removed		
Lebo, Mathilda	Wife of the half granduncle		
Lehman, Susannah	Wife of the 3rd great-grandfather		
Leid, Malinda	Wife of the 3rd cousin once removed		
Leininger, George	Husband of the great-grandaunt		
Leininger, George	1st cousin twice removed	VI	4
Lenker, Catherine	Wife of the 1st cousin twice removed		
Lenker, Catherine	Wife of the 1st cousin twice removed		
Lenker, Hannah	Wife of the 1st cousin 3 times removed		
Lenker, Lydia A	Wife of the 2nd cousin twice removed		
Lentz, Allen C.	Half 2nd cousin	VI	3
Lentz, Annie Louise	Half 2nd cousin	VI	3
Lentz, Charles Warren	Half 2nd cousin	VI	3
Lentz, Clair Riegle	Half 2nd cousin once removed	VII	4
Lentz, Daniel C.	Half 2nd cousin	VI	3
Lentz, Edwin	Half 2nd cousin	VI	3
Lentz, Eugene Clinton	Half 2nd cousin once removed	VII	4
Lentz, Henry H.	Half 2nd cousin	VI	3
Lentz, James Edwin	Half 2nd cousin	VI	3
Lentz, John Calvin	Husband of the half 1st cousin once removed		
Lentz, John Philip	Half 2nd cousin	VI	3
Lentz, Joseph Harry	Half 2nd cousin	VI	3
Lentz, Katie E.	Half 2nd cousin	VI	3
Lentz, Paul Jacob	Half 2nd cousin once removed	VII	4
Lentz, Raymond Andrew	Half 2nd cousin	VI	3
Lentz, Richard Riegle	Half 2nd cousin once removed	VII	4
Lentz, Robert Calvin	Half 2nd cousin once removed	VII	4
Lentz, William Benjamin	Half 2nd cousin once removed	VII	4
Leopald, Elizabeth L.	Wife of the half 2nd cousin once removed		
Lerch	Wife of the 2nd cousin once removed		
Lesher, Anna	Wife of the half 1st cousin once removed		
Lesher, Samuel	Husband of the half 3rd cousin once removed		
Lewis, Minnie Pearl	Wife of the 6th cousin		

Name	Relationship with Dwight Eisenhower	Civil	Canon
Lewis, Sarah Griffin	Wife of the 2nd cousin 4 times removed		
Lightner, Lavina	Wife of the half 1st cousin 3 times removed		
Lingle, Virginia Arlene	Wife of the half 3rd cousin 4 times removed		
Link, Elizabeth Ida	Grandmother	II	2
Linville, Nancy Ann	Wife of the 1st cousin 5 times removed		
Lionberger, John	Husband of the 3rd great-grandaunt		
Little, Elizabeth	Wife of the 2nd cousin 4 times removed		
Little, Henry	Husband of the 4th cousin twice removed		
Living	Half 2nd cousin 3 times removed	IX	6
LIVING	Wife of the half 2nd cousin once removed		
LIVING	Wife of the half 2nd cousin once removed		
Living	Half 2nd cousin 3 times removed	IX	6
Living	Half 2nd cousin 3 times removed	IX	6
Living	Half 2nd cousin 3 times removed	IX	6
Living	Half 2nd cousin 3 times removed	IX	6
Living	Husband of the half 2nd cousin 3 times removed		
Living	Half 2nd cousin 4 times removed	X	7
Living	Half 2nd cousin 4 times removed	X	7
Living	Half 2nd cousin 4 times removed	X	7
LIVING	Half 2nd cousin once removed	VII	4
Living	Half 2nd cousin 4 times removed	X	7
LIVING	Wife of the half 2nd cousin once removed		
Living	Half 2nd cousin twice removed	VIII	5
LIVING	Wife of the half 2nd cousin once removed		
LIVING	Wife of the half 2nd cousin once removed		
LIVING	Wife of the half 2nd cousin once removed		
LIVING	Wife of the half 2nd cousin once removed		
LIVING	Wife of the half 2nd cousin once removed		
Living	Wife of the 4th cousin 4 times removed		
Living	Wife of the 4th cousin 3 times removed		
Lizzie	Wife of the 6th cousin		
Lizzie	Half 1st cousin once removed	V	3
Locke, Rebecca	Wife of the 2nd cousin 4 times removed		
Loftis, Dimple	Wife of the 6th cousin once removed		
Long, Anna	Wife of the uncle		
Lowe, Allen D.	Husband of the half 3rd cousin 3 times removed		
Lowe, Amanda Jane	Wife of the half 3rd cousin once removed		
Lowery, Alice	Wife of the 4th cousin twice removed		
Lowery, Amy Emma Gist	Wife of the 3rd cousin 3 times removed		
Lowery, Crocket	5th cousin once removed	XIII	7
Lowery, D. Charles	5th cousin once removed	XIII	7
Lowery, Dudley	5th cousin once removed	XIII	7
Lowery, Eli	6th cousin	XIV	7
Lowery, James B.	Husband of the 4th cousin twice removed		
Lowery, Jimmie	6th cousin	XIV	7
Lowery, Seth	5th cousin once removed	XIII	7
Lowry, D. Charles Sr.	Husband of the 4th cousin twice removed		
Lowry, Mary	5th cousin once removed	XIII	7
Lucinda	Wife of the half 3rd cousin		
Lyddon, Alta May	Wife of the half 3rd cousin twice removed		
Machamer, Charles A.	Husband of the 3rd cousin		
Machamer, Charlotte M.	3rd cousin once removed	IX	5
Magrill, Alice Evelyn	Wife of the 6th cousin once removed		
Mann, Durcilla	Wife of the half 2nd cousin once removed		
Mann, Lyda	Wife of the 5th cousin once removed		
Marckley, John	Husband of the 2nd cousin twice removed		
Margaret	Wife of the 4th cousin twice removed		
Margaret, Rebecca	Wife of the 2nd cousin twice removed		
Margaretha	1st cousin twice removed	VI	4
Martin, Betsey	Wife of the 3rd cousin 3 times removed		
Martin, Emma Elizabeth	Wife of the 6th cousin		
Martin, Noah B	Husband of the 1st cousin		
Martz, Harriet L.	Wife of the 2nd cousin once removed		
Mary	Wife of the 3rd cousin 3 times removed		
Mather, Richard	5th great-grandfather	VII	7
Matter, Aaron	2nd cousin twice removed	VIII	5
Matter, Aaron Franklin	3rd cousin	VIII	4
Matter, Abraham	1st cousin twice removed	VI	4
Matter, Adam	Great-granduncle	V	4
Matter, Adda Louella	3rd cousin once removed	IX	5
Matter, Amanda	2nd cousin once removed	VII	4

Name	Relationship with Dwight Eisenhower	Civil	Canon
Matter, Amos	3rd cousin once removed	IX	5
Matter, Andrew G Curton	Half 1st cousin once removed	V	3
Matter, Ann Elizabeth	3rd cousin once removed	IX	5
Matter, Anna	1st cousin twice removed	VI	4
Matter, Anna Catharina	Great-grandaunt	V	4
Matter, Anna Catharine	1st cousin 3 times removed	VII	5
Matter, Anna Catherina	Great-grandaunt	V	4
Matter, Anna Maria	Great-grandaunt	V	4
Matter, Anna Maria	1st cousin 3 times removed	VII	5
Matter, Anna Maria	1st cousin twice removed	VI	4
Matter, Anna Maria	3rd cousin once removed	IX	5
Matter, Arthur Guy	3rd cousin once removed	IX	5
Matter, Balthasar	Great-granduncle	V	4
Matter, Balthaser	1st cousin 3 times removed	VII	5
Matter, Benjamin	1st cousin twice removed	VI	4
Matter, Benjamin	3rd cousin once removed	IX	5
Matter, Benjamin Franklin	3rd cousin once removed	IX	5
Matter, Benneville	1st cousin twice removed	VI	4
Matter, Caleb Wheeler	Half 1st cousin once removed	V	3
Matter, Carrie Minerva	3rd cousin	VIII	4
Matter, Catharina	Half grandaunt	IV	3
Matter, Catherine	1st cousin 3 times removed	VII	5
Matter, Catherine	Great-grandaunt	V	4
Matter, Catherine	2nd cousin twice removed	VIII	5
Matter, Charles	1st cousin twice removed	VI	4
Matter, Christian	1st cousin 3 times removed	VII	5
Matter, Christian	2nd cousin once removed	VII	4
Matter, Christianna	1st cousin twice removed	VI	4
Matter, Christopher	1st cousin twice removed	VI	4
Matter, Christopher	1st cousin twice removed	VI	4
Matter, Clara Ida Adeline	3rd cousin	VIII	4
Matter, Clinton Jodus	Half 1st cousin once removed	V	3
Matter, Conrad	2nd cousin twice removed	VIII	5
Matter, Cora Ann	3rd cousin once removed	IX	5
Matter, Cunrath	1st cousin twice removed	VI	4
Matter, Daniel	Husband of the 1st cousin 3 times removed		
Matter, Daniel	1st cousin 3 times removed	VII	5
Matter, Daniel	1st cousin twice removed	VI	4
Matter, Daniel	2nd cousin once removed	VII	4
Matter, Daniel D	2nd cousin once removed	VII	4
Matter, David	1st cousin twice removed	VI	4
Matter, David J	2nd cousin twice removed	VIII	5
Matter, Delila	1st cousin twice removed	VI	4
Matter, Edward	1st cousin twice removed	VI	4
Matter, Elias Elsworth	3rd cousin once removed	IX	5
Matter, Elisabeth	Great-grandaunt	V	4
Matter, Elisabeth	1st cousin 3 times removed	VII	5
Matter, Elisabeth	1st cousin twice removed	VI	4
Matter, Elisabeth	Half grandaunt	IV	3
Matter, Elisabeth	1st cousin twice removed	VI	4
Matter, Elisabeth	1st cousin twice removed	VI	4
Matter, Elizabeth	2nd cousin twice removed	VIII	5
Matter, Elizabeth	1st cousin 3 times removed	VII	5
Matter, Elizabeth	4th great-grandmother	VI	6
Matter, Elizabeth	1st cousin twice removed	VI	4
Matter, Elizabeth	2nd cousin twice removed	VIII	5
Matter, Ellen Elizabeth	2nd cousin once removed	VII	4
Matter, Emanuel	1st cousin twice removed	VI	4
Matter, Emanuel	3rd cousin once removed	IX	5
Matter, Emma Iona	3rd cousin once removed	IX	5
Matter, Estella Hannah	3rd cousin once removed	IX	5
Matter, Eva	Great-grandaunt	V	4
Matter, George	1st cousin 3 times removed	VII	5
Matter, George Daniel	Great-granduncle	V	4
Matter, George Washington	Half granduncle	IV	3
Matter, Georgianna	Great-grandaunt	V	4
Matter, Gideon	2nd cousin twice removed	VIII	5
Matter, Hannah	1st cousin 3 times removed	VII	5
Matter, Hannah Elizabeth	Half 1st cousin once removed	V	3
Matter, Hannah Lorena	3rd cousin once removed	IX	5
Matter, Heinrich	Great-grandfather	III	3

Name	Relationship with Dwight Eisenhower	Civil	Canon
Matter, Henry	3rd cousin once removed	IX	5
Matter, Henry	3rd cousin	VIII	4
Matter, Ida Alice	3rd cousin once removed	IX	5
Matter, Infant	Great-grandaunt/uncle	V	4
Matter, Infant A	Half 1st cousin once removed	V	3
Matter, Infant B	Half 1st cousin once removed	V	3
Matter, Isaac Jacob	1st cousin 3 times removed	VII	5
Matter, Isaac Newton	3rd cousin once removed	IX	5
Matter, Isaac Walter	3rd cousin	VIII	4
Matter, Isabella Amelia	Half 1st cousin once removed	V	3
Matter, Jacob	1st cousin 3 times removed	VII	5
Matter, Jacob	Great-granduncle	V	4
Matter, Jacob	1st cousin 3 times removed	VII	5
Matter, Jacob	3rd cousin once removed	IX	5
Matter, James	2nd cousin twice removed	VIII	5
Matter, James	1st cousin twice removed	VI	4
Matter, Johann George	Great-granduncle	V	4
Matter, Johann Michael	Great-granduncle	V	4
Matter, Johann Solomon	Great-granduncle	V	4
Matter, Johannes	2nd great-granduncle	VI	5
Matter, Johannes	Great-granduncle	V	4
Matter, Johannes	1st cousin 3 times removed	VII	5
Matter, Johannes Adams	3rd great-grandfather	V	5
Matter, John	3rd cousin once removed	IX	5
Matter, John Elias	3rd cousin	VIII	4
Matter, John George	Husband of the 2nd great-grandaunt		
Matter, John L.	2nd cousin once removed	VII	4
Matter, John Michael	2nd great-grandfather	IV	4
Matter, John Philip	Husband of the 1st cousin 3 times removed		
Matter, Jonas	Great-granduncle	V	4
Matter, Jonathan	2nd cousin twice removed	VIII	5
Matter, Jonathan	2nd cousin twice removed	VIII	5
Matter, Jonathon	1st cousin twice removed	VI	4
Matter, Joseph	2nd cousin twice removed	VIII	5
Matter, Joseph	1st cousin twice removed	VI	4
Matter, Joseph	2nd cousin twice removed	VIII	5
Matter, Joseph	3rd cousin once removed	IX	5
Matter, Joseph M.	1st cousin 3 times removed	VII	5
Matter, Julia	1st cousin 3 times removed	VII	5
Matter, Katharina Anna	1st cousin twice removed	VI	4
Matter, Laura A	3rd cousin once removed	IX	5
Matter, Lavina Magdalena	1st cousin twice removed	VI	4
Matter, Leah	2nd cousin twice removed	VIII	5
Matter, Leah	1st cousin twice removed	VI	4
Matter, Leah Jane	2nd cousin once removed	VII	4
Matter, Levi	1st cousin twice removed	VI	4
Matter, Lewis	1st cousin twice removed	VI	4
Matter, Lydia Jane	2nd cousin twice removed	VIII	5
Matter, Mabel Irene	3rd cousin once removed	IX	5
Matter, Margaret	1st cousin 3 times removed	VII	5
Matter, Margaret	1st cousin twice removed	VI	4
Matter, Margareta Rebecca	Grandmother	II	2
Matter, Martin	1st cousin twice removed	VI	4
Matter, Mary	1st cousin twice removed	VI	4
Matter, Mary Ann	Half grandaunt	IV	3
Matter, Mary Anna	2nd cousin twice removed	VIII	5
Matter, Mary Ellen	Half 1st cousin once removed	V	3
Matter, Michael	1st cousin 3 times removed	VII	5
Matter, Michael	Great-granduncle	V	4
Matter, Michael	1st cousin twice removed	VI	4
Matter, Michael	2nd cousin once removed	VII	4
Matter, Michael	2nd cousin once removed	VII	4
Matter, Moses	2nd cousin twice removed	VIII	5
Matter, Moses	2nd cousin twice removed	VIII	5
Matter, Moses	Half granduncle	IV	3
Matter, Nicholas	Half granduncle	IV	3
Matter, Oliver	3rd cousin once removed	IX	5
Matter, Orson Eugene	3rd cousin once removed	IX	5
Matter, Peter	1st cousin 3 times removed	VII	5
Matter, Regina	Great-grandaunt	V	4
Matter, Reuben	1st cousin twice removed	VI	4

Name	Relationship with Dwight Eisenhower	Civil	Canon
Matter, Robert Elmer	3rd cousin once removed	IX	5
Matter, Salome	1st cousin 3 times removed	VII	5
Matter, Sara	1st cousin twice removed	VI	4
Matter, Sarah	1st cousin 3 times removed	VII	5
Matter, Sarah	2nd cousin twice removed	VIII	5
Matter, Sarah	Half grandaunt	IV	3
Matter, Sarah	1st cousin twice removed	VI	4
Matter, Sarah	2nd cousin twice removed	VIII	5
Matter, Sarah	2nd cousin once removed	VII	4
Matter, Sarah	Wife of the 2nd cousin twice removed		
Matter, Sarah Ann	1st cousin twice removed	VI	4
Matter, Sarah Ellen	2nd cousin once removed	VII	4
Matter, Simon	1st cousin twice removed	VI	4
Matter, Solomon	1st cousin twice removed	VI	4
Matter, Sophia	Great-grandaunt	V	4
Matter, Susan	2nd cousin twice removed	VIII	5
Matter, Susan	1st cousin 3 times removed	VII	5
Matter, Susan Emily	2nd cousin twice removed	VIII	5
Matter, Susanna	Great-grandaunt	V	4
Matter, Susanna	1st cousin twice removed	VI	4
Matter, Susanna	1st cousin 3 times removed	VII	5
Matter, Susanna	1st cousin twice removed	VI	4
Matter, Theodore Nathaniel	Half 1st cousin once removed	V	3
Matter, Thomas	Half granduncle	IV	3
Matter, William	1st cousin 3 times removed	VII	5
Matter, William	3rd cousin once removed	IX	5
Matter, William Elmer	3rd cousin	VIII	4
Matter, William Henry	2nd cousin twice removed	VIII	5
Matter, William Isaac	3rd cousin once removed	IX	5
Maugridge	7th great-grandfather	IX	9
Maugridge	7th great-grandmother	IX	9
Maugridge, John Milton	6th great-grandfather	VIII	8
Maugridge, Mary	5th great-grandmother	VII	7
Maurer, Ida Celara	Wife of the 3rd cousin once removed		
May, George	4th cousin twice removed	XII	7
May, Hinton	4th cousin twice removed	XII	7
May, Ira	4th cousin twice removed	XII	7
May, John	Husband of the 3rd cousin 3 times removed		
May, John	4th cousin twice removed	XII	7
May, Richard	4th cousin twice removed	XII	7
May, William	4th cousin twice removed	XII	7
Maye, Elizabeth Hannah	Wife of the 3rd cousin once removed		
Mayfield, m	Husband of the half 3rd cousin 5 times removed		
Mazzie	Wife of the 3rd cousin once removed		
Mc Clain, Mary	Wife of the 3rd cousin 3 times removed		
McAlarney, Joseph C.	Husband of the 2nd cousin twice removed		
McAlarney, M. Wilson	Husband of the 2nd cousin twice removed		
McCorkle, Margaret	Wife of the half 2nd cousin once removed		
McCormick, Cydia	Wife of the 5th cousin once removed		
McCoy, B. H.	Husband of the 3rd cousin once removed		
McCoy, Hugh Franklin	Husband of the half 2nd cousin once removed		
McCoy, Martin Lee	Half 3rd cousin	VIII	4
McCoy, Mary	Wife of the 3rd cousin 3 times removed		
McCoy, Matilda Josephine	Half 3rd cousin	VIII	4
McCoy, Washington	Half 3rd cousin	VIII	4
McDonald, Nancy Anna	Wife of the great-granduncle		
McGlasson, Abslom	Husband of the 5th cousin once removed		
McGlasson, Emma J.	Wife of the 5th cousin once removed		
McKay, Bessie	Half 3rd cousin once removed	IX	5
McKay, James E.	Husband of the half 2nd cousin twice removed		
McKay, Jennie E.	Half 3rd cousin once removed	IX	5
McKinney, Catherine	Wife of the 2nd cousin 3 times removed		
McLallen, Orron Treat	Husband of the 5th cousin once removed		
McMains, Alta Nina	Wife of the half 3rd cousin 3 times removed		
McMullen, J. A.	Husband of the 4th cousin twice removed		
McNabb, William Alexander	Husband of the half 2nd cousin once removed		
McQuitty, Almirinda	4th cousin twice removed	XII	7
McQuitty, David	Husband of the 3rd cousin 3 times removed		
Mercer, Louisa Jane	Wife of the half 3rd cousin twice removed		
Merchant, Martha Jane	Wife of the 3rd cousin 3 times removed		
Meredith, Maggie	Wife of the 5th cousin once removed		

Name	Relationship with Dwight Eisenhower	Civil	Canon
Merwin, Henry C.	Husband of the 5th cousin once removed		
Metcalf, Uri	Wife of the half 3rd cousin once removed		
Meyer, Christian	Husband of the half great-grandaunt		
Meyer, Hannah	Wife of the 2nd cousin twice removed		
Michael, Lydia	Wife of the 1st cousin 3 times removed		
Michalko, Mary	Wife of the 4th cousin twice removed		
Mikel	Half 3rd cousin twice removed	X	6
Mikel	Half 3rd cousin twice removed	X	6
Mikel	Half 3rd cousin twice removed	X	6
Mikel	Half 3rd cousin 3 times removed	XI	7
Mikel	Half 3rd cousin twice removed	X	6
Mikel	Half 3rd cousin once removed	IX	5
Mikel	Half 2nd cousin once removed	VII	4
Mikel	Half 2nd cousin once removed	VII	4
Mikel	Half 3rd cousin 3 times removed	XI	7
Mikel	Half 3rd cousin twice removed	X	6
Mikel, ?	Half 1st cousin twice removed	VI	4
Mikel, Aaron D.	Half 3rd cousin once removed	IX	5
Mikel, Abraham Lee	Half 3rd cousin	VIII	4
Mikel, Ada Ethel	Half 3rd cousin 3 times removed	XI	7
Mikel, Alfred	Half 3rd cousin once removed	IX	5
Mikel, Angeline	Half 3rd cousin twice removed	X	6
Mikel, Anna M.	Half 3rd cousin twice removed	X	6
Mikel, Arthur Milton	Half 3rd cousin once removed	IX	5
Mikel, Barbara	Half 1st cousin twice removed	VI	4
Mikel, Barnum B.	Half 3rd cousin twice removed	X	6
Mikel, Benjamin F.	Half 3rd cousin	VIII	4
Mikel, Betheny Louisa	Half 3rd cousin	VIII	4
Mikel, Beulah	Half 3rd cousin 3 times removed	XI	7
Mikel, Carl V	Half 3rd cousin once removed	IX	5
Mikel, Casper	Half 3rd cousin twice removed	X	6
Mikel, Charity Ann	Half 3rd cousin twice removed	X	6
Mikel, Charles Edward	Half 3rd cousin twice removed	X	6
Mikel, Charles Homer	Half 3rd cousin twice removed	X	6
Mikel, Charles Milton	Half 3rd cousin	VIII	4
Mikel, Charles O.	Half 3rd cousin twice removed	X	6
Mikel, Charles W.	Half 3rd cousin once removed	IX	5
Mikel, Charlie Frank	Half 3rd cousin twice removed	X	6
Mikel, Chester Paul	Half 3rd cousin 3 times removed	XI	7
Mikel, Christian M.	Husband of the half great-grandaunt		
Mikel, Cleo Edward	Half 3rd cousin 3 times removed	XI	7
Mikel, Clora Alice	Half 3rd cousin 3 times removed	XI	7
Mikel, Cornelia H.	Half 3rd cousin twice removed	X	6
Mikel, David H.	Half 1st cousin twice removed	VI	4
Mikel, David Hugh	Half 2nd cousin once removed	VII	4
Mikel, David Hugh	Half 3rd cousin	VIII	4
Mikel, David J.	Half 3rd cousin once removed	IX	5
Mikel, Dora Bell	Half 3rd cousin twice removed	X	6
Mikel, Dorcas E	Half 3rd cousin 3 times removed	XI	7
Mikel, Edward B.	Half 3rd cousin once removed	IX	5
Mikel, Eliza	Half 3rd cousin once removed	IX	5
Mikel, Eliza Ellen	Half 3rd cousin twice removed	X	6
Mikel, Elizabeth	Half 3rd cousin twice removed	X	6
Mikel, Ellen J.	Half 3rd cousin once removed	IX	5
Mikel, Elwyn Arthur	Half 3rd cousin twice removed	X	6
Mikel, Emaline Lena	Half 3rd cousin twice removed	X	6
Mikel, Emily J.	Half 3rd cousin once removed	IX	5
Mikel, Emma	Half 3rd cousin twice removed	X	6
Mikel, Emmar	Half 3rd cousin once removed	IX	5
Mikel, Eugene	Half 3rd cousin 3 times removed	XI	7
Mikel, Eva Adelma	Half 3rd cousin 3 times removed	XI	7
Mikel, Evan L	Half 3rd cousin 3 times removed	XI	7
Mikel, Florence Eva	Half 3rd cousin twice removed	X	6
Mikel, Frank	Half 3rd cousin twice removed	X	6
Mikel, Fred Caswell	Half 3rd cousin once removed	IX	5
Mikel, Fred Lane	Half 3rd cousin once removed	IX	5
Mikel, G. W.	Half 3rd cousin once removed	IX	5
Mikel, Generva E.	Half 3rd cousin twice removed	X	6
Mikel, Genie M.	Half 3rd cousin 3 times removed	XI	7
Mikel, George Evert	Half 3rd cousin twice removed	X	6
Mikel, George M.	Half 3rd cousin once removed	IX	5

Name	Relationship with Dwight Eisenhower	Civil	Canon
Mikel, George Washington	Half 3rd cousin twice removed	X	6
Mikel, George William	Half 3rd cousin twice removed	X	6
Mikel, Gladys Melvina	Half 3rd cousin twice removed	X	6
Mikel, Grace	Half 3rd cousin twice removed	X	6
Mikel, Hannah	Half 2nd cousin once removed	VII	4
Mikel, Harry	Half 3rd cousin twice removed	X	6
Mikel, Henry Samuel	Half 3rd cousin twice removed	X	6
Mikel, Homer W	Half 3rd cousin twice removed	X	6
Mikel, Howley B.	Half 3rd cousin twice removed	X	6
Mikel, Hugh D.	Half 3rd cousin once removed	IX	5
Mikel, Hugh Frank	Half 3rd cousin	VIII	4
Mikel, Ida Belle	Half 3rd cousin twice removed	X	6
Mikel, James	Half 3rd cousin twice removed	X	6
Mikel, James	Half 3rd cousin	VIII	4
Mikel, James F.	Half 3rd cousin 3 times removed	XI	7
Mikel, James Harvey	Half 3rd cousin once removed	IX	5
Mikel, James King	Half 3rd cousin	VIII	4
Mikel, James P.	Half 3rd cousin	VIII	4
Mikel, James Purvis	Half 3rd cousin once removed	IX	5
Mikel, James T.	Half 3rd cousin once removed	IX	5
Mikel, James T.	Half 3rd cousin twice removed	X	6
Mikel, Jean Lurena	Half 3rd cousin twice removed	X	6
Mikel, Jesse Boone	Half 3rd cousin twice removed	X	6
Mikel, Jesse William	Half 3rd cousin twice removed	X	6
Mikel, Jimmie	Half 3rd cousin once removed	IX	5
Mikel, John	Half 1st cousin twice removed	VI	4
Mikel, John	Half 3rd cousin	VIII	4
Mikel, John	Half 3rd cousin twice removed	X	6
Mikel, John C.	Half 3rd cousin once removed	IX	5
Mikel, John D.	Half 3rd cousin twice removed	X	6
Mikel, John H.	Half 3rd cousin twice removed	X	6
Mikel, John L.	Half 3rd cousin once removed	IX	5
Mikel, John Noah	Half 3rd cousin once removed	IX	5
Mikel, John Noah	Half 3rd cousin twice removed	X	6
Mikel, John S.	Half 3rd cousin	VIII	4
Mikel, John S.	Half 2nd cousin once removed	VII	4
Mikel, Joseph	Half 3rd cousin	VIII	4
Mikel, Joseph	Half 3rd cousin twice removed	X	6
Mikel, Joseph A	Half 3rd cousin once removed	IX	5
Mikel, Joseph N.	Half 3rd cousin	VIII	4
Mikel, Joseph P.	Half 3rd cousin once removed	IX	5
Mikel, Judith Isabell	Half 3rd cousin	VIII	4
Mikel, Kenneth	Half 3rd cousin twice removed	X	6
Mikel, Laura	Half 3rd cousin once removed	IX	5
Mikel, Lela Clifton	Half 3rd cousin once removed	IX	5
Mikel, Leslie L	Half 3rd cousin 3 times removed	XI	7
Mikel, Levander L.	Half 3rd cousin once removed	IX	5
Mikel, Lewis	Half 3rd cousin once removed	IX	5
Mikel, Linda	Half 3rd cousin once removed	IX	5
Mikel, Louise Lewellen	Half 3rd cousin twice removed	X	6
Mikel, Lousia	Half 3rd cousin 3 times removed	XI	7
Mikel, Lucinda	Half 2nd cousin once removed	VII	4
Mikel, Lucy	Half 3rd cousin once removed	IX	5
Mikel, Lucy Adeline	Half 3rd cousin once removed	IX	5
Mikel, Lydia Lottie	Half 3rd cousin twice removed	X	6
Mikel, Margaret	Half 3rd cousin once removed	IX	5
Mikel, Margaret	Half 3rd cousin twice removed	X	6
Mikel, Margaret Alvira	Half 3rd cousin once removed	IX	5
Mikel, Marquerette Marie	Half 3rd cousin twice removed	X	6
Mikel, Marshall	Half 3rd cousin once removed	IX	5
Mikel, Martha	Half 3rd cousin once removed	IX	5
Mikel, Martha America	Half 3rd cousin	VIII	4
Mikel, Martha J.	Half 3rd cousin once removed	IX	5
Mikel, Mary Alice	Half 3rd cousin twice removed	X	6
Mikel, Mary E.	Half 3rd cousin twice removed	X	6
Mikel, Mary Frances	Half 3rd cousin twice removed	X	6
Mikel, Mary Frances	Half 3rd cousin twice removed	X	6
Mikel, Mary Jane	Half 3rd cousin	VIII	4
Mikel, Merle A	Half 3rd cousin 3 times removed	XI	7
Mikel, Millie	Half 3rd cousin once removed	IX	5
Mikel, Milton S.	Half 3rd cousin twice removed	X	6

Name	Relationship with Dwight Eisenhower	Civil	Canon
Mikel, Moses Loren	Half 2nd cousin once removed	VII	4
Mikel, Myrtie Bell	Half 3rd cousin once removed	IX	5
Mikel, Myrtle	Half 3rd cousin 3 times removed	XI	7
Mikel, Nancy J.	Half 3rd cousin	VIII	4
Mikel, Ned Edward?	Half 3rd cousin	VIII	4
Mikel, Nettie	Half 3rd cousin 3 times removed	XI	7
Mikel, Nettie J.	Half 3rd cousin twice removed	X	6
Mikel, Noah	Half 3rd cousin once removed	IX	5
Mikel, Noah W.	Half 3rd cousin once removed	IX	5
Mikel, Oda F.	Half 3rd cousin twice removed	X	6
Mikel, P. Boone	Half 3rd cousin once removed	IX	5
Mikel, Polly A.	Half 3rd cousin once removed	IX	5
Mikel, Polly Ellen	Half 3rd cousin once removed	IX	5
Mikel, Posie H.	Half 3rd cousin twice removed	X	6
Mikel, Rebecca	Half 2nd cousin once removed	VII	4
Mikel, Rebecca Adaline	Half 3rd cousin	VIII	4
Mikel, Reitty Belle	Half 3rd cousin twice removed	X	6
Mikel, Richard	Half 3rd cousin twice removed	X	6
Mikel, Ruth	Half 3rd cousin 3 times removed	XI	7
Mikel, Sally J.	Half 3rd cousin twice removed	X	6
Mikel, Samuel	Half 3rd cousin	VIII	4
Mikel, Samuel	Half 3rd cousin once removed	IX	5
Mikel, Samuel	Half 3rd cousin once removed	IX	5
Mikel, Sarah	Half 2nd cousin once removed	VII	4
Mikel, Sarah F.	Half 3rd cousin once removed	IX	5
Mikel, Sarah Jane	Half 3rd cousin twice removed	X	6
Mikel, Sidney	Half 3rd cousin	VIII	4
Mikel, Susan	Half 3rd cousin	VIII	4
Mikel, Sydney Fulton	Half 3rd cousin	VIII	4
Mikel, Theodore	Half 3rd cousin once removed	IX	5
Mikel, Thomas M.	Half 3rd cousin	VIII	4
Mikel, Traverse	Half 3rd cousin 3 times removed	XI	7
Mikel, W. A.	Half 3rd cousin once removed	IX	5
Mikel, W. M.	Half 3rd cousin twice removed	X	6
Mikel, Wallace Stanley	Half 3rd cousin twice removed	X	6
Mikel, Walter S	Half 3rd cousin twice removed	X	6
Mikel, Walter Sherman	Half 3rd cousin once removed	IX	5
Mikel, Warren	Half 3rd cousin 3 times removed	XI	7
Mikel, Warren C.	Half 3rd cousin twice removed	X	6
Mikel, Wesley	Half 3rd cousin once removed	IX	5
Mikel, Whitaker W.	Half 3rd cousin	VIII	4
Mikel, Willard L.	Half 3rd cousin twice removed	X	6
Mikel, William	Half 3rd cousin	VIII	4
Mikel, William	Half 3rd cousin once removed	IX	5
Mikel, William Albert	Half 3rd cousin twice removed	X	6
Mikel, William H.	Half 3rd cousin twice removed	X	6
Mikel, William L.	Half 3rd cousin once removed	IX	5
Mikel, William M.	Half 3rd cousin 3 times removed	XI	7
Mikel, William Silas	Half 3rd cousin	VIII	4
Mikel, Zula Hale	Half 3rd cousin once removed	IX	5
Mildenberger, Anna Catherina	4th great-grandmother	VI	6
Miller, America Susie	Wife of the half 3rd cousin once removed		
Miller, Barbara	Wife of the great-grandfather		
Miller, Benjamin	Husband of the half grandaunt		
Miller, Daniel A.	Husband of the half 1st cousin once removed		
Miller, Henry	Husband of the 1st cousin 3 times removed		
Miller, John	Half 1st cousin once removed	V	3
Miller, Lovina	Wife of the 2nd cousin once removed		
Miller, Sallie	Wife of the 3rd cousin 3 times removed		
Miller, Samuel H.	Husband of the half 3rd cousin once removed		
Miller, Sarah Elizabeth	Wife of the 3rd cousin 3 times removed		
Miller, Susan	Half 1st cousin once removed	V	3
Milliken, Sallie J.	Wife of the 5th cousin once removed		
Milton	7th great-grandfather	IX	9
Milton, Mary Susan Mean	6th great-grandmother	VIII	8
Miner, G. L.	Husband of the 4th cousin twice removed		
Minkler, Mary Lucinda	Wife of the 4th cousin twice removed		
Minnich, Aaron Frank	Husband of the 3rd cousin		
Minnich, Anna Elizabeth	3rd cousin once removed	IX	5
Minnich, Arthur Franklin	3rd cousin once removed	IX	5
Minnich, Carrie	3rd cousin	VIII	4

Name	Relationship with Dwight Eisenhower	Civil	Canon
Minnich, Catherine	1st cousin twice removed	VI	4
Minnich, Child	1st cousin twice removed	VI	4
Minnich, Daniel	1st cousin twice removed	VI	4
Minnich, Debra Louise	3rd cousin 3 times removed	XI	7
Minnich, Donald Mark	3rd cousin once removed	IX	5
Minnich, Elizabeth	1st cousin twice removed	VI	4
Minnich, Erma Estella	3rd cousin once removed	IX	5
Minnich, Harold Leroy	3rd cousin once removed	IX	5
Minnich, Johannes	1st cousin twice removed	VI	4
Minnich, John Arthur	3rd cousin twice removed	X	6
Minnich, Lynn Arlington	3rd cousin once removed	IX	5
Minnich, Marlin Oswald	3rd cousin once removed	IX	5
Minnich, Mary Frances	3rd cousin once removed	IX	5
Minnich, Myrtle Irene	3rd cousin once removed	IX	5
Minnich, Peter	Husband of the great-grandaunt		
Minnich, Peter	1st cousin twice removed	VI	4
Minnich, Robert David	3rd cousin once removed	IX	5
Minnich, Russell Leo	3rd cousin once removed	IX	5
Minnich, Sarah	1st cousin twice removed	VI	4
Minnich, Sarah Caroline	3rd cousin once removed	IX	5
Minnich, Son	3rd cousin once removed	IX	5
Minnich, William Grant	3rd cousin once removed	IX	5
Minnick, Maude May	Wife of the 5th cousin once removed		
Minton, Lucy	Half 3rd cousin	VIII	4
Minton, Martha Elizabeth	Half 3rd cousin	VIII	4
Minton, Shadrack	Husband of the half 2nd cousin once removed		
Mintum, Louisa Bethany	Wife of the half 2nd cousin once removed		
Mitchell, Isabella	Wife of the half 1st cousin twice removed		
Mitchell, Jennie Eleanor	Wife of the 3rd cousin once removed		
Mitchell, William F.	Husband of the 5th cousin once removed		
Mogridge, Jane	5th great-grandaunt	IX	8
Mogridge, Johan	5th great-grandaunt	IX	8
Mogridge, John	5th great-granduncle	IX	8
Mogridge, Nicholas	5th great-granduncle	IX	8
Molko, Mary Elizabeth	Wife of the 3rd cousin once removed		
Mollie	Wife of the half 3rd cousin twice removed		
Moore, Leanna Jane	Wife of the 5th cousin once removed		
Moore, Tom F.	Husband of the 4th cousin twice removed		
Moretz, Ada Belle	Wife of the half 3rd cousin once removed		
Morgan, Charity	3rd cousin 3 times removed	XI	7
Morgan, Cyrus	3rd cousin 3 times removed	XI	7
Morgan, Daniel	3rd cousin 3 times removed	XI	7
Morgan, Elizabeth	3rd cousin 3 times removed	XI	7
Morgan, George	3rd cousin 3 times removed	XI	7
Morgan, Hannah	3rd cousin 3 times removed	XI	7
Morgan, John	Husband of the 2nd cousin 4 times removed		
Morgan, John	3rd cousin 3 times removed	XI	7
Morgan, Joseph	3rd cousin 3 times removed	XI	7
Morgan, Malinda	Wife of the 4th cousin twice removed		
Morgan, Martha	3rd cousin 3 times removed	XI	7
Morgan, Mary	3rd cousin 3 times removed	XI	7
Morgan, Nancy	3rd cousin 3 times removed	XI	7
Morgan, Sarah	3rd cousin 3 times removed	XI	7
Morgan, Sarah	Wife of the 4th great-granduncle		
Morgan, William	3rd cousin 3 times removed	XI	7
Morris, Mary Polly	Wife of the 2nd cousin 4 times removed		
Morris, Mary Virginia	Wife of the 6th cousin		
Moser, John	Husband of the half 1st cousin 3 times removed		
Motter, Leonard	1st cousin twice removed	VI	4
Moyer, Isaac	Husband of the 2nd cousin twice removed		
Moyer, Kenneth Richard	Husband of the half 2nd cousin once removed		
Moyer, Living	Half 2nd cousin twice removed	VIII	5
Moyer, Living	Half 2nd cousin twice removed	VIII	5
Moyer, Living	Half 2nd cousin twice removed	VIII	5
Muir, Malinda	Wife of the 3rd cousin 3 times removed		
Musser, Beulah E	1st cousin	IV	2
Musser, Christian O	Husband of the aunt		
Musser, Florence	1st cousin	IV	2
Myers, Christian	Husband of the half 2nd cousin once removed		
Myers, Henry	Half 3rd cousin	VIII	4
Myers, Mary	Wife of the half great-granduncle		

Name	Relationship with Dwight Eisenhower	Civil	Canon
Myers, Sarah	Half 3rd cousin once removed	IX	5
Nancy	Wife of the 2nd cousin 4 times removed		
Nella	1st cousin twice removed	VI	4
Neumeister, Morris L.	Husband of the 3rd cousin once removed		
New, Emily	Wife of the 3rd cousin 3 times removed		
Newcomer, ?	Half 3rd cousin 4 times removed	XII	8
Newcomer, ?	Half 3rd cousin 4 times removed	XII	8
Newcomer, Ethel L.	Half 3rd cousin 3 times removed	XI	7
Newcomer, Georgie F.	Half 3rd cousin 3 times removed	XI	7
Newcomer, Grace L.	Half 3rd cousin 3 times removed	XI	7
Newcomer, Larena Jane	Half 3rd cousin 4 times removed	XII	8
Newcomer, Minnie E.	Half 3rd cousin 3 times removed	XI	7
Newcomer, Nellie Mae	Half 3rd cousin 3 times removed	XI	7
Newcomer, Oscar	Half 3rd cousin 3 times removed	XI	7
Newcomer, William M.	Husband of the half 3rd cousin twice removed		
Newman, John	Husband of the 3rd cousin 3 times removed		
Nichols, Elizabeth	Wife of the half 2nd cousin once removed		
Niemann, Frank	Ex-husband of the half 3rd cousin 4 times removed		
Nilsson, Gunner	Husband of the 4th cousin once removed		
Nilsson, Lisa Britt	4th cousin twice removed	XII	7
Nimrod	Husband of the 3rd cousin 3 times removed		
Nincehelser, ?	Husband of the 1st cousin once removed		
Nissly, Martin	Husband of the 3rd great-grandaunt		
Nixon, Julie	Wife of the grandson		
Norris	Husband of the 3rd cousin 3 times removed		
Norris, George William	5th cousin once removed	XIII	7
Norris, James Davis	5th cousin once removed	XIII	7
Norris, Jesse Albert	5th cousin once removed	XIII	7
Norris, Katherine Ann	4th cousin twice removed	XII	7
Norris, Louisa Sophia	5th cousin once removed	XIII	7
Norris, Mary Caroline	5th cousin once removed	XIII	7
Norris, Thomas Cecil	Husband of the 4th cousin twice removed		
Norris, Thomas Cecil	5th cousin once removed	XIII	7
Norris, Thomas K.	4th cousin twice removed	XII	7
Norris, Virginia L.	5th cousin once removed	XIII	7
Novinger, Catherine	Half 1st cousin once removed	V	3
Novinger, Elizabeth	Half 1st cousin once removed	V	3
Novinger, James	Half 1st cousin once removed	V	3
Novinger, John D.	Half 1st cousin once removed	V	3
Novinger, Joseph	Husband of the half grandaunt		
Novinger, Mary Ann	Half 1st cousin once removed	V	3
Novinger, Samuel P.	Half 1st cousin once removed	V	3
Null, Elizabeth	Wife of the half 1st cousin twice removed		
Oehrle, Anna Margaret Early	Wife of the half 1st cousin twice removed		
Officer, Henrietta Lancaster	Wife of the 3rd cousin 3 times removed		
Orndorf, Sarah	Wife of the 1st cousin 3 times removed		
Orndorff, Leah Jane	Wife of the half 1st cousin once removed		
Orndorff, Lydia	Wife of the half granduncle		
Orndorff, Mary Ann	Wife of the half granduncle		
Orwig, Elizabeth E.	Wife of the 2nd cousin twice removed		
Osborn, Elizabeth Lurena	Wife of the half 3rd cousin		
Osborn, James	Husband of the half 3rd cousin		
Otis, Albert J.	5th cousin once removed	XIII	7
Otis, Elmer	Husband of the 4th cousin twice removed		
Otis, Francis I.	5th cousin once removed	XIII	7
Otis, Joseph F.	5th cousin once removed	XIII	7
Otis, Margraet M.	5th cousin once removed	XIII	7
Otis, Martha M. S.	5th cousin once removed	XIII	7
Otis, Mary B.	5th cousin once removed	XIII	7
Overcash, Rosanna	Wife of the half 2nd cousin once removed		
Paffenberger, Adam R.	2nd cousin twice removed	VIII	5
Paffenberger, Amanda	2nd cousin twice removed	VIII	5
Paffenberger, Daniel Lloyd	3rd cousin once removed	IX	5
Paffenberger, Jennie Isabelle	3rd cousin once removed	IX	5
Paffenberger, John	Husband of the 1st cousin 3 times removed		
Palmer, Sarah A.	Wife of the 2nd cousin twice removed		
Patsy	3rd cousin 3 times removed	XI	7
Patsy	3rd cousin 3 times removed	XI	7
Patsy	Wife of the half 3rd cousin		
Patterson, Mark B.	Husband of the half 3rd cousin		
Patton, Martha Jane	Wife of the 3rd cousin 3 times removed		

Name	Relationship with Dwight Eisenhower	Civil	Canon
Patton, Susannah	Wife of the 4th cousin twice removed		
Patty	Wife of the 2nd cousin 4 times removed		
Paul, Anna Catharina	Wife of the 2nd great-granduncle		
Paul, Anna Maria	Wife of the great-granduncle		
Paul, Mary Ellen	Wife of the 3rd cousin once removed		
Pearce, Nira	Wife of the half 3rd cousin twice removed		
Peek, Elkana	Husband of the 6th cousin		
Peek, Mertie Lee	6th cousin once removed	XV	8
Peffer, James	Husband of the 4th cousin 3 times removed		
Peffer, Living	4th cousin 4 times removed	XIV	9
Peffer, Living	4th cousin 4 times removed	XIV	9
Peffer, Living	4th cousin 4 times removed	XIV	9
Penn, Anna Belle	Wife of the 4th cousin twice removed		
Pennington, Daniel	2nd cousin 4 times removed	X	7
Pennington, George	Husband of the 6th cousin		
Pennington, Hubert	6th cousin once removed	XV	8
Pennington, Richard	Husband of the 1st cousin 5 times removed		
Perry, Ann	Wife of the 2nd cousin 4 times removed		
Perseponko, Margaret T.	Wife of the 3rd cousin once removed		
Phillips, Elizabeth	Wife of the 3rd cousin 3 times removed		
Phillips, Nathan	Husband of the 3rd cousin 3 times removed		
Pierson, Catherine	Wife of the 3rd cousin 3 times removed		
Plank, Catherine	Wife of the half great-granduncle		
Plowman, Charles E	Husband of the 2nd cousin twice removed		
Poffenberger, Alvin Joseph Adam	3rd cousin once removed	IX	5
Poffenberger, Flora Jennie May	4th cousin	X	5
Poffenberger, Hattie L	4th cousin	X	5
Poffenberger, June Madeline	4th cousin once removed	XI	6
Poffenberger, Roby Earl	4th cousin	X	5
Poffenberger, Roy Alvin	4th cousin	X	5
Pohren, Joyce Eleanor	Ex-wife of the half 3rd cousin 4 times removed		
Polly	3rd cousin 3 times removed	XI	7
Polly	Wife of the half 2nd cousin once removed		
Polly	Wife of the 3rd cousin 3 times removed		
Polly	Wife of the 1st cousin 4 times removed		
Poole, Carl Dick	Husband of the half 3rd cousin 4 times removed		
Poteicher, Mary	Wife of the 3rd cousin once removed		
Power, John	Husband of the 2nd cousin 4 times removed		
Power, Mary	3rd cousin 3 times removed	XI	7
Prescott, Julia	Wife of the half 2nd cousin twice removed		
Proctor, Leona Margery	Wife of the half 1st cousin once removed		
Pyke, Abraham Solomon	Half 2nd cousin	VI	3
Pyke, Anna C	Half 2nd cousin	VI	3
Pyke, Anna Jane	Half 1st cousin once removed	V	3
Pyke, Catherine E	Half 2nd cousin	VI	3
Pyke, Cora	Half 2nd cousin	VI	3
Pyke, Elizabeth	Half 2nd cousin	VI	3
Pyke, Elizabeth Rebecca	Half 1st cousin once removed	V	3
Pyke, Ernest James	Half 2nd cousin	VI	3
Pyke, Franklin Milton	Half 2nd cousin	VI	3
Pyke, Harry M	Half 2nd cousin	VI	3
Pyke, Isaac Lesher	Half 2nd cousin	VI	3
Pyke, Jacob Frederick	Half 1st cousin once removed	V	3
Pyke, Jacob Herb	Half 2nd cousin	VI	3
Pyke, John Albert	Half 2nd cousin	VI	3
Pyke, John David	Half 1st cousin once removed	V	3
Pyke, Lilly M	Half 2nd cousin	VI	3
Pyke, Mary Ann	Half 1st cousin once removed	V	3
Pyke, Rhoda Leah	Half 2nd cousin	VI	3
Pyke, Samuel	Husband of the half grandaunt		
Pyke, Samuel Frederick	Half 2nd cousin	VI	3
Pyke, Samuel Peter	Half 1st cousin once removed	V	3
Pyke, Samuel Wesley	Half 2nd cousin	VI	3
Pyke, Sarah Catherine	Half 1st cousin once removed	V	3
Pyke, Susan	Half 1st cousin once removed	V	3
Pyke, Susan	Half 2nd cousin	VI	3
Pyke, William Franklin	Half 2nd cousin	VI	3
Raeger, Emme Yama	Wife of the 3rd cousin once removed		
Rager, Edythe	Wife of the half 1st cousin once removed		
Randall, Mary Ann	Wife of the 3rd cousin 3 times removed		
Randall, Zeralda	Wife of the 3rd cousin 3 times removed		

Name	Relationship with Dwight Eisenhower	Civil	Canon
Randolph, Jackie	6th cousin twice removed	XVI	9
Randolph, Mary Ann	Wife of the 3rd cousin 3 times removed		
Rau, Eve	2nd cousin 3 times removed	IX	6
Rau, John	Husband of the 1st cousin 4 times removed		
Rau, John,Jr	2nd cousin 3 times removed	IX	6
Raven, Guy Lamond	Husband of the 6th cousin		
Ray, Horace E.	Husband of the 3rd cousin once removed		
Rebecca	Wife of the 3rd cousin 3 times removed		
Rebecca	Grandmother	II	2
Rebuck, Charles	Husband of the 3rd cousin once removed		
Reed, Jane	Wife of the half 2nd cousin once removed		
Reid, ?	Half 3rd cousin twice removed	X	6
Reid, James W.	Husband of the half 3rd cousin once removed		
Reid, Joseph H.	Half 3rd cousin twice removed	X	6
Reigel, Benjamin	Husband of the 2nd cousin twice removed		
Reigle, Susanna Catharine	Wife of the great-granduncle		
Reynolds, Catherine	Wife of the 3rd cousin 3 times removed		
Rickert, Ann J.	3rd cousin once removed	IX	5
Rickert, Benjamin F.	3rd cousin once removed	IX	5
Rickert, Elizabeth	2nd cousin twice removed	VIII	5
Rickert, Emma Jane	Wife of the 3rd cousin once removed		
Rickert, George M .	3rd cousin once removed	IX	5
Rickert, Hannah	2nd cousin twice removed	VIII	5
Rickert, Heinrich	Husband of the 1st cousin 3 times removed		
Rickert, James M.	3rd cousin once removed	IX	5
Rickert, John	2nd cousin twice removed	VIII	5
Rickert, John H.	3rd cousin once removed	IX	5
Rickert, Jonas H.	2nd cousin twice removed	VIII	5
Rickert, Lucetta	2nd cousin twice removed	VIII	5
Rickert, Mary	2nd cousin twice removed	VIII	5
Rickert, Rebecca	2nd cousin twice removed	VIII	5
Rickert, Sarah	2nd cousin twice removed	VIII	5
Rickert, William Henry	2nd cousin twice removed	VIII	5
Ridenhour, Esther	Wife of the half 2nd cousin once removed		
Rider, Catherine	Wife of the 1st cousin 4 times removed		
Riegle, Minnie Mae	Wife of the half 2nd cousin		
Ritzman, Anna Maria	1st cousin twice removed	VI	4
Ritzman, Catherine	Wife of the great-granduncle		
Ritzman, Johannes	Husband of the great-grandaunt		
Ritzman, Susanna	Wife of the 1st cousin 3 times removed		
Roach, F E	Husband of the half 1st cousin once removed		
Robbins, Zena Fern	Wife of the half 3rd cousin once removed		
Roberson, J. A.	Half 3rd cousin once removed	IX	5
Roberson, Theophilus	Husband of the half 3rd cousin		
Roberts, Maria Louise	Wife of the 3rd cousin 3 times removed		
Robinson, Annie	Wife of the half 1st cousin twice removed		
Robinson, John Thomas	Husband of the 6th cousin		
Robinson, Virginia Evelyn	6th cousin once removed	XV	8
Rock, Ollie B	Wife of the 1st cousin		
Rock, Viola C	Wife of the 1st cousin		
Rockey, Paul Warren	Husband of the 2nd cousin twice removed		
Roemer, Sophia	Wife of the half 1st cousin once removed		
Romberger, Aaron Dewilla	3rd cousin once removed	IX	5
Romberger, Adam	3rd great-granduncle	VII	6
Romberger, Adam	1st cousin 4 times removed	VIII	6
Romberger, Adam	2nd great-granduncle	VI	5
Romberger, Adam	2nd cousin 3 times removed	IX	6
Romberger, Adam	2nd cousin twice removed	VIII	5
Romberger, Albert Morris	Husband of the half 2nd cousin		
Romberger, Alfred D	2nd cousin twice removed	VIII	5
Romberger, Alice J.	3rd cousin twice removed	X	6
Romberger, Amanda	Half 1st cousin 3 times removed	VII	5
Romberger, Anna	Wife of the 3rd cousin		
Romberger, Anna Catharina	2nd great-grandaunt	VI	5
Romberger, Anna Catharina	1st cousin 3 times removed	VII	5
Romberger, Anna M.	Half 1st cousin 3 times removed	VII	5
Romberger, Anna Maria	1st cousin 4 times removed	VIII	6
Romberger, Anna Maria	2nd great-grandmother	IV	4
Romberger, Anna Maria	1st cousin 3 times removed	VII	5
Romberger, Anna Mary	1st cousin 3 times removed	VII	5
Romberger, Anna Mary	3rd cousin twice removed	X	6

Name	Relationship with Dwight Eisenhower	Civil	Canon
Romberger, Ararh	2nd cousin 3 times removed	IX	6
Romberger, Balsar	3rd cousin twice removed	X	6
Romberger, Balthaser	3rd great-grandfather	V	5
Romberger, Balthaser	2nd great-granduncle	VI	5
Romberger, Balthaser H	2nd cousin twice removed	VIII	5
Romberger, Balthaser W.	1st cousin 3 times removed	VII	5
Romberger, Baltzer	2nd great-granduncle	VI	5
Romberger, Barbara	Half 1st cousin 4 times removed	VIII	6
Romberger, Barbara	1st cousin 3 times removed	VII	5
Romberger, Barbara	2nd cousin 3 times removed	IX	6
Romberger, Bengohan	1st cousin 3 times removed	VII	5
Romberger, Benner	3rd cousin twice removed	X	6
Romberger, Betsy	2nd cousin 3 times removed	IX	6
Romberger, Caroline C.	Half 1st cousin 3 times removed	VII	5
Romberger, Catharina	1st cousin 3 times removed	VII	5
Romberger, Catherine	2nd cousin 3 times removed	IX	6
Romberger, Catherine	1st cousin 3 times removed	VII	5
Romberger, Catherine	Half 1st cousin 3 times removed	VII	5
Romberger, Catherine	3rd cousin twice removed	X	6
Romberger, Catherine	3rd cousin twice removed	X	6
Romberger, Charles	3rd cousin once removed	IX	5
Romberger, Charles E	3rd cousin once removed	IX	5
Romberger, Charles E.	2nd cousin twice removed	VIII	5
Romberger, Charles Oscar	Half 2nd cousin	VI	3
Romberger, Christian	Half 1st cousin 3 times removed	VII	5
Romberger, Christina	1st cousin 3 times removed	VII	5
Romberger, Clara Louise	2nd cousin twice removed	VIII	5
Romberger, Conrad	2nd cousin twice removed	VIII	5
Romberger, Cyrus	2nd cousin 3 times removed	IX	6
Romberger, Cyrus	2nd cousin twice removed	VIII	5
Romberger, Daniel	2nd cousin 3 times removed	IX	6
Romberger, Daniel	1st cousin 3 times removed	VII	5
Romberger, Daniel	1st cousin 3 times removed	VII	5
Romberger, Daniel	Half 1st cousin 3 times removed	VII	5
Romberger, Daniel	3rd cousin once removed	IX	5
Romberger, Daniel D.	1st cousin 3 times removed	VII	5
Romberger, Darin Eugene	3rd cousin once removed	IX	5
Romberger, David	1st cousin 3 times removed	VII	5
Romberger, David	3rd cousin twice removed	X	6
Romberger, David	3rd cousin once removed	IX	5
Romberger, Edward	Half 1st cousin 3 times removed	VII	5
Romberger, Edward	2nd cousin twice removed	VIII	5
Romberger, Elisabeth	1st cousin 3 times removed	VII	5
Romberger, Elisabeth	Half 1st cousin 4 times removed	VIII	6
Romberger, Elisabeth	2nd cousin 3 times removed	IX	6
Romberger, Elisabeth	3rd cousin twice removed	X	6
Romberger, Elizabeth	1st cousin 4 times removed	VIII	6
Romberger, Elizabeth	2nd cousin 3 times removed	IX	6
Romberger, Elizabeth	1st cousin 3 times removed	VII	5
Romberger, Elizabeth	2nd cousin 3 times removed	IX	6
Romberger, Elizabeth	1st cousin 3 times removed	VII	5
Romberger, Elizabeth	3rd cousin twice removed	X	6
Romberger, Ellen	3rd cousin twice removed	X	6
Romberger, Emanuel	Half 1st cousin 3 times removed	VII	5
Romberger, Emma C	3rd cousin once removed	IX	5
Romberger, Esther	2nd cousin 3 times removed	IX	6
Romberger, Eva	1st cousin 4 times removed	VIII	6
Romberger, Eva	1st cousin 3 times removed	VII	5
Romberger, Eva	2nd cousin 3 times removed	IX	6
Romberger, Eva Margaret	1st cousin 3 times removed	VII	5
Romberger, Fanny	2nd cousin 3 times removed	IX	6
Romberger, Fanny	2nd cousin 3 times removed	IX	6
Romberger, Franklin	3rd cousin twice removed	X	6
Romberger, George	3rd cousin twice removed	X	6
Romberger, George	2nd cousin 3 times removed	IX	6
Romberger, George B.	2nd cousin 3 times removed	IX	6
Romberger, George Bartholomew	1st cousin 4 times removed	VIII	6
Romberger, George Bartholomus	Half 3rd great-granduncle	VII	6
Romberger, George Franklin	3rd cousin once removed	IX	5
Romberger, George H	2nd cousin twice removed	VIII	5
Romberger, George John	1st cousin 3 times removed	VII	5

Name	Relationship with Dwight Eisenhower	Civil	Canon
Romberger, George Washington	3rd cousin twice removed	X	6
Romberger, Gilbert	2nd cousin 3 times removed	IX	6
Romberger, Gilbert	2nd cousin twice removed	VIII	5
Romberger, Hanna Lydia	Half 1st cousin 3 times removed	VII	5
Romberger, Hannah	1st cousin 3 times removed	VII	5
Romberger, Hannah	1st cousin 3 times removed	VII	5
Romberger, Hannah	2nd cousin twice removed	VIII	5
Romberger, Hannah	3rd cousin once removed	IX	5
Romberger, Hannah R	3rd cousin once removed	IX	5
Romberger, Harvey D	3rd cousin once removed	IX	5
Romberger, Heinrich	2nd great-granduncle	VI	5
Romberger, Henry	2nd cousin twice removed	VIII	5
Romberger, Henry Ammon	3rd cousin once removed	IX	5
Romberger, Henry F.	Half 1st cousin 3 times removed	VII	5
Romberger, Henry Marshall	2nd cousin twice removed	VIII	5
Romberger, Howard Henry	2nd cousin twice removed	VIII	5
Romberger, Isaac	1st cousin 3 times removed	VII	5
Romberger, Isaac	3rd cousin twice removed	X	6
Romberger, Jacob	1st cousin 4 times removed	VIII	6
Romberger, Jacob	2nd cousin 3 times removed	IX	6
Romberger, Jacob	Half 2nd great-granduncle	VI	5
Romberger, Jacob	2nd cousin 3 times removed	IX	6
Romberger, Jacob	3rd cousin twice removed	X	6
Romberger, Jacob J.	Half 1st cousin 3 times removed	VII	5
Romberger, James	3rd cousin twice removed	X	6
Romberger, James Frank	Half 2nd cousin	VI	3
Romberger, James M	3rd cousin once removed	IX	5
Romberger, James W	3rd cousin once removed	IX	5
Romberger, Jane	3rd cousin twice removed	X	6
Romberger, Jennie	3rd cousin once removed	IX	5
Romberger, Johann Bartholomus	4th great-grandfather	VI	6
Romberger, Johannes	Half 3rd great-granduncle	VII	6
Romberger, Johannes	1st cousin 4 times removed	VIII	6
Romberger, Johannes	2nd great-granduncle	VI	5
Romberger, John	2nd cousin 3 times removed	IX	6
Romberger, John	2nd cousin 3 times removed	IX	6
Romberger, John	2nd cousin 3 times removed	IX	6
Romberger, John	Half 1st cousin 3 times removed	VII	5
Romberger, John	3rd cousin once removed	IX	5
Romberger, John A.	3rd cousin twice removed	X	6
Romberger, John Ambrose	2nd cousin twice removed	VIII	5
Romberger, John B.	Half 1st cousin 3 times removed	VII	5
Romberger, John G	2nd cousin twice removed	VIII	5
Romberger, John G.	3rd cousin twice removed	X	6
Romberger, John G.	3rd cousin twice removed	X	6
Romberger, John H.	3rd cousin twice removed	X	6
Romberger, John Henry	Husband of the half 1st cousin once removed		
Romberger, John S.	3rd cousin twice removed	X	6
Romberger, John W.	3rd cousin twice removed	X	6
Romberger, Jonas	1st cousin 3 times removed	VII	5
Romberger, Jonas	2nd cousin twice removed	VIII	5
Romberger, Jonas Allen	3rd cousin once removed	IX	5
Romberger, Jonathon	Half 1st cousin 3 times removed	VII	5
Romberger, Joseph	Half 2nd great-granduncle	VI	5
Romberger, Joseph	3rd cousin twice removed	X	6
Romberger, Joseph	3rd cousin twice removed	X	6
Romberger, Joseph	3rd cousin twice removed	X	6
Romberger, Joseph D.	Half 1st cousin 3 times removed	VII	5
Romberger, Josiah	Half 1st cousin 3 times removed	VII	5
Romberger, Josiah	2nd cousin twice removed	VIII	5
Romberger, Julianna	1st cousin 3 times removed	VII	5
Romberger, Lavina	3rd cousin twice removed	X	6
Romberger, Leah H	2nd cousin twice removed	VIII	5
Romberger, Levi A.	2nd cousin 3 times removed	IX	6
Romberger, Luther	2nd cousin twice removed	VIII	5
Romberger, Lydia Ann	1st cousin 3 times removed	VII	5
Romberger, Mabel Catherine	Half 2nd cousin	VI	3
Romberger, Maggie	3rd cousin once removed	IX	5
Romberger, Margaret	2nd cousin 3 times removed	IX	6
Romberger, Margaret	2nd cousin 3 times removed	IX	6
Romberger, Margaretha	2nd cousin 3 times removed	IX	6

Name	Relationship with Dwight Eisenhower	Civil	Canon
Romberger, Margaretta Mary	1st cousin 4 times removed	VIII	6
Romberger, Maria Catherine	Half 3rd great-grandaunt	VII	6
Romberger, Maria Eva	3rd great-grandaunt	VII	6
Romberger, Maria Magdalena	Half 3rd great-grandaunt	VII	6
Romberger, Martha E.	3rd cousin twice removed	X	6
Romberger, Martin	2nd cousin 3 times removed	IX	6
Romberger, Mary	2nd cousin 3 times removed	IX	6
Romberger, Mary	2nd cousin 3 times removed	IX	6
Romberger, Mary	2nd cousin 3 times removed	IX	6
Romberger, Mary	Half 1st cousin 3 times removed	VII	5
Romberger, Mary	2nd cousin twice removed	VIII	5
Romberger, Mary	3rd cousin twice removed	X	6
Romberger, Mary	Half 1st cousin 3 times removed	VII	5
Romberger, Mary A.	3rd cousin twice removed	X	6
Romberger, Mary Agatha	3rd cousin once removed	IX	5
Romberger, Mary C.	3rd cousin twice removed	X	6
Romberger, Mary Elizabeth	3rd cousin once removed	IX	5
Romberger, Mary Elizabeth	Half 2nd cousin	VI	3
Romberger, Michael	2nd cousin 3 times removed	IX	6
Romberger, Miriam	3rd cousin twice removed	X	6
Romberger, Nancy	2nd cousin 3 times removed	IX	6
Romberger, Nancy	1st cousin 3 times removed	VII	5
Romberger, Oliver S.	3rd cousin twice removed	X	6
Romberger, Polly	1st cousin 3 times removed	VII	5
Romberger, Rebecca	1st cousin 3 times removed	VII	5
Romberger, Regis	3rd cousin twice removed	X	6
Romberger, Reuben	2nd cousin 3 times removed	IX	6
Romberger, Sallie	3rd cousin once removed	IX	5
Romberger, Samuel	3rd cousin twice removed	X	6
Romberger, Samuel	Half 2nd great-granduncle	VI	5
Romberger, Samuel	2nd cousin 3 times removed	IX	6
Romberger, Samuel	2nd cousin twice removed	VIII	5
Romberger, Samuel B	2nd cousin twice removed	VIII	5
Romberger, Samuel Oscar	3rd cousin once removed	IX	5
Romberger, Sarah	2nd cousin 3 times removed	IX	6
Romberger, Sarah	2nd cousin twice removed	VIII	5
Romberger, Sarah	Half 1st cousin 3 times removed	VII	5
Romberger, Sarah	3rd cousin twice removed	X	6
Romberger, Sarah Conrad	Half 1st cousin 3 times removed	VII	5
Romberger, Sarah Elizabeth	3rd cousin once removed	IX	5
Romberger, Sarah Salome	1st cousin 3 times removed	VII	5
Romberger, Simon	Half 1st cousin 3 times removed	VII	5
Romberger, Susan	2nd cousin twice removed	VIII	5
Romberger, Susan	3rd cousin twice removed	X	6
Romberger, Susan	2nd cousin twice removed	VIII	5
Romberger, Susanna	1st cousin 3 times removed	VII	5
Romberger, Susanna	1st cousin 3 times removed	VII	5
Romberger, Susanna	Half 1st cousin 3 times removed	VII	5
Romberger, Susanna	Half 1st cousin 3 times removed	VII	5
Romberger, Susannah	Half 2nd great-grandaunt	VI	5
Romberger, Thaddeus	3rd cousin twice removed	X	6
Romberger, Thomas Pyke	Half 2nd cousin	VI	3
Romberger, William	Half 1st cousin 3 times removed	VII	5
Romberger, William	3rd cousin twice removed	X	6
Romberger, William	3rd cousin once removed	IX	5
Romberger, William F.	2nd cousin 3 times removed	IX	6
Ross, Elisabeth	Wife of the 2nd cousin 3 times removed		
Rossiter, Mary Ann	Wife of the half 3rd cousin		
Roueche, Arthur Bradford	Grandnephew	IV	3
Roueche, Berton	Husband of the niece		
Row, Elisabeth	Wife of the 2nd cousin 3 times removed		
Row, Isabella	Wife of the great-granduncle		
Rowe, Joseph	Husband of the great-grandaunt		
Ruddell, Harrison C.	Husband of the half 3rd cousin 3 times removed		
Ruffner, Elizabeth	Wife of the 3rd great-granduncle		
Ruhl, ?	Husband of the half 1st cousin 3 times removed		
Ryan	6th cousin once removed	XV	8
Ryan, Alva L.	Husband of the 6th cousin		
Ryan, Elmer William	6th cousin once removed	XV	8
Ryan, Hattie Gwendolyn	6th cousin once removed	XV	8

Name	Relationship with Dwight Eisenhower	Civil	Canon
Ryan, Ruth Marie	6th cousin once removed	XV	8
Ryan, Virginia Elizabeth	6th cousin once removed	XV	8
Sailor, Ida	Wife of the 5th cousin once removed		
Sally	Half 2nd cousin twice removed	VIII	5
Salomon	1st cousin twice removed	VI	4
Sassman, ?	Husband of the half 1st cousin 3 times removed		
Schaeffer, Joan Mardell	Wife of the 3rd cousin twice removed		
Schaffer, John	Husband of the 3rd cousin once removed		
Scheideman, m	Husband of the 1st cousin once removed		
Schmidt, Anna Maria Elizabeth	Wife of the 2nd great-grandfather		
Schneider, Susanna	Wife of the half 3rd great-granduncle		
Scholl	5th cousin once removed	XIII	7
Scholl	5th cousin once removed	XIII	7
Scholl	5th cousin once removed	XIII	7
Scholl	4th cousin twice removed	XII	7
Scholl	4th cousin twice removed	XII	7
Scholl	4th cousin twice removed	XII	7
Scholl	4th cousin twice removed	XII	7
Scholl, ?	4th cousin twice removed	XII	7
Scholl, ?	5th cousin once removed	XIII	7
Scholl, Ambrose	5th cousin once removed	XIII	7
Scholl, Anna May	6th cousin	XIV	7
Scholl, Annie Mary	6th cousin once removed	XV	8
Scholl, Caroline	4th cousin twice removed	XII	7
Scholl, Catherine	4th cousin twice removed	XII	7
Scholl, Celia	3rd cousin 3 times removed	XI	7
Scholl, Charity Ann	3rd cousin 3 times removed	XI	7
Scholl, Charlotte	4th cousin twice removed	XII	7
Scholl, Charlotte F.	4th cousin twice removed	XII	7
Scholl, Cyrus	4th cousin twice removed	XII	7
Scholl, Daniel Boone	4th cousin twice removed	XII	7
Scholl, Daniel Boone	3rd cousin 3 times removed	XI	7
Scholl, Delcina	4th cousin twice removed	XII	7
Scholl, Deward	4th cousin twice removed	XII	7
Scholl, Dudley	3rd cousin 3 times removed	XI	7
Scholl, Dulceney	4th cousin twice removed	XII	7
Scholl, Edward A.	4th cousin twice removed	XII	7
Scholl, Edward B.	3rd cousin 3 times removed	XI	7
Scholl, Edward Boone	3rd cousin 3 times removed	XI	7
Scholl, Edward Boone	4th cousin twice removed	XII	7
Scholl, Effie A.	6th cousin	XIV	7
Scholl, Elizabeth	4th cousin twice removed	XII	7
Scholl, Elizabeth	4th cousin twice removed	XII	7
Scholl, Elizabeth T.	5th cousin once removed	XIII	7
Scholl, Elledge	4th cousin twice removed	XII	7
Scholl, Elmer Joseph	6th cousin	XIV	7
Scholl, Emily Anna	5th cousin once removed	XIII	7
Scholl, Emma	5th cousin once removed	XIII	7
Scholl, Frances Elizabeth	5th cousin once removed	XIII	7
Scholl, Francis Marion	4th cousin twice removed	XII	7
Scholl, George W.	5th cousin once removed	XIII	7
Scholl, Harley Richard	6th cousin	XIV	7
Scholl, Herbert Edward	6th cousin	XIV	7
Scholl, Hulda	5th cousin once removed	XIII	7
Scholl, Isahi	4th cousin twice removed	XII	7
Scholl, James M.	4th cousin twice removed	XII	7
Scholl, James M.	5th cousin once removed	XIII	7
Scholl, Jesse Albert	6th cousin	XIV	7
Scholl, Jesse B.	5th cousin once removed	XIII	7
Scholl, Jesse Boone	3rd cousin 3 times removed	XI	7
Scholl, Jesse Bryan	3rd cousin 3 times removed	XI	7
Scholl, John	3rd cousin 3 times removed	XI	7
Scholl, John F.	5th cousin once removed	XIII	7
Scholl, John R.	5th cousin once removed	XIII	7
Scholl, Joseph	4th cousin twice removed	XII	7
Scholl, Joseph	4th cousin twice removed	XII	7
Scholl, Joseph	3rd cousin 3 times removed	XI	7
Scholl, Joseph	3rd cousin 3 times removed	XI	7
Scholl, Joseph B.	4th cousin twice removed	XII	7
Scholl, Joseph Sr.	Husband of the 2nd cousin 4 times removed		
Scholl, Josephine L.	4th cousin twice removed	XII	7

Name	Relationship with Dwight Eisenhower	Civil	Canon
Scholl, Julia	4th cousin twice removed	XII	7
Scholl, Julia Ann	4th cousin twice removed	XII	7
Scholl, Lavina	5th cousin once removed	XIII	7
Scholl, Leah	3rd cousin 3 times removed	XI	7
Scholl, Lena Florence	6th cousin	XIV	7
Scholl, Levisa	4th cousin twice removed	XII	7
Scholl, Louisa	3rd cousin 3 times removed	XI	7
Scholl, Lucy	5th cousin once removed	XIII	7
Scholl, Lydia	4th cousin twice removed	XII	7
Scholl, Lydia Ann	3rd cousin 3 times removed	XI	7
Scholl, Lydia C.	5th cousin once removed	XIII	7
Scholl, Malinda	3rd cousin 3 times removed	XI	7
Scholl, Marcia	3rd cousin 3 times removed	XI	7
Scholl, Marcus	4th cousin twice removed	XII	7
Scholl, Marcus	3rd cousin 3 times removed	XI	7
Scholl, Martha	3rd cousin 3 times removed	XI	7
Scholl, Martha E.	4th cousin twice removed	XII	7
Scholl, Martha Jane	5th cousin once removed	XIII	7
Scholl, Mary	5th cousin once removed	XIII	7
Scholl, Mary	3rd cousin 3 times removed	XI	7
Scholl, Mary Ann	Wife of the half 3rd cousin		
Scholl, Mary Mural	6th cousin	XIV	7
Scholl, Mary S.	5th cousin once removed	XIII	7
Scholl, Mary Susan	5th cousin once removed	XIII	7
Scholl, Nancy E.	5th cousin once removed	XIII	7
Scholl, Nelson	4th cousin twice removed	XII	7
Scholl, Orley	6th cousin	XIV	7
Scholl, Perry	Half 3rd cousin once removed	IX	5
Scholl, Peter	3rd cousin 3 times removed	XI	7
Scholl, Peter	Husband of the 1st cousin 5 times removed		
Scholl, Peter Boone	5th cousin once removed	XIII	7
Scholl, Peter Morgan	3rd cousin 3 times removed	XI	7
Scholl, Peter Morgan	4th cousin twice removed	XII	7
Scholl, Sarah E.	5th cousin once removed	XIII	7
Scholl, Sarah H.	5th cousin once removed	XIII	7
Scholl, Septimus	3rd cousin 3 times removed	XI	7
Scholl, Susan A.	5th cousin once removed	XIII	7
Scholl, Tamar A.	5th cousin once removed	XIII	7
Scholl, Telitha	4th cousin twice removed	XII	7
Scholl, William	3rd cousin 3 times removed	XI	7
Scholl, William A.	5th cousin once removed	XIII	7
Scholl, William Boone	4th cousin twice removed	XII	7
Scholl, William Elledge	6th cousin	XIV	7
Scholl, William P.	4th cousin twice removed	XII	7
Scholl, William T.	5th cousin once removed	XIII	7
Scholl, William Wallace	4th cousin twice removed	XII	7
Schoonover, Eleanor	Wife of the half 2nd cousin once removed		
Schreffler, Hannah	Wife of the 1st cousin 3 times removed		
Schrock, Emma	Wife of the 4th cousin		
Schuler, John	Husband of the 4th cousin		
Schupp, Catherina	Wife of the 1st cousin 3 times removed		
Schupp, Isaac	Husband of the 2nd cousin twice removed		
Schupp, John H.	3rd cousin once removed	IX	5
Schupp, Nathaniel P.	3rd cousin once removed	IX	5
Schupp, Sarah	3rd cousin once removed	IX	5
Schwab	Wife of the 1st cousin twice removed		
Schwab, Anna Mary	Wife of the 1st cousin 3 times removed		
Scott, Catherine	Wife of the 4th cousin twice removed		
Scott, Edward Alfred	Husband of the half 3rd cousin 4 times removed		
Scott, Mary J.	Wife of the half 3rd cousin		
Seig, Samuel	Husband of the half 1st cousin twice removed		
Sellers, ?	Wife of the 2nd cousin 3 times removed		
Shade, Edna Alice	Sister-in-law		
Shaffer, John	Husband of the 3rd cousin once removed		
Shaffetall, Catherine	Wife of the half 1st cousin once removed		
Shaw, Caroline	Wife of the 2nd cousin twice removed		
Sheesley, Anna	Half 1st cousin once removed	V	3
Sheesley, David	Husband of the half grandaunt		
Sheesley, Rebecca	Half 1st cousin once removed	V	3
Sheesley, Sarah Etta	Half 1st cousin once removed	V	3
Shobe, Anna Bell	5th cousin once removed	XIII	7

Name	Relationship with Dwight Eisenhower	Civil	Canon
Shobe, George Rodney	5th cousin once removed	XIII	7
Shobe, Larkin Daniel	5th cousin once removed	XIII	7
Shobe, Mary Virginia	5th cousin once removed	XIII	7
Shobe, Solomon	Husband of the 4th cousin twice removed		
Shomper, Beatrice	Wife of the 3rd cousin once removed		
Shomper, Catherine R.	3rd cousin once removed	IX	5
Shomper, Daniel	Husband of the 2nd cousin twice removed		
Shomper, John Adam	3rd cousin once removed	IX	5
Shomper, Lawrence	3rd cousin once removed	IX	5
Shoop, Darrell E	Husband of the 3rd cousin twice removed		
Shore, Mary Francis Elizabeth	Wife of the half 3rd cousin once removed		
Shores, Elnore	Wife of the 4th cousin twice removed		
Sierer, Amelia Rachel	Wife of the 4th cousin once removed		
Sierer, Elizabeth	Wife of the 2nd great-granduncle		
Simmons, J. Will	Husband of the 5th cousin once removed		
Simpson, Anna	Ex-wife of the 2nd cousin 4 times removed		
Singer, ?	Husband of the half 1st cousin 3 times removed		
Sitlinger, Claude Albert	4th cousin once removed	XI	6
Sitlinger, Cora Gertrude	4th cousin twice removed	XII	7
Sitlinger, Dorothy Delilah	4th cousin once removed	XI	6
Sitlinger, Edward LeRoy Aaron	4th cousin twice removed	XII	7
Sitlinger, Harold Thurston	4th cousin twice removed	XII	7
Sitlinger, Jacob	Husband of the 4th cousin		
Sitlinger, Jacob Charles	4th cousin twice removed	XII	7
Sitlinger, Kathleen Mildred	4th cousin twice removed	XII	7
Sitlinger, Lester Ray	4th cousin twice removed	XII	7
Sitlinger, Living	4th cousin 3 times removed	XIII	8
Sitlinger, Living	4th cousin 3 times removed	XIII	8
Sitlinger, Living	4th cousin 3 times removed	XIII	8
Sitlinger, Living	4th cousin 3 times removed	XIII	8
Sitlinger, Living	4th cousin 4 times removed	XIV	9
Sitlinger, Living	4th cousin 4 times removed	XIV	9
Sitlinger, Living	4th cousin 4 times removed	XIV	9
Sitlinger, Living	4th cousin 4 times removed	XIV	9
Sitlinger, Ray Edwin	4th cousin once removed	XI	6
Smink, Anna Elizabeth Gisels	Half 2nd cousin twice removed	VIII	5
Smink, Carrie Estelle	Half 2nd cousin twice removed	VIII	5
Smink, Elmer E.	Half 2nd cousin twice removed	VIII	5
Smink, Frank Alfred	Half 2nd cousin twice removed	VIII	5
Smink, Harry Abraham Lincoln	Half 2nd cousin twice removed	VIII	5
Smink, Isaac Allison	Husband of the half 1st cousin 3 times removed		
Smink, Isaac Wilson	Half 2nd cousin twice removed	VIII	5
Smink, John William Henry	Half 2nd cousin twice removed	VIII	5
Smink, Joseph Werkman	Half 2nd cousin twice removed	VIII	5
Smink, Julia Ann	Half 2nd cousin twice removed	VIII	5
Smink, Minnie A.	Half 2nd cousin twice removed	VIII	5
Smink, Sara A. E.	Half 2nd cousin twice removed	VIII	5
Smink, Sidney Ann	Half 2nd cousin twice removed	VIII	5
Smith, ?	Wife of the 2nd cousin twice removed		
Smith, Charles	Husband of the 1st cousin 5 times removed		
Smith, Florence	Wife of the 2nd cousin twice removed		
Smith, Hilda Jean	6th cousin twice removed	XVI	9
Smith, John	Wife of the half 2nd cousin once removed		
Snyder, Kathryn McIntyre	Sister-in-law		
Snyder, Veronica	Wife of the 1st cousin twice removed		
Speaks, Lucretia	Wife of the half 3rd cousin		
Spencer, Benjamin Davies	Husband of the 4th cousin twice removed		
Spilman, Mary Maurine	Wife of the half 3rd cousin 4 times removed		
Spotts, Robert	Husband of the 4th cousin		
Spurgeon, ?	Half 3rd cousin 5 times removed	XIII	9
Spurgeon, ?	Half 3rd cousin 6 times removed	XIV	10
Spurgeon, Lorene I.	Wife of the half 3rd cousin 4 times removed		
Spurgeon, Lowell A.	Husband of the half 3rd cousin 4 times removed		
Spurgeon, Shari	Half 3rd cousin 6 times removed	XIV	10
Stanberry, ?	Half 3rd cousin once removed	IX	5
Stanberry, ?	Half 3rd cousin once removed	IX	5
Stanberry, Arthur	Half 3rd cousin once removed	IX	5
Stanberry, Emmet	Half 3rd cousin once removed	IX	5
Stanberry, Gordie	Half 3rd cousin once removed	IX	5
Stanberry, Harrison David	Half 3rd cousin once removed	IX	5
Stanberry, John	Half 3rd cousin once removed	IX	5

Name	Relationship with Dwight Eisenhower	Civil	Canon
Stanberry, Joshua Senter	Husband of the half 3rd cousin		
Stanberry, Nancy	Half 3rd cousin once removed	IX	5
Stanberry, Sarah A.	Half 3rd cousin once removed	IX	5
Stanberry, Virginia	Half 3rd cousin once removed	IX	5
Stanberry, William E.	Half 3rd cousin once removed	IX	5
Stanford, Vincent	Husband of the 3rd cousin once removed		
Stauffer, William	Husband of the half 1st cousin once removed		
Steckley, Lewis	Husband of the 1st cousin		
Stephens, Andrew J.	Husband of the half 2nd cousin once removed		
Stephens, Ella	Half 3rd cousin	VIII	4
Stephens, Harry C.	Half 3rd cousin	VIII	4
Stephens, J. David	Half 3rd cousin	VIII	4
Stephens, Orlanda	Half 3rd cousin	VIII	4
Stephens, Scott	Half 3rd cousin	VIII	4
Stephenson, Nancy J.	Wife of the half 3rd cousin		
Stephenson, Sam White	Husband of the half 3rd cousin once removed		
Stevens, Phoebe	Wife of the 3rd cousin 3 times removed		
Stevenson, Sam M.	Husband of the 5th cousin once removed		
Steward, Anita Heather	Wife of the 3rd cousin 3 times removed		
Stewart, ?	Half 3rd cousin 4 times removed	XII	8
Stewart, ?	Half 3rd cousin 4 times removed	XII	8
Stewart, Charles Ferney	6th cousin	XIV	7
Stewart, Dale	Half 3rd cousin 5 times removed	XIII	9
Stewart, David	Half 3rd cousin 5 times removed	XIII	9
Stewart, Disa	Wife of the 3rd cousin 3 times removed		
Stewart, Elizabeth	Wife of the 3rd cousin 3 times removed		
Stewart, James Francis	Husband of the 5th cousin once removed		
Stewart, John	Husband of the 1st cousin 5 times removed		
Stewart, John	Half 3rd cousin 5 times removed	XIII	9
Stewart, John Thomas	Husband of the half 3rd cousin twice removed		
Stewart, Linda	Half 3rd cousin 5 times removed	XIII	9
Stewart, Lucinda Elizabeth	Wife of the half 3rd cousin once removed		
Stewart, Ole W.	Half 3rd cousin 3 times removed	XI	7
Stewart, Percey DeWitte	6th cousin once removed	XV	8
Stewart, Robert B	Husband of the half 3rd cousin 4 times removed		
Stewart, Walter C.	Half 3rd cousin 3 times removed	XI	7
Stith, Mary E.	Wife of the half 2nd cousin once removed		
Story, Tom	Husband of the half 3rd cousin		
Stout, John Franklin	Husband of the half 2nd cousin twice removed		
Stover, ?	3rd great-grandaunt	VII	6
Stover, ?	5th great-grandmother	VII	7
Stover, Abraham	3rd great-grandfather	V	5
Stover, Barbara	3rd great-grandaunt	VII	6
Stover, Christian	5th great-grandfather	VII	7
Stover, Daniel	2nd great-grandfather	IV	4
Stover, Daniel	Great-grandfather	III	3
Stover, Henry	2nd great-granduncle	VI	5
Stover, Ida Elizabeth	Mother	I	1
Stover, Jacob	4th great-grandfather	VI	6
Stover, Jacob	3rd great-granduncle	VII	6
Stover, Jeremiah	2nd great-granduncle	VI	5
Stover, Simon P	Grandfather	II	2
Strole, Dale	Half 2nd cousin	VI	3
Strole, Dean E	Half 2nd cousin	VI	3
Strole, Elmer	Half 2nd cousin	VI	3
Strole, Freda	Half 2nd cousin	VI	3
Strole, George Luther	Husband of the half 1st cousin once removed		
Strole, Mabel	Half 2nd cousin	VI	3
Strole, Paul L.	Half 2nd cousin	VI	3
Strubel, ?	4th great-grandfather	VI	6
Strubel, Frederich	3rd great-granduncle	VII	6
Struble, Anna	3rd great-grandmother	V	5
Stuppy, Ludwig	Husband of the 3rd cousin once removed		
Stuppy, Maria Theresa	4th cousin	X	5
Sullivan, Doris	Wife of the half 3rd cousin 4 times removed		
Summers, Sarah Brubridge	Wife of the 5th cousin once removed		
Susannah	Wife of the half 2nd cousin once removed		
Sutton, Lucinda E.	Wife of the half 3rd cousin once removed		
Swab, Sarah	Wife of the 1st cousin twice removed		
Swaggart, Henry	Husband of the half 2nd cousin once removed		
Swigert, m	Wife of the 4th cousin twice removed		

Name	Relationship with Dwight Eisenhower	Civil	Canon
Swinney, Margaret Minerva	Wife of the half 2nd cousin once removed		
Syrena	Wife of the 4th cousin twice removed		
Tate, Bell	Wife of the 4th cousin twice removed		
Tate, Henry	Husband of the 4th cousin twice removed		
Tate, Lucy Jane	Wife of the 4th cousin twice removed		
Tate, Maud Price	Wife of the 5th cousin once removed		
Tate, Warren	Husband of the 4th cousin twice removed		
Tatman, Anna Belle	Wife of the 6th cousin		
Taylor, Living	Wife of the 4th cousin 4 times removed		
Terry, Walter Alex	Husband of the 6th cousin once removed		
Thacker, Anne Elizabeth	4th cousin twice removed	XII	7
Thacker, George Washington	Husband of the 3rd cousin 3 times removed		
Thacker, James R.	4th cousin twice removed	XII	7
Thacker, Jane L.	4th cousin twice removed	XII	7
Thacker, Mary	4th cousin twice removed	XII	7
Thacker, Sarah	4th cousin twice removed	XII	7
Thacker, William Washington	4th cousin twice removed	XII	7
Thompson, Barbara Jean	Daughter-in-law		
Thompson, John H.	Husband of the half 3rd cousin 3 times removed		
Thompson, William S.	Husband of the half 3rd cousin 3 times removed		
Thrush, Barbara Isabelle	Wife of the half 3rd cousin once removed		
Timmons, Mary C.	Wife of the 3rd cousin once removed		
Toler, Edgar F.	Half 3rd cousin once removed	IX	5
Toler, Robert N.	Husband of the half 3rd cousin		
Toler, William L.	Half 3rd cousin once removed	IX	5
Tomey, Chreryl	Half 3rd cousin 5 times removed	XIII	9
Tomey, Eugene Stewart	Half 3rd cousin 4 times removed	XII	8
Tomey, Eugene Stewart	Half 3rd cousin 5 times removed	XIII	9
Tomey, Jack Phillip	Half 3rd cousin 4 times removed	XII	8
Tomey, Jack W	Half 3rd cousin 5 times removed	XIII	9
Tomey, Jeffrey Keith	Half 3rd cousin 5 times removed	XIII	9
Tomey, John	Half 3rd cousin 5 times removed	XIII	9
Tomey, Karen	Half 3rd cousin 5 times removed	XIII	9
Tomey, Kristen	Half 3rd cousin 5 times removed	XIII	9
Tomey, Laurann	Half 3rd cousin 5 times removed	XIII	9
Tomey, Lisa	Half 3rd cousin 5 times removed	XIII	9
Tomey, Max Allen	Half 3rd cousin 5 times removed	XIII	9
Tomey, Max H	Half 3rd cousin 4 times removed	XII	8
Tomey, Michael	Half 3rd cousin 5 times removed	XIII	9
Tomey, Mitchell	Half 3rd cousin 5 times removed	XIII	9
Tomey, Paul Austin	Husband of the half 3rd cousin 3 times removed		
Tomey, Pauline Annette	Half 3rd cousin 4 times removed	XII	8
Tomey, Rex Whitacre	Half 3rd cousin 4 times removed	XII	8
Tomey, William Joseph	Half 3rd cousin 4 times removed	XII	8
Tool, m	Husband of the 2nd cousin twice removed		
Towles, James Oliver	Husband of the half 3rd cousin twice removed		
Towles, May E.	Wife of the half 3rd cousin twice removed		
Traut, Anna Maria	3rd great-grandmother	V	5
Travitz, Johannes	Husband of the 1st cousin twice removed		
Travitz, Katie L.	3rd cousin	VIII	4
Travitz, Simon	2nd cousin once removed	VII	4
Tribble, Andrew	Husband of the 3rd cousin 3 times removed		
Tribble, Peter	3rd cousin 3 times removed	XI	7
Tribble, Peter Burris	Husband of the 2nd cousin 4 times removed		
Trivitte, Mary Jane	Wife of the half 3rd cousin		
Troutman, Lena	Wife of the 1st cousin 3 times removed		
Turner, Anna Maupin	Wife of the 3rd cousin 3 times removed		
Turner, Elizabeth	Wife of the 2nd cousin 4 times removed		
Turner, Nancy Jane	Wife of the 4th cousin twice removed		
Turner, William A.	Husband of the 6th cousin		
Umholtz, Anna Maria	Wife of the 1st cousin 3 times removed		
Umholtz, John	Husband of the 3rd cousin		
Underhill, Emily Hart	Wife of the 4th cousin twice removed		
Unfug, Conrad Otto	Husband of the 4th cousin twice removed		
Unger, David	Husband of the half 1st cousin twice removed		
Unger, John George	Half 2nd cousin once removed	VII	4
Uppey	7th great-grandfather	IX	9
Uppey, Sarah	6th great-grandmother	VIII	8
Van Bibber, Chloe	Wife of the 2nd cousin 4 times removed		
Van Bibber, Isaac	Husband of the 3rd cousin 3 times removed		
Van Bibber, Olive	Wife of the 2nd cousin 4 times removed		

Name	Relationship with Dwight Eisenhower	Civil	Canon
Van Cleve, Jane	Wife of the 1st cousin 5 times removed		
Vandine, Lena V.	Wife of the half 2nd cousin once removed		
VanHoose, John Sr.	Husband of the 2nd cousin 4 times removed		
Wade, Liltra Ann	Wife of the half 3rd cousin		
Wadsworth, John Caton	Husband of the 4th cousin twice removed		
Wagner, Helena	Wife of the 1st cousin 3 times removed		
Wagoner, Nancy A.	Wife of the half 3rd cousin		
Walborn, Augustus George	Husband of the half 1st cousin 3 times removed		
Walker, Jennet	Wife of the half 1st cousin twice removed		
Walker, John	Husband of the half 2nd cousin once removed		
Wallace, John	5th cousin once removed	XIII	7
Wallace, Mary	5th cousin once removed	XIII	7
Wallace, Mathew	Husband of the 4th cousin twice removed		
Wallace, Thomas Jefferson	5th cousin once removed	XIII	7
Waller, Eliza	Wife of the 4th cousin twice removed		
Walters, Joseph McEwen	Husband of the half 3rd cousin twice removed		
Waltz, ?	Husband of the half 1st cousin 3 times removed		
Ward	Husband of the 5th cousin once removed		
Ward, Minnie Louise	6th cousin	XIV	7
Warner, Angela Sanford	5th cousin once removed	XIII	7
Warner, Thoedore Fulton	4th cousin twice removed	XII	7
Warner, Wynkoop	Husband of the 3rd cousin 3 times removed		
Weatherford, Bertha J.	6th cousin	XIV	7
Weatherford, Franklin Ambrose	6th cousin	XIV	7
Weatherford, Guy Ulysses	6th cousin	XIV	7
Weatherford, Harbart Lancaster	Husband of the 5th cousin once removed		
Weatherford, Mary Effie	6th cousin	XIV	7
Weatherford, Stella E.	6th cousin	XIV	7
Weatherford, Winfred Lee	6th cousin	XIV	7
Weaver, Jacob	Husband of the 1st cousin 3 times removed		
Webb, John	Husband of the half 1st cousin twice removed		
Webb, John	Husband of the 4th great-grandaunt		
Weiser, Catherine E.	Wife of the half 1st cousin 3 times removed		
Weiss, John	Husband of the 1st cousin 3 times removed		
Welborn, Nancy E.	Wife of the half 3rd cousin		
Welch, Martha Ella	Wife of the half 3rd cousin once removed		
Wells, Horton	Husband of the 3rd cousin 3 times removed		
Werner, Anna Maria	Wife of the 2nd great-granduncle		
Westrope, John	Husband of the 2nd cousin 4 times removed		
Wetzel, Aaron	Husband of the aunt		
Wetzel, Della Mae	1st cousin	IV	2
Wetzel, Franklin Jacob	1st cousin	IV	2
Wetzel, Grace Pearl	1st cousin	IV	2
Wetzel, Harper	1st cousin	IV	2
Wetzel, Janny R.	1st cousin	IV	2
Wetzel, Minnie M.	1st cousin	IV	2
Wetzel, Otto Robert	1st cousin	IV	2
Wetzel, Raymond	1st cousin	IV	2
Wetzel, Sarah A.	1st cousin	IV	2
Wetzel, Vernon	1st cousin	IV	2
Wharton, John A	Husband of the half 1st cousin once removed		
Wharton, Mary Scrogin	Wife of the 1st cousin 5 times removed		
Whitacre, ?	Half 3rd cousin 6 times removed	XIV	10
Whitacre, ?	Half 3rd cousin 6 times removed	XIV	10
Whitacre, ?	Half 3rd cousin 6 times removed	XIV	10
Whitacre, ?	Half 3rd cousin 5 times removed	XIII	9
Whitacre, ?	Half 3rd cousin 5 times removed	XIII	9
Whitacre, ?	Half 3rd cousin 5 times removed	XIII	9
Whitacre, ?	Half 3rd cousin 6 times removed	XIV	10
Whitacre, ?	Half 3rd cousin 6 times removed	XIV	10
Whitacre, ?	Half 3rd cousin 6 times removed	XIV	10
Whitacre, ?	Half 3rd cousin 4 times removed	XII	8
Whitacre, ?	Half 3rd cousin 4 times removed	XII	8
Whitacre, ?	Half 3rd cousin 6 times removed	XIV	10
Whitacre, ?	Half 3rd cousin 6 times removed	XIV	10
Whitacre, ?	Half 3rd cousin 5 times removed	XIII	9
Whitacre, ?	Half 3rd cousin 5 times removed	XIII	9
Whitacre, Alta Effie	Half 3rd cousin 3 times removed	XI	7
Whitacre, Bonnie Beth	Half 3rd cousin 5 times removed	XIII	9
Whitacre, Carroll D.	Half 3rd cousin 4 times removed	XII	8

Name	Relationship with Dwight Eisenhower	Civil	Canon
Whitacre, Charles Newton	Half 3rd cousin 3 times removed	XI	7
Whitacre, Chester Oral	Half 3rd cousin 3 times removed	XI	7
Whitacre, Ella L.	Half 3rd cousin 4 times removed	XII	8
Whitacre, Essie Elizabeth	Half 3rd cousin 3 times removed	XI	7
Whitacre, Estel L.	Half 3rd cousin 4 times removed	XII	8
Whitacre, Geneva B.	Half 3rd cousin 4 times removed	XII	8
Whitacre, Glen N.	Half 3rd cousin 4 times removed	XII	8
Whitacre, Harold O.	Half 3rd cousin 4 times removed	XII	8
Whitacre, Hugh W.	Half 3rd cousin 4 times removed	XII	8
Whitacre, Ida Berniece	Half 3rd cousin 3 times removed	XI	7
Whitacre, Jane	Half 3rd cousin 5 times removed	XIII	9
Whitacre, Joan A	Half 3rd cousin 4 times removed	XII	8
Whitacre, John George	Half 3rd cousin 4 times removed	XII	8
Whitacre, John Leslie	Half 3rd cousin 3 times removed	XI	7
Whitacre, John Morgan	Husband of the half 3rd cousin twice removed		
Whitacre, Kay	Half 3rd cousin 5 times removed	XIII	9
Whitacre, Ken	Half 3rd cousin 5 times removed	XIII	9
Whitacre, Kenneth Omer	Half 3rd cousin 3 times removed	XI	7
Whitacre, Lowell	Half 3rd cousin 4 times removed	XII	8
Whitacre, Melody	Half 3rd cousin 5 times removed	XIII	9
Whitacre, Minnie Estella	Half 3rd cousin 3 times removed	XI	7
Whitacre, Naomi Vernadean	Half 3rd cousin 3 times removed	XI	7
Whitacre, Olen Aubry	Half 3rd cousin 3 times removed	XI	7
Whitacre, Omer Charles	Half 3rd cousin 4 times removed	XII	8
Whitacre, Opal Lydia	Half 3rd cousin 3 times removed	XI	7
Whitacre, Ralph	Half 3rd cousin 4 times removed	XII	8
Whitacre, Ray M	Half 3rd cousin 4 times removed	XII	8
Whitacre, Richard Allen	Half 3rd cousin 4 times removed	XII	8
Whitacre, Sarah	Wife of the half 2nd cousin once removed		
Whitacre, Vernon Jewell	Half 3rd cousin 3 times removed	XI	7
White, Clara Ada	Wife of the half 3rd cousin 3 times removed		
White, Jesse	Husband of the 3rd cousin 3 times removed		
Whited, Mary	Wife of the half 2nd cousin twice removed		
Whitely, Franklin	Husband of the 4th cousin twice removed		
Wicoff, John	Husband of the 2nd cousin 4 times removed		
Wiest, Catharine	3rd cousin once removed	IX	5
Wiest, Catherine	3rd cousin once removed	IX	5
Wiest, Charles	3rd cousin once removed	IX	5
Wiest, Charles A.	3rd cousin once removed	IX	5
Wiest, Charles W.	4th cousin	X	5
Wiest, Clayton L.	4th cousin	X	5
Wiest, Corinne	4th cousin	X	5
Wiest, Daniel Merkel	Husband of the 2nd cousin twice removed		
Wiest, Daughter	3rd cousin once removed	IX	5
Wiest, Daughter	3rd cousin once removed	IX	5
Wiest, David	3rd cousin once removed	IX	5
Wiest, David	3rd cousin once removed	IX	5
Wiest, Edward	4th cousin	X	5
Wiest, Ella Amanda	Wife of the 2nd cousin twice removed		
Wiest, Ella Amanda	Wife of the 2nd cousin twice removed		
Wiest, Ella May	3rd cousin once removed	IX	5
Wiest, George	4th cousin	X	5
Wiest, Grace	3rd cousin once removed	IX	5
Wiest, Harry	4th cousin	X	5
Wiest, Harry	Husband of the 1st cousin 3 times removed		
Wiest, Hattie	3rd cousin once removed	IX	5
Wiest, Henry	Husband of the 1st cousin 3 times removed		
Wiest, Henry	2nd cousin twice removed	VIII	5
Wiest, Jacob	2nd cousin twice removed	VIII	5
Wiest, Jefferson	3rd cousin once removed	IX	5
Wiest, Jefferson	3rd cousin once removed	IX	5
Wiest, Laurence Orwig	3rd cousin once removed	IX	5
Wiest, Lily	3rd cousin once removed	IX	5
Wiest, Lovetta	3rd cousin once removed	IX	5
Wiest, Loyetta	4th cousin	X	5
Wiest, Luisianna	3rd cousin once removed	IX	5
Wiest, Lusianna	3rd cousin once removed	IX	5
Wiest, Margaret	4th cousin	X	5
Wiest, Maude	3rd cousin once removed	IX	5
Wiest, Oliver	2nd cousin twice removed	VIII	5
Wiest, Paul	4th cousin	X	5

Name	Relationship with Dwight Eisenhower	Civil	Canon
Wiest, Pauline Minerva	4th cousin	X	5
Wiest, Rebecca	2nd cousin twice removed	VIII	5
Wiest, Russell	4th cousin	X	5
Wiest, Ruth	3rd cousin once removed	IX	5
Wiest, Sally	4th cousin	X	5
Wiest, Samuel L.	2nd cousin twice removed	VIII	5
Wiest, Warren Orwig	3rd cousin once removed	IX	5
Wiest, William	4th cousin	X	5
wife, Living	Wife of the 4th cousin 3 times removed		
Wilbert, Amanda E.	Half 1st cousin once removed	V	3
Wilbert, Clara R.	Half 1st cousin once removed	V	3
Wilbert, Emeline	Half 1st cousin once removed	V	3
Wilbert, John H.	Half 1st cousin once removed	V	3
Wilbert, Lydia A.	Half 1st cousin once removed	V	3
Wilbert, Mary	Half 1st cousin once removed	V	3
Wilbert, May	Half 1st cousin once removed	V	3
Wilbert, Phillip	Husband of the half grandaunt		
Wilbert, Sarah Jane	Half 1st cousin once removed	V	3
Wilcox, David	Husband of the 2nd cousin 4 times removed		
Wilcoxson, David	2nd cousin 4 times removed	X	7
Wilcoxson, Elizabeth	2nd cousin 4 times removed	X	7
Wilcoxson, George	2nd cousin 4 times removed	X	7
Wilcoxson, Isaac	2nd cousin 4 times removed	X	7
Wilcoxson, Isreal	2nd cousin 4 times removed	X	7
Wilcoxson, John	2nd cousin 4 times removed	X	7
Wilcoxson, John D.	Husband of the 1st cousin 5 times removed		
Wilcoxson, Nancy	2nd cousin 4 times removed	X	7
Wilcoxson, Rachel	2nd cousin 4 times removed	X	7
Wilcoxson, Sarah	2nd cousin 4 times removed	X	7
Wilcoxson, William	2nd cousin 4 times removed	X	7
Willcoxson, Elizabeth	2nd cousin 4 times removed	X	7
Willden, Don Edward	Half 3rd cousin 3 times removed	XI	7
Willden, Elmer Sherman	Half 3rd cousin 3 times removed	XI	7
Willden, Esther Corilla	Half 3rd cousin 3 times removed	XI	7
Willden, Leona Gladys	Half 3rd cousin 3 times removed	XI	7
Willden, Mark	Husband of the half 3rd cousin twice removed		
Williams, Caroline	Wife of the 5th cousin once removed		
Williams, Ernest T.	Husband of the 6th cousin		
Williard, George R.	Husband of the half grandaunt		
Wilson, Mildred Elizabeth	Wife of the half 2nd cousin		
Wilson, William	Husband of the 3rd cousin 3 times removed		
Windsor, Cordie	Wife of the 5th cousin once removed		
Withers	Husband of the 4th cousin twice removed		
Witmer, Catharine	2nd cousin twice removed	VIII	5
Witmer, Jonas	2nd cousin twice removed	VIII	5
Witmer, Josiah	2nd cousin twice removed	VIII	5
Witmer, Samuel	Husband of the 1st cousin 3 times removed		
Witmer, Sarah	2nd cousin twice removed	VIII	5
Witter, Amanda	1st cousin	IV	2
Witter, Bessie	1st cousin	IV	2
Witter, Harry	1st cousin	IV	2
Witter, John J	Husband of the aunt		
Witter, Johnnie	1st cousin	IV	2
Witter, Mamie Stella	1st cousin	IV	2
Witter, Martha Rebecca	1st cousin	IV	2
Witter, Ray I	1st cousin	IV	2
Witter, Sadie	1st cousin	IV	2
Witter, Susie A	1st cousin	IV	2
Wolf, Abraham	Husband of the half 1st cousin twice removed		
Wood	Husband of the half great-grandaunt		
Wood, Liddia	Wife of the half 3rd cousin twice removed		
Woodside, Jacob	Husband of the 1st cousin 3 times removed		
Worick, m	Husband of the 2nd cousin twice removed		
Workman, Catherine	Half 1st cousin 3 times removed	VII	5
Workman, Edward	Half 2nd cousin twice removed	VIII	5
Workman, Elizabeth	Half 1st cousin 3 times removed	VII	5
Workman, Hariet	Half 2nd cousin twice removed	VIII	5
Workman, Henry	Half 1st cousin 3 times removed	VII	5
Workman, Israel	Half 2nd cousin twice removed	VIII	5
Workman, Jacob	Half 1st cousin 3 times removed	VII	5
Workman, John	Half 1st cousin 3 times removed	VII	5

Name	Relationship with Dwight Eisenhower	Civil	Canon
Workman, John	Half 2nd cousin twice removed	VIII	5
Workman, Joseph	Half 2nd cousin twice removed	VIII	5
Workman, Joseph	Husband of the half 2nd great-grandaunt		
Workman, Joseph R.	Half 1st cousin 3 times removed	VII	5
Workman, Kitty	Half 2nd cousin twice removed	VIII	5
Workman, Levi	Half 2nd cousin twice removed	VIII	5
Workman, Levina	Half 2nd cousin twice removed	VIII	5
Workman, Nancy	Half 1st cousin 3 times removed	VII	5
Workman, Sarah	Half 2nd cousin twice removed	VIII	5
Yeager, Susan	Wife of the 2nd cousin twice removed		
Yeartz, Florence	Wife of the 3rd cousin once removed		
Yerger, Living	Wife of the 4th cousin 4 times removed		
Yerges, Anna Mary	Wife of the 2nd cousin twice removed		
Yohe, Clarence	Husband of the 3rd cousin once removed		
Young, Daniel W.	Husband of the 5th cousin once removed		
Young, Daniel W.	6th cousin	XIV	7
Young, Kate	6th cousin	XIV	7
Young, Levi	Husband of the 5th cousin once removed		
Young, Maggie	6th cousin	XIV	7
Young, Mallie	6th cousin	XIV	7
Young, Mourning Ann	Wife of the 4th cousin twice removed		
Young, Nannie	6th cousin	XIV	7
Young, William Archibald	Husband of the 5th cousin once removed		
Zerb, Mamie	Wife of the 3rd cousin once removed		
Zimmerman, Ruth	Wife of the 3rd cousin once removed		

Lawrence Knorr, MBA PMP CCP, born 1964, is an amateur genealogist with deep roots in the Pennsylvania Dutch Region. Lawrence's "real" jobs are as Director of Information Systems for Giant Food Stores, LLC of Carlisle, PA and as an adjunct professor at Harrisburg University, Harrisburg, PA. Lawrence holds a Bachelor's degree in Business/Economics (History Minor) from Wilson College and a Masters of Business Administration from Penn State. He is also a Certified Computer Professional and Project Management Professional. Lawrence lives with his wife Tammi and has two daughters.

Lawrence has been involved in genealogical research for fifteen years, and is or has been a member of several related organizations:

National Genealogical Society
Pennsylvania German Society
Berks County Genealogical Society
Pennsylvania Heritage Society
Palatines to America - Pennsylvania Chapter
Sons of the American Revolution
Mahanoy & Mahantango Historical & Preservation Society
Derry Township Historical Society
Manheim Historical Society

Other recently (or soon to be) published works by Lawrence include:

71 Years of Marriage: The Ancestors, Descendents and Relations of George and Alice Knorr of Reading, PA (2002)

The Shellems of Philadelphia (2003)

The Relations of Milton Snavely Hershey (2004, 2005, 2008)

The Descendants of Hans Peter Knorr (2007)

A Pennsylvania Mennonite and the California Gold Rush: The Journal and Letters of David Baer Hackman (2008)

The Relations of Major General John Fulton Reynolds (to be published 2010)

The Relations of the Reverand Isaac Faust Stiehly (to be published 2010)

Index of Individuals

William Eugene: 189, 230
William Henry: 176, 189, 230
William Linville: 158, 163, 164, 171, 230
William R.: 181, 230
William Randall: 170, 230
William T.: 167, 230
Zeralda Engleton: 170, 230

Bordner -
Elizabeth Bordner: 119, 230
John: 119, 230
John W.: 119, 230
William Henry Harrison: 119, 230

Boschen -
Jeanne Anne: 75, 212, 230

Bowers -
Susan Jane: 51, 148, 149, 230

Bowman -
?: 112, 231
Elizabeth: 51, 231
Esther M.: 95, 136
Isaac: 135, 231
Philip: 19, 85, 125, 231

Boyer -
Lottie: 56, 231
Samuel B.: 127, 231

Bradley -
Harry: 73, 205, 231
John L.: 73, 76, 205, 212, 213, 231

Bragg -
Martha: 56, 57, 231

Brandt -
Jacob M: 61, 99, 141, 153, 231
Orville E: 62, 99, 141, 153, 231
Preston L: 62, 99, 141, 153, 231
Victor O: 62, 99, 141, 153, 231

Brechbill -
Abram E: 53, 93, 133, 150, 231

Brehm -
Eldred H: 60, 98, 140, 152, 231
Faithe Marie: 60, 98, 140, 152, 231
Irma Aurelia: 60, 98, 140, 152, 231
Samuel W: 60, 98, 140, 152, 231
Zena Leroy: 60, 98, 140, 152, 231

Bressler -
Elizabeth: 129, 231

Brower -
Elias: 48, 231

Brown -
Addie L.: 59, 231
Arminda: 54, 231
Benjamin F.: 49, 231
Charles F.: 201, 231
Cintha M.: 59, 231
David A.: 49, 60, 66, 231
Delphia: 55, 231
Elizabert: 112, 231
Emil: 67, 231
Fred E.: 66, 231
Hannah: 176, 231

Horace Charles: 67, 231
Howard: 67, 231
Ira W.: 66, 231
John: 197, 231
John: 54, 231
John W.: 49, 59, 231
Joseph: 49, 60, 231
Julia: 49, 231
Laura E.: 49, 231
Lawsen: 197, 231
Linville Lee: 67, 231
Lucy: 49, 231
Lula J.: 59, 231
Maria: 49, 231
Martha: 55, 231
Martha: 49, 231
Martha E.: 49, 231
Martishe R.: 49, 231
Mary: 49, 59, 231
Mary: 56, 231
Mary B.: 59, 231
Micajah: 55, 231
Rebecca: 54, 231
Roy M.: 60, 231
Samuel: 49, 231
Samuel Smith: 60, 66, 231
Sarah: 49, 231
Settie: 67, 231
Walter E.: 95, 137, 231
William: 49, 231
William M.: 60, 231
Winfred Tate: 67, 231

Bruce -
(name: Arthur Morris): 96, 138

Brunk -
m: 74, 210, 231

Bryan -
Unnamed: 158, 231
Abner: 158, 231
Abner: 162, 231
Daniel: 163, 231
Daniel: 163, 231
Daniel Boone: 158, 163, 231
David: 167, 168, 232
Drucilla: 167, 232
Elizabeth: 163, 232
Elizabeth: 158, 232
Elizabeth: 167, 232
Hannah: 158, 232
Iciline Archibald: 168, 232
James: 167, 232
John: 158, 232
John: 167, 168, 232
Joseph: 163, 232
Louis: 163, 232
Martha: 158, 171, 232
Mary: 163, 232
Mary: 158, 232
Mary: 163, 232
Mary: 167, 232
Melcina Callaway: 168, 232
Morgan: 167, 168, 177, 232
Phoebe: 163, 232
Phoebe: 158, 232

Phoebe: 162, 232
Rebecca: 159, 232
Rebecca: 157, 232
Sallie: 163, 232
Samuel: 162, 232
Samuel: 163, 232
Samuel: 158, 162, 232
Samuel: 167, 232
Sarah: 158, 162, 232
Susan: 167, 232
Thomas: 163, 232
Thomas: 163, 232
William: 158, 232
William: 162, 232
William K.: 167, 232
William Sr.: 157, 158, 232
William Turner: 163, 232
Willis: 167, 168, 232

Bryant -
William: 156, 232

Buffington -
Alfred Peter: 54, 151, 232
Alice P: 54, 151, 232
Annie E: 54, 151, 232
Benjamin: 116, 232
Bertie: 54, 151, 232
Cornelius: 116, 232
Dorothy Pauline: 62, 67, 153, 154, 232
Eldred Leroy: 54, 151, 232
Elisabeth: 116, 126, 127, 232
Ethel M: 54, 151, 232
Isaiah T.: 127, 232
Jacob: 116, 232
John G: 54, 151
Josiah: 116, 127, 232
Laura J: 54, 151, 232
Mabel E: 54, 151, 232
Meta: 54, 151, 232
Roland McKinley: 54, 62, 67, 151, 153, 154, 232
Roland R: 62, 153, 232
Solomon: 116, 232
Solomon: 116, 232
Susanna: 116, 232

Bullock -
Eliza Naomi: 199, 206, 209, 232
Francis Marion: 199, 206, 232
Ida Myrtle: 209, 214, 215, 232
Ida Pauline: 199, 209, 215, 232
Joseph: 199, 209, 214, 215, 232
Mamie Lou: 209, 232
Martha Ann: 199, 209, 214, 232
Mary Ollie: 199, 208, 209, 232
Nannie Joe: 209, 215, 232
Sarah Edith: 209, 232
Willie Ruth: 209, 233

Burgin -
Mella B.: 66, 193, 233

Burkett -
George Park: 49, 233

Burris -
Lula: 203, 233

Button -

288

Jacob: 27, 80, 109, 251
Jacob: 111, 251
Jacob: 88, 251
James: 84, 251
James: 81, 115, 251
Johann George: 24, 80, 82, 109, 115, 251
Johann Michael: 23, 24, 80, 81, 85, 91, 109, 114, 115, 124, 131, 132, 251
Johann Solomon: 26, 80, 83, 109, 116, 251
Johannes: 29, 80, 83, 84, 87, 88, 94, 100, 101, 103, 104, 251
Johannes: 23, 80, 81, 84, 88, 109, 114, 123, 129, 251
Johannes: 110, 251
Johannes Adams: 22, 29, 80-104, 109, 251
John: 87, 251
John Elias: 89, 129, 251
John George: 30, 110, 251
John L.: 85, 124, 251
John Michael: 18, 22, 23, 29, 30, 80-103, 109, 251
John Philip: 111, 251
Jonas: 25, 80, 109, 251
Jonathan: 84, 251
Jonathan: 83, 251
Jonathon: 82, 115, 251
Joseph: 83, 87, 94, 100, 101, 103, 104, 251
Joseph: 82, 115, 251
Joseph: 83, 88, 251
Joseph: 88, 251
Joseph M.: 110, 251
Julia: 81, 251
Katharina Anna: 81, 115, 251
Laura A: 88, 251
Lavina Magdalena: 82, 115, 251
Leah: 84, 251
Leah: 82, 115, 251
Leah Jane: 84, 123, 251
Levi: 81, 85, 91, 114, 124, 131, 132, 251
Lewis: 82, 115, 251
Lydia Jane: 83, 251
Mabel Irene: 88, 251
Margaret: 81, 251
Margaret (aka: Margaretha): 81, 114, 249, 251
Margareta Rebecca (aka: Rebecca): 10, 13, 14, 17, 19, 46, 82, 86, 91-93, 98, 99, 101, 102, 116, 125, 132-134, 139-144, 147, 189, 251, 259
Martin: 81, 115, 251
Mary (aka: Nella): 82, 115, 251, 257
Mary Ann: 20, 82, 116, 251
Mary Anna: 83, 88, 251
Mary Ellen: 87, 126, 251
Michael: 110, 251
Michael: 26, 80, 83, 87, 93, 100,

109, 116, 126, 134, 141, 251
Michael: 82, 115, 251
Michael: 85, 124, 251
Michael: 87, 93-95, 100, 126, 134, 137, 141, 251
Moses: 84, 251
Moses: 83, 251
Moses: 20, 82, 116, 251
Nicholas: 20, 82, 116, 251
Oliver: 87, 251
Orson Eugene: 88, 251
Peter: 81, 251
Regina: 27, 80, 109, 251
Reuben: 82, 115, 251
Robert Elmer: 88, 252
Salome: 111, 252
Sara: 82, 115, 252
Sarah: 110, 118, 252
Sarah: 84, 252
Sarah: 20, 82, 116, 252
Sarah: 82, 115, 252
Sarah: 83, 252
Sarah: 84, 123, 252
Sarah: 128, 252
Sarah Ann: 82, 115, 252
Sarah Ellen: 85, 91, 124, 132, 252
Simon: 81, 84, 88, 114, 123, 129, 252
Solomon (aka: Salomon): 83, 116, 252, 263
Sophia: 25, 80, 109, 252
Susan: 84, 252
Susan: 81, 252
Susan Emily: 83, 252
Susanna: 27, 80, 109, 252
Susanna: 82, 115, 252
Susanna: 111, 252
Susanna: 83, 116, 252
Theodore Nathaniel: 87, 126, 252
Thomas: 19, 82, 115, 252
William: 81, 84, 252
William: 88, 252
William Elmer: 89, 129, 252
William Henry: 83, 88, 252
William Isaac: 88, 252
Maugridge -
Unnamed: 252
Unnamed: 252
John Milton: 34, 155, 252
Mary: 33, 34, 155, 252
Maurer -
Ellen Amanda: 89, 130
Ida Celara: 135, 252
May -
George: 170, 252
Hinton: 170, 252
Ira: 170, 252
John: 170, 252
John: 170, 252
Richard: 170, 252
William: 170, 252
Maye -
Elizabeth Hannah: 88, 252

Mayfield -
m: 75, 212, 252
Mazzie -
(name: Mary C. Timmons): 127, 252, 267
Mc Clain -
Mary: 172, 252
McAlarney -
Joseph C.: 117, 252
M. Wilson: 117, 252
McCorkle -
Margaret: 44, 252
McCormick -
Cydia: 199, 252
McCoy -
B. H.: 128, 252
Hugh Franklin: 50, 252
Martin Lee: 50, 252
Mary (aka: Polly): 172, 252, 258
Matilda Josephine: 50, 252
Washington: 50, 252
McCulley -
Caroline: 89, 100, 130, 141
McDonald -
Nancy Anna: 21, 40, 252
McGlasson -
Abslom: 184, 252
Emma J.: 184, 252
McKay -
Bessie: 129, 252
James E.: 129, 252
Jennie E.: 129, 252
McKinney -
Catherine: 121, 252
McLallen -
Orron Treat: 189, 252
McMains -
Alta Nina: 71, 204, 252
McMullen -
J. A.: 173, 252
McNabb -
William Alexander: 45, 252
McQuitty -
Almirinda: 171, 252
David: 171, 252
Melusky -
Anna: 95, 137
Mercer -
Louisa Jane: 69, 195, 252
Merchant -
Martha Jane: 170, 171, 252
Meredith -
Maggie: 198, 252
Merwin -
Henry C.: 178, 253
Messner -
Daniel C.: 89, 130
Metcalf -
Uri: 64, 186, 253
Meyer -
Christian: 40, 253
Hannah: 88, 253

www.ingramcontent.com/pod-product-compliance
Lightning Source LLC
Chambersburg PA
CBHW081357270326
41930CB00015B/3331